Southern Italy

Naples & Campania
p65

Puglia, Basilicata & Calabria
p139

Sicily
p197

Brett Atkinson, Cristian Bonetto, Gregor Clark,
Duncan Garwood, Brendan Sainsbury, Nicola Williams

Contents

CAPPELLA PALATINA P204

STREET STALL, AMALFI P127

PROCIDA P119

Contents

COVID-19

We have re-checked every business in this book before publication to ensure that it is still open after the COVID-19 outbreak. However, the economic and social impacts of COVID-19 will continue to be felt long after the outbreak has been contained, and many businesses, services and events referenced in this guide may experience ongoing restrictions. Some businesses may be temporarily closed, have changed their opening hours and services, or require bookings; some unfortunately could have closed permanently. We suggest you check with venues before visiting for the latest information.

Right:
Positano (p121)

WELCOME TO
Southern Italy

Offering relaxing balance compared to other busier parts of Europe, southern Italy is a destination where travellers are virtually mandated to slow down upon arrival. I love negotiating less-busy coastal roads scented with pine forests and exploring more remote ancient archeological sites – often its own exercise in solitude and quiet reflection. When I'm ready to join the party, Naples, Lecce and Palermo all feature a vibrant cosmopolitan focus on culture and cuisine, and there's always new discoveries to be found amid the labyrinthine laneways of my favourite hill towns including baroque Noto, elegant Ostuni and gritty Cosenza.

By Brett Atkinson, Writer
🐦 @travelwriternz 📷 @travelwriternz
For more about our writers, see p320

Southern Italy

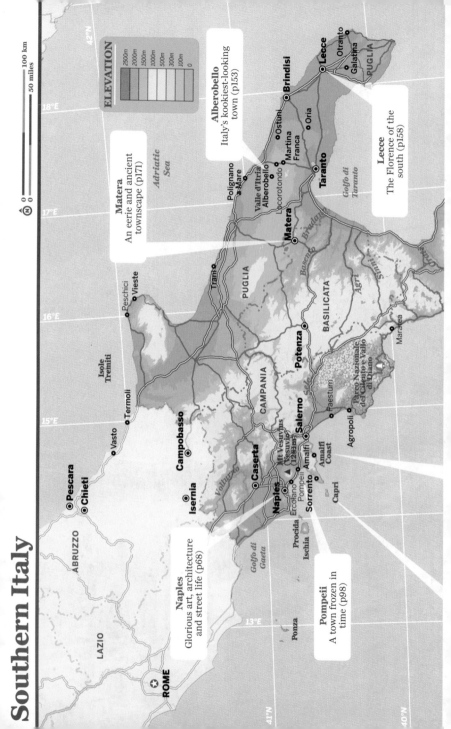

Naples
Glorious art, architecture and street life (p68)

Pompeii
A town frozen in time (p98)

Matera
An eerie and ancient townscape (p171)

Alberobello
Italy's kookiest-looking town (p153)

Lecce
The Florence of the south (p158)

ELEVATION
2500m
2000m
1500m
1000m
500m
300m
100m
0

LAZIO

ABRUZZO

Pescara
Chieti

Termoli
Vasto

Campobasso

Isernia

MOLISE

Golfo di
Gaeta

Ponza

Procida
Ischia

Naples
Caserta
Mt Vesuvius
(1281m)
Ercolano
Pompeii
Sorrento
Amalfi
Amalfi
Coast
Capri

Salerno

CAMPANIA

Volturno

Paestum

Agropoli

Parco Nazionale
del Cilento e Vallo
di Diano

Maratea

Peschici
Vieste

Isole
Tremiti

Trani

PUGLIA

Polignano
a Mare

Valle d'Itria
Alberobello
Locorotondo
Martina
Franca
Ostuni

Potenza

BASILICATA

Matera

Bradano

Basento

Agri

Sinni

Taranto

Golfo di
Taranto

Oria

Brindisi

Lecce

Otranto

Galatina

PUGLIA

Adriatic
Sea

ROME

Sele

0   100 km
0   50 miles

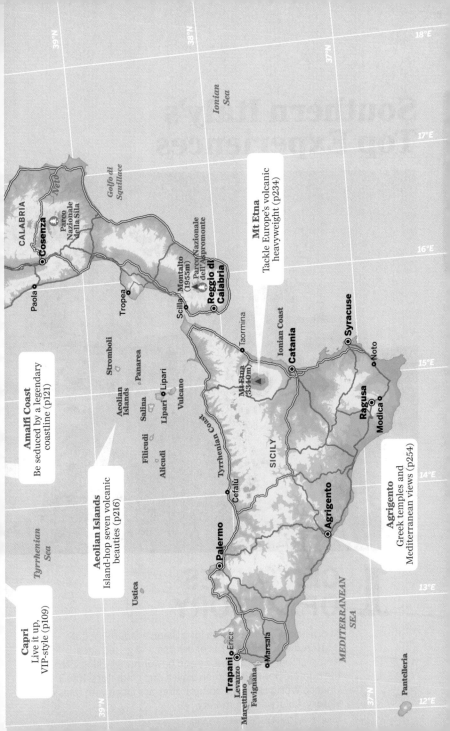

Southern Italy's Top Experiences

Capri
Live it up, VIP-style (p109)

Amalfi Coast
Be seduced by a legendary coastline (p121)

Aeolian Islands
Island-hop seven volcanic beauties (p216)

Mt Etna
Tackle Europe's volcanic heavyweight (p234)

Agrigento
Greek temples and Mediterranean views (p254)

CALABRIA

Cosenza
Parco Nazionale della Sila
Paola
Aspromonte
Parco Nazionale dell'Aspromonte
Montalto (1955m)
Scilla
Reggio di Calabria
Tropea
Veto
Golfo di Squillace
Ionian Sea

SICILY

Palermo
Ustica
Cefalù
Tyrrhenian Coast
Aeolian Islands
Stromboli
Panarea
Salina
Filicudi
Alicudi
Lipari
Lipari
Vulcano
Taormina
Ionian Coast
Mt Etna (3340m)
Catania
Syracuse
Noto
Ragusa
Modica
Agrigento
Trapani
Erice
Levanzo
Marettimo
Favignana
Marsala
Pantelleria

Tyrrhenian Sea

MEDITERRANEAN SEA

39°N
38°N
37°N
39°N
37°N
18°E
17°E
16°E
15°E
14°E
13°E
12°E

Southern Italy's Top Experiences

1 CENTURIES OF HISTORY

At civilisation's crossroads for millennia, southern Italy is littered with the detritus of diverse and gilded ages; from Carthaginian invasions and power-hungry kings, to the humble hopes of Roman slaves and gladiators. Its 13 Unesco World Heritage cultural sites are laced with tales of victory, failure and humanity.

Above: Chiesa di San Pietro Caveoso (p173), Matera

Ghostly Pompeii

Frozen in its death throes, the sprawling, time-warped ruins of Pompeii (pictured right) hurtle you 2000 years into the past. Wander through chariot-grooved Roman streets and elegantly frescoed villas and bathhouses, food stores, markets, theatres and even an ancient brothel. p98

Valley of the Temples

Few archaeological sites evoke the past like Agrigento's Valley of the Temples (pictured above). Overlooking the Mediterranean, its stoic temples belonged to the once-great Greek city of Akragas. To conjure the ghosts of the past, roam the ruins late in the afternoon, when crowds have thinned and the wind whistles hauntingly between the columns. p254

Villa Romana del Casale

Superb mosaics (pictured above) offer memories of the past at central Sicily's 3rd-century Villa Romana del Casale. The privileged life of a Roman co-emperor – including hunting scenes and murals of sumptuous feasts – is brought to life in stunning detail. p251

2 COASTAL JOURNEYS

Perfect for confident drivers behind the wheel of a zippy Fiat 500, coastal road trips around southern Italy include the bucket-list experience of the Amalfi Coast, exploring the clifftop coves and bays of Puglia's Salento region, and a meandering route through the quieter Tyrrhenian coast towns of Calabria. Be sure to plan a leisurely schedule, taking time to discover a few surprises along the way.

Above: Amalfi (p127)

Amalfi Coast

Italy's most celebrated coastline is a gripping strip: mountains plunge into creamy blue sea in a prime-time scene of precipitous crags, sun-bleached villages and lush woodland. Between sea and sky, mountaintop hiking trails deliver Tyrrhenian panoramas fit for a god. p121

Coastal Salento

Best explored on a leisure-ly DIY road trip on quieter back roads, Salento, the southern tip of Italy's heel combines historic Otranto, the walled city of Castro, and Gallipoli's labyrinthine whitewashed promontory. p158

Top: Near Otranto (p166)

Tyrrhenian Surprises

An emerging favourite of Italian travellers, Calabria's southern Tyr-rhenian coast is enlivened by a trio of spectacular hilltop towns. Journey down the coastal road to mix and match a journey featuring Pizzo, Scilla and Tropea. p192

Bottom: Santa Maria dell'Isola (p193), Tropea

3 EXCEPTIONALLY GOOD EATING

Southern Italy's dedication to food is utterly forgivable, as this is the country's culinary cornucopia, a sun-drenched platter of produce and flavours. From pizza in Naples to chilli-spiked *salsiccie* (sausages) in the wilds of Basilicata and Calabria, the options are both mouth-watering and deliciously overwhelming. Maybe a bowl of fragrant couscous in Sicily, or the freshest of seafood in Salento? Whatever you choose, you'll definitely be back for seconds.

Puglia

Southeastern Italy's sun-baked landscape and a serrated Adriatic coastline combine for hearty *cucina povera* in Puglia, and briny-fresh seafood including sea urchins, oysters and prawns. p142

Below: *Fritto misto* (mixed fish fry)

CAM024 / SHUTTERSTOCK ©

Naples

From perfectly-charred pizza to a potent espresso – best enjoyed at a laneway bar – eating and drinking is an obsession in Naples. Leave room for dessert of delicious Neapolitan sweets and pastries. p86

Sicily

Centuries of culinary influence from both conquerors and colonisers have left their mark on the food of Sicily. Arab, Greek and Saracen traditions all combine with the freshest of local produce p197

Right: Mercato di Ballarò (p204), Palermo

4 ISLAND ESCAPES

LEOKS / SHUTTERSTOCK ©

IMAGERIE / GETTY IMAGES ©

Take advantage of a comprehensive armada of ferries to journey beyond the mainland of southern Italy, venturing to holiday hotspots like Capri and Procida – Italy's Capital of Culture for 2022 – or further afield to craggy volcanic islets and forested archipelagos. Off Sicily's west coast, the Isole Egadi (Egadi Islands) are popular for clifftop hiking and good diving and snorkelling.

Above: Procida (p119)

GARY YIM / SHUTTERSTOCK ©

Capri

Capri has been seducing mortals for millennia and even the summer hordes can't quite dilute its ethereal magic. Travellers on the Grand Tour waxed lyrical, and celebrities continue to moor their yachts in its turquoise waters. p109

Aeolian Islands

Build an exciting and spectacular Aeolian itinerary around seven volcanic outcrops, among them the thermal hotspot of Vulcano, vine-laced Salina, and fiery, lava-spewing Stromboli. p216

Isole Tremiti

Reached from the whitewashed hilltop port towns of Vieste and Peschici on Puglia's Promontorio del Gargano, this remote trio of islands combines excellent diving, forest walking and an interesting medieval history. p152

5 COMPELLING CITIES

Discover an enthralling amalgam of fascinating history and contemporary urban culture in the cities of southern Italy. Layers of heritage and architecture provide echoes of those who conquered and colonised across the ages, while narrow laneways, restored mansions and quiet squares all showcase a new breed of innovative chefs, colourful street art, and bars and cafes definitely at their best during the *aperitivi* hour of late afternoon.

MIKOLAJN / GETTY IMAGES ©

Naples

The alleyways of Naples (pictured above) lead to palm-fringed boulevards; crumbling facades mask baroque naves; and cultish shrines flank street art murals and a wave of hip new bars, eateries and galleries. p68

Lecce

With its own homegrown baroque architectural style, *barocco leccese*, Lecce boasts a stunning roll-call of churches and *palazzi*, while superb museums tell the story of Salento. p158

Top: Basilica di Santa Croce

Palermo

An addictive blend of faded elegance, urban edge and modern reinvention, uncovering the centuries of civilisation infusing the Sicilian capital is an ideal project for curious and mindful travellers. p201

Above: Cattedrale di Palermo (p204)

6 LABYRINTHINE HILL TOWNS

MKOS83 / SHUTTERSTOCK ©

MARCO RUBINO / SHUTTERSTOCK ©

DAVID IONUT / SHUTTERSTOCK ©

I JUST TRY TO TELL MY EMOTIONS AND TAKE YOU AROUND THE WORLD / GETTY IMAGES ©

Matera

An extraordinary and ancient city, Matera and its Unesco World Heritage–listed *sassi* (cave dwellings; rainwater gathering system pictured top), were once a symbol of Basilicata's abject poverty. Now these cavernous dwellings are repurposed as on-point eateries, bars and stylish accommodation. p171

Alberobello

The *trulli* (whitewashed circular buildings with coneshaped roofs; pictured bottom) of Alberobello, tumble down the slopes like an army of hatted gnomes, and in the 21st century have been reborn as cafes, bars and hotels. p153

Locorotondo

White-washed laneways enlivened with crimson accents of geranium flowers all lead uphill to the compact main square in Locorotondo. On the town's slopes, wine bars offer views across Puglia's verdant Valle d'Itria. p155

Experience a remarkable blend of inspired architecture and spectacular natural locations in the hill towns of southern Italy. Beyond the popular locations of Matera, Alberobello and Locorotondo, Ostuni crowns a Salento hilltop for Adriatic views, while Sicily's Noto and Ragusa are both adorned with the design excesses of baroque *palazzi*. Visit at dusk to see the town's golden sandstone softly glowing in late-afternoon light.

7 OUTDOOR ADVENTURES

Rugged mountains, fiery volcanoes and electric-blue grottoes all conspire to make southern Italy a giant adventure playground for active travellers. Raft down Calabria's river Lao, scale the oft-steaming volcanoes of Stromboli and Mt Etna, or mountain bike and dive around Puglia. Opportunities to raise a sweat in the region's spectacular outdoors may be many, but there is one constant: landscapes that are beautiful, diverse, and just a little ethereal.

Promontorio del Gargano

Negotiate forested coastal roads to northern Puglia for hiking and mountain biking in the Foresta Umbra, or diving into prehistoric sea caves along the region's idiosyncratic coastline (pictured below). p148

MORENOOU / SHUTTERSTOCK ©

Parco Nazionale del Pollino

Spanning both Basilicata and Calabria, this rugged national park (pictured above) is popular for river-rafting, canyoning and paragliding. The park's mountains are shrouded with ancient forests. p184

Explore Mt Etna

Towering above Sicily's Ionian Coast, the slopes of Mount Etna (pictured right) are part of the Parco dell'Etna, an area encompassing prized vineyards, hiking trails through alpine forests, and a forbiddingly ink-black summit. p234

8 BEACH LIFE ITALIAN-STYLE

FERNANDO FERNÁNDEZ BAUNA / GETTY IMAGES ©

MICHAEL HEFFERNAN / LONELY PLANET ©

STUART WILSON / SHUTTERSTOCK ©

With a few thousand km of coastline and many islands waiting to be explored, southern Italy is packed with beach experiences. Partner a blend of Cefalù's vacation vibe and Torre Salsa's remote wilderness with an exciting boat trip past sea caves to the quiet beaches of Puglia's Promontorio del Gargano, or find your own slice of coastal paradise on the Aeolian Islands.

Cefalù

Spend the day in Cefalù, along its arcing town beach (pictured above) before retiring late afternoon for *aperitivi* refreshments followed by a leisurely meal amid the town's historic laneways. p214

Ischia

Catch water taxis or tackle coastal walking trails to the best beaches on the island. Natural hot springs warm the sand at Spiaggia di Maronti, while more remote Punta Caruso offers deep, clear water near a rocky headland. p115

Torre Salsa

Negotiate a bumpy un-sealed road to this beauti-fully deserted beach in a compact nature reserve in southwest Sicily. Take in mountain views from well-marked walking trails before refreshing with a swim. p258

Need to Know

For more information, see Survival Guide (p293)

Currency
Euro (€)

Language
Italian

Visas
Generally not required for stays of up to 90 days (or at all for EU nationals); some nationalities need a Schengen visa.

Money
ATMs widely available. Credit cards accepted in most hotels and restaurants.

Mobile Phones
Local SIM cards can be used in European, Australian and some unlocked US phones. Other phones must be set to roaming.

Time
Central European Time (GMT/UTC plus one hour)

When to Go

Dry climate
Warm to hot summer, mild winters

Lecce
GO All year; summer for parties

Naples
GO All year

Maratea
GO May–Oct

Aeolian Islands
GO May, Jun & Sep

Palermo
GO Sep–Oct

High Season
(Jul–Aug)
➡ Queues and crowds at big sights and beaches, especially in August.
➡ High levels of traffic congestion in tourist areas, including the Amalfi Coast.
➡ A good period for cultural events and festivals in tourist areas.

Shoulder
(Apr–Jun & Sep–Oct)
➡ Good deals on accommodation.
➡ Spring best for wildflowers and local produce, with numerous festivals too.
➡ Autumn offers the grape harvest and warm weather without the crowds.

Low Season
(Nov–Mar)
➡ Prices can be 30% lower than in high season (except major holidays).
➡ Many sights, hotels and restaurants close in coastal and mountainous areas.
➡ Christmas feasting and colourful Carnevale.

Useful Websites

Lonely Planet (www.lonely planet.com/italy) Destination information, hotel reviews and more.

Trenitalia (www.trenitalia.com) Italian railways website.

Agriturismi (www.agriturismi.it) Guide to farm accommodation.

Italia (www.italia.it) Italy's official tourism website.

The Local (www.thelocal.it) English-language news from Italy, including travel-related stories.

Important Numbers

From outside Italy, dial your international access code, Italy's country code (39), then the number (including the '0').

Italy's country code	☎39
International access code	☎00
Ambulance	☎118
Police	☎112, 113
Fire	☎115

Exchange Rates

Australia	A$1	€0.63
Canada	C$1	€0.69
Japan	¥100	€0.76
New Zealand	NZ$1	€0.61
UK	UK£1	€1.16
US	US$1	€0.87

For current exchange rates, see www.xe.com.

Daily Costs

Budget:
Less than €100

➡ Dorm bed: €15–30

➡ Double room in a budget hotel: €60–110

➡ Pizza or pasta: €6–15

Midrange: €100–250

➡ Double room in a hotel: €100–220

➡ Local restaurant dinner: €25–50

➡ Admission to museum: €4–15

Top end:
More than €250

➡ Double room in a four- or five-star hotel: €200–450

➡ Top restaurant dinner: €50–150

➡ Opera ticket: €40–200

Opening Hours

Banks 8.30am to 1.30pm and 2.45pm to 4pm Monday to Friday.

Restaurants noon to 3pm and 7.30pm to 11pm or midnight; many close one day per week.

Cafes 7am to 8pm, later if offering evening bar service.

Bars and clubs 10pm to 4am or 5am.

Shops 9.30am to 1.30pm and 4pm to 7.30pm or 8pm Monday to Saturday. Some also open Sunday and several close Monday morning.

Arriving in Southern Italy

Capodichino airport (Naples) A shuttle bus to the centre of Naples (€5, 15 to 35 minutes) runs every 10 to 20 minutes from 6am to 11.20pm. Taxi fares range from €18 to €27, depending on your destination, and take around 30 minutes.

Karol Wojtyła airport (Palese airport; Bari) A shuttle bus to central Bari (€4, 30 minutes) runs roughly hourly from 5.35am to 12.10am. Trains (€5, 20 minutes) run every 15 to 60 minutes from 5am to 11.30pm. A taxi costs (€25) and takes around 20 minutes.

Falcone-Borsellino airport (Palermo) A shuttle bus to central Palermo (€6.30, 50 minutes) runs half-hourly from 5am to 12.30am (1am in summer). Trains (€5.90, one hour) run every 15 to 60 minutes. A taxi (€35 to €45) takes between 30 and 60 minutes.

Safe Travel

Despite Mafia notoriety, southern Italy is generally not a dangerous place. Consider the following tips for a stress-free stay.

➡ Be vigilant about pickpockets at train stations and ferry terminals, on buses and at markets (especially those in Naples, Palermo and Catania).

➡ If carrying a bag or camera, wear the strap across your body and away from the road – moped thieves can swipe a bag and be gone in seconds.

➡ In major cities, roads that appear to be for one-way traffic often have special lanes for buses travelling in the opposite direction, so always look both ways before stepping out.

For much more on **getting around**, see p304

PLAN YOUR TRIP NEED TO KNOW

First Time Southern Italy

For more information, see Survival Guide (p293)

Checklist

→ Ensure your passport is valid for at least six months past your departure date from Italy

→ Check airline baggage restrictions

→ Organise travel insurance

→ Make bookings for accommodation and entertainment

→ Inform your credit-/debit-card company of your travels

→ Check whether you can use your mobile (cell) phone in Italy

→ Check requirements for hiring a car

What to Pack

→ Hat, sunglasses, sunscreen and comfortable walking shoes

→ Electrical adapter and phone charger

→ A detailed driving map for southern Italy's rural back roads

→ A smart outfit and shoes for higher-end restaurants

→ Phrasebook, for ordering and charming

Top Tips for Your Trip

→ Visit in the shoulder season (spring and autumn) for good weather and thinner crowds.

→ If driving, get off the main roads where possible: some of the most stunning scenery is on secondary or tertiary roads.

→ Avoid restaurants with touts and a *menu turistico* (tourist menu).

→ At archaeological sites, watch out for touts posing as legitimate guides.

→ Queue-jumping is common; be polite but assertive.

What to Wear

Appearances matter in Italy. In the cities, suitable wear for men is generally trousers (including stylish jeans) and shirts or polo shirts, and for women skirts, trousers or dresses. Shorts, T-shirts and sandals are fine in summer and at the beach, but a long-sleeved shirt is more suitable for dining out in restaurants. A light sweater or waterproof jacket is useful in spring and autumn, and sturdy, comfortable shoes are good when visiting archaeological sites.

Sleeping

Southern Italy has a varied range of accommodation and it's generally a good idea to book in advance. This is especially important if visiting coastal resort towns in July and August, when booking three or more months ahead is advised.

Hotels Span cheap-and-charmless to chic-and-boutique.

Agriturismi and masserie Family-friendly farm stays range from rustic farmhouses to luxe country estates.

B&Bs Anything from rooms in family houses to good-value studio apartments.

Pensioni Similar to hotels, though *pensioni* are generally of one- to three-star quality.

Hostels Many *ostelli* offer both dorms and private rooms with bathroom.

Money

➡ Though widely accepted, the use of credit cards is not as ubiquitous in southern Italy as it is in some other parts of Europe, the UK, the US and Australia. Always have some cash on hand.

➡ Note that using your credit card in ATMs can be costly. Every time you withdraw cash, you'll typically be charged a withdrawal fee as well as a conversion charge. Fees can sometimes be reduced by withdrawing cash from banks affiliated with your home banking institution; check with your bank.

➡ Always inform your bank of your travel plans to avoid your card being blocked for payments made in unusual locations.

Bargaining

Gentle haggling is common in outdoor markets; in all other instances you're expected to pay the stated price.

Tipping

Italians are not big tippers. Use the following as a rough guide:

Bars In cafes, locals often place a €0.10 or €0.20 coin on the bar when ordering coffee. Consider leaving small change when ordering drinks.

Hotels Tip porters about €5 at high-end hotels.

Restaurants Service (servizio) is generally included in restaurant bills – if it's not, a euro or two is fine in pizzerias, 10% in restaurants.

Taxis Optional, but most people round up to the nearest euro.

Language

English is not as widely spoken in southern Italy as it is in northern Europe. In the main tourist centres you can get by, but in the countryside it will be helpful to master a few basic phrases. This will improve your experience no end, especially when ordering in restaurants, some of which have no written menu. It's also a good way of connecting with the locals, leading to a richer, more personal experience of the region and its people. For more on language, see p308.

 What's the local speciality?
Qual'è la specialità di questa regione?
kwa·le la spe·cha·lee·ta dee kwes·ta re·jo·ne

A bit like the rivalry between medieval Italian city-states, these days the country's regions compete in speciality foods and wines.

 Which combined tickets do you have?
Quali biglietti cumulativi avete?
kwa·lee bee·lye·tee koo·moo·la·tee·vee a·ve·te

Make the most of your euro by getting combined tickets to various sights; they are available in all major Italian cities.

 Where can I buy discount designer items?
C'è un outlet in zona? che oon owt·let in zo·na

Discount fashion outlets are big business in major cities – get bargain-priced seconds, samples and cast-offs for la bella figura.

 I'm here with my husband/boyfriend.
Sono qui con il mio marito/ragazzo.
so·no kwee kon eel mee·o ma·ree·to/ra·ga·tso

Solo women travellers may receive unwanted attention in some parts of Italy; if ignoring fails have a polite rejection ready.

Etiquette

Italy is a surprisingly formal society; the following tips will help avoid awkward moments.

Greetings Greet people in shops, restaurants and bars with a buongiorno (good morning) or buonasera (good evening); kiss both cheeks and say come stai (how are you) to friends. Use 'lei' (formal 'you') in polite company; use 'tu' (informal 'you') with friends and children. With older people, only use first names if invited.

Asking for help Say mi scusi (excuse me) to attract attention; use permesso (permission) to pass someone in a crowded space.

Religious etiquette Cover shoulders, torso and thighs when visiting religious sites and never intrude on a church service.

Dining out Dress smartly when eating out at restaurants.

At the table Eat pasta with a fork, not a spoon; it's OK to eat pizza with your hands. Summon the waiter by saying mi scusi (excuse me). When dining in an Italian home, bring a small gift of dolci (sweets) from a pasticceria (pastry shop) or wine, and dress well.

Scheduling Take official opening hours and timetables with a grain of salt.

What's New

It's been a tough few years for southern Italy, with COVID-19, wildfires, volcanic eruptions and a geographic location at the nexus of the 21st-century's refugee crisis. Despite the Mezzogiorno's extreme tribulations, hope remains strong, especially for the return of travellers to experience the region's singular beauty and cultural and culinary attractions.

Capital of Culture

Throughout 2022, the compact Italian island of Procida will take centre stage as Italy's Capital of Culture. Located in the Bay of Naples and adorned with pastel-painted houses and idyllic bays, Procida is the first island to be awarded the prestigious honour. Key to Procida's winning bid was the island's emphasis on low impact tourism – defined as 'sustainable travel and leisure activities that directly benefit local communities and are respectful of wildlife, local people and their cultures' – and a focus on its rich artisanal heritage. Cultural events will span the year with plans for more than 40 diverse cultural projects involving almost 250 artists and eight regenerated cultural spaces.

Taranto's time to shine

Following the southwestern Puglian city's successful hosting of the SailGP yachting regatta in June 2021, Taranto is embarking on more initiatives to drive awareness of the region's second-largest city as a cultural, sporting and tourism destination. Leading up to Taranto's hosting of the Mediterranean Games in 2026, key projects include a sparkling new stadium for the city's beloved Taranto F.C. and the reinvigoration of the sprawling Palazzo Archita, a brick-red 18th-century edifice that dominates the eastern edge of Piazza Garibaldi. Plans for the historic building include an art gallery, cafes and restaurants and a cultural centre. Inspired by the renaissance of other industrial cities like Bilbao and Pittsburgh – Taranto's gritty

LOCAL KNOWLEDGE

WHAT'S HAPPENING IN SOUTHERN ITALY

Brett Atkinson, Lonely Planet writer

Despite being impacted a few months later than northern Italian regions like Lombardy, COVID-19's social devastation and death toll were tragically only slightly lower in the south. Other recent challenges have included forest wildfires in Puglia, Calabria and Sicily in August 2021, and an increase in the numbers of migrants, mainly escaping sub-Saharan Africa, Pakistan and Syria, arriving on the island of Lampedusa during the calmer seas of mid-2021. Challenges from the natural realm included Mount Etna erupting more than 50 times during 2021, with the volcanic island of Stromboli always keen to provide a supporting role.

With tourism limited throughout much of 2020 and 2021, the economic toll on southern Italy has been severe, but the summer and autumn of 2021 saw a positive turnaround driven by Matera's starring role in the new James Bond film, *No Time to Die*, an 80% COVID-19 vaccination rate across the country by October 2021, and the' security provided by Italy's Green Pass digital certificate guaranteeing vaccination status.

heritage includes the massive Ilva steel-works - other projects include the restoration and repopulation of Taranto's Città Vecchia (Old Town), built on the city's even older Greek foundations, and the modernisation of the Mar Grande waterfront to link the city's three very diverse precincts.

Future underwater discoveries

Presented at the Mediterranean Exchange of Archeological Tourism in Salerno in November 2021, the Mediterranean Underwater Cultural Heritage plan comprises linking underwater archeological sites across several Mediterranean countries including Greece, Turkey, Israel, Egypt and Italy. It's envisaged a pan-Mediterranean itinerary suitable for visiting snorkellers and divers will be developed, with southern Italian underwater destinations to feature including Sicily's Isole Egadi, northern Puglia's Isole Tremiti, and Capo Rizzuto near the Magna Graecia heritage of Crotone (p189) in Calabria.

Michelin-starred restaurants

Southern Italy was again well represented in Michelin's 2021 guide to Europe's best restaurants with new additions to the list including Ristorante Lorelei in Sorrento, and Casa Sgarra in the Puglian port city of Trani. Established favourites retaining their Michelin recognition include Vitoantonio Lombardo (p176) in Basilicata's Matera, and the Sicilian hill town culinary success stories of Accursio (p248) in Modica and Ristorante Duomo (p251) in Ragusa.

New hotels in heritage hotels

With an eye on the travel industry post-COVID-19, a few new luxury hotels opened around the region in 2021. Overlooking the Gulf of Palermo, Villa Igiea is a re-imagining of an historical Art Nouveau palazzo once owned by Sicily's entrepreneurial Florio family, while Four Seasons' San Domenico Palace re-opened in a 14th-century convent in the forested hills above Taormina.

LISTEN, WATCH & FOLLOW

For inspiration and up-to-date news, visit www.lonelyplanet.com/italy

Italy Magazine (www.italymagazine.com) Culture and lifestyle webzine.

Katie Parla (www.katieparla.com) Culinary-themed blog posts and guides.

Italian Wine Podcast (www.italianwinepodcast.com) Tales from Italian winemakers.

Sauced & Found (www.saucedandfound.com) Food and travel on the Amalfi Coast and surrounds.

Insta @weareinpuglia Inspiring shots of Puglia.

FAST FACTS

Food trend Gourmet versions of traditional street food

World Heritage sites 15 (plus 12 'Tentative' sites)

Foreign-born residents 4.4%

Population 16.9 million

NAPLES   LOS ANGELES   ITALY

= 200 people per sq km

Inspiration for future travels

At a time when travel to southern Italy was compromised, various books were published in 2021 to inspire future exploration of the region. *Sicilia: A love letter to the food of Sicily*, by British chef Ben Tish showcases the culinary influences of the various civilisations that have washed over the Mediterranean's biggest island, while *Sicily: Wines and Wine Routes* is the definitive guide to one of Europe's most dynamic winemaking scenes. *Gennaro's Limoni* by chef Gennaro Contaldo presents recipes showcasing the plump and luscious lemons of Campania's Amalfi Coast.

Accommodation

Find more accommodation reviews throughout the On the Road chapters (from p63)

Accommodation Types

Agriturismo and masseria Working farm or winery with rooms; usually family-run and often with evening dining. Properties run the gamut from simple, rustic country houses with farm animals to luxe estates with designer interiors, gourmet restaurants and swimming pools.

Albergo A hotel, which comes in a range of options from simple and family-run to business, historic and unapologetically opulent.

B&B A small guesthouse offering bed and breakfast; double rooms usually have a private bathroom. Morning food options can sometimes be little more than pre-packaged *cornetti* (Italian croissants), biscuits, jam, coffee and tea.

Pensione A small, family-run guesthouse offering B&B; the owners live on-site.

Ostello A hostel offering dorm beds and rooms to budget travellers. Private rooms may come with en suite bathroom.

Castello Literally a castle but in reality anything from a converted outbuilding on a farm to a fully fledged castle with crenellated towers.

Rifugio Usually a simple mountain hut for outdoors enthusiasts.

PRICE RANGES

The following price ranges refer to a double room with breakfast and private bathroom in high season.

€ less than €110

€€ €110–200

€€€ more than €200

Best Places to Stay

Best on a Budget

Finding a double room in an appealing B&B for under €80 is common in most southern cities. Rates rise in exclusive destinations like the Amalfi Coast and Taormina. Consider opting for a less famous, often more authentic alternative – for instance, Procida over Capri.

Best budget choices:

➡ Magma Home, Naples (p85)

➡ Casale Giancesare Villa Agricola, Paestum (p135)

➡ Pensione Tranchina, Scopello (p261)

➡ h-sa Guesthouse, Matera (p175)

➡ Bozzi 1910, Bari (p144)

Best for Families

The south's extraordinary mix of historic and natural drawcards offers a plethora of family holiday experiences, from cultural and culinary to active and adventurous. While self-contained apartments provide families with autonomy in the towns and cities, rural farm stays (known as *agriturismi* or *masserie*) offer space and, often, fun activities, from cycling and horse riding to cooking lessons.

Best family accommodation:

➡ Albergo Labotte, Vieste (p149)

➡ Agriturismo I Moresani, Cilento (p137)

➡ Donnaciccina, Tropea (p194)

➡ Fattoria Mosè, Agrigento (p254)

➡ Hotel Villa Eva, Capri (p113)

Best for Solo Travellers

Naples' gregarious locals, buzzing bars and vibrant street life make the city perfect for solo travellers. Significant university populations, good bars and regular musical events also give Bari, Cosenza, Lecce and Catania particular appeal. Consider staying at proper B&Bs and *pensioni,* where your hosts can quickly become newfound friends.

Best for solo travellers:

➡ Magma Home, Naples (p85)

➡ Urban Oasis, Lecce (p161)

➡ B&B Casa Pimpolini, Bari (p144)

➡ B&B Faro, Catania (p231)

Best for Unique Settings

Southern Italy's rich, varied history is echoed in its idiosyncratic slumber offerings. Unique options include a converted medieval castle on Ischia, gnome-like *trulli* (conical-roofed houses) in the Valle d'Itria, upgraded *sassi* (cave dwellings) in Matera, and opulent baroque *palazzi* in the Val di Noto. Art-themed digs are also dotted across the south, some serving up rooms designed by homegrown and international artists.

Best for unique settings:

➡ Trullidea, Alberobello (p154)

➡ Seven Rooms Villadorata, Noto (p246)

➡ Hotel Il Belvedere, Matera (p175)

➡ Albergo Il Monastero, Ischia (p117)

➡ Asmundo di Gisira, Catania (p231)

Noto (p243)

Airbnb (airbnb.com) Average nightly price of €80 for an entire place, with plentiful options under €50.

Camping.it (www.camping.it) Directory of campsites throughout Italy.

Monastery Stays (www.monasterystays.com) Monastic sleeps in Campania and Sicily.

Booking

Book well ahead if travelling at Easter or in the summer. Some hotels may impose a multinight stay, usually beach hotels in July and August. From November to Easter, many places on the coast shut down. Accommodation in cities and larger towns usually remains open all year.

Lonely Planet (lonelyplanet.com/hotels) You'll find independent reviews, as well as recommendations on the best places to stay.

Slumber Tax

Cities and towns in Italy charge a *tassa di soggiorno* (hotel occupancy tax) on top of advertised hotel rates. Expect to pay an extra €1 to €7 per night; children usually pay a discounted rate or may be completely exempt from the tax depending on the destination. The maximum number of nights that the tax is charged can also vary between cities and regions. It's always a good idea to confirm whether taxes are included when booking.

Getting Around

For more information, see Transport (p304)

Travelling by Car

Exploring southern Italy by car offers incomparable freedom and autonomy, allowing you to easily access smaller villages, remote beaches and rural landscapes not well serviced by buses and trains. Major toll routes, such as the A16 and A14 from Naples to Bari, the A18 from Messina to Catania and the A20 between Messina and Palermo, are fast, modern and well signposted. Speed limits top out at 130km/h, making for quick connections between major cities. While the south's back roads can be narrow, twisting and poorly maintained, they often compensate with beautiful landscapes. One place where driving is not recommended is in major urban areas, where narrow streets, traffic and limited parking can make for a stressful experience.

Car Hire

International rental agencies are well represented in southern Italy, with offices at the main airports (including Naples, Bari, Palermo and Catania) and in several city centres. Advance reservations made through travel booking websites usually offer the best deals.

Driving Conditions

Southern Italy's autostrade (motorways) are generally well maintained, as is the network of smaller national highways such as the SS18 and the SS267 in Campania, the SS172 in Puglia and the SS113 in Sicily. On smaller rural roads, conditions can

RESOURCES

Automobile Club d'Italia (ACI; www.aci.it). Round-the-clock emergency breakdown services (phone 80 31 16 or 800 116800).

Touring Club Italiano (www.touringclubstore.com) Publishes high-quality regional and city maps, including 1:200,000 maps of Campania and Basilicata, Puglia, Calabria and Sicily.

Autostrade per l'Italia (www.autostrade.it) Information about Sicily's autostrade (motorways), including road closures, traffic conditions and toll-booth locations.

deteriorate, with impediments such as potholes and poor signage becoming more frequent.

Tolls

Tolls are commonly charged on motorways – pay at the booth when exiting. It's advisable to carry some small change with you, as a few booths are automated and will not accept credit cards. To calculate toll rates for your itinerary, log onto www.autostrade.it and click 'Traffico, percorsi e pedaggi'.

No Car?

Bus

Several regional bus companies offer service throughout southern Italy, including SITA, FlixBus, Interbus, SAIS, STP Brindisi and AST. Buses offer better service than trains on certain routes, including Palermo to Syracuse, Catania to Taormina and Trapani to Palermo. They also provide access to areas not serviced by rail, including the Amalfi Coast and a handful of towns in the Parco Nazionale del Pollino and Parco Nazionale dell'Aspromonte.

Train

Southern Italy's rail network, operated mainly by Trenitalia (www.trenitalia.com), is less extensive and less efficient than in the north. That said, it does offer an enjoyable, practical alternative to driving, especially along the main routes that connect cities like Naples and Reggio Calabria, Bari and Taranto, as well as Palermo and Catania. Other key destinations easily reached by train include the Valle d'Itria, Lecce, Tropea, Syracuse, Noto, Modica and Ragusa.

Boat

Frequent ferries and hydrofoils run year-round to the Bay of Naples islands, with seasonal services along the Amalfi Coast. Year-round services reach Sicily's offshore islands and the Isole Tremiti off Puglia.

Key mainland ports include Naples for Capri, Ischia and Procida, Sorrento and Salerno for the Amalfi Coast, and Termoli for the Isole Tremiti. Notable ports in Sicily include Milazzo for the Aeolian Islands, Palermo for Ustica, Trapani for Pantelleria and the Egadi Islands, and Porto Empedocle for Lampedusa and the Pelagic Islands.

Air

Regularly scheduled commercial air travel within southern Italy is limited. Convenient routes include Naples to Palermo and Catania, as well as Palermo, Catania and Trapani to Pantelleria and Lampedusa.

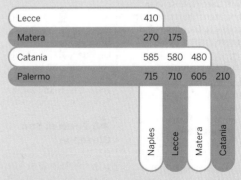

DRIVING FAST FACTS

➡ Drive on the right.

➡ All vehicle occupants must wear a seatbelt.

➡ Minimum age for a full licence is 18 years.

➡ Maximum speed 130 km/h on autostrade (motorways), 90km/h on secondary highways, 50km/h in built-up areas.

➡ Blood alcohol limit 50mg per 100ml (0.05%).

Road Distances (in kilometres)

	Naples	Lecce	Matera	Catania
Lecce	410			
Matera	270	175		
Catania	585	580	480	
Palermo	715	710	605	210

Month by Month

TOP EVENTS

Settimana Santa, March/April

Maggio dei Monumenti, May

Ravello Festival, July & August

Festival della Valle d'Itria, July & August

La Notte della Taranta, August

February

Short and accursed is how Italians describe February. It might still be chilly down south, but almond trees start to blossom and Carnevale season brightens things up with confetti, costumes and sugar-dusted treats.

🎭 Carnevale

In the period leading up to Ash Wednesday, many southern towns stage pre-Lenten carnivals. One of the most flamboyant is the Carnevale di Acireale (www.carnevaleacireale. it), the elaborate and whimsical floats of which are famous throughout the country.

March

Sunny, rainy and windy all at once, March's capricious weather lends it the local nickname *Marzo pazzo* (Crazy March). While spring officially starts on 21 March, the main holiday season kicks off with Easter week.

🎭 Settimana Santa

Processions and passion plays mark Easter Holy Week across the south. Notable processions take place in Procida (Campania), Sorrento (p106; Campania), Taranto (Puglia) and Trapani (Sicily). Processions and Passion plays mark Easter Holy Week across the south. On Good Friday and the Thursday preceding it, hooded penitents walk through Sorrento (p106). On Procida, Good Friday sees wooden statues and life-size tableaux carted across the island for the Procession of the Misteri.

🎭 Festa di San Giuseppe

On the weekend before or after the Feast of St Joseph (March 19), Scicli (p248) commemorates the biblical flight into Egypt with a colourful two-day festival. On the Saturday, locals dressed as medieval farmers ride horses adorned with spectacular floral mantles.

May

The month of roses and early summer produce, May is the perfect time to travel, especially for walkers. The weather is warm but not too hot, and prices remain good value across the south.

☆ Ciclo di Rappresentazioni Classiche

Ancient intrigue in an evocative Sicilian setting, the Festival of Greek Theatre (www. indafondazione.org) brings Syracuse's 5th-century-BC amphitheatre to life with performances from Italy's acting greats. The season runs from early May to early July.

☆ Maggio dei Monumenti

As the weather warms up, Naples rolls out a mammoth, month-long program of art exhibitions, concerts, performances and tours around the city (p84). Many historical and architectural treasures

usually off-limits to the public are open and free to visit.

June

The temperature cranks up quickly, beach *lidi* open in earnest and some of the big summer festivals commence. Adding to the celebratory vibe is a national holiday on 2 June, the Anniversary of the Republic.

☆ Napoli Teatro Festival Italia

From early June to mid-July, Naples celebrates all things performance, with theatre, dance and literary events (p84; www.napoliteatrofestival.it) staged in conventional and unconventional venues across town. Works range from the classic to the contemporary, both Italian and international.

☆ Taormina Arte

Opera, dance, theatre and live-music performances are staged at Taormina's panoramic Teatro Greco from June to September, with big-name performers from all over the world (p225; www.taoarte.it).

July

School is out and urban Italians everywhere are heading to the mountains or beaches for their summer holidays. Prices and temperatures rise, the beach is in full swing, but numerous cities host summer art festivals.

Top: Sagra della Madonna della Bruna (p175), Matera

Bottom: Carnevale di Acireale

✨ Sagra della Madonna della Bruna

A week-long celebration (p175) of Matera's patron saint that culminates on 2 July with a colourful procession that sees the Madonna della Bruna escorted around town in a papier-mâché-adorned chariot. The chariot is ultimately torn to pieces by the crowd, who take home the scraps as souvenirs.

☆ Ravello Festival

Perched high above the Amalfi Coast, Ravello draws world-renowned artists during its eponymous festival (p130; www.ravellofestival.com), which runs in July and August and covers everything from music and dance to film and art exhibitions. Several events take place in the beautiful gardens of Villa Rufolo.

☆ Festival della Valle d'Itria

From mid-July to early August, the town of Martina Franca sets toes a-tapping with its esteemed music festival (p156; www.festivaldellavalleditria.it). The focus is on musical theatre, especially opera, though concertos and other recitals also abound.

August

August is hot, expensive and crowded. Everyone is on holiday, and while it may no longer be true that everything is shut,

Top: Sicilian cous cous

Bottom: Nativity scene, Naples

many businesses and restaurants do close for part of the month.

🎭 La Notte della Taranta

Puglia celebrates its hypnotic *pizzica* dance with the Night of the Taranta (www. lanottedellataranta.it), a festival held in and around the Puglian town of Melpignano. Dancing aside, the event also showcases Salento's folk-music traditions.

📅 Ferragosto

After Christmas and Easter, Ferragosto is Italy's biggest holiday. While it now marks the Feast of the Assumption, even the ancient Romans honoured their pagan gods on Feriae Augusti. Naples lets loose with particular fervour.

September

This is a glorious month in the south. As summer wanes into autumn, the grape harvest begins. Adding to the culinary excitement are the many local *sagre* (food festivals), celebrating regional produce and traditions.

🍴 Cous Cous Fest

The Sicilian town of St Vito celebrates multiculturalism and its famous

fish couscous at this 10-day event in mid- to late September (www. couscousfest.it). Highlights include an international couscous cook-off, tastings and live world-music gigs.

October

Businesses in the outer islands and mainland coastal resorts begin to curtail services. Meanwhile, the chestnut harvest and wild mushroom seasons begin in earnest in the mountains.

🎭 Scale del Gusto

For three days in October, Ragusa's squares, streets and Unesco-listed buildings not usually open to the public become evocative settings for this buzzing celebration (p250; www.scaledelgusto. it) of Sicilian food and artisan food producers. The programme includes masterclasses, pop-up restaurants, music and art.

☆ Le Vie dei Tesori

During this eight-week, island-wide 'Open House' (www.leviedeitesori.com/ festival-le-vie-dei-tesori) – lasting from mid-September to early November – a vast array of venues open their doors to celebrate Sicily's cultural heritage.

November

The advent of winter creeps down the peninsula in November, but there's plenty going on. This is the time for the chestnut harvest, mushroom picking and All Saints' Day.

📅 Ognissanti

Celebrated all over Italy as a national holiday, All Saints' Day on 1 November commemorates the Saint Martyrs, while All Souls' Day, on 2 November, is set aside to honour the deceased.

December

The days of alfresco living are at an end. Yet, despite the cooler days and longer nights, looming Christmas festivities warm things up with festive street lights, nativity scenes and Yuletide specialities.

🎭 Natale

The weeks preceding Christmas are studded with religious events. Many churches set up nativity scenes known as *presepe*. While Naples is especially famous for these, you'll find impressive tableaux in many southern towns, including Erice in Sicily.

GLENN VAN DER KNIJFF/GETTY IMAGES ©

Plan Your Trip
Itineraries

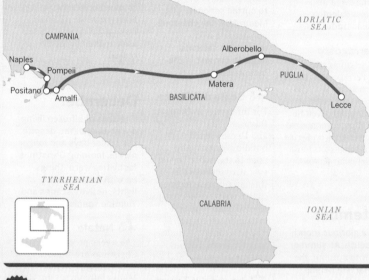

ADRIATIC
SEA

CAMPANIA

Alberobello

Naples

Pompeii

PUGLIA

Positano

Matera

Amalfi

BASILICATA

Lecce

TYRRHENIAN
SEA

CALABRIA

IONIAN
SEA

10 DAYS Southern Highlights

An easy introduction to some of southern Italy's must-see wonders, this 10-day overview covers everything from cosmopolitan city culture to ancient ruins, superlative coastal scenery and World Heritage–listed architecture.

Pique your appetite with two heady days in **Naples**, an urban wild child bursting with glorious art, architecture, street life and flavours. You'll be kept busy exploring its bounty of cultural treasures, which include Caravaggio masterpieces at Pio Monte della Misericordia, Palazzo di Capodimonte

and the Galleria d'Italia – Palazzo Zevallos Stigliano, as well as stirring baroque frescoes in churches such as the Duomo and Chiesa del Gesù Nuovo. The city's Cappella Sansevero is home to the *Cristo velato* (Veiled Christ), widely considered one of Italy's finest sculptures.

Spend day three roaming the time-warped ruins of **Pompeii**, among them communal baths, private residences, shops and even a brothel etched with ancient graffiti. Leap back into the present and continue to **Positano**, the Amalfi Coast's undisputed pinup town. Lap up two days

Cattedrale di Sant'Andrea (p127), Amalfi

here, hiring a boat for a spot of coastal cruising or hiking the breathtaking Sentiero degli Dei (Path of the Gods).

On day six, continue east along the Amalfi Coast, stopping briefly in atmospheric **Amalfi** to view its iconic Sicilian Arab–Norman cathedral, the oldest part dating from the early 10th century. Continue on your way to the city of **Matera** in time for dinner, then spend the following day exploring its one-of-a-kind, Unesco–lauded *sassi* (former cave dwellings). Swap *sassi* for World Heritage-listed *trulli* (conical-roofed abodes) in **Alberobello** the following day. Late evening is the best time to experience the town's historic Rione Monti quarter, home to more than 1000 *trulli*. Spend the night, then hit the road one last time to the university city of **Lecce**, dubbed the 'Florence of the South'. It's quixotic baroque buildings make for an extravagant epilogue to your southern overview.

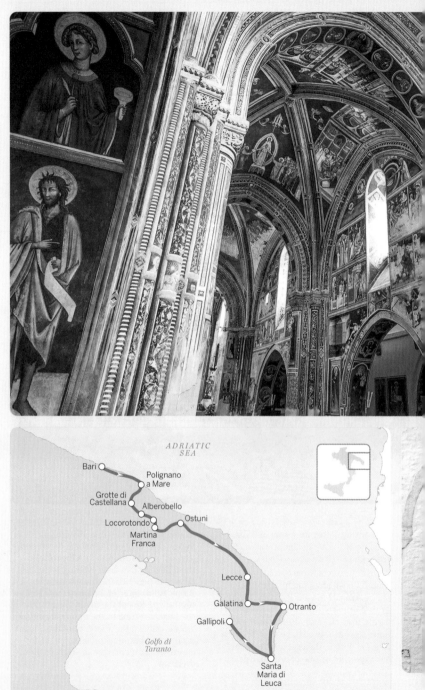

ADRIATIC SEA

Bari
Polignano a Mare
Grotte di Castellana
Alberobello
Locorotondo
Martina Franca
Ostuni
Lecce
Galatina
Otranto
Gallipoli
Golfo di Taranto
Santa Maria di Leuca

Perfect Puglia

Puglia is one of Italy's most seductive regions, its abundance of history and one-of-a-kind architecture melded with an enviable coastline and one of Italy's simplest, healthiest cuisines.

Start your explorations in dynamic **Bari**, roaming its ancient historic centre and huge Romanesque basilica; the latter is a pilgrimage site for both Catholic and Orthodox Christians. Strike out south, via **Polignano a Mare**, to the jaw-dropping limestone **Grotte di Castellana**. Italy's longest network of subterranean caves, its most famous feature is the Grotta Bianca (White Grotto), Mother Nature's alabaster take on Gothic architecture.

From here, a two- to three-day drive south will take you through some of the finest towns in the celebrated Valle d'Itria. Among these is **Alberobello**, with its hobbit-like, World Heritage–listed *trulli*, wine-producing **Locorotondo**, beautiful baroque **Martina Franca** and chic, whitewashed **Ostuni**, the latter home to some particularly outstanding restaurants.

Next up is inimitable **Lecce**, dubbed the 'Florence of the South' for its operatic architectural ensembles and scholarly bent. Hire a bike and spend at least three or four days exploring its wealth of cultural assets. Among these is the obsessively detailed Basilica di Santa Croce and the Museo Faggiano, the latter a veritable layer cake of archaeology stretching back to the 5th century BC.

From Lecce, move on to **Galatina**, its 14th-century basilica awash with astounding frescoes. Head east to the fortified port of **Otranto**, whose own 11th-century cathedral stands out for its extraordinary 12th-century floor mosaic. If the weather is warm, enjoy a little downtime on the inviting beaches of the Baia dei Turchi, then push south along the wild, vertiginous coastline to **Santa Maria di Leuca**, the very tip of the Italian stiletto. Finally, conclude your adventure in the walled island city of **Gallipoli**, feasting on raw sea urchin and octopus in its elegant town centre.

Top: Basilica di Santa Caterina d'Alessandria (p167), Galatina

Bottom: Locorotondo (p155)

Sicily to Calabria

15 DAYS

Ancient cultures and natural beauty collide in this two-week adventure. From Greek temples and Norman cathedrals to rugged mountains and coveted coastal resorts, strike out on a gripping journey through Italy's southern extremes.

Fly into **Palermo** and take two days to savour the city's cross-cultural food, markets and architecture. Soak up the glittering, 12th-century Cappella Palatina, snoop around the revamped archaeological museum, and detour to nearby **Monreale** to marvel at its mosaic-encrusted Norman cathedral. On day three, day trip west to the 5th-century-BC ruins of **Segesta**, one of Italy's most remarkable ancient sites.

From Palermo, head east to eye-candy **Cefalù** on day four. Spend a night – just enough time to admire its commanding Arab–Norman cathedral and crystalline sea. Come day five, shoot through to **Taormina**, a long-time haunt of poets, painters and hopeless romantics. The town was once Sicily's Byzantine capital and its sweeping ancient Greek theatre is the island's second largest. Allow two nights and consider hiking up nearby **Mt Etna** on one of your days.

Day seven sees you catching a ferry from Messina to **Reggio Calabria** in time to see the *Bronzi di Riace* at the Museo Nazionale di Reggio Calabria. The finest examples of ancient Greek sculpture in existence, the bronze sculptures are southern Italy's answer to Florence's *David*. Rest your head in tiny Gambarie, using the town as your base as you explore the wild beauty of the **Parco Nazionale dell'Aspromonte** over the next two days.

Come day 10, head back down to the Tyrrhenian coast. Lunch on fresh swordfish in castle-capped **Scilla**, continuing through to dazzling **Tropea**, Calabria's coastal darling. Spend two nights recharging your weary bones, lazily ambling its labyrinthine streets and catching some of the south's finest sunsets. Restored, continue north to the gritty yet erudite city of **Cosenza** on day 12. After taking in its impressively preserved medieval core on day 13, hit Camigliatello Silano for two nights, concluding your adventure with soul-lifting hikes through the alpine beauty of the **Parco Nazionale della Sila**.

Top: Cefalù (p214)
Bottom: *Stigghiola* (stuffed goat's intestines)

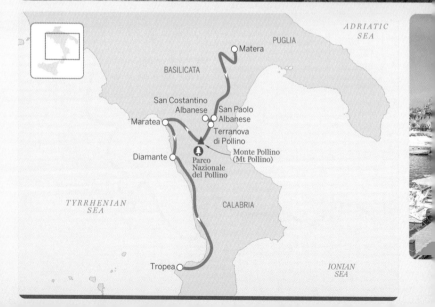

Matera

PUGLIA

ADRIATIC SEA

BASILICATA

San Costantino
Albanese

San Paolo
Albanese

Maratea

Terranova
di Pollino

Monte Pollino
(Mt Pollino)

Diamante

Parco
Nazionale
del Pollino

*TYRRHENIAN
SEA*

CALABRIA

Tropea

*IONIAN
SEA*

9 DAYS The Deep South

This itinerary touches some of the deepest, rawest, most surreal corners of the south, from a cave-studded city to rare Albanian mountain villages. Add a dose of sparkling Tyrrhenian blue and you have a journey guaranteed to get under your skin.

Start this soulful journey in the cave city of **Matera**, one of Europe's most unusual settlements. Spend a couple of days exploring its famous *sassi*, as well as the *chiese rupestri* (cave churches) on a hike along the Gravina. The dynamic Casa Noha museum offers valuable insight into both the *sassi* and the city's poverty-stricken past.

From Matera, escape south to the **Parco Nazionale del Pollino** for an invigorating fix of nature. Base yourself in **Terranova di Pollino** for four days, hiking through pine woods and beech forest to Basilicata's highest peak, Monte Pollino. Spanning alpine meadows and deep river canyons, the national park harbours rare stocks of roe deer, wild cats, wolves and birds of prey, among them the Egyptian vulture. It's also home to the curious Albanian villages of **San Paolo Albanese** and **San Costantino Albanese**, where you may just find yourself dancing to the *zampogne* (double-chantered pipes). Another of the park's unexpected treasures is the rare Bosnian pine tree, *pino loricato*.

Lungs filled with mountain air, it's time to head west to the gorgeous coastal jewel of **Maratea**. Pass a couple of days relaxing in the town's crystalline Tyrrhenian waters and sailing to nearby grottoes and coves. Back in town, kick back at local bars and feast on fresh seafood. Recharged, it's time to head south to Calabria on the SS18 coastal road. If it's September, you might catch a chilli-eating competition in **Diamante**. Otherwise, keep moving until you reach Calabria's most arresting coastal town, **Tropea**. An ancient settlement whose past rulers have included Arabs, Normans, Swabians and Anjous, its piercing views and sunsets make for a beautiful, soul-soothing wrap-up.

Top: The *sassi* (p171), Matera
Bottom: Maratea (p178)

The Grand Tour

3 WEEKS

Covering Campania, Basilicata, Calabria and Sicily, this three-week trip is rich in both blockbuster sights and off-the-beaten-track highlights.

Commence with three days in **Naples**, roaming its secret catacombs, baroque churches and palatial Museo di Capodimonte, one of Italy's great art galleries. Take an easy day trip to the formidable royal palace of **Caserta** or to the ill-fated ancient towns of **Pompeii** or **Herculaneum**. Whichever you choose, treat yourself to two romantic days on **Capri**, making time for quiet hikes, the spectacular Grotta Azzurra and the unforgettable views from atop Monte Solaro. Sail across to **Sorrento** for a night, then hit the fabled Amalfi Coast on day six, allowing two days in see-and-be-seen **Positano** and a further night in **Amalfi** or hilltop **Ravello**. Travel back in time roaming millennia-old Greek temples in **Paestum** on day nine before continuing to fellow World Heritage marvel **Matera** and its otherworldly abodes.

Come day 12, it's time to escape to the wilds of the **Parco Nazionale del Pollino**. With Terranova di Pollino as your base, spend three days hiking through invigorating woods and exploring the curious Albanian villages of San Paolo Albanese and San Costantino Albanese. Both towns were founded in the 16th century by ethnic Albanian refugees (*Arbëreshë*) who left Koroni in Greece during its Ottoman occupation.

Slide down to Calabria's Tyrrhenian coastline on day 15, home to seaside show-off **Tropea**. Allow two nights of waterside *dolce vita* (sweet life) before catching a ferry from Villa San Giovanni to Sicily on day 17. Allow yourself another two days of coastal slumming in chi-chi **Taormina**, home to a 3rd-century-BC theatre and a world-class summertime arts festival. If you can pull yourself away on day 19, wrap things up with a couple of days exploring **Syracuse**, described by Roman philosopher Cicero as the 'greatest Greek city and the most beautiful of them all'. Its Hellenic past lives on at the Parco Archeologico della Neapolis, considered to be one of Sicily's most important archaeological sites.

Top: Tropea (p193)
Bottom: Tempio di Cerere, Paestum (p134)

Caserta
Naples
Herculaneum
Pompeii
Ravello/Amalfi
Positano
Sorrento
Capri
Paestum
PUGLIA
Matera
ADRIATIC SEA
BASILICATA
Parco Nazionale del Pollino
TYRRHENIAN SEA
CALABRIA
Aeolian Islands
Tropea
IONIAN SEA
Mt Etna
Taormina
SICILY
Syracuse

Parco Nazionale dell'Aspromonte (p189)

Plan Your Trip

Activities

Southern Italy lays claim to some of the country's most dramatic, breathtaking terrain. For active types, this means endless possibilities for high-octane adventure and blissful relaxation. Whatever you're itching for – be it a dive off the Amalfi Coast, a hike in the wilds of Calabria's Parco Nazionale del Pollino or a muscle-soothing soak on a volcanic Aeolian beach – the Mezzogiorno delivers.

Best Activities

ANTONIO ARICO/SHUTTERSTOCK ©

Diving & Snorkelling

Witness the underwater wonders of Lipari, Filicudi, Ustica or Isola Bella in Sicily.

Sailing Trips

Explore the coves and grottoes of Campania's Amalfi Coast and Bay of Naples islands, Puglia's Promontorio del Gargano or Sicily's Riserva Naturale dello Zingaro.

Hiking

Climb into the Madonie mountains above Cefalù, lose yourself in the rugged peaks of Calabria, or view the fabled Amalfi Coast from mountain paths.

Rafting & Kayaking

Ride wild rapids in Calabria's Parco Nazionale del Pollino or soften the pace with an urban kayaking trip along the Neapolitan coastline.

Thermal Therapy

De-stress in natural hot springs on the Campanian island of Ischia or wallow in therapeutic mud on the Aeolian island of Vulcano.

Volcano Viewing

Watch Stromboli's nocturnal fireworks from the summit or a boat, or teeter on the edges of Etna or Vesuvius.

Hiking & Walking

The south's attention-grabbing scenery makes for some unforgettable hikes. For spectacular sea views in Campania, hit the Amalfi Coast (p121) and Sorrento Peninsula, where age-old paths such as the Sentiero degli Dei (Path of the Gods) disappear into wooded mountains and ancient lemon groves.

To the surprise of many, both Capri (p109) and Ischia (p115) offer some spectacular walks that will see you enjoying the islands away from the crowds. Delightful though precipitous trails lead you out of

Capri Town to a Roman villa and a natural rock arch, or for a more arduous route you can follow a chain of forts and take in the western coast.

Southeast of the Amalfi Coast, the Parco Nazionale del Cilento, Vallo di Diano e Alburni (p135) serves up relaxing walks and more challenging hikes, reliable guides and excellent maps. This remarkable wilderness area is home to around 3000 registered botanical species, as well as a number of rare birds, including the golden eagle and seacrow.

The park's most famous feature, however, is an incredible series of caves. Among these are the Grotte di Castelcivita (p135) and Grotte di Pertosa-Auletta (p136), their Gothic-like stalagmites and stalactites yours to explore on regular speleological tours.

Crossing the border between Calabria and Basilicata is the Parco Nazionale del Pollino (p184), Italy's largest national park. Claiming the richest repository of flora and fauna in the south, its varied landscapes range from deep river canyons to alpine meadows. Calabria's other national parks – the Sila (p185) and Aspromonte (p188) – offer similarly dramatic hiking, particularly the area around Sersale in the Sila, studded with waterfalls and the possibility of trekking through the Valli Cupe canyon.

Close to the heel of the stiletto in the sun-baked region of Puglia, the Parco della Murgia Materana, part of the Matera (p171) Unesco World Heritage site, is full of fascinating cave churches and is great for birdwatching.

With its unique and varied topography, Sicily provides unforgettable walking opportunities. Take your pick of volcano hikes in Sicily; the mother of them all is Mt Etna (p234), but there's a whole host of lesser volcanoes on the Aeolian Islands, from the slumbering Vulcano (p219), where you can descend to the crater floor, to a three-hour climb to the summit of Stromboli (p222) to see it exploding against the night sky. On Salina you can clamber up extinct volcano Monte Fossa delle Felci (p221) for staggering views of symmetrically aligned volcanic peaks. From Etna you can also trek across into the Parco Naturale Regionale delle Madonie (p215) or on Sicily's northwestern coast you can track the shoreline in the Riserva Naturale

ZIP-LINE FLIGHTS

How do angels fly? At the speed of light, apparently. Il Volo dell'Angelo (Flight of the Angel; p177) in Basilicata is one of the world's longest (1452m) and fastest (120km/h) zip lines, racing you between two villages: Castelmezzano and Pietrapertosa! If you want to amp up the adventure, this is the ultimate high-wire thrill.

dello Zingaro (p261). Tour agency **Sicilian Experience** (www.sicilianexperience.com) offers a number of guided and self-guided walking tours on the island, including from the Madonie mountains down to the coastal town of Cefalù.

Italian Parks (www.parks.it) lists walking trails through each of southern Italy's national parks, and provides updates on its marine parks and other protected areas. Italy's major walking club, the Club Alpino Italiano (www.cai.it), lists a handful of mountain huts found in southern Italy on its website – follow the *rifugi e bivacchi* link and click on the specific region you plan on visiting. Members of organisations such as the New Zealand Alpine Club, Fédération française des clubs alpins et de montagne and Deutscher Alpenverein can enjoy discounted rates for accommodation and meals. Also note that backcountry or wild camping is not permitted in Italy; if you want to pitch a tent, you'll have to do so at a private campsite.

For detailed information on hiking routes in Sicily and on Campania's Amalfi Coast and Bay of Naples islands, check out the reliable Cicerone (www.cicerone.co.uk) series of walking guides.

Diving & Snorkelling

Sparkling waters make diving and snorkelling popular activities on southern coasts, especially from May to October. Just off Campania's Sorrento Peninsula, Punta Campanella is an 11-sq-km marine reserve well known for its underwater grottoes and abundant sea life.

Across the Tyrrhenian Sea, divers from around the world head to the offshore Sicilian island of Ustica (p208) to explore its magnificent underwater sites. The island's western shores are home to a protected marine reserve that is divided into three zones. Highlights include the underwater archaeological trail off Punta Cavazzi, where artefacts including anchors and Roman amphorae can be admired. Other popular dive sites are the Scoglio del Medico, an outcrop of basalt riddled with caves and gorges that plunge to great depths; and Secca di Colombara, a magnificent rainbow-coloured display of sponges and gorgonias.

There are good dives off most of the Aeolians, with some of the best surrounding the main island of Lipari (p216). Seasonal diving operators can be found across the Aeolian islands.

West of Palermo, the Riserva Naturale dello Zingaro (p261) is also great for diving. **Cetaria Diving Centre** (www.cetaria.it) in Scopello organises guided dives in the waters off the nature reserve between April and October, visiting underwater caves and shipwrecks; it also offers boat excursions with snorkelling.

Near Taormina, the WWF-protected reserve of Isola Bella (p225) also has some good diving. Here, **Nike Diving Centre** (www.diveniketaormina.com) offers a range of diving and snorkelling packages, as well as kayak and stand-up paddleboard hire.

Sailing

Southern Italy has a proud maritime tradition and you can hire a paddle boat or sleek yacht across its coasts. Sailors of all levels are catered for: experienced skippers can island-hop around Sicily or along the Amalfi Coast on chartered yachts, while weekend boaters can explore hidden coves in rented dinghies, for which you need no experience – though be sure you understand the instructions before you set off!

On the Amalfi Coast (p121), prime swimming spots are often only accessible by boat. It's a similar story on the islands of Capri (p109), Ischia (p115) and Procida (p119).

In Puglia, the Promontorio del Gargano (p148) is studded with beautiful

Top: Il Volo dell'Angelo, Pietrapertosa (p177)

Bottom: Marina Corricella, Procida (p118)

BEST BEACHES

Scala dei Turchi (p258) A dazzling white outcropping shaped like a staircase, with beaches on either side, perfect for wading or diving off the rocks.

Torre Salsa (p258) Perfect for fans of wild, unspoiled coastline, this off-the-beaten-track gem is part of a WWF-administered nature reserve.

Spiaggia di Cefalù (p214) A lovely, family-friendly expanse of sand backed by a dramatic promontory and one of Sicily's prettiest medieval towns.

Spiaggia Valle Muria (p216) Fabulously far from civilisation, save for its cavelike beachside bar, this cliff-backed beach is one of the Aeolians' finest.

Spiaggia dei Faraglioni (p261) Scopello's rough-pebbled beach has shimmering turquoise waters backed by towering rock formations.

Isola Bella (p225) Facing the island preserve of the same name, this pebbly beach below Taormina is tucked into a supremely picturesque cove.

Baia di Sorgeto (p115) Catch a water taxi to this toasty thermal beach on Ischia.

coastal grottoes. The promontory's sea-side town of Vieste is home to numerous boat operators offering seasonal tours of the coast's caves and striking rock formations.

Boat trips of all kinds can be organised along Sicily's coast and in the outer islands. San Vito Lo Capo–based Buena Vida (www.buenavida.it) runs sailing and other boat excursions to the Riserva Naturale dello Zingaro and the Egadi Islands. Off Sicily's northeastern coast, the cobalt waters of the Aeolian Islands (p216) are perfect for idle island-hopping.

Reputable yacht-charter companies that cover southern Italy include Bareboat Sailing Holidays (www.bareboatsailing holidays.com).

Rafting & Kayaking

One of the best spots for whitewater sports in the south is Calabria's Parco Nazionale del Pollino (p184). Here, the Lao river rapids provide exhilarating rafting, as well as canoeing and canyoning. Trips can be arranged in Scalea.

Across the sea, Sicily in Kayak (p220) offers kayaking tours around Vulcano and the other Aeolian islands, ranging from half a day to an entire week. It also offers sailing and stand-up paddleboarding excursions.

A number of other operators on the Aeolians organise round-the-island and inter-island boat trips exploring the islands' sea grottoes and secluded swimming spots.

Back on the Italian mainland, **Kayak Napoli** (www.kayaknapoli.com) offers a refreshingly different take on Naples, with great kayaking tours of the Neapolitan coastline for all levels. The tours tick off usually inaccessible ruins, neoclassical villas, gardens and grottoes from the water. It also offers stand-up paddleboarding tours.

Rock Climbing

Arrampicata (climbing) is increasingly popular in Sicily. San Vito Lo Capo is the island's rock-climbing capital, luring climbers with its variety of challenging crags and the **San Vito Climbing Festival** (www.sanvitoclimbingfestival.it), a four-day event held in October or early November.

Other leading climbing destinations include Mt Etna, the limestone pinnacles of Rocche di Crasto in the Nebrodi Mountains, and multiple sites in the Madonie mountains including Monte D'Oro outside Collesano, La Rocca di Sciara near Caltavuturo, Rocca di Sant'Otiero near Petralia Sottana and Passo Scuro outside Castelbuono.

Horse Riding

Horse riding experiences are available across Italy's south. Horse Riding Tour Naples (p95) runs daily morning and afternoon horse-riding tours of the

Parco Nazionale del Vesuvio (weather permitting), offering a novel way to explore Italy's most infamous volcano. The Neapolitan outfit also offers transfers to and from Naples, Pompeii or Ercolano (Herculaneum), making the tours especially accessible for those without their own set of wheels.

Further south in Calabria, CST Tropea (p194) offers multilevel horseback excursions of the woods, meadows and olive groves to the east of Tropea. The tours include a small picnic, featuring fresh cheese, bread and other local edibles. Across the border in Basilicata, hotspot destination Matera is where you'll find the suitably named horseback-riding outfit Eldorado Ranch (p174), which runs memorable gallops through the Gravina gorge or Cripta del Peccato Originale, the latter dubbed the 'Sistine Chapel' of Matera's churches for its remarkable 8th-century frescoes.

Tour operators aside, numerous *agriturismi* (farm stays) across the southern regions offer horseback adventures for those seeking a unique way to experience the Mezzogiorno's bucolic landscapes.

Ischia (p115)

Birdwatching

Given its prime position on the migratory flight path between Africa and Europe, Sicily is a great place for birdwatching. April and September are the best months. Hotspots include the following:

Riserva Naturale dello Zingaro (p261) A nature reserve with over 40 species, including the rare Bonelli eagle, hawks, buzzards, kestrels, swifts and Imperial crows, as well as the 'Greek partridge of Sicily'.

Riserva Naturale di Vendicari (☑0931 46 88 79; www.riserva-vendicari.it; ☷7am-8pm Apr-Oct, to 5pm Nov-Mar) **FREE** A short drive south of Noto, these wetlands are home to flamingos, herons, spoonbills, cranes, ducks, cormorants and collared pratincoles.

Lingua Salina's lagoon attracts huge numbers of birds in April; scores of Eleonora's falcons *(Falco eleonorae)* return to nest here.

Companies offering birdwatching tours in Sicily include UK-based **Nature Trek** (www.naturetrek.co.uk) and **Limosa Holidays** (www.limosaholidays.co.uk).

Spas

The upside of southern Italy's volcanic activity is a string of natural spa experiences. In Campania, the verdant island of Ischia (p115) is considered one of the world's richest hydrothermal areas. Its spas include Negombo (p116), which combines lush botanical gardens with over a dozen mineral pools and a private beach. On Ischia's southern side, warm thermal waters at Baia di Sorgeto (p116) make a soak in the sea toasty at any time of the year.

Neapolitan *casatiello* (bread stuffed with salami, pancetta and hard cheeses)

Plan Your Trip

Eat & Drink Like a Local

Italy is a gastronomic powerhouse, and the country's south claims many of its most venerated exports, from Gragnano pasta and San Marzano tomatoes to buffalo mozzarella and cannoli (pastry shells with a sweet filling of ricotta or custard). Here, businesses still close for lunch and Sunday pranzo (lunch) remains a long, sacred family affair. Famished? You've come to the right place.

The Year in Food

While *sagre* (local food festivals) go into overdrive in autumn, there's never a bad time to raise your fork in southern Italy.

Spring (Mar–May)

Come for asparagus, artichokes and Easter specialities like Naples' *casatiello:* rustic-style bread stuffed with Neapolitan salami, pancetta and hard cheeses.

Summer (Jun–Aug)

Aubergines, peppers, berries and fresh seafood by the sea. Beat the heat with Sicilian *granite* (ices made with coffee, fresh fruit, pistachios or almonds).

Autumn (Sep–Nov)

Hearty chestnuts, mushrooms and game. In September, celebrate fish couscous at San Vito's famous Cous Cous Fest.

Winter (Dec–Feb)

Time for festive treats like Campania's *raffioli* (sponge and marzipan biscuits) and Sicily's *cobaita* (hard, sesame-seed confectionery).

Food Experiences

So much produce, so many specialities, so little time! Fine-tune your culinary radar with the following edible musts.

Meals of a Lifetime

Accursio, Modica (p248) Show-stopping, Michelin-starred Sicilian in an intimate setting in Modica.

Il Frantoio, Ostuni (p158) Legendary eight-course lunches at an olive grove-fringed Puglian *masseria* (working farm).

Il Focolare, Ischia (p117) A carnivorous, Slow Food stalwart, especially famous for its *coniglio all'ischitana* (Ischian-style rabbit).

President, Pompeii (p104) Playful, Michelin-acclaimed reinterpretations of Campanian cuisine.

Vitoantonio Lombardo, Matera (p176) Thrilling, contemporary flavours in one of the world's oldest settlements.

La Bettolaccia, Trapani (p260) Serving western Sicily's famous fish couscous and other Slow Food classics.

Al Trabucco da Mimì, Peschici (p152) Sterling seafood and a spectacular clifftop setting on Puglia's Promontorio del Gargano.

Nangalarruni, Castelbuono (p215) Mountain mushrooms form the menu's backbone at this intimate dining room in Sicily's Madonie mountains.

Cheap Treats

Arancini Deep-fried Sicilian rice balls stuffed with *ragù* (meat sauce), tomato and vegetables.

Crocchè Deep-fried, mozzarella-filled potato croquettes.

Pizza fritta Neapolitan fried pizza dough stuffed with salami, dried lard cubes, smoked *provola* (provolone) cheese, ricotta and tomato.

Sgagliozze Deep-fried polenta cubes served street-side in Bari.

Pane e panelle Palermo chickpea fritters on a sesame roll.

Mozzarella di bufala Silky, snow-white mozzarella made with local buffalo milk.

Gelato The best Italian gelato uses seasonal ingredients and natural colours.

Dare to Try

Pani ca meusa A Palermo sandwich of beef spleen and lungs dipped in boiling lard.

Sanguinaccio Hearty pig's-blood sausage, particularly popular in Calabria and Basilicata.

Cavallo Puglia's Salento region is famous for its horse meat. Taste it in dishes like *pezzetti di cavallo* (horse-meat casserole with tomato, celery, carrot and bay leaf).

Stigghiola A classic Sicilian dish of grilled sheep's or goat's intestines stuffed with onions and parsley, and seasoned with salt or lemon.

Spaghetti ai ricci Pasta in an orange-tinted sauce made from the reproductive organs of sea urchins, especially popular in Sicily and Puglia.

'Mpanatigghiu A traditional Sicilian pastry from Modica, filled with minced meat, almonds and the town's famous chocolate.

Sfogliatella (sweetened ricotta pastry)

Local Specialities

The Italian term for civic pride is *campanilismo,* but a more accurate word would be *formaggismo:* loyalty to the local cheese. Clashes among medieval duchies and principalities involving castle sieges and boiling oil have been replaced by competition in speciality foods and wine. Keep reading for a gut-rumbling overview of the Mezzogiorno's culinary nuances.

Campania

In Naples, tuck into Italy's best pizza, a wood-fired masterpiece of thin charred crust and slightly chewy dough. According to the official, non-profit Associazione Verace Pizza Napoletana (Real Neapolitan Pizza Association), genuine Neapolitan pizza should be cooked at 485°C (905°F) in a double-domed, wood-fired oven using oak, ash, beech or maple timber. Its on-the-go sibling is the surprisingly light *pizza fritta:* fried pizza dough stuffed with salami, dried lard cubes, smoked *provola* cheese, ricotta and tomato.

Vegetarian decadence comes in the form of *parmigiana di melanzana* (fried aubergine layered with hard-boiled eggs, mozzarella, onion, tomato sauce and basil), while the city's signature *spaghetti alla puttanesca* (whore's spaghetti) blends tomatoes and black olives with capers, anchovies and (in some cases) a dash of red chilli. Altogether more virtuous is Campania's unique *friarielli,* a bitter vegetable similar to broccoli rabe, *saltata in padella* (pan-fried), spiked with *peperoncino* (red chilli) and often served with rustic *salsiccia di maiale* (pork sausage).

At the sweeter end of the spectrum are *sfogliatella* (sweetened ricotta-filled pastry), *babà* (rum-soaked sponge cake) and *pastiera* (latticed tart filled with ricotta, cream, candied fruits and cereals flavoured with orange-blossom water).

Caserta and the Cilento region produce Italy's finest *mozzarella di bufala* (buffalo mozzarella), made using the milk of locally reared black water buffaloes. While the mozzarella from both areas is superb, some aficionados argue that Paestum's version has a more delicate flavour than its rival from Caserta. Best eaten when freshly made that morning, its sweet flavour and luscious texture is nothing short of a revelation. And while its most common form is round and fresh, *mozzarella di bufala* also comes in a twisted, plait form *(treccia),* as well as smoked *(affumicata).* Its most decadent variation is *burrata,* a mozzarella filled with a wickedly buttery cream. Burrata itself was invented in the neighbouring region of Puglia; the swampy fields around Foggia are famed for their buffalo-milk goodness.

Cow's-milk mozzarella is a star ingredient in Capri's refreshing *insalata caprese* (mozzarella, tomato and basil salad). The neighbouring island of Ischia is famed for its succulent *coniglio all'ischitana,* claypot-cooked local rabbit with garlic, chilli, tomato, basil, thyme and white wine.

Sorrento serves up sizzling *gnocchi alla sorrentina* (oven-baked gnocchi drizzled

ANTONMARIA GALANTE/SHUTTERSTOCK ©

Parmigiana di melanzana (fried aubergine layered with parmesan, mozzarella, ham and tomato sauce)

with mozzarella and *parmigiano reggiano* cheese) and ricotta-stuffed cannelloni, while the Amalfi Coast is famous for two larder essentials: Cetara's *colatura di alici* (an intense anchovy essence) and Salerno's Colline Salernitane DOP olive oil.

Puglia, Basilicata & Calabria

The heartland of *cucina povera* (poor-man's cuisine), Italy's deep south delivers back-to-basics brilliance.

Carbolicious Puglian snacks include *puccia* (bread with olives) and ring-shaped *taralli* (pretzel-like biscuits), while bread-crumbs lace everything from *strascinati con la mollica* (pasta with breadcrumbs and anchovies) to *tiella di verdure* (baked vegetable casserole). Vegetables play a leading role in Puglian cuisine, with herbi-vorous classics including *maritata,* a dish of boiled chicory, escarole, celery and fennel layered alternatively with *pecorino* (sheep's-milk cheese) and pepper and cov-ered in broth.

Puglia's coastline delivers spiky *ricci di mare* (sea urchins), caught south of Bari in spring and autumn. They might be a challenge to crack open, but once you've

dipped your bread into the delicate, dark-red roe, chances are you'll be glad that you persisted. Easier to slurp are *zuppa di pesce* (fish soup), *riso cozze e patate* (baked rice, mussels and potatoes) and *polpo in umido* or *alla pignata* (steamed octopus teamed with garlic, onion, tomatoes, pars-ley, olive oil, black pepper, bay leaves and cinnamon).

Puglia is also southern Italy's *olio* (oil) heavyweight. The region produces around 40% of Italy's olive oil, much of it from Puglia's north. It's a fine match for the region's equally esteemed *pane* (bread). Its wood-fired variety is the stuff of legend, usually made from hard durum wheat (like pasta), with a russet-brown crust, an eggy-golden interior and a distinctively fine flavour. The best comes from Altamura, where it's thrice-risen, getting even better with time.

Basilicata and Calabria have a knack for salami and sausages – pigs here are prized and fed on natural foods such as acorns. Basilicata's *lucanica* or *lucanega* sausage is seasoned with fennel, pepper, *peperon-cino* and salt, and eaten fresh – roasted on a coal fire – or dried, or preserved in olive oil. The drooling continues with *soppressata,* the pork sausage from Rivello made from finely chopped pork grazed in pastures, dried and pressed and kept in extra-virgin olive oil, and *pezzenta* ('beggars' – probably a reference to their peasant origins), made from pork scraps and spicy Senise peppers. Across the border, the Calabrians turn pig's fat, organ meats and hot *peperoncino* into spicy, cured *'nduja,* a spreadable sausage.

In August, look out for red aubergines, unique to Rotonda and Basilicata but originally from Africa. Spicy and bitter, they're often dried, pickled or preserved in oil and served as antipasti. When autumn comes, the mountains yield delicious *funghi* (mushrooms) of all shapes and sizes. A favourite of the ancient Romans was the small, wild umbel oyster mushroom, eaten fried with garlic and parsley or accompanying lamb or vegetables. One of the best spots for a little mushroom hunting is Calabria's Parco Nazionale della Sila, which even hosts a *fungo*-focused *sagra* (local festival).

For a year-round treat, nibble on provolone, a semi-hard, wax-rind cheese. Though now commonly produced in the northern Italian regions of Lombardy and the Veneto, its roots lie firmly in Basilicata. Like mozzarella, the cheese is made using the *pasta filata* method, which sees the curd heated until it becomes stringy *(filata).* Aged two to three months, *provolone dolce* is milder and sweeter than the more piquant *provolone piccante,* which is aged for more than four months.

WHAT TO BOOK
•••••••••••••••••••••••••••••••••••••
Avoid disappointment with the following simple tips.

➡ Book high-end and popular restaurants, especially for Friday and Saturday evenings and Sunday lunch.

➡ In major tourist centres, always book restaurants in the summer high season and during Easter and Christmas.

➡ Book culinary and wine courses, such as Lecce's Awaiting Table (p160) and Matera's Cook'n Fun at Mary's (p174) at least a month or two in advance.

Sicily

Sicily's history as a cultural crossroads shines through its sweet and sour flavours. The Saracens brought the aubergine and spiced up dishes with saffron and sultanas. These ancient Arab and North African influences endure in western Sicily's fragrant fish couscous, as well as the island's spectacular sweets. Sink your teeth into *cannoli, cuccia* (grain, honey and ricotta cake), *malvasia e sesamini* (orange-scented sesame cookies with sweet Malvasia wine) and the queen of Sicilian desserts, the *cassata* (made with ricotta, sugar, vanilla, diced chocolate and candied fruits). Almonds are put to heavenly use in *pasta di mandorle* (almond cookies) and *frutti della Martorana,* marzipan sweets shaped to resemble fruits or vegetables. Both Arab and New World influences flavour Modica's famous chocolate, worked at low temperature using an ancient method to give it a distinctly grainy texture. Another Modican speciality worth seeking out is *pasta che paddunedda,* a comforting dish of veal meatballs and noodles in broth. The origins of ice cream lie in the Arab *sarbat* (sherbet), a concoction of sweet fruit syrups chilled with iced water, later developed into granita (where crushed ice was mixed with anything from fruit juice to coffee and almond milk) and *cremolata* (fruit syrups chilled with iced milk), the forerunner to gelato.

Sicily's Norman invaders live on in *pasta alla Norma* (pasta with basil, aubergine, ricotta and tomato), while the island's bountiful seafood shines in staples like *pasta con le sarde* (pasta with sardines, pine nuts, raisins and wild fennel), Palermo's *sarde a beccafico alla palermitana* (sardines stuffed with anchovies, pine nuts, currants and parsley) and Messina's *agghiotta di pesce spada* (swordfish flavoured with pine nuts, sultanas, garlic, basil and tomatoes). Swordfish also gets top billing in *involtini di pesce spada* (thinly sliced swordfish fillets rolled up and filled with breadcrumbs, tomatoes, olives and capers). The finest capers hail from the island of Pantelleria, while the most prestigious pistachios are grown around Bronte, a town just west of Mt Etna.

Then there are Sicily's finger-licking *buffitieri* (hot street snacks), among them *sfincione* (spongy, oily pizza made with *caciocavallo* cheese, tomatoes, onions and

Top: *Sfincione* (a type of Sicilian pizza)

Bottom: Pasta with sardines

occasionally anchovies) and Palermo's *pane e panelle* (fried chickpea-flour fritters, often served in a roll). Other doughy morsels include *calzone* (a pocket of pizza-like dough baked with ham, cheese or other stuffings), *impanata* (bread-dough snacks stuffed with meat, vegetables or cheese) and *scaccie* (discs of bread dough spread with a filling and rolled up into a crêpe). Queen of the street scene, however, is the ubiquitous *arancino* (rice ball stuffed with meat or cheese, coated with breadcrumbs and fried).

Southern Wines

Winemaking in the south dates back to the Phoenicians. The Greeks introduced Campania to its now-famous Greco (Greek) grape, and dubbed the south 'Enotria' (Wineland).

Campania

Lauded producers such as Feudi di San Gregorio, Mastroberardino, Villa Matilde, Pietracupa and Terredora have returned to their roots, cultivating ancient grape varieties like the red Aglianico (thought to be the oldest cultivated grape in Italy) and the whites Falanghina, Fiano and Greco (all growing long before Mt Vesuvius erupted in AD 79). Keeping them company is a growing list of reputable organic, biodynamic and low-intervention wineries, among them I Cacciagalli, Cantina Giardino, Casebianche,

Cautiero, Il Cancelliere and Pierluigi Zampaglione (Il Don Chisciotte).

Taurasi, a full-bodied Aglianico wine, sometimes known as the Barolo of the south, is one of southern Italy's finest labels. One of only four in the region to carry Italy's top quality rating, DOCG (Denominazione di Origine Controllata e Garantita; Controlled and Guaranteed Denomination of Origin), it goes perfectly with barbecued and boiled meats. The other three wines to share this honour are Aglianico del Taburno, a full-bodied red from the Benevento area, as well as Fiano di Avellino and Greco di Tufo, both whites and both from the Avellino area.

Other *vino*-producing areas include Ischia, whose wines were the first to receive DOC (Denominazione di Origine Controllata) status, the Campi Flegrei (home to DOC-labelled Piedirosso and Falanghina vines) and the Cilento region, home to the DOC Cilento bianco (Cilento white) and to the Aglianico Paestum. Mt Vesuvius' most famous drop is the Lacryma Christi (Tears of Christ), a blend of locally grown Falanghina, Piedirosso and Coda di Volpe grapes.

Puglia & Basilicata

The different characteristics of these regions' wines reflect their diverse topography and terroir. In Puglia there are vast, flat acreages of vineyards, while Basilicata's vineyards tend to be steep and volcanic.

It's the Pugliese reds that gain most plaudits. The main grapes grown are the

---

THE CULT OF CAFFÈ

According to the Neapolitans, it's the local water that makes their coffee stronger and better than any other in Italy. While the magic formula is up for debate, there's no doubt that Naples brews the country's thickest, richest espresso. Indeed, coffee plays a venerable role in Neapolitan cultural identity. Celebrated Neapolitan folk songs include ''O cafè' (Oh, coffee) and 'A tazza 'e cafè' (The cup of coffee), while Italian design company Alessi pays tribute to the city's distinctive stovetop coffee maker with its own *Caffettiera napoletana* (Neapolitan coffee maker), designed by prolific Neapolitan artist Riccardo Dalisi.

Locals still favour the Arabica and Robusta blends that deliver a dense *crema*, a higher caffeine jolt, a longer shelf life and, crucially, a price point everyone can afford. Chances are you'll be savouring it on your feet. In Naples, as in the rest of Italy, drinking coffee at a bar is usually a moment to pause, but rarely linger. It's a stand-up swirl and gulp, an exchanged *buongiorno* or *buona sera* with the barista, and a hop back onto the street. But don't be fooled – the speed with which it's consumed does not diminish its cultural importance.

Salad with *burrata* (cream filled buffalo mozzarella)

Primitivo (a clone of the zinfandel grape), Negroamaro, Nero di Troia and Malvasia. While Negroamaro reaches its peak in the Salento – particularly around Salice, Guagnano and Copertino – the area around Manduria is well known for its high-quality Primitivi, produced by the likes of internationally renowned winemaker Gianfranco Fino. That said, clued-in oenophiles also praise the lesser-known town of Gioia del Colle, whose higher altitude produces a distinctly thinner Primitivo, which some argue is more elegant. It's here that you'll find some of the region's most exciting organic and low-intervention wineries, among them Cantine Cristiano Guttarolo, Plantamura and Pietraventosa.

Almost all Pugliese reds work perfectly with pasta, pizza, meats and cheeses. Pugliese whites have less cachet; however, those grown on the Murge, particularly Locorotondo and Martina, are good, clean, fresh-tasting wines, while those from Gravina are a little weightier. They are all excellent with fish.

In Basilicata the red wine of choice is made from the Aglianico grape, the best being produced in the Vulture region. It is the volcanic terroir that makes these wines so unique and splendid. Basilicata, like Puglia, has seen a renaissance in recent years with much investment, such as that of oenologist Donato D'Angelo at his eponymous winery at Rionero in Vulture.

Sicily

Although Sicily is one of the largest wine-producing regions in Italy, it has only recently begun enjoying the international acclaim its wines deserve.

The most common varietal is Nero d'Avola, a robust red similar to syrah (shiraz). Vintages are produced by numerous Sicilian wineries, including Planeta, which has six estates around the island; Donnafugata in western Sicily; Azienda Agricola COS and Azienda Agricola Arianna Occhipinti in southeastern Sicily; and Azienda Agricola G Milazzo near Agrigento. Try Planeta's Plumbago, Donnafugata's Mille e una Notte, COS's Nero di Lupo, and Milazzo's Maria Costanza and Terre della Baronia Rosso.

The Sangiovese-like Nerello Mascalese and Nerello Cappuccio are used in the popular Etna Rosso DOC, a dark-fruited, medium-bodied wine that pairs perfectly with lamb and goat's-milk cheeses. Winemaker Frank Cornelissen uses Nerello Mascalese to produce his powerful, smoky IGT Magma, made using grapes grown on Mt Etna's northern slope.

There is only one Sicilian DOCG, Cerasuolo di Vittoria, a blend of Nero d'Avola and Frappato grapes. Feudi del Pisciotto and COS make especially fine versions. The two grape varietals also conspire in Arianna Occhipinti's celebrated SP68 Rosso.

Sicily produces no shortage of standout *bianchi* (whites), with the island's common white varietals including Carricante, chardonnay, Grillo, Inzolia, Cataratto, Grecanico and Corinto. Superb drops include Tasca d'Almerita's Nozze d'Oro Inzolia and sauvignon blend and Palmento Costanzo's Etna Bianco di Sei.

Sicily's dessert wines are also impressive. The Aeolian island of Salina is renowned for its Malvasia, a honey-like wine produced by award-winning wineries such

as Azienda Agricola Biologica Caravaglio. In western Sicily, Marsala is famous for its eponymous sweet wine, made to an exceptional standard at local wineries Cantine Florio and Cantine Pellegrino. Further south, the far-flung island of Pantelleria produces Italy's most famous Moscato (muscat), the Passito di Pantelleria. Deep amber in colour, its taste is an extraordinary mélange of apricots and vanilla.

How to Eat & Drink Like a Local

With your appetite piqued, it's time for the technicalities of eating *all'italiana*.

When to Eat

Colazione (breakfast) A continental affair, often little more than a pre-work espresso, accompanied by a *cornetto* (Italian croissant) or *brioche* (breakfast pastry). In Sicily, your brioche might be filled with gelato or dipped in *granita* (flavoured crushed ice).

Pranzo (lunch) A sacred time, with most businesses closing for *la pausa* (afternoon break). Traditionally the main meal of the day, lunch usually consists of a *primo* (first course), *secondo* (second course) and *dolce* (dessert). Standard restaurant times are noon to 3pm, though most locals don't lunch before 1pm.

Aperitivo Especially popular in larger cities like Naples, Palermo and Catania, post-work drinks usually take place between 7pm and 9pm, when the price of your drink includes complimentary savoury snacks.

Cena (dinner) Traditionally a little lighter than lunch, though still a main meal. Standard restaurant times are 7.30pm to around 11pm, though many southern Italians don't sit down to dinner until 9pm or even later.

Where to Eat

Ristorante (restaurant) Formal service and refined dishes.

Trattoria Cheaper than a restaurant, with more relaxed service and home-style classics.

Osteria Historically a tavern focused on wine; the modern version is often an intimate trattoria or wine bar offering a handful of dishes.

Enoteca Wine bars often serve snacks or meals to accompany your tipple.

TABLE MANNERS

➡ Cardinal sins: skipping or being late for lunch.

➡ *Buon appetito* is what you say before eating. *Salute!* (Cheers!) is the toast used for alcoholic drinks – always make eye contact when toasting.

➡ Never order a coffee *with* your lunch or dinner.

➡ Eat spaghetti with a fork, not a spoon.

➡ Don't eat bread with your pasta; using it to wipe any remaining sauce from your plate (called *fare la scarpetta*) is fine.

➡ Unless you have hollow legs, don't accept a second helping of that delicious *primo* – you might not have room for the *secondo*, *dolce*, *sopratavola* (raw vegetables) and fruit.

➡ Whoever invites usually pays. Splitting *il conto* (the bill) is common enough; itemising it is not.

➡ If invited to someone's house, bring wine or a tray of *dolcetti* from a local *pasticceria* (pastry shop).

FESTIVE FAVOURITES

Culinary indulgence is the epicentre of any southern celebration, and major holidays are defined by their specialities. Lent is heralded by Carnevale (Carnival), a time for *sanguinaccio* (blood pudding made with dark chocolate and cinnamon), *chiacchiere* (fried biscuits sprinkled with icing sugar) and Sicily's *mpagnuccata* (deep-fried dough tossed in soft caramel).

Around 19 March (St Joseph's Feast Day), expect to eat *zeppole* (fritters topped with lemon-scented cream, sour cherry and dusting sugar) in Naples and Bari, and *crispelle di riso* (citrus-scented rice fritters dipped in honey) in Sicily.

Lent specialities like Sicilian *quaresimali* (hard, light almond biscuits) give way to Easter lamb and *colomba* (dove-shaped cake). The dominant ingredient at this time is egg, used to make Naples' legendary *pastiera* (shortcrust pastry tart filled with ricotta, cream, candied fruits and cereals flavoured with orange water).

If you're in Palermo around late October, before Ognissanti (All Souls' Day), you'll see stalls selling *frutti della Martorana,* named after the church that first began producing them. These marzipan biscuits, shaped to resemble fruits (or whatever takes the creator's fancy), are part of a Sicilian tradition that dates back to the Middle Ages.

Come Christmas, it's time for national staples like Milan's *panettone* (yeasty cake studded with raisins and dried fruit), Verona's simpler, raisin-free *pandoro* (dusted with vanilla-flavoured icing sugar) and Siena's *panforte* (chewy, flat cake made with candied fruits, nuts, chocolate, honey and spices). Neapolitans throw caution (and scales) to the wind with *raffioli* (sponge and marzipan biscuits), *struffoli* (tiny fried pastry balls dipped in honey and sprinkled with colourful candied sugar) and *pasta di mandorla* (marzipan), while their Sicilian cousins toast to the season with *cucciddatu* (ring-shaped cake made with dried figs, nuts, honey, vanilla, cloves, cinnamon and citrus fruits). Not that the Sicilians stop there, further expanding waistlines with *buccellati* (dough rings stuffed with minced figs, raisins, almonds, candied fruit and/or orange peel).

Agriturismo A working farmhouse offering food made with farm-grown produce.

Pizzeria Cheap grub, cold beer and a convivial vibe. The best pizzerias are often crowded: be patient.

Tavola calda Cafeteria-style spots serving cheap pre-made food like pasta and roast meats.

Friggitoria Simple, takeaway businesses specialising in deep-fried street snacks like *arancini*, *crocchè* and tempura-style vegetables.

Menu Decoder

Menù alla carta Choose whatever you like from the menu.

Menù di degustazione Degustation menu, usually consisting of six to eight 'tasting size' courses.

Menù turistico The 'tourist menu' usually signals mediocre fare – steer clear!

Piatto del giorno Dish of the day.

Antipasto A hot or cold appetiser. For a tasting plate of different appetisers, request an *antipasto misto* (mixed antipasto).

Primo First course, usually a substantial pasta, rice or *zuppa* (soup) dish.

Secondo Second course, often *carne* (meat) or *pesce* (fish).

Contorno Side dish, usually *verdura* (vegetable).

Dolce Dessert, including *torta* (cake).

Sopratavola Raw vegetables such as fennel or chicory eaten after a meal.

Frutta Fruit, usually the epilogue to a meal.

Nostra produzione Made in-house.

Surgelato Frozen, usually used to denote fish or seafood that's not freshly caught.

Plan Your Trip
Family Travel

Southern Italians adore *bambini* (children) and fawning locals are as common as espresso, olive groves and Vespas. On the flip side, Italy's southern regions offer few special amenities for little ones, which means a little planning goes a long way.

Keeping Costs Down

Accommodation

Apartment rental is easy to find and works best for families who want to self-cater. Many hotels and *pensioni* (guesthouses) offer reduced rates for children or will add an additional bed or cot on request (usually for an extra 30% or so). Campgrounds are relatively economical and many offer kids' activities in July and August.

Sightseeing

At state-run museums and sites, admission is free for under-18s; EU citizens aged between 18 and 25 pay €2 for tickets. Many other museums and monuments offer reduced admission for children. All state-run museums and sites are free for 20 days a year, including the first Sunday of each month between October and March.

Eating

Children can get a *mezza porzione* (half portion) at many *trattorie* (informal restaurant or tavern) and restaurants. Southern Italy's *mercati* (markets) are a great, affordable way to sample the regions' culinary bounty. Pick up fresh bread, cheeses, olives, smoked meats, fruit and vegetables for a picnic or home-cooked meal.

Children Will Love...

Outdoor Thrills

Aeolian Islands (p216) Seven tiny volcanic islands off Sicily with everything from spewing lava to black-sand beaches.

Mt Vesuvius (p95) Play 'spot the landmark' from the summit of Naples' formidable, slumbering volcano.

Ischia (p115) Catch a water taxi to a bubbling thermal beach or pool-hop at a verdant spa resort.

Parco Nazionale del Pollino (p184) Kids over 10 can join the grown-ups for white-water-rafting adventures in Calabria's wilds.

Maratea (p178) Shallow, sandy beaches and a very walkable town centre.

Brushes with History

Tunnel Galleria Borbonica (p81) Escape routes, hideouts and vintage smugglers' cars bring wartime Naples to life.

Herculaneum (p93) Smaller and better preserved than Pompeii, Herculaneum is easier to visit in a shorter time.

Valley of the Temples (p254) Agrigento's astounding Greek temples come with picnic-friendly grounds and space to move.

Castel del Monte (p147) Puglia's octagonal 13th-century castle boasts Europe's very first flush toilet.

Villa Romana del Casale (p251) Mosaics of wild beasts and youthful gymnasts capture young minds at Piazza Armerina's ancient Roman hunting villa.

Kooky Kicks

Cimitero delle Fontanelle (p84) Tour Naples' bizarre Fontanelle Cemetery, stacked with skulls, shrines and fantastical tales.

Alberobello (p153) Was that Snow White? Imagination runs riot in this World Heritage–listed town in Puglia, famous for its cone-roofed *trulli* abodes.

Matera (p171) Relive *The Flintstones* exploring Matera's Unesco-protected *sassi* (stone houses carved out of caves and cliffs).

Teatro dei Pupi (p237) Syracuse's little Sicilian puppet theatre brings old tales to vivid life.

Region by Region

Naples & Campania

Subterranean escape routes (p81), catacombs (p82) and Graeco-Roman ruins (p74) will ignite a sense of adventure in Naples, as will walking along the crater of Mt Vesuvius (p95) or exploring the volcano's slopes on horseback (p95). An easy day trip from Naples or Sorrento, Pompeii (p98) and its more compact rival Herculaneum (p93) bring history to life with their ancient homes, shops, bathhouses and theatres. Capri's glittering Grotta Azzurra (p112) will have little ones feeling like they've stepped into a Disney animation, while on Ischia, both kids and grown-ups will love the alfresco thermal pools at spa oasis Negombo (p116). For something a little more action packed, explore ancient caves in the Cilento, home to the Grotte di Castelcivita (p135) and the Grotte di Pertosa-Auletta (p136).

Puglia, Basilicata & Calabria

Storybook villages await in Puglia's Valle d'Itria (p153), where traditional *trulli* seem pulled straight out of a fairy tale. Young travellers will find more storybook déjà vu at Puglia's medieval Castel del Monte (p147), a Unesco-lauded castle reputedly home to Europe's first flushing loos. Excellent beaches, the chance to explore offshore islands and sea cliffs, and opportunities for hiking and mountain biking make Vieste (p148) on Puglia's Promontorio del Gargano another great family destination. Soft sand and sparkling waters also beckon in Calabria's

ORIREDMOUSE/GETTY IMAGES ©

Valley of the Temples (p254), Agrigento

Tropea (p193), while further inland the mountains of Calabria and Basilicata offer a plethora of active thrills, from hiking and mountain biking to high-speed zipline rides (p178), water tubing (p184) and white-water rafting (p184).

Sicily

Fire up the imagination with tales of conquest and pillage at Agrigento's World Heritage–listed Valley of the Temples (p254), or seek out fantastical beasts in the Roman mosaics at Villa Romana del Casale (p251). Gluttons can ride the funicular to Erice to sample sugary almond sweets at the legendary Pasticceria di Maria Grammatico (p262) or channel Willy Wonka in cocoa-obsessed Modica, home to esteemed chocolate purveyor Antica Dolceria Bonajuto (p249). Crystalline waters make for summertime bliss at beaches like Spiaggia di Cefalù (p214), while sea caves set the scene for memorable kayaking (p220) jaunts on the island of Vulcano. In Palermo, catch a puppet show at Teatro dei Pupi di Mimmo Cuticchio (p212) or take in some real-life theatrics at the city's larger-than-life Mercato di Ballarò (p204).

Good to Know

Look out for the 🚼 icon for family-friendly suggestions throughout this guide.

Weather Spring, early summer and autumn are generally best for families with small children. High summer temperatures can make life miserable for little ones – although good beaches and the occasional gelato should make this more bearable.

Baby essentials Pharmacies and supermarkets (some closed Sundays) sell baby formula, nappies (diapers), ready-made baby food and sterilising solutions. Fresh cow's milk is sold in cartons in supermarkets.

Prams and strollers Cobbled stones and potholes can make pushing a stroller challenging. Consider purchasing an ergonomic baby carrier before leaving home.

Dining out Southern Italian families eat late and few restaurants open before 7pm. Children are warmly welcomed, though high chairs (*seggioloni*) are not always available.

Car travel Children under 150cm or 36kg must be buckled into an appropriate child seat for their weight and are not allowed in the front passenger seat. Car seats for infants and children are available from most car-rental agencies but should always be booked in advance.

Public transport Discounts are sometimes available for child passengers. In some cases, young children travel free if accompanied by a paying adult. Check at the tourist office. Inter-city trains and buses are safe, convenient and relatively inexpensive.

Useful Resources

Lonely Planet Kids (www.lonelyplanetkids.com) Loads of activities and great family-travel blog content.

Italia Kids (www.italiakids.com) Family travel and lifestyle guide to Italy, packed with practical tips and accommodation listings.

Context Travel (www.contexttravel.com) Superb guided walks for families in Naples.

Ciao Bambino (www.ciaobambino.com) Tours, activities, recommendations and planning advice, put together by family-travel experts.

Baby Friendly Boltholes (www.babyfriendly bolholes.co.uk) Search for stylish, child-friendly accommodation in Puglia and Sicily.

Kids' Corner

Say What?

Hello.	Buongiorno bwon·*jor*·no
Goodbye.	Arrivederci. a·ree·ve·*der*·chee
Thank you.	Grazie. *gra*·tsye
Yes./No.	Sì./No. see/no
My name is ...	Mi chiamo ... mee *kya*·mo ...

Did You Know? ℹ

- Southern Italy is home to three active volcanoes.

- Sicilians eat ice cream in a brioche for breakfast.

Have You Tried?

'Mpanatigghi
Sweet biscuits filled with chocolate, spices...and minced beef.

ROSARIO SCALIA/GETTY IMAGES ©

Regions at a Glance

Home to A-list coastal destinations like Capri and the Amalfi Coast, not to mention the cultural riches of Naples, it's not surprising that Campania has traditionally played southern Italy's leading role.

Puglia and Basilicata have become the darlings of in-the-know travellers, both regions famed for their gorgeous beaches, fantastic food, architectural quirks and authentic festivals. While off-the-radar Calabria may lack big-hitter sights and cosmopolitan cities, it's well compensated by its rugged natural beauty, adventure sports and spicy, earthy cuisine.

Like Campania, Sicily offers an enviable repertoire of landscapes, from volcanic peaks and vine-laced slopes to irresistible beaches. It's also home to some of Italy's greatest Graeco-Roman temples and amphitheatres, baroque architecture, food and wine.

Naples & Campania

History
Food & Wine
Scenery

Ancient Ruins

Sitting beneath Mt Vesuvius, Neapolitans abide by the motto *carpe diem* (seize the day). And why not? All around them – at Pompeii, Herculaneum and the Campi Flegrei – they have reminders that life is short. Further afield, Paestum's stoic Greek temples defy the test of time.

Standout Specialities

Campania claims some of Italy's most iconic bites: pizza, pasta, San Marzano tomatoes, *sfogliatelle* (sweet ricotta pastries) and vibrant Falanghina wine. Head to the Cilento for buffalo mozzarella and up Ischia's hills for pit-reared *coniglio* (rabbit), slow-cooked with wild herbs.

Stunning Coastline

From the Amalfi Coast's citrus-fringed panoramas to Ischia's subtropical gardens and Capri's dramatic cliffs, the views from this coastline are as famous as its holidaying celebrities. Add thermal beaches and glittering grottoes, and the appeal is as crystal clear as the sea itself.

p65

Puglia, Basilicata & Calabria

Beaches
Outdoor Activities
Food & Wine

Sand & Sun

Lapped by turquoise waters, Italy's southern coasts are the stuff of Instagram dreams. Lounge beneath white cliffs on the Promontorio del Gargano, gaze at violet sunsets in Tropea and spend summer on the golden beaches of Otranto and Gallipoli.

Pure Adrenalin

With its crush of spiky mountains, Basilicata and Calabria are top spots to go wild. Burst through the clouds in mountaintop Pietrapertosa, white-water raft down the Lao river, pick bergamot in the Aspromonte and keep an eye out for Apennine wolves.

Vibrant Flavours

Puglia turned its poverty into a culinary art: sample wholesome, vegetable-based pasta dishes like *orecchiette con le cime di rape* ('little ears' pasta with turnip greens), taste-test creamy *burrata* (cheese made from mozzarella and cream), and raise a toast with a rustic Salento red.

p139

Sicily

Food & Wine
History
Outdoor Activities

A Bountiful Larder

Sicilian cuisine seduces seafood lovers and sets sweet tooths on edge. Tuna, sardines, swordfish and shellfish come grilled, fried or seasoned with mint or wild fennel. Desserts, laden with citrus fruits, ricotta and nuts, include Arab–Italian dishes such as *cannoli* (pastry shells filled with sweetened ricotta), while libations span luscious Nero d'Avola and silky Marsala.

Temples & Tesserae

A Mediterranean crossroads for centuries, Sicily keeps history buffs busy with its cache of Greek temples, Roman and Byzantine mosaics, Phoenician statues, Norman–Romanesque castles and art-nouveau villas.

Volcanic Highs

Sicily's restless geology gives outdoor activities a thrilling edge. Pamper weary muscles in warm volcanic waters, hike the Aeolian Islands' dramatic coastlines or take in the natural firework displays of volcanic Stromboli and Etna.

p197

On the Road

POPULATION
5.71 million

**POPULATION
DENSITY: NAPLES**
8,306 per sq km

BEST PIZZA
Concettina Ai Tre
Santi (p86)

BEST VIEW
Seggiovia del Monte
Solaro (p112)

BEST SPA
Negombo (p116)

WHEN TO GO

May Best month to
visit. Warm days,
with many special
events.

Jun & Sep Summer
heat without the
August crowds and
traffic.

Aug Hottest month;
many shops and
restaurants close for
a few weeks.

Positano (p121)
JOCRZH/SHUTTERSTOCK

Naples & Campania

C ampania is a rich *ragù* of Arabesque street life, decadent palaces, pastel-hued villages and aria-inspiring vistas.

Few corners of Europe can match the cultural conundrums here. Should you spend the morning waltzing through chandeliered Bourbon bedrooms or the frescoed villa of a Roman emperor's wife? And which of Caravaggio's canvases shouldn't you miss: the multiscene masterpiece inside Naples' Pio Monte della Misericordia, or the artist's swansong inside the city's belle époque Palazzo Zevallos?

Campania's mountains and coastline offer their own plethora of options, from horse-riding the slopes of Mt Vesuvius to sailing the Amalfi Coast and soaking in thermal waters on Ischia.

Naples & Campania Highlights

1 Pompeii (p98)
Channelling the ancients on the ill-fated streets of this erstwhile Roman city.

2 Grotta Azzurra (p112) Being bewitched by Capri's ethereal blue cave.

3 Sentiero degli Dei (p125) Walking with the gods on the Amalfi Coast.

4 Cappella Sansevero (p73) Re-evaluating artistic ingenuity in Naples.

5 Procida (p119) Lunching by lapping waves on the pastel-hued smallest island of the Bay of Naples.

6 Negombo (p116) Indulging in a little thermal therapy on Ischia.

7 Villa Rufolo (p130) Attending a concert at this dreamy Ravello villa and its cascading gardens.

8 Reggia di Caserta (p92) Pretending you're royalty at this monumental Unesco-listed palace complex.

9 Paestum (p134) Admiring ancient Hellenic ingenuity in the colossal ruins of Magna Graecia.

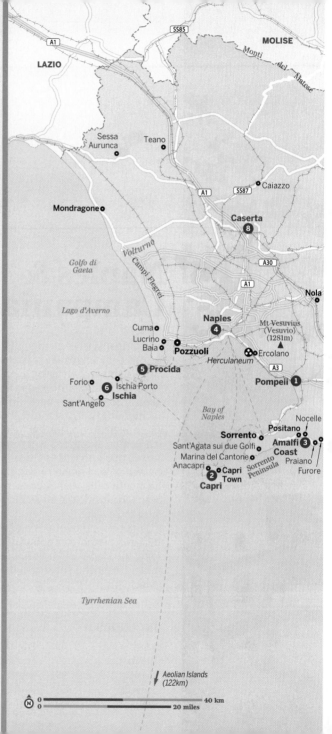

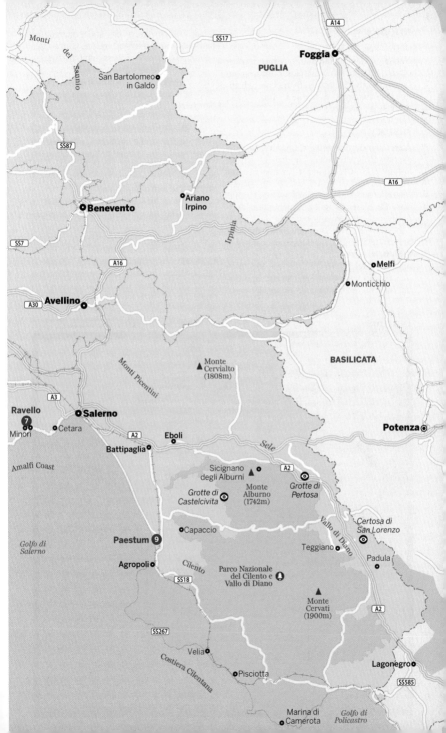

NAPLES

 081 / POP 966.145

Naples is raw, high-octane energy, a place of soul-stirring art and panoramas, spontaneous conversations and unexpected, inimitable elegance. Welcome to Italy's most unlikely masterpiece.

History

After founding nearby Cuma in the 8th century BCE, the Greeks settled the city in around 680 BCE, calling it Parthenope. Under the Romans, the area became an ancient Miami of sorts: a sun-soaked spa region that drew the likes of Virgil. Dampening the bonhomie was Mt Vesuvius' eruption in 79 CE.

Naples fell into Norman hands in 1139 before the French Angevins took control a century later, boosting the city's cred with the mighty Castel Nuovo (p81). By the 16th century, Naples was under Spanish rule and riding high on Spain's colonial riches. By 1600,

it was Europe's largest city and a burgeoning baroque beauty adorned by artists like Luca Giordano, Jusepe de Ribera and Caravaggio.

Despite a devastating plague in 1656, Naples soared under the Bourbons (1734–1860), with epic constructions such as the Teatro San Carlo (p89) and the Reggia di Caserta (p92) sealing the city's showcase reputation.

An ill-fated attempt at republican rule in 1799 was followed by a short stint under the French and a final period of Bourbon governance before nationalist rebel Giuseppe Garibaldi inspired the city to snip off the puppet strings and join a united Italy in 1860.

The Nazis took Naples in 1943, but they were quickly forced out by a series of popular uprisings between 26 and 30 September, famously known as the *Quattro giornate di Napoli* (Four Days of Naples). Led by locals, especially by young *scugnizzi* (Neapolitan for 'street urchins') and ex-soldiers, the street battles paved the way for the Allies to enter the city on 1 October.

Naples

After setting up a provisional government in Naples, the Allies were confronted with an anarchic mass of troops, German prisoners of war and bands of Italian fascists all competing with the city's starving population for food. Overwhelmed, Allied authorities turned to the underworld for assistance. As long as the Allies agreed to turn a blind eye to their black-market activities, the Mafia was willing to help. And so the Camorra (Neapolitan Mafia) was given a boost.

On 23 November 1980, a devastating earthquake struck the mountainous area of Irpinia, 100km east of Naples. The quake, which left more than 2700 people dead and thousands more homeless, caused extensive damage in Naples. It is believed that US$6.4 billion of the funds that poured into the region to assist the victims and rebuilding ended up in the pockets of the Camorra.

In 2011, Neapolitan voters elected the city's current mayor, Luigi de Magistris, a youthful former public prosecutor and vocal critic of both the Mafia and government corruption. Determined to improve the city's liveability, de Magistris has pushed through a number of initiatives, including the transformation of the Lungomare from a traffic-clogged thoroughfare into a pedes-trian and bike-friendly waterfront strip.

While De Magistris is not without his critics, his progressive, anticorruption agenda has hit the right note with many Neapolitans. In 2016, the Gen-X independent was re-elected city mayor, beating rival Gianni Lettieri of the centre-right Forza Italia party.

Naples

◉ Sights

◉ Centro Storico

★ **Museo Archaeologico Nazionale** MUSEUM
See p70.

★ **Complesso Monumentale
di Santa Chiara** BASILICA
(Map p72; ☑ 081 551 66 73; www.monasterodisanta chiara.it; Via Santa Chiara 49c; basilica free, Complesso Monumentale adult/reduced €6/4.50; ⊙ basilica 7.30am-1pm & 4.30-8pm, Complesso Monumentale 9.30am-5.30pm Mon-Sat, 10am-2.30pm Sun; Ⓜ Dante) Vast, Gothic and cleverly deceptive, the mighty **Basilica di Santa Chiara** stands at the heart of this tranquil monastery complex. The church was severely damaged in WWII: what you see today is a 20th-century recreation of Gagliardo Primario's 14th-century original. Adjoining it are the basilica's **cloisters**, adorned with brightly coloured 17th-century majolica tiles and frescoes.

While the Angevin porticoes date back to the 14th century, the cloisters took on their current look in the 18th century thanks to the landscaping work of Domenico Antonio Vaccaro. The walkways that divide the central garden of lavender and citrus trees are lined with 72 ceramic-tiled octagonal columns connected by benches. Painted by Donato and Giuseppe Massa, the tiles depict various rural scenes, from hunting sessions to vignettes of peasant life. The four internal walls are covered with soft, whimsical 17th-century frescoes of Franciscan tales.

Adjacent to the cloisters, a small and elegant **museum** of mostly ecclesiastical props also features the excavated ruins of a 1st-century spa complex, including a remarkably well-preserved *laconicum* (sauna).

Commissioned by Robert of Anjou for his wife Sancia di Maiorca, the monastic complex was built to house 200 monks and the tombs of the Angevin royal family. Dissed as a 'stable' by Robert's ungrateful son Charles of Anjou, the basilica received a luscious baroque makeover by Domenico Antonio Vaccaro, Gaetano Buonocore and Giovanni Del Gaizo in the 18th century. It took a direct hit during an Allied air raid on 4 August 1943 and its reconstruction was completed in 1953. Features that did survive the fire resulting from the bombing include part of a 14th-century fresco to the left of the main door and a chapel containing the tombs of the Bourbon kings from Ferdinand I to Francesco II.

TOP SIGHT
MUSEO ARCHAEOLOGICO NAZIONALE

The stuff history dreams are made of, Naples' Museo Archeologico Nazionale houses an extraordinary collection of ancient art and artefacts. Its assets include many of the finest frescoes, mosaics and epigraphs from the ancient settlements below Mt Vesuvius, not to mention the largest single sculpture from antiquity unearthed to date, the epic *Toro Farnese* (Farnese Bull).

Toro Farnese & Hercules

The undisputed star of the ground-floor Farnese collection of colossal Greek and Roman sculptures is the *Toro Farnese* (Farnese Bull). Mentioned in the *Natural History* of Pliny the Elder, the early-3rd-century masterpiece – most likely a Roman copy of a Greek original – is the largest single sculpture recovered from antiquity. Unearthed in Rome in 1545, the piece was restored by Michelangelo before being escorted to Naples by warship in 1788. Sculpted from a single block of marble, the masterpiece depicts the humiliating demise of Dirce, Queen of Thebes, tied to a raging bull and violently dragged to her death. Directly opposite the work is mighty *Ercole* (Hercules), also discovered at Rome's Baths of Caracalla, albeit without his legs. Michelangelo commissioned Guglielmo della Porta to sculpt replacement pins. The original legs were later uncovered and reinstated by the Bourbons. An inscription on the rock below Hercules' club attributes the work to Athenian sculptor Glykon.

DON'T MISS

→ Toro Farnese & Hercules statues

→ Alexander the Great mosaic from the Casa del Fauno

→ Gabinetto Segreto (Secret Chamber)

→ Frescoes of *Perseus and Andromeda*, *Theseus the Liberator*, *Bacchus and Vesuvius* and the *Riot between Pompeians and Nucerians*.

→ Villa dei Papiri sculptures

PRACTICALITIES

→ Map p72

→ ☑ 848 800288

→ www.museoarcheologico napoli.it

→ Piazza Museo Nazionale 19

→ adult/reduced €18/2

→ ⊙ 9am-7.30pm Wed-Mon

→ Ⓜ Museo, Piazza Cavour

Mezzanine Mosaics & Ancient Erotica

The museum's mezzanine level is awash with precious mosaic panels, most of which hail from ancient Pompeii. Room LIX is home to the playful *Scena di commedia: Musici ambulanti*, depicting four roaming musicians, as well as the allegorical *Memento mori*, in which a skull represents death, a butterfly the soul, and the wheel fate. The mosaics in rooms LX and LXI are even more impressive. Once adorning the largest home in Pompeii, the Casa del Fauno, they include an action-packed mural of Alexander the Great in battle against Persian king Darius III. Considered one of the most important works of art from antiquity, it's a precise copy of a famous Hellenistic painting from the second half of the 4th century BCE. The mosaics found in the Casa del Fauno were created by lauded craftsmen from Alexandria, Egypt, active in Italy between the end of the 2nd century BCE and the beginning of the 1st century BCE. The mezzanine is also home to the Gabinetto Segreto (Secret Chamber), a small, once-scandalous collection of erotically themed artworks and objects. Its most famous piece is a marble sculpture of the mythical half-goat, half-man Pan copulating with a nanny goat. The collection's bounty of erect members is testament to the common use of phallic symbols in Roman homes, considered symbols of good fortune, success and fertility.

First-Floor Frescoes & Sculptures

The 1st floor is a tour-de-force of ancient frescoes, pottery, glassware and sculpture. From the Sala del Meridione, the collection commences with frescoes retrieved from Vesuvian villas. Room LXXII is home to the largest known depiction of Perseus and Andromeda, in which the hero rescues his young bride after slaying a sea monster. More beast slaying occurs in Room LXXIII, home to a notable depiction of *Theseus the Liberator*. In Room LXXV, *Bacchus and Vesuvius* is believed to represent Vesuvius as it looked before the eruption of 79 CE, with one summit instead of two. A notorious clash between rival spectators at Pompeii's amphitheatre in 59 CE is captured in Room LXXVIII's *Riot between Pompeians and Nucerians*. At the end of the building is a collection of impressive sculptures found at the Villa dei Papiri. Room CXVI houses the five bronzes known collectively as the *Daughters of Danaus*. Dating from the Augustan period (27 BCE–14 CE), the figures represent mythical siblings condemned to pouring water for eternity after murdering their cousins (and bridegrooms) to appease their father, who sought revenge on his own sibling, Aegyptus.

BASEMENT TREASURES

The museum's basement claims one of the world's most important collections of ancient Greek, Italic and Latin epigraphs (stone inscriptions), representing both public and private life in ancient times. Adjoining it is a collection of Egyptian treasures, which, in Italy, is outshone only by Turin's Museo Egizio.

Before tackling the collection, consider investing in the *National Archaeological Museum of Naples* (€12), published by Electa; if you want to concentrate on the highlights, audio guides (€5) are available in English.

MUSEUM ARCHITECTURE

The museum occupies the Palazzo degli Studi, built in the late 16th century as a cavalry barracks. It was extended and modified over the centuries by architects including Giulio Cesare Fontana, the son of the late-Renaissance architect Domenico Fontana. The building's pièce de résistance is its 1st-floor Salone della Meridiana (Hall of the Sundial), featuring a vault fresco by Pietro Bardellino honouring King Ferdinand IV and Maria Carolina of Austria.

Central Naples

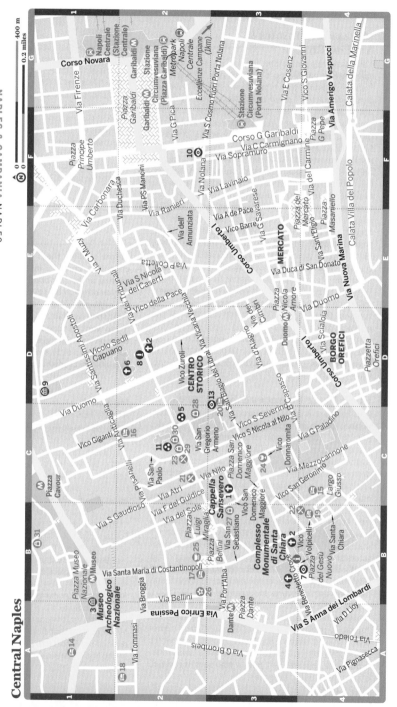

Central Naples

The church forecourt makes a cameo in Pier Paolo Pasolini's film *Il Decameron* (The Decameron), itself based on Giovanni Boccaccio's 14th-century novel.

★**Cappella Sansevero**   CHAPEL
(Map p72; ☑081 551 84 70; www.museo sansevero.it; Via Francesco de Sanctis 19; adult/reduced €7/5; ◷9am-7pm Wed-Mon; Ⓜ Dante) It's in this Masonic-inspired baroque chapel that you'll find Giuseppe Sanmartino's incredible sculpture, *Cristo velato* (Veiled Christ), its marble veil so realistic that it's tempting to try to lift it and view Christ underneath. It's one of several artistic wonders that include Francesco Queirolo's sculpture *Disinganno* (Disillusion), Antonio Corradini's *Pudicizia* (Modesty) and riotously colourful frescoes by Francesco Maria Russo that have remained untouched since their creation in 1749.

Originally built around the end of the 16th century to house the tombs of the di Sangro family, the chapel was given its current baroque fit-out by Prince Raimondo di Sangro, who, between 1749 and 1766, commissioned the finest artists to adorn the interior. In Queirolo's *Disinganno*, the man trying to untangle himself from a net represents Raimondo's father, Antonio, Duke of Torremaggiore. After the premature death of his wife, Antonio abandoned the young Raimondo, choosing instead a life of travel and hedonistic pleasures. Repentant in his later years, he returned to Naples and joined the priesthood, his attempt to free himself from sin represented in Queirolo's masterpiece.

Even more poignant is Antonio Corradini's *Pudicizia,* whose veiled female figure pays tribute to Raimondo's mother, Cecilia Gaetani d'Aquila d'Aragona. Raimondo was only 11 months old when she died, and the statue's lost gaze and broken plaque represent a life cruelly cut short.

The chapel's original polychrome marble flooring was badly damaged in a major collapse involving the chapel and the neighbouring Palazzo dei di Sangro in 1889. Designed by Francesco Celebrano, the flooring survives in fragmentary form in the passageway leading off from the chapel's right side. The passageway leads to a staircase, at the bottom of which you'll find two meticulously preserved human arterial systems – one of a man, the other of a woman. Debate still circles the models: are the arterial systems real or reproductions? And if they are real, just how was such an incredible state of preservation achieved? More than two centuries on, the mystery surrounding the alchemist prince and his abilities lives on.

Queues here can be notoriously long so consider purchasing your ticket online in advance for fast-track entry into the chapel; it's worth the extra €2 booking fee, especially during peak holiday periods.

Chiesa del Gesù Nuovo CHURCH

(Map p72; ☑ 081 557 81 51; Piazza del Gesù Nuovo; ⊙ 7.15am-12.45pm & 4-8pm Mon-Sat, 8am-2pm & 4-9pm Sun; ⓂDante) The extraordinary Chiesa del Gesù Nuovo is an architectural Kinder Surprise. Its shell is the 15th-century, Giuseppe Valeriani–designed facade of Palazzo Sanseverino, converted to create the 16th-century church. Inside, *piperno*-stone sobriety gives way to a gob-smacking blast of baroque that could make the Vatican blush: a vainglorious showcase for the work of top-tier artists such as Francesco Solimena, Luca Giordano and Cosimo Fanzago.

The church is the final resting place of much-loved local saint Giuseppe Moscati (1880–1927), a doctor who served the city's poor. Adjacent to the right transept, the Sale di San Giuseppe Moscati (Rooms of St Joseph Moscati) include a recreation of the great man's study, complete with the armchair in which he died. Scan the walls for *ex-voti*, gifts offered by the faithful for miracles purportedly received. The church itself received a miracle of sorts on 4 August 1943, when a bomb dropped on the site failed to explode. Its shell is aptly displayed beside the *ex-voti*.

The church flanks the northern side of beautiful Piazza del Gesù Nuovo, a favourite late-night hang-out for students and lefties. At its centre soars Giuseppe Genuino's lavish Guglia dell'Immacolata (Piazza del Gesù Nuovo), an obelisk built between 1747 and 1750. On 8 December, the Feast of the Immacolata, a firefighter scrambles up to the top to place a wreath on the statue of the Virgin Mary.

Via San Gregorio Armeno STREET

(Map p72; ⓂDante) Dismissed by serious collectors, this narrow street nonetheless remains famous across Italy for its *pastori* (nativity-scene figurines). Connecting Spaccanapoli with Via dei Tribunali, the *decumanus maior* (main road) of ancient Neopolis, its clutter of shops and workshops peddle everything from doting donkeys to kitsch celebrity caricatures. At No 8 you'll find the workshop of Ferrigno (☑ 081 552 31 48; www.arteferrigno.com), whose terracotta figurines are the most famous and esteemed on the strip.

Complesso Monumentale di San Lorenzo Maggiore ARCHAEOLOGICAL SITE

(Map p72; ☑ 081 211 08 60; www.laneapolissotterrata.it; Via dei Tribunali 316; church free, museum & excavations guided tour adult/reduced €10/7.50; ⊙ church 8am-7pm, excavations & museum 9.30am-5.30pm; ⓂDante) The basilica at this richly layered religious complex is deemed one of Naples' finest medieval buildings. Aside from Ferdinando Sanfelice's facade, the Cappella al Rosario and the Cappellone di Sant'Antonio, its baroque makeover was stripped away last century to reveal its austere, Gothic elegance. Beneath the basilica is a sprawl of extraordinary Graeco-Roman ruins, accessible on a one-hour guided tour.

Napoli Sotterranea ARCHAEOLOGICAL SITE

(Underground Naples; Map p72; ☑ 081 29 69 44; www.napolisotterranea.org; Piazza San Gaetano 68; adult/reduced €10/8; ⊙ English tours 10am, noon, 2pm, 4pm & 6pm; ⓂDante) This evocative guided tour leads you 40m below street level to explore Naples' ancient labyrinth of aqueducts, passages and cisterns.

The passages were originally hewn by the Greeks to extract tufa stone used in construction and to channel water from Mt Vesuvius. Extended by the Romans, the network of conduits and cisterns was more recently used as an air-raid shelter in WWII. Part of the tour takes place by candlelight via extremely narrow passages – not suitable for expanded girths!

★ Pio Monte della Misericordia CHURCH, MUSEUM

(Map p72; ☑ 081 44 69 44; www.piomontedellamisericordia.it; Via dei Tribunali 253; adult/reduced €7/5; ⊙ 9am-6pm Mon-Sat, to 2.30pm Sun; ⓂPiazza Cavour) The 1st-floor gallery of this octagonal, 17th-century church delivers a satisfying, digestible collection of Renaissance and baroque art, including works by Francesco de Mura, Jusepe de Ribera, Andrea Vaccaro and Paul van Somer. It's also home to contemporary artworks by Italian and foreign artists, each inspired by Caravaggio's masterpiece *Le sette opere di Misericordia* (The Seven Acts of Mercy). Considered by many to be the most important painting in Naples, you'll find it above the main altar in the ground-floor chapel.

Magnificently demonstrating the artist's chiaroscuro style, which had a revolutionary impact in Naples, *Le sette opere di Misericordia* was considered unique in its ability to illustrate the various acts in one seamlessly choreographed scene. Pio Monte della Misericordia's archives are home to the *Declaratoria del 14 Ottobre 1607,* an original church document acknowledging payment of 400 ducats to Caravaggio for the painting. A photocopy of the document is on display in the 1st-floor gallery, where you can also view the painting from the gallery's Sala del Coretto (Coretto Room).

On the opposite side of the street stands the **Guglia di San Gennaro** (Piazza Riario Sforza). Dating back to 1636, with stonework by Cosimo Fanzago and a bronze statue by Tommaso Montani, the obelisk is a soaring *grazie* (thank you) to the city's patron saint for protecting Naples from the 1631 eruption of Mt Vesuvius.

★**Duomo** CATHEDRAL
(Map p72; ☎081 44 90 97; Via Duomo 149; cathedral/baptistry free/€2; ☉cathedral 8.30am-1.30pm & 2.30-7.30pm Mon-Sat, 8.30am-1.30pm & 4.30-7.30pm Sun, baptistry 8.30am-12.30pm & 3.30-6.30pm Mon-Sat, 8.30am-1pm Sun, Cappella di San Gennaro 8.30am-1pm & 3-6.30pm Mon-Sat, 8.30am-1pm & 4.30-7pm Sun; ◻147, 182, 184 to Via Foria, Ⓜ Piazza Cavour) Whether you go for Giovanni Lanfranco's fresco in the Cappella di San Gennaro (Chapel of St Janarius), the 4th-century mosaics in the baptistry, or the thrice-annual miracle of San Gennaro, do not miss Naples' cathedral. Kick-started by Charles I of Anjou in 1272 and consecrated in 1315, it was largely destroyed in a 1456 earthquake. It has had copious nips and tucks over the subsequent centuries.

Among these is the gleaming neo-Gothic facade, only completed in 1905. Step inside and you'll immediately notice the central nave's gilded coffered ceiling, studded with late-mannerist art. The high sections of the nave and the transept are the work of baroque overachiever Luca Giordano.

Off the right side of the nave, the **Cappella di San Gennaro** (also known as the Chapel of the Treasury) was designed by Theatine priest and architect Francesco Grimaldi, and completed in 1646. The most sought-after artists of the period worked on the chapel, creating one of Naples' greatest baroque legacies. Highlights here include Jusepe de Ribera's gripping canvas *St Gennaro Escaping the Furnace Unscathed* and Giovanni Lanfranco's dizzying dome fresco. Hidden away in a strongbox behind the altar is a 14th-century silver bust in which sit the skull of San Gennaro and the two phials that hold his miraculously liquefying blood.

The next chapel eastwards contains an urn with the saint's bones and a cupboard full of femurs, tibias and fibulas. Below the high altar is the **Cappella Carafa**, a Renaissance chapel built to house yet more of the saint's remains.

Off the left aisle lies the 4th-century **Basilica di Santa Restituta**, the subject of an almost complete makeover after the earthquake of 1688. From it you can access the **Battistero di San Giovanni in Fonte**. It is Western Europe's oldest baptistry and is encrusted with fragments of glittering 4th-century mosaics.

The Duomo's subterranean **archaeological zone**, which includes fascinating remains of Greek and Roman buildings and roads, remains closed indefinitely.

MADRE GALLERY
(Museo d'Arte Contemporanea Donnaregina; Map p72; ☎081 1973 7254; www.madrenapoli.it; Via Settembrini 79; adult/reduced €8/4; ☉10am-7.30pm Mon & Wed-Sat, to 8pm Sun; Ⓜ Piazza Cavour) When *Madonna and Child* overload hits, reboot at Naples' museum of modern and contemporary art. In the lobby, French conceptual artist Daniel Buren sets the mood with his playful, mirror-panelled installation *Work in Situ*, with other specially commissioned installations from heavyweights like Anish Kapoor, Rebecca Horn and Sol LeWitt on level one. Level two houses the bulk of MADRE's permanent collection of painting, sculpture, photography and installations from other prolific 20th- and 21st-century artists, designers and architects.

Mercato di Porta Nolana MARKET
(Porta Nolana; ☉8am-2pm; ◻R2 to Corso Umberto I, Ⓜ Garibaldi) Naples at its most vociferous and intense, the Mercato di Porta Nolana is a heady, gritty street market where bellowing fishmongers and greengrocers collide with fragrant delis and bakeries, contraband cigarette vendors and Bangladeshi takeaways and grocery stores. Dive in for anything from luscious tomatoes and mozzarella to golden-fried street snacks, cheap luggage and bootleg CDs.

◉ **Vomero**

★**Certosa e Museo di San Martino** MONASTERY, MUSEUM
(Map p76; ☎081 229 45 03; www.polomusealecampania.beniculturali.it/index.php/certosa-e-museo; Largo San Martino 5; adult/reduced €6/3; ☉8.30am-7.30pm Tue & Thu-Sat, to 6.30pm Sun; Ⓜ Vanvitelli, ◻Montesanto to Morghen) The high point (quite literally) of the Neapolitan baroque, this charterhouse-turned-museum was built as a Carthusian monastery between 1325 and 1368. Centred on one of the most beautiful cloisters in Italy, it has been decorated, adorned and altered over the

Quartieri Spagnoli, Santa Lucia & Chiaia

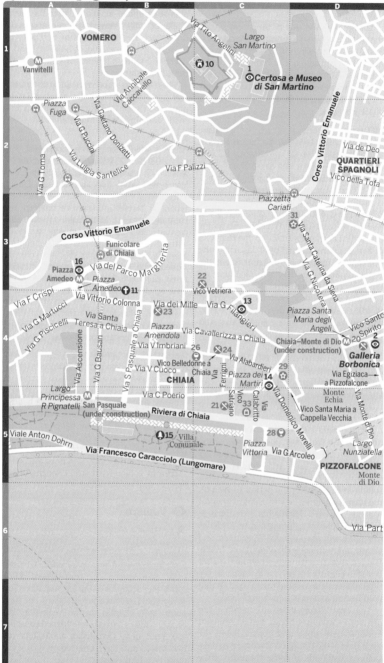

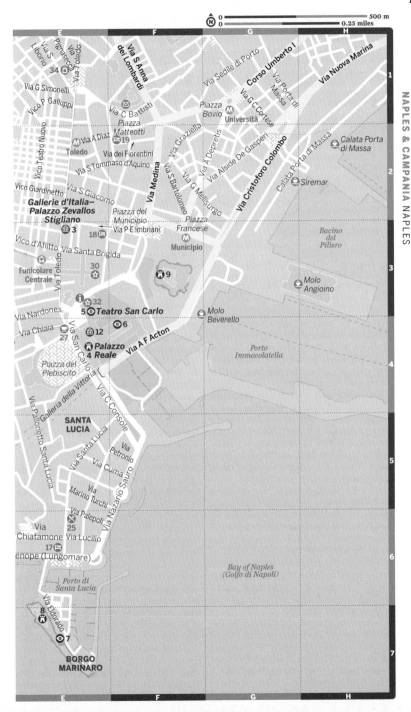

Quartieri Spagnoli, Santa Lucia & Chiaia

centuries by some of Italy's finest talent, most importantly architect Giovanni Antonio Dosio in the 16th century and baroque sculptor Cosimo Fanzago a century later. Nowadays, it's a superb repository of Neapolitan and Italian artistry.

The monastery's **church** and the sacristy, treasury and chapter house that flank it contain a feast of frescoes and paintings by some of Naples' greatest 17th-century artists, among them Battista Caracciolo, Jusepe de Ribera, Guido Reni and Massimo Stanzione. In the nave, Cosimo Fanzago's inlaid marble work is simply extraordinary.

Adjacent to the church, the **Chiostro dei Procuratori** is the smaller of the monastery's two cloisters. A grand corridor on the left leads to the larger **Chiostro Grande** (Great Cloister). Originally designed by Dosio in the late 16th century and added to by Fanzago, it's a sublime composition of Tuscan-Doric porticoes, marble statues and vibrant camellias. The balustrade marks the Certosa's small cemetery, adorned with skulls created by Fanzago.

Just off the Chiostro dei Procuratori, the **Sezione Navale** documents the history of the Bourbon navy from 1734 to 1860, and features a small yet extraordinary collection of royal barges. The **Sezione Presepiale** – which faces the refectory – houses a whimsical collection of rare Neapolitan *presepi*

(nativity scenes) from the 18th and 19th centuries, including the colossal 19th-century Cuciniello creation, which covers one wall of what used to be the monastery's kitchen. The **Quarto del Priore** in the southern wing houses the bulk of the monks' historic picture collection, as well as one of the museum's most famous sculptures, the tender *Madonna col Bambino e San Giovannino* (Madonna and Child with the Infant John the Baptist). The piece is the work of Pietro Bernini, father of the more famous Gian Lorenzo Bernini. Also noteworthy is a statue of St Francis of Assisi by 18th-century master sculptor Giuseppe Sanmartino, creator of the *Cristo velato* (Veiled Christ) housed in Naples' Cappella Sansevero.

A pictorial history of Naples is told in **Immagini e Memorie della Città e del Regno** (Images and Memories of the City and Kingdom of Naples). Here you'll find portraits of historic characters; antique maps, including a 35-panel copper map of 18th-century Naples in Room 45; and rooms dedicated to major historical events such as the eruption of Mt Vesuvius and the Revolt of the Masaniello (Room 36) and the plague (Room 37). Room 32 boasts the beautiful *Tavola Strozzi* (Strozzi Table); its fabled depiction of maritime Naples in the second half of the 15th century is one of the city's most celebrated historical records.

It's worth noting that some sections of the museum are only open at various times of the day; see the website for specific times.

Below the Certosa is the imposing **Sotterranei Gotici** (Gothic basement). The austere vaulted space holds around 150 marble sculptures and epigraphs.

Castel Sant'Elmo CASTLE

(Map p76; ☎ 081 558 77 08; www.polomuseale campania.beniculturali.it/index.php/il-castello; Via Tito Angelini 22; adult/reduced Wed-Mon €5/2.50, Tue €2.50/1.25; ☉castle 8.30am-7.30pm daily, museum 9.30am-5pm Wed-Mon, reduced hours winter; Ⓜ Vanvitelli, Ⓖ Montesanto to Morghen) Star-shaped Castel Sant'Elmo was originally a church dedicated to St Erasmus. Some 400 years later, in 1349, Robert of Anjou turned it into a castle before Spanish viceroy Don Pedro de Toledo had it further fortified in 1538. Used as a military prison until the 1970s, it's now famed for its jaw-dropping panorama, which takes in much of the city, its bay, islands and beyond. It's also known for its **Museo del Novecento**, dedicated to 20th-century Neapolitan art.

◉ Via Toledo & Quartieri Spagnoli

★**Gallerie d'Italia – Palazzo Zevallos Stigliano** GALLERY

(Map p76; ☎ 081 42 50 11; www.palazzozevallos. com; Via Toledo 185; adult/reduced €5/3; ☉10am-7pm Tue-Fri, to 8pm Sat & Sun; Ⓜ Municipio) Built for a Spanish merchant in the 17th century and reconfigured in belle-époque style by architect Luigi Platania in the early 20th century, Palazzo Zevallos Stigliano houses a compact yet stunning collection of Neapolitan and Italian art spanning the 17th to early 20th centuries. Star attraction is Caravaggio's mesmerising swansong, *The Martyrdom of St Ursula* (1610). Completed weeks before the artist's lonely death, the painting depicts a vengeful king of the Huns piercing the heart of his unwilling virgin-bride-to-be, Ursula.

La Pignasecca MARKET

(Via Pignasecca; ☉8am-1pm; Ⓜ Toledo) Naples' oldest street market is a multisensory escapade into a world of wriggling seafood, fragrant delis and clued-up *casalinghe* (homemakers) on the hunt for perfect produce. Fresh produce aside, the market's street-side stalls flog everything from discounted perfume and linen to Neapolitan hip-hop CDs and oh-so-snug nonna slippers.

◉ Santa Lucia & Chiaia

★**Palazzo Reale** PALACE

(Royal Palace; Map p76; ☎081 40 05 47; www. coopculture.it; Piazza del Plebiscito 1; adult/reduced €6/3; ☉9am-8pm Thu-Tue; ☐R2 to Via San Carlo, Ⓜ Municipio) Envisaged as a 16th-century monument to Spanish glory (Naples was under Spanish rule at the time), the magnificent Palazzo Reale is home to the **Museo del Palazzo Reale**, a rich and eclectic collection of baroque and neoclassical furnishings, porcelain, tapestries, sculpture and paintings, spread across the palace's royal apartments.

Among the many highlights is the **Teatrino di Corte**, a lavish private theatre created by Ferdinando Fuga in 1768 to celebrate the marriage of Ferdinand IV and Marie Caroline of Austria. Incredibly, Angelo Viva's statues of Apollo and the Muses set along the walls are made of papier mâché.

Sala (Room) VIII is home to a pair of vivid, allegorical 18th-century French tapestries representing earth and water respectively. Further along, Sala XII will leave you sniggering at the 16th-century canvas *Gli esattori delle imposte* (The Tax Collectors). Painted by Dutch artist Marinus Claeszoon Van Reymerswaele, it confirms that attitudes to tax collectors have changed little in 500 years. Sala XIII used to be Joachim Murat's study in the 19th century, but was used as a snack bar by Allied troops in WWII. Meanwhile, what looks like a waterwheel in Sala XXIII is actually a nifty rotating reading desk made for Queen Maria Carolina of Austria by Giovanni Uldrich in the 18th century.

The Cappella Reale (Royal Chapel) houses an 18th-century *presepe napoletano* (Neapolitan nativity scene). Fastidiously detailed, its cast of *pastori* (nativity-scene figurines) were crafted by a series of celebrated Neapolitan artists, including Giuseppe Sanmartino, creator of the *Cristo velato* (Veiled Christ) sculpture in the Cappella Sansevero.

The palace is also home to the **Biblioteca Nazionale di Napoli** (National Library; ☎081 781 91 11; www.bnnonline.it; ☉8.30am-7pm Mon-Fri, to 1.30pm Sat, papyrus exhibition by appointment only, Sezione Lucchesi Palli 8.30am-6.45pm Mon-Thu, to 3.30pm Fri) **FREE**, its own priceless treasures including at least 2000 papyri discovered at Herculaneum. You will need to email the library a month ahead to organise a viewing of its ancient papyri, retrieved from Herculaneum. Thankfully, you won't need to book ahead to view the library's exquisite **Biblioteca Lucchesi Palli** (Lucchesi

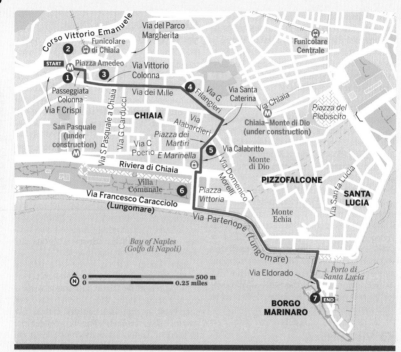

City Walk
An Architectural Saunter

START PIAZZA AMEDEO
END CASTEL DELL'OVO
LENGTH 2.2KM; 1.5 HOURS

Begin the walk outside Piazza Amedeo metro station on **1 Piazza Amedeo.** Just off its northern end stands former hotel **2 Villa Maria** (Map p76; Via del Parco Margherita 1; Ⓜ Piazza Amedeo), one of Naples' finest examples of art nouveau architecture. From the southeast side of Piazza Amedeo, slip into Via Vittorio Colonna (which becomes Via dei Mille). To your left you'll pass the unapologetically baroque **3 Chiesa di Santa Teresa a Chiaia** (Map p76; ☑ 081 41 42 63; Via Vittorio Colonna 22; ⊙ 7.30-11am Mon-Sat, 8.30am-noon & 5-7.30pm Sun), designed by Cosimo Fanzago and home to paintings by Luca Giordano. Via dei Mille eventually kinks southeast, becoming Via Filangieri. It's here that you'll find art nouveau **4 Palazzo Mannajuolo** (Map p76; Via Filangieri 36; ⊙ 8am-9pm; ⊑ E6 to Piazza dei Martiri). Wander inside to admire its

spiral staircase, famously featured in *Napoli velata* (Naples in Veils), a film by prolific Turkish-Italian director Ferzan Özpetek. Continue along Via Filangieri, then turn right into Via Santa Caterina. The street leads to dashing **5 Piazza dei Martiri,** its 19th-century centrepiece dedicated to Neapolitan martyrs. The monument's four lions represent the anti-Bourbon uprisings of 1799, 1820, 1848 and 1860. At No 30 is Palazzo Calabritto, designed by architect Luigi Vanvitelli, most famous for his monumental Reggia di Caserta. Head south on exclusive Via Calabritto, cross busy Piazza Vittoria – which flanks former Bourbon garden **6 Villa Comunale** (Map p76; Piazza Vittoria; ⊙ 7am-midnight) – and turn left into Via Partenope (Lungomare), a pedestrianised seafront promenade popular with everyone from love-struck teens to boisterous families. The strip leads to Via Eldorado and the ancient islet of Borgo Marinaro, home to the **7 Castel dell'Ovo** and its silver screen–worthy rooftop views.

Palli Library; closed Saturday). Crafted by some of Naples' most celebrated 19th-century artisans, it's home to numerous fascinating artistic artefacts, including letters by composer Giuseppe Verdi. Bring photo ID to enter the Biblioteca Nazionale. Theatre and opera fans can buy the combination ticket (€11) for entry to both the Palazzo Reale and adjoining MeMus theatre museum.

★ **Galleria Borbonica** HISTORIC SITE
(Map p76; ☏ 081 764 58 08, 366 2484151; www.galleriaborbonica.com; Vico del Grottone 4; 1hr standard tour adult/reduced €10/5; ⊙ standard tour 10am, noon, 3pm & 5pm Fri-Sun; ☐ R2 to Via San Carlo, Ⓜ Chiaia-Monte di Dio) Traverse five centuries along Naples' Bourbon Tunnel. Conceived by Ferdinand II in 1853 to link the Palazzo Reale to the barracks and the sea, the never-completed escape route is part of the 17th-century Carmignano Aqueduct system, itself incorporating 16th-century cisterns. The standard tour does not require prebooking, though the Adventure Tour (85 minutes; adult/reduced €15/10) and adults-only Speleo Light Tour (90 minutes; €15) do.

MeMus MUSEUM
(Museum & Historical Archive of the Teatro San Carlo; Map p76; http://memus.squarespace.com; Palazzo Reale, Piazza del Plebiscito; adult/reduced €6/5; ⊙9am-7pm Mon, Tue & Thu-Sat, to 3pm Sun; ☐ R2 to Via San Carlo, Ⓜ Municipio) Located inside the Palazzo Reale (p79) – purchase tickets at the palace ticket booth – MeMus hosts long-running temporary exhibitions linked to the rich history of Europe's oldest working opera house, the Teatro San Carlo (p89). Exhibitions showcase everything from original stage-design sketches, costumes, posters and letters, to the personal artefacts of legends of the theatre and opera world.

Castel Nuovo CASTLE
(Map p76; ☏ 081 795 77 22; Piazza Municipio; adult/reduced €6/3; ⊙8.30am-6pm Mon-Sat, 10am-1pm Sun; Ⓜ Municipio) Locals know this 13th-century castle as the Maschio Angioino (Angevin Keep), and its Cappella Palatina is home to fragments of frescoes by Giotto; they're on the splays of the Gothic windows. You'll also find Roman ruins under the glass-floored Sala dell'Armeria (Armoury Hall). The castle's upper floors (closed on Sunday) house a collection of mostly 17th- to early-20th-century Neapolitan paintings. The top floor houses the more interesting works, including landscape paintings by Luigi Crisconio and a watercolour by architect Carlo Vanvitelli.

The history of the castle stretches back to Charles I of Anjou, who upon taking over Naples and the Swabians' Sicilian kingdom found himself in control not only of his new southern Italian acquisitions but also of possessions in Tuscany, northern Italy and Provence (France). It made sense to base the new dynasty in Naples, rather than Palermo in Sicily, and Charles launched an ambitious construction program to expand the port and city walls. His plans included converting a Franciscan convent into the castle that still stands in Piazza Municipio.

Christened the Castrum Novum (New Castle) to distinguish it from the older Castel dell'Ovo and **Castel Capuano**, it was completed in 1282, becoming a popular hang-out for the leading intellectuals and artists of the day – Giotto repaid his royal hosts by painting much of the interior. Of the original structure, however, only the Cappella Palatina remains; the rest is result of Aragonese renovations two centuries later, as well as a meticulous restoration effort prior to WWII.

The two-storey Renaissance triumphal arch at the entrance – the **Torre della Guardia** – commemorates the victorious entry of Alfonso I of Aragon into Naples in 1443, while the stark stone **Sala dei Baroni** (Hall of the Barons) is named after the barons slaughtered here in 1486 for plotting against King Ferdinand I of Aragon. Its striking ribbed vault fuses ancient Roman and Spanish late-Gothic influences.

Castel dell'Ovo CASTLE
(Map p76; ☏ 081 795 45 92; Borgo Marinaro; ⊙9am-7.30pm Mon-Sat, to 2pm Sun Apr-Oct, reduced hours Nov-Mar; ☐ E6, 128 to Via Santa Lucia) FREE Built by the Normans in the 12th century, Naples' oldest castle owes its name (Castle of the Egg) to Virgil. The Roman scribe reputedly buried an egg on the site where the castle now stands, warning that when the egg breaks, the castle (and Naples) will fall. Thankfully, both are still standing, and walking up to the castle's ramparts will reward you with a breathtaking panorama.

Used by the Swabians, Angevins and Alfonso of Aragon, who modified it to suit his military needs, the castle sits on the rocky, restaurant-lined 'island' of **Borgo Marinaro**. According to legend, the heartbroken siren Partenope washed ashore here after failing to seduce Ulysses with her song. It's also where the Greeks first settled the city in the 7th century BCE, calling the island Megaris. Its commanding position wasn't wasted on the

 TOP SIGHT
SUBTERRANEAN NAPLES

Lurking beneath Naples' loud and greasy streets is one of the world's most thrilling urban wonderlands, a silent, mostly undiscovered sprawl of Greek-era grottoes, paleo-Christian burial chambers, catacombs and ancient ruins. Search out these places for a glimpse of the city's fascinating *sottosuolo* (underground).

History

Speleologists (cave specialists) estimate that about 60% of Neapolitans live and work above this *sottosuolo* network. Since the end of WWII, some 700 cavities have been discovered, from original Greek-era grottoes to palaeo-Christian burial chambers and royal Bourbon escape routes. According to the experts, this is simply a prelude, with another 2 million sq metres of troglodytic treats to unfurl.

Naples' dedicated caving geeks are quick to tell you that their underworld is one of the largest and oldest on earth. Sure, Paris might claim a catacomb or two, but its subterranean offerings don't come close to this giant's 2500-year history.

And what a history it is. Naples' most famous saint, San Gennaro, was interred in the Catacombe di San Gennaro in the 5th century. A century later, in 536, Belisario and his troops caught Naples by surprise by storming the city through the ancient tunnels. According to legend, Alfonso of Aragon used the same trick in 1442, undermining the city walls by using an underground passageway leading into a tailor's shop and straight into town. Even the city's dreaded Camorra has got in on the act. In 1992 the notorious Stolder clan was busted for running a subterranean drug lab, with escape routes heading straight to the clan boss's pad.

GIANNIS PAPANIKOS/SHUTTERSTOCK ©

DON'T MISS

➡ Early-Christian frescoes at the Catacombe di San Gennaro

PRACTICALITIES

➡ Map p68

➡ ☎ 081 744 37 14

➡ www.catacombe dinapoli.it

➡ Via Capodimonte 13

➡ adult/reduced €9/6

➡ ⊙ 1hr tours hourly 10am-5pm Mon-Sat, to 2pm Sun

➡ 🚌 R4, 178 to Via Capodimonte

Catacombe di San Gennaro

Naples' oldest and holiest catacombs harbour three types of ancient tombs, including the open-room *cubiculum* preferred by the city's wealthiest denizens. One of these features an especially beautiful funerary fresco of a mother, father and child: it's made up of three layers of fresco, one commissioned for each death. From the 5th to the 9th centuries, the remains of San Gennaro – Naples' most famous patron saint – were buried in the catacombs' *basilica minore* (minor basilica). The painting on the side of San Gennaro's tomb – depicting the saint with Mt Vesuvius and Mt Somma in the background – is the first known image of San Gennaro as Naples' protector. Lovingly restored, the catacombs now also host occasional special events, including theatrical and live-music performances; see the website for updates.

Galleria Borbonica

During WWII, Naples' subterranean cisterns and former quarries were turned into civilian shelters. The lakes of rubbish that had filled many of them were compacted and covered, old passageways were enlarged, toilets were built and new staircases were erected. As bombs showered the city above, tens of thousands took refuge in the dark, damp spaces below. One of these spaces was the Galleria Borbonica (p81). Used as an air-raid shelter and makeshift hospital, the restored labyrinth rekindles the past with evocative wartime artefacts, from toys and stretchers to moving graffiti.

Complesso Monumentale di San Lorenzo Maggiore

Architecture and history buffs shouldn't miss this richly layered religious complex (pictured; p74), whose subterranean ruins include ancient bakeries, wineries, laundries and barrel-vaulted rooms that once formed part of ancient Neapolis' two-storey *macellum* (market). The onsite Museo dell'Opera di San Lorenzo Maggiore includes a model of the area as it appeared in ancient times, while the 13th-century basilica itself upcycles ancient columns in its nave. Catherine of Austria, who died in 1323, is buried here in a beautiful mosaic tomb. Legend has it that this was where Boccaccio first fell for Mary of Anjou, the inspiration for his character Fiammetta, while the poet Petrarch called the adjoining convent home in 1345.

NEED TO KNOW

For more on Naples' underground wonders check out www.napoli unplugged.com/ locations-category/ subterranean-naples.

For a gourmet break from your underground adventuring, head to the famed Da Ettore (p87), near the Tunnel Borbonico.

TOURS

Tours of the Catacombe di San Gennaro are run by the Cooperativa Sociale Onlus 'La Paranza' (p84), whose ticket office is to the left of the **Chiesa di Madre di Buon Consiglio** (Map p68; ☑ 081 741 00 06; Via Capodimonte 13), a snack-sized replica of St Peter's in Rome completed in 1960. Tickets can also be purchased in advance online. The cooperative also runs a fascinating Sunday-morning walking tour called *Il Miglio Sacro* (The Holy Mile; adult/ reduced €15/13), which explores the neighbouring Sanità district. The Holy Mile tour must be prebooked and is offered in Italian unless requested in English, French or Spanish in advance; see the website for details.

Roman general Lucullus either, who had his villa here long before the castle hit the skyline. Views aside, the castle is also the setting for temporary art exhibitions, special events, and no shortage of posing brides and grooms.

◉ Capodimonte & La Sanità

★ Catacombe di San Gennaro HISTORIC SITE
See p82.

★ Museo di Capodimonte MUSEUM
(Map p68; ☏ 081 749 91 11; www.museocapod imonte.beniculturali.it; Via Miano 2; adult/reduced €12/8; ⊙ 8.30am-7.30pm Thu-Tue; ☐ R4, 178 to Via Capodimonte, ☐ Shuttle Capodimonte) Originally designed as a hunting lodge for Charles VII of Bourbon, the monumental Palazzo di Capodimonte was begun in 1738 and took more than a century to complete. It's now home to the Museo di Capodimonte, southern Italy's largest and richest art gallery. Its vast collection – much of which Charles inherited from his mother, Elisabetta Farnese – was moved here in 1759 and ranges from exquisite 12th-century altarpieces to works by Botticelli, Caravaggio, Titian and Warhol.

The gallery is spread over three floors and 160 rooms; for most people, a full morning or afternoon is enough for an abridged best-of tour. The 1st floor includes works by greats such as Michelangelo, Raphael and Titian, with highlights including Masaccio's *Crocifissione* (Crucifixion), Botticelli's *Madonna col Bambino e due angeli* (Madonna with Child and Angels), Bellini's *Trasfigurazione* (Transfiguration) and Parmigianino's *Antea*, all of which are subject to room changes within the museum.

The floor is also home to the royal apartments, a study in regal excess. The **Salottino di Porcellana** (Room 52) is an outrageous example of 18th-century chinoiserie, its walls and ceiling dense with whimsically themed porcelain 'stucco'. Originally created between 1757 and 1759 for the Palazzo Reale in Portici, it was transferred to Capodimonte in 1867.

Upstairs, the 2nd-floor galleries display work by Neapolitan artists from the 13th to the 19th centuries, including de Ribera, Giordano, Solimena and Stanzione. It's also home to some spectacular 16th-century Belgian tapestries. The piece that many come to see, however, is Caravaggio's *Flagellazione* (Flagellation of Christ; 1607–10), which hangs in reverential solitude in Room 78. Rooms 88 to 95 are dedicated to paintings of the Neapolitan baroque period.

Accessed from the 2nd floor, a small mezzanine level hosts a rotating selection of modern works from artists including Andy Warhol, Mimmo Jodice and John Armleder.

Once you've finished in the museum, the **Real Bosco di Capodimonte** (www. boscodicapodimonte.it; ⊙ 7am-7.30pm Apr-Sep, to 6pm Feb, Mar & Oct, to 5pm Nov-Jan;) FREE – the palace's 134-hectare estate – provides a much-needed breath of fresh air.

The museum offers a convenient, hourly shuttle-bus service, Shuttle Capodimonte, that runs between central Naples and the museum. Buses depart from Piazza Trieste e Trento (opposite Teatro San Carlo) and stop at Piazza Dante and the Museo Archeologico Nazionale en route. Tickets (which include museum entry) can be purchased directly on the bus.

★ Cimitero delle Fontanelle CEMETERY
(Map p68; ☏ 081 1925 6964; www.cimitero fontanelle.com; Via Fontanelle 80; ⊙ 10am-5pm; ☐ C51 to Via Fontanelle, Ⓜ Materdei) FREE Holding about eight million human bones, the ghoulish Fontanelle Cemetery was first used during the 1656 plague, before becoming Naples' main burial site during the 1837 cholera epidemic. At the end of the 19th century it became a hot spot for the *anime pezzentelle* (poor souls) cult, in which locals adopted skulls and prayed for their souls. Lack of information at the site makes joining a tour much more rewarding; reputable outfits include **Cooperativa Sociale Onlus 'La Paranza'** (Map p68; ☏ 081 744 37 14; www. catacombedinapoli.it; Via Capodimonte 13; ⊙ information point 10am-5pm Mon-Sat, to 2pm Sun; ☐ R4, 178 to Via Capodimonte).

★ Festivals & Events

Maggio dei Monumenti CULTURAL
(www.comune.napoli.it; ⊙ May) A month-long cultural feast, with a bounty of concerts, performances, exhibitions, guided tours and other events across Naples. The festival program is usually released on the Comune di Napoli (Naples City Council) website.

★ Napoli Teatro Festival Italia THEATRE
(www.napoliteatrofestival.it; ⊙ Jun/Jul) One month of local and international theatre, dance and performance art, staged in conventional and unconventional venues.

Wine & The City WINE
(www.wineandthecity.it; ⊙ May) A 10-day celebration of regional vino, with free wine tastings and cultural events in palaces,

museums, boutiques and eateries across the city.

Festa di San Gennaro
RELIGIOUS

(Duomo; ⊘ Sat before 1st Sun in May, 19 Sep, 16 Dec) The faithful flock to the Duomo to witness the miraculous liquefaction of San Gennaro's blood three times a year.

🛏 Sleeping

Where to slumber? The *centro storico* (historic centre) is studded with important churches and sights, artisan studios and student-packed bars. Seafront Santa Lucia delivers grand hotels, while sceney Chiaia is best for fashionable shops and *aperitivo* bars. The lively, laundry-strung Quartieri Spagnoli is within walking distance of all three neighbourhoods.

★ The Church
B&B €

(Map p72; ☑081 1952 9272; www.thechurch.it; San Biagio dei Librai 39; d €50-100, tr €70-130; ✳️☎; 🚇R2 to Corso Umberto I) On the 4th floor of an anecdote-rich 16th-century *palazzo*, this intimate, cultured B&B is decorated with contemporary Neapolitan photography and cleverly upcycled objects, from coffee percolators turned plant pots to an African tek tree turned bookshelf. The four minimalist rooms are equally whimsical; the top-floor room is the most coveted and comes with a striking in-room shower and private terrace.

★ Magma Home
B&B €

(Map p72; ☑320 4360272, 338 3188914; http:// magmahome.it; Via San Giuseppe dei Nudi 18; d €70-150; ✳️☎; 🅜Museo) 🖋 Contemporary artworks, cultural soirées and impeccable hospitality plug you straight into Naples' cultural scene at Magma. Its eight rooms – each designed by a local artist – intrigue with their mix of Italian design classics, upcycled materials and specially commissioned artworks. There's a large, contemporary communal kitchen and living area, plus two inviting rooftop terraces with views of the city and Mt Vesuvius.

★ Schiara
B&B €

(Map p72; ☑081 033 09 77, 338 9264453; www. maisonsdecharme.it; Vico Volpicelli 20; s €30-85, d €50-100, tr €65-110, q €80-125; ✳️@☎; 🅜Dante) Freshly minted B&B Schiara offers five contemporary rooms, each with en-suite bathroom and playful artisan details inspired by southern Italian themes. The 'Miti' room comes with its own in-room soaking tub, while the upstairs 'Riti' room has a kitchenette and private rooftop terrace. All guests have access to a gorgeous outdoor terrace and communal rooftop garden with sunbeds and bewitching views.

★ Dimora dei Giganti
B&B €

(Map p72; ☑081 033 09 77, 338 9264453; www. maisonsdecharme.it/dimoradeigiganti; Vico Giganti 55; s €40-60, d €55-80, tr €70-95, q €85-105; 🅿✳️☎; 🅜Piazza Cavour, Museo) Run by a warm and personable team, this urbane B&B offers four colour-coordinated bedrooms with specially commissioned sculptural lamps, ethnic-inspired furnishings and designer bathrooms. It has a modern kitchen, a cosy lounge and a charming majolica-tiled terrace. Best of all, its quiet side-street location is only steps away from the buzzing heart of the *centro storico*.

B&B Arte e Musei
B&B €

(Map p72; ☑081 1950 4479, 333 6962469; www. facebook.com/bnbarteemusei; Via Salvator Rosa 345; s €40-70, d €60-120, tr €80-150; ✳️☎; 🅜Museo, Piazza Cavour) Close to the Museo Archeologico Nazionale, this artful B&B is adorned with Neapolitan-themed paintings and ceramics by gracious owner and artist Federica. Both the double and triple room include a small balcony and spotless en-suite bathroom, while the smaller single room (with double bed) has its private bathroom in the hallway.

★ Atelier Inès
B&B €€

(Map p68; ☑349 4433422; www.atelierinesgallery.com; Via dei Cristallini 138; d €135-170; ✳️☎; 🚇C51, C52 to Via dei Vergini, 🅜Piazza Cavour) A stylish, eclectic oasis in the earthy Sanità district, this three-suite B&B is a homage to the late Neapolitan sculptor and designer Annibale Oste, whose **workshop** (www.annibaleoste.com/esperienza-oste; ⊘ usually 9am-6pm Mon-Fri) shares a leafy courtyard. Everything from the lamps and spiral towel racks to the one-of-a-kind sculptural bedheads are Oste's whimsical designs, complemented by heavenly mattresses, a choice of pillows, and Vietri-ceramic bathrooms with satisfyingly hot water.

Neapolitan Trips
HOSTEL €€

(Map p76; ☑B&B 081 551 8977, hostel 081 1836 6402, hotel 081 1984 5933; www.neapolitantrips. com; Via dei Fiorentini 10; hostel dm €15-35, B&B d €45-90, hotel d €80-160; ✳️☎; 🅜Toledo) Neapolitan Trips is a unique beast, with a clean, next-gen hostel on one floor, and both B&B and hotel rooms on another. The hostel is the standout, boasting a hip communal lounge-bar complete with electric guitars, amps and a piano for impromptu evening jams, a modern guest kitchen with complimentary pasta to cook, and mixed-gender dorms with USB ports by each bed.

★ Hotel Piazza Bellini   BOUTIQUE HOTEL €€

(Map p72; ☑ 081 45 17 32; www.hotelpiazza bellini.com; Via Santa Maria di Costantinopoli 101; d €90-190; ❄@☎; Ⓜ Dante) Only steps from the bars and nightlife of Piazza Bellini, this sharp, hip hotel occupies a 16th-century *palazzo,* its pure-white spaces spiked with original majolica tiles, vaulted ceilings and *piperno*-stone paving. Rooms are modern and functional, with designer fittings, fluffy duvets and chic bathrooms with excellent showers. Four rooms on the 5th and 6th floors feature panoramic terraces.

Check the hotel website for decent discounts.

Decumani Hotel de Charme   BOUTIQUE HOTEL €€

(Map p72; ☑ 081 551 81 88; www.decumani.it; Via San Giovanni Maggiore Pignatelli 15; d from €116; ❄@☎; Ⓜ Università) This classic boutique hotel occupies the former *palazzo* of Cardinal Sisto Riario Sforza, the last bishop of the Bourbon kingdom. Its simple, stylish 42 rooms feature high ceilings, parquet floors, 19th-century furniture and modern bathrooms with spacious showers. Deluxe rooms crank up the *dolce vita* with personal hot tubs. The pièce de résistance, however, is the property's breathtaking baroque salon.

★ La Ciliegina Lifestyle Hotel   BOUTIQUE HOTEL €€€

(Map p76; ☑ 081 1971 8800; www.cilieginahotel .it; Via PE Imbriani 30; d from €200; ❄@☎; Ⓜ Municipio) An easy walk from the hydrofoil terminal, this chic, contemporary slumber spot is a hit with fashion-conscious urbanites. Spacious white rooms are splashed with blue and red accents, each with top-of-the-range Hästens beds, flat-screen TVs and marble-clad bathrooms with a water-jet jacuzzi shower (one junior suite has a jacuzzi tub).

Breakfast in bed or on the rooftop terrace, which comes with sunbeds, hot tub and a view of Vesuvius. Complimentary iPad use is a nice touch, and it's always a good idea to check the hotel website for decent discounts.

Grand Hotel Vesuvio   HOTEL €€€

(Map p76; ☑ 081 764 00 44; www.vesuvio.it; Via Partenope 45; d from €260; ❄@☎; ☐128, E6 to Via Santa Lucia) Known for hosting legends – past guests include Rita Hayworth and Humphrey Bogart – this five-star veteran seduces with its dripping Murano chandeliers, period antiques and strangely appealing, faded glory. Rooms are a suitable mix of luxury linen sheets, sumptuous mattresses and Echia spa products, though it's the sea-view rooms that really justify the price of slumbering here.

Count your lucky stars at the rooftop bar and restaurant, which is better for sunset drinks than a forgettable dinner.

✖ Eating

Naples is one of Italy's gastronomic darlings, and the bonus of a bayside setting makes for some seriously memorable meals. While white linen, candlelight and €50 bills are readily available, some of the best bites await in the city's spit-and-sawdust trattorias, where two courses and house wine can cost under €20.

★ Concettina Ai Tre Santi   PIZZA €

(Map p68; ☑ 081 29 00 37; www.pizzeriao liva.it; Via Arena della Sanità 7; pizzas from €5; ⊘ noon-midnight Mon-Sat, to 5pm Sun; ☎; Ⓜ Piazza Cavour, Museo) Head in by noon (or 7.30pm at dinner) to avoid a long wait at this hot-spot pizzeria, made famous thanks to its young, driven *pizzaiolo* Ciro Oliva. The menu is an index of fastidiously sourced artisanal ingredients, used to top Ciro's flawless, wood-fired bases. Traditional Neapolitan pizza aside, you'll also find a string of creative seasonal options.

These might include the slider-like *Annarella,* its pizza-dough buns filled with artichoke prepared three ways (boiled, creamed and fried), *provola* (provolone cheese), *culatello* (cured ham) and lemon peel. The pizzeria includes a casual takeaway outlet next door, though the pizzas at the latter are not quite as spectacular.

Pasticceria Mennella   PASTRIES €

(Map p76; ☑ 081 42 60 26; www.pasticceria mennella.it; Via Carducci 50-52; pastries from €1.50; ⊘ 6.30am-9.30pm Mon-Fri, to 10.30pm Sat, 7am-9.30pm Sun; Ⓜ Piazza Amedeo) If you eat only one sweet treat in Naples (good luck with that!), make it Mennella's spectacular *frolla al limone,* a shortbread pastry filled with heavenly lemon cream. Just leave room for the *mignon* (bite-size) version of its *sciù* (choux pastry) with *crema di nocciola* (hazelnut cream). Before you go feeling guilty, remember that everything is free of preservatives and artificial additives.

Mennella also makes its own almond milk, a sweet, refreshing must for lovers of marzipan flavour. If you're more in the mood for a cold treat, you'll find a branch of Mennella's exceptional gelateria across the street at number 45.

★ Pizzeria Starita
PIZZA €

(Map p68; ☑ 081 557 36 82; www.pizzeriestarita.it; Via Materdei 28; pizzas from €4; ⊙ noon-3.30pm & 7pm-midnight Tue-Sun; ⓂMaterdei) The giant fork and ladle hanging on the wall at this historic pizzeria were used by Sophia Loren in *L'oro di Napoli,* and the kitchen made the *pizze fritte* sold by the actress in the film. While the 60-plus pizza varieties include a tasty *fiorilli e zucchine* (zucchini, zucchini flowers and *provola),* our allegiance remains to its classic *marinara.*

Serafino
SICILIAN €

(Map p72; ☑ 081 557 14 33; Via dei Tribunali 44; arancini, cannoli €2.50; ⊙ 10.30am-10.30pm Mon-Thu, to midnight Fri-Sun) A veritable porthole to Sicily, this takeaway stand peddles authentic island street food. Savoury bites include various types of *arancini* (deep-fried rice balls), among them *al ragù* (with meat sauce) and *alla Norma* (with fried aubergine and ricotta). The real reason to head here, however, is for the crisp, flawless cannoli, filled fresh with silky Sicilian ricotta and sprinkled with pistachio crumbs. Bliss.

Pizzeria Gino Sorbillo
PIZZA €

(Map p72; ☑ 081 44 66 43; www.sorbillo.it; Via dei Tribunali 32; pizzas from €4; ⊙ noon-3.30pm & 7-11.30pm Mon-Sat; ⓂDante) Day in, day out, this cult-status pizzeria is besieged by hungry hordes. While debate may rage over whether Gino Sorbillo's pizzas are the best in town, there's no doubt that his giant, wood-fired discs – made using organic flour and tomatoes – will have you licking fingertips and whiskers. Head in superearly or prepare to wait.

★ Da Ettore
NEAPOLITAN €€

(Map p76; ☑ 081 764 35 78; Via Gennaro Serra 39; meals €25; ⊙ 1-3pm & 8-10pm Tue-Sat, 1-3pm Sun; ; R2 to Via San Carlo, ⓂChiaia-Monte di Dio) This homey, eight-table trattoria has an epic reputation. Scan the walls for famous fans like comedy great Totò, and a framed passage from crime writer Massimo Siviero, who mentions Ettore in one of his tales. The draw is solid regional cooking, which includes one of the best *spaghetti alle vongole*

(spaghetti with clams) in town. Book two days ahead for Sunday lunch.

★ Salumeria
NEAPOLITAN €€

(Map p72; ☑ 081 1936 4649; www.salumeria upnea.it; Via San Giovanni Maggiore Pignatelli 34/35; sandwiches from €5.50, meals around €30; ⊙ 12.30-5pm & 7.15pm-midnight Thu-Tue; ; ⓂDante) Small producers, local ingredients and contemporary takes on provincial Campanian recipes drive bistro-inspired Salumeria. Nibble on quality charcuterie and cheeses or fill up on artisanal *panini,* hamburgers or Salumeria's sublime *ragù napoletano* (pasta served in a rich tomato-and-meat sauce slow-cooked over two days). Even the ketchup here is made in-house, using DOP Piennolo tomatoes from Vesuvius.

Pescheria Mattiucci
SEAFOOD €€

(Map p76; ☑ 081 251 2215; www.pescheriamat tiucci.com; Vico Belledonne a Chiaia 27; crudo €25, cooked dishes €12-15; ⊙ 12.30-3pm & 7-10.30pm Tue-Sat; E6 to Piazza dei Martiri, ⓂPiazza Amedeo) Run by brothers Francesco, Gennaro and Luigi, this local Chiaia fishmonger transforms daily into a wonderfully intimate, sociable seafood eatery. Perch yourself on a bar stool, order a vino, and watch the team prepare your superfresh, tapas-style *crudo* (raw seafood) to order. You'll also find a number of simple, beautifully cooked surf dishes.

If they're on the menu, order the scampi with fresh pineapple and mustard as well as the salted *alici* (anchovies), the latter served with toasted bread and butter. For the best experience, go early in the week, when the crowds are thin and the ambience *much* more relaxed.

★ L'Ebbrezza di Noè
ITALIAN €€

(Map p76; ☑ 081 40 01 04; www.lebbrezzadi noe.com; Vico Vetriera 9; meals €35-40, cheese & charcuterie platters €10; ⊙ 6-11pm Tue-Thu, to midnight Fri & Sat, 1-3pm Sun; ; ⓂPiazza Amedeo) A wine shop by day, 'Noah's Drunkenness' transforms into an intimate culinary hot spot by night. Slip inside for *vino* and conversation with sommelier Luca at the bar, or settle into one of the bottle-lined dining rooms for seductive, market-driven dishes such as house special *paccheri fritti* (fried pasta stuffed with aubergine and served with fresh basil and a rich tomato sauce).

Dialetti
ITALIAN €€

(Map p76; ☑ 081 248 1158; www.facebook.com/ DialettiNapoli; Vico Satriano 10; meals around

€32; ◷noon-3.30pm & 6pm-midnight Mon-Sat; ⊙; 🚌128, 140, 151 to Riviera di Chiaia) On-point Dialetti takes its cues from cities like New York, London and Sydney. You'll find a snug, vintage-pimped lounge corner at the front, a communal dining table with views of the glassed-in kitchen, and a softly lit dining room beyond it. Service is attentive and the daily changing menu champions gorgeous ingredients, cooked beautifully and with subtle contemporary tweaks.

Ristorantino dell'Avvocato NEAPOLITAN €€

(Map p76; ☑081 032 00 47; www.ilristorantinodellavvocato.it; Via Santa Lucia 115-117; meals €40-45; ◷noon-3pm & 7.30-11pm Tue-Sat, noon-3pm Sun; ⊙; 🚌128, E6 to Via Santa Lucia) This elegant yet welcoming restaurant is a favourite of Neapolitan gastronomes. Apple of their eye is affable lawyer turned head chef Raffaele Cardillo, whose passion for Campania's culinary heritage merges with a knack for subtle, refreshing twists – think coffee papardelle served with mullet *ragù*.

The degustation menus (€50 to €60) are good value. Book ahead.

🍷 Drinking & Nightlife

Although Neapolitans aren't big drinkers, Naples offers an increasingly varied selection of venues in which to imbibe. You'll find well-worn wine bars and a new wave of options focused on craft beer, cocktails and even speciality coffee. The main hubs are the *centro storico* and Chiaia. The former is generally cheaper and more alternative, the latter more fashionable and scene-y.

★ L'Antiquario COCKTAIL BAR

(Map p76; ☑081 764 53 90; www.facebook.com/AntiquarioNapoli; Via Gaetani 2; ◷7.30pm-2.30am; 🚌151, 154 to Piazza Vittoria) If you take your cocktails seriously, slip into this sultry, speakeasy-inspired den. Wrapped in art nouveau wallpaper, it's the domain of Neapolitan barkeep Alex Frezza, a finalist at the 2014 Bombay Sapphire World's Most Imaginative Bartender Awards. Straddling classic and contemporary, the drinks are impeccable, made with passion and meticulous attention to detail. Live jazz-centric tunes add to the magic on Wednesdays.

★ Barril BAR

(Map p76; ☑393 9814362; www.barril.it; Via G Fiorelli 11; ◷7pm-2am Tue-Thu & Sun, to 3am Fri & Sat; ⊙; Ⓜ Piazza Amedeo) From street level, stairs lead down to this softly lit, buzzing garden bar, where grown-up, fashionable types mingle among birdcage seats and vintage Cinzano posters. Fresh cocktails include giant, creamy piña coladas, and you'll also find over 40 gins with numerous tonic waters for a customised G&T. Bites include cheese and charcuterie platters, plus a decent selection of complimentary *aperitivo*-time snacks.

★ Caffè Gambrinus CAFE

(Map p76; ☑081 41 75 82; www.grancaffegambrinus.com; Via Chiaia 1-2; ◷7am-1am Sun-Fri, to 2am Sat; 🚌R2 to Via San Carlo, Ⓜ Municipio) Gambrinus is Naples' oldest and most venerable cafe, serving superlative Neapolitan coffee under flouncy chandeliers. Oscar Wilde knocked back a few here and Mussolini had some rooms shut to keep out left-wing intellectuals. Sit-down prices are steep, but the *aperitivo* nibbles are decent and sipping a *spritz* or a luscious *cioccolata calda* (hot chocolate) in its belle-époque rooms is something worth savouring.

Shanti Art Musik Bar BAR

(Map p72; ☑081 551 49 79; www.facebook.com/ShantiSPACCANapoli; Via Giovanni Paladino 56; ◷10.30am-2.30am Mon-Wed, 11am-3am Thu-Sat; ⊙; Ⓜ Dante) Under Tibetan prayer flags, shabby Shanti draws a cosmopolitan crowd of arty and indie types, both local and foreign. While the place serves lunchtime grub, head here in the evenings, when party people congregate at upcycled, candlelit tables to chat, flirt and party well into the night. Drinks are well priced.

Spazio Nea CAFE

(Map p72; ☑081 45 13 58; www.spazionea.it; Via Costantinopoli 53; ◷9am-2am, to 3am Fri & Sat; ⊙; Ⓜ Dante) Aptly skirting bohemian Piazza Bellini, this whitewashed gallery features its own cafe-bar speckled with books, flowers, cultured crowds and al fresco seating at the bottom of a baroque staircase. Eye up exhibitions of contemporary Italian and foreign art, then kick back with a *caffè* or a *spritz*. Check Nea's Facebook page for upcoming readings, live-music gigs or DJ sets.

☆ Entertainment

Although Naples is no London or Milan on the entertainment front, it does offer world-class opera, ballet, classical music and jazz, thought-provoking theatre and in-the-know DJs. To see what's on, scan Italian-language *Corriere del Mezzogiorno* (https://corriere delmezzogiorno.corriere.it/napoli) or *La Repubblica* (http://napoli.repubblica.it), or ask at the tourist office.

★**Teatro San Carlo** OPERA, BALLET
(Map p76; ☑box office 081 797 23 31; www.teatro
sancarlo.it; Via San Carlo 98f; ☺box office 10am-9pm
Mon-Sat, to 6pm Sun; ☐R2 to Via San Carlo, ⓂMu-
nicipio) San Carlo's opera season runs from
November or December to June, with occasional summer performances. Sample prices:
a place in the 6th tier (from €35), the stalls
(€75 to €130) or the side box (from €40). Ballet season runs from late October to April or
early May; tickets range from €30 to €110. Although the original 1737 theatre burnt down
in 1816, Antonio Niccolini's 19th-century reconstruction is pure Old World opulence. If
you can't make it to a performance, consider
taking one of the 45-minute guided tours of
the venue; tickets (adult/reduced €9/7) can
be purchased at the theatre up to 15 minutes
before each tour begins.

★**Stadio San Paolo** FOOTBALL
(Piazzale Vincenzo Tecchio; Ⓜ Napoli Campi Flegrei)
Naples' football team, Napoli, is the fourth
most supported in Italy after Juventus, AC
Milan and Inter Milan, and watching it play
in the country's third-largest stadium is a
rush. The season runs from late August to
late May; seats cost from around €20 to
€100. Tickets are available from selected
tobacconists, the agency inside **Feltrinelli** (Map p76; ☑081 032 23 62; www.azzurroser
vice.net; La Feltrinelli bookstore, Piazza dei Martiri
23; ☺11am-2pm & 3-8pm Mon-Sat; ☐E6 to Piazza
dei Martiri), or **Box Office** (Map p76; ☑081 551
91 88; www.boxofficenapoli.it; Galleria Umberto I 17;
☺9.30am-8pm Mon-Fri, 10am-1.30pm & 4.30-8pm
Sat; ☐R2 to Piazza Trieste e Trento, ⓂMunicipio);
bring photo ID. On match days, tickets are
also available at the stadium itself.

**Centro di Musica Antica
Pietà de' Turchini** CLASSICAL MUSIC
(Map p76; ☑081 40 23 95; www.turchini.it;
Via Santa Caterina da Siena 38; adult/reduced
€10/7; ☐Centrale to Corso Vittorio Emanuele)
Classical-music buffs are in for a treat at this
beautiful deconsecrated church, an evocative setting for concerts of mostly 17th- to
19th-century Neapolitan works. Upcoming
concerts are listed on the venue's website.
Note that some concerts are held at other
venues, including the Palazzo Zevallos Stigliano (p79).

Bourbon Street JAZZ
(Map p72; ☑338 8253756; www.bourbon
streetjazzclub.com; Via Bellini 52; ☺8.30pm-2am
Tue-Thu & Sun, to 3am Fri & Sat; closed Jul-early
Sep; ⓂDante) Bourbon Street is one of the

top spots for live jazz and blues, drawing
a mixed crowd of seasoned jazz nerds and
rookies. Acts are mostly local, with Wednesday, Thursday and Sunday nights featuring
'JamJazz' sessions, when musicians hit the
stage for impromptu collaborations. Check
the venue's Facebook page (Bourbon Street
Napoli Jazz Club) to see who's up next.

🛍 **Shopping**

★**Omega** FASHION & ACCESSORIES
(Map p72; ☑081 29 90 41; www.omegasrl.com; Via
Stella 12; ☺8.30am-6pm Mon-Fri; ⓂPiazza Cavour,
Museo) Despite hiding away on the 3rd floor
of a nondescript building, Paris, New York
and Tokyo know all about this family-run
glove factory, whose clients include Dior and
Hermes. Omega's men's and women's leather
gloves are meticulously handcrafted using a
traditional 25-step process, and best of all,
they retail for a fraction of the price charged
by the luxury fashion houses.

Expect to pay between €30 and €110 for
a pair of gloves, depending on the style. The
workshop is now run by the fourth and fifth
generations of the family: affable Mauro
Squillace and his son Alberto. Mauro offers
free 45-minute tours of the workshop and
glove-making process if he's not busy, and
no reservations are necessary to drop by the
place, whether to shop or simply take a peek.

★**Bottega 21** FASHION & ACCESSORIES
(Map p72; ☑081 033 55 42; www.bottegaventu
no.it; Vico San Domenico Maggiore 21; ☺9.30am-
8pm Mon-Sat) Top-notch Tuscan leather and
traditional, handcrafted methods translate
into coveted, contemporary leather goods at
Bottega 21. Block colours and clean, simple
designs underline the range, which includes
stylish totes, handbags, backpacks and duf-
fel bags, as well as wallets and coin purses,
unisex belts, gloves, sandals, tobacco pouch-
es and, occasionally, notebook covers.

There's a second branch further down the
street at No 11.

★**E Marinella** FASHION & ACCESSORIES
(Map p76; ☑081 764 32 65; www.emarinella.
com; Via Riviera di Chiaia 287; ☺6.30am-8pm
Mon-Sat, 9am-1pm Sun; ☐C25 to Piazza Vittoria,
E6 to Piazza dei Martiri) One-time favourite of
Luchino Visconti and Aristotle Onassis, this
pocket-sized, vintage boutique is *the* place
for prêt-à-porter and made-to-measure silk
ties in striking patterns and hues. Match
them with an irresistible selection of luxury

accessories, including shoes, heritage colognes and scarves for female style queens.

★ **La Scarabattola** ARTS & CRAFTS
(Map p72; ☑ 081 29 17 35; www.lascarabattola.it; Via dei Tribunali 50; ☉ 10.30am-2pm & 3.30-7.30pm Mon-Fri, 10am-8pm Sat; Ⓜ Dante) La Scarabattola's handmade sculptures of *magi* (wise men), devils and Neapolitan folk figures constitute Jerusalem's official Christmas crèche, and the artisanal studio's fans also include fashion designer Stefano Gabbana and Spanish royalty. Figurines aside, sleek ceramic creations (like Pulcinella-inspired place-card holders) inject Neapolitan folklore with refreshing contemporary style.

Limonè FOOD & DRINKS
(Map p72; ☑ 081 29 94 29; www.limoncellodi napoli.it; Piazza San Gaetano 72; ☉ 11am-8.30pm; Ⓜ Dante) For a take-home taste of Napoli, stock up on a few bottles of Limonè's homemade *limoncello* (lemon liqueur), made with organic lemons from the Campi Flegrei. For something a little sweeter, opt for the *crema di limone*, a gorgeous lemon liqueur made with milk. Other take-home treats include lemon pasta and risotto, lemon-infused chocolate, jars of rum-soaked *babà*, even lemon-infused grappa.

Ask nicely for a sample of the liqueurs. If the shop isn't too busy, you might even get shown the foundations of an ancient Greek temple hidden out the back.

❶ Information

MEDICAL SERVICES

Loreto Mare Hospital (Ospedale San Maria di Loreto Nuovo; ☑ 081 254 21 11; www.aslnapoli centro.it/818; Via Vespucci 26; ☐ 154 to Via Vespucci) Central-city hospital with an emergency department.

Pharmacy (Napoli Centrale; ☉ 7am-9.30pm Mon-Sat (to 9pm in winter), 8am-9pm Sun; Ⓜ Garibaldi, Ⓡ Napoli Centrale) Pharmacy inside the main train station.

POST

Main Post Office (Map p76; ☑ 081 428 98 14; www.poste.it; Piazza Matteotti 2; ☉ 8.20am-7pm Mon-Fri, to 12.30pm Sat; Ⓜ Toledo) Naples' curvaceous main post office is famous for its fascist-era architecture.

TOURIST INFORMATION

Tourist Information Office (Map p72; ☑ 081 551 27 01; www.inaples.it; Piazza del Gesù Nuovo 7; ☉ 9am-5pm Mon-Sat, to 1pm Sun; Ⓜ Dante) In the *centro storico*.

Tourist Information Office (Map p76; ☑ 081 40 23 94; www.inaples.it; Via San Carlo 9; ☉ 9am-5pm Mon-Sat, to 1pm Sun; ☐ R2 to Via San Carlo, Ⓜ Municipio) At Galleria Umberto I, directly opposite Teatro San Carlo.

❶ Getting There & Away

AIR

Naples International Airport (Capodichino; ☑ 081 789 62 59; www.aeroportodinapoli.it; Viale F Ruffo di Calabria), 7km northeast of the city centre, is southern Italy's main airport. It's served by a number of major airlines and low-cost carriers, including easyJet, which operates flights to Naples from London, Paris, Amsterdam, Vienna, Berlin and several other European cities.

BOAT

Fast ferries and hydrofoils for Capri, Ischia, Procida and Sorrento depart from **Molo Beverello** (Map p76; Ⓜ Municipio) in front of Castel Nuovo; hydrofoils for Capri, Ischia and Procida also sail from Mergellina.

High-speed ferry and hydrofoil operators include the following:

Alilauro (☑ 081 497 22 38; www.alilauro.it; Molo Beverello) Runs up to six daily services to/from Naples and Sorrento (€13). Also runs up to 10 daily services to/from Naples and Ischia (€20).

Caremar (☑ 081 1896 6690; www.caremar. it; Molo Beverello) Operates up to four daily services between Naples and Capri (€18). Also runs up to six daily services to/from Naples and Ischia (€18) and up to eight daily services to/from Procida (€14.50).

Navigazione Libera del Golfo (NLG; ☑ 081 552 07 63; www.navlib.it; Marina Grande) Runs up to nine daily services to/from Naples and Capri (from €19). Also runs one daily services to/from Naples and Sorrento (€13).

SNAV (☑ 081 428 55 55; www.snav.it; Molo Beverollo, Naples) Runs up to nine daily services between Naples and Capri (from €22.50). Also runs up to eight daily services to Ischia (from €20) and up to four daily services to Procida (from €17.50).

Slow ferries for Sicily, the Aeolian Islands and Sardinia sail from **Molo Angioino** (Map p76; Ⓜ Municipio), which is right beside Molo Beverello, and neighbouring **Calata Porta di Massa** (Map p76; Ⓜ Municipio). Car ferries to Ischia and Procida also depart from Calata Porta di Massa.

Slow-ferry operators include the following:

Caremar (☑ 081 1896 6690; www.caremar.it; Molo Beverello) Runs ferries to/from Naples and Capri (from €12.50) three times daily. Runs up to eight times daily to/from Naples and

Ischia (€12.50) and up to seven times daily to/from Naples and Prodica (€10.50).

Medmar (📞 081 333 44 11; www.medmar group.it; Calata Porta di Massa, Naples) Runs ferries to/from Naples and Ischia (from €12.50) three times daily.

Siremar (Map p76; 📞 800 627414; www.sire-mar.it; Calata Porto di Massa, Naples) Operates overnight ferries to the Isole Eolie (Aeolian Islands) and Milazzo in Sicily (from €57.50) twice weekly.

SNAV (www.snav.it; Calata Porta di Massa) Runs to/from Naples and the Isole Eolie (Aeolian Islands) several times weekly (from €58) from June to early September.

Tirrenia (📞 199 303040; www.tirrenia.it; Calata Porta di Massa) Runs ferries from Naples to Cagliari in Sardinia (from €47) twice weekly. Also runs once daily from Naples to Palermo in Sicily (from €56.50).

BUS

Most national and international buses leave from **Metropark Napoli Centrale** (Map p72; 📞 800 650006; Corso Arnaldo Lucci; Ⓜ Garibaldi), on the southern side of Napoli Centrale train station. The bus station is home to **Biglietteria Vecchione** (📞 331 88969217; Corso Arnaldo Lucci, Terminal Bus Metropark; ⊗ 6.30am-9.15pm Mon-Fri, to 7pm Sat, 7am-7pm Sun; Ⓜ Garibaldi), a ticket agency selling national and international bus tickets.

Metropark Napoli Centrale serves numerous bus companies offering regional and inter-regional services, among them FlixBus (https://global.flixbus.com), **CLP** (📞 081 531 17 07; www.clpbus.it; Metropark Napoli Centrale, Corso Arnaldo Lucci), **Marino** (📞 080 311 23 35; www.marinobus.it; Metropark Napoli Centrale, Corso Arnaldo Lucci), **Miccolis** (📞 080 531 53 34; www.miccolis-spa.it; Metropark Napoli Centrale, Corso Arnaldo Lucci) and **SAIS** (📞 091 617 11 41; www.saistrasporti.it; Metropark Napoli Centrale, Corso Arnaldo Lucci). It also serves **Fiumicino Express** (📞 391 3998081; www.fiumicino express.com), which runs to and from Rome's Fiumicino and Ciampino airports via Caserta.

The bus stop for **SITA Sud** (📞 342 6256442; www.sitasudtrasporti.it) services to the Amalfi Coast is just around the corner on Via Galileo Ferraris (in front of the hulking Istituto Nazionale della Previdenza Sociale office building).

CAR & MOTORCYCLE

Naples is on the north–south Autostrada del Sole, the A1 (north to Rome and Milan) and the A3 (south to Salerno and Reggio di Calabria).

Among other locations, the following car-rental agencies have branches at Naples International Airport:

Avis (📞 081 28 40 41; www.avisautonoleggio.it; Piazza Garibaldi 92, Starhotels Terminus; ⊗ 8am-7.30pm Mon-Fri, 8.30am-4.30pm Sat, 9am-1pm Sun)

Europcar (📞 081 780 56 43; www.europcar.it; Naples International Airport (Capodichino); ⊗ 7.30am-11.30pm)

Hertz (📞 081 20 28 60; www.hertz.it; Corso Arnaldo Lucci 171; ⊗ 8.30am-1pm & 2.30-7pm Mon-Fri, 8.30am-1pm Sat)

Maggiore (📞 081 28 78 58; www.maggiore.it; Napoli Centrale; ⊗ 8.30am-7.30pm Mon-Fri, to 6pm Sat, to 12.30pm Sun)

For scooter rental, contact **Vespa Sprint** (📞 081 764 34 52; http://vespasprint.it/noleggio-vespa-scooter-napoli; Via Santa Lucia 36, Naples; scooter hire per day from €60; ⊗ 8am-8pm Mon-Sat, 10am-6pm Sun), in the city's Santa Lucia district.

TRAIN

Naples is southern Italy's rail hub and on the main Milan–Palermo line, with good connections to other Italian cities and towns.

The city's main train station is **Napoli Centrale** (Stazione Centrale; 📞 081 554 31 88; Piazza Garibaldi), just east of the centro storico. From here, the national rail company **Trenitalia** (📞 892021; www.trenitalia.com) runs regular direct services to Rome (2nd class €13 to €48, 70 minutes to three hours, around 66 daily). High-speed private rail company **Italo** (📞 892020; www.italotreno.it) also runs daily direct services to Rome (2nd class €15 to €40, 70 minutes, around 20 daily). Most Italo services stop at Roma Termini and Roma Tiburtina stations.

ⓘ Getting Around

BUS

ANM (📞 800 639525; www.anm.it) operates city buses in Naples. There's no central bus station, but most buses pass through Piazza Garibaldi. Buses generally run from around 5.30am to about 11pm, depending on the route and day. Some routes do not run on Sunday. A small number of routes run through the night, marked with an 'N' before their route number.

Useful city routes include the following:

140 Santa Lucia to Posillipo (via Mergellina)

154 Port area to Chiaia (along Via Volta, Via Vespucci, Via Marina, Via Depretis, Via Acton, Via Morelli and Piazza Vittoria)

C51 Piazza Cavour to La Sanità (along Via Foria, Via Vergini, Via Sanità and Via Fontanelle)

E6 Piazza Trieste e Trento to Chiaia (along Via Monte di Dio, Via Santa Lucia, Via Morelli, Piazza dei Martiri and Via Filangieri)

R2 Napoli Centrale to Piazza Trento e Trieste (along Corso Umberto I and Piazza Municipio)

R4 Via Toledo to Capodimonte (via Piazza Dante and Via Santa Maria di Costantinopoli)

FUNICULAR

Three services connect central Naples to Vomero, while a fourth connects Mergellina to Posillipo. All operate from 7am to 10pm daily. ANM transport tickets are valid on funicular services.

Funicolare Centrale (www.anm.it; ⊙7am-10pm) Travels from Piazzetta Augusteo to Piazza Fuga.

Funicolare di Chiaia (www.anm.it; ⊙7am-10pm) Travels from Via del Parco Margherita to Via Domenico Cimarosa.

Funicolare di Montesanto (www.anm.it; ⊙7am-10pm) Travels from Piazza Montesanto to Via Raffaele Morghen.

Funicolare di Mergellina (www.anm.it; ⊙7am-10pm) Connects the waterfront at Via Mergellina with Via Manzoni.

METRO

Metro Line 1 (Linea 1; www.anm.it) Runs from Garibaldi (Stazione Centrale) to Vomero and the northern suburbs via the city centre. Useful stops include Duomo and Università (southern edge of the *centro storico*), Municipio (hydrofoil and ferry terminals), Toledo (Via Toledo and Quartieri Spagnoli), Dante (western edge of the *centro storico*) and Museo (National Archaeological Museum).

Metro Line 2 (Linea 2; www.trenitalia.com) Runs from Gianturco to Garibaldi (Stazione Centrale) and on to Pozzuoli. Useful stops include Piazza Cavour (La Sanità and northern edge of *centro storico*), Piazza Amedeo (Chiaia) and Mergellina (Mergellina ferry terminal). Change between Lines 1 and 2 at Garibaldi or Piazza Cavour (known as Museo on Line 1).

Metro Line 6 (Linea 6; www.anm.it) Expected to open in 2022. When completed, it will run from Municipio to Mostra, with useful stops

---

WORTH A TRIP

REGGIA DI CASERTA

Italy's swansong to the baroque, the colossal **Reggia di Caserta** (Palazzo Reale; ☑0823 44 80 84; www.reggiadicaserta.beniculturali.it; Viale Douhet 22, Caserta; adult/reduced €12/6; ⊙palace 8.30am-7.30pm Wed-Mon, park to 7pm Wed-Mon Apr-Sep, reduced hours Oct-Mar, Giardino Inglese to 6pm Wed-Mon Apr-Sep, reduced hours Oct-Mar; ℝCaserta) began life in 1752 after Charles VII ordered a palace to rival Versailles. Not one to disappoint, Neapolitan architect Luigi Vanvitelli delivered a palace bigger than its French rival. With its 1200 rooms, 1790 windows, 34 staircases and 250m-long facade, it was reputedly the largest building in 18th-century Europe.

Vanvitelli's immense staircase leads up to the Royal Apartments, lavishly decorated with frescoes, art, tapestries, period furniture and crystal.

The back rooms off the Sala di Astrea (Room of Astraea) house an extraordinary collection of historic wooden models of the Reggia, along with architectural drawings and early sketches of the building by Luigi Vanvitelli and his son, Carlo. The apartments are also home to the Mostra Terrea Motus, an underrated collection of international modern art commissioned after the region's devastating earthquake in 1980. Among the contributors are US heavyweights Cy Twombly, Robert Mapplethorpe and Keith Haring, as well as local luminaries like Mimmo Paladino and Jannis Kounellis.

The complex has appeared in numerous films, including *Mission: Impossible III, Star Wars: Episode 1 – The Phantom Menace,* and *Star Wars: Episode II – Attack of the Clones,* moonlighting as Queen Amidala's palace in the latter two.

To clear your head afterwards, explore the elegant landscaped park, which stretches for some 3km to a waterfall and a fountain of Diana. Within the park is the famous Giardino Inglese (English Garden), a romantic oasis of intricate pathways, exotic flora, pools and cascades. Bicycle hire (from €4) is available at the back of the palace building, as are pony-and-trap rides (€50 for 40 minutes, up to five people).

If you're feeling peckish, consider skipping the touristy palace cafeteria for local cafe **Martucci** (☑0823 32 08 03; www.facebook.com/martucci.caffe; Via Roma 9, Caserta; pastries from €1.50, sandwiches from €3.50, salads €7.50; ⊙5am-10.30pm; 🕿), located 250m east of the complex.

Regular trains connect Naples to Caserta (€3.40, 30 to 50 minutes); always plan ahead and check times online before hitting the station. Caserta train station is located directly opposite the palace grounds. If you're driving from Naples, exit the A1 (E45) at Caserta Sud and follow signs for Caserta and the Reggia.

including Chiaia–Monte di Dio (just west of Piazza del Plebiscito), San Pasquale (Chiaia and the Lungomare) and Mergellina.

TAXI

Official taxis are white and metered. Always ensure the meter is running.

The minimum starting fare is €3.50 (€6.50 on Sunday), with a baffling range of additional charges, all of which are listed at www.taxi napoli.it/tariffe. These extras include the following:

➡ €1.50 for a radio taxi call

➡ €4 for an airport run

➡ €5 for trips starting at the airport and €0.50 per piece of luggage in the boot (trunk). Guide dogs, wheelchairs and strollers are carried free of charge.

There are taxi stands at most of the city's main piazzas. Book a taxi by calling any of the following companies:

Consortaxi (☑ 081 22 22; www.consortaxi. com)

Radio Taxi Partenope (☑ 081 01 01; www. radiotaxilapartenope.it)

Taxi Napoli (☑ 081 88 88; www.taxinapoli.it)

SOUTH OF NAPLES

Herculaneum (Ercolano)

Ercolano is an uninspiring Neapolitan suburb that's home to one of Italy's best-preserved ancient sites: Herculaneum. A superbly conserved fishing town, the site is smaller and less daunting than Pompeii, allowing you to visit without the nagging feeling that you're bound to miss something.

⊙ Sights

★ Ruins of Herculaneum   ARCHAEOLOGICAL SITE

(☑ 081 777 70 08; http://ercolano.beniculturali.it; Corso Resina 187, Ercolano; adult/reduced €13/2; ⊙ 8.30am-7.30pm, last entry 6pm Apr-Oct, 8.30am-5pm, last entry 3.30pm Nov-Mar; **P**; **R** Circumvesuviana to Ercolano–Scavi) Herculaneum harbours a wealth of archaeological finds, from ancient advertisements and stylish mosaics to carbonised furniture and terror-struck skeletons. Indeed, this superbly conserved Roman fishing town of 4000 inhabitants is easier to navigate than Pompeii, and can be explored with a map and highly recommended audio guide (€8).

To reach the ruins from Ercolano–Scavi train station, walk downhill to the very end of Via IV Novembre and through the archway across the street. The path leads down to the ticket office, which lies on your left. Ticket purchased, follow the walkway around to the actual entrance to the ruins, where you can also hire audio guides.

Herculaneum's fate runs parallel to that of Pompeii. Destroyed by an earthquake in 62 CE, the 79 CE eruption of Mt Vesuvius saw it submerged in a 16m-thick sea of mud that essentially fossilised the city. This meant that even delicate items, such as furniture and clothing, were discovered remarkably well preserved. Tragically, the inhabitants didn't fare so well; thousands of people tried to escape by boat but were suffocated by the volcano's poisonous gases. Indeed, what appears to be a moat around the town is in fact the ancient shoreline. It was here in 1980 that archaeologists discovered some 300 skeletons, the remains of a crowd that had fled to the beach only to be overcome by the terrible heat of clouds surging down from Vesuvius.

The town itself was rediscovered in 1709 and amateur excavations were carried out intermittently until 1874, with many finds carted off to Naples to decorate the houses of the well-to-do or ending up in museums. Serious archaeological work began again in 1927 and continues to this day; with much of the ancient site buried beneath modern Ercolano, it's slow going.

Note that at any given time some houses will invariably be shut for restoration.

Casa d'Argo   ARCHAEOLOGICAL SITE

(Argus House) This noble house would originally have opened onto Cardo II (as yet unearthed). Its porticoed garden opens onto a *triclinium* (dining room) and other residential rooms.

Casa dello Scheletro   ARCHAEOLOGICAL SITE

(House of the Skeleton) The modest Casa dello Scheletro features five styles of mosaic flooring, including a design of white arrows at the entrance to guide the most disoriented of guests. In the internal courtyard, don't miss the skylight, complete with the remnants of an ancient security grill. Of the house's mythically themed wall mosaics, only the faded ones are originals; the others now reside in Naples' Museo Archeologico Nazionale (p70).

Terme Maschili   ARCHAEOLOGICAL SITE

(Men's Baths) The Terme Maschili were the men's section of the **Terme del Foro** (Forum Baths). Note the ancient latrine to the left of the entrance before you step into the *apodyterium* (changing room), complete with bench for waiting patrons and a nifty wall shelf for sandal and toga storage. While those after a bracing soak would pop into the *frigidarium* (cold bath) to the left, the less stoic headed straight into the *tepadarium* (tepid bath) to the right. The sunken mosaic floor here is testament to the seismic activity preceding Mt Vesuvius' catastrophic eruption. Beyond this room lies the *caldarium* (hot bath), as well as an exercise area.

Decumano Massimo ARCHAEOLOGICAL SITE
Herculaneum's ancient high street is lined with shops, and fragments of advertisements; look for the wall fresco advertising wines by colour code and price per weight. Note the one to the right of the Casa del Salone Nero. Further east along the street, a crucifix found in an upstairs room of the **Casa del Bicentenario** (Bicentenary House) provides possible evidence of a Christian presence in pre-Vesuvius Herculaneum.

Casa del Bel Cortile ARCHAEOLOGICAL SITE
(House of the Beautiful Courtyard) The Casa del Bel Cortile is home to three of the 300 skeletons discovered on the ancient shore by archaeologists in 1980. Almost two millennia after the volcanic eruption, it's still poignant to see the forms of what are understood to be a mother, father and young child huddled together in the last, terrifying moments of their lives.

**Casa di Nettuno
e Anfitrite** ARCHAEOLOGICAL SITE
(House of Neptune & Amphitrite) This aristocratic pad takes its name from the extraordinary mosaic in the *triclinium* (dining room), which also features a mosaic-encrusted *nymphaeum* (fountain and bath as a shrine to the water nymph). The warm colours in which the sea god and his nymph bride are depicted hint at how lavish the original interior must have been.

**Casa del Tramezzo
di Legno** ARCHAEOLOGICAL SITE
(House of the Wooden Partition) Unusually, this house features two atria, which likely belonged to two separate dwellings that were merged in the 1st century CE. The most famous relic here is a wonderfully well-preserved wooden screen, separating the atrium from the *tablinum,* where the owner talked business with his clients. The second room off the left side of the atrium features the remains of an ancient bed.

**Casa dell'Atrio
a Mosaico** ARCHAEOLOGICAL SITE
(House of the Mosaic Atrium; ⊘ closed for restoration) An ancient mansion, the House of the Mosaic Atrium harbours extensive floor tilework, although time and nature have left the floor buckled and uneven. Particularly noteworthy is the black-and-white chessboard mosaic in the atrium.

Casa del Gran Portale ARCHAEOLOGICAL SITE
(House of the Large Portal) Named after the brick Corinthian columns that flank its main entrance, the House of the Large Portal is home to some well-preserved wall paintings.

Casa dei Cervi ARCHAEOLOGICAL SITE
(House of the Stags) The Casa dei Cervi is an imposing example of a Roman noble family's house that, before the volcanic mud slide, boasted a seafront address. Constructed around a central courtyard, the two-storey villa contains murals and some beautiful still-life paintings. Waiting for you in the courtyard is a diminutive pair of marble deer assailed by dogs, and an engaging statue of a drunken, peeing Hercules.

Terme Suburbane ARCHAEOLOGICAL SITE
(Suburban Baths) Marking Herculaneum's southernmost tip is the 1st-century-CE Terme Suburbane, one of the best-preserved Roman bath complexes in existence, with deep pools, stucco friezes and bas-reliefs looking down upon marble seats and floors. This is also one of the best places to observe the soaring volcanic deposits that smothered the ancient coastline.

MAV MUSEUM
(Museo Archeologico Virtuale; ✐081 777 68 43; www.museomav.com; Via IV Novembre 44; adult/reduced €10/8; ⊘9am-5.30pm daily Mar-May, 10am-6.30pm daily Jun-Sep, to 4pm Tue-Sun Oct-Feb; ⋈; ⍰Circumvesuviana to Ercolano–Scavi) Using computer-generated recreations, this 'virtual archaeological museum' brings ruins such as Pompeii's forum and Capri's Villa Jovis back to virtual life. Some of the displays are in Italian only. The short documentary gives an overview of the history of Mt Vesuvius and its infamous eruption in 79 CE... in rather lacklustre 3D. The museum is on the main street linking Ercolano–Scavi train station to the ruins of Herculaneum.

🍴 Eating

Viva Lo Re NEAPOLITAN €€
(✐081 739 02 07; www.vivalore.it; Corso Resina 261, Ercolano; meals €32; ⊘noon-3.30pm & 7.30-

11.30pm Tue-Sat, noon-3.30pm Sun; 🐭) Whether you're after an inspired meal or a simple glass of vino, this refined yet relaxed *osteria* (casual tavern) is a solid choice. The wine list is extensive and impressive, while the menu offers competent, produce-driven regional cooking with subtle modern twists. For an appetite-piquing overview, start with the multitaste *antipasto Viva Lo Re*.

The *osteria* lies 500m southeast of the Herculaneum ruins on Corso Resina; dubbed the *Miglio d'Oro* (Golden Mile) for its once glorious stretch of 18th-century villas.

❶ Information

Tourist Office (☑ 081 788 13 75; Via IV Novembre 44; ☺ 9am-2pm Mon-Fri & 2.30-5pm Tue & Thu; ☒ Circumvesuviana to Ercolano–Scavi) Ercolano's tourist office is in the same building as MAV, between the Circumvesuviana Ercolano–Scavi train station and the Herculaneum *scavi* (ruins).

❶ Getting There & Away

If travelling by **Circumvesuviana** (☑ 800 211388; www.eavsrl.it) train (€2.20 from Naples or €2.90 from Sorrento), get off at Ercolano–Scavi and walk 500m downhill to the ruins – follow the signs for the *scavi* down the main street, Via IV Novembre.

If driving from Naples, the A3 runs southeast along the Bay of Naples. To reach the ruins of Herculaneum, exit at Ercolano Portico and follow the signs to car parks near the site. From Sorrento, head north along the SS145, which spills onto the A3.

From mid-March to early November, tourist train *Campania Express* runs four times daily between Naples (Porta Nolana and Piazza Garibaldi Circumvesuviana stations) and Sorrento, stopping at Ercolano–Scavi and Pompei Scavi–Villa dei Misteri en route. One-day return tickets from Naples to Ercolano (€7) or from Sorrento to Ercolano (€11) can be purchased at the stations or online at **EAV** (☑ 800 211388; www.eavsrl.it).

Mt Vesuvius

Rising formidably beside the Bay of Naples, Mt Vesuvius forms part of the Campanian volcanic arch, a string of active, dormant and extinct volcanoes that include the Campi Flegrei's Solfatara and Monte Nuovo, and Ischia's Monte Epomeo. Infamous for its explosive Plinian eruptions and surrounding urban sprawl, it's also one of the world's most carefully monitored volcanoes. Another full-scale eruption would be catastrophic. More than half a million people live in the so-called 'red zone', the area most vulnerable to pyroclastic flows and crushing pyroclastic deposits in a major eruption. Yet, despite government incentives to relocate, few residents are willing to leave.

⊙ Sights

Mt Vesuvius   VOLCANO

(☑ 081 239 56 53; www.parconazionaledelvesuvio.it; crater adult/reduced €10/8; ☺ crater 9am-6pm Jul & Aug, to 5pm Apr-Jun & Sep, to 4pm Mar & Oct, to 3pm Nov-Feb, ticket office closes 1hr before crater) Since exploding into history in 79 CE, Vesuvius has blown its top more than 30 times. What redeems this slumbering menace is the spectacular panorama from its crater, which takes in Naples, its world-famous bay, and part of the Apennine Mountains. Vesuvius is the focal point of the **Parco Nazionale del Vesuvio** (Vesuvius National Park), with nine nature walks around the volcano – download a simple map from the park's website. **Horse Riding Tour Naples** (☑ 345 8560306; www.horseridingnaples.com; guided tour €60) also runs daily horse-riding tours.

The mountain is widely believed to have been higher than it currently stands, claiming a single summit rising to about 3000m rather than the 1281m of today. Its violent outburst in 79 CE not only drowned Pompeii in pumice and pushed the coastline back several kilometres but also destroyed much of the mountain top, creating a huge caldera and two new peaks. The most destructive explosion after that of 79 CE was in 1631, while the most recent was in 1944.

❶ Getting There & Away

Vesuvius can be reached by bus from Pompeii and Ercolano.

The cheapest option is to catch the public **EAV** (☑ 800 211388; www.eavsrl.it) bus service, which departs from Piazza Anfiteatro in Pompeii and stops outside Pompei Scavi–Villa dei Misteri train station en route. Buses depart every 50 minutes from 8am to 3.30pm and take around 50 minutes to reach the summit car park. Once here, purchase your entry ticket to the summit area (adult/reduced €10/8) and follow the 860m gravel path up to the crater (roughly a 25-minute climb). In Pompeii, ignore any touts telling you that the public bus only runs in summer; they are merely trying to push private tours. Bus tickets cost €3.10 one-way and can be purchased on board.

1. Complesso Monumentale di San Lorenzo Maggiore (p74), Naples 2. Tempio di Cerere (p134), Paestum 3. Pompeii (p98) 4. Mosaic, Herculaneum (p93)

GMAS/SHUTTERSTOCK©

ALYSTA/SHUTTERSTOCK©

Historical Riches

Few Italian regions can match Campania's historical legacy. Colonised by the ancient Greeks and loved by the Romans, it's a sun-drenched repository of A-list antiquities, from World Heritage wonders to lesser-known archaeological gems.

Subterranean Naples

Eerie aqueducts, mysterious burial crypts and ancient streetscapes: beneath Naples' hyperactive streets lies a wonderland of Graeco-Roman ruins (p82). For a taste, head below the Complesso Monumentale di San Lorenzo Maggiore (p74) or follow the leader on a tour of the evocative Catacombe di San Gennaro (p82).

Paestum

Great Greek temples never go out of vogue and those at Paestum (p134) are among the greatest outside Greece itself. With the oldest structures stretching back to the 6th century BC, this place makes Rome's Colosseum feel positively modern.

Pompeii

Short of stepping into the Tardis, Pompeii (p98) is your best bet for a little time travel. Locked in ash for centuries, its excavated streetscapes offer a tangible encounter with the ancients and their daily lives. It has everything from luxury homes to a racy brothel.

Herculaneum

A bite-sized Pompeii, Herculaneum (p93) is even better preserved than its nearby rival. This is the place to delve into the details, from once-upon-a-time shop advertisements and furniture, to vivid mosaics and even an ancient security grille.

In Ercolano, private company **Vesuvio Express** ([✆] 081 739 36 66; www.vesuvioexpress. it; Piazzale Stazione Circumvesuviana, Ercolano; return incl admission to summit €20; ⊙ every 40min, 9.30am-5pm Jul & Aug, to 4pm Apr-Jun & Sep, to 2.10pm Oct-Mar) runs buses to the summit car park from Piazzale Stazione Circumvesuviana, outside Ercolano–Scavi train station. A word of warning: this company has received very mixed reviews, with numerous claims of unreliability from travellers.

When the weather is bad the summit path is shut and bus departures are suspended.

If travelling by car, exit the A3 at Ercolano Portico and follow signs for the Parco Nazionale del Vesuvio. From the summit car park (€5), a shuttle bus (return €3) reaches the ticket office and entry point further up the volcano.

Pompeii

Modern-day Pompeii (Pompei in Italian) may feel like a nondescript satellite of Naples, but it's here that you'll find Europe's most compelling archaeological site: the ruins of Pompeii. Sprawling and haunting, the site is a stark reminder of the destructive forces that lie deep inside Vesuvius.

◉ Sights

Terme Suburbane ARCHAEOLOGICAL SITE
Just outside ancient Pompeii's city walls, this 1st-century-BCE bathhouse is famous for several erotic frescoes that scandalised the Vatican when they were revealed in 2001. The panels decorate what was once the *apodyterium* (changing room). The room leading to the colourfully frescoed *frigidarium* (cold bath) features fragments of stuccowork, as well as one of the few original roofs to survive at Pompeii. Beyond the *tepadar-*

ium (tepid bath) and *caldarium* (hot bath) rooms are the remains of a heated outdoor swimming pool. The bathhouse was closed at the time of research.

Tempio di Apollo ARCHAEOLOGICAL SITE
(Temple of Apollo) The oldest and most important of Pompeii's religious buildings, the Tempio di Apollo largely dates from the 2nd century BCE, including the striking columned portico. Fragments remain of an earlier version dating from the 6th century BCE. The statues of Apollo and Diana (depicted as archers) on either side of the portico are copies; the originals are housed in Naples' Museo Archeologico Nazionale (p70).

Basilica ARCHAEOLOGICAL SITE
The basilica was the 2nd-century-BCE seat of Pompeii's law courts and exchange. The semicircular apses would later influence the design of early Christian churches.

Foro ARCHAEOLOGICAL SITE
A huge rectangle flanked by limestone columns, the *foro* was ancient Pompeii's main piazza, as well as the site of gladiatorial games before the Anfiteatro (p101) was constructed. The buildings surrounding the forum are testament to its role as the city's hub of civic, commercial, political and religious activity. At its northern end are the remains of the **Tempio di Giove** (Capitolium), the heart of religious life in Pompeii.

Granai del Foro ARCHAEOLOGICAL SITE
(Forum Granary) The Granai del Foro is now used to store hundreds of amphorae and a number of body casts that were made in the late 19th century by pouring plaster into the hollows left by disintegrated bodies. Among these casts is a pregnant slave; the belt

---

OFF THE BEATEN TRACK

OPLONTIS

Buried beneath the unappealing streets of Torre Annunziata, **Oplontis** ([✆] 081 857 53 47; www.pompeiisites.org; Via dei Sepolcri, Torre Annunziata; adult/reduced incl Boscoreale €7/2; ⊙ 8.30am-7.30pm, last entry 6pm Apr-Oct, 8.30am-5pm, last entry 3.30pm Nov-Mar; [R] Circumvesuviana to Torre Annunziata) was once a blue-ribbon seafront suburb under the administrative control of Pompeii. First discovered in the 18th century, only two of its houses have been unearthed; only one, Villa Poppaea, is open to the public. This villa is a magnificent example of an *otium* villa (a residential building used for rest and recreation), thought to have belonged to Sabina Poppaea, Nero's second wife. Particularly outstanding are the richly coloured 1st-century wall paintings in the *triclinium* (dining room) and *calidarium* (hot bath) in the west wing. Marking the villa's eastern border is a garden with a swimming pool (17m by 61m). The villa is a straightforward 300m walk from Torre Annunziata Circumvesuviana train station.

Old Pompeii

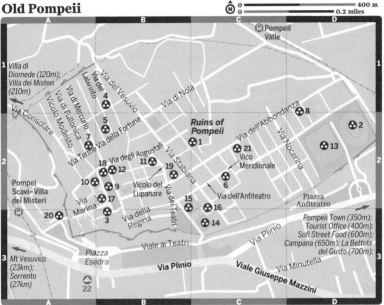

Old Pompeii

around her waist would have displayed the name of her owner.

Macellum ARCHAEOLOGICAL SITE
Dating from the 2nd century BCE, the *macellum* was the city's main produce market. Note the 12 bases at the centre of the market, which were once stands for the timber poles that supported the market's conical roof. Surviving frescoes reveal some of the goods for sale, including prawns.

Casa dei Vettii ARCHAEOLOGICAL SITE
The Casa dei Vettii is home to a famous depiction of Priapus with his gigantic phallus

balanced on a pair of scales...much to the anxiety of many a male observer. The image symbolised the impressive wealth of its sibling owners, Aulus Vettius Restitutus and Aulus Vettius Conviva, who made their fortune trading in wine and agricultural produce.

Via dell'Abbondanza ARCHAEOLOGICAL SITE
(Street of Abundance) The Via dell'Abbondanza was one of ancient Pompeii's main streets. The elevated stepping stones allowed people to cross the street without stepping into the waste that washed down the thoroughfare.

TOP SIGHT
RUINS OF POMPEII

The ruins of Pompeii are a veritable time machine, hurling visitors back to the time of emperors and Latin chatter. Here, time remains paused at 79 CE, the city's frescoed homes, businesses and baths still waiting for their occupants to return. Few archaeological sites offer such an intimate connection to the past, and few are as deeply haunting and evocative.

A Site Reborn

An injection of both national and EU funding over the past decade has fuelled Pompeii's ongoing rehabilitation, turning the once-forlorn site into a hub of archaeological activity and restoration work. Ongoing digs in Cardio V, located to the north of the main archaeological park, have unearthed numerous news-worthy treasures in recent years, including one of Pompeii's most elaborate domestic shrines. While these most recent discoveries may not yet be accessible to the public, Campania's top archaeological drawcard is not short of highlights, including the following.

Villa dei Misteri

This restored, 90-room villa is one of the most complete structures left standing in Pompeii. The Dionysiac frieze, the most important fresco still on-site, spans the walls of the large dining room. One of the largest paintings from the ancient world, it vividly depicts the initiation of a bride-to-be into the cult of Dionysus, the Greek god of wine. A farm for much of its life, the villa's vino-making area is still visible at its northern end.

DON'T MISS

➡ Dionysiac frieze inside Villa dei Misteri

➡ Stucco decoration in the Terme Stabiane

➡ Canine floor mosaic at Casa del Poeta Tragico

➡ Anfiteatro

PRACTICALITIES

➡ ☎ 081 857 53 47

➡ www.pompeiisites.org

➡ entrances at Porta Marina & Piazza Anfiteatro

➡ adult/reduced €16/2

➡ ⊙ 9am-7.30pm Mon-Fri, from 8.30am Sat & Sun, last entry 6pm Apr-Oct, 9am-5.30pm Mon-Fri, from 8.30am Sat & Sun, last entry 3.30pm Nov-Mar

➡ ⊞ Circumvesuviana to Pompei Scavi–Villa dei Misteri

Casa del Poeta Tragico

The 1st-century-CE Casa del Poeta Tragico (House of the Tragic Poet) features the world's first-known 'beware of the dog' – *cave canem* – warnings. Visible through a protective glass panel, the floor mosaic is one of the best preserved at the ruins. The house itself is featured in Edward Bulwer-Lytton's 1834 novel *The Last Days of Pompeii*.

Terme Stabiane

At this typical 2nd-century-BCE bathing complex, bathers would enter from the vestibule, stop off in the vaulted *apodyterium* (changing room), and then pass through to the *tepidarium* (tepid bath) and *caldarium* (hot bath). Particularly impressive is the stuccoed vault in the men's changing room, complete with whimsical images of *putti* (winged babies) and nymphs.

Casa del Menandro

Better preserved than the larger Casa del Fauno, luxurious Casa del Menandro has an outstanding, elegant peristyle (a colonnade-framed courtyard; pictured) beyond its beautifully frescoed atrium. On the peristyle's far right side a doorway leads to a private bathhouse, lavished with exquisite frescoes and mosaics. The central room off the far end of the peristyle features a striking fresco of the ancient Greek dramatist Menander, after whom the rediscovered villa was named.

Lupanare

Ancient Pompeii's only dedicated brothel, Lupanare is a tiny two-storey building with five rooms on each floor. Its collection of raunchy frescoes was a menu of sorts for clients. The walls in the rooms are carved with graffiti – including declarations of love and hope written by the brothel workers – in various languages.

Anfiteatro

Gladiatorial battles thrilled up to 20,000 spectators at the grassy anfiteatro (Amphitheatre). Built in 70 BCE, it's the oldest known Roman amphitheatre in existence. In 59 CE, the venue witnessed violent clashes between spectators from Pompeii and Nucera, documented in a fresco now found in Naples' Museo Archeologico Nazionale.

TOURS

You'll almost certainly be approached by a guide outside the *scavi* (excavations) ticket office: note that authorised guides wear identification tags. If considering a guided tour of the ruins, reputable tour operators include Yellowsudmarine Food Art & Tours (☑ 329 1010328; www.yellowsudmarine.com; 2hr Pompeii guided tour €150, plus entrance fee) and Walks of Italy (www.walksofitaly.com; 3hr Pompeii guided tour per person €59), both of which also offer excursions to other areas of Campania.

Buy your ticket online to avoid long queues, especially in high season, and allow at least three or four hours (longer if you want to go into detail).

THEATRE AT THE RUINS

In the summer, Naples' Teatro Stabile presents an acclaimed season of classical theatre at Pompeii's ancient Teatro Grande. See the theatre company's website (www.teatrostabile napoli.it/pompeii-thea trum-mundi) for more details.

Tragedy in Pompeii

24 AUGUST AD 79

8am Buildings including the **❶ Terme Suburbane** and the **❷ Foro** are still undergoing repair after an earthquake in AD 63 caused significant damage to the city. Despite violent earth tremors overnight, residents have little idea of the catastrophe that lies ahead.

Midday Peckish locals pour into the **❸ Thermopolium di Vetutius Placidus**. The lustful slip into the **❹ Lupanare**, and gladiators practise for the evening's planned games at the **❺ Anfiteatro**. A massive boom heralds the eruption. Shocked onlookers witness a dark cloud of volcanic matter shoot some 14km above the crater.

3pm–5pm Lapilli (burning pumice stone) rains down on Pompeii. Terrified locals begin to flee; others take shelter. Within two hours, the plume is 25km high and the sky has darkened. Roofs collapse under the weight of the debris, burying those inside.

25 AUGUST AD 79

Midnight Mudflows bury the town of Herculaneum. Lapilli and ash continue to rain down on Pompeii, bursting through buildings and suffocating those taking refuge within.

4am–8am Ash and gas avalanches hit Herculaneum. Subsequent surges smother Pompeii, killing all remaining residents, including those in the **❻ Orto dei Fuggiaschi**. The volcanic 'blanket' will safeguard frescoed treasures like the **❼ Casa del Menandro** and **❽ Villa dei Misteri** for almost two millennia.

Villa dei Misteri
Home to the world-famous *Dionysiac Frieze* fresco. Other highlights at this villa include *trompe l'oeil* wall decorations in the *cubiculum* (bedroom) and Egyptian-themed artwork in the *tablinum* (reception).

Villa di Diomede

Casa del Poeta Tragico
Porta Ercolano
Casa del Fauno

Basilica
Tempio di Apollo

Porta Marina ❶

Terme del Foro

Macellum

Teatro Grande

Quadriportico dei Teatri
Porta di Stabia
Teatro Piccolo

Foro
An ancient Times Square of sorts, the forum sits at the intersection of Pompeii's main streets and was closed to traffic in the 1st century AD. The plinths on the southern edge featured statues of the imperial family.

TOP TIPS

➡ Visit in the afternoon.
➡ Allow three hours.
➡ Wear comfortable shoes and a hat.
➡ Bring drinking water.
➡ Don't use flash photography.

Lupanare

The prostitutes at this brothel were often slaves of Greek or Asian origin. Mattresses once covered the stone beds and the names engraved in the walls are possibly those of the workers and their clients.

Thermopolium di Vetutius Placidus

The counter at this ancient snack bar once held urns filled with hot food. The *lararium* (household shrine) on the back wall depicts Dionysus (the god of wine) and Mercury (the god of profit and commerce).

Casa dei Vettii

Porta del Vesuvio

EYEWITNESS ACCOUNT

Pliny the Younger (AD 61–c 112) gives a gripping, first-hand account of the catastrophe in his letters to Tacitus (AD 56–117).

Porta di Nola

Casa della Venere in Conchiglia

Porta di Sarno

3

7

6

Grande Palestra

5

Tempio di Iside

Orto dei Fuggiaschi

The Garden of the Fugitives showcases the plaster moulds of 13 locals seeking refuge during Vesuvius' eruption – the largest number of victims found in any one area. The huddled bodies make for a moving scene.

Casa del Menandro

This dwelling most likely belonged to the family of Poppaea Sabina, Nero's second wife. A room to the left of the atrium features Trojan War paintings and a polychrome mosaic of pygmies rowing down the Nile.

Anfiteatro

Magistrates, local senators and the games' sponsors and organisers enjoyed front-row seating at this veteran amphitheatre, home to gladiatorial battles and the odd riot. The parapet circling the stadium featured paintings of combat, victory celebrations and hunting scenes.

Teatro Grande
ARCHAEOLOGICAL SITE

The 2nd-century-BCE Teatro Grande was a huge 5000-seat theatre carved into the lava mass on which Pompeii was originally built. The site hosts the annual Pompeii Theatrum Mundi (www.teatrostabilenapoli.it/pompeii-theatrum-mundi; ⊘ Jun-Jul), a summer season of classical theatre.

Quadriportico dei Teatri
ARCHAEOLOGICAL SITE

Behind the Teatro Grande's stage, the porticoed Quadriportico dei Teatri was initially used as a place for the audience to stroll between acts and later as a barracks for gladiators.

Teatro Piccolo
ARCHAEOLOGICAL SITE

(Odeon) The Teatro Piccolo was once an indoor theatre renowned for its acoustics.

Casa della Venere in Conchiglia
ARCHAEOLOGICAL SITE

(House of the Venus Marina, House of Venus in a Shell) Casa della Venere in Conchiglia harbours a lovely peristyle looking onto a small, manicured garden. It's here in the garden that you'll find the large, striking Venus fresco, after which the house is named. Venus – whose hairstyle in this depiction reflects the style popular during Emperor Nero's reign – was the patron goddess of the city.

Palestra Grande
ARCHAEOLOGICAL SITE

Lithe ancients kept fit at the Palestra Grande, an athletics field with an impressive portico dating from the Augustan period. Used both as a training ground for gladiators and as a meeting centre for youth associations, its huge, portico-flanked courtyard includes the remains of a swimming pool. The site is now used to host temporary exhibitions.

Antiquarium
MUSEUM

Pompeii's small museum hosts rotating exhibitions showcasing the site's archaeological finds and exploring various aspects of ancient Roman culture. The space also includes an impressive multimedia presentation that digitally reconstructs a number of ancient Pompeii's buildings, making it a helpful stop before roaming the ruins themselves.

🛏 Sleeping & Eating

Although the town of Pompeii has a number of mainly nondescript hotels, you're better off basing yourself in Sorrento or Naples and exploring the ruins as an easy day trip.

★ President
CAMPANIAN €€€

(☏081 850 72 45; www.ristorantepresident.it; Piazza Schettini 12; meals €80, tasting menus €80-120; ⊘noon-3.30pm & 7pm-late Tue-Sun; 🚆FS to Pompei, Circumvesuviana to Pompei Scavi–Villa dei Misteri) At the helm of this Michelin-starred standout is charming owner-chef Paolo Gramaglia, whose passion for local produce, history and culinary whimsy translates into bread made to ancient Roman recipes, yellowtail carpaccio with bitter orange and citrus zest, lemon emulsion and buffalo mozzarella, or impeccably glazed duck breast lifted by vinegar cherries, orange sauce and nasturtium. The menu's creative and visual brilliance is matched by sommelier Laila Buondonno's swoon-inducing wine list, which features around 600 drops from esteemed and lesser-known Italian winemakers; best of all, the staff are happy to serve any bottle to the value of €100 by the glass.

Note: if you plan on catching a *treno regionale* (regional train) back to Naples from nearby Pompei station (a more convenient option than the Pompei Scavi–Villa dei Misteri station on the Circumvesuviana train line), check train times first as the last service from Pompei can depart as early as 9.53pm.

❶ Getting There & Away

To reach the *scavi* (ruins) by **Circumvesuviana** (☏800 211388; www.eavsrl.it) train (€2.80 from Naples, 36 minutes; €2.40 from Sorrento, 30 minutes), alight at Pompei Scavi–Villa dei Misteri station, located beside the main entrance at Porta Marina. Regional trains (www.trenitalia.com) stop at Pompei station in the centre of the modern town.

From mid-March to mid-October, tourist train *Campania Express* runs four times daily between Naples (Porta Nolana and Piazza Garibaldi Circumvesuviana stations) and Sorrento, stopping at Ercolano–Scavi, Torre Annunziata (Oplontis), Pompei Scavi–Villa dei Misteri, Castellammare and Vico Equense en route. One-day return tickets from Naples to Pompei (€11, 29 minutes) or from Sorrento to Pompei (€7, 24 minutes) can be purchased at the stations or online at **EAV** (☏800 211388; www.eavsrl.it).

If driving from Naples, head southeast on the A3, using the Pompei exit and following the signs to Pompei Scavi. Car parks are clearly marked and vigorously touted. Close to the ruins, **Camping Spartacus** (☏081 862 40 78; www.campingspartacus.it; Via Plinio 127; adult/child per night €7.50/4, car/camper/caravan €5/10/12; 🛜🚻) offers good-value, all-day parking (€5). This is a much cheaper option than the main car park located directly north of the Circumvesuviana train station.

From Sorrento, head north along the SS145, which connects to the A3 and Pompei.

Sorrento

📍 081 / POP 16,400

A small resort with a big reputation, Sorrento is a town of lemons, high-pedigree hotels and plunging cliffs that cut through the heart of the historical core.

The town's longstanding popularity stems from its location at the western gateway to the Amalfi. It's also on the train line to Pompeii and has regular fast-ferry connections to Naples and Capri.

Tourism has a long history here. It was a compulsory stop on the 19th-century 'Grand Tour' and interest in the town was first sparked by the poet Byron, who inspired a long line of holidaying literary geniuses – including Goethe, Dickens and Tolstoy – to sample the Sorrentine air. The romance persists. Wander through Piazza Tasso on any given Sunday and you'll be exposed to one of Italy's finer *passeggiate* (strolls), snaking past palatial hotels, magnificent marquetry shops and simple Campanian restaurants serving *gnocchi alla sorrentina* finished off with a shot of ice-cold *limoncello*.

◉ Sights

Museo Correale di Terranova   MUSEUM

(📍 081 878 18 46; www.museocorreale.it; Via Correale 50; adult/reduced €8/5; ⊙ 9.30am-6.30pm Mon-Sat, to 1.30pm Sat) East of the city centre, this wide-ranging museum is well worth a visit whether you're a clock collector, an archaeological egghead or into delicate ceramics. In addition to the rich assortment of 16th- to 19th-century Neapolitan arts and crafts (including extraordinary examples of marquetry), you'll discover Japanese, Chinese and European ceramics, clocks, fans and, on the ground floor, ancient and medieval artefacts. Among these is a fragment of an ancient Egyptian carving uncovered in the vicinity of Sorrento's **Sedile Dominova** (Via San Cesareo).

Chiesa & Chiostro
di San Francesco   CHURCH

(📍 081 878 12 69; Via San Francesco; ⊙ 7am-7pm) Located next to the Villa Comunale Park, this church is best known for the peaceful 14th-century cloister abutting it, which is accessible via a small door from the church. The courtyard features an Arabic portico and interlaced arches supported by octagonal pillars. Replete with bougainvillea and birdsong, they're built on the ruins of a 7th-century monastery. Upstairs in the

Sorrento International Photo School, the **Gallery Celentano** (📍 344 0838503; www.raffaelecelentano.com; adult/reduced €3.50/free; ⊙ 10am-9pm Mar-Dec) exhibits black-and-white photographs of Italian life and landscapes by contemporary local photographer Raffaele Celentano. The cloisters host classical-music concerts in the summer.

Museo Bottega
della Tarsia Lignea   MUSEUM

(📍 081 877 19 42; Via San Nicola 28; adult/reduced €8/5; ⊙ 10am-6.30pm Apr-Oct, to 5pm Nov-Mar) Since the 18th century, Sorrento has been famous for its *intarsio* (marquetry) furniture, made with elaborately designed inlaid wood. Some wonderful historical examples can be found in this museum, many of them etched in the once fashionable picaresque style. The museum, housed in an 18th-century palace complete with beautiful frescoes, also has an interesting collection of paintings, prints and photographs depicting the town and the surrounding area in the 19th century.

Duomo   CATHEDRAL

(📍 081 878 22 48; Corso Italia; ⊙ 8am-12.30pm & 4.30-9pm) Sorrento's cathedral features a striking exterior fresco, a triple-tiered bell tower, four classical columns and an elegant majolica clock. Inside, take note of the marble bishop's throne (1573), as well as both the wooden choir stalls and stations of the cross, decorated in the local *intarsio* (marquetry) style. Although the cathedral's original structure dates from the 15th century, the building has been altered several times, most recently in the early 20th century when the current facade was added.

🏃 Activities

★ **Nautica Sic Sic**   BOATING

(📍 081 807 22 83; www.nauticasicsic.com; Via Marina Piccola 43, Marina Piccola; ⊙ Apr-Oct) Seek out the best beaches by rented boat, with or without a skipper. This outfit rents a variety of motor boats, starting at around €50 per hour or from €150 per day plus fuel. It also organises boat excursions and wedding shoots.

Bagni Regina Giovanna   SWIMMING

Sorrento lacks a decent beach, so consider heading to Bagni Regina Giovanna, a rocky beach with clear, clean water about 2km west of town, amid the ruins of the Roman Villa Pollio Felix. It's possible to walk here (follow Via Capo), but wear good shoes as it's a bit of a scramble. Alternatively, you can

Sorrento

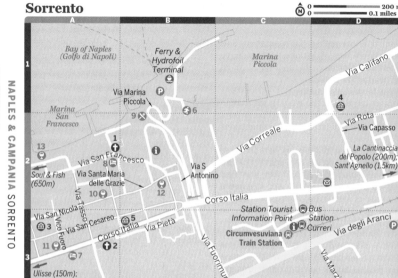

Sorrento

◉ Sights

◉ Activities, Courses & Tours

⬛ Sleeping

◉ Eating

◉ Drinking & Nightlife

take the SITA Sud bus headed for Massa Lubrense to save your strength.

Ulysse Day Spa   SPA
(☏081 807 35 81; www.spaulysse.it; Via del Mare 22; ⏱baths 11am-10pm Mon, Wed & Fri, 3-10pm Tue & Thu, 11am-8pm Sat, 10am-7pm Sun, massage centre 9am-8pm Mon-Sat, 10am-7pm Sun) Ischia might be the spa capital of Campania, but Sorrento gets its oar in with the Ulysse where you can unwind in the spa (€25) or rev up in the gym (€10). There's also a long massage and beauty menu (extra cost). Spa facilities include an indoor pool and a jacuzzi, plus a cave-like Turkish bath and a chill-out lounge. The centre shares digs with deluxe hostel Ulisse.

✦✦ Festivals & Events

Settimana Santa   RELIGIOUS
(Holy Week) Famed throughout Italy; the first procession takes place at midnight on the Thursday preceding Good Friday, with robed and hooded penitents in white; the second occurs on Good Friday, when participants wear black robes and hoods to commemorate the death of Christ.

Sant'Antonino   RELIGIOUS
(⏱14 Feb) The city's patron saint, Sant'Antonino, is remembered annually with processions and huge markets. The saint is credited with having saved Sorrento during WWII when Salerno and Naples were heavily bombed.

⌖ Sleeping

Accommodation is thick on the ground in Sorrento, although if you're arriving in high summer (July and August), you'll need to book ahead. Most of the big city-centre hotels are geared towards package tourism and prices are correspondingly high. There are, however, some excellent choices, particularly on Via Capo, the coastal road west of the centre.

Ulisse HOSTEL €

(☏ 081 877 47 53; www.ulissedeluxe.com; Via del Mare 22; dm from €35, d from €139; ❄️❄️🛜🏊) Although it calls itself a hostel, the Ulisse is about as far from a backpackers' pad as a hiking boot from a stiletto. Most rooms are plush, spacious affairs with swish if bland fabrics, gleaming floors and large en-suite bathrooms. There are two single-sex dorms, and quads for sharers. Breakfast is included in some rates but costs €10 with others. At the adjacent wellness centre Ulysse Day Spa guests get to use the facilities for a daily rate of €10.

Nube d'Argento CAMPGROUND €

(☏ 081 878 13 44; www.nubedargento.com; Via Capo 21; camping per 2 people, car & tent €26-42, 2-person bungalows €70-95, 4-person bungalows €100-130; ☺late Mar-early Jan; 🛜🏊) Remarkably central for a campground, this sloping affair set in a ravine above the Maria Grande has pitches and wooden chalet-style bungalows spread out beneath a canopy of olive trees – a source of much-needed summer shade – and the facilities are excellent. Kids in particular will enjoy the open-air swimming pool, table-tennis table, slides and swings.

Hotel Cristina HOTEL €€

(☏ 081 878 35 62; www.hotelcristinasorrento.it; Via Privata Rubinacci 6, Sant'Agnello; d/tr/q from €150/220/240; ☺Mar-Oct; ❄️❄️🛜🏊) Located high above Sant'Agnello, this hotel has superb views, particularly from the swimming pool. The spacious rooms have sea-view balconies and combine inlaid wooden furniture with contemporary flourishes such as Philippe Starck chairs. There's an in-house restaurant and a free shuttle bus to/from Sorrento's Circumvesuviana train station.

Casa Astarita B&B €€

(☏ 081 877 49 06; www.casastarita.com; Corso Italia 67; d €90-140, tr €115-165; ❄️🛜) Housed in an 18th-century *palazzo* (mansion) on Sorrento's main strip, this charming B&B has a colourful, eclectic look with original vaulted ceilings, brightly painted doors and tiled floors. Its eight rooms are simple but well equipped, with breakfast served on a large rustic table in the B&B's central parlour.

★Palazzo Marziale BOUTIQUE HOTEL €€€

(☏ 081 807 44 06; www.palazzomarziale.com; Largo San Francesco 2; d/ste from €220/455; ❄️🛜) From cascading vines, Chinese porcelain urns and Persian rugs in the lobby lounge, to antique furniture, *objets* and artworks in the hallways, and inlaid wood in the lift, this sophisticated, 11-room hideaway is big on details. The family's elegant tastes extend to the rooms, resplendent with high ceilings, chaise longues and classy mattresses and linens.

La Tonnarella HOTEL €€€

(☏ 081 878 11 53; www.latonnarella.com; Via Capo 31; d €160-300, ste €333-410; ☺Apr-Oct & Christmas; ❄️❄️@🛜) A splendid choice atop a cliff to the west of town, La Tonnarella is a dazzling canvas of majolica tiles, antiques and chandeliers. Rooms, most with their own balcony or small terrace, continue the sumptuous classical theme with traditional furniture and discreet mod cons. The hotel also has its own lift-accessible private beach and a highly regarded terrace restaurant.

⚒ Eating

The centre of town heaves with bars, cafes, trattorias, restaurants and even the odd kebab takeaway shop. Many places, particularly those with waistcoated waiters stationed outside (or eateries displaying sun-bleached photos of the dishes), are tourist traps serving bland food at inflated prices. Don't leave without a dose of *gnocchi alla sorrentina* (gnocchi with tomato sauce and mozzarella).

La Cantinaccia del Popolo NEAPOLITAN €

(☏ 366 1015497; Vico Terzo Rota 3; meals €21; ☺11am-3pm & 7-11pm Tue-Sun) Festooned with garlic and with cured hams hanging from the ceiling, this down-to-earth favourite proves that top-notch produce and simplicity are the keys to culinary success. A case in point is the *spaghetti al pomodoro*, a basic dish of pasta and tomato that bursts with flavour, vibrancy and balance. For extra authenticity, it's served directly to you in the pan.

La Cantinaccia's also plies its own cured meats and some interesting Campanian cheeses straight out of the glass deli counter.

Acqu' e Sale NEAPOLITAN €€
(☑081 1900 5967; www.acquesale.it; Piazza Marinai D'Italia 2; pizzas from €7, meals €35-40; ☺7am-11.30pm; ☎) This so-called 'water and salt' restaurant with a dazzling blue-and-white interior is right next to the ferry terminal. Seafood here is worth getting excited about and it also offers fine Neapolitan-style pizzas with a creative choice of bases, including a very local lemon-flavoured option (*al limone*).

With its generous opening times and proximity to the port, Acqu' e Sale is a good place to catch a last-minute breakfast before heading across the water.

Soul & Fish SEAFOOD €€
(☑081 878 21 70; www.soulandfish.com; Via Marina Grande 202; meals €38-46; ☺noon-2.30pm & 7-10.30pm, closed Nov-Easter; ☎) Soul & Fish has a hipper vibe than Marina Grande's no-nonsense seafood restaurants. Your bread comes in a bag, your dessert might come in a Kilner jar and your freshly grilled fish with a waiter ready to slice it up before your eyes. The decor is more chic beach shack than sea-shanty dive bar, with wooden decks, director chairs and puffy cushions.

🍷 Drinking & Nightlife

⭐**D'Anton** LOUNGE
(☑333 1543706; Piazza Sant'Antonino 3/4; ☺10am-11pm mid-Mar–early Jan, to 1.30am summer; ☎) Welcome to a very Italian concept: a cocktail bar doubling up as an interior-design store. That elegant sofa you're sipping a negroni on is for sale. So is that glistening chandelier and that enchanting mirror. Add them to your drinks bill if you're feeling flush, or just admire the candelabras and lampshades over savoury *antipasti* and wicked chocolate-and-almond cake.

Bollicine WINE BAR
(☑081 878 46 16; Via Accademia 9; ☺6pm-late Mar-Nov; ☎) The wine list at this unpretentious bar with a dark, woody interior includes all the big Italian names and a selection of interesting local labels. If you can't decide what to go for, the amiable bar staff will advise you. There's also a small menu of *panini* (sandwiches), bruschettas and one or two pasta dishes.

Cafè Latino BAR
(☑081 877 37 18; www.cafelatinosorrento.it; Vico Fuoro 4a; ☺10am-1am Easter-Oct; ☎) Think locked-eyes-over-cocktails time. This is the place to impress your date with cocktails (€8) on the candlelit terrace, surrounded by orange, lemon and banana trees. Sip a spicy Hulk (vodka, grapefruit, sugar cane and jalapeño) or a glass of chilled white wine. If you can't drag yourselves away, you can also eat here (pizzas from €7, meals around €40).

La Pergola BAR
(☑081 878 10 24; www.bellevue.it; Hotel Bellevue Syrene, Piazza della Vittoria 5; ☺10.30am-11pm) When love is in the air, put on your best Italian shoes and head for a predinner libation at the Hotel Bellevue Syrene's swoon-inducing terrace bar–restaurant. With its commanding clifftop view across the Bay of Naples towards Mt Vesuvius, it never fails to glam up an otherwise ordinary evening.

ℹ️ Information

Main Tourist Office (☑081 807 40 33; www.sorrentotourism.com; Via Luigi de Maio 35; ☺9am-7pm Mon-Sat, to 1pm Sun Jun-Oct, 9am-4pm Mon-Fri, to 1pm Sat Nov-May; ☎) In the Circolo dei Forestieri (Foreigners' Club); lists ferry and train times. Ask for the useful publication *Surrentum*, published monthly from March to October.

Post Office (www.poste.it; Corso Italia 210; ☺8.20am-7pm Mon-Fri, to 12.30pm Sat) Just north of the train station.

ℹ️ Getting There & Away

BOAT

Sorrento is the main jumping-off point for Capri and also has ferry connections to Naples and Amalfi coastal resorts during the summer months from its **ferry and hydrofoil terminal** (Via Luigi de Maio).

Caremar (☑081 807 30 77; www.caremar.it) Runs fast ferries to Capri (€14.40, 25 minutes, four daily).

Alilauro (☑081 807 18 12; www.alilauro.it) Runs year-round hydrofoils to Naples (€13, 20 minutes, up to six daily) and Capri (€20.50, 20 minutes, up to 13 daily), as well as seasonal services to Ischia (€23, one hour, two to three daily), Positano (€20, 30 minutes, two daily) and Amalfi (€21, 50 minutes, two daily).

BUS

SITA Sud (www.sitasudtrasporti.it) buses serve Naples, the Amalfi Coast and Sant'Agata, leaving from the **bus station** (Piazza Giovanna Battista de Curtis) across from the entrance to the Circumvesuviana train station. Buy tickets at the station or from shops bearing the blue SITA sign.

TRAIN

Sorrento is the last stop on the **Circumvesuviana** (☑ 800 211388; www.eavsrl.it) line from Naples. Trains run every 30 minutes for Naples (€3.90, 70 minutes), via Pompeii (€2.40, 30 minutes) and Ercolano (€2.90, 50 minutes).

THE ISLANDS

Capri

☑ 081 / POP 14,120

Capri is beautiful – seriously beautiful. There's barely a grubby building or untended garden to blemish the splendour. Steep cliffs rise majestically from an impossibly blue sea; elegant villas drip with wisteria and bougainvillea; even the trees seem to be carefully manicured.

Long a preserve of celebrities and the super-rich, this small, precipitous island off the west end of the Sorrento Peninsula has a tangible deluxe feel. Your credit card can get a lot of exercise in its expensive restaurants and museum-quality jewellery shops – a cappuccino alone can cost €7. But, regardless of this, Capri is worth visiting, whatever your budget. Glide silently up craggy Monte Solaro on a chairlift. Relive erstwhile poetic glories in Villa Lysis. Find a quiet space in the sinuous lanes of Anacapri. In the process, you'll enjoy some sublime moments.

◉ Sights

◉ Capri Town & Around

With its whitewashed stone buildings and tiny, car-free streets, Capri Town exudes a cinematic air. A diminutive model of upmarket Mediterranean chic, it's a well-tended playground of luxury hotels, expensive bars, smart restaurants and high-end boutiques. In summer the centre swells with crowds of camera-wielding day trippers and yacht-owning playboys (and girls), but don't be put off from exploring the atmospheric and ancient side streets, where the crowds quickly thin. The walk east out of town to Villa Jovis is especially wonderful.

★ **Villa Jovis**   RUINS
(Jupiter's Villa; Via A Maiuri; adult/reduced €6/4; ⊙ 10am-7pm Jun-Sep, to 6pm Apr, May & Oct, to 4pm Mar, Nov & Dec, closed Jan & Feb) Villa Jovis was the largest and most sumptuous of 12

Roman villas commissioned by Roman Emperor Tiberius (14–37 CE) on Capri, and his main island residence. This vast complex, now reduced to ruins, famously pandered to the emperor's supposedly debauched tastes, and included imperial quarters and extensive bathing areas set in dense gardens and woodland. It's located a 45-minute walk east of Capri Town along Via Tiberio.

The villa's spectacular location posed major headaches for Tiberius' architects. The main problem was how to collect and store enough water to supply the villa's baths and 3000-sq-metre gardens. The solution they eventually hit upon was to build a complex canal system to transport rainwater to four giant storage tanks, whose remains you can still see today.

Beside the ticket office, which closes 45 minutes before site closing time, is the 330m-high **Salto di Tiberio** (Tiberius' Leap), a sheer cliff from where, as the story goes, Tiberius had out-of-favour subjects hurled into the sea. True or not, the stunning views are real enough; if you suffer from vertigo, tread carefully.

★ **Villa Lysis**   HISTORIC BUILDING
(www.villalysiscapri.com; Via Lo Capo 12; €2; ⊙ 10am-7pm Thu-Tue Jun-Aug, to 6pm Apr, May, Sep & Oct, to 4pm Nov & Dec) This beautifully melancholic art-nouveau villa is set on a clifftop on Capri's northeast tip and was the one-time retreat of French poet Jacques d'Adelswärd-Fersen, who came to Capri in 1904 to escape a gay sex scandal in Paris. Unlike other stately homes, the interior has been left almost entirely empty; this is a place to let your imagination flesh out the details. It's a 40-minute walk from Piazza Umberto I and rarely crowded.

One notable curiosity is the 'Chinese room' in the basement, which includes a semicircular opium den with a swastika emblazoned on the floor. Fersen became addicted to opium following a visit to Ceylon in the early 1900s; the swastika is the Sanskrit symbol for well-being. Equally transfixing is the sun-dappled garden, a triumph of classical grandiosity half given over to nature.

The €2 entry fee includes an explanatory pamphlet available in Italian and English. Afterwards, it is possible to take a steep, winding path, the **Sentiero delle Calanche**, to Villa Jovis (20 minutes away).

Fersen's scandal-plagued life ended in 1923 with a lethal cocaine-champagne cocktail.

Capri

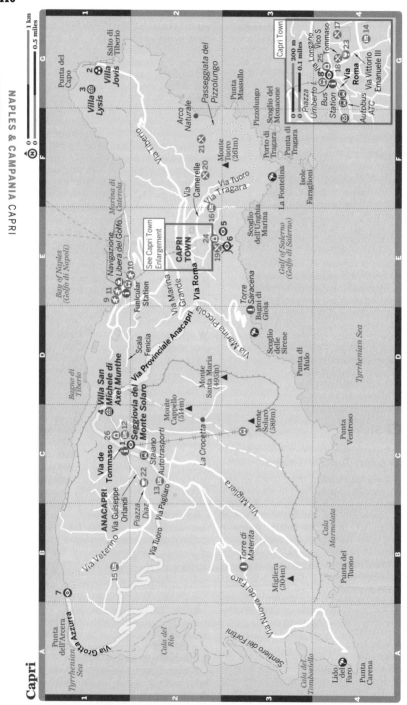

Tyrrhenian Sea

Punta dell'Arcera

Via Grotta Azzurra

Punta del Capo

Salto di Tiberio

Villa Jovis

Villa Lysis

Via Tiberio

Arco Naturale

Passeggiata del Pizzolungo

Punta Massullo

Marina di Caterola

Bay of Naples (Golfo di Napoli)

Bagno di Tiberio

Villa San Michele di Axel Munthe

Navigazione Libera del Golfo

Funicular Station

Monte Tuoro (261m)

Via Tuoro

Via Camerelle

Via Tragara

Pizzolungo

Porto di Tragara

Punta di Tragara

Scoglio del Monacone

La Fontelina

Isole Faraglioni

CAPRI TOWN

See Capri Town Enlargement

Via Roma

Scoglio dell'Unghia Marina

Gulf of Salerno (Golfo di Salerno)

Scala Fenicia

Via Marina Grande

Via Marina Piccola

Torre Saracena

Bagni di Gioia

Scoglio delle Sirene

Tyrrhenian Sea

Punta di Mulo

Seggiovia del Monte Solaro

Via de Tommaso

ANACAPRI

Via Guiseppe Orlandi

Piazza Diaz

Staiano Autotrasporti

Via Pagliaro

Via Tuoro

Monte Santa Maria (495m)

Monte Cappello (514m)

La Crocetta

Monte Solaro (589m)

Via Migliera

Punta Ventroso

Via Veterino

Torre di Materita

Migliera (304m)

Cala Marmolata

Punta del Tuono

Punta dell'Arcera

Via Nuove del Faro

Sentiero dei Fortini

Cala del Rio

Cala del Tombosiello

Lido del Faro

Punta Carena

Via Provinciale Anacapri

Capri Town

Piazza Umberto I

Bus Station

Via Longano

Vico S Tommaso

Via Roma

Autobus ATC

Via Vittorio Emanuele III

Capri

Giardini di Augusto   GARDENS
(Gardens of Augustus; €1; ⊙ 9am-7.30pm summer, reduced hours rest of year) As their name suggests, these gardens near the Certosa di San Giacomo were founded by Emperor Augustus. Rising in a series of flowered terraces, they lead to a lookout point offering breathtaking views over to the **Isole Faraglioni**, a group of three limestone stacks rising out of the sea.

From the gardens, pretty, hairpin **Via Krupp** winds down to Marina Piccola and past a bust of Vladimir Lenin overlooking the road from a nearby platform. The Russian revolutionary visited Capri in 1908, during which he was famously snapped engaged in a game of chess with fellow revolutionary Alexander Bogdanov. Looking on in the photograph is Russian writer Maxim Gorky, who called the island home between 1906 and 1909.

Certosa di San Giacomo   MONASTERY
(☑ 081 837 62 18; Viale Certosa 40; adult/reduced €6/2; ⊙ 10am-6pm Tue-Sun Apr-Sep, to 3pm Oct-Mar) Founded in 1363, this substantial monastery is generally considered to be the finest remaining example of Caprese architecture and today houses a school, a library, a temporary exhibition space and a museum with some evocative 17th-century paintings. Be sure to look at the cloisters, which have a real sense of faded glory (the smaller is 14th-century, the larger 16th-century).

To get here take Via Vittorio Emanuele III, east of Piazza Umberto I, which meanders down to the monastery.

The monastery's history is a harrowing one: it became the stronghold of the island's powerful Carthusian fraternity and was viciously attacked during Saracen pirate raids in the 16th century. A century later, monks retreated here to avoid the plague and were rewarded by an irate public (whom they should have been tending), who tossed corpses over the walls. There are some soothing 17th-century frescoes in the church, which will hopefully serve as an antidote as you contemplate the monastery's dark past.

Piazza Umberto I   PIAZZA
Located beneath the 17th-century clock tower and framed by see-and-be-seen cafes, this showy, open-air salon is central to your Capri experience, especially in the evening when the main activity in these parts is dressing up and hanging out. Be prepared for the cost of the front-row seats – the moment you sit down for a drink, you're going to pay handsomely for the grandstand views (around €7 for a cappuccino and €18 for a couple of glasses of white wine).

⊙ Anacapri & Around

Traditionally Capri Town's more subdued neighbour, Anacapri is no stranger to tourism. The focus is largely limited to Villa San Michele di Axel Munthe and the souvenir shops on the main streets. Delve further, though, and you'll discover that Anacapri is still, at heart, the laid-back, rural village that it's always been.

★ **Seggiovia del**
Monte Solaro   CABLE CAR
(☑ 081 837 14 38; www.capriseggiovia.it; Via Capscuro; single/return €8/11; ☺ 9.30am-5pm May-Oct, 9am-4pm Mar & Apr, to 3.30pm Nov-Feb) Sitting in an old-fashioned chairlift above the white houses, terraced gardens and hazy hillsides of Anacapri as you rise to the top of Capri's highest mountain, the silence broken only by a distant dog barking or your own sighs of contentment, has to be one of the island's most sublime experiences. The ride takes an all-too-short 13 minutes, but when you get there, the views, framed by dismembered classical statues, are outstanding.

★ **Villa San Michele**
di Axel Munthe   MUSEUM, GARDENS
(☑ 081 837 14 01; www.villasanmichele.eu; Via Axel Munthe 34; €8; ☺ 9am-6pm May-Sep, reduced hours rest of year) The former home of Swedish doctor, psychiatrist and animal-rights advocate Axel Munthe, San Michele di Axel Munthe should be included on every visitor's itinerary. Built on the site of the ruins of a Roman villa, the gardens make a beautiful setting for a tranquil stroll, with pathways flanked by immaculate flowerbeds. There are also superb views from here, plus some fine photo props in the form of Roman sculptures.

🏃 Activities

Banana Sport   BOATING
(☑ 348 5949665; Marina Grande; 2hr/day rental 5-person boat €80/220; ☺ May–mid-Oct) Located on the eastern edge of the waterfront, Banana Sport hires out five-person motorised dinghies, allowing you to explore secluded coves and grottoes. You can also visit the popular swimming spot **Bagno di Tiberio** (€10), a small inlet west of Marina Grande; it's said that Tiberius once swam here.

★ **Capri Whales**   BOATING
(☑ 081 837 58 33; www.capriwhales.it; Marina Grande 17; 2hr private boat tours from per boat €150, day trip to Positano from €650, boat hire 2hr/full day €100/250, children under 6yr free; ☺ year-round; 🚼) A congenial business based on the main quay offering guided boat tours

---

GROTTA AZZURRA

Capri's most famous attraction is the **Grotta Azzurra** (Blue Grotto; €14; ☺ 9am-5pm), an unusual sea cave illuminated by an otherworldly blue light. The easiest way to visit is to take a boat **tour** (☑ 081 837 56 46; www.motoscafisticapri.com; Private Pier 0; Grotta Azzurra/island trip €15/€18) from Marina Grande; tickets include the return boat trip, but the rowing boat into the cave and admission are paid separately. Beautiful though it is, the Grotta is extremely popular in the summer. The crowds, coupled with long waiting times and tip-hungry guides, can make the experience underwhelming for some.

The grotto had long been known to local fisherfolk when it was rediscovered by two Germans – writer August Kopisch and painter Ernst Fries – in 1826. Subsequent research revealed that Emperor Tiberius had built a quay in the cave around 30 CE, complete with a *nymphaeum* (shrine to the water nymph). Remarkably, you can still see the carved Roman landing stage towards the rear of the cave.

Measuring 54m by 30m and rising to a height of 15m, the grotto is said to have sunk by up to 20m in prehistoric times, blocking every opening except the 1.3m-high entrance. And this is the key to the magical blue light. Sunlight enters through a small underwater aperture and is refracted through the water; this, combined with the reflection of the light off the white sandy seafloor, produces the vivid blue effect to which the cave owes its name.

The Grotta can also be accessed from land. Take a bus from Marina Grande to Anacapri and then another bus to the road's end at Grotta Azzurra. From here, a staircase leads down to a small dock where rowing boats await to take passengers into the adjacent cave.

Bear in mind that the time actually spent in the Grotta during a tour amounts to 10 minutes maximum. The singing row-boat 'captains' are included in the price, so don't feel any obligation if they push for a tip.

The grotto is closed if the sea is too choppy and swimming in it is forbidden, although you can swim outside the entrance.

of the island as well as longer full-day trips to Positano. Alternatively, you can hire your own boat for three hours or a full day. Trips are family-friendly, with a child life vest and water toys provided.

🛏 Sleeping

You can't fully discover Capri in one day; stay the night and you'll see the island in a different light. Accommodation is strictly seasonal, which means bed space is tight and, in general, costly – although there are a few relative bargains to be had, mainly in Anacapri. At the top end of the market, you'll find some of Italy's most opulent hotels. Book well ahead in the summer.

★ Casa Mariantonia   BOUTIQUE HOTEL €€
(☑ 081 837 29 23; www.casamariantonia.com; Via Orlandi 80, Anacapri; d €120-300; ☺ late Mar-Oct; **P ❄ 🛜 🌊**) A family-run boutique hotel with a history (*limoncello di Capri* was supposedly invented here), boasting nine fabulous rooms, a giant swimming pool, a prestigious restaurant and a heavyweight list of former guests – philosopher Jean-Paul Sartre among them. If the tranquillity, lemon groves and personal *pensione* feel doesn't sooth your existential angst, nothing will.

Hotel Villa Eva   HOTEL €€
(☑ 081 837 15 49; www.villaeva.com; Via La Fabbrica 8, Anacapri; d €120-200; tr €150-220; apt per person €60-90; ☺ Apr-Oct; **❄ @ 🛜 🌊**) Villa Eva is all about the garden, which is lush and immense. This is about as bucolic as it gets in Capri. The 10-room villa is fairly self-contained, with a swimming pool, a snack bar, and sunny rooms and apartments. Whitewashed domes, terracotta floors, stained-glass windows and vintage fireplaces add character, while the location ensures peace and quiet.

★ Capri Palace   HOTEL €€€
(☑ 081 978 01 11; www.capripalace.com; Via Capodimonte 2b, Anacapri; d/ste from €410/1070; ☺ mid-Apr–mid-Oct; **❄ 🛜 🌊**) This really lives up to the 'palace' in its name – a regal mix of chicness, opulence and unashamed luxury that takes the concept of *la dolce vita* to dizzying heights. Lily-white communal areas set the scene for the lavish guestrooms – some even have their own terraced garden and private plunge pool with Warhol-esque motifs decorating the tiles.

★ La Minerva   BOUTIQUE HOTEL €€€
(☑ 081 837 70 67; www.laminervacapri.com; Via Occhio Marino 8, Capri Town; d €190-650; ☺ late Mar-early Nov; **❄ 🛜 🌊**) This gleaming establishment is a model of Capri style and considered by many to be one of the best hotels in Italy. The 19 rooms, which cascade down the hillside, feature ravishing blue and white ceramic tiles, silk drapes and cool 100% linen sheets, while terraces come with sun loungers, jacuzzis and obligatory sea views.

And then there's the gorgeous pool, surrounded by a veritable arboretum of trees, as well as the genteel lobby bar with its unique cocktails, and the general pinch-yourself atmosphere of pure bliss.

Room prices start at €190 and head north, but there's one single room (€100 to €140) and a cheaper double (from €140) available without views.

Grand Hotel Quisisana   HOTEL €€€
(☑ 081 837 07 88; www.quisisana.com; Via Camerelle 2, Capri Town; r from €360; ☺ Apr–mid-Oct; **❄ 🛜 🌊**) The Quisisana is Capri's most prestigious address, just a few espadrille-clad steps from Piazza Umberto I. A slumber palace since the 19th century, it's a bastion of unashamed opulence, with two swimming pools, a fitness centre and spa, restaurants, bars and subtropical gardens. Rooms are suitably palatial, with off-white colour schemes and mostly classic, conservative furniture.

🍴 Eating

Traditional Campanian food served in traditional trattorias is what you'll mainly find on Capri. Prices are high but drop noticeably the further you get from Capri Town. The island's culinary gift to the world is *insalata caprese*, a salad of fresh tomatoes, basil and silky mozzarella drizzled with olive oil.

Many restaurants, like hotels, close over winter and reopen at Easter.

Gelateria Buonacore   FAST FOOD €
(☑ 081 837 78 26; Via Vittorio Emanuele III 35, Capri Town; snacks €2-10, gelato from €2.50; ☺ 8am-midnight Jul-Sep, reduced hours rest of year, closed Tue Oct-Jun; **♿**) Ideal for quick takeaways, this popular, down-to-earth snack bar does a roaring trade in savoury and sweet treats. Hit the spot with *panini* (sandwiches), stuffed peppers, waffles and the legendary ice cream. Hard to beat, though, are the delicate but filling *sfogliatelle*

(cinnamon-infused ricotta in a puff-pastry shell; €2.50) and the feather-light speciality *caprilu al limone* (lemon and almond cakes).

★ La Palette
ITALIAN €€

(☑ 081 837 72 83; www.lapalette.it; Via Matermània 36; meals from €35; ⊙ 11am-midnight Apr-early Nov) Local Caprese ingredients are combined into the most flavour-filled, creative dishes possible here. Expect the delights of zucchini flowers stuffed with ricotta, fresh and tangy octopus salad, and an aubergine *parmigiana* that seems to taste so much better than everyone else's. An easy 10-minute walk from Capri Town, it has swooningly romantic bay views.

★ È Divino
ITALIAN €€

(☑ 081 837 83 64; www.edivinocapri.com/divino; Via Sella Orta 10a, Capri Town; meals €33-48; ⊙ 8pm-1am daily Jun-Aug, 12.30-2.30pm & 7.30pm-midnight Tue-Sun rest of year; ☏) Proudly eccentric (what other restaurant has a bed in its dining room?), this diligent purveyor of Slow Food is a precious secret to those who know it. Whether dining among lemon trees in the garden or among antiques, chandeliers and contemporary art (and that bed!) inside, expect a thoughtful, regularly changing menu dictated by what's fresh from the garden and market.

Le Grottelle
ITALIAN €€

(☑ 081 837 57 19; Via Arco Naturale 13; meals €30-40; ⊙ noon-2.30pm & 7-11pm Fri-Wed summer, noon-3pm Fri-Wed Apr, May & Oct, closed Nov-Mar; ☏) This is a great place to impress someone – not so much for the food, which is decent enough, but for the dramatic setting: its two dining areas are set in a cave and on a hillside terrace with sea views. Dishes are rustic, from homemade *fusilli* pasta with shrimps and courgettes to rabbit with onions, garlic and rosemary.

★ Il Geranio
SEAFOOD €€€

(☑ 081 837 06 16; www.geraniocapri.com; Via Matteotti 8, Capri Town; meals €45-50; ⊙ noon-3pm & 7-11pm mid-Apr–mid-Oct) Time to pop the question or quell those predeparture blues? The terrace at this sophisticated spot offers heart-stealing views over the pine trees to Isole Faraglioni. Seafood is the speciality, particularly the salt-baked fish. Other fine choices include octopus salad and linguine with saffron and mussels. Book at least three days ahead for a terrace table in high season.

Drinking & Nightlife

Taverna Anema e Core
CLUB

(☑ 329 4742508; www.anemaecore.com; Via Sella Orta 39e, Capri Town; ⊙ 11pm-late Jun-Aug, closed Wed Apr, May, Sep & Oct, closed rest of year) Behind a humble exterior is one of the island's most famous nightspots, run by the charismatic Guido Lembo. This smooth and sophisticated bar-club attracts an appealing mix of superchic and casually dressed punters, here for the relaxed atmosphere and regular live music, including unwaveringly authentic Neapolitan guitar strumming and singing.

Caffè Michelangelo
CAFE

(☑ 333 7784331; Via Orlandi 138, Anacapri; ⊙ 8am-2am Jul & Aug, to 1am Sep-Jun, closed Thu Nov & Dec; ☏) On a street flanked by tasteful shops and near two lovely piazzas, this is the best place in Anacapri to park your gluteus maximus for a bit of tourist-watching. Rate the passing parade over a *spritz con Cynar*, a less-sweet take on the classic Aperol *spritz*, made using a herbacious Italian bitter liqueur. It also does wine by the glass.

Shopping

★ La Parisienne
FASHION & ACCESSORIES

(☑ 081 837 02 83; www.laparisiennecapri.it; Piazza Umberto I 7, Capri Town; ⊙ 9am-10pm) First opened in 1906 (yes, that is not a misprint!) and best known for introducing Capri pants in the 1960s – famously worn by Audrey Hepburn, who bought them here – La Parisienne can run you up a made-to-measure pair within a day. It also sells off-the-hook Capri pants (from €250).

Jackie O was a customer, and Clark Gable apparently favoured the fashions here, particularly the Bermuda shorts, which (believe it or not) were considered quite raffish in their day.

Limoncello Capri
Canale Massimo
DRINKS

(☑ 081 837 29 27; www.limoncello.com; Via Capodimonte 27, Anacapri; ⊙ 9am-7.30pm, closed mid-Jan–mid-Feb) Don't be put off by the gaudy yellow display: this historic shop stocks some of the island's best *limoncello*. In fact, it was here that the drink was first concocted (or at least that is the claim). Apparently, the grandmother of current owner Massimo made the tot as an after-dinner treat for the guests in her small guesthouse.

Carthusia I Profumi di Capri COSMETICS
(☑ 081 837 53 93; www.carthusia.it; Via Matteotti 2d, Capri Town; ⊙ 9am-8pm Apr-Sep, to 5pm rest of year) Allegedly, Capri's famous floral perfume was established in 1380 by the prior of the Certosa di San Giacomo. Caught unawares by a royal visit, he displayed the island's most beautiful flowers for the queen. Changing the water in the vase, he discovered a floral scent. This became the base of the classic perfume now sold at this smart laboratory outlet.

ℹ Information

Post Office (www.poste.it; Via Roma 50, Capri Town; ⊙ 8.20am-7pm Mon-Fri, to 12.30pm Sat; ☎) Located just west of the bus terminal.

Tourist Office (☑ 081 837 06 34; www.capritourism.com; Banchina del Porto; ⊙ 8.30am-4.15pm, closed Sat & Sun Jan-Mar & Nov) Can provide a map of the island, plus accommodation listings, ferry timetables and other useful information.

ℹ Getting There & Away

The two major ferry routes to Capri are from Naples and Sorrento, although there are also seasonal connections with Ischia and the Amalfi Coast (Amalfi, Positano and Salerno).

Caremar (☑ 081 837 07 00; www.caremar.it; Marina Grande) Operates hydrofoils and ferries to/from Naples (€12.50 to €18, 40 minutes to 1¼ hours, up to seven daily) and hydrofoils to/from Sorrento (€14.40, 25 minutes, four daily).

Navigazione Libera del Golfo (NLG; ☑ 081 552 07 63; www.navlib.it; Marina Grande) Operates hydrofoils to/from Naples (from €19, 45 minutes, up to nine daily).

SNAV (☑ 081 428 55 55; www.snav.it; Marina Grande) Operates hydrofoils to/from Naples (from €22.50, 45 minutes, up to nine daily).

ℹ Getting Around

BUS

Autobus ATC (☑ 081 837 04 20; Bus Station, Via Roma, Capri Town; tickets €2, day pass €6) Runs buses between Marina Grande, Capri Town, Marina Piccola and Anacapri.

Staiano Autotrasporti (☑ 081 837 24 22; www.staianotourcapri.com; Bus Station, Viale de Tommaso, Anacapri; tickets €2) Runs regular buses to the Grotta Azzurra and Punta Carena *faro* (lighthouse) from Anacapri.

FUNICULAR

Funicular (Via Colombo 18; tickets €2; ⊙ 6.30am-9.30pm) The first challenge facing visitors is how to get from Marina Grande to Capri Town. The most enjoyable option is the funicular, if only for the evocative en-route views over the lemon groves and surrounding countryside. The ticket booth in Marina Grande is not at the funicular station itself; it's behind the tourist office (turn right onto Via Marina Grande from the ferry port). Note that the funicular usually closes from January through March for maintenance; a substitute bus service is in place during this period.

SCOOTER

Capri Scooter (☑ 338 3606918, 081 362 00 83; www.capriscooter.com; Via Marina Grande 280, Marina Grande; per 2/24hr €30/65) If you're looking to hire a scooter at Marina Grande, stop here. There's another outlet in **Anacapri** (☑ 081 837 38 88; www.capriscooter.com; Piazza Barile 20, Anacapri; per 2/24 hr €30/65).

TAXI

Taxi (☑ in Anacapri 081 837 11 75, in Capri Town 081 837 66 57) From Marina Grande, a taxi costs from €17 to Capri Town and from €23 to Anacapri; from Capri Town to Anacapri costs around €18. These rates include one bag per vehicle. Each additional bag (with dimensions exceeding 40cm by 20cm by 50cm) costs an extra €2.

Ischia

☑ 081 / POP 64,110

The volcanic outcrop of Ischia is the most developed and largest of the islands in the Bay of Naples. An early colony of Magna Graecia, first settled in the 8th century BCE, Ischia today is famed for its thermal spas, manicured gardens, striking Aragonese castle and unshowy, straightforward Italian airs – a feature also reflected in its food. Ischia is a refreshing antidote to glitzy Capri.

Most visitors head straight for the north-coast towns of Ischia Porto, Ischia Ponte, Forio and Lacco Ameno. Of these, Ischia Porto boasts the best bars, while Forio and Lacco Ameno have the prettiest spas and gardens. On the calmer south coast, the car-free perfection of Sant'Angelo offers a languid blend of a cosy harbour and lazy beaches. In between the coasts lies a less-trodden landscape of chestnut forests, vineyards and volcanic rock, loomed over by Monte Epomeo, Ischia's highest peak.

⊙ Sights

★ **Castello Aragonese** CASTLE
(Aragon Castle; ☑ 342 9618566, 081 99 28 34; www.castelloaragoneseischia.com; Rocca del Castello, Ischia Ponte; adult/reduced €10/6; ⊙ 9am-sunset)

LOCAL KNOWLEDGE

ISCHIA'S BEST BEACHES

Spiaggia dei Maronti Long, sandy and very popular; the sand here is warmed by natural steam geysers. Reach the beach by bus from Barano, by water taxi from Sant'Angelo (€3 one way) or on foot along the path leading east from Sant'Angelo.

Baia di San Montano Due west of Lacco Ameno, this gorgeous bay is the place for warm, shallow, crystal-clear waters. You'll also find the Negombo spa park here. Take the bus to Lacco Ameno and walk the last 500m.

Baia di Sorgeto (Via Sorgeto) Not a beach as such, but an intimate cove complete with bubbling thermal spring. Perfect for a winter dip. Catch a water taxi from Sant'Angelo (€5 one way) or get here on foot from the town of Panza.

Spiaggia dei Pescatori (Fishermen's Beach; 🖪) Wedged between Ischia Porto and Ischia Ponte is the island's most down-to-earth and popular seaside strip; it's perfect for families. It's accessible by the island's main bus line.

Punta Caruso Located on Ischia's northwestern tip, this secluded rocky spot is perfect for a swim in clear, deep water. To get here, follow the walking path that leads off Via Guardiola down to the beach. Not suitable for children or when seas are rough.

There are castles and then there's Ischia's Castello Aragonese, a veritable fort-city set on its own craggy islet, looking like a cross between Harry Potter's Hogwarts and Mont Saint Michel. While Syracusan tyrant Gerone I built the first fortress here in 474 BCE, the bulk of the current structure dates from the 1400s, when King Alfonso of Aragon gave the older Angevin fortress a thorough makeover, building the fortified bastions, current causeway and access ramp cut into the rock.

★ **La Mortella** GARDENS
(Place of the Myrtles; ☑ 081 98 62 20; www.la mortella.it; Via F Calese 39; adult/reduced €12/10; ☺ 9am-7pm Tue, Thu, Sat & Sun Apr–early Nov) A symphony of plants, La Mortella (the myrtles) is the former home and gardens of the late British composer William Walton (1902–83) and his Argentine wife, Susana. Designed by Russell Page and inspired by the Moorish gardens of Spain's Alhambra, it is recognised as one of Italy's finest botanical gardens. Stroll among terraces, pools, palms, fountains and more than 1000 rare and exotic plants from all over the world.

The lower section of the garden is humid and tropical, while the upper level features Mediterranean plants and beautiful views over Forio and the coast.

The Waltons first came here in 1949 to establish a new home where they subsequently entertained such venerable house guests as Sir Laurence Olivier, Maria Callas and Charlie Chaplin. Walton's life is commemorated in a small on-site museum, while his ashes are buried beneath a monument in the garden's upper reaches. The gardens host chamber-music recitals and concerts and there's also a rather elegant cafe where you can enjoy a cup of tea amid the greenery.

Monte Epomeo MOUNTAIN
To anyone of average fitness, an ascent of Ischia's slumbering volcanic peak is practically obligatory. The views from the rocky summit are superb. And, if that's not enough, a rustic restaurant sheltered beneath a precipitous crag lures hikers with what is possibly the best tomato bruschetta in the viewable vicinity (which, on a clear day, is a long way).

The quickest way to climb Epomeo is from the village of Fontana located on the island's southern flank. The route (signposted from a bend in the road where the bus stops) weaves up a paved road, diverts onto a track and finishes on a steep-ish path. Total distance: 2.5km.

🏃 Activities

★ **Negombo** SPA
(☑ 081 98 61 52; www.negombo.it; Baia di San Montano; all day adult/reduced €35/23, from 3.30pm €23/19; ☺ 8.30am-7pm mid-Apr–early Oct) This is arguably the best thermal spa on an island full of them, courtesy of its multifaceted attractions. Sure, there are the Zen-like thermal pools, a hammam and private beach, but Negombo is also part of the Grandi Giardini Italiani network, home to more than 500 exotic plant species. Furthermore,

it ranks as an 'art park' with avant-garde sculptures incorporated into the greenery.

Attractive pools (13 of them) are arranged amid floral foliage, plus there's a Japanese labyrinth pool for weary feet, a decent *tavola calda* (snack bar), and a full range of massage and beauty treatments. A private beach on the Baia di San Montano lies out front, meaning Negombo tends to draw a younger crowd than many other Ischian spa spots.

Those arriving by car or scooter can park all day on-site (car/scooter €5/€3).

Ischia Diving   DIVING
(☑ 081 98 18 52; www.ischiadiving.net; Via Iasolino 106, Ischia Porto; single dive €40) This well-established diving outfit offers some attractively priced dive packages, such as five dives including equipment for €180.

🛌 Sleeping

Camping Mirage   CAMPGROUND €
(☑ 347 3781562; www.campingmirage.it; Via Maronti 37, Spiaggia dei Maronti, Barano d'Ischia; camping 2 people, car & tent €38-46; ☺ Apr-Oct; ℗) Located on Spiaggia dei Maronti, one of Ischia's best beaches, and within walking distance of Sant'Angelo, this shady campground offers 50 places, as well as showers, laundry facilities, a bar and a restaurant dishing up local speciality *tubettoni, cozze e pecorino* (pasta with mussels and sheep cheese).

Hotel Noris   HOTEL €
(☑ 081 99 13 87; www.norishotel.it; Via Sogliuzzo 2, Ischia Ponte; d €50-150; ☺ Easter–mid-Oct; ✳🛜) This place has a great price and a great position within easy strolling distance of the Ponte sights. Comfortable, decent-sized rooms are decked out in blue and white, and breakfast is a generous Continental buffet. If you can, take a front room with a balcony for views towards Procida and partial glimpses of the magnificent Castello Aragonese.

Semiramis Hotel de Charme   HOTEL €€
(☑ 081 90 75 11; www.hotelsemiramisischia.it; Via Giovanni Mazzella 236, Forio; d €143-215; ☺ mid-Apr–mid-Oct; ℗✳🛜🏊) A few minutes' walk from the Poseidon spa complex, this bright hotel has a tropical-oasis feel with its outdoor thermal pools surrounded by lofty palms. Rooms are large and beautifully tiled in the traditional yellow-and-turquoise pattern, and the garden is equally glorious, with fig trees, vineyards and sea views.

★ **Albergo Il Monastero**   HOTEL €€
(☑ 081 99 24 35; www.albergoilmonastero.it; Castello Aragonese, Rocca del Castello, Ischia Ponte; s €65-90, d €105-145; ☺ mid-April–mid-Oct; ✳🛜) Monastery stays offer some of Italy's best bargains but you know you're onto something really special when the digs are inside Ischia's huge castle. The former monks' cells here still have a certain appealing sobriety about them, with their dark-wood furniture, white walls and vintage terracotta tiles. Elsewhere, the hotel exudes a pleasing sense of space and style.

Relax and enjoy the vaulted ceilings, plush sofas, antiques and contemporary art by the late owner and artist Gabriele Mattera. There are no TVs but the views more than make up for this.

🍴 Eating

★ **La Casereccia**   CAMPANIAN €€
(☑ 081 98 77 56; www.lacasereccia.com; Via Baiola 269; meals €28-40; ☺ 1-3pm & 7.30pm-1am, closed Mon-Wed Feb) Safe in the hands of Mamma Tina, Casereccia delivers plenty of full-flavoured *casereccia* (homemade food). The very Ischian menu pushes seafood, doughy pizzas, island-produced wine and that much vaunted local speciality – *coniglio* (rabbit). Try it either roasted or packaged in delicate ravioli. It's a little out of town on the flanks of Monte Epomeo, but worth the detour.

★ **Il Focolare**   ITALIAN €€
(☑ 081 90 29 44; www.trattoriailfocolare.it; Via Creajo al Crocefisso 3, Barano d'Ischia; meals €30-35; ☺ 12.30-2.45pm Thu-Sun & 7.30-11.30pm daily Jun-Oct, closed Wed Nov-May, closed Feb) A good choice for those seeking a little turf instead of surf, this is one of the island's best-loved restaurants. Family run, homely and rustic, it has a solidly traditional meat-based menu with steaks, lamb cutlets and specialities including *coniglio all'Ischitana* (typical local rabbit dish with tomatoes, garlic and herbs). On the sweet front, the desserts are homemade and exquisite.

Owner Riccardo D'Ambra (who runs the restaurant together with his wife, Loretta, and their children) is a leading local advocate of the Slow Food movement. If you want seafood, coffee or soft drinks, you'll have to go elsewhere; they're not on the menu here.

★ **Ristorante Pietratorcia**   ITALIAN €€
(☑ 081 90 72 32; www.ristorantepietratorcia.it; Via Provinciale Panza 401; menus €35, wine

LOCAL KNOWLEDGE

ISCHIA ON A FORK

If you wanted to stick the best parts of Ischian cuisine on a fork, you'd need to make it a big one. The island's insularity and rich volcanic soil have thrown up a rich melange of recipes over the years, many of them subtly different from dishes found elsewhere in Campania.

A popular Ischian starter is *caponata*. Unlike Sicilian *caponata* (made with aubergines), the Ischian dish resembles tomato bruschetta with added tuna and olives. It was originally a poor person's food, made for farmers out in the fields from the leftovers of the previous day's stale bread.

For the main course, there's an enticing choice between land and sea. Classic seafood dishes adhere to a cooking method known as *acqua pazza* (crazy water): white fish poached in a herb-heavy broth with locally grown *pomodorini* (cherry tomatoes), garlic and parsley. Typical local fish include *pesce bandiera* (sailfish), the flat castagna, lampuga and *palamide* (a small tuna). Smaller seafood, such as squid, prawns and anchovies, are best enjoyed fried in a *frittura di parzana* (meaning 'from the trawler') and served simply with lemon.

Plump local *pomodorini* reappear in the most classic of all Ischian dishes, *coniglio all'ischitana*, a rabbit stew cooked on the hob in a large terracotta pot with a sauce of olive oil, unpeeled garlic, tomato, chilli, basil, thyme and white wine. Traditionally, rabbits were caught wild, but by the late 20th century cage-bred rabbits had become standard fare on Ischia. In recent years, in a nod to the Slow Food movement, farmers have started to return to rearing rabbits *di fossa* (semiwild in burrows).

Despite its high population density and limited agricultural terrain, Ischia still supports an estimated 800 hectares of vineyards, most of them terraced on the lower slopes of Monte Epomeo. Wine production in Ischia goes back to the ancient Greeks and the island harbours some of Italy's oldest DOCs. With fish or pasta, try a Forastera or a Biancolella (both whites). With the rich *coniglio all'ischitana* go for a ruby red Piedirosso.

If you've room for dessert, opt for chocolate and almond cake (an import from nearby Capri), helped down with an obligatory ice-cold limoncello.

degustations from €20; ⊗11am-2pm & 5.30pm-midnight Tue-Sun Easter-Oct; 🐾) Enjoying a bucolic setting among tumbling vines, wild fig trees and rosemary bushes, this A-list winery is a showcase for Ischian cooking. Tour the old stone cellars, sip a local drop and eye up a competent, seasonal turf-and-surf menu that is led by rabbit, served with pasta or slow-cooked island style with wine and potatoes. Book ahead in high season.

The CD and CS buses stop within metres of the winery's entrance; ask the driver to advise you when to alight.

Montecorvo ITALIAN €€
(📞081 99 80 29; www.montecorvo.it; Via Montecorvo 33; meals €30; ⊗7.30pm-midnight daily yr round, 12.30-3pm Sun mid-Sep–mid-Jun, closed Wed Nov-Mar; 🐾) Part of the dining room at hillside Montecorvo is tunnelled into a cave, while the verdant terrace offers spectacular sunset views. Owner Giovanni prides himself on the special dishes he makes daily.

There's an emphasis on grilled meat and fish, and an especially popular dish of local rabbit, cooked in a woodfired oven.

❶ Information

Tourist Office (📞081 507 42 31; www.info ischiaprocida.it; Via Iasolino 7, Ischia Porto; ⊗9am-2pm & 3-8pm Mon-Sat Apr-Sep, 9am-2pm Mon-Fri Oct-Mar) A slim selection of maps and brochures, next to the ferry port.

❶ Getting There & Away

Hydrofoils and ferries are the most likely way of getting to the islands. Note that services departing to/from Positano and Amalfi operate solely from around May to September or October. At other times of the year, you will have to catch services from Naples or Sorrento. In Naples, hydrofoils leave from Molo Beverello, with slower ferries leaving from the adjacent Calata Porta Massa. Generally, there is no need to book: just turn up around 35 minutes before departure in case there's a queue.

Ischia's main ferry terminal is in Ischia Porto. However, there are also other smaller terminals in Casamicciola and Forio.

Caremar (⌘ 081 98 48 18; www.caremar.it; Via Iasolino) Operates up to six daily hydrofoils from Naples to Ischia Porto (€17.90, 45 minutes) and Procida (€8.70, 20 minutes), as well as ferries.

Alilauro (⌘ 081 497 22 42; www.alilauro.it) Operates hydrofoils from Naples to Ischia Porto (€20.10, 50 minutes, up to 12 daily) and up to six hydrofoils daily between Forio and Naples (€21.50). There are also two daily ferries to Sorrento (€22.90, one hour) from Ischia Porto.

SNAV (⌘ 081 428 55 55; www.snav.it) Operates hydrofoils from Naples to the Ischian town of Casamicciola (€20.20 to €21.20, one hour, five daily).

ℹ Getting Around

Ischia's main circular highway can get clogged with traffic in the height of summer. This, combined with the penchant the local youth have for overtaking on blind corners and the environmental impact of just too many cars, means that you may want to consider riding the excellent network of buses (cheap!) or hopping in a taxi (not cheap!) to get around. The distance between attractions and the lack of pavements on the busy roads makes walking unappealing.

The island's main **bus station** (cnr Via Iasolino & Via della Foce) is a one-minute walk west of the **ferry and hydrofoil terminal** (Via Iasolino), at Ischia Porto, with buses servicing all other parts of the island.

Procida

⌘ 081 / POP 10,465

The Bay of Naples' smallest island is also its best-kept secret. Off the mass-tourist radar, Procida is like the Portofino prototype and is refreshingly real. August aside – when beach-bound mainlanders flock to its shores – its narrow, sun-bleached streets are the domain of the locals: kids clutch fishing rods, parents push prams and old seafolk swap yarns. Here, the hotels are smaller, fewer waiters speak broken German and the island's welcome hasn't been changed by a tidal wave of visitors.

If you have the time, Procida is an ideal place to explore on foot. The most compelling areas (and where you will also find most of the hotels, bars and restaurants) are Marina Grande, Marina Corricella and Marina di Chiaiolella. Beaches are not plentiful here, apart from the Lido di Procida,

where, aside from August, you shouldn't have any trouble finding some towel space.

◉ Sights

Abbazia di San Michele Arcangelo
CHURCH, MUSEUM

(⌘ 334 8514252, 334 8514028; www.abbaziasanmicheleprocida.it; Via Terra Murata 89, Terra Murata; ◷10am-12.45pm Mon-Sat, from 10.30am Sun) **FREE** Soak up the dizzying bay views at the belvedere before exploring the adjoining Abbazia di San Michele Arcangelo. Built in the 11th century and remodelled between the 17th and 19th centuries, this one-time Benedictine abbey houses a small museum with some arresting pictures created in gratitude by shipwrecked sailors, plus a church with a spectacular coffered ceiling and an ancient Greek alabaster basin converted into a font.

The church apse features four paintings by Neapolitan artist Nicola Russo. Dating back to 1690, these works include a depiction of St Michael the Archangel protecting Procida from Saracen attack on 8 May 1535. The painting is especially fascinating for its depiction of Marina Grande in the 16th century. Free guided tours can be arranged between April and October.

Isola di Vivara
ISLAND

(⌘ 347 7858256; www.comune.procida.na.it; adult/reduced €10/5; ◷guided tours 10am & 3pm Fri-Sun) Linked to Procida by pedestrian bridge, pocket-sized Vivara is what remains of a volcanic crater dating back some 55,000 years. The island is home to unique flora and abundant birdlife, while archaeological digs have uncovered traces of a Bronze-Age Mycenaean settlement as well as pottery fragments dating back to early Greek colonisation. Book online 15 days in advance.

🏃 Activities

Blue Dream Yacht Charter Boating
BOATING

(⌘ 081 896 05 79, 339 5720874; www.bluedreamcharter.com; Via Emanuele 14, Marina Grande; 6/8-person yacht per week from €1600/2800) If you have 'champagne on the deck' aspirations, you can always charter your very own yacht or catamaran from here.

Sprint
CYCLING

(⌘ 339 8659600; www.sprintprocida.com; Via Roma 28, Marina Grande; standard/electric bike per day €10/20; 🖐) One of several bike-hire places on the port at Marina Grande. Bikes are an excellent way of exploring this small, relatively flat island.

🕝 Tours

Cesare Boat Trips
BOATING

(📞 333 4603877; 2½hr tour per person €25; ☺ Mar-Oct) On the harbour at Marina Corricella, ask for friendly Cesare in your best Italian. Check at one of the beach bars or by La Gorgonia restaurant – he won't be far away. Cesare runs some great boat trips.

🎭 Festivals & Events

Procession of the Misteri
RELIGIOUS

Good Friday sees a solemn procession when a wooden statue of Christ and the Madonna Addolorata, along with life-size plaster and papier-mâché tableaux illustrating events leading to Christ's crucifixion, are carted across the island. Men dress in blue tunics with white hoods, while many of the young girls dress as the Madonna.

The procession starts in the Piazza dei Martiri, just behind Marina della Corricella.

🛏 Sleeping

Bed & Breakfast La Terrazza
B&B €

(📞 081 896 00 62; Via Faro 26, Marina Grande; s €50-70, d €75-90; ☺ Easter-Oct; 🛜) Attractive budget option tucked into one of the timeless lanes that characterise central Procida, the Terrazza is run by an equally timeless couple who rent three compact rooms with low ceilings and carefully chosen seafaring decor. The highlight is the broad terracotta-tiled roof terrace where generous breakfasts are served.

⭐ Hotel La Vigna
BOUTIQUE HOTEL €€

(📞 081 896 04 69; www.albergolavigna.it; Via Principessa Margherita 46, Terra Murata; d €110-180, ste €160-230; ☺ Easter-Oct; 🅿❄🛜🐾) Enjoying a discreet cliffside location, this crenelated 18th-century villa is a gorgeous retreat, complete with rambling garden, vines and swimming pool. Five of the spacious, simply furnished rooms offer direct access to the garden. The hotel also has its own vineyard, produces its own wine (served in a chic wine bar) and offers wine therapy treatments at its small spa.

Casa Sul Mare
HOTEL €€

(📞 081 896 87 99; www.lacasasulmare.it; Salita Castello 13, Marina Corricella; d €126-162; ☺ early Mar-Oct; ❄🛜) A crisp, white-washed place

with the kind of evocative views that helped make *The Talented Mr. Ripley* such a memorable film (parts were filmed in Procida). Overlooking the pastel-hued fishing village of Marina Corricella, near the ruined Castello d'Avalos, its rooms are simple yet elegant, with fetching tiled floors, wrought-iron bedsteads and the odd piece of antique furniture.

The hotel treats its guests well: during summer there's a boat service to the nearby Spiaggia della Chiaia (Chiaia Beach), and the morning cappuccino, courtesy of Franco, may be the best you'll find outside Turin.

🍴 Eating

Prime waterfront dining here needn't equal an overpriced disappointment, with portside trattorias serving fresh, classic food. Several inland trattorias use home-grown produce and game in their cooking. Try the zesty *insalata al limone,* a lemon salad infused with chilli oil. Marina Grande is the place to mix with the fisherfolk at one of the earthy local bars.

⭐ Da Mariano
ITALIAN €

(📞 081 896 73 50; Marina di Chiaiolella; meals €20-25; ☺ noon-3pm & 7pm-midnight Easter-Nov; 🛜) Hugely popular with locals, thanks to simple yet perfectly executed dishes like stuffed calamari and *spaghetti alle vongole* (spaghetti with clams). The fish, including swordfish, is jumping fresh, and you eat looking out at the bay. Round off a meal with the signature *la Procidana,* a *caprese*-style cake made with white chocolate and the juice and rind of local lemons.

Da Giorgio
TRATTORIA €

(📞 081 896 79 10; Via Roma 36, Marina Grande; meals €24; ☺ noon-3pm & 7-11.30pm Mar-Oct, closed Tue Nov-Feb) A retro, no-frills neighbourhood trattoria close to the port. The menu holds few surprises, but the ingredients are fresh; try the *spaghetti con frutti di mare* (seafood spaghetti) with some spongy *casareccio* (home-style) bread.

ℹ Information

Pro Loco (📞 081 010 07 24; www.prolocodi procida.it; Via Roma, Stazione Marittima, Marina Grande; ☺ 10am-1pm daily, 3-5pm Sat & Sun Apr-Oct) Located at the Ferry & Hydrofoil Ticket Office, this modest office has sparse printed information but should be able to advise on activities, accommodation and the like.

❶ Getting There & Away

The **Ferry & Hydrofoil Terminal** (Via Roma, Stazione Marittima, Marina Grande) is in Marina Grande.

Caremar (☑ 081 896 72 80; www.caremar.it; Via Roma, Stazione Marittima, Marina Grande) Operates hydrofoils to/from Naples (€14.50, 40 minutes, up to eight daily) and Ischia (from €13, 20 minutes, up to six daily). It also runs slower ferries to/from both destinations.

SNAV (☑ 081 428 55 55; www.snav.it; Via Roma, Stazione Marittima, Marina Grande) Operates up to four hydrofoils daily to/from Naples (from €17.50, 25 minutes).

THE AMALFI COAST

The Amalfi Coast is one of Italy's most memorable destinations. Here, mountains that plunge into the sea in a nail-biting vertical scene of precipitous crags, cliff-clinging abodes and verdant woodland.

Its string of fabled towns read like a Hollywood cast list. There's jet-set favourite Positano, a pastel-coloured cascade of chic boutiques, spritz-sipping pin-ups and sun-kissed sunbathers. Further east, ancient Amalfi lures with its Arabic-Norman cathedral, while mountaintop Ravello stirs hearts with its cultured villas and Wagnerian connection. To the west lies Amalfi Coast gateway Sorrento, a handsome clifftop resort that has miraculously survived the onslaught of package tourism.

The region also boasts well-marked hiking trails providing the chance to escape the star-struck coastal crowds.

❶ Getting There & Away

BOAT

Year-round hydrofoils run between Naples and Sorrento (€13, 20 minutes, up to six daily), as well as between Sorrento and Capri (€20.50, 20 minutes, up to 13 daily). From around April/May to October, ferry services connect Sorrento to Positano (€20, 30 minutes, two daily) and Amalfi (€21, 50 minutes, two daily), from where ferries continue to Salerno.

BUS

The Circumvesuviana train runs from Naples' Piazza Garibaldi to Sorrento, from where there is a regular and efficient **SITA Sud** (www.sitasudtrasporti.it) bus service to Positano, Amalfi and Salerno.

TRAIN

The **Circumvesuviana** (☑ 800 211388; www.eavsrl.it) runs every 30 minutes between Naples' Garibaldi station (beside Napoli Centrale station) and Sorrento (€3.90, 70 minutes). Trains stop in Ercolano (Herculaneum) and Pompeii en route. **Trenitalia** (☑ 892021; www.trenitalia.com) runs frequent services between Napoli Centrale station and Salerno (€4.70, 40 minutes).

Positano

☑ 089 / POP 3915

Dramatic, deluxe and more than a little dashing, Positano is the Amalfi Coast's front-cover splash, with vertiginous houses tumbling down to the sea in a cascade of sun-bleached peach, pink and terracotta. No less photo-worthy are its steep streets and steps, flanked by wisteria-draped hotels, smart restaurants and fashionable retailers.

Look beyond the facades and the fashion, however, and you will find reassuring signs of everyday reality: crumbling stucco, streaked paintwork and even, on occasion, a faint whiff of drains. There's still a southern-Italian-holiday feel about the place, with sunbathers eating pizza on the beach, kids pestering parents for gelato and chic *signore* from Milan browsing the boutiques. The fashionista history runs deep – *moda Positano* was born here in the '60s and the town was the first in Italy to import bikinis from France.

◉ Sights & Activities

Positano's most memorable sight is its pyramidal townscape, with pastel-coloured houses stacked up on the hillsides.

Getting around town is largely a matter of walking. If your knees can take the slopes, dozens of narrow alleys and stairways make strolling around relatively straightforward and joyously traffic-free. The easy option is to take the local bus to the top of the town and wind your way down on foot.

Chiesa di Santa Maria Assunta CHURCH
(☑ 089 87 54 80; Piazza Flavio Gioia; ⊗ 9am-noon & 4-7pm Mon-Sat) Omnipresent in most Positano photos is the colourful majolica-tiled dome of its main church (and the town's only real sight). If you are visiting at a weekend you will probably have the added perk of seeing a wedding; it's one of the most

NAPLES & CAMPANIA POSITANO

Positano

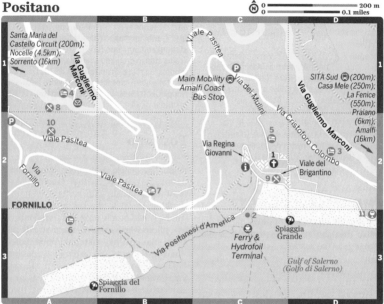

Positano

popular churches in southern Italy for ex-
changing vows.

The church is known for a 13th-century
Byzantine *Black Madonna and Child* above
the main altar. The icon was supposedly
stolen from Constantinople by pirates and
smuggled west.

Santa Maria del Castello Circuit   HIKING
For those travelling on foot, there's no real
way out of Positano that doesn't involve
climbing steep stone staircases – lots of 'em!
The advantage of this particular circuitous
route is that it enjoys a bit of shade in its
early stages as you plod heavenward amid a
thick and gnarly holm-oak forest.

The walk starts on the main coast road
(SS163) close to the Montepertuso turn-off

by a ruined building and climbs steeply
through trees before breaking into dryer
Mediterranean scrub higher up. The coastal
views open out as the path (#333a) traverses the hills above Positano, with the hulk of
Monte Sant'Angelo standing sentinel in the
background. Turn left 2km up the ascent
and then right at the top to join a wider
trail towards the hike's high point; the tiny
village of Santa Maria del Castello (670m)
is accessible by diverting along a narrow,
paved road. At this ancient crossing point
around 5km into the hike, you'll find a small
bar and a church. Take the narrow road back
down to the main path; turn left (trail #333),
proceed around the headland and then head
right on a path that leads steeply down via a
series of well-constructed staircases to Pos-

itano, visible in all its glory directly below. The walk ends beside the Bar Internazionale (p126) in Upper Positano. The total distance is 9km.

L'Uomo e il Mare BOATING
(📞089 81 16 13; www.escursioniluomoeilmare.it; ⏰9am-8pm Easter-Oct) Offers a range of tours, including Capri and Amalfi day trips (from €65 to €80), out of a kiosk near the ferry terminal. It also organises private sunset tours to Li Galli, complete with champagne (from €200 for up to 12 people). Private tours should be organised at least a day in advance.

🛏 Sleeping

Positano is a glorious place to stay, but be aware that prices are, overall, high. Like everywhere on the Amalfi Coast, it gets very busy in summer, so book ahead, particularly on weekends and in July and August. Ask at the tourist office about rooms or apartments in private houses.

Villa Nettuno HOTEL €
(📞089 87 54 01; www.villanettunopositano.com; Viale Pasitea 208; d €80-150; ⏰Apr-Oct; ❄️🛜) Hidden behind a barrage of perfumed foliage, lofty Villa Nettuno is not short on charm. Go for one of the original rooms in the 300-year-old part of the building, decked out in robust rustic decor and graced with a communal terrace. Bathrooms are a little old fashioned, but this place is all about the view.

Pensione Maria Luisa PENSION €€
(📞089 87 50 23; www.pensionemarialuisa.com; Via Fornillo 42; d €129-179; ⏰Mar-Oct; ❄️@🛜) Carlo the ceramicist is the main man at Maria Luisa; he's an extremely congenial (and multilingual) host who'll make your stay in glitzy Positano feel pleasantly homely. Simple rooms have extravagant views over town (get one with a balcony) and handy fridges, and there's a small rooftop terrace. It's in the Fornillo neighbourhood, a short walk via steps from the beach. Breakfast is €8 extra.

Hostel Brikette HOSTEL €€
(📞089 87 58 57; www.hostel-positano.com; Via Guglielmo Marconi 358; dm €40-73, d €160-220; ⏰mid-Mar–mid-Oct; ❄️🛜) Though more expensive than most hostels, cheerful Brikette is relatively cheap by Positano standards as long as you opt for a dorm. The top-of-the-town building has wonderful views and a range of sleeping options, from doubles

to three different types of dorm. Premium dorms have private bathrooms and terraces; all have handy bunk-side USB sockets and reading lights.

La Fenice B&B €€
(📞089 87 55 13; www.lafenicepositano.com; Via Gugliemo Marconi 8; d €180; ⏰Easter-Oct; ❄️🛜🏊) With hand-painted Vietri tiles, high ceilings and the odd piece of antique furniture, the rooms at this friendly family-run place are simple but smart; most have their own balcony or terrace with dreamy views. As with everywhere in Positano, you'll need to be good at stomping up and down steps to stay here – it's 1km east of the town centre.

Albergo California HOTEL €€
(📞089 87 53 82; www.hotelcaliforniapositano.it; Via Cristoforo Colombo 141; d €160-250; ⏰Mar-mid-Oct; P❄️🛜) If you were to choose the best place to take a quintessential Positano photo, it might be from the balcony of this hotel. But the view isn't all you get. The rooms in the older part of this grand 18th-century palace are magnificent, with original ceiling friezes and decorative doors. Rooms are simply decorated but tasteful, spacious and minimalist.

⭐Hotel Palazzo Murat HOTEL €€€
(📞089 87 51 77; www.palazzomurat.it; Via dei Mulini 23; d from €310; ⏰late Mar-early Nov; ❄️@🛜🏊) Positano personified. Hidden behind an ancient wall away from the tourists who surge along the pedestrian thoroughfares daily, this magnificent hotel occupies the 18th-century *palazzo* (mansion) that the one-time king of Naples used as his summer residence. Rooms are regal quarters (one even has a crown over the bed) with sumptuous antiques, original oil paintings and gleaming marble.

🍴 Eating

Positano excels in deluxe restaurants with fine food and romantic settings, but you can also get by on a budget if you know where to look. Generally, the nearer you get to the seafront, the more expensive everything becomes. Many places close over winter, making a brief reappearance for Christmas and New Year.

⭐C'era Una Volta TRATTORIA, PIZZA €
(📞089 81 19 30; Via Marconi 127; meals €20-30; ⏰noon-3pm Wed-Mon, 6-11pm daily) Calling like a siren to any cash-poor budget traveller

who thought Positano was for celebs only, this heroically authentic trattoria at the top of town specialises in honest, down-to-earth Italian grub. No need to look further than the *gnocchi alla sorrentina* (gnocchi in a tomato and basil sauce) and Caprese salad. Pizzas start at €4.50; beer €2. In Positano, no less!

It also runs a free shuttle to/from anywhere in Positano in the summer.

La Cambusa
SEAFOOD €€

(☑089 87 54 32; www.lacambusapositano.com; Piazza Vespucci 4; meals €40; ◐noon-11pm, closed Nov-mid-Dec; ☜) Sporting summery pastel hues and a seafront terrace, La Cambusa is on the front line, which, given the number of cash-rich tourists in these parts, could equal high prices for less-than-average food. Happily, that is not the case. Ingredients are top-notch and shine brightly in dishes such as homemade crab-filled ravioli and seafood risotto.

★ Casa Mele
ITALIAN €€€

(☑089 81 13 64; www.casamele.com; Via Guglielmo Marconi 76; tasting menus €75-100; ◐7pm-midnight Tue-Sun Apr-Nov; ☜) Something of a rarity in this land of traditional trattorias, Casa Mele is one of those cool contemporary restaurants with a lengthy tasting menu and food presented as art – and theatre. The slick open kitchen is a window into a high-powered food laboratory from which emerge whimsical pastas, delicate fish in subtle sauces, and outstanding desserts. Service is equally sublime.

★ Donna Rosa
ITALIAN €€€

(☑089 81 18 06; www.drpositano.com; Via Montepertuso 97-99, Montepertuso; meals €45-65; ◐11am-2pm & 5.30-10pm Wed-Mon Apr-Oct, closed lunch Aug) Once a humble trattoria, Donna Rosa is now considered an Amalfi Coast classic despite its out-of-the-way location in the village of Montepertuso. The reason? Jolly good food served by three generations of the original Rosa's family and a nod of admiration from that well-known food-campaigning Italophile, Jamie Oliver. Reservations are highly recommended for dinner and obligatory for lunch.

Next2
ITALIAN €€€

(☑089 812 35 16; www.next2.it; Viale Pasitea 242; meals €65, 6-course menu €80; ◐6.30-11pm Apr-Oct; ☜) Local produce and polished takes on tradition underscore sophisticated Next2. Standouts include the signature *conchigli-*

oni ripieni di ragù alla bolognese e stracciatella, shell-shaped pasta served with pork-mince *ragù* and *stracciatella* cheese. The kitchen boasts a top-range charcoal oven, put to fine use in dishes like tender octopus and mackerel with chickpea purée and cherry tomatoes. In summer, reserve a table on the terrace.

🍷 Drinking & Nightlife

Music on the Rocks
CLUB

(☑089 87 58 74; www.musicontherocks.it; Via Grotte dell'Incanto 51; cover charge €10-30; ◐10pm-4am Apr-Oct; ☜) This is one of the town's few genuine nightspots and one of the best clubs on the coast. The venue is dramatically carved into the tower at the eastern end of Spiaggia Grande. Join a lively crowd and some of the region's top DJs spinning anything from mainstream house to retro disco.

ℹ Information

Post Office (www.poste.it; Via Guglielmo Marconi 318; ◐8.20am-1.45pm Mon-Fri, to 12.45pm Sat) On the main highway passing through town.

Tourist Office (☑089 87 50 67; www.azienda turismopositano.it; Via Regina Giovanna 13; ◐8.30am-5pm Mon-Sat, to 3pm Sun) Provides lots of information, from sightseeing and tours to transport information. Also supplies a free hiking map.

ℹ Getting There & Away

BOAT

Positano has excellent ferry connections to the coastal towns and islands between April and October from its ferry and hydrofoil terminal.

TraVelMar (☑089 87 29 50; www.travelmar. it) Sails to numerous coastal destinations between April and October, including Amalfi (€8, 25 minutes, six daily) and Salerno (€12, 70 minutes, six daily). To reach Minori (€11), Maiori (€11) and Cetara (€12), transfer in Amalfi.

Lucibello Positano (☑089 87 50 32; www. lucibello.it) Operates three daily services to Capri (€22, 30 minutes) from mid-April to mid-October.

BUS

About 16km west of Amalfi and 18km from Sorrento, Positano is on the main SS163 coastal road. There are two Sita Sud main bus stops: coming from Sorrento and the west, the first stop you come to is opposite Bar Internazionale; arriving from Amalfi and the east, the stop is at the top of Via Cristoforo Colombo. To get into

WALK OF THE GODS

The Sentiero degli Dei (Path of the Gods) is the best-known walk on the Amalfi Coast for two reasons: first, it's spectacular from start to finish; and second, unlike most Amalfi treks, it doesn't involve inordinate amounts of stair-climbing. The walk starts in the village of Bomerano (a subdivision of Agerola), easily accessible from Amalfi town by SITA bus.

Beginning in the main square, where several cafes supply portable snacks, follow the red-and-white signs along Via Pennino. The start of the walk proper is marked by a **monument** inscribed with quotes by Italo Calvino and DH Lawrence. Views of terraced fields quickly open out as the path contours around a cliff-face and passes beneath the overhanging **Grotta del Biscotto** (Biscuit Cave). From here, the trail continues its traverse of the mountainside with some minor undulations. Periodically it dips into thickets of trees and sometimes you'll be required to negotiate rockier sections, but, in the main, the going is relatively easy.

The first main landmark after the Grotta is a path junction at **Colle Serra**. Here you get a choice between a low route or a high route. The low route is more exposed and threads its way through vineyards and rockier sections, with magnificent views of Praiano below. Roughly 800m along its course, it is possible to make a short diversion south to the **San Domenico Monastery**. The more popular high route (#327a) sticks to the rocky heights with broad, sweeping vistas. Both paths converge at a point called **Cisternulo**, 1.5km further on. Just below Colle Serra, a path from the Sentiero degli Dei's alternative start in Praiano joins the main trail. Bear in mind that starting in Praiano involves a thigh-challenging climb up 1000 steps before you reach the trail proper.

After Cisternulo, the path kinks around some half-obscured grotte (caves) and descends into the Valle Grarelle before climbing back up to the finish point in the tiny village of **Nocelle**. A small kiosk selling cold drinks and coffee, served on a charming terrace, greets you as you enter the village. Alternatively, head a little further through the village to Piazza Santa Croce, where a stall dispenses freshly squeezed orange and lemon juice.

From here you have three options: 1) take stairs (around 1500 of them!) down through the village to be deposited on the coast road 2km east of Positano; 2) catch a bus from the end of Nocelle's one interconnecting road to Positano – small minibuses run by Mobility Amalfi Coast (p126) depart 10 times a day; 3) a much nicer if longer option – especially if you're weary of steps at this point – is to continue along the path that leads west out of Nocelle towards Montepertuso. Don't miss the huge hole in the centre of the cliff at Montepertuso where it looks as though an irate giant has punched through the slab of limestone. In Montepertuso cut down past the church via a series of staircases to hit the northern fringes of Positano.

The CAI (Club Alpino Italiano; Italian Alpine Club) has a website dedicated to the Monti Lattari area (www.caimontilattari.it). Alternatively, the best printed map is from the cart&guide series (map #3) and available in most local bookshops/newsagents (€5). If you prefer a guided hike, reliable local guides include American **Frank Carpegna** (www.positanofrankcarpegna.com), a longtime resident here, and **Zia Lucy** (www.zialucy.it).

The Sentiero degli Dei is not advised for acute vertigo sufferers – if in doubt, take the less exposed upper path (#327a). The trail itself (Bomerano to Nocelle) measures just under 6km one-way, but you'll add on another 3km if you continue by foot to Positano at the end. Bring a rucksack and plenty of water, and wear proper walking shoes. You may want to pack swimming gear too and end the walk with a refreshing plunge into the sea.

Inclement weather and/or landslides can sometimes lead to trail closures. Check ahead. Tourist offices in Praiano (p127) and **Bomerano** (☑ 081 879 10 64; Piazza Paolo Capasso, Bomerano; ☺ 8am-1pm & 3-8pm Easter-Sep, 8am-1pm & 2-7pm rest of year; ☎) can provide more guidance.

town from the former, follow Viale Pasitea; from the latter (a far shorter route), take Via Cristoforo Colombo. When departing, buy bus tickets at **Bar Internazionale** (Via Guglielmo Marconi 306; ⊙7am-1am) or from the **tabaccheria** (☑089 81 21 33; Via Cristoforo Colombo 5; ⊙9.30am-9pm) at the bottom of Via Cristoforo Colombo.

SITA Sud (www.sitasudtrasporti.it) runs up to 28 daily buses to Sorrento (€2, one hour). It also runs up to 25 daily services to Amalfi (€2, 50 minutes), from where buses continue east to Salerno.

Nocelle

☑089 / POP 140

A tiny, still relatively isolated mountain village, located 2km southeast of Montepertuso, Nocelle (450m) commands some of the most spectacular views on the entire coast. A world apart from touristy Positano, it's a sleepy, silent place where not much ever happens and where the small population of residents are happy to keep it that way. The Sentiero degli Dei officially ends here.

Very handy as you stumble off the Sentiero degli Dei with wobbly legs, Villa della Quercia (☑089 812 34 97; http://villa laquercia.com; Via Nocelle 5; d €75-85; ⊙Apr–mid-Oct; 🗟) is a delightful B&B in a former hilltop monastery in Nocelle. It comes armed with a tranquil garden and spectacular, goat's-eye views of the coast. All six simple rooms have a terrace or balcony for languid lounging and the hosts welcome you with small-village friendliness. To reach the property, catch a local bus (€1.30) from Amalfi to Nocelle. The B&B is about a 10-minute walk from the bus stop.

Modest Trattoria Santa Croce (☑089 81 12 60; www.ristorantesantacrocepositano.com; Via Nocelle 19; meals €22; ⊙noon-3.30pm & 7-9.30pm Apr-Oct) has spectacular views over the coast and is located just past the finishing post on the Sentiero degli Dei. The menu is short and traditional, with a mix of good (if not memorable) surf-and-turf dishes such as rustic lentil soup, tagliatelle alla genovese (pasta with a rich, onion-based Neapolitan sauce) and freshly caught fish with local herbs.

ⓘ Getting There & Away

Small minibuses run by **Mobility Amalfi Coast** (☑089 81 30 77) depart for Positano (€1.30, 30 minutes) via Montepertuso 10 times a day. Catch the bus from the end of Nocelle's one inter-

connecting road. Note that tickets purchased onboard (as opposed to those purchased from *tabaccheria* shops) cost €1.80.

A taxi to/from Positano costs an extortionate €35 to €40: avoid.

It's a 3km walk to Positano – downhill all the way.

Praiano

☑089 / POP 2020

An ancient fishing village, a low-key summer resort and, increasingly, a popular centre for the arts, Praiano is a delight. With no centre as such, its whitewashed houses pepper the verdant ridge of Monte Sant'Angelo as it slopes towards Capo Sottile. Formerly an important silk-production centre, it was a favourite of the Amalfi *doges* (dukes), who made it their summer residence.

Praiano is glued to a steep bluff 120m above sea level and exploring it inevitably involves lots of steps. There are also several trails that start from town, including a dreamy walk – particularly romantic at sunset – that leaves from beside the San Gennaro church, descending due west to the Spiaggia della Gavitelli, via 300 steps, and carrying on to the medieval defensive Torre di Grado. The town also acts as an alternative starting point for the Sentiero degli Dei (Path of the Gods; p125).

The spread-out settlement stretches east and down to the sea at Marina di Praia, a sheltered cove with restaurants, a beach and a couple of diving operators.

🛏 Sleeping & Eating

Fish and seafood dominate the menus in this old fishing town. Its most famous traditional dish is *totani e patate alla praianese*, a soulful combination of soft calamari rings, sliced potato, *datterini* tomatoes, garlic, croutons, *peperoncino* (chilli) and parsley.

Hotel Onda Verde   HOTEL €€€

(☑089 87 41 43; www.hotelondaverde.com; Via Terramare 3, Praiano; d from €250; ⊙Apr-Oct; P✳🗟☀) The 'Green Wave' enjoys a commanding cliffside position overlooking secluded Marina di Praia. The interior is tunnelled into the stone cliff face, which makes it wonderfully cool in the height of summer. Elegant rooms have lashings of white linen, satin bedheads, Florentine-inspired furniture and majolica-tiled floors.

Some spoil guests with terraces and deckchairs for panoramic contemplation.

The **restaurant** (⌨ 089 87 41 43; www.on daverde.it; Via Terramare 3; meals €38; ⊙12.30-9.30pm Apr-Nov) comes highly recommended.

Da Armandino SEAFOOD €€
(⌨ 089 87 40 87; Via Praia 1, Marina di Praia; meals €35; ⊙1-4pm & 7pm-midnight Apr-Nov) Seafood-lovers should head for this widely acclaimed, no-frills restaurant located in a former boatyard on the beach at Marina di Praia. Da Armandino is great for fish fresh off the boat. There's no menu; just opt for the dish of the day – it's all excellent.

The holiday atmosphere and appealing setting – at the foot of sheer cliffs towering up to the main road – round things off nicely.

Drinking & Nightlife

★Africana Famous Club CLUB
(⌨ 089 81 11 71; www.africanafamousclub.com; Via Terramare 2; €10-35; ⊙10pm-late May-Sep, bar opens 8pm; ☎) All Amalfi nightlife converges in the unlikely setting of Marina di Praia. But this is no run-of-the-mill nightclub: Africana's been going since the '60s, when Jackie Kennedy was a regular guest. It has an extraordinary cave setting (complete with natural blowholes), a mix of DJs and live music, plus a glass dance floor with fish swimming beneath your feet.

ⓘ Information

Tourist Office (⌨ 089 87 45 57; www.praiano. org; Via G Capriglione 116b; ⊙9am-1pm & 4.30-8.30pm Mon-Sat) Can provide maps and information for the area's hiking trails.

ⓘ Getting There & Away

SITA Sud (www.sitasudtrasporti.it) runs up to 27 daily buses to Sorrento (€2.40, 1¼ hours). It also runs up to 25 daily services to Amalfi (€1.30, 25 minutes) from where buses continue east to Salerno. Reduced services on Sunday.

Amalfi

⌨ 089 / POP 5100

It is hard to grasp that pretty little Amalfi, with its sun-filled piazzas and small beach, was once a maritime superpower with a population of more than 70,000. For one thing, it's not a big place – you can easily walk from one end to the other in about 20 minutes. For another, there are very few historical buildings of note. The explanation is chilling: most of the old city, and its inhabitants, simply slid into the sea during an earthquake in 1343.

Despite this, the town exudes history and culture, most notably in its over-sized Byzantine-influenced cathedral and diminutive Paper Museum. And while the permanent population is now a fairly modest 5000 or so, the numbers swell significantly during summer.

Just around the headland, neighbouring **Atrani** is a dense tangle of whitewashed alleys and arches centred on an agreeably lived-in piazza and small scimitar of beach; don't miss it.

⊙ Sights & Activities

★Cattedrale di Sant'Andrea CATHEDRAL
(⌨ 089 87 35 58; Piazza del Duomo; adult/reduced €3/1 between 10am-5pm; ⊙7.30am-8.30pm, closed Nov-Mar) A melange of architectural styles, Amalfi's cathedral is a bricks-and-mortar reflection of the town's past as an 11th-century maritime superpower. It makes a striking impression at the top of a sweeping 62-step staircase. Between 10am and 5pm, the cathedral is only accessible through the adjacent **Chiostro del Paradiso** (⌨ 089 87 13 24; adult/reduced €3/1; ⊙9am-7.45pm Jul & Aug, shorter hours Sep-early Jan & Mar-Jun, closed early Jan & Feb), part of a four-section museum, incorporating the cloisters, the 9th-century Basilica del Crocefisso, the crypt of St Andrew and the cathedral itself. Outside these times, you can enter the cathedral for free.

The cathedral dates in part from the early 13th century. Its striped facade has been rebuilt twice, most recently at the end of the 19th century. It was constructed next to an older cathedral, the Basilica del Crocefisso, to which it long remained interconnected. The still-standing basilica now serves as a museum.

The cathedral was originally built to house the relics of St Andrew the Apostle, which arrived here from Constantinople in 1208. Architecturally the building is a hybrid. The Sicilian Arabic-Norman style predominates outside, particularly in the two-tone masonry, mosaics and 13th-century bell tower. The huge bronze doors, the first of their type in Italy, were commissioned by a local noble and made in Syria before being shipped to Amalfi. The interior is primarily baroque with some fine statues at the altar, along with some interesting 12th- and 13th-century mosaics.

Museo della Carta
MUSEUM

(Paper Museum; ☑089 830 45 61; www.museo dellacarta.it; Via delle Cartiere 23; adult/reduced €4/2.50; ☺10am-6.30pm daily Mar-Oct, to 4pm Tue-Sun Nov-late Jan) Amalfi's Paper Museum is housed in a rugged, cave-like 13th-century paper mill (the oldest in Europe). It lovingly preserves the original paper presses, which are still in full working order, as you'll see during the 30-minute guided tour (in English). The tour explains the original cotton-based paper production and the subsequent wood-pulp manufacturing. Afterwards you might be inspired to pick up some of the stationery sold in the gift shop, including calligraphy sets and paper pressed with flowers.

Grotta dello Smeraldo
CAVE

(admission €5; ☺9am-4pm) Four kilometres west of Amalfi, this grotto is named after the eerie emerald colour that emanates from the water. Stalactites hang down from the 24m-high ceiling, while stalagmites grow up to 10m tall. Buses regularly pass the car park above the cave entrance (from where you take a lift or stairs down to the rowing boats). Alternatively, Coop Sant'Andrea (☑089 87 31 90; www.coopsantandrea.com; Lungomare dei Cavalieri 1) runs boats from Amalfi (€10 return, plus cave admission). Allow 1½ hours for the return trip.

Amalfi Marine
BOATING

(☑338 3076125; www.amalfiboatrental.com; Spiaggia del Porto, Lungomare dei Cavalieri 7) Amalfi Marine hires out boats (without a skipper from €220 per day per boat excluding petrol; maximum six passengers). Private day-long tours with a skipper start from €600.

🛏 Sleeping

Despite its reputation as a day-trip destination, Amalfi has plenty of places to stay. It's not especially cheap, though, and most hotels are in the midrange to top-end price bracket. Always try to book ahead, as the summer months are very busy and many places close over winter. If you're coming by car, consider a hotel with a car park, as finding on-street parking can be especially painful.

Albergo Sant'Andrea
HOTEL €

(☑089 87 11 45; www.albergosantandrea.it; Salita Costanza d'Avalos 1; s/d €70/100; ☺Mar-Dec;

❉❧) Enjoy the atmosphere of busy Piazza del Duomo from the comfort of your own room. This modest two-star place has basic rooms with brightly coloured tiles and coordinating fabrics. Double glazing has helped cut down the piazza hubbub, which can reach fever pitch in high season – this is one place to ask for a room with a (cathedral) view.

★ DieciSedici
B&B €€

(☑089 87 22 52; www.diecisedici.it; Piazza Municipio 10-16; d from €145; ☺Mar-Oct; ❉) DieciSedici (1016) dresses up an old medieval palace in the kind of style that only the Italians can muster. The half-dozen rooms dazzle with chandeliers, mezzanine floors, glass balconies and gorgeous linens. Two rooms (the Junior Suite and Family Classic) come complete with kitchenettes. All have satellite TV, air-con and Bose sound systems.

Breakfast is laid on in a cafe in the nearby Piazza del Duomo.

Residenza del Duca
HOTEL €€

(☑089 873 63 65; www.residencedelduca.it; Via Duca Mastalo II 3; d from €135; ☺mid-Mar–Oct; ❉❧) This family-run hotel has just six rooms, all of them light, sunny and prettily furnished with antiques, majolica tiles and the odd chintzy cherub. The jacuzzi showers are excellent. Call ahead if you are carrying heavy bags, as it's a seriously puff-you-out staircase climb to reach here and a luggage service is included in the price.

Hotel Lidomare
HOTEL €€

(☑089 87 13 32; www.lidomare.it; Largo Duchi Piccolomini 9; s/d €65/145; ❉❧) This gracious, old-fashioned, family-run hotel has no shortage of character. The large, luminous rooms have an air of gentility, with their appealingly haphazard decor, vintage tiles and fine antiques. Some have spa baths, others have sea views and a balcony; some have both. Rather unusually, breakfast is laid out on top of a grand piano.

Hotel Centrale
HOTEL €€

(☑089 87 26 08; www.amalfihotelcentrale.it; Largo Duchi Piccolomini 1; d/tr/q €159/180/220; ❉❧) Central it is, with small, functional rooms berthed in a building accessed via a tiny little piazza in the *centro storico*. The joy is not the rooms themselves (which are visually boring), but the window seat they offer over the buzzing Piazza del Duomo below. Be sure to ask for a front-facing room with a balcony.

Hotel Luna Convento HOTEL €€€
(🖉089 87 10 02; www.lunahotel.it; Via Pantaleone Comite 33; d from €340; ⊙mid-Mar–Dec; P✳@ 🛉🏊) This former convent was founded by St Francis in 1222 and has been a hotel for some 170 years. Rooms in the original building are in the former monks' cells, but there's nothing poky about the bright tiles, balconies and seamless sea views. The newer wing is equally beguiling, with religious frescoes over the beds. The cloistered courtyard is magnificent.

✖ Eating

La Pansa CAFE €
(🖉089 87 10 65; www.pasticceriapansa.it; Piazza del Duomo 40; cornetti from €1, pastries from €1.80; ⊙7.30am-midnight Wed-Mon, closed early Jan-early Feb) A marbled and mirrored fifth-generation cafe on Piazza del Duomo where black-bow-tied waiters serve minimalist Italian breakfasts: freshly made *cornetti* (croissants), full-bodied espresso and deliciously frothy cappuccino. Standout pastries include the crisp, flaky *coda di aragosta con crema di limone*, a lobster-tail-shaped concoction filled with a rich yet light lemon-custard cream.

Le Arcate ITALIAN €€
(🖉089 87 13 67; www.learcateatrani.it; Largo Orlando Buonocore, Atrani; pizzas from €6, meals €30; ⊙12-3.30pm & 7-11pm daily Jul & Aug, closed Mon Sep-Jun; 🛉) If you've had it with the tourist tumult of Amalfi, try temporarily relocating to its quieter cousin Atrani to eat al fresco at one of its traditional restaurants. Arcate is right on the seafront with huge parasols shading its sprawl of tables, and a dining room in a stone-walled natural cave.

★Ristorante La Caravella ITALIAN €€€
(🖉089 87 10 29; www.ristorantelacaravella.it; Via Matteo Camera 12; meals €50-90, tasting menus €50-135; ⊙noon-2.30pm & 7-11pm Wed-Mon; ✳) A restaurant of artists, art and artistry, Caravella once hosted Andy Warhol. No surprise that it doubles up as a de-facto gallery with frescoes, creative canvases and a ceramics collection. And then there's the food on the seven-course tasting menu, prepared by some of the finest culinary Caravaggios in Italy.

Despite its fame, Michelin-starred Caravella, in business since 1959, remains an unpretentious and discreet place that's true to its seafood roots.

Not to be missed are the anchovy croquettes, fish with fennel and sun-dried tomatoes and – the *Mona Lisa* on the menu – a fine lemon *soufflé*. The wine list is, arguably, the best on the Amalfi Coast. Reservations essential.

ℹ Information

Post Office (www.poste.it; Corso delle Repubbliche Marinare 31; ⊙8.20am-7pm Mon-Fri, to 12.30pm Sat) Next door to the tourist office.

Tourist Office (🖉089 87 11 07; www.amalfitouristoffice.it; Corso delle Repubbliche Marinare 27; ⊙8.30am-1pm & 2-6pm Mon-Sat Apr-Oct, 8.30am-1pm Mon-Sat Nov-Mar; 🛉) Just off the main seafront road in a small courtyard.

ℹ Getting There & Away

BOAT

The ferry terminal is a simple affair with several ticket offices located a short hop from the bus station on the seafront.

TraVelMar (🖉089 87 29 50; www.travelmar.it) Runs a reliable April to October water taxi to/from Positano (€8, 25 minutes, daily), Minori (€3, 10 minutes, seven daily), Cetara (€5, 40 minutes, six daily) and Salerno (€8, 35 minutes, up to 12 daily).

Alilauro (🖉081 497 22 38; www.alilauro.it) Runs ferries to Sorrento (€21, one hour, two daily) via Positano, and to Capri (€24, 1¼ hours, one daily) from around April to October.

BUS

Amalfi's **bus station** (Lungomare dei Cavalieri) in Piazza Flavio Gioia is little more than a car park, but it is the main transport nexus on the coast.

SITA Sud (🖉342 6256442; www.sita sudtrasporti.it; Piazza Flavio Gioia) runs up to 27 buses daily to Ravello (€1.30, 25 minutes). Eastbound, it runs up to 20 buses daily to Salerno (€2.40, 1¼ hours) via Maiori (20 minutes). Westbound, it runs up to 25 buses daily to Positano (€2, 40 minutes) via Praiano (€1.30, 25 minutes). Many continue to Sorrento (€2.90, 1¾ hours).

You can buy tickets from the *tabacchi* (tobacconist) on the corner of Piazza Flavio Gioia and Via Duca Mansone I (the side street that leads to Piazza del Duomo).

Ravello

🖉089 / POP 2490

It cured Richard Wagner's writer's block, provided inspiration for DH Lawrence as he nurtured the plot of *Lady Chatterley's*

Lover, and impressed American writer Gore Vidal so much that he stayed for 30 years and became an honorary local. Ravello has a metamorphic effect on people.

Founded in the 5th century as a sanctuary from barbarian invaders fresh from sacking Rome, this lofty Amalfi town was built, in contrast to other Amalfi settlements, up on a hill rather than down on the coast. It's second only to Positano in its style and glamour.

Ravello's refinement is exemplified in the town's polished main piazza, where debonair diners relax under the canopies of alfresco cafes. It's also reflected in its lush villas (many now turned into palatial hotels), manicured gardens and one of Italy's finest musical festivals (thank Wagner's wife for that).

◎ Sights

Even if you have absolutely no sense of direction and a penchant for going round in circles, it's difficult to get lost in this town; everything is clearly signposted from the main Piazza Duomo. Explore the narrow backstreets, however, and you will discover glimpses of a quieter, traditional lifestyle: dry-stone walls fronting simple homes surrounded by overgrown gardens, neatly planted vegetable plots and basking cats.

★Villa Rufolo   GARDENS
(☑089 85 76 21; www.villarufolo.it; Piazza Duomo; adult/reduced €7/5; ⊙9am-9pm summer, reduced hours winter, tower museum 10am-7pm summer, reduced hours winter) To the south of Ravello's cathedral, a 14th-century tower marks the entrance to this villa, famed for its beautiful cascading gardens. Created by a Scotsman, Sir Francis Neville Reid, in 1853, they are truly magnificent, commanding divine panoramic views packed with exotic colours, artistically crumbling towers and luxurious blooms. Note that the gardens are at their best from May till October; they don't merit the entrance fee outside those times.

The villa was built in the 13th century for the wealthy Rufolo dynasty and was home to several popes as well as King Robert of Anjou. Wagner was so inspired by the gardens when he visited in 1880 that he modelled the garden of Klingsor (the setting for the second act of the opera *Parsifal*) on them.

The 13th-century Torre Maggiore (Main Tower) now houses the Torre-Museo, an interactive museum that sheds light on the villa's history and characters. Among the latter is Reid, the Scottish botanist who purchased and extensively restored the property in the 19th century. The museum also showcases art, archaeological finds and ceramics linked to the villa. Stairs inside the tower lead up to an outdoor viewing platform, affording knockout views of the villa and the Amalfi Coast.

Today Villa Rufolo's gardens stage world-class concerts during the town's annual arts festival.

★Villa Cimbrone   GARDENS
(☑089 85 74 59; www.hotelvillacimbrone.com/gardens; Via Santa Chiara 26; adult/reduced €7/4; ⊙9am-sunset) If you could bottle up a take-away image of the Amalfi, it might be the view from the Belvedere of Infinity, classical busts in the foreground, craggy coast splashed with pastel-shaded villages in the background. It's yours to admire at this refashioned 11th-century villa (now an upmarket hotel) with sublime gardens. Open to the public, the gardens were mainly created by a British peer, Ernest Beckett, who reconfigured them with rose-beds, temples and a Moorish pavilion in the early 1900s.

The villa (also owned by Beckett) was something of a bohemian retreat in its early days; it was frequented by Greta Garbo and her lover Leopold Stokowski as a secret hideaway. Other illustrious former guests include Virginia Woolf, Winston Churchill, DH Lawrence and Salvador Dalí. The house and gardens sit atop a crag that's a 10-minute walk south of Piazza Duomo.

☆☆ Festivals & Events

★Ravello Festival   PERFORMING ARTS
(☑089 85 84 22; www.ravellofestival.com; ⊙Jul-Aug) The Ravello Festival – established in 1953 – turns much of the town centre into a stage. Events range from orchestral concerts and chamber music to ballet performances, film screenings and exhibitions. The festival's most celebrated (and impressive) venue is the overhanging terrace in the Villa Rufolo gardens.

⛏ Sleeping

Ravello is an upmarket town and the accommodation reflects this, both in style and in price. There are some superb top-end hotels, several lovely midrange places and a fine *agriturismo* (farm stay) nearby. Book well ahead for summer – especially if you're planning to visit during the music festival.

Agriturismo Monte Brusara　　AGRITURISMO €
(☑089 85 74 67; www.montebrusara.com; Via Monte Brusara 32; d €94-100; ⊗yr-round; 🐾) 🍃 A working farm, this mountainside *agriturismo* (farm stay) is located a tough half-hour walk of about 1.5km from Ravello's centre (call ahead to arrange to be picked up). It's especially suited to families or those who simply want to escape the crowds and drink in the bucolic views.

Villa Casale　　APARTMENT €€
(☑340 9479909; www.ravelloresidence.it; Via Orso Papice 4; apt €99-206, ste €179-280; ❄🐾🏊) Practically next to the Villa Rufolo and enjoying the same glamorous view, Villa Casale consists of a handful of elegant suites and apartments arranged around a large pool. Top billing goes to the suites, graced with antiques and occupying the original 14th-century building. All the suites and apartments come with a self-contained kitchen and the property has tranquil gardens.

⭐**Belmond Hotel Caruso**　　HOTEL €€€
(☑089 85 88 01; www.grandluxuryhotels.com; Piazza San Giovanni del Toro 2; d from €935; ⊗mid-Apr-Oct; 🅿❄🐾🏊) There can be no better place to swim than the Caruso's sensational infinity pool. Seemingly set on the edge of a precipice, its blue waters merge with the sea and sky to magical effect. Inside, the sublimely restored 11th-century *palazzo* (mansion) is no less impressive, with 15th-century vaulted ceilings, high-class ceramics and Moorish arches doubling as window frames.

🍴 Eating

Babel　　CAFE €
(☑089 858 62 15; Via Trinità 13; meals €20; ⊗11.30am-5pm & 6.30-10.30pm daily May-Sep, closed Wed late Mar, Apr & Oct, closed Nov-late Mar; 🐾) A cool little deli-cafe with a compact menu of what you could call 'Italian tapas', affordable bites including Italian *gazpacho* (cold soup), bruschetta, dry polenta and creative salads with combos such as lemon and orange with goat's cheese and chestnut honey. It offers an excellent range of local wines, smooth jazz on the sound system, and Vietri-school ceramics for sale.

Da Salvatore　　ITALIAN €€
(☑089 85 72 27; Via della Repubblica 2; meals €38-45, pizzas from €5; ⊗12.30-3pm & 7.30-10pm Tue-Sun Easter-Nov) Located just before the bus stop, Da Salvatore doesn't merely rest on the laurels of its spectacular terrace views.

This is one of the coast's best restaurants, serving arresting dishes that showcase local produce with creativity, flair and whimsy; your premeal *benvenuto* (welcome) may include an *aperitivo* of Negroni encased in a white-chocolate ball.

ℹ️ Information

Tourist Office (☑089 85 70 96; www.ravellotime.it; Piazza Fontana Moresca 10; ⊗9am-7pm summer, to 5pm rest of year) Shares digs with the police station. Provides brochures and maps, and can also assist with accommodation.

ℹ️ Getting There & Away

From the bus stop on the eastern side of Amalfi's Piazza Flavio Gioia, **SITA Sud** (☑342 6256442; www.sitasudtrasporti.it) runs up to 27 buses daily to Ravello (€1.30, 25 minutes).

SALERNO & THE CILENTO

Salerno

☑089 / POP 133,970

Salerno may initially seem like a bland big city, but the place has a charming, if gritty, individuality, especially around its ostensibly tatty *centro storico*, where medieval churches and neighbourhood trattorias echo with the addictive bustle of southern Italy. The city has invested in various urban-regeneration programs centred on this historic neighbourhood, which features a tree-lined seafront promenade widely considered to be one of the cheeriest and most attractive in Italy.

⦿ Sights

Although Salerno is a sprawling town, you can easily visit it in one day and on foot, as the main sights (castle aside) are concentrated in and around the historic centre. Don't miss having a walk along the seafront promenade.

⭐**Duomo**　　CATHEDRAL
(☑089 23 13 87; www.cattedraledisalerno.it; Piazza Alfano; ⊗8.30am-8pm Mon-Sat, 8.30am-1pm & 4-8pm Sun) One of Campania's strangely under-the-radar sights, Salerno's impressive cathedral is considered by aficionados to be the most beautiful medieval church in Italy. Built by the Normans in the 11th century and later aesthetically remodelled in the

18th century, it sustained severe damage in a 1980 earthquake. It is dedicated to San Matteo (St Matthew), whose remains were reputedly brought to the city in 954 and now lie beneath the main altar in the vaulted crypt.

Take special note of the magnificent main entrance, the 12th-century **Porta dei Leoni**, named after the marble lions at the foot of the stairway. It leads through to a beautiful, harmonious courtyard, surrounded by graceful arches and overlooked by a 12th-century bell tower. Carry on through the huge bronze doors (similarly guarded by lions), which were cast in Constantinople in the 11th century. When you come to the three-aisled interior, you will see that it is largely baroque, with only a few traces of the original church. These include parts of the transept and choir floor and the two raised pulpits in front of the choir stalls. Throughout the church you can see highly detailed 13th-century mosaic work redolent of the extraordinary early-Christian mosaics in Ravenna.

In the right-hand apse, don't miss the **Cappella delle Crociate** (Chapel of the Crusades), containing powerful frescoes and more wonderful mosaics. It was so named because crusaders' weapons were blessed here. Under the altar stands the tomb of 11th-century pope Gregory VII.

Museo Archeologico Provinciale MUSEUM
(☎089 23 11 35; www.museoarcheologicosalerno.it; Via San Benedetto 28; adult/reduced €4/2; ⏲9am-7.30pm Tue-Sun) The province's restored and revitalised main archaeological museum is an excellent showcase for the excavated history of the surrounding area, dating back to cave dwellers and the colonising Greeks. The pièce de résistance is the 1st-century BCE *Testa bronzea di Apollo* (bronze head of Apollo). Showcased in its own small room upstairs, the head is thought to have been part of a larger statue; it was found by a fisherman in the Gulf of Salerno in 1930.

Castello di Arechi CASTLE
(☎089 296 40 15; www.ilcastellodiarechi.it; Via Benedetto Croce; adult/reduced €4/2; ⏲9am-5pm Tue-Sat, to 3.30pm Sun) Hop on bus 19 from Piazza XXIV Maggio to visit Salerno's most famous landmark, the forbidding Castello di Arechi, dramatically positioned 263m above the city. Originally a Byzantine fort, it was built by the Lombard duke of Benevento, Arechi II, in the 8th century and subsequently modified by the Normans and Aragonese, most recently in the 16th century.

Sleeping

The little accommodation that Salerno offers is fairly uninspiring, although, conveniently, there are several reasonable hotels in the town centre. Prices tend to be considerably lower than on the Amalfi Coast.

Ostello Ave Gratia Plena HOSTEL €
(☎089 23 47 76; www.ostellodisalerno.it; Via dei Canali; dm/s/d €16/45/65; @📶) Housed in a 16th-century convent, Salerno's excellent HI hostel is right in the heart of the *centro storico* action. Inside, there's a charming central courtyard and a range of bright rooms, from dorms to great-bargain doubles with private bathroom. The 2am curfew is for dorms only.

Hotel Montestella HOTEL €€
(☎089 22 51 22; www.hotelmontestella.it; Corso Vittorio Emanuele II 156; d €90-125, tr €95-160; ❄@📶) Within walking distance of just about anywhere worth going to, the modern, if slightly bland, Montestella is on Salerno's main pedestrian thoroughfare, halfway between the *centro storico* and train station. Although some rooms are quite small, all are light and contemporary, with firm beds and patterned feature walls.

Eating

Cicirinella ITALIAN €€
(☎089 22 65 61; Via Genovesi 28; meals €25; ⏲8pm-midnight daily, 1-3pm Sat & Sun; 📶) This place, tucked behind the cathedral, has that winning combination of an earthy and inviting atmosphere and unfailingly good, delicately composed dishes. Exposed stone, shelves of wine and an open-plan kitchen set the scene for traditional Campanian cuisine like pasta with seafood and chickpeas, or a mussel soup that tastes satisfyingly of the sea.

Sant'Andrea ITALIAN €€
(☎328 727274; www.ristorantesantandrea.it; Piazza Sedile del Campo 58; pizzas €4-6, meals €25-30; ⏲12.30-3pm & 8pm-midnight Tue-Sun; 📶) There's an earthy southern Italian flavour at this classic old-town trattoria with its terrace surrounded by historic houses decorated with last night's pajamas hung out to dry. Choices are more innovative than you would expect, and include such seafood dishes as

Salerno

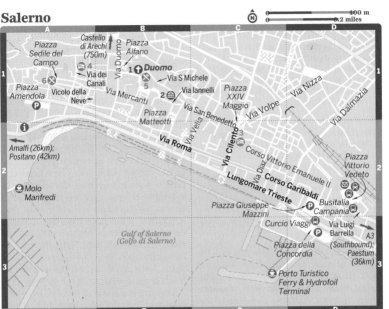

squid with porcini mushrooms and cuttle-fish with creamed vegetables.

ℹ Information

Post Office (Piazza Vittorio Veneto 7; ⊙8.20am-1.30pm Mon-Fri, to 12.30pm Sat) Beside the train station.

Tourist Office (☑089 23 14 32; Lungomare Trieste 7; ⊙9am-7pm Mon-Sat) Located right on the promenade. Has limited information.

ℹ Getting There & Away

BOAT

TraVelMar (☑089 87 29 50; www.travelmar.it) Sails seasonally to Amalfi (€8, 35 minutes, 12 daily) and Positano (€12, 70 minutes, eight daily), as well as to Cetara (€5, 15 minutes, six daily), Maiori (€7, 30 minutes, six daily) and Minori (€7, 40 minutes, six daily).

Alicost (☑Mon-Fri 089 87 14 83, Sat & Sun 089 948 36 71; www.alicost.it) Runs one daily seasonal ferry service to Capri (€25.40, 2¼ hours) via Minori (€7), Amalfi (€8) and Positano (€12).

Navigazione Libera del Golfo (NLG; www.navlib.it) Runs one daily hydrofoil service to Capri (€26) from Easter to mid-October.

TraVelMar services depart from the **Porto Turistico**, 200m down the pier from Piazza della Concordia. You can buy tickets from the booths by the embarkation point. Alicost and Navigazi-

one Libera del Golfo services depart from **Molo Manfredi**, 1.8km further west.

BUS

SITA Sud (www.sitasudtrasporti.it) buses for Amalfi depart at least hourly from the bus station on Piazza Vittorio Veneto, beside the train station, stopping en route at Vietri sul Mare, Cetara, Maiori and Minori. For Pompeii, take **Busitalia Campania** (☑089 984 72 86; www.fsbusitaliacampania.it) bus 4 from nearby Corso Garibaldi (at the corner of Via Luigi Barrella). For the south coast and Paestum, take bus 34 from Piazza della Concordia near the Porto Turistico ferry terminal. Bus 34 runs roughly every one to two hours from Monday to Saturday, with no service on Sunday.

CAR & MOTORCYCLE

Salerno is on the A3 between Naples and Reggio di Calabria; the A3 is toll-free from Salerno south. Take the Salerno exit and follow signs to the *centro*. If you want to hire a car, there's a **Europcar** (☑ 089 258 07 75; www.europcar. com; Via Clemente Mauro 18; ⊘ 8.30am-1pm & 2.30-6.30pm Mon-Fri, 8.30am-1pm Sat) agency not far from the train station.

TRAIN

Salerno is a major stop on southbound routes to Calabria, and the Ionian and Adriatic coasts. From the **train station** (Piazza Vittorio Veneto) there are regular services to Naples (from €4.70, 35 to 45 minutes), Rome (Intercity from €30.50, three hours) and Agropoli (€3.40, 40 minutes).

Cilento Coast

The Cilento stretch of coastline may lack the sophistication of the Amalfi Coast, but it too has a string of craggy, sun-bleached towns, among them popular Agropoli, gleaming white Palinuro, charming Castellabate and the evocative ruined temples of Paestum. The Cilento can even afford to have a slight air of superiority when it comes to its beaches: a combination of secluded coves and long stretches of golden sand with fewer overpriced ice creams and sunbeds. Yet Campania's southern bookend is about more than its waterside appeal. It's here that you'll find the ancient Greek temples of Paestum and a large coastal tract of the Parco Nazionale del Cilento, Vallo di Diano e Alburni, also a Unesco World Heritage site.

Paestum

Paestum is home to one of Europe's most glorious archaeological zones. Deemed a World Heritage site by Unesco, it includes three of the world's best-preserved ancient Greek temples, as well as an engrossing museum crammed with millennia-old frescoes, ceramics and daily artefacts. Among these is the iconic *Tomba del tuffatore* (Tomb of the Diver) funerary fresco.

Paestum – or Poseidonia as the city was originally called, in honour of Poseidon, the Greek god of the sea – was founded in the 6th century BCE by Greek settlers and fell under Roman control in 273 BCE. Decline set in following the demise of the Roman Empire. Savage raids by the Saracens and periodic outbreaks of malaria forced the steadily dwindling population to abandon the city altogether.

Today, Paestum offers visitors a vivid, to-scale glimpse of the grandeur and sophistication of the area's past life.

◉ Sights

★ **Paestum's Temples**   ARCHAEOLOGICAL SITE
(Area Archeologica di Paestum; ☑ 0828 81 10 23; www.museopaestum.beniculturali.it; adult/reduced incl museum €12/2, ruins only €8/2; ⊘ 8.30am-7.30pm daily, last entry 6.50pm, museum closed Mon) Very different to Pompeii, Paestum's ruins are smaller, older, more Greek and – crucially – a lot less overrun. Consequently, it is possible to steal some reflective moments here as the sun slants across the giant Doric columns of this once great city of Magna Graecia (the Greek colony that once covered much of southern Italy). Take the train to Paestum station. Buy your tickets in the museum, just east of the site, before entering from the main entrance at the northern end.

Paestum was probably founded by Greeks from Sybaris in the 6th century BCE. It later became a Roman city, but was abandoned in the Middle Ages. The ruins were rediscovered in the 1760s, but not fully unearthed and excavated until the 1950s.

The first structure is the 6th-century-BCE **Tempio di Cerere** (Temple of Ceres); originally dedicated to Athena, it served as a Christian church in medieval times.

As you head south, you can pick out the basic outline of the large rectangular forum, the heart of the ancient city. Among the partially standing buildings are the vast domestic housing area and, further south, the amphitheatre. Both provide evocative glimpses of daily life here in Roman times. In the former houses you'll see mosaic floors, and a marble *impluvium* (cistern) that stood in the atrium and collected rainwater.

The **Tempio di Nettuno** (Temple of Neptune), dating from about 450 BCE, is the largest and best preserved of the three temples at Paestum; only parts of its inside walls and roof are missing. The two rows of double-storied columns originally divided the outer colonnade from the *cella,* or inner chamber, where a statue of the temple deity would have been displayed. Despite its commonly used name, many scholars believe that the temple was actually dedicated to the Greek goddess Hera, sister and wife of Greek god Zeus.

Almost next door, the so-called basilica (a temple to the goddess Hera) is Paestum's oldest surviving monument. Dating from the middle of the 6th century BCE, it's a magnificent sight, with nine columns across and 18 along the sides. Ask someone to take your photo next to one of the columns: it's a good way to appreciate the scale.

Save time for the museum (☑0828 81 10 23; adult/reduced incl temples €9.50/4.75; ☺8.30am-7.30pm, last entry 6.50pm, closes 1.40pm 1st & 3rd Mon of month), which covers two floors and houses a collection of interesting bas-relief friezes, plus numerous frescoes dating back to the 5th century BCE.

The archaeological site and adjoining museum are particularly evocative in spring when they are surrounded by scarlet poppies.

🛏 Sleeping & Eating

There are various restaurants in close proximity to the ruins at Paestum, most serving mediocre food at inflated prices. A much better alternative is Nonna Sceppa, located around 4km northwest of the ruins. Alternatively, head south to Agropoli for more options or book ahead to dine at one of the Cilento's rustic *agriturismi* (farm stays).

★ **Casale Giancesare**
Villa Agricola   B&B €
(☑0828 199 96 14; www.casalegiancesare.com/en; Via Giancesare 8, Capaccio Paestum; s €50-120, d €60-150, 4-person apt from €80-185; [P][✱][@] [🛜][🛎]) A 19th-century former farmhouse, this elegantly decorated, stone-clad B&B is run by the delightful Voza family, who will happily ply you with their homemade wine, *limoncello* and marmalades; they even make their own olive oil. The B&B is located 2.5km from Paestum and is surrounded by vineyards and olive and mulberry trees; views are marvellous, particularly from the swimming pool.

There are seven farmhouse-chic rooms and three apartments on offer.

Nonna Sceppa   ITALIAN €€
(☑0828 85 10 64; Via Laura 53; meals €35; ☺12.30-3pm & 7.30-11pm Fri-Wed; [🛜][🛎]) Seek out the superbly prepared, robust dishes at Nonna Sceppa, a family-friendly restaurant that's gaining a reputation throughout the region for excellence. Dishes are firmly seasonal and, during summer, concentrate on fresh seafood, like the refreshingly simple grilled fish with lemon. Other popular choices include risotto with zucchini and artichokes, and spaghetti with lobster.

❶ Information

Tourist Office (☑0828 81 10 16; www.info paestum.it; Via Magna Grecia 887; ☺9am-1pm & 2-4pm) Across the street from the archaeological site, this helpful tourist office offers a map of the archaeological site, as well as information on the greater Cilento region.

❶ Getting There & Away

Trains run around 16 times daily from Salerno to Paestum (€2.90, 30 minutes). The temples are a pleasant 10-minute stroll from the station.

Busitalia Campania (www.fsbusitalia campania.it) bus 34 goes to Paestum from Piazza della Concordia in Salerno (€2.70, one hour). Bus 34 runs roughly every one to two hours from Monday to Saturday, with no service on Sunday.

Parco Nazionale del Cilento e Vallo di Diano

Proving the perfect antidote to the holiday mayhem further north, the Parco Nazionale del Cilento, Vallo di Diano e Alburni combines dense woods and flowering meadows, with dramatic mountains, rivers and waterfalls. It is the second-largest national park in Italy, covering 1810 sq km, including 80 towns and villages. To get the best out of the park, you will probably need a car, although the coastal strip from Castellabate down to Palinuro has reasonable pubic transport. The Cilento is known for its orchids, vast underground cave complexes and handsome hilltop villages. Sitting on the cusp of the park proper are the ruins of Paestum and the Certosa di San Lorenzo, both crucial to it gaining Unesco World Heritage status in 1998.

Compared to the Amalfi, the Cilento is not so well set up for tourism and the network of walking trails is less well marked. If in doubt, join a guided excursion.

◉ Sights

★ **Grotte di Castelcivita**   CAVE
(☑0828 77 23 97; www.grottedicastelcivita.com; Piazzale N Zonzi, Castelcivita; adult/reduced €10/8; ☺standard tours 10.30am, noon, 1.30pm & 3pm, 4.30pm & 6pm Apr-Sep, 10.30am, noon, 1.30pm & 3pm Mar & Oct; [P][🛎]) The grottoes are

fascinating, otherworldly caves that date from prehistoric times: excavations have revealed that they were inhabited 42,000 years ago, making them the oldest known settlement in Europe. Don't forget a jacket, and leave the high heels at home, as paths are wet and slippery. Hard hats (provided) and a certain level of fitness and mobility are required. Located 40km southeast of Salerno on the northwest cusp of the national park, the complex is refreshingly noncommercial.

Although it extends over 4800m, only around half of the complex is open to the public. The one-hour tour winds through a route surrounded by extraordinary stalagmites and stalactites, and a mesmerising play of colours, caused by algae, calcium and iron, which tint the naturally sculpted rock shapes.

The tour culminates in a cavernous lunar landscape – think California's Death Valley in miniature – called the Caverna di Bertarelli. The caves are still inhabited – by bats – and visitors are instructed not to take flash photos for fear of disturbing them.

Certosa di San Lorenzo   MONASTERY
(✆ 0975 7 77 45; www.polomusealecampania.be niculturali.it; Viale Certosa, Padula; adult/reduced €6/3; ⏰ 9am-7pm Wed-Mon) A giant among monasteries, even by Italian standards, the Certosa di San Lorenzo dates from 1306 and covers 250,000 sq metres. Numerologists can get a kick out of ticking off the supposed 320 rooms and halls, 2500m of corridors, galleries and hallways, 300 columns, 500 doors, 550 windows, 13 courtyards, 100 fireplaces, 52 stairways and 41 fountains – in other words, it is *huge*. The monastery is just outside the hillside town of Padula.

As it is unlikely that you will have time to see everything, be sure to visit the highlights, including the vast central courtyard (a venue for summer classical-music concerts), the magnificent wood-panelled library, frescoed chapels, and the kitchen with its grandiose fireplace and famous tale: apparently this is where the legendary 1000-egg omelette was made in 1534 for Charles V's passing army. Unfortunately, the historic frying pan is not on view – just how big was it, one wonders.

Within the monastery you can also peruse the modest collection of ancient artefacts at the **Museo Archeologico Provinciale della Lucania Occidentale** (✆ 0975 7 71 17; Certosa di San Lorenzo, Viale Certosa, Padula; ⏰ 9am-7pm Wed-Mon; ♿) FREE.

Grotte di Pertosa-Auletta   CAVE
(✆ 0975 39 70 37; www.grottedipertosa-auletta. it; Pertosa; guided visits adult/reduced 100min €20/15, 60min €13/10; ⏰ tour times vary, see website; P ♿) (Re)discovered in 1932, the Grotte di Pertosa-Auletta date back 35 million years. Used by the Greeks and Romans as places of worship, the caves burrow for some 2500m, with long underground passages and lofty grottoes filled with stalagmites and stalactites. The first part of the tour is a boat (or raft) ride on the river; you disembark just before the waterfall (phew!) and continue on foot for around 800m, surrounded by marvellous rock formations and luminous crystal accretions.

🏃 Activities

The park has 15 listed nature trails that vary from 1km to 8km in length. But this isn't the Amalfi. Don't expect abundant signage, well-trodden paths and a surfeit of trail-side cafes selling cappuccinos or lemonade.

The countryside in the park can be dramatic, and in spring you'll experience real flower power: delicate narcissi, wild orchids and tulips hold their own among blowsier summer drifts of brilliant yellow ox-eye daisies and scarlet poppies.

Thickets of silver firs, wild chestnuts and beech trees add to the sumptuous landscape, as do the dramatic cliffs, pine-clad mountains and fauna, including wild boars, badgers and wolves and, for bird-watchers, the increasingly rare golden eagle.

Even during the busier summer season, the sheer size of the park means that hikers are unlikely to meet others on the trail to swap tales and muesli bars – so getting lost could become a lonely, not to mention dangerous, experience if you haven't done some essential planning before striding out. In theory, the tourist offices should be able to supply you with a guide to the trails. In reality, they frequently seem to have run out of copies. Failing this, you can buy the *Parco Nazionale del Cilento, Vallo di Diano e Alburni: Carta Turistica e dei Sentieri* (Tourist and Footpath Map; €7) or the excellent *Monte Stella: Walks & Rambles in Ancient Cilento,* published by the Comunita' Montana Alento Monte Stella (€3). Most of the *agriturismi* (farm stays) in the park can also organise guided treks.

A popular self-guided hike, where you are rewarded with spectacular views, is a climb of Monte Alburno (1742m). There's a choice of two trails, both of which are clearly marked from the centre of the small town of Sicignano degli Alburni and finish at the mountain's peak. Allow approximately four hours for either route. The less experienced may prefer to opt for a guide.

Another good access area for hikers is the Trentova-Tresino (Via Fontana dei Monaci; [P]) nature reserve just south of Agropoli, which has four well-marked coastal walks and a visitor centre.

There are some excellent *agriturismi* (farm-stay accommodation) here that offer additional activities, including guided hikes, painting courses and horse-riding.

🛏 Sleeping & Eating

⭐ **Agriturismo i Moresani**   AGRITURISMO €
(☑0974 90 20 86; www.agriturismoimoresani. com; Località Moresani; d €90-110; ☉Mar-Oct; ❄🛜🛝) ✔ For tranquillity and fabulous food, head to this family-run *agriturismo* 1.5km west of Casal Velino. The setting is bucolic: rolling hills interspersed with grapevines, grazing pastures and olive trees. The sprawling farm produces its own *caprino* goat's cheese, wine, olive oil and preserves, and home-grown organic products are the protagonists in its notable restaurant. The rooms themselves are simple and classic in style.

Trattoria degli Ulivi   ITALIAN €
(☑334 2595091; www.tavolacaldadegliulivi.it; Viale Certosa, Padula; set menus €10-16; ☉11am-4pm Wed-Mon; 🛜) After your marathon walk through the endless corridors of the Certoza di San Lorenzo, head to this uncomplicated restaurant, a short 50m stumble from the main entrance. The decor is canteen-like, but the daily specials are affordable, flavour-filled and generously proportioned. It serves snacks as well as four-course blow-out lunches.

ℹ Information

Alpine Rescue (☑118) For emergencies.

Parks.it (www.parks.it/parco.nazionale. cilento/Eindex.php) Useful online information about the national park.

Sicignano degli Alburni Pro Loco (☑0828 97 37 55; www.scoprisicignano.it; Piazza Plebiscito 13, Sicignano degli Alburni; ☉9am-1.30pm & 2.30-5pm Mon-Sat) Tourist information office with very basic info on the national park.

Tourist Office (p135) In Paestum; this office has info on the Parco Nazionale del Cilento.

ℹ Getting There & Away

SITA Sud (www.sitasudtrasporti.it) Runs three daily services between Salerno and Pertosa (Monday to Saturday), two of which continue to Polla. It also runs one daily bus between Salerno and Castelcivita (weekdays only).

Busitalia Campania (☑089 984 72 86; www. fsbusitaliacampania.it) Runs daily buses between Salerno, Agropoli, Castellabate and Acciaroli.

Infante Viaggi (☑089 82 57 65; www.agenzia infanteviaggi.it) A twice-weekly bus runs to/from Rome stopping in Salerno, Sicignano degli Alburni, Padula and Palinuro.

AT A GLANCE

POPULATION
6.4 million

CAPITAL
Bari

BEST TRABUCCO
Al Trabucco da Mimì
(p152)

BEST ECO-HOTEL
Palazzo Papaleo
(p167)

**BEST
THRILL-SEEKING**
Il Volo dell'Angelo
(p178)

WHEN TO GO
Apr–Jun Spring wild-
flowers are blooming:
perfect for hiking in
Parco Nazionale del
Pollino.

Jul & Aug Summer
beach weather and
festivals in towns
such as Lecce and
Matera.

Sep & Oct Thinner
crowds, mild weather
and mushrooms
sprouting in Parco
Nazionale della Sila.

Puglia, Basilicata & Calabria

T he Italian boot's heel (Puglia), instep (Basilicata) and toe (Calabria) are where the 'Mezzogiorno' (southern Italy) shows all its throbbing intensity. Long stereotyped as the poorer, more passionate cousins of Italy's sophisticated northerners, these regions are finally being appreciated for their true richness. You *will* see washing on weather-worn balconies, scooters speeding down medieval alleys and ancient towns crumbling under Mediterranean suns. But look past the pasta-advert stereotypes and you'll find things altogether more complex and wonderful: gritty, unsentimental cities with pedigrees stretching back thousands of years, dramatically broken coastlines that have harboured fisherfolk and pirates for millennia, and above all, proud and generous people who are eager to share these delights with you.

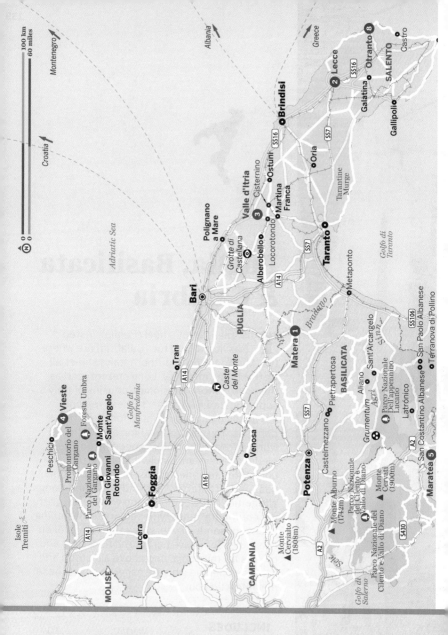

Puglia, Basilicata & Calabria Highlights

1 Matera (p171)
Marvelling at the contrast between miserable caves and soaring cathedrals in this ancient city.

2 Lecce (p158)
Learning to love the ornate excesses of the city's baroque architecture.

3 Valle d'Itria (p153) Eating the best of Mediterranean cuisine in the valley's gorgeous hill towns.

4 Vieste (p148)
Searching for early morning photo ops around the cream-coloured lanes of this divine coastal town.

5 Maratea (p178)
Driving with the top down and the sea in your nostrils around an impossibly

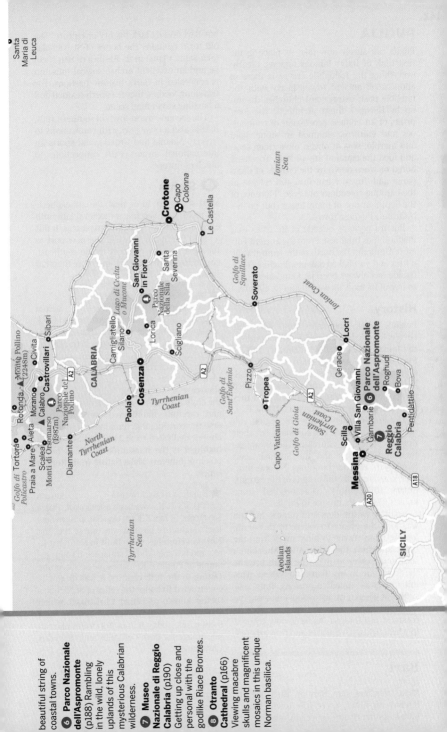

PUGLIA

Ionian Sea

Santa Maria di Leuca

Golfo di Tortora
Policastro
Praia a Mare
Rotonda ● Aieta ● Monte Pollino (2248m)
Morano ● Civita
Scalea ● Calabro ● Castrovillari
Monti di Orsomarso (1987m)
Parco Nazionale del Pollino
Diamante ●
Sibari

Camigliatello Silano ● Lago di Cecita o Mucone
CALABRIA
Paola ● **Cosenza**
San Giovanni in Fiore
Lorica ● Parco Nazionale della Sila
Scigliano ● Santa Severina
A2

Crotone ✪ Capo Colonna
Le Castella

North Tyrrhenian Coast

Tyrrhenian Coast

Tyrrhenian Sea

Golfo di Sant'Eufemia
Pizzo ●
Tropea ●
Golfo di Gioia
Capo Vaticano
South Tyrrhenian Coast
Scilla ● Villa San Giovanni
Messina ● Gambarie ●
Reggio Calabria
A3
Pentidattilo ●

Soverato ●
Golfo di Squillace
Ionian Coast

Locri ●
Gerace ●
Parco Nazionale dell'Aspromonte ❻
Roghudi ●
Bova ●
❼

A20
A18

Aeolian Islands

SICILY

beautiful string of coastal towns.

❻ Parco Nazionale dell'Aspromonte
(p188) Rambling in the wild, lonely uplands of this mysterious Calabrian wilderness.

❼ Museo Nazionale di Reggio Calabria (p190)
Getting up close and personal with the godlike Riace Bronzes.

❽ Otranto Cathedral (p166)
Viewing macabre skulls and magnificent mosaics in this unique Norman basilica.

PUGLIA

Puglia can surely now take its place in the first rank of Italy's famous regions. Clearly, everything the Italophile craves is there in abundance: ancient towns heavy with the tangible past; extravagant churches dreamt up by Europe's finest architects; the footprints of an endless procession of conquerors and cultures, stamped in stone, gold and marble; seas of olives; olive-green seas; and food the equal of any in Italy. Travellers bored or worn down by the crowds of Campania and Tuscany can find still release in the baroque splendour of Lecce, 'Florence of the South', or one of many lesser (but no less beautiful) Pugliese towns.

But it's perhaps outside of its cities that Puglia shines brightest. From the ancient Forest of Umbra in the north to the fruitful Valle d'Itria and sun-baked Salento, Puglia's countryside has always been its foundation – the source of its food, its wealth and its culture.

History

Puglia's Greek vibe dates from when the Greeks founded a string of settlements along the Ionian coast in the 8th century BCE. A form of Greek dialect (Griko) is still spoken in some towns southeast of Lecce. Historically, the major city was Taras (Taranto), settled by Spartan exiles who dominated until they were defeated by the Romans in 272 BCE.

The long coastline made the region vulnerable to conquest. The Normans left their fine Romanesque churches, the Swabians their fortifications and the Spanish their flamboyant baroque buildings. No one, however, knows exactly the origins of the extraordinary 16th-century conical-roofed stone houses, the *trulli*, unique to Puglia.

Apart from invaders and pirates, malaria was long the greatest scourge of the south, forcing many towns to build away from the coast and into the hills. After Mussolini's seizure of power in 1922, the south became the front line in his 'Battle for Wheat'. This initiative was aimed at making Italy self-sufficient when it came to food, following the sanctions imposed on the country after its conquest of Ethiopia. Puglia is now covered in wheat fields, olive groves and fruit arbours.

Bari

📞 0805 / POP 324,200

Most travellers skip Bari on their way to Puglia's big-hitter, Lecce (the towns have a long-standing rivalry, especially over soccer),

but Bari doesn't lack history or culture. The old town contains the bones of St Nicholas (aka Santa Claus) in its Basilica di San Nicola, and an excellent archaeological museum is concealed in Bari's historic bastions. For travelling foodies, there's superb seafood and a bustling street food scene.

The second-largest town in southern Italy, Bari is also a busy port with connections to Greece, Albania and Croatia, and sports an international airport with connections to much of Europe.

⊙ Sights

Most sights are in or near the atmospheric old town, Bari Vecchia, a medieval labyrinth of tight alleyways and graceful piazzas. It fills a small peninsula between the new port to the west and the old port to the southeast, cramming in 40 churches and more than 120 shrines.

★ Museo Archeologico di Santa Scolastica
MUSEUM

(Piazzale Cristoforo Colombo; adult/reduced €5/3; ⊙10am-5pm Wed-Sat & Mon, 10am-2pm Sun) Housed in a well-preserved 16th-century defensive bastion, this excellent museum features a superbly curated overview of the historic origins of Bari. Interactive features showcase a fascinating timeline including the city's Bronze Age and Hellenistic periods, and carefully illuminated walkways traverse the considerable remains of a medieval church dedicated to St Paul and St John. A highlight is the museum's collection of sepulchral funerary slabs dating from Roman times.

★ Basilica di San Nicola
BASILICA

(📞 080 573 71 11; www.basilicasannicola.it; Piazza San Nicola; ⊙7am-8.30pm Mon-Sat, to 10pm Sun) Bari's signature basilica was one of the first Norman churches to be built in southern Italy, and is a splendid (if square and solid) example of Pugliese-Romanesque architecture. Dating to the 12th century, it was originally constructed to house the relics of St Nicholas (better known as Father Christmas), which were stolen from Turkey in 1087 by local fishing folk. Today, it is an important place of pilgrimage for both Catholics and Orthodox Christians.

Cathedral
CATHEDRAL

(📞080 521 06 05; www.arcidiocesibaribitonto.it; Piazza dell'Odegitria; ⊙8am-7pm Mon-Sat, 8-10am & 11am-7pm Sun) Built over the original Byzantine church, the 12th- to 13th-century

Bari

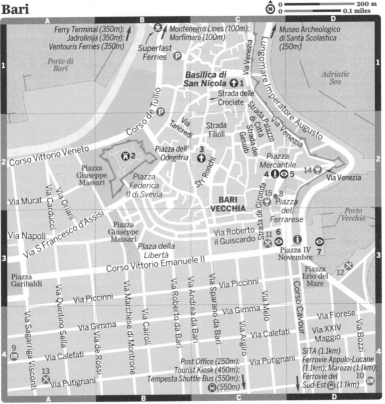

Bari

◎ Top Sights
1 Basilica di San Nicola C1

◎ Sights
2 Castello Svevo...................................... B2
3 Cathedral C2
4 Colonna della Giustizia......................... C2
  Museo del Succorpo della
  Cattedrale ....(see 3)
5 Piazza Mercantile C2
6 Spazio Murat C3
7 Teatro Margherita................................ D3

◎ Activities, Courses & Tours
8 Velo Service.. C2

◎ Sleeping
9 B&B Casa Pimpolini...............................A4
10 Bozzi 1910 ....D4

◎ Eating
11 Mastro Ciccio.......................................C3
12 Seafood Market....................................D3
13 Terranima..A4

◎ Drinking & Nightlife
14 La Bitta...D2
15 Reverso Unconventional
   Bistrot C2

Romanesque cathedral, dedicated to San Sabino, is technically Bari's most important church, although its fame pales alongside San Nicola. Inside, the plain walls are punctuated with deep arcades and the eastern window is a tangle of plant and animal motifs. The highlight lies in the subterrane-

an **Museo del Succorpo della Cattedrale** (€adult/reduced €3/2; ◎9.30am-4pm Mon, Wed, Sat & Sun, to 12.30pm Tue, Thu & Fri), where excavations have revealed remnants left over from an ancient Christian basilica and various Roman ruins.

Teatro Margherita
ARTS CENTRE

(Piazza IV Novembre; ☺vary by exhibition) Originally constructed from 1912 to 1914, this historic theatre was restored and reopened in 2018 and is now used for travelling art and photographic exhibitions. To see inside the beautifully restored interior, ask at the nearby tourist information office if any exhibitions are currently scheduled.

Spazio Murat
CULTURAL CENTRE

(www.facebook.com/spaziomurat; Piazza del Ferrarese; ☺11am-8pm Tue-Sun) Check out this repurposed heritage building for an ever-changing series of interesting and innovative cultural and art displays, part of the nexus of galleries and exhibition spaces taking shape near the edge of Bari's harbour.

Castello Svevo
CASTLE

(Swabian Castle; ☑080 521 37 04; Piazza Federico II di Svevia; adult/reduced €9/3.50; ☺8.30am-7.30pm Wed-Mon) Roger the Norman originally built this castle in the 12th century over the ruins of a Byzantine structure. Later, Frederick II of Swabia built over the existing castle, leaving intact the two towers of the Norman structure that still stand. The bastions, with corner towers overhanging the moat, were added in the 16th century during the Aragonese rule. Excavation is ongoing and the largely sparse interior is used for occasional art and sculpture exhibitions.

Piazza Mercantile
PIAZZA

This beautiful piazza is fronted by the Sedile, the headquarters of Bari's Council of Nobles. In the square's northeast corner is the Colonna della Giustizia (Column of Justice), where debtors were once tied and whipped.

🎇 Festivals & Events

Festa di San Nicola
RELIGIOUS

(☺7-9 May) The Festival of St Nicholas is Bari's biggest annual shindig, celebrating the 11th-century arrival of St Nicholas' relics from Turkey. On the first evening a procession leaves Castello Svevo for the Basilica di San Nicola. The next day there's a deafening fly-past and a fleet of boats carries the statue of St Nicholas along the coast.

🛏 Sleeping

Most of Bari's hotels tend to be bland and overpriced. B&Bs and rental apartments are generally a better option.

Bozzi 1910
APARTMENT €

(☑328 8167829; www.bozzi1910.com; Via Bozzi 39; s/d from €60/85; ☎) Four stylish studio apartments are in a heritage building near Bari's waterfront. Well-equipped kitchenettes include coffee machines, bathrooms are modern and include laundry facilities, and interesting art enlivens the walls. The friendly owners can also arrange transfers from Bari airport or to the train station. The location is quiet, but it's just a short stroll to good bars and restaurants.

B&B Casa Pimpolini
B&B €

(☑333 9580740, 0805 21 99 38; www.casapimpolini.com; Via Calefati 249; s €50-65, d €75-90; ✳🤖) This lovely B&B in Bari's new town is within easy walking distance to shops, restaurants and Bari Vecchia (the old town). The two rooms are warm and welcoming, and the superb homemade breakfast is an absolute treat. Great value and great hospitality from the friendly, well-travelled owner, Dyria.

🍴 Eating

Seafood Market
SEAFOOD €

(Molo San Nicola 6; ☺11am-2pm Mon-Sat) Just maybe Puglia's freshest raw seafood is served outside at simple tables by Bari's wise-cracking fisherfolk. Around €5 will buy a plateful, and local custom is to devour it with a frosty bottle of Peroni beer. An essential Bari experience.

Mastro Ciccio
SANDWICHES €

(☑0805 21 00 01; www.facebook.com/mastrociccio bari; Corso Emanuele 15; from €5; ☺9am-midnight) 🍴 Top-notch salads and panini sandwiches crammed with local products including octopus, ham, buffalo mozzarella cheese and pistachios make Mastro Ciccio a great place for lunch or a less formal, good-value dinner. Order at the counter and combine your snack with a beer or glass of wine.

Terranima
PUGLIAN €€

(☑0805 21 97 25, 334 6608618; www.terranima.com; Via Putignani 213; meals €30-35; ☺noon-3pm daily, 7-11pm Mon-Sat) Peep through the lace curtains into the cool interior of this rustic trattoria, where worn flagstone floors and period furnishings make you feel like you're dining in someone's front room. The menu features fabulous regional offerings such as veal, lemon and caper meatballs, and *sporcamuss,* a sweet flaky pastry.

🍷 Drinking & Nightlife

La Bitta
CRAFT BEER

(☑391 7703075; www.facebook.com/labittanew; Via Manfredi Re 36; ☺11am-3am) Our favourite of the bars and cafes along narrow Via Manfredi Re on the edge of Bari's old town. Six beer taps feature a rotating selection and the fridge is packed with top drops from top Italian breweries including CR/AK and Extraomnes. La Bitta's music is usually great and the friendly bar staff can rustle up cheese and charcuterie platters.

Reverso Unconventional Bistrot   WINE BAR
(☑347 9123522; www.facebook.com/reversobis trot; Strada Vallisa 79; ⊙7pm-late Tue-Sun; 🛜) Tucked away in a laneway in Bari Vecchia, the cosy Reverso combines an excellent Puglian wine list, interesting bar snacks and platters, and a welcoming and inclusive vibe. Drop by to see if any live music is scheduled, often from Thursday to Saturday from around 9pm.

ℹ Information

From Piazza Aldo Moro, in front of the main train station, streets heading north will take you to Corso Vittorio Emanuele II, which separates the old and new parts of the city.

Hospital (☑800 34 93 49; Piazza Cesare 11)
Post Office (☑0805 25 01 50; Piazza Umberto I 33a; ⊙8.30am-7pm Mon-Fri, to 12.30pm Sat)
Tourist information office (www.viaggiarein puglia.it; Piazza del Ferrarese 29; ⊙9am-7.30pm) English is spoken at this very helpful office – a good source of information on bus and train travel to Matera and Alberobello.
Tourist Kiosk (☑0805 82 14 11; Piazza Aldo Moro 32; ⊙9am-1pm & 3-7pm Mon-Sat) Convenient to Bari's central train station and packed with information on the city and Puglia generally.

ℹ Getting There & Away

AIR

Bari's **Karol Wojtyła Airport** (☑0805 80 02 00; www.aeroportidipuglia.it; Viale Ferrari), 10km northwest of the city centre, is served by a host of international and budget airlines, including easyJet, Alitalia and Ryanair.

Pugliairbus (www.aeroportidipuglia.it) connects Bari airport with Foggia and Brindisi airports. It also has services to Matera, Vieste and Taranto.

BOAT

Ferries run from Bari to Albania, Croatia, Greece and Montenegro. All boat companies have offices at the **ferry terminal**, accessible on bus 20 from the main train station. Fares vary considerably among companies and it's easier to book with a travel agent such as **Morfimare** (☑0805 7 98 15; www.morfimare.it; Corso de Tullio 36-40).

The main companies and their routes:
Jadrolinija (☑0805 27 54 39; www.jadrolinija. hr; Nuova Stazione Marittima di Bari) For

Dubrovnik, Croatia (from €55, 10 hours, up to six times per week) and Bar, Montenegro (from €59, 10 hours, two per week).
Montenegro Lines (☑382 30 31 11 64; www. montenegrolines.net; Corso de Tullio 36) For Bar (Montenegro, from €59, 10 hours, two per week) and Dubrovnik (Croatia, from €59, 10 hours, up to six times per week).
Superfast (☑0805 28 28 28; www.superfast. com; Corso de Tullio 6) For Corfu (from €75, nine hours), Igoumenitsa (from €64, 10 hours) and Patras (from €64) in Greece.
Ventouris Ferries (☑080 876 14 51; www.ven touris.gr; Nuova Stazione Marittima di Bari) For Corfu, Cephalonia and Igoumenitsa (Greece; from €74, 10 hours) and daily ferries to Durrës (Albania; from €75, nine hours).

BUS

Intercity buses leave from two main locations. From Via Capruzzi, south of the main train station, **SITA** (☑0805 79 01 11; www.sitabus.it) covers local destinations. **Ferrovie Appulo-Lucane** (☑0805 72 52 29; http://ferrovie appulolucane.it) buses serving Matera (€4.90, 1¾ hours, six daily) also depart from here, plus **Marozzi** (☑0805 79 02 11; www.marozzivt.it) buses for Rome (from €34.50, 4½ to 5½ hours, six daily – note that the overnight bus departs from Piazza Moro in front of the railway station) and other long-distance destinations.

Buses operated by **Ferrovie del Sud-Est** (FSE; ☑0805 46 21 11; www.fseonline.it) leave from Largo Ciaia, south of Piazza Aldo Moro and service the following places:
Alberobello (€5, 1½ hours, hourly); continues to Locorotondo (€5.70, 1¾ hours) and Martina Franca (€5.70, two hours)
Grotte di Castellana (€2.80, one hour, frequent)
Taranto (from €8.60, three hours with change, four per day)

TRAIN

A web of train lines spreads out from Bari. Note that there are fewer services on the weekend.

From the **Bari Centrale Station** (☑0805 24 43 86), Trenitalia trains go to Puglia and beyond: Destinations include Brindisi (from €8.60, one hour, frequent and Rome (from €40, four hours, four per day).

Ferrovie Appulo-Lucane (☑0805 72 52 29; http://ferrovieappulolucane.it) serves Matera (€5, 1¾ hours, 12 daily) and Potenza (€11.60, 3¾ hours, four daily).

Ferrovie del Sud-Est (FSE; ☑0805 46 21 11; www.fseonline.it) trains leave from the southern side of the station where they have their own separate ticket office: Destinations include:
Alberobello (€5, 1¾ hours, hourly)
Martina Franca (€5.70, 3¼ hours, five per day)
Taranto (from €6.40, 2½ hours, nine daily)

WORTH A TRIP

GROTTE DI CASTELLANA

These spectacular limestone caves, 40km southeast of Bari, are Italy's longest natural subterranean network. The interlinked galleries contain an incredible range of underground landscapes, with extraordinary stalactite and stalagmite formations. The highlight is the Grotta Bianca (White Grotto), an eerie alabaster cavern hung with stiletto-thin stalactites. 'Speleonights' take small torch-wielding groups into the caves after dark, among the bats, beetles, and crustacea that live there.

There are two tours in English: a 1km, 50-minute tour that doesn't include the Grotta Bianca (€12, on the half hour); and a 3km, two-hour tour (€16, on the hour) that does include it. Temperatures inside the cave average 18°C, so take a light jacket.

In the same complex, you'll also find a speleology **museum** (☑ 080 499 82 30; www.grottedicastellana.it; ⊙ 9.30am-1pm & 3.30-6.30pm mid-Mar–Oct, 10am-1pm Nov–mid-Mar) **FREE** and an **observatory** (☑ 080 499 82 13; www.osservatorio.grottedicastellana.it; adult/6-14yr €5/3; ⊙ tours by appointment Jul & Aug).

Grotte di Castellana can be reached by rail from Bari on the FSE Bari–Taranto train line (€3.20, 1¼ hours, roughly hourly).

❶ Getting Around

Central Bari is compact – a 15-minute walk will take you from Piazza Aldo Moro to the old town. For the ferry terminal, take bus 20 (tickets €1.50) from Piazza Moro.

Street parking is migraine-inducing. There's a large parking area (€1) south of the main port entrance; otherwise, there's a large multistorey car park between the main train station and the FSE station. Another car park is on Via Zuppetta, opposite Hotel Adria.

TO/FROM THE AIRPORT

To and from the airport, the most direct option is to catch the **train** (www.ferrovienordbarese.it; Piazza Aldo Moro; to Bari Centrale's Ferrovie Nord terminal (€5, 20 minutes, 6am to midnight). Another option is to take the **Tempesta shuttle bus** (www.autoservizitempesta.it), also from Bari Centrale (€4, 30 minutes, hourly), with pickups at Piazza Garibaldi and the corner of Via Andrea da Bari and Via Calefati. A taxi trip from the airport to town costs around €25.

Around Bari

The *Terra di Bari*, or 'land of Bari', surrounding the capital is rich in olive groves and orchards, and has an impressive architectural history, with some magnificent cathedrals, an extensive network of castles along its coastline, charming seaside towns like Trani and the mysterious inland Castel del Monte.

Trani

☑ 0883 / POP 56,100

Known as the 'Pearl of Puglia', beautiful Trani has a sophisticated feel, particularly in summer when well-heeled visitors pack the array of marina-side bars. The marina is the place to promenade and watch the white yachts and fishing boats in the harbour, while the historic centre, with its medieval churches, glossy limestone streets, historic Jewish quarter and faded yet charming *palazzi* is an enchanting area to explore. But it's the cathedral, pale against the deep-blue sea, that is the town's most arresting sight.

◉ Sights

Cathedral   CATHEDRAL
(www.cattedraletrani.it; Piazza del Duomo; campanile €5; ⊙ 8.30am-12.30pm & 3.30-7pm Mon-Sat, 9am-12.30pm & 4-8.30pm Sun Apr-Oct, shorter hours Nov-Mar) This dramatic seafront cathedral is dedicated to St Nicholas the Pilgrim, a Greek Christian who wandered through Puglia crying '*Kyrie eleison*' ('Lord, have mercy'). First thought to be a simpleton, he was posthumously revered after several miracles attributed to him occurred. Below the church is the **crypt**, a forest of ancient columns that predates the current structure, and where the bones of St Nicholas are kept beneath the altar. You can also visit the **campanile** (bell tower).

Castello   CASTLE
(☑ 080 528 52 49; www.castelloditrani.beniculturali.it; Piazza Manfredi 16; adult/reduced €5/2.50; ⊙ 8am-7pm) Two hundred metres north of the cathedral is one of Trani's major landmarks, the vast, almost modernist Swabian castle built by Frederick II in 1233. Charles V later strengthened the fortifications and it was used as a prison from 1844 to 1974. While the moat is now dry, the ingenious engineers originally devised a system allowing the level of seawater in it to be precisely controlled.

Scolanova Synagogue   SYNAGOGUE

(☑ 0883 48 17 99; Via Scolanova 23; ⊘ hours vary) This synagogue, one of four once established in Trani's ancient Jewish quarter, has been reborn after over 600 years. Persecutions, forced conversions and confiscations periodically beset the Jews of Trani, culminating in their forced expulsion in 1510. This 13th-century synagogue was converted to a Christian church in an earlier wave of hate, around 1380. Abandoned by the mid-20th century, it has been deconsecrated and returned to life as the Jewish house of worship it originally was.

Ognissanti Church   CHURCH

(Via Ognissanti; ⊘ hours vary) Traditionally (but controversially) thought to be built by the Knights Templar in the 12th century, this church became a place of blessing for those setting out on Crusade. Legend has it that it was in this austere and dignified building that the knights of the First Crusade swore allegiance to their leader, Bohemond I of Antioch, before setting off to 'liberate' the Holy Lands. Whatever the truth, it's a treasured example of Pugliese-Romanesque architecture of the period.

🛏 Sleeping

B&B Centro Storico Trani   B&B €

(☑ 0883 50 61 76; www.bbtrani.it; Via Leopardi 28; s/d €40/60; 🕿) This simple, old-fashioned B&B inhabits the 14th-century Palazzo Moro-la in the old Jewish quarter, and is run by a lovely elderly couple. It's basic, but the rooms are large and 'Mama' makes a mean *crostata* (jam tart). There's a terrace, laundry and wi-fi in communal areas.

Palazzo Filisio   HOTEL €€

(☑ 0883 50 09 31; www.palazzofilisio.it; Piazza Addazi 2; d/ste €145/190; 🅿 ❄ 🕿) A lovely building facing the cathedral and the Adriatic, the 18th-century Palazzo Filisio houses this charmingly understated grand hotel. Stylish rooms have been renovated with colours referencing the cobalt Adriatic and the location is superb. The in-house Regia restaurant (meals €60) maintains the upmarket vibe with dishes such as risotto with prawns, asparagus and black truffle.

🍴 Eating

Paninart   SEAFOOD €

(Via Statuti Marittimi 78; meals €7-12; ⊘ noon-3pm & 6-11.30pm; 🕿) This compact and happening spot soundtracked by classic soul music combines good-value gourmet salads and *panini* sandwiches with a thoughtful selection of local wines and Puglian craft beers. There's brilliant harbourfront seating outside and excellent service from the young waitstaff. Try the U Purp sandwich, crammed with tender lemon-marinated octopus.

★ Corteinfiore   SEAFOOD €€

(☑ 0883 50 84 02; www.corteinfiore.it; Via Ognissanti 18; meals €40-45; ⊘ 1-2.15pm Tue-Sun,

---

WORTH A TRIP

FREDERICK II'S TOY CASTLE

You'll see **Castel del Monte** (☑ 0883 56 99 97; www.casteldelmonte.beniculturali.it; adult/reduced €10/3.50; ⊘ 10.30am-7.30pm Apr-Sep, 9am-6.30pm Oct-Mar), an inhumanly exact geometric shape on a hilltop, from miles away. Mysterious and perfectly octagonal, it's one of southern Italy's most talked-about landmarks and a Unesco World Heritage Site. No one knows why Frederick II built it – there's no nearby town or strategic crossroads. It was not built to defend anything, as it has no moat or drawbridge, no arrow slits, and no trapdoors for pouring boiling oil on invaders.

Some theories claim that, according to mid-13th-century beliefs in geometric symbolism, the octagon represented the union of the circle and square, of God-perfection (the infinite) and human-perfection (the finite). The castle was therefore nothing less than a celebration of the relationship between humanity and God.

The castle has eight octagonal towers. Its interconnecting rooms have decorative marble columns and fireplaces, and the doorways and windows are framed in corallite stone. Many of the towers have washing rooms with what are thought to be Europe's first flushing loos – Frederick II, like the Arab world he admired, set great store by cleanliness. Audio guides (€3) are a worthwhile investment to maximise your visit.

To get to the castle without a car, take the Ferrovia Bari-Nord train from Bari to Andria, then bus number 6 from Andria station to the castle (35 minutes, five daily, April to October only). The castle is about 35km from Trani; there's no parking, but a nearby site charges €5 for a car, and €1 for a shuttle up the short, steepish 500m to the castle.

WORTH A TRIP

POLIGNANO A MARE

Located around 34km south of Bari on the S16 coastal road, Polignano a Mare is spectacularly built on the edge of a craggy ravine pockmarked with caves. The town is thought to be one of the most important ancient settlements in Puglia and was later inhabited by successive invaders ranging from the Huns to the Normans. On Sunday the *logge* (balconies) are crowded with day trippers from Bari who come here to view the crashing waves, visit the caves and crowd out the *cornetterias* (shops specialising in Italian croissants) in the atmospheric *centro storico*. Polignano Made in Love (☑ 080 321 77 58; www.polignanomadeinlove.com; Via Anemone 39; tours per person €25-100) offers a wide range of culinary experiences, including cookery classes, as well as biking tours, SUP (stand-up paddleboarding) and boat trips exploring the spectacular coastline. The town is also home to MINT Cucina Fresca (www.mintcucinafresca.com; Via San Benedetto 32; meals €25-35; ⏱ 12.30-2.30pm & 7-10pm Tue-Sat, 12.30-4pm Sun; ☑) ✎ , a notable eatery known for its vegetarian focus.

Regular trains (€2.50, 35 minutes) link Bari Centrale to Polignano a Mare.

8-10.15pm Tue-Sat) The decking, stiff table-cloths and marquee setting of this famed Trani seafood restaurant set hopes racing, and the food, wine and service deliver in full. Expect lots of seafood, and expect it to be excellent: try the *frutti di mari antipasti,* or the Gallipoli prawns with candied lemon. Also rents delightful rooms (double €120) decked out in pale colours.

ℹ Information

Tourist Office (☑ 0883 58 88 30; https://viaggiareinpuglia.it; 1st fl, Palazzo Palmieri, Piazza Trieste 10; ⏱ 10.30am-12.30pm & 5.30-7.30pm Mon-Sat) Located 200m south of the cathedral. Offers free guided walking tours most days in the peak season at 8pm.

ℹ Getting There & Away

STP (☑ 0883 49 18 00; www.stpspa.it) has frequent bus services to Bari (€4.20, 45 minutes). Services depart from **Bar Stazione** (Piazza XX Settembre 23), which has timetables and tickets.

Trani is on the main train line between Bari (€3.20, 30 to 45 minutes, frequent) and Foggia (€6.50, 40 to 50 minutes, frequent).

Promontorio del Gargano

The coast surrounding this expansive promontory seems permanently bathed in a pink-hued, pearly light, providing a painterly contrast to the sea, which softens from intense to powder blue as the evening draws in. It's one of Italy's most beautiful corners, encompassing white limestone cliffs, fairytale grottoes, sparkling sea, ancient forests, rare orchids and tangled, fragrant maquis (dense scrub vegetation).

Once connected to what is now Dalmatia (in Croatia), the 'spur' of the Italian boot has more in common with the land mass across the sea than with the rest of Italy. Creeping urbanisation was halted in 1991 by the creation of the Parco Nazionale del Gargano (www.parcogargano.gov.it) FREE. Aside from its magnificent national park, the Gargano is home to pilgrimage sites and the lovely seaside towns of Vieste and Peschici.

Vieste

☑ 0884 / POP 13,950

Like a young belle who's beautiful without even realising it, the town of Vieste clings modestly to a spectacular promontory on the Gargano Promontory. It resembles nothing so much as a cross between Naples and Dubrovnik, with a bit of Puglian magic mixed in. The narrow alleys of the old town, draped with lines of drying clothes and patrolled by slinking cats and the odd friendly dog, are atmospheric day or night, high or low season. Wedged up against the old town is the equally unpretentious new town, ghostly in winter, but packed with holidaying humanity in summer, especially during the *passeggiata* (evening stroll).

Vieste is strategically placed atop the steep Pizzomunno cliffs between two sweeping sandy beaches. The gritty harbour offers water sports, while the surrounding Parco Nazionale del Gargano is perfect for cycling and hiking.

◎ Sights

Cathedral   CATHEDRAL
(Via Duomo; ⏱ 7.30am-noon & 4-11pm) Built by the Normans on the ruins of a Vesta temple,

this 11th-century 'co-cathedral' (so called because its bishopric is shared with another) is in Pugliese-Romanesque style with a fanciful tower that resembles a cardinal's hat. Of note are its beautiful paintings, swirling interior columns and Latin-inscribed altar.

Chianca Amara HISTORIC SITE
(Bitter Stone; Via Cimaglia) Vieste's most gruesome sight is this worn and polished stone where thousands were beheaded when Turks sacked Vieste in the 16th century.

Activities

Superb sandy beaches surround the town: in the south are **Spiagga del Castello**, **Cala San Felice** and **Cala Sanguinaria**; due north, head for the area known as **La Salata**. **Diving** is popular around the promontory's rocky coastline, which is filled with marine grottoes. From May to September fast boats zoom to the **Isole Tremiti.**

For **hiking** ideas, pick up a *Guida al Trekking sul Gargano* brochure from the tourist office. A section of walk 4 is doable from Vieste. It starts 2.5km south of town off the Lungomare Enrico Mattei, where a track cuts up through olive groves into increasingly wild terrain.

Tours

Motobarca Desirèe BOATING
(☎360 262386; www.grottemarinegargano.com; Lungomare Vespucci; adult/child €23/10; ⊙Apr-Oct) These boat tours of the various caves, arches and *trabucchi* (Pugliese fishing structures) that characterise the Gargano coast are spectacular, though the boats can get crowded. There are two departures a day (9am and 2.30pm); buy tickets port-side. Other boat operators offer similar trips.

Explora Gargano CYCLING
(☎340 7136864, 0884 70 22 37; www.exploragargano.it/contatti.html; Vieste-Peschici km 5.5; tours from €50) To get off the beach for a day or two, take one of the many tours on offer at Explora Gargano. As well as hiking and mountain biking (half day from €70) in the Foresta Umbra, it offers quad tours and 4WD safaris.

Sleeping

Albergo Labotte B&B €
(☎0884 70 75 13; Lungomare Mattei 14; d from €60; P 📶) With a location opposite Vieste's main beach, Albergo Labotte is well placed for a convenient stay. All rooms have been refurbished to a modern and very comfortable standard and there is also off-street, secure parking. The owners don't speak much English, but they are unfailingly friendly and helpful. Bathrooms are particularly spacious.

B&B Rocca sul Mare B&B €
(☎0884 70 27 19; www.roccasulmare.it; Via Mafrolla 32; r from €80; 📶) In a former convent in the old quarter, this is a popular, charming and reasonably priced place with comfortable high-ceilinged rooms. There's also a rooftop terrace with panoramic views, a suite with a steam bath and simple, tasty meals (€25 for four courses). Bike hire is available, and your hosts can arrange fishing trips and cook your catch that evening.

Relais Parallelo 41 B&B €€
(☎0884 35 50 09; www.bbparallelo41.it; Via Forno de Angelis 3; r €120; ⊙Mar-Oct; ❄📶) This small B&B in an updated *palazzo* in the midst of the old town has five renovated rooms decorated with hand-painted ceilings, luxurious beds and super modern bathrooms. Breakfasts consist of a buffet, and the reception area acts as a mini information centre for local activities. Note that there are minimum stays in July and August.

Eating & Drinking

Osteria degli Archi ITALIAN €€
(☎0884 70 51 99; www.osteriadegliarchivieste.it; Via Ripe 2; meals €35-40; ⊙noon-2.30pm & 7-11pm) A classy cut above other Vieste restaurants, Osteria degli Archi offers innovative spins on established flavours and recipes. Standout dishes include tartare of red tuna and gossamer-light ravioli stuffed with smoked cheese, mint and fennel. Wine bottles lining the stone walls hint at the restaurant's excellent wine list with many Puglian and Salento labels available. Bookings recommended on summer weekends.

Carpenter WINE BAR
(☎320 6989512; Via Seggio 9; ⊙11am-late Apr-Oct; 📶) Vieste's go-to for *aperitivi* is this popular spot where locals line their refreshing drinks up on a rustic sea wall. Look forward to ocean views on the edge of the old town and a selection of Italian craft beers and wine. During the day it's a more laid-back espresso bar. The location used to be a carpenter's workshop.

Information

POST OFFICE

Post Office (☎0884 70 28 49; Via Vittorio Veneto 7; ⊙8.30am-7pm Mon-Sat)

TOURIST INFORMATION

Tourist Office (☑ 0884 70 88 06; Piazza Garibaldi; ⊙ 8am-8pm Mon-Sat) You can weigh yourself down with useful brochures here.

ⓘ Getting There & Away

BOAT

Vieste's port is to the north of town, about a five-minute walk from the tourist office. In summer, several companies, including **Linee Marittime Adriatico** (☑ 0884 96 20 23; Corso Garibaldi 32), head to the Isole Tremiti. Tickets can be bought port-side and at agencies in town.

BUS

From Piazzale Manzoni, where intercity buses terminate, a 10-minute walk east along Viale XXIV Maggio, which becomes Corso Fazzini, brings you into the old town and the Marina Piccola's attractive promenade. In summer buses terminate at Via Verdi, a 300m walk from the old town down Via Papa Giovanni XXIII.

SITA (☑ 0881 35 20 11; www.sitabus.it) buses run between Vieste and Foggia via Manfredonia. There are also services to Monte Sant'Angelo (€5) via Macchia Bivio Monte.

From May to September, **Pugliairbus** (☑ 080 580 03 58; www.aeroportidipuglia.it) runs a service (€20, three hours, four daily) to the Gargano, including Vieste and Peschici, from Bari airport.

Monte Sant'Angelo

☑ 0884 / POP 12,550 / ELEV 796M

One of Europe's most important pilgrimage sites, this isolated mountain-top town has an extraordinary atmosphere. Pilgrims have been coming here for centuries – and so have the hustlers, pushing everything from religious kitsch to parking spaces.

THE RICH FLAVOURS OF CUCINA POVERA

In Italy's less wealthy 'foot', traditional recipes evolved through economic necessity rather than experimental excess. Local people used whatever ingredients were available to them, plucked directly from the surrounding soil and seas, and kneaded and blended using recipes passed down through generations. The result is called cucina povera (literally 'food of the poor'), which, thanks to a recent global obsession with farm-to-table purity, has become increasingly popular.

If there is a mantra for cucina povera, it is 'keep it simple'. Pasta is the south's staple starch. Made with just durum wheat and water (and no eggs, unlike some richer northern pastas) it is most commonly sculpted into orecchiette ('little ears') and used as the starchy platform on which to serve whatever else might be growing readily and inexpensively. For the same reasons, vegetables feature prominently: eggplants, mushrooms, tomatoes, artichokes, olives and many other staple plants grow prodigiously in these climes and are put to good use in the dishes.

Meat, though present in cucina povera, is used more sparingly than in the north. Lamb and horsemeat predominate and are usually heavily seasoned. Unadulterated fish is more common, especially in Puglia, which has a longer coastline than any other mainland Italian region. Popular fish dishes incorporate mussels, clams, octopus (in Salento), swordfish (in northern Calabria), cod and prawns.

A signature Pugliese primi (first course) is orecchiette con cima di rape, a gloriously simple blend of rapini (a bitter green leafy veg with small broccoli-like shoots) mixed with anchovies, olive oil, chilli peppers, garlic and pecorino. Another popular orecchiette accompaniment is ragù di carne di cavallo (horsemeat), sometimes known as ragù alla barese. Bari is known for its starch-heavy riso, patate e cozze, a surprisingly delicious marriage of rice, potatoes and mussels that is baked in the oven. Another wildly popular vegetable is wild chicory, which, when combined with a fava bean purée, is reborn as fave e cicorie.

Standard cheeses of the south include burrata, which has a mozzarella-like shell and a gooey centre, and pecorino di filiano, a sheep's-milk cheese from Basilicata. There are tons of bread recipes, but the horn-shaped crusty bread from Matera is king.

Recommended traditional restaurants include Terranima (p144) in Bari and Alle due Corti (p163) in Lecce. Awaiting Table (p160) in Lecce and Charming Tours (p154) in Alberobelllo offer cookery classes, and tours with **Velo Service** in Bari (☑ 389 6207353; www.veloservice.org; Strada Vallisa 81; tours from €15; ⊙ 10am-7pm) and Lecce (p161) explore the region's hearty street food.

The object of devotion is the Santuario di San Michele. Here, in 490 CE, St Michael the Archangel is said to have appeared in a grotto to the Bishop of Siponto.

During the Middle Ages, the sanctuary marked the end of the Route of the Angel, which began in Mont St-Michel (in Normandy) and passed through Rome. In 999 the Holy Roman Emperor Otto III made a pilgrimage to the sanctuary to pray that prophecies about the end of the world in the year 1000 would not be fulfilled. His prayers were answered, the world staggered on and the sanctuary's fame grew.

The sanctuary has been a Unesco World Heritage Site since 2011.

◉ Sights

Santuario di San Michele   CAVE
(☑ 0884 56 11 50; www.santuariosanmichele.it; Via Reale Basilica; ⊙ 7.30am-7.30pm Jul-Sep, shorter hours rest of year) **FREE** Over the centuries this sanctuary has expanded to incorporate a large complex of religious buildings that overlay its original shrine. The double-arched entrance vestibule at street level stands next to a distinctive octagonal bell tower built by Carlo I of Naples in 1282. As you descend the staircase inside, look for the 17th-century pilgrims' graffiti. The grotto/shrine where St Michael is said to have left a footprint in stone is located at the bottom of the staircase.

Because of St Michael's footprint, it became customary for pilgrims to carve outlines of their feet and hands into the stone. Etched Byzantine bronze and silver doors, cast in Constantinople in 1076, open into the grotto itself. Inside, a 16th-century statue of the Archangel Michael covers the site of St Michael's footprint. Audio guides cost €3, and it's €5 to get into the museum (or €7 for both together).

Tomba di Rotari   TOMB
(☑ 0884 56 11 50; Largo Tomba di Rotari; €1; ⊙ 9am-noon & 3-7pm Apr-Oct, to 4.30pm Nov-Mar) A short flight of stairs opposite the Santuario di San Michele leads to a 12th-century baptistry with a deep sunken basin for total immersion. You enter the baptistry through the facade of the **Chiesa di San Pietro** with its intricate rose window squirming with serpents – all that remains of the church, destroyed in a 19th-century earthquake. The Romanesque portal of the adjacent 11th-century **Chiesa di Santa Maria Maggiore** has some fine bas-reliefs.

Castle   CASTLE
(☑ 0884 56 54 44; Largo Roberto Giuscardo 2; €2; ⊙ 9am-1pm & 2.30-7pm) At the highest point of Monte Sant'Angelo is this rugged fastness, first built by Orso I, who later became Doge of Venice, in the 9th century. One 10th-century tower, Torre dei Giganti, survives, but most of what you can see are Norman, Swabian and Aragonese additions. The views alone are worth the admission.

🛏 Sleeping & Eating

Hotel Michael   HOTEL €
(☑ 0884 56 55 19; Via Reale Basilica 86; s/d €50/65; 🖥) A small hotel with shuttered windows, located on the main street across from the Santuario di San Michele, this traditional place has spacious rooms and walls spruced up with devotional art. Ask for a room with a view, or just enjoy it as you breakfast on the rooftop terrace.

Casa li Jalantuúmene   TRATTORIA €€
(☑ 0884 56 54 84; www.li-jalantuumene.it; Piazza de Galganis 5; meals €45; ⊙ noon-3pm & 7.30-10.30pm Wed-Mon; ☑) This renowned restaurant owned by chef Gegè Mangano serves excellent fare in an intimate setting. The seasonal menu always features good vegetarian options, there's a select wine list and, in summer, tables spill onto the piazza. There are also four suites on-site (from €100), decorated in traditional Pugliese style. Chef Gegè has also opened an informal **wine bar** (☑ 087 97 63 21; Via Gambadoro 27; ⊙ 7.30pm-late) nearby.

ℹ Getting There & Away

SITA (☑ 0881 35 20 11; www.sitasudtrasporti. it) buses run to and from Foggia (€7, 1½ hours, four daily) and Vieste via Macchia Bivio Monte.

Peschici

☑ 0884 / POP 4500
Perched above a turquoise sea and tempting beach, Peschici is another cliff-clinging Amalfi lookalike. Its tight-knit old walled town of whitewashed houses acts as a hub to a wider resort area. The small town gets crammed in summer, so book in advance. Boats zip across to the Isole Tremiti in high season, and there are a couple of excellent places to eat.

◉ Sights

Castello di Peschici   CASTLE
(adult/reduced €4/2; ⊙ 9.30am-1.30pm & 4-9pm Jun-Sep) Peschici's medieval hilltop castle stands sentinel over the town's port, and in-

side there is a fascinating Museum of Torture with replicas of some of history's most devious and chilling methods to extract information through extreme coercion.

🛏 Sleeping & Eating

Peschici's ample accommodation stocks can come under stress when it seems half of Puglia heads to Gargano in August.

Locanda al Castello B&B €€
(☑0884 96 40 38; www.peschicialcastello.it; Via Castello 29; s/d €70/120; P ❄ 🛜) Staying here is like entering a large, welcoming family home. It's by the cliffs with fantastic views and it's air-conditioned, should you visit in the height of summer. Enjoy hearty home cooking in the restaurant (meals €25) while the owners' kids run around playing football – indoors!

⭐Al Trabucco da Mimì SEAFOOD €€
(☑0884 96 25 56; www.altrabucco.it; Localita Punta San Nicola; meals €40-45; ⊙12.30-2pm & 7-11pm Easter-Oct) Mimì sadly passed away in 2016, but his extended family keep this delightful place ticking. Sitting on wooden trestles beneath the *trabucco* (a traditional Pugliese wooden fishing platform) you'll eat the freshest seafood, prepared with expertise but no fuss, as you watch the sun sink behind Peschici. Local Gargano craft beers complete a relaxed experience. Bookings are recommended for weekends.

There are three simple rooms for rent, at €50 per person. There's also occasional live music (usually jazz) and *aperitivo* in summer.

Porta di Basso ITALIAN €€€
(☑0884 35 51 67; www.portadibasso.it; Via Colombo 38; menus €45-60; ⊙noon-2.30pm & 7-11pm, closed Jan & Feb) 🌿 Superb views of the ocean drop away from the floor-to-ceiling windows beside intimate alcove tables at this adventurous and stylish clifftop restaurant. Choose from one of three degustation menus, and prepare to be delighted by dishes such as smoked bluefish with Jerusalem artichokes, foie gras and honey vinegar.

ℹ Information

Tourist Office (☑0884 96 49 66; Via Magenta 3; ⊙10am-1pm & 4.30-7pm Mon-Sat)

ℹ Getting There & Away

The bus terminal is beside the sports ground, uphill from the main street, Corso Garibaldi.

From April to September, ferry companies, including Linee Marittime Adriatico (p150),

serve the Isole Tremiti (adult/child €30/18, 1½ hours). Day trips to the islands are also possible daily during July and August, and around key holiday weekends.

Foresta Umbra

The 'Forest of Shadows' is the Gargano's enchanted interior – thickets of tall, epic trees interspersed with picnic spots bathed in dappled light. It's the last remnant of Puglia's ancient forests: Aleppo pines, oaks, yews and beech trees cloak the hilly terrain. More than 65 different types of orchid have been discovered here, and the wildlife includes roe deer, wild boar, foxes, badgers and the increasingly rare wild cat. Walkers and mountain bikers will find plenty of well-marked trails within the forest's 5790 sq km.

There is a small *centro visitatori* in the middle of Foresta Umbra that houses a **museum and nature centre** (SP52bis, Foresta Umbra; €1.50; ⊙9.30am-6.30pm mid-Apr–mid-Oct, 4-10pm Easter) with fossils, photographs, and stuffed animals and birds. Half-day guided hikes are available by reservation (€10 per person) and you can hire bikes (per hour/day €5/25) and buy walking maps (€2.50). The centre is on SP52bis close to the junction with SP528.

In the middle of the Foresta Umbra, 5km north of the visitor centre on the way to Vico di Gargano, cosy **Rifugio Sfilzi** (☑338 3345544; www.rifugiosfilzi.com; SP528; adult €45, incl half-/full board €85/100, child 4-12 incl full board €50) offers eight rooms with three- and four-bed configurations, making them ideal for groups or families. It also has a small shop selling locally made products such as jams and oils, and a cafe-restaurant with home-made cake and coffee. Three-course menus (€525) are also available.

ℹ Getting There & Away

You'll need your own transport to get in and out of the forest.

Isole Tremiti

POP 490

This beautiful archipelago of three islands, 36km offshore, is a picturesque composition of ragged cliffs, sandy coves and thick pine woods, surrounded by the glittering dark-blue sea.

Unfortunately, the islands are no secret, and in July and August some 100,000 holidaymakers head over. If you want to savour the islands in tranquillity, visit during the shoulder season. In the low season most tourist facilities close down and the few permanent residents resume their quiet and isolated lives.

The islands' main facilities are on San Domino, the largest and lushest island, formerly used to grow crops. It's ringed by alternating sandy beaches and limestone cliffs; inland grows thick maquis flecked with rosemary and foxglove. The centre harbours a nondescript small town with several hotels.

Small San Nicola island is the traditional administrative centre; a castle-like cluster of medieval buildings rises up from its rocks. The third island, Capraia, is uninhabited.

◉ Sights

San Domino ISLAND

Head to San Domino for walks, grottoes and coves. It has a pristine, marvellous coastline and the islands' only sandy beach, **Cala delle Arene**. Alongside the beach is the small cove **Grotta dell'Arene**, with calm clear waters for swimming. You can also take a boat trip (around €20 from the port) around the island to explore the grottoes: the largest, Grotta del Bue Marino, is 70m long. A tour of all three islands costs around €25.

Diving in the translucent sea is another option with **Tremiti Diving Center** (☑337 648917; www.tremitidivingcenter.com; Via Federico II, Villaggio San Domino; 1-tank day-/night-dive from €40/50). There's an undemanding, but enchanting, walking track around the island, starting at the far end of the village.

San Nicola ISLAND

Medieval buildings thrust out of San Nicola's rocky shores, the same pale-sand colour as the barren cliffs. In 1010, Benedictine monks founded the **Abbazia e Chiesa di Santa Maria** here; for the next 700 years the islands were ruled by a series of abbots who accumulated great wealth.

Capraia ISLAND

The third of the Isole Tremiti, Capraia (named after the wild caper plant) is uninhabited. Birdlife is plentiful, with impressive flocks of seagulls. There's no organised transport, but trips can be negotiated with local fishing folk.

🛏 Sleeping & Eating

La Casa di Gino B&B €€

(☑0882 46 34 10; www.hotel-gabbiano.com; Via dei Forni, San Nicola; d €140-165; ﹡) A tranquil accommodation choice on San Nicola, away from the frenzy of San Domino, this B&B run by the Hotel Gabbiano has stylish white-on-white rooms. Great views and quiet space to amble or relax are two of its most delightful aspects.

Hotel Gabbiano HOTEL €€

(☑0882 46 34 10; www.hotel-gabbiano.com; Via Garibaldi 5, Villaggio San Domino; d from €120; ﹡🛜) An established icon on San Nicola and run for decades by the same Neapolitan family, this smart hotel has pastel-coloured rooms with balconies overlooking the town and the sea. It also has a seafood restaurant, spa and gym.

Architiello SEAFOOD €€

(☑0882 46 30 54; Via Salita delle Mura 5, San Domino; meals €30-35; ☺noon-3pm & 7.30-11pm Apr-Oct) A class act with a sea-view terrace, this place specialises in – what else? – fresh fish.

ℹ Getting There & Away

Boats for the Isole Tremiti depart from several points on the Italian mainland: Manfredonia, Vieste and Peschici in summer, and Termoli in nearby Molise year-round. Most boats arrive at San Domino. Small boats regularly make the brief crossing to San Nicola (€6 return) in high season; from October to March a single boat makes the trip after meeting the boat from the mainland.

Valle d'Itria

Between the Ionian and Adriatic coasts rises the great limestone plateau of the Murgia (473m). It has a strange karst geology: the landscape is riddled with holes and ravines through which small streams and rivers gurgle, creating what is, in effect, a giant sponge. At the heart of the Murgia lies the idyllic Valle d'Itria.

The rolling green valley is criss-crossed by drystone walls, vineyards, almond and olive groves, and winding country lanes. This is the part of Puglia most visited by foreign tourists and is the best served by hotels and luxury *masserias* (working farms) or manor farms.

Alberobello

☑080 / POP 10,750

Unesco World Heritage Site Alberobello resembles an urban sprawl – for gnomes. The *zona dei trulli* on the westernmost of the town's two hills is a dense mass of 1500 beehive-shaped houses, white-tipped as if

Side text: PUGLIA, BASILICATA & CALABRIA VALLE D'ITRIA

dusted by snow. These drystone buildings are made from local limestone; none are older than the 14th century.

The town is named after the primitive oak forest Arboris Belli (beautiful trees) that once covered this area. It's an amazing place, but also something of a tourist trap – from May to October busloads of tourists pile into *trullo* homes, drink in *trullo* bars and shop in *trullo* shops. Try to visit in the morning to avoid the arrival of tourist buses and the inevitable throng of visitors.

If you park in Lago Martellotta, follow the steps up to Piazza del Popolo, where the Belvedere Trulli lookout offers fabulous views over the whole higgledy-piggledy picture.

⊙ Sights

Rione Monti   AREA
Within the old town quarter of Rione Monti more than 1000 *trulli* cascade down the hillside, many of which are now souvenir shops. The area is surprisingly quiet and atmospheric in the late evening, once the day trippers have left and the gaudy stalls have been stashed away.

Rione Aia Piccola   AREA
On the eastern side of Via Indipendenza is Rione Aia Piccola. This neighbourhood is much less commercialised than Rione Monti, with 400 *trulli,* many still used as family dwellings. You can climb up for a rooftop view at many shops, although most do have a strategically located basket for donations.

Trullo Sovrano   MUSEUM
(☑080 432 60 30; www.trullosovrano.eu; Piazza Sacramento 10; adult/reduced €1.50/1; ⊙10am-1.30pm & 3.30-7pm Apr-Oct, to 6pm Nov-Mar) Trullo Sovrano dates in parts to the early 17th century, and is Alberobello's only two-floor *trullo.* Built by a wealthy priest's family, it's now a small 'living' museum recreating *trullo* life, with sweet, rounded rooms that include a recreated bakery, bedroom and kitchen. The souvenir shop here has a wealth of literature on the town and surrounding area, plus Alberobello recipe books.

☞ Tours

Charming Tours   FOOD & DRINK
(☑080 432 38 29; www.charmingtours.it; Piazza Sacramento 8; tours per person from €120) Offering food-based tours and cookery classes in Alberobello and the surrounding region. Shopping at food markets, cheese-making and visits to local farms can all be arranged,

and cultural and historical tours to destinations including Matera, Lecce and Otranto are available. Ask about special tours negotiating Valle d'Itria's sleepy rural byways on a retro Vespa or in a vintage Fiat 500.

🛏 Sleeping

Casa Albergo Sant'Antonio   HOTEL €
(☑080 432 29 13; www.santantonioalbergo.com; Via Isonzo 8a; s/d/tr/q €53/80/95/110; 🐾) Excellent value right in the heart of the Rione Monti neighbourhood, this simple hotel is in an old monastery located next to a unique *trulli*-style church with a conical roof. The tiled rooms are relatively monastic and spartan, but will do the trick for the unfussy.

Trullidea   RENTAL HOUSE €€
(☑080 432 38 60; www.trullidea.it; Via Monte Sabotino 24; trulli from €140; 🐾) Based on the *albergo diffuso* concept, Trullidea has numerous renovated, quaint, cosy and atmospheric *trulli* in Alberobello's historic centre available on a self-catering, B&B, or half- or full-board basis. Half-board is €30 person, and a buffet breakfast is included in the price.

🍴 Eating

Trattoria Amatulli   TRATTORIA €
(☑080 432 29 79; Via Garibaldi 13; meals €20-25; ⊙12.30-3pm & 7.30-11.30pm Tue-Sun) The cheerily cluttered interior of this excellent trattoria is papered with photos of smiley diners, obviously put in the best mood by dishes like *orecchiette scure con cacioricotta pomodoro e rucola* ('little ears' pasta with cheese, tomato and arugula). Wash it down with the surprisingly drinkable house wine, only €5 a litre. It won't add much to an invariably reasonable bill.

Trattoria Terra Madre   VEGETARIAN €€
(☑080 432 38 29; www.trattoriaterramadre.it; Piazza Sacramento 17; meals €26-57; ⊙12.15-2.45pm & 7.15-9.45pm Tue-Sat, 12.15-2.45pm Sun; 🍴) 🌿 Vegetables take pride of place in Italian kitchens, especially at this enthusiastic vegetarian-ish (some meat is served) restaurant. The farm-to-table ethos rules – most of what you eat comes from the organic garden outside. Start with the huge vegetable antipasti and save room for *primi* like *capunti* 'Terra Madre' (pasta with eggplant, zucchini and peppers) and the perfect house-baked desserts.

ℹ Information

The main **tourist information office** (☑080 432 28 22; www.prolocoalberobello.it; Monte Nero 1; ⊙9am-7pm) is in the *zona dei trulli.*

There is another smaller **tourist office** (📋 080 432 51 71; cnr Via Independenza & Largo Martellotta; ⊙10am-1pm & 3-6pm) that opens only during peak times.

ℹ️ Getting There & Away

Alberobello is easily accessible from Bari (€5, 1½ hours, hourly) on the FSE Bari–Taranto train line. From the station, walk straight ahead along Via Mazzini, which becomes Via Garibaldi, to reach Piazza del Popolo (a journey of around 500m).

Locorotondo

📋 080 / POP 14,160

Locorotondo is endowed with a whisper-quiet pedestrianised *centro storico,* where everything is shimmering white aside from the blood-red geraniums that tumble from the window boxes. Situated on a hilltop on the Murge Plateau, it's a *borgo più bella d'Italia* (see http://borghipiubellid italia.it) – that is, it's rated as one of the most beautiful towns in Italy. There are few 'sights' as such – rather, the town itself is a sight. The streets are paved with smooth ivory-coloured stones, with the church of **Santa Maria della Graecia** as their sun-baked centrepiece.

From **Villa Comunale**, a public garden, you can enjoy panoramic views of the surrounding valley. You enter the compact historic quarter directly across from here.

Not only is this deepest *trulli* country, it's also the liquid heart of the Pugliese wine region. Sample some of the local *verdeca* at Controra.

🛌 Sleeping

Locorotondo and the surrounding country are blessed with it comes to quality accommodation. If you're going to stay on a *masseria* or in a *trullo* whilst in Puglia, this is the place to do it.

Truddhi   AGRITURISMO €
(📋 080 443 13 26; www.truddhi.com; Contrada Trito 161; d per 5 nights from €440; ᴘ🐾) This charming cluster of 11 self-catering *trulli* in the hamlet of Trito near Locorotondo is surrounded by olive groves and vineyards. It's a tranquil place and you can take cooking courses (per day €80) with Mino, a lecturer in gastronomy. The *trulli* sleep between two and six people, depending on size.

★ Sotto le Cummerse   APARTMENT €€
(📋080 4313298; www.sottolecummerse.it; Via Vittorio Veneto 138; apt incl breakfast from €125; ✳️🐾)

At this *albergo diffuso* (dispersed hotel) you'll stay in one of 13 tastefully furnished apartments scattered throughout Locorotondo's *centro storico*. The apartments are traditional buildings that have been beautifully restored and furnished, and you can book activities such as horse riding, cooking classes and historical tours. A delightful base for exploring the Valle d'Itria.

🍽️ Eating & Drinking

Quanto Basta   PIZZA €
(📋 080 431 28 55; www.facebook.com/qbpizzeria; Via Morelli 12; pizza €6-13; ⊙12.30-3pm & 7.30-11.30pm; 🐾) Craft beer and pizza make an excellent combination at this quietly stylish old town restaurant with wooden tables, soft lighting and stone floors. It's hard to stop at *quanto basta* (just enough) when the pizza, carpaccio, salads and antipasti are so good, to say nothing of the lovely Itrian wines. Try the superb Golosa pizza with local Itrian almonds and sausage.

La Taverna del Duca   TRATTORIA €€
(📋 080 431 30 07; www.tavernadelducascatigna.it; Via Papatodero 3; meals €38; ⊙noon-3pm & 7.30pm-midnight Tue-Sat, noon-3pm Sun & Mon) In a narrow side street off Piazza Vittorio Emanuele, this well-regarded trattoria serves robust Itrian fare such as pork cheek in a *primitivo* reduction and donkey stew. If they sound daunting, there's always Puglia's favourite pasta (*orecchiette*), thick vegetable soup and other more familiar foods.

Controra   WINE BAR
(📋 339 6874169; www.facebook.com/controralo corotondo; Via Nardelli 67; ⊙noon-late) Treat this laid-back little place either as a sandwich shop or wine bar, sampling *prosit* (sparkling rose), *verdeca* and other niche wines of the Valle d'Itria, all partnered with amazing sandwiches, platters of regional produce, and Locorotondo's uniformly stunning views of olive groves and *trulli*. Welcome to the best seats in town.

ℹ️ Information

Tourist Office (📋 080 431 30 99; www.prolo colocorotondo.it; Piazza Emanuele 27; ⊙9am-1pm & 5-7pm) Offers free internet access. Only open Saturday and Sunday outside peak season.

ℹ️ Getting There & Away

Locorotondo is easily accessible via frequent trains from Bari (€5.70, 1½ to two hours) on the FSE Bari–Taranto train line.

PUGLIA, BASILICATA & CALABRIA VALLE D'ITRIA

Cisternino

📋 080 / POP 11,600

An appealing, whitewashed hilltop town, slow-paced Cisternino has a charming *centro storico* beyond its bland modern outskirts; with its kasbah-like knot of streets, it has been designated as one of the country's *borghi più belli* (most beautiful towns). Beside its 13th-century Chiesa Matrice and Torre Civica there's a pretty communal garden with rural views. If you take Via Basilioni next to the tower you can amble along an elegant route right to the central piazza, Vittorio Emanuele.

✕ Eating

Micro   VEGETARIAN €

(📋 340 5315463; www.facebook.com/micropuglia; Via Santa Lucia 53; meals €20-25; ☉ 10am-3pm & 6-11pm Wed-Mon; 🖈) 🍃 This charismatic little juice bar/lunch spot is the necessary counterbalance to the meaty excesses Cisternino is famous for. Market-fresh vegetables and herbs arrive each morning and are turned into soups, salads, torte, vegetarian sushi and more. There are some choices for carnivores, but for once it's they who are the afterthought. Organic wines and Italian craft beers complete the picture.

Rosticceria L'Antico Borgo   BARBECUE €€

(📋 080 444 64 00; www.rosticceria-lanticoborgo. it; Via Tarantini 9; meals €30-35; ☉ 6.30-11pm daily summer, Mon-Sat winter) A classic *fornello pronto* (half butcher's shop, half trattoria), this is the place for a cheerful, no-frills meat fest. The menu is brief, listing a few simple pastas and various meat options (priced per kilo), including Cisternino's celebrated *bombette* (skewered pork wrapped around a piece of cheese). Choose your roast meat and eat it with red wine, chips and salad.

❶ Getting There & Away

Cisternino is accessible by regular FSE trains from Bari (€5, 45 minutes). STP Brindisi runs hourly buses between Cisternino and Ostuni.

Martina Franca

📋 080 / POP 49,030

The old quarter of this town is a picturesque scene of winding alleys, blinding white houses and blood-red geraniums. There are graceful baroque and rococo buildings here too, plus airy piazzas and curlicue ironwork balconies that almost touch above the narrow streets. This town is the highest in the

Murgia, and was founded in the 10th century by refugees fleeing the Arab invasion of Taranto. It only started to flourish in the 14th century when Philip of Anjou granted tax exemptions (*franchigie,* hence Franca); the town became so wealthy that a castle and defensive walls complete with 24 solid bastions were built.

⊙ Sights

The best way to appreciate Martina Franca's beauty is to wander around the narrow lanes and alleyways of the *centro storico.*

Passing under the baroque Arco di Sant'Antonio at the western end of pedestrianised Piazza XX Settembre, you emerge into Piazza Roma, dominated by the imposing, 17th-century rococo Palazzo Ducale (📋 080 480 57 02; Piazza Roma 28; ☉ 9am-8pm Mon-Fri, from 10am Sat & Sun mid-Jun–Sep, shorter hours rest of year) FREE, whose upper rooms have semirestored frescoed walls and host temporary art exhibitions.

From Piazza Roma, follow the fine Corso Vittorio Emanuele, with baroque townhouses, to reach Piazza Plebiscito, the centre's baroque heart. The piazza is overlooked by the 18th-century Basilica di San Martino, its centrepiece a statue of city patron, St Martin, swinging a sword and sharing his cloak with a beggar.

✦ Festivals & Events

Festival della Valle d'Itria   MUSIC

(📋 080 480 51 00; www.festivaldellavalleditria.it; event tickets from €15; ☉ Jul & Aug) This summer music festival takes over Martina Franca's venues from mid-July to early August. Musical theatre, especially opera, tops the bill, but concertos and other recitals also abound. For information, contact the Centro Artistico Musicale Paolo Grassi in the Palazzo Ducale.

🛏 Sleeping & Eating

B&B San Martino   B&B €

(📋 080 48 56 01; www.bandbsanmartino.com; Via Abate Fighera 32; s/d €33/85; ❋ 🏊) A stylish B&B in a historic palace with rooms overlooking gracious Piazza XX Settembre. The rooms have exposed stone walls, shiny parquet floors, wrought-iron beds and small kitchenettes and there's a compact pool to take a dip in when it's hot.

Cibando   BISTRO €

(📋 080 798 42 22; https://cibando.business.site; Piazza Roma 18; platters from €10; ☉ 11am-3pm & 6pm-late) A friendly delicatessen and cafe showcasing Slow Food ingredients, Cibando is a good place to try the area's renowned smoked burrata cheese and *capocollo* (pork neck salami). Local wines and interesting craft brews on tap reinforce the proclamation on the door, *Non abbiamo birre normali!* (We don't have normal beers!)

⭐ **Nausikaa** ITALIAN €€
(📞080 485 82 75; www.ristorantenausikaa.it; Vico Arco Fumarola 2; meals €35; ⏲noon-3pm Tue-Sun, 7.30-11.30pm Tue-Sat) Tucked away down a dogleg alley off Martina Franca's main pedestrian drag is this lovely little modern Italian place, run by brothers Francesco and Martino. Tradition is not sacrificed to forward-thinking, and vice versa – a 'caprese' salad, for instance, is stuffed inside a silky pasta bundle, anointed with 'basil pearls'. The Puglia-focused wine list is a joy.

ℹ️ Information

Tourist Office (📞080 480 57 02; www.agenziapugliapromozione.it; Piazza XX Settembre 3; ⏲10.30am-1.30pm & 4.30-7pm Jul & Aug, shorter hours rest of year)

ℹ️ Getting There & Away

The FSE train station is downhill from the historic centre. From the train station, go right along Viale della Stazione, continue along Via Alessandro Fighera to Corso Italia, then continue to the left along Corso Italia to Piazza XX Settembre.

FSE (📞080 546 21 11; www.fseonline.it) trains run to/from Bari (€5.70, 2¼ hours, hourly) and Taranto (€2.50, 50 minutes, four per day). Buses run to Alberobello (€1.10, 20 minutes, frequent).

Ostuni

📞0831 / POP 31.150

Chic Ostuni shines like a pearly white tiara, extending across three hills with the magnificent gem of a cathedral as its sparkling centrepiece. It's the end of the *trulli* region and the beginning of the hot, dry Salento. With some excellent restaurants, stylish bars and swish yet intimate places to stay, it's packed in summer.

Ostuni is surrounded by olive groves, so this is the place to buy some of the region's DOC 'Collina di Brindisi' olive oil – either delicate, medium or strong – direct from producers.

🔘 Sights & Activities

The surrounding countryside is perfect for cycling. **Ciclovagando** (📞330 985255; www.

ciclovagando.com; Via Savoia 19, Mesagne; bike rental per day from €20), based in Mesagne, 30km south of Ostuni, rents basic and high-end bikes at reasonable rates, and will deliver them free within a 10km radius of its office in Mesagne (any further and there is a charge). It also guides half- and full-day tours (€35/70), including bike rental and helmets, with a choice of three or four itineraries, departing daily from Lecce, Matera, Trani and Castellana Grotte.

Museo di Civiltà Preclassiche della Murgia MUSEUM
(📞0831 33 63 83; www.ostunimuseo.it; Via Cattedrale 15; adult/reduced €5/3; ⏲10am-7pm) Located in the Convento delle Monacelle, the museum's most famous exhibit is Delia, a 25,000-year-old expectant mother. Pregnant at the time of her death, her well-preserved skeleton was found in a local cave. Many of the finds here come from the Palaeolithic burial ground, now the **Parco Archeologico e Naturale di Arignano** (⏲10am-1pm Sun, or by appointment).

Cathedral CATHEDRAL
(Piazza Beato Giovanni Paolo II; by donation; ⏲9am-noon & 3.30-7pm) Dedicated to the Assumption of the Virgin Mary, Ostuni's dramatic 15th-century cathedral has an unusual Gothic-Romanesque-Byzantine facade with a frilly rose window and an inverted gable. The 18th-century sacred art covering the ceiling and altars is well worth stepping inside to see.

🎎 Festivals & Events

La Cavalcata RELIGIOUS
Ostuni's annual feast day is held on 26 August, when processions of horsemen dressed in glittering red-and-white uniforms (resembling Indian grooms on their way to be wed) follow the statue of Sant'Oronzo around town.

🛏️ Sleeping

Le Sole Blu B&B €
(📞0831 30 38 56; https://bed-and-breakfast-sole blu-ostuni.business.site; Corso Vittorio Emanuele II 16; d & apt €70) Located in the 18th-century (rather than medieval) part of town, Le Sole Blu only has one room available: it's large, fully renovated and has a separate entrance. The two self-catering apartments nearby are also excellent value. It's just a short stroll to good cafes and Ostuni's shimmering marble main square.

La Terra
HOTEL €€

(📞0831 33 66 51; www.laterrahotel.it; Via Petrarolo 16; d from €130; P 🕸 🛜) This 13th-century former *palazzo* offers atmospheric and stylish accommodation with original niches, dark-wood beams and furniture, and contrasting light stonework and whitewash. There's a colonnaded terrace, wi-fi throughout, a more-than-decent restaurant and a truly cavernous bar – tunnelled out of a cave.

★ Il Frantoio
AGRITURISMO €€€

(📞0831 33 02 76; www.masseriailfrantoio.it; SS16 km 874, Ostuni; d €220; P 🕸 @ 🛜 🚖) Stay at this charming, whitewashed farmhouse and estate where the owners still live and work producing high quality olive oil. Even if you're not staying here, book in for one of the marathon eight-course lunches – the food is local, organic and superb. Il Frantoio's swimming pool is welcome on warmer Puglian days.

🍴 Eating

Osteria Ricanatti
ITALIAN €€

(📞0831 1561831; Corso Cavour 37; meals €35-45; ⏰noon-3pm & 7-11pm Wed-Mon) Puglian classics are given a thoroughly modern makeover at the stylish and elegant Osteria Ricanatti. Seafood is often the star, including superb tuna and octopus, while the savvy chef also has a winning way with local vegetables like eggplant and zucchini. The optional five-course menu (€35) is good value. Delve into the wine list with a few top Salento varietals.

Porta Nova
ITALIAN €€€

(📞0831 33 89 83; www.ristoranteportanova.com; Via Petrarolo 38; meals €50-55; ⏰12.30-3.30pm & 7.30-11pm) Scenically installed in the Aragonese fortifications, this terraced restaurant is a special occasion charmer. Seafood is wonderful here, with a whole section of the menu devoted to *crudo mare* (raw fish). Ease into what will be a splendid hour or so of indulgence with sea-bass carpaccio, then ramp it up with rosemary-scented Gallipoli prawns on beech-smoked potato.

ℹ Information

Tourist Office (📞0831 30 12 68, 0831 33 96 27; Corso Mazzini 6; ⏰8am-2pm & 3-8pm)

ℹ Getting There & Away

STP Brindisi (www.stpbrindisi.it) buses run to Brindisi (€3.10, 50 minutes, six daily) and to Martina Franca (€2.10, 45 minutes, three daily), leaving from Piazza Italia in the newer part of Ostuni.

Trains run frequently to Brindisi (€2.90, 25 minutes) and Bari (€5.70, 50 minutes). A half-hourly local bus covers the 2.5km between the station and town.

Salento

The Penisola Salentina, better known simply as Salento, is hot, dry and remote, retaining a flavour of its Greek past. It stretches across Italy's heel from Brindisi to Taranto and down to Santa Maria di Leuca. Here the lush greenery of Valle d'Itria gives way to flat, ochre-coloured fields hazy with wildflowers in spring, and endless olive groves.

Lecce
📞0832 / POP 95,000

Bequeathed with a generous stash of baroque buildings by its 17th-century architects, Lecce has a completeness and homogeneity that other southern Italian metropolises lack. Indeed, so distinctive is Lecce's architecture that it has acquired its own moniker, *barocco leccese* (Lecce baroque), an expressive and hugely decorative incarnation of the genre replete with gargoyles, asparagus columns and cavorting gremlins. Swooning 18th-century traveller Thomas Ashe thought it 'the most beautiful city in Italy', but the less-impressed Marchese Grimaldi said the facade of Basilica di Santa Croce made him think a lunatic was having a nightmare.

👁 Sights

Lecce has more than 40 churches and at least as many *palazzi,* all built or renovated between the 17th and 18th centuries, giving the city an extraordinary cohesion. Two of the main proponents of *barocco leccese* (the craziest, most lavish decoration imaginable) were brothers Antonio and Giuseppe Zimbalo, who both had a hand in the fantastical Basilica di Santa Croce.

Admission fees are charged for a selection of the city's most popular churches. Full tickets (€9) cover admission to the Cathedral, Basilica di Santa Croce, Chiesa di San Matteo, Chiesa di Santa Chiara and the Museo Diocesano d'Arte Sacra, while a secondary ticket (€3) allows admission to only two of these.

★ Basilica di Santa Croce
BASILICA

(📞0832 24 19 57; Via Umberto I; full ticket incl admission to 4 other churches €9, incl admission to 1 other church €3; ⏰9am-9pm) It seems that hallucinating stonemasons have been at work on the basilica. Sheep, dodos, cherubs and beasties writhe across the facade, a swirling magnificent allegorical feast. Throughout the 16th and 17th centuries, a team of artists under Giuseppe Zimbalo laboured to work the building up to this pitch. The interior is more conventionally baroque, and deserves a look. Spare a thought for the expelled Jewish families whose land the basilica was built on.

Piazza del Duomo
PIAZZA

Piazza del Duomo is a baroque feast, the city's focal point and a sudden open space amid the surrounding enclosed lanes. During times of invasion the inhabitants of Lecce would barricade themselves in the square, which has conveniently narrow entrances. Lecce's 12th-century cathedral, Palazzo Vescoville (Episcopal Palace) and museum of sacred art (☑ 0832 24 47 64; http://museo.diocesilecce.org; full ticket incl admission to 4 other churches €9, incl admission to 1 other church €3; ⊙ 9am-9pm) face one another in silent dignity across the square.

Cathedral
CATHEDRAL

(☑ 0832 30 85 57; Piazza del Duomo; full ticket incl admission to 4 other churches €9, incl admission to 1 other church €3; ⊙ 9am-9pm) Giuseppe Zimbalo's 1659 reconstruction of Lecce's original 12th-century cathedral is recognised as being among his finest work. Zimbalo, Lecce's famous 17th-century architect, was also responsible for the thrusting, tiered bell tower, 72m high. The cathedral is unusual in that it has two facades, one on the western end and the other, more ornate, facing the piazza. It's framed by the 17th-century Palazzo Vescovile (Episcopal Palace) and the 18th-century Seminario, designed by Giuseppe Cino.

★ Museo Faggiano
MUSEUM

(☑ 0832 30 05 28; www.museofaggiano.it; Via Grandi 56/58; €5; ⊙ 9.30am-8pm) Descend through Lecce's rich historical strata in this fascinating home-turned-museum, where sewerage excavations led to the chance discovery of an archaeological treasure trove. The deepest finds take you all the way back to the Messapii culture of the 5th century BCE; you then ascend through Roman crypts, medieval walls, Jewish insigna and Knights Templar symbols in the rooftop tower.

Museo Ebraico
MUSEUM

(Jewish Museum Lecce; ☑ 0832 24 70 16; www.palazzotaurino.com; Via Umberto 9; adult/reduced €5/4; ⊙ 10am-1pm & 3-7pm Mon-Sat, 10.30am-1.30pm Sun) This fascinating museum outlines the Jewish history of Lecce and the greater Salento region. Entry is by 30-minute guided tour only, running every 45 minutes from 10am to 1pm and 3pm to 6.15pm. Excellent maps (€1.50) covering other nearby Jewish heritage sites are a good option for self-drive travellers. On Thursday evenings at 6.30pm the museum hosts *Sarah's Stories* (€12), a poignant spoken-word and audiovisual performance by Italian actor, Giustina de Iaco. Booking ahead is recommended.

MUST
GALLERY

(Museo Storico Citta di Lecce; ☑ 0832 24 10 67; www.mustlecce.it; Via degli Ammirati 11; adult/reduced €4.50/2.50; ⊙ noon-7pm Tue-Sun) The beautifully restored 15th-century Monastery of Santa Chiara houses this civic museum and gallery, and has a great view of the Roman theatre from the back window. Exhibits focus on the history of Lecce, from the Messapians of 2500 years ago to the present day, while the work of modern Leccese artists hangs in the ground-floor gallery.

Castello di Carlo V
CASTLE

(☑ 0832 24 65 17; www.castellocarlov.it; Via XXV Luglio; adult/reduced €10/8; ⊙ 9am-8.30pm Mon-Fri, from 9.30am Sat & Sun, closes later in summer) While the Normans built the original castle in the 12th century, it became associated with the Spanish Holy Roman Emperor Charles V, who enlarged it in the 16th century. Bound within enormous trapezoidal walls cornered with stout bastions, it is Puglia's largest castle, and has been used as a prison, court, military barracks and now the headquarters of Lecce's cultural authorities. You can wander around inside, catch a recital, and visit the on-site papier-mâché museum.

Museo Provinciale Sigismondo Castromediano
MUSEUM

(☑ 0832 68 35 03; www.facebook.com/MuCastromediano; Viale Gallipoli 30; ⊙ 8.30am-7.30pm Mon-Sat, 9am-1pm Sun) FREE This museum stylishly covers 10,000 years of history, from Palaeolithic and Neolithic bits and bobs to a handsome display of Greek and Roman jewels, weaponry and ornaments. The stars of the show are the Messapians, whose jaunty Mycenaean-inspired jugs and bowls date back 2500 years. There's also an interesting collection of 15th- to 18th-century paintings.

Roman Amphitheatre
AMPHITHEATRE

(Piazza Sant'Oronzo) Below the ground level of the piazza is this restored 2nd-century-CE amphitheatre, discovered in 1901 by

PUGLIA, BASILICATA & CALABRIA SALENTO

Lecce

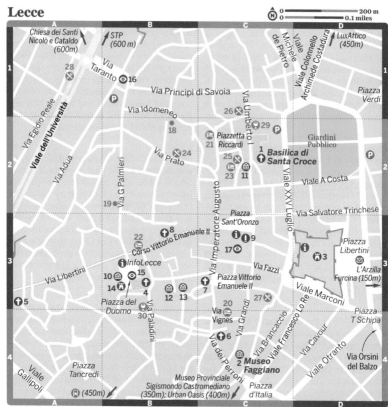

construction workers. It was excavated in the 1930s to reveal a perfect horseshoe that actually extends under the rest of the square to originally seat 15,000. A little colonised by weeds, it's nonetheless an impressive centrepiece to Lecce's main communal square. Walking tours available at the nearby tourist office (p163) include the history of the amphitheatre.

Museo Teatro Romano   MUSEUM
(☑0832 27 91 96; Via degli Ammirati 5; adult/reduced €3/2; ◎9.30am-1pm Mon-Sat) Exhibiting artefacts revealed during the excavation of the adjacent Roman theatre, this museum also has displays recreating classical Roman life, including a reconstruction of Roman Lupiae (Lecce). The museum is housed in a handsome 17th-century *palazzo*.

Colonna di Sant'Oronzo   MONUMENT
(Piazza Sant'Oronzo) Two Roman columns once marked the end of the Appian Way in Brindisi. When one of them crumbled in 1582

some of the pieces were rescued and subsequently donated to Lecce (the base and capital remain in Brindisi). The old column was rebuilt in 1666 with a statue of Lecce's patron saint placed on top. Sant'Oronzo is venerated for supposedly saving the city of Brindisi from a 1656 plague.

Porta Napoli   GATE
The main city gate, Porta Napoli, was erected in 1548 in anticipation of a state visit from Charles V. It's a typically bombastic effort by Gian dell'Acaja (builder of Lecce's fortified walls), who modelled it on a Roman triumphal arch and gave it a pointy pediment carved with toy weapons and an enormous Spanish coat of arms.

🍴 Courses

Awaiting Table   COOKING
(☑334 7676970; www.awaitingtable.com; Via Idomeneo 41; day/week €265/1995) Silvestro Silvestori's splendid culinary and wine school

Lecce

provides day- or week-long courses with market shopping, tours, tastings, noteworthy lecturers and lots of hands-on cooking. Week-long courses are held in Silvestro's home, but you'll need to arrange your own accommodation. Book well in advance.

🖙 Tours

Velo Service TOURS
(📞 389 6207353; www.veloservice.org; Via Palmieri 32; tours from €15; ⏰ 10am-7pm) Offers various guided tours of Lecce including street food, papier mâché and shopping. Alternative ways to negotiate the city include by bicycle, in a rickshaw, by foot or on a Segway. Velo Service can also arrange tours exploring Puglia's olive oil scene. Booking ahead is recommended for all tours. Bicycle rental is also available along with ideas for day excursions.

🛏 Sleeping

Urban Oasis HOSTEL €
(📞 0832 30 00 50; www.urbanoasishostel.com; Via Cataldi 3; dm/d from €17/45; 🗖) Lecce's only hostel is a winner, with options including dorms for a maximum of six guests, and stylish double and triple rooms. Bathrooms are uniformly modern and there's a hip vibe enlivened by colourful decor. At the rear of the building is a wonderful garden perfect for end-of-day drinks.

B&B Idomeneo 63 B&B €
(📞 333 9499838; www.bebidomeneo63.it; Via Idomeneo 63; d/ste €80/120; 🗖) Be treated like a VIP

at this wonderfully curated B&B in the midst of Lecce's baroque quarter, complete with six colour-coded rooms and a funky entrance lounge. Decked out boutique-hotel style, it manages to seamlessly incorporate features like stone ceiling arches. The two 'apartments', with kitchenettes, are great value.

Azzurretta B&B B&B €
(📞 0832 24 22 11; www.bblecce.it; Via Vignes 2; d/tr €80/90; 🅿 🗖) Tullio runs this arty B&B located in a historic *palazzo*. Of the four rooms, ask for the large double with a balcony, wooden floors and vaulted ceiling. Massage is available in your room or on the roof terrace – also a splendid place to take a sundowner. You get a cafe voucher for breakfast.

There is also a tiny studio flat, which is a little dark but a good option if you're self-catering on a budget.

Palazzo Rollo B&B €
(📞 0832 30 71 52; www.palazzorollo.it; Corso Vittorio Emanuele II 14; s/d/ste from €75/90/100; 🅿 ❄ @) This tastefully restored 17th-century *palazzo* – the Rollo family seat for more than 200 years – makes a delightful base from which to explore Lecce. The grand B&B suites (with kitchenettes) have high curved ceilings and chandeliers, while contemporary studios downstairs open onto a courtyard. There are also self-catering apartments (from €120) and a rooftop garden.

Centro Storico B&B B&B €
(📞 328 8351294, 0832 24 27 27; www.centrostoricolecce.it; Via Vignes 2; s/d/ste €70/90/110;

LECCE'S NOTABLE CHURCHES

Lecce's unique baroque style is perhaps best seen in its churches; the city harbours dozens of them.

Chiesa dei Santi Nicolò e Cataldo (Via Cimitero; ⊗ 9am-noon & 5-7pm Jun-Aug, shorter hours rest of year) Located in the monumental cemetery outside the city walls, this outstanding church was built by the Normans in 1180. It got caught up in the city's baroque frenzy and was revamped in 1716 by the prolific Giuseppe Cino, who retained the Romanesque rose window and portal. The 16th-century fresco cycles inside tell stories from the saints' lives.

Chiesa di Santa Chiara (Piazzetta Vittorio Emanuele II; full ticket incl admission to 4 other churches €9, incl admission to 1 other church €3; ⊗ 9am-9pm) A 15th-century church given a baroque makeover between 1687 and 1691. Inside, every niche and surface swirls with twisting columns and ornate statuary. The ceiling is 18th-century Leccese *cartapestra* (papier mâché) masquerading as wood.

Chiesa di Sant'Irene (Corso Vittorio Emanuele II; ⊗ 7.30-11am & 4-6pm) Dedicated to Lecce's former patron saint and modelled on Rome's Basilica di Sant'Andrea della Valle, this church was completed in 1639. Inside you'll find a magnificent pair of mirror-image baroque altarpieces, facing each other across the transept.

Chiesa di San Matteo (Via dei Perroni 29; full ticket incl admission to 4 other churches €9, incl admission to 1 other church €3; ⊗ 9am-9pm) Known by the locals as Santa Maria della Luce, this graceful little church bears the fingerprints of Giuseppe Zimbalo, as much of baroque Lecce does. The famed architect completed the building, with its elaborate facade and more restrained interior, when the original architect died before completion.

Chiesa del Rosario (Via Libertini 5; ⊗ 8.30-11.30am & 5-6pm) Also known as the Chiesa di San Giovanni Battista (Church of John the Baptist), this elaborately fronted church was prodigious Leccese architect Giuseppe Zimbalo's last commission. He died before it was completed, and a quick-fix wooden roof was put up, instead of the dome he had intended.

P ❄ 🛜) This friendly and well-run B&B located in the 16th-century Palazzo Astore features big rooms, double-glazed windows and a classy heritage makeover with sparkling bathrooms and stylish furniture. Perfect for end of day relaxation, the huge rooftop terrace has sunloungers, views of Lecce's rooftops and a popular Jacuzzi. Vouchers are provided for breakfast at a nearby cafe.

LuxAttico B&B €€
(📞 328 1233450; https://luxattico.it; Via Lubello Formoso 2; s/d €90/120; P 🛜) Hosted by the friendly Luisa, LuxAttico has stylish rooms in a quiet residential area a short walk from Lecce's historic centre. Breakfast includes Lecce's finest baked goods, and there's a sunny terrace with views across the rooftops to Lecce's cathedral. There's a handy car park in the building (per day €5), and Luisa can recommend the best of Lecce's restaurants.

Patria Palace Hotel HOTEL €€
(📞 0832 24 51 11; http://patriapalace.com; Piazzetta Riccardi 13; d from €127; P ❄ @ 🛜) This sumptuous hotel is traditionally Italian with large mirrors, dark-wood furniture and wistful murals. The location is wonderful, the bar gloriously art deco with a magnificent carved ceiling, and the shady roof terrace has views over the Basilica di Santa Croce. The attached restaurant, **Atenze** (meals €50; ⊗ 12.30-3pm & 7-11pm), is one of Lecce's finest.

★ **Masseria Trapana** AGRITURISMO €€€
(📞 0832 18 32 101; www.trapana.com; Strada Vicinale Masseria Trapana 9; ste from €600; P ❄ 🛜) Surrounded by citrus groves, this modern reinvention of a 16th-century farmhouse is 12km north of Lecce. Ten suites combine with shared areas enlivened by Oriental textiles, and the Moroccan-style firepit is ideal for *aperitivi*. A subterranean vault houses a romantic plunge pool, the property makes its own mandarin liqueur, and excellent Puglian cuisine and superb breakfasts both feature.

🍴 Eating

La Succursale PIZZA €
(📞 391 4977749; www.facebook.com/lasuccursale.lecce; Viale dell'Università 15; pizza €7-10; ⊗ 6pm-midnight Tue-Sun) Lecce is an important university town and this boisterous pizzeria

combining gourmet pizzas with decent wine and craft beer is hugely popular with local students. Grab a table outside in warmer weather and feast on wood-fired goodness.

Baldo Gelato GELATO €
(📷 328 0710290; www.facebook.com/Baldogelato; Via Idomeneo 78; medium cone or cup €3; ⊘ 11am-10pm Mon-Thu, to midnight Fri-Sun) The couple behind Baldo Gelato make the best gelato in Lecce, hands down. The dark chocolate may be the most intensely chocolatey thing you've ever put in your mouth.

★ La Cucina di Mamma Elvira PUGLIAN €€
(📷 331 5795127; www.mammaelvira.com; Via Maremonti 33; meals €30-35; ⊘ 12.30pm-midnight) An offshoot of the stylish Enoteca Mamma Elvira, 'The Kitchen' makes use of a bigger space than that available to its older sibling to deliver more ambitious and substantial food. There's a focus on Pugliese wine, simply augmented by a seasonal menu that offers seafood antipasti, lovely vegetarian options, robust Pugliese pastas and more. Booking ahead is recommended.

L'Arzilla Furcina ITALIAN €€
(📷 391 3320419; www.larzillafurcina.it; Via Bacile 25; meals €30-35; ⊘ 7.30-11.30pm Tue-Sun, 12.30-2.30pm Tue, Thu & Sun) Tucked away down a shopping street in Lecce's new town, L'Arzilla Furcina is a stylish space showcasing seasonal and local ingredients and Salento wines. Traditional Puglian recipes are given a modern spin and could feature local seafood such as *cozze* (mussels). Thoroughly unpretentious and friendly service also makes it worth the short detour from Lecce's historic centre.

Alle due Corti PUGLIAN €€
(📷 0832 24 22 23; www.alleduecorti.com; Via Prato 42; meals €30-35; ⊘ 12.30-2pm & 7.30-11pm Mon-Sat, closed Jan) Rosalba de Carlo, a noted repository of Salento gustatory wisdom, is the presiding authority in this authentic-as-it gets Pugliese kitchen. 'The Two Courts' keeps it strictly seasonal and local, dishing up classics such as *ciceri e tria* (crisply fried pasta with chickpeas) and *turcineddhi* (offal of kid) in a relaxed environment.

🍷 Drinking & Nightlife

★ Quanta Basta COCKTAIL BAR
(📷 347 0083176; www.facebook.com/quantobasta lecce; Via Paladini 17; ⊘ 8pm-2am Thu-Tue) Just maybe Lecce's best Negroni cocktail is a fine reason to adjourn to Quanta Basta's outdoor tables for your nightly *aperitivi* session. Further rationale is provided by friendly service

from the hip, bearded bartenders and a superb location framed by twilight shadows, historic architecture and Lecce's beautiful golden light.

★ Enoteca Mamma Elvira WINE BAR
(📷 0832 169 20 11; www.mammaelvira.com; Via Umberto I 19; ⊘ 8am-3am; 📞) All you need to know about Salento wine will be imparted by the hip staff at this cool joint near the Santa Croce church. Taster glasses are dispatched liberally if you order snacks. You'll need to order a few if you're going to properly research the 250+ Pugliese wines it stocks. Italian craft beers also feature.

ℹ Information

MEDICAL SERVICES
Hospital (Ospedale Vito Fazzi; 📷 0832 66 11 11; Piazza Filippo) About 2km south of the centre on the Gallipoli road.

POST
Post Office (Piazza Libertini 5; ⊘ 8.30am-7pm Mon-Fri, to 12.30pm Sat)

TOURIST INFORMATION
InfoLecce (📷 0832 52 18 77; www.infolecce. it; Piazza del Duomo 2; ⊘ 9.30am-1.30pm & 3.30-7.30pm Mon-Fri, 10am-1.30pm & 3.30-7pm Sat & Sun) Independent and helpful tourist information office. Has guided tours and bike rental (per hour/day €3/15).

Puglia Blog (www.thepuglia.com) An informative site run by Fabio Ingrosso with articles on culture, history, food, wine, accommodation and travel in Puglia.

Tourist Office (📷 0832 24 20 99; Piazza Sant'Oronzo; ⊘ 10am-1pm & 4-6pm) One of two main government-run offices. The other is in **Castello di Carlo V** (📷 0832 24 65 17; ⊘ 9am-8.30pm Mon-Fri, 9.30am-8.30pm Sat & Sun, closes later in summer).

ℹ Getting There & Away

BUS
The city bus terminal is located to the north of Porta Napoli. Brindisi is best reached by train.

Pugliairbus (www.aeroportidipuglia.it/home pagebrindisi) Connects with Brindisi airport (€7.50, 40 minutes, nine daily).

STP (📷 0832 35 91 42; www.stplecce.it) Runs buses to Gallipoli (€4.40, 1¼ hours, frequent) and Otranto (€4.40, one hour, frequent) from the **STP bus station** (📷 800 43 03 46; Viale Porta D'Europa).

TRAIN
The main train station, 1km southwest of Lecce's historic centre, runs frequent services.

Bari from €10.80, 1½ to two hours
Bologna from €53.50, 7½ to 9½ hours
Brindisi from €2.90, 30 minutes
Naples from €49.30, 5½ hours (transfer in Caserta)
Rome from €56, 5½ to nine hours

FSE trains head to Otranto, Gallipoli and Martina Franca; the ticket office is located on platform 1.

Brindisi

☑ 0831 / POP 87,800

Like all ports, Brindisi has its seamy side, but it's also surprisingly slow paced and balmy, particularly along the palm-lined Corso Garibaldi and the promenade stretching along the interesting *lungomare* (seafront).

The town was the end of the ancient Roman road Via Appia, down whose length trudged weary legionnaires and pilgrims, crusaders and traders, all heading to Greece and the Near East.

⊙ Sights

★ **Tempio di San Giovanni al Sepolcro**　　　CHURCH
(☑ 0831 52 30 72; Piazzetta San Giovanni al Sepolcro; ⊙ 8am-2pm & 2.30-8.30pm) FREE This 12th-century church, a brown bulk of Norman stone conforming to the circular plan the Templars so loved, is a wonderfully evocative structure, austere and bare. You'll see vestigial medieval frescoes on the walls, and glimpses of the crypt below. The church was a popular stop for Crusaders travelling to and from the Holy Land. Don't miss the expansive gardens at the rear of the building.

Museo Archeologico Provinciale Ribezzo　　　MUSEUM
(☑ 0831 56 55 01; Piazza del Duomo 6; adult/reduced €5/3; ⊙ 9.30am-1.30pm Wed-Sat, 9.30am-1.30pm & 3.30-6.30pm Tue) This superb museum has several floors of well-documented exhibits (in English), including some 3000 bronze sculptures and fragments in Hellenistic Greek style. There are also terracotta figurines from the 7th century, underwater archaeological finds, and Roman statues and heads (not always together).

Cathedral　　　CATHEDRAL
(Piazza del Duomo; ⊙ 8am-9pm Mon-Fri & Sun, to noon Sat) This 12th-century cathedral was substantially remodelled after an earthquake in 1743. You can see how the original Romanesque structure may have looked by studying the nearby Porta dei Cavalieri Templari, a fanciful portico with pointy arches – it's all that remains of a medieval Knights Templar church that once also stood here.

Porta dei Cavalieri Templari　　　RUINS
After the Romans, the next big event to hit Brindisi was the Crusades during the 12th and 13th centuries. The Porta dei Cavalieri Templari, an exotic-looking portico with pointy arches, is thought to be all that remains of the Knights Templar's main church (although some doubt has been cast on that by recent scholarship). It stands beside the cathedral in the heart of the small historic quarter.

Roman Column　　　MONUMENT
(Via Colonne) The gleaming white column above a sweeping set of sun-whitened stairs leading to the waterfront promenade marks the terminus of the Roman Via Appia at Brindisi. Originally there were two columns, but one was presented to the town of Lecce back in 1666 as thanks to Sant'Oronzo for having relieved Brindisi of the plague.

Palazzo Granafei-Nervegna　　　MUSEUM
(Via Duomo 20; ⊙ 8am-8.30pm) FREE This 16th-century Renaissance-style palace is named for the two different families who owned it. The building is of interest because it houses the huge ornate capital that used to sit atop one of the Roman columns that marked the end of the Appian Way (the rest of the column is in Lecce). Also on site are Brindisi's tourist office, a pleasant cafe, a bookshop, exhibition spaces and the archaeological remains of a Roman *domus* (house).

🛏 Sleeping & Eating

Hotel Orientale　　　HOTEL €
(☑ 0831 56 84 51; www.hotelorientale.it; Corso Garibaldi 40; r €99; P ❄ 🛜) This sleek, modern hotel overlooks the long palm-lined *corso*. Rooms are pleasant, the location is good and it has a small fitness centre, private car park and (rare) cooked breakfast option.

Numero Primo　　　ITALIAN €€
(☑ 0831 179 55 37; www.vinotecanumeroprimo.it; Viale Regina Margherita 46; meals €25-30; ⊙ 11am-3pm & 6pm-midnight Tue-Sun) This stylish glass pavilion along Brindisi's seafront is the showcase restaurant for Puglia's Tenute Rubino winery. Local seafood like octopus and tuna is harnessed for the concise menu and there's also more hearty fare like gourmet

Brindisi

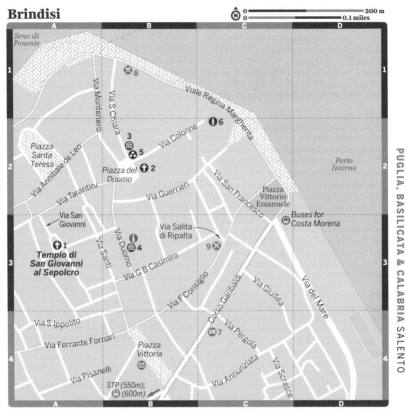

burgers. The attentive waitstaff have good recommendations on wine matches from Tenute Rubino's diverse range. See www.tenuterubino.com for details about cellar tours.

Trattoria Pantagruele TRATTORIA €€
(☏ 0831 56 06 05; www.facebook.com/brindisitrattoria; Via Salita di Ripalta 1; meals €33; ☉ 12.30-2.30pm Mon-Sat, 7.30-10.30pm Mon-Fri) Named after the Rabelaisian giant Pantagruel, this trattoria three blocks from the waterfront serves excellent fish and grilled meats. Expect fresh anchovies in season, and homemade pasta in all seasons. Begin with the Mare e Terra (Sea & Land) *antipasti*, and we can recommend the raw prawns with *salmoriglio* (a condiment with lemon juice, olive oil, garlic and fresh herbs).

ℹ Information

Post Office (☏ 0831 22 55 95; Piazza Vittoria 10; ☉ 8.30am-7pm Mon-Fri, to 12.30pm Sat)

Brindisi

⊙ Top Sights
1 Tempio di San Giovanni al
   Sepolcro A3

⊙ Sights
2 Cathedral.. B2
3 Museo Archeologico Provinciale
   Ribezzo B2
4 Palazzo Granafei-Nervegna................ B3
5 Porta dei Cavalieri Templari B2
6 Roman Column.................................... C2

⊑ Sleeping
7 Hotel Orientale C4

⊗ Eating
8 Numero Primo B1
9 Trattoria Pantagruele C3

Tourist Office (☏ 0831 52 30 72; www.visit brindisi.it; Via Duomo 20, Palazzo Granafei-Nervegna; ☉ 10am-6pm Mon, 8am-8pm Tue-Sun; ☏)

ⓘ Getting There & Away

AIR

From Brindisi's small **airport** (BDS; ☑ 0831 411 74 06; www.aeroportidipuglia.it; Contrada Baroncino) there are domestic flights to Rome, Bologna, Naples, Turin and Milan. Airlines include Alitalia, Ryanair and easyJet. There are also direct flights from London Stansted with Ryanair.

BOAT

Ferries, all of which take vehicles, leave Brindisi for Greece and Albania.

Ferry companies have offices at Costa Morena (the newer port), which is 4km from the train station. A free bus connects the two.

Grimaldi Lines (☑ 0831 54 81 16; www.grimaldi-lines.com; Costa Morena Terminal) Frequent year-round ferries to Igoumenitsa (from €41, nine hours), Corfu (from €41, seven hours) and Patras (from €55, 17 hours) in Greece.

Red Star Ferries (☑ 0831 57 52 89; www.directferries.co.uk/red_star_ferries.htm; Costa Morena Terminal) To Vlorë in Albania, once a day (€42, five hours).

BUS

Pugliairbus (www.aeroportidipuglia.it) Services to Bari airport (€10, 1¾ hours) and Lecce (€7.50, 40 minutes) from Brindisi's airport.

Ferrovie del Sud-Est Buses serving local towns leave from Via Bastioni Carlo V, in front of the train station.

Marozzi (☑ 0831 52 16 84; www.marozzivt.it) Runs to Rome's Stazione Tiburtina (from €28, 6½ to 8½ hours, four daily) from Viale Arno.

STP Brindisi (www.stpbrindisi.it) Buses go regularly to Ostuni (€3.20, 50 minutes, frequent), Lecce (€6.30, 35 minutes, nine daily) and other towns throughout the Salento. Most leave from Via Bastioni Carlo V, in front of the train station.

TRAIN

Brindisi's train station has regular services to the following destinations:

Bari from €8.60, 1¼ hours

Lecce from €2.90, 30 minutes

Milan from €43.80, 8½ to 11 hours

Rome from €28, eight to 12 hours

Taranto from €5, one hour

ⓘ Getting Around

Major and local car-rental firms are represented at the airport. To reach the airport by bus, take the STP-run **Cotrap** (☑ 800 232042; www.stpbrindisi.it; ticket €1) bus from Via Bastioni Carlo V.

A free minibus connects the train station and old ferry terminal with Costa Morena. It departs two hours before boat departures. You'll need a valid ferry ticket.

Otranto

☑ 0836 / POP 5750

Bloodied and bruised by an infamous Turkish massacre in 1480, Otranto is best appreciated in its amazing cathedral, where the bones of 813 martyrs are displayed in a glass case behind the altar. The city has back-heeled quite a few invaders over the centuries and been brutally kicked by others – most notably the Turks. Sleuth around its compact old quarter and you can peel the past off in layers – Greek, Roman, Turkish and Napoleonic.

⊙ Sights

★ Cathedral   CATHEDRAL

(☑ 0836 80 27 20; Piazza Basilica; ⊙ 7am-noon & 3-8pm, shorter hours in winter) Mosaics, skulls, crypts and biblical-meets-tropical imagery: Otranto's cathedral is like no other in Italy. It was built by the Normans in the 11th century, incorporating Romanesque, Byzantine and early Christian styles with their own, and has been given a few facelifts since. Covering the entire floor is its pièce de résistance, a vast 12th-century mosaic of a stupendous tree of life balanced on the back of two elephants.

Castello Aragonese Otranto   CASTLE

(☑ 0836 21 00 94; www.castelloaragoneseotranto.com; Piazza Castello; adult/reduced €6/4; ⊙ 10am-8pm) Built in the late 15th century, when Otranto was more populous and important than today, and not long after the Ottoman raid that resulted in the execution of hundreds, the castle is a blunt and grim structure, well preserved internally and offering views from the outer walls. It is also famous from Horace Walpole's *The Castle of Otranto* (1764), recognised as the first Gothic novel. Ask about guided tours (adult/reduced €3/2) of the castle's underground area.

L'Approdo   PUBLIC ART

Dubbed *L'Approdo* (The Landing) and located in Otranto's new port area, this striking installation by the Greek artist Costas Varostos was erected in 2012. Sheathed in shards of green glass, it is based on the rusting infrastructure of the *Kateri i Rades,* a boat that foundered near Otranto in 1997 with the loss of 87 Albanian asylum seekers. More than 20 years after the tragedy, *L'Approdo* remains a poignant memorial to those seeking refuge across the Mediterranean in southern Europe.

Chiesa di San Pietro
CHURCH

(Via San Pietro; ⊙10am-noon & 4-8pm Jun-Sep, by request rest of year) The origins of this church are uncertain, but some think they may be as remote as the 5th century. The present structure seems to be a product of the 10th century, to which the oldest of the celebrated frescoes decorating its three apses dates.

🏃 Activities

There are some great beaches north of Otranto, especially Baia dei Turchi, with its translucent blue water. South of Otranto a spectacular rocky coastline makes for an impressive drive down to Castro. To see what goes on underwater, speak to Scuba Diving Otranto (✆0836 80 27 40; www.scubadiving.it; Via del Porto 1; 1-/2-tank dive incl equipment €48/75; ⊙7am-10pm).

🛏 Sleeping

Palazzo de Mori
B&B €€

(✆0836 80 10 88; www.palazzodemori.it; Bastione dei Pelasgi; d €160; ⊙Apr-Oct; ❄@) In Otranto's historic centre, this charming B&B serves fabulous breakfasts on the sun terrace overlooking the port. The rooms are decorated in soothing white on white.

★ Palazzo Papaleo
HOTEL €€€

(✆0836 80 21 08; www.hotelpalazzopapaleo.com; Via Rondachi 1; r from €230; P❄@🖥) Located next to the cathedral, this sumptuous hotel has magnificent rooms with original frescoes, exquisitely carved antique furniture and walls washed in soft greys, ochres and yellows. Soak in the panoramic views while enjoying the rooftop spa, or steam yourself pure in the hammam. The staff are exceptionally friendly.

🍴 Eating

SoFish
SEAFOOD €

(✆331 9867387; Corso Garibaldi 39; meals €10-15; ⊙noon-11pm) A modern update on a traditional *friggitoria,* SoFish features excellent fried seafood, good salads – the one with huge slabs of seared tuna almost overflows the plate – and a concise drinks list with Salento wines by the glass and a rather good selection of Italian craft beers. The fried calamari and octopus are both also very good.

★ L'Altro Baffo
SEAFOOD €€

(✆0836 80 16 36; www.laltrobaffo.com; Via Cenobio Basiliano 23; meals €40-45; ⊙12-2.30pm & 7.30pm-midnight Tue-Sun) This elegant modern restaurant near the castle stands out

in Otranto's competitive dining scene. It stays in touch with Pugliese and Italian principles, but ratchets things up several notches: the 'carbonara' made with sea-urchin roe is a daring instant classic. The menu is mainly seafood, but vegetarian dishes are anything but afterthoughts.

ℹ Information

Tourist Office (✆0836 80 14 36; Castello Aragonese Otranto; ⊙9am-1pm & 3-6pm) Located in the entrance to the castle.

ℹ Getting There & Away

Otranto can be reached from Lecce by FSE train (€3.50, 1½ hours). It is on a small branch line, which necessitates changing in Maglie and sometimes Zollino too. Services are reduced on Sundays. By bus, STP links directly from Lecce (€4.40, one hour, frequent).

Castro

✆0836 / POP 2450

One of Salento's most striking coastal settlements, the walled commune of Castro has a pedigree that predates the Romans, who gave it the name *Castrum Minervae,* or 'Minerva's Castle'. The castle and walls that remain today date to the 16th-century rule of the Aragonese, who built atop foundations laid by the Angevins and Byzantines before them. The charming old town, which also has a 12th-century cathedral, the remains of a Byzantine church and a clifftop piazza with delightful sea views, sits above a marina and terraced olive groves leading to a limestone coast riddled with spectacular caves.

◉ Sights

Grotta Zinzulusa
CAVE

(☑0836 94 38 12; Via Zinzulusa; adult/reduced €6/3; ☺9.30am-7pm Jul & Aug, shorter hours rest of year; 🅿) An aperture on the Ionian coast below Castro leads into this magnificent cave, one of the most significant coastal limestone karst formations in Italy. The portion accessible to the public stretches hundreds of metres back from the cliff face, terminating in a chamber grand enough to justify the sobriquet 'Il Duomo'. Divided into three distinct geomorphological sections, Zinzulusa is home to endemic crustacea and other 'living fossils' known nowhere else on the planet.

Castello Aragonese
CASTLE

(☑0836 94 70 05; Via Sant Antonio 1; adult/reduced €2.50/2; ☺10am-1pm & 3-7.30pm) Primarily the work of the Aragonese who ruled southern Italy in the 16th century, this sturdy redoubt retains elements built by the Angevins in previous centuries, on earlier Byzantine foundations. Partly ruinous by the 18th century, it's been restored, and now houses a small museum, exhibiting archaeology uncovered in Castro and the surrounding area. Its prize piece is a torso of the goddess Minerva (Athena), buried at the ancient city gates.

❶ Getting There & Away

STP Lecce runs a daily bus between Castro and Lecce (€4, 90 minutes).

Gallipoli

☑ 0833 / POP 20.700

Like Taranto, Gallipoli is a two-part town: the modern hub is based on the mainland, while the older *centro storico* inhabits a small island that juts out into the Ionian Sea. With a raft of serene baroque architecture usurped only by Lecce, it is, arguably, the prettiest of Salento's smaller settlements.

◉ Sights

Gallipoli has some fine beaches, including the **Baia Verde**, just south of town. Nature enthusiasts will want to take a day trip to **Parco Regionale Porto Selvaggio**, about 20km north – a protected area of wild coastline with walking trails among the trees and diving off the rocky shore.

Cattedrale di Sant'Agata
CATHEDRAL

(www.cattedralegallipoli.it; Via Duomo 1; ☺hours vary) On the island, Gallipoli's 17th-century cathedral is a baroque beauty that could compete with anything in Lecce. Not surprisingly, Giuseppe Zimbalo, who helped beautify Lecce's Santa Croce basilica, worked on the facade.

Frantoio Ipogeo
HISTORIC SITE

(☑0833 26 42 42; Via Antonietta de Pace 87; €1.50; ☺10am-1pm & 3-6pm) This is only one of some 35 olive presses buried in the tufa rock below the town. It was here, between the 16th and early 19th centuries, that local workers pressed Gallipoli's olive oil, which was then stored in one of the 2000 cisterns carved beneath the old town.

🛏 Sleeping

Insula
B&B €

(☑329 8070056, 0833 20 14 13; www.bbinsula gallipoli.it; Via Antonietta de Pace 56; d €80; ☺Apr-Oct; ❋ @) A magnificent 16th-century building houses this memorable B&B. The five rooms share the same princely atmosphere with antiques, vaulted high ceilings and cool pastel paintwork. Directly adjacent to the cathedral, it couldn't be any more central.

Hotel Palazzo del Corso
HOTEL €€€

(☑0833 26 40 40; www.hotelpalazzodelcorso.it; Corso Roma 145; r/ste €220/370; 🅿 ❋ 🛰 ⛱) It's worth forking out a bit extra for this beautiful town hotel, if you fancy a bit of luxury. The rooms are furnished distinctively enough to avoid looking too corporate, there's a gym and a fantastic terrace complete with a small swimming pool.

🍴 Eating

Gallipoli is famous for its red prawns and its soothing *spumone* layered gelato.

Baguetteria de Pace
SANDWICHES €

(www.facebook.com/baguetteriadepace; Via Sant'Angelo 8; baguettes €6-8; ☺11am-3pm & 7-11pm) The Italian art of making exceptional sandwiches is practised assiduously here. Choose the dense Italian bread (or a baguette if you're feeling fluffy) and have the friendly staff stuff it with top-notch smallgoods, cheeses, vegetables and whatever else takes your fancy. Especially good is the black pork salami with local burrata cheese. Salento wines and craft beer are also available.

La Puritate
SEAFOOD €€€

(☑0833 26 42 05; Via Sant'Elia 18; meals €50; ☺12.30-3pm & 7.30-10.30pm, closed Wed winter) Book ahead to ensure your table at *the* place for fish in this seafood-loving town. Anything fishy is good (especially the prawns, swordfish and tuna) and the picture windows allow splendid views of the waters whence it came.

Taranto

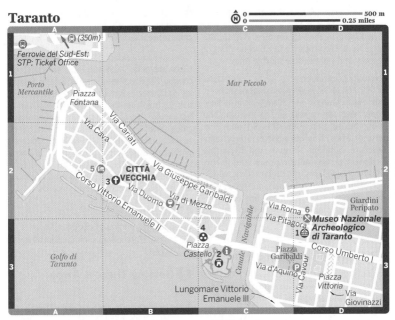

ℹ Information

Tourist Office (☑ 0833 26 25 29; Via Antonietta de Pace 86; ☉ 8am-9pm summer, 8am-1pm & 4-9pm Mon-Sat winter) Near the cathedral in the old town.

ℹ Getting There & Away

FSE (www.fseonline.it) buses and trains head direct to Lecce (€4.40, 1¾ hours, frequent).

Taranto

☑ 099 / POP 199,560

Not generally considered to be on the tourist circuit, Taranto is rimmed by modern industry, including a massive steelworks, and is home to Italy's second biggest naval base after La Spezia. Thanks to an illustrious Greek and Roman history, it has been bequeathed with one of the finest Magna Graecia museums in Italy. For this reason alone, it's worth a stopover.

◉ Sights

★ Museo Nazionale Archeologico di Taranto
MUSEUM

(☑ 099 453 21 12; www.museotaranto.org; Via Cavour 10; adult/reduced €5/2.50; ☉ 9am-7.30pm) Sitting unassumingly in a side street in Taranto's new town is one of Italy's most important archaeological museums, chiefly dedicated to the archaeology of ancient Taras

---

Taranto

◉ **Top Sights**
1 Museo Nazionale Archeologico di
   Taranto D3

◎ **Sights**
2 Castello Aragonese C3
3 Cathedral B2
4 Temple of Poseidon C3

🛏 **Sleeping**
5 Hotel Akropolis A2

🍴 **Eating**
6 Trattoria al Gatto Rosso D3

🍷 **Drinking & Nightlife**
7 Cibo per la Mente B2

(Taranto). It houses, among other artefacts, the largest collection of Greek terracotta figures in the world. Also on display are fine collections of 1st-century-BCE glassware, classic black-and-red Attic vases and stunning gold and jewellery from Magna Graecia, such as a 4th-century-BCE bronze and terracotta crown.

Cathedral
CATHEDRAL

(Piazza Duomo; ☉ 4.30-7.30pm daily, 7.30am-noon Sat & Sun) The 11th-century cathedral is one of Puglia's oldest Romanesque buildings and an extravagant treat. It's dedicated to San Cataldo, an Irish monk who lived and was buried here in the 7th century. Within, the Capella di San Cataldo is a baroque riot of frescoes and polychrome marble inlay.

Castello Aragonese — CASTLE

(☑ 099 775 34 38; www.castelloaragonesetaranto. com; Piazza Castello; ⊙ 9.30am-1.30pm summer, shorter hours rest of year) FREE Guarding the swing bridge that joins the old and new parts of town, this impressive 15th-century structure, built on Norman and Byzantine predecessors, was once a prison and is currently occupied by the Italian navy, which has restored it. Multilingual and free guided tours, mandatory to get inside, are led by naval officers throughout the day. Opposite are the two remaining columns of the ancient Temple of Poseidon.

✯ Festivals & Events

Le Feste di Pasqua — RELIGIOUS
Taranto is famous for its Holy Week celebrations – the biggest in the region – when bearers in Ku Klux Klan–style robes carry icons around the town. There are three processions: the Perdoni, celebrating pilgrims; the Addolorata (lasting 12 hours but covering only 4km); and the Misteri (even slower at 14 hours to cover 2km).

🛏 Sleeping

Hotel Akropolis — HOTEL €€
(☑ 099 470 41 10; www.hotelakropolis.it; Vico Seminario 3; s/d/ste €90/120/160; ❄ @ ☎) If Taranto's richly historic yet crumbling old town is ever to be reborn, it will be due to businesses such as this hotel – a converted medieval palazzo with a heavy Greek theme. It offers 13 stylish cream-and-white rooms, beautiful majolica-tiled floors, a panoramic rooftop terrace and an atmospheric bar and restaurant, decked out in stone, wood and glass.

🍴 Eating & Drinking

Trattoria al Gatto Rosso — TRATTORIA €€
(☑ 340 5337800, 099 452 98 75; www.ristorante gattorosso.com; Via Cavour 2; meals €35-40; ⊙ 12.30-3pm & 7.30-11pm Tue-Sun) Unsurprisingly, seafood is the thing at the Red Cat. Relaxed and unpretentious, its heavy tablecloths, deep wine glasses and solid cutlery set the scene for full enjoyment of dishes such as spaghetti with local clams and slow-cooked swordfish with eggplant caponata (sweet-and-sour vegetable salad). Rooms at

Gatto Rosso's adjacent Baylon Guesthouse are stylish and colourful and include an excellent breakfast.

Cibo per la Mente — BAR
(Caffe Letterario; ☑ 099 400 75 20; www.facebook. com/pg/CiboPerLaMenteTaranto; Palazzo Gennarini, Via Duomo; ⊙ 9am-11pm Mon-Thu, to 1am Fri & Sat; ☎) Inspiring the reinvigoration of Taranto's centro storico is this cool and compact cafe. Local cats mooch around on bench seats outside, while the interior adorned with books and quirky prints of David Bowie is good for a coffee or cocktail. Light snacks are available, and the space is used occasionally for live music and literary events.

ℹ Information

Tourist office (☑ 334 2844098; Castello Aragonese; ⊙ 9am-8pm summer, shorter hours rest of year)

ℹ Getting There & Away

BUS
Buses heading north and west depart from Porto Mercantile. **FSE** (☑ 080 546 21 11; www. fseonline.it) buses go to Bari (€8.60, 3¼ hours, four per day); **STP** (☑ 080 975 26 19) buses go to Lecce, with a change at Monteparano (€6.80, two hours, four daily).

Marozzi (☑ 080 5799 0211; www.marozzivt. it) has express services serving Rome's Stazione Tiburtina (from €32, six to eight hours, four daily); **Autolinee Miccolis** (☑ 099 470 44 51; www.busmiccolis.it) serves Naples (from €16, four hours, three daily).

The bus **ticket office** (⊙ 6am-1pm & 2-7pm) is at Porto Mercantile.

TRAIN
From **Taranto Centrale** (Piazza Moro), Trenitalia and FSE trains go to the following destinations:

Bari €8.60, 1¼ hours, frequent

Brindisi €5, one hour, frequent

Rome from €52.50, six hours, five daily

AMAT (☑ 099 452 67 32; www.amat.taranto. it) buses run between the train station and the new city.

BASILICATA

Much of Basilicata is an otherworldly landscape of mountain ranges, trackless forests and villages that seem to sprout organically from the granite. Not easily penetrated, it is strategically located, and has been dominated by the Lucanians, Greeks, Romans,

Germans, Lombards, Byzantines, Saracens, Normans and others. Being the plaything of such powers has not been conducive to a quiet or happy fate.

In the north the landscape is a fertile zone of gentle hills and deep valleys; the interior is dominated by the Lucanian Apennines and the Parco Nazionale del Pollino. The Tyrrhenian coast is a fissured wonderland of rocky coves and precariously sited villages. Here, Maratea is one of Italy's most charming seaside resorts.

But it is inland Matera, where primitive *sassi* (caves) lurk under grand cathedrals, that is Basilicata's most precious gem. The third-oldest continuously inhabited city in the world, it's intriguing, breathtaking and tragic in equal measures.

History

Basilicata spans Italy's 'instep', and is landlocked apart from slivers of Tyrrhenian and Ionian coastline. It was known to the Greeks and Romans as Lucania, after the Lucani tribe who lived here as far back as the 5th century BCE. The name survives in the 'Lucanian Dolomites', 'Lucanian cooking' and elsewhere. The Greeks also prospered in ancient Basilicata, possibly settling along the coastline at Metapontum and Erakleia as far back as the 8th century BCE. Roman power came next, and the Punic Wars between that expanding power and Carthage. Hannibal, the ferocious Carthaginian general, rampaged through the region, making the city of Grumentum his base.

In the 10th century, the Byzantine Emperor Basil II (976–1025) bestowed his title, 'Basileus', on the region, overthrew the Saracens in southern Italy and reintroduced Christianity. The pattern of war and overthrow continued throughout the Middle Ages right up until the 19th century, as the Normans, Hohenstaufens, Angevins and Bourbons ceaselessly tussled over this strategic location. As talk of the Italian unification began to gain ground, Bourbon-sponsored loyalists took to Basilicata's mountains to oppose political change. Ultimately, they became the much-feared bandits of local lore who make scary appearances in writings from the late 19th and early 20th centuries. In the 1930s, Basilicata was used as a kind of open prison for political dissidents – most famously the painter, writer and doctor Carlo Levi – sent into exile to remote villages by the fascists.

Matera

0835 / POP 60,350 / ELEV 405M

Matera, Basilicata's jewel, may be the world's third-longest continuously inhabited human settlement. Natural caves in the tufa limestone, exposed as the Gravina cut its gorge, attracted the first inhabitants perhaps 7000 years ago. More elaborate structures were built atop them. Today, looking across the gorge to Matera's huddled *sassi* (cave dwellings) it seems you've been transported back to the ancient Holy Land.

Old Matera is split into two sections – the Sasso Barisano and the Sasso Caveoso – separated by a ridge upon which sits Matera's gracious *duomo* (cathedral). The *sassi*, many little more than one-room caves, once contained such appalling poverty and unthinkable living conditions that in the 1950s Matera was denounced as the 'Shame of Italy', and the *sassi*-dwellers were moved on. Only in later decades has the value of this extraordinarily built environment been recognised, and in 2019 the city was recognised as a European Capital of Culture.

◉ Sights

The two *sassi* districts – the more restored, northwest-facing Sasso Barisano and the more impoverished, northeast-facing Sasso Caveoso – are both extraordinary, riddled with serpentine alleyways and staircases, and dotted with frescoed *chiese rupestri* (cave churches) created between the 8th and 13th centuries. Modern Matera still contains some 3000 habitable caves.

The *sassi* are accessible from several points. There's an entrance off Piazza San Francisco, or take Via delle Beccherie to Piazza del Duomo and follow the tourist itinerary signs to enter either Barisano or Caveoso. Sasso Caveoso is also accessible from Via Ridola.

For a great photograph, head out of town for about 3km on the Taranto–Laterza road and follow signs for the *chiese rupestri*. This takes you up on the Murgia Plateau to the belvedere (Contrada Murgia Timone), from where you have fantastic views of the plunging ravine and Matera.

◉ Sasso Barisano

★ Chiesa San Pietro Barisano   CHURCH
(342 0319991; www.oltrelartematera.it; Piazza San Pietro Barisano; adult/reduced €3.50/2.50, incl Chiesa di Santa Lucia alle Malve & Chiesa di Santa

Matera

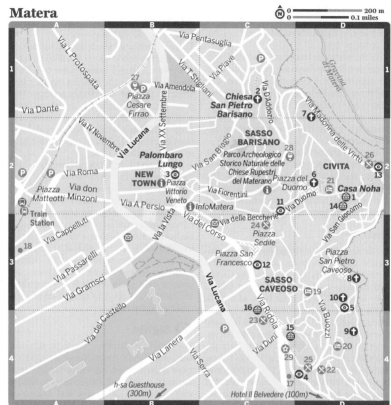

Maria di Idris €7/5; ⊙9am-8pm Apr-Oct, 10am-5pm Nov-Mar) Dating in its earliest parts to the 12th century, St Peter's, the largest of Matera's rupestrian churches, overlays an ancient honeycomb of niches where corpses were placed for draining. At the entrance level can be found 15th- and 16th-century frescoes of the Annunciation and a variety of saints. The empty frame of the altarpiece graphically illustrates the town's troubled recent history: the church was plundered when Matera was partially abandoned in the 1960s and '70s.

Chiesa di Madonna delle Virtù
& Chiesa di San Nicola dei Greci   CHURCH

(☑377 4448885; www.caveheritage.it; Via Madonna delle Virtù; ⊙10am-8pm Jun-Sep, shorter hours rest of year) **FREE** This monastic complex, one of the most important monuments in Matera, comprises dozens of chambers carved into the tufa limestone over two floors. Chiesa di Madonna delle Virtù was built in the 10th or

11th century and restored in the 17th. Above it, the simple Chiesa di San Nicola dei Greci is rich in frescoes. The complex was used in 1213 by Benedictine monks of Palestinian origin. The churches are sometimes used for art installations (admission charges apply).

⊙ Sasso Caveoso

★Casa Noha   MUSEUM

(☑0835 33 54 52; www.fondoambiente.it/casa-noha-eng; Recinto Cavone 9; adult/reduced €6/2; ⊙9am-7pm Apr-Oct, shorter hours rest of year) Highly recommended as a precursor to visiting the *sassi* themselves, this wonderful 25-minute multimedia exhibit, spread across three rooms of a 16th-century family home donated to the Fondo Ambiente Italiano, relates the astonishing and often painful social history of the town and its *sassi*. Your appreciation of Matera's unique history and renaissance, and the tribulations of the *sassi* dwellers, will be transformed.

Matera

Museo della Scultura
Contemporanea   MUSEUM
(MUSMA; ☑ 366 9357768; www.musma.it; Via San Giacomo; adult/reduced €5/3.50; ⊙ 10am-8pm Apr-Sep, to 6pm Oct-Mar) The setting of this fabulous museum of contemporary sculpture – deeply recessed caves and the frescoed rooms of the 16th-century Palazzo Pomarici – is as extraordinary as the exhibits. Italian sculpture from the late 19th century to the present day is the principal focus, but you can also see beautiful examples of graphic art, jewellery and ceramics.

Chiesa di San Pietro Caveoso   CHURCH
(☑ 0835 31 15 10; Piazza San Pietro Caveoso 1; ⊙ Mass 7pm Mon-Sat, 11am & 7pm Sun) FREE The only church in the *sassi* not dug into the tufa rock, Chiesa di San Pietro Caveoso was originally built in 1300 and has a 17th-century Romanesque-baroque facade and frescoed timber ceiling.

Chiesa di Santa Maria di Idris   CHURCH
(☑ 344 2763197; www.oltrelatematera.it; Piazza San Pietro Caveoso; adult/reduced €3.50/2.50, incl Chiesa San Pietro Barisano & Chiesa di Santa Lucia alle Malve €7/5; ⊙ 9am-8pm Apr-Oct, 10am-5pm Nov-Mar) Dug into the Idris rock, this church has an unprepossessing facade, but the narrow corridor communicating with the recessed church of San Giovanni in Monterrone is richly decorated with 12th- to 17th-century frescoes.

Chiesa di Santa Lucia alle Malve   CHURCH
(☑ 342 0919624; www.oltrelatematera.it; Rione Malve; adult/reduced €3.50/2.50, incl Chiesa San Pietro Barisano & Chiesa di Santa Maria di Idris €7/5; ⊙ 9am-8pm Apr-Oct, 10am-5pm Nov-Mar) Dating to the 8th century, when it was built as the Benedictine Order's first foothold in Matera, this cliff-face church has a number of 13th-century frescoes, including an unusual breastfeeding Madonna. The church originally comprised three aisles, with two later adapted as dwellings.

Casa-Grotta di Vico Solitario   HISTORIC SITE
(€3; ⊙ 9.30am-late) For a glimpse of life in old Matera, visit this historic *sasso* off Via Bruno Buozzi. There's a bed in the middle, a loom, a room for manure and a section for a pig and a donkey. You also have access to a couple of neighbouring caves: in one there's, a black-and-white film depicting gritty pre-restoration Matera.

◎ New Town

The nucleus of the new town is **Piazza Vittorio Veneto**, an excellent, bustling meeting point for a *passeggiata* (sociable evening stroll). It's surrounded by elegant churches and richly adorned *palazzi* with their backs deliberately turned on the *sassi*: an attempt by the bourgeois to block out the shameful poverty the *sassi* once represented.

★ **Palombaro Lungo**   HISTORIC SITE

(☑ 339 3638332; Piazza Vittorio Veneto; guided tour €3; ⊙ 10am-1pm & 3-6pm) This giant cistern, arguably as magnificent as a subterranean cathedral, is one of Matera's great sights. Lying under the city's main square with arches carved out of the existing rock, it is mind-boggling in its scale and ingenuity, and was still supplying water to Materans within living memory. Book ahead for a 25-minute tour with the multilingual guides, who explain its conception and history (English-language tours generally leave at 10.30am, 12.30pm, 3.30pm and 5.30pm).

Museo Nazionale d'Arte Medievale e Moderna della Basilicata   MUSEUM

(☑ 0835 25 62 11; www.musei.basilicata.benicul turali.it; Piazzetta Pascoli 1, Palazzo Lanfranchi; adult/reduced €3/1.50; ⊙ 9am-8pm Thu-Tue, from 11am Wed) The Palazzo Lanfranchi, built as a seminary incorporating an earlier church in the 17th century, now houses this intriguing museum of sacred and contemporary art. The stars of the show here are Carlo Levi's paintings, including the panoramic mural *Lucania '61* depicting peasant life in biblical technicolour. There are also some centuries-old sacred art from the *sassi*.

Cathedral   CATHEDRAL

(☑ 0835 33 29 08; www.matera-irsina.chiesacat tolica.it; Piazza del Duomo; ⊙ 9am-7pm) Set high up on a spur between the two natural bowls of the *sassi*, the wan, graceful exterior of the 13th-century Pugliese-Romanesque cathedral makes the neobaroque excess with-

in all the more of a surprise. Following 13 years of renovation, it's possible once again to admire the ornate capitals, sumptuous chapels, 17th-century frescoes, 13th-century Byzantine Madonna and two 12th-century frescoed crypts, uncovered in the works. Note the pediments mounted on the cathedral's altars, which come from Greek temples at Metaponto.

Museo Nazionale Ridola   MUSEUM

(☑ 0835 31 00 58; www.musei.basilicata.benicul turali.it; Via Ridola 24; adult/reduced €2.50/1.25; ⊙ 9am-8pm Tue-Sun, 2-8pm Mon) This impressive collection includes local Neolithic finds and some remarkable Greek pottery, such as the *Cratere Mascheroni*, a huge urn more than 1m high.

🏃 Activities

Eldorado Ranch   HORSE RIDING

(☑ 328 7610502; www.eledoradoranch.it; Strada Statale 7; 1hr ride €30; ⊙ 9am-7pm) A few kilometres south of Matera, this well-run horseback-riding outfit takes tours (one to two hours) through the Gravina gorge, or south, to the Cripta del Peccato Originale. It's a delightful day trip outside Matera, if you're here for a while.

🎓 Courses

Cook'n Fun at Mary's   COOKING

(☑ 320 6936553; www.cooknfunatmarys.com; Via Monsignor Macco 67a; per person €100) Fresh produce from the kitchen garden is the foundation of the traditional Lucanian recipes taught in Mary's relaxed domestic kitchen.

EXPLORING THE GRAVINA GORGE

In the picturesque landscape of the Murgia Plateau, the Matera Gravina cuts a rough gouge in the earth, a 200m-deep canyon pockmarked with abandoned caves and villages and roughly 150 mysterious *chiese rupestri* (cave churches). The area is protected as the Parco della Murgia Materana, an 80-sq-km wild park formed in 1990 and, since 2007, included in Matera's Unesco World Heritage Site. You can hike from the *sassi* into the gorge; steps lead down from the parking place near the Monasterio di Santa Lucia (Via Madonna delle Virtù; ⊙ 7.30am-1pm & 5-8.30pm). At the bottom of the gorge you have to ford a river and then climb up to the belvedere on the other side; this takes roughly two hours.

Cave churches accessible from the belvedere include San Falcione, Sant'Agnese and Madonna delle Tre Porte. The belvedere is connected by road to the Jazzo Gattini (p177) visitor centre, housed in an old sheepfold. Guided hikes can be organised here, as can walks to the nearby Neolithic village of Murgia Timone. For longer forays into the park, including a long day trek to the town of Montescaglioso, consider a guided hike with Ferula Viaggi (☑ 0835 33 65 72; www.ferulaviaggi.it; Via Cappelluti 34; ⊙ 9am-1.30pm & 3.30-7pm Mon-Sat). Beware: paths and river crossings in the park can be treacherous during and after bad weather.

Classes are in English, and culminate in a meal and glass of wine.

👉 Tours

Amy Weideman
TOURS

(☑ 339 2823618; www.materatours.net; half-day tour for 1-3 people €80, for 4 or more people €100) Amy Weideman offers an English-speaking expat's perspective on her adopted home of Matera, with tours ranging from 2½ hours to full-day excursions and trips further afield (to the delightful hilltop towns of Pietrapertosa and Castelmezzano, for example). Highly recommended.

Altieri Viaggi
TOURS

(☑ 346 6453440, 0835 31 43 59; www.altieriviaggi.it; Via Ridola 61; ⊘ 9am-9pm) Runs tours around the *sassi* and rupestrian churches of Matera and the Parco della Murgia, starting from €20 for a 50-minute tour (minimum four people). Altieri also offers plenty of other trips, including hiking and *sassi* tours by *ape calessino* (autorickshaw). Tours usually end with a tasting of typical local products.

🎊 Festivals & Events

Sagra della Madonna della Bruna
RELIGIOUS

(⊘ 2 Jul) This week-long celebration of Matera's patron saint has 14th-century roots. The culminating day, 2 July, begins at dawn with the colourful 'Procession of Shepherds', in which an image of the Virgin is carried through Matera's neighbourhoods. The finale is the *assalto al carro,* when the crowd descends on the ornately decorated main float and tears it to pieces.

🛏 Sleeping

Matera's unique appeal has seen accommodation options mushroom across the *sassi* and the new town. Take your pick: a smartly refurbished *sasso,* a room in a repurposed *palazzo,* or something more modern in the new town. Cheaper options can still be found.

h-sa Guesthouse
B&B €

(☑ 340 7062574; Via Pasquale Vena 87; d from €80; 🅿 ❄ 🖥) In a quiet residential neighbourhood around 1km walk from central Matera, the modern h-sa Guesthouse is an excellent option if you're travelling with a car. There's plenty of free off-street parking, and the friendly family owners provide an excellent breakfast. In warmer weather, stylish rooms open onto leafy gardens with outdoor seating and places to relax. Book through online booking websites.

La Dolce Vita B&B
B&B €

(☑ 328 7111121, 0835 31 03 24; www.ladolcevitamatera.it; Rione Malve 51; r €80; 🖥) 🚲 This delightful, ecofriendly B&B in Sasso Caveoso comprises two self-contained apartments with solar panels, rainwater recycling, a scenic terrace and cool, comfortable furnishings. Owners Vincenzo and Carla are passionate about Matera and are mines of information on the *sassi.*

Il Vicinato
B&B €

(☑ 380 1828935; www.ilvicinato.com; Piazzetta San Pietro Caveoso 7; s/d €60/90; ❄ 🖥) Run by Luigi and Teresa, 'The Neighbourhood' is wonderfully located in Sasso Caveoso, in a building dating in parts to around 1600. Rooms are decorated in clean modern lines, with views across to the Murgia Plateau. As well as the standard rooms, there's a room with a balcony and a small apartment, each with an independent entrance.

⭐ Hotel Il Belvedere
HOTEL €€

(☑ 0835 31 17 02; www.hotelbelvedere.matera.it; Via Casalnuovo 133; d from €135; ❄ 🖥) This cave boutique looks unremarkable from its street-side perch on the edge of the Sasso Caveoso, but you'll feel your jaw start to drop as you enter its luxurious entrails and spy the spectacle of Old Matera sprawling below a jutting terrace. Cavernous rooms sport mosaics, mood lighting and curtained four-poster beds. Two-night minimums apply in August.

Palazzo Viceconte
HOTEL €€

(☑ 0835 33 06 99; www.palazzoviceconte.it; Via San Potito 7; d/ste from €158/220; ❄ 🖥) You won't have trouble spotting the palatial features at this 17th-century *palazzo* near the cathedral with superb views of the *sassi* and gorge. The 14 rooms are elegantly furnished, the bathrooms all have baths and the rooftop terrace has panoramic views. Be king (or queen) for a day (or more) amid the courtyards, salons, frescoed ceilings and antiques.

Corte San Pietro
BOUTIQUE HOTEL €€€

(☑ 0835 31 08 13; www.cortesanpietro.it; Via Buozzi 97; d €230; ❄ 🖥) Located in Sasso Caveoso, the family-owned Corte San Pietro is one of Matera's most comfortable boutique hotels. Each room is a different shape and size, designed to fit the idiosyncratic cave location, and the shadow and light interplay of the interior is sometimes used to showcase interesting art installations.

WORTH A TRIP

CRIPTA DEL PECCATO ORIGINALE

A fascinating Benedictine site dating to the Lombard period, the **Cripta del Peccato Originale** (✆320 3345323; www.criptadelpeccatooriginale.it; Contrada Pietrapenta; adult/reduced €10/8; ⊘10am-1.30pm & 4-7.30pm Tue-Sun Apr-Sep, shorter hours rest of year) houses well-preserved 8th-century frescoes – depicting vivid scenes from both Old and New Testaments – that have earned it a reputation as the 'Sistine Chapel' of Matera's cave churches. It's 7km south of Matera: all visits must be booked through the website, then joined at the ticket office (at Azienda Agricola Dragone on Contrada Pietrapenta) 30 minutes prior to the scheduled starting time.

✖ Eating

★**I Vizi degli Angeli**   GELATO €
(✆0835 31 06 37; www.ivizidegliangeli.it; Via Ridola 36; medium cone €23; ⊘noon-11pm Thu-Tue) 'The Angels' Vices', an artisanal gelato 'laboratory' on the busy promenade of Via Domenico Ridola, is Matera's best. Alongside classics such as pistachio, you'll find experimental flavours such as grapefruit with pink pepper and thyme and mallow, which taste even better than they read.

enoteca dai tosi   ITALIAN €€
(✆0835 31 40 29; www.enotecadaitosi.it; Via Buozzi 12; meals €30-35; ⊘noon-3pm & 7pm-late Wed-Mon) Easily Matera's most spectacular wine bar and restaurant, enoteca dai tosi's subterranean space enlivened with shimmering green glass is a top place to partner wines from southern Italy with a concise selection of shared plates. Standout tapas-style dishes include fava bean and chicory croquettes and the stuffed calamari with zucchini. Tasting platters (€12 to €28) of cheese and charcuterie are good value.

La Gatta Buia   ITALIAN €€
(✆0835 25 65 10; www.lagattabuia.eu; Via delle Beccherie 90-92; meals €38; ⊘1-3pm & 7.30-11pm) With a sleekly decorated bar and dining areas and a menu that goes beyond Basilicatan classics, 'The Good Cat' is another feather in the cap of Matera's increasing sophistication. Wines from Lombardy, Piedmont and Abruzzo join the local drops to help you wash

down veal cheeks braised in Aglianico wine, or Sicilianesque pasta with cod, raisins, pine nuts, tomatoes and olives.

L'Abbondanza Lucana   ITALIAN €€
(✆0835 33 45 74; Via Buozzi 11; meals €45; ⊘noon-3pm Tue-Sun, 7-11pm Tue-Sat) The paradoxical bounty of Lucania's *cucina povera* is laid out before you in this stone cellar in Sasso Caveoso. For a fantastic introduction to a range of *prodotti tipici* from the region, start with the Lucanian tasting plate, laden with delights such as wild boar, baked ricotta and a soup of chestnuts with Sarconi's famous beans.

★**Vitoantonio Lombardo**   ITALIAN €€€
(✆0835 33 54 75; www.vlristorante.it; Via Madonna delle Virtu 13/14; meals €85-130; ⊘12.30-2pm & 7.30-10pm Thu-Mon, 7.30-10pm Wed) Degustation menus from five to 12 courses provide a sumptuous experience of elevated Italian cuisine at Matera's most innovative restaurant. Menu options include lamb with fennel, lemon and liquorice, and a dessert of ravioli with salted ricotta cheese and a basil and tomato sorbet. Yes, it's pricey, but it will be the Materan meal you remember the most. Bookings essential.

☗ Drinking & Nightlife

Options for drinking and socialising have mushroomed, along with Matera's renaissance. You'll find wine bars, pubs and *enotecas* along Via Domenico Ridola, Via Fiorentini, Via San Biagio and Via delle Beccherie, and also dotted throughout the *sassi*.

★**Malto & Luppolo**   CRAFT BEER
(✆327 4405292; www.facebook.com/maltoeluppolomatera; Piazza Firrao 25; ⊘6pm-midnight Tue-Sun) A short walk from Piazza Vittorio Veneto but off the tourist trail is this warm and welcoming bar specialising in Italian craft beer. Four rotating taps feature regular surprises and the bar fridge has interesting tipples like a nectarine-flavoured sour beer. The friendly owner's English is better than he thinks.

Vicolo Cieco   WINE BAR
(✆338 8550984; www.facebook.com/vicolocieco salsamenteria; Via Fiorentini 74; ⊘6pm-2am Tue-Thu, from noon Fri-Sun) Matera's renaissance and relaxed vitality come to the fore at this wine bar in a typical cave-house off Sasso Barisano's main drag. The eccentric decor signals its friendly, upbeat spirit – retro jukeboxes, a wall-mounted Scalextric track,

chairs cut in half and glued to the wall in the name of art, and a chandelier of repurposed cutlery.

★ Entertainment

★ Area 8   LIVE MUSIC
(☑ 333 3369788; http://area8.it; Via Casalnuovo 15; ☺ 7.30pm-3am Wed-Sun) This unusual cafe/bar and 'nano-theatre' is a production agency by day, but comes alive four nights a week to host film screenings, live music, product launches and other events beneath its beautiful creamy arches.

ℹ️ Information

POST

Post Office (☑ 0835 25 70 40; Via del Corso 15; ☺ 8am-1.30pm Mon-Fri, to 12.30pm Sat; ☎)
Post Office (☑ 0835 24 55 32; Via Passarelli 13B; ☺ 8.30am-7pm Mon-Fri, to 12.30pm Sat; ☎)

TOURIST INFORMATION

Basilicata Turistica (www.aptbasilicata.it) is the official tourist website with useful information on history, culture, attractions and sights. Sassiweb (www.sassiweb.it) is another informative website on Matera. Quite a few private operators also advertise themselves as tourist information offices. They're there to sell tours, generally, but can still give good (if not impartial) advice.

InfoMatera (☑ 0835 68 02 54; Piazza Veneto 39; ☺ 9am-8pm) This private operator in Matera's new town offers advice on sights, accommodation, tours and more.

Jazzo Gattini (☑ 0835 33 22 62; www.ceamatera.it; Contrada Murgia Timone; ☺ 9.30am-2.30pm & 4-6.30pm Apr-Oct, shorter hours rest of year) Home to the visitor centre of the Parco della Murgia Materana.

Parco Archeologico Storico Naturale delle Chiese Rupestri del Materano (☑ 0835 33 61 66; www.parcomurgia.it; Via Dolori 10; ☺ 9.30am-6.30pm) For info on Parco della Murgia Materana.

Tourist Information Centre (Basilicata Open Space; www.basilicataturistica.it; Piazza Vittorio Veneto, Palazzo dell'Annunziata; ☺ 9am-9pm) Centrally located. Includes galleries focusing on Matera's history.

ℹ️ Getting There & Away

BUS

The bus station is south of Piazza Matteotti, next to the subterranean **train station** (Piazza Matteotti).

Marino (www.marinobus.it) For Naples (€12, 4¾ hours, six daily).

Marozzi (☑ 06 225 21 47; www.marozzivt.it) For Rome (€30, six to seven hours, five daily), Siena (€39, 8¼ hours, one daily), Florence (€43, 9½ hours, one daily) and Pisa (€48, 11¾ hours, one daily).

Pugliairbus (☑ 080 579 02 11; www.aeroportidipuglia.it) For Bari airport (€6, 1¼ hours, five daily).

SITA (☑ 0835 38 50 07; www.sitabus.it) For Taranto (from €8, 1¾ hours, three daily).

TRAIN

Ferrovie Appulo-Lucane (FAL; ☑ 800 050500; http://ferrovieappulolucane.it) For Bari (€5, 1¾ hours).

Appennino Lucano

The Appennino Lucano (Lucanian Apennines) bite Basilicata in half like a row of jagged teeth. Sharply rearing up south of Potenza, they protect the lush Tyrrhenian coast and leave the Ionian shores gasping in the semi-arid heat. Much of the area is protected by the **Parco Nazionale Dell'Appennino Lucano**, inaugurated in 2007 and the second-youngest of Italy's 25 national parks.

Aside from its gorgeous mountain terrain, the park's most iconic site is the abandoned Roman town of **Grumentum**, 75km south of Potenza and just outside the town of Grumento Nova. In the granite eyries of Pietrapertosa and Castelmezzano, it can also lay claim to two of Italy's most strikingly situated hill towns.

Castelmezzano & Pietrapertosa

The two mountaintop villages of Castelmezzano (elevation 985m) and Pietrapertosa (elevation 1088m), ringed by the Lucanian Dolomites, are spectacular. Basilicata's highest villages, they're often swathed in cloud, making you wonder why anyone would build here, in a territory best suited to goats.

Castelmezzano is surely one of Italy's most theatrical villages: the houses huddle along an impossibly narrow ledge that falls away in gorges to the Rio di Caperrino. **Pietrapertosa** is possibly even more amazing: the Saracen fortress at its pinnacle is difficult to spot as it is carved out of the mountain. Despite difficulties of access, the towns can be swarmed by Italian tourists on weekends and holidays. Foreign visitors are scarcer.

You can 'fly' between these two dramatic settlements courtesy of Il Volo dell'Angelo, two heart-in-mouth zip lines across the void. Another option is to walk 7km across the valley on the Sentiero Sette Pietre (Path of the Seven Stones).

🏃 Activities

★ Il Volo dell'Angelo
ADVENTURE SPORTS

(Angel's Flight; ☑ Castelmezzano 0971 98 60 20, Pietrapertosa 0971 98 31 10; www.volodellangelo.com; s €35-42, couples €63-75; ⊙ 9.30am-6.30pm May-Oct) The extraordinary situation of Pietrapertosa and Castelmezzano, two steepling Basilicatan hill towns, is the inspiration behind 'Angel's Flight', two zip lines running over 1400m between the peaks, dropping over 100m and reaching speeds of up to 120km/h. Tandem flights are possible, providing the couple's combined weight doesn't exceed 150kg. It's only open daily in August; check the website for details.

Dolomiti Discovery
ADVENTURE SPORTS

(☑ 320 8696246; www.dolomitidiscovery.it; Via Provinciale 4; ⊙ tours from €30) Operates self-drive quad bike excursions around the area with the option of riding in a 4WD with a driver. Also supplies climbing gear for tackling nearby Via Ferrata courses and provides advice on walking the 7km Sentiero Sette Pietre (Path of the Seven Stones) linking Castelmezzano and Pietrapertosa. Ask about organising a quad bike transfer from Pietrapertosa back to Castelmezzano.

🛏 Sleeping & Eating

La Casa di Penelope e Cirene
B&B €

(☑ 338 3132196; Via Garibaldi 32, Pietrapertosa; d €75) This delightful B&B, the 'House of Penelope and Cirene', offers just two handsomely furnished rooms in the heart of Pietrapertosa. There's a sitting room, kitchenette, and great views over the Lucanian Dolomites.

Al Becco della Civetta
RISTORANTE €€

(☑ 0971 98 62 49; www.beccodellacivetta.it; Vico I Maglietta 7, Castelmezzano; meals €35-40; ⊙ 1-3pm & 8-10pm) Don't miss this authentic Lucano restaurant in Castelmezzano, which serves excellent regional cuisine based on seasonal local ingredients. It also offers 22 traditionally furnished, simple white-washed rooms (doubles €80), some with lots of dark wood, others with vivid murals, and many with fabulous views. Booking recommended.

ℹ Getting There & Away

SITA SUD (☑ 0971 50 68 11; www.sitasudtrasporti.it) bus 102 runs twice a day between Potenza and Castelmezzano (€5, 80 minutes) but you'll probably want your own wheels to explore properly.

Maratea
POP 5100

A sparkling, sun-drenched contrast to Basilicata's rugged interior, Maratea is a pure delight. In fact a disparate collection of placid coastal villages, rather than a single place, it's the centrepiece of Basilicata's Tyrrhenian coast. Embellished with lush vegetation, riven by rock-walled coves below well-tended hillside villages, Maratea's joys might be compared to those of the Amalfi. Perhaps the biggest, most welcome disparity is the number of tourists – far fewer here, and notably fewer non-Italians. You can climb the steep hill above Maratea to see the ruins of the prior settlement, take boat cruises and fishing trips, poke around venerable hilltop churches (44 of them), or just kick back with a coffee in a perfectly photogenic piazza, watching the sun play on the waters below.

ℹ ORIENTATION

What is usually referred to as Maratea is actually a collection of small settlements split into several parts, some of them walkable if you're relatively fit and the weather co-operates. Maratea's main train station sits roughly in the middle.

The **Porto** is clustered around a small harbour and is about a 10-minute walk below the station (towards the sea). The 'village' of **Fiumicello** is in the same direction, but reached by turning right rather than left once you've passed under the railway bridge. The main historic centre, known as **Maratea Borgo**, is perched in the hills behind. A bus leaves every 30 minutes or so from the station, or you can walk up a series of steps and paths (approximately 5km; the town is always visible). It has plenty of cafes and places to eat. The **Marina di Maratea** is located 5km south along the coast and has its own separate train station. The village of **Acquafredda** is 8km in the other direction, kissing the border of Campania.

GRUMENTUM

The **Parco Archeologico di Grumentum** (☑ 0975 6 50 74; Contrada Spineta, Grumento Nova; incl museum €2.50; ⊙ 9am-1hr before sunset Tue-Sun, from 2pm Mon; P) – sometimes known as Basilicata's 'Little Pompeii' – contains remains of a theatre, an amphitheatre, Roman baths, a forum, two temples and a *domus* (villa) with mosaic floors. Knowing something of its history ratchets up the interest: among its illustrious inhabitants was Hannibal, who made it his headquarters in the 3rd century BC. Its swansong came when the Saracen invasions of the 10th century forced its abandonment in favour of Grumento Nova, on a nearby hill.

Many of the artefacts found here are on display at the nearby and moderately interesting **Museo Nazionale dell'Alta Val d'Agri** (☑ 0975 6 50 74; www.musei.basilicata. beniculturali.it/; Contrada Spineta, Grumento Nova; incl archaeological site €2.50; ⊙ 9am-8pm Tue-Sun, 2-8pm Mon; P).

PUGLIA, BASILICATA & CALABRIA MARATEA

◉ Sights & Activities

The deep green hillsides that encircle this tumbling conurbation offer excellent walking trails, providing a number of easy day trips to the surrounding hamlets of Acquafredda and Fiumicello, with its small sandy beach. The tourist office in Maratea Borgo's main square can provide an excellent map. Other activities including boating and kayaking.

Maratea Superiore　　RUINS
FREE The ruins of the original settlement of Maratea, supposedly founded by the Greeks, are situated at a higher elevation than the current village on a rocky escarpment just below the Christ the Redeemer statue. Abandoned houses with trees growing in their midst, some thought to be over 1000 years old, have long been given over to nature.

Statue of Christ the Redeemer　　STATUE
The symbol of Maratea, visible from multiple vantage points along the coast, this 22m-high statue of Christ faces inland towards the Basilica di San Biagio. Slightly smaller than Rio's Christ the Redeemer, it's made of concrete faced with Carrara marble and sits atop 644m-high Monte San Biagio. A dramatic winding asphalt road leads to the top, although it's more fun to walk the steep path (number 1) that starts off Via Cappuccini in Maratea Borgo.

Fly Maratea　　ADVENTURE SPORTS
(☑ 333 7957286; www.flymaratea.it) This affiliation of local tour operators offers a range of different activities including coastal kayaking, mountain biking, trekking and paragliding. Check the website for contact details of specific guides specialising in each option. The local tourist office can also usually arrange introductions.

☞ Tours

Nautilus Escursioni　　BOATING
(☑ 334 3545085; www.facebook.com/Maratea Escursioni; Porto di Maratea; ⊙ tours adult/child from €25/10) Friendly boat skipper and an excellent option to help you explore the spectacular surrounding coastline.

🛏 Sleeping

Locanda delle Donne Monache　　HOTEL €€
(☑ 0973 87 61 39; www.locandamonache.com; Via Mazzei 4, Maratea Borgo; d/ste €180/300; ⊙ Apr-Oct; P ❄ @ 🛜 🛏) Overlooking the *borgo* (medieval hamlet), this exclusive hotel is in a converted 18th-century convent with a suitably lofty setting. It's a hotchpotch of vaulted corridors, terraces and gardens fringed with bougainvillea and lemon trees. The rooms are elegantly decorated in pastel shades and there's a fitness centre, Jacuzzi and a stunning panoramic outdoor pool.

Hotel Villa Cheta Elite　　HOTEL €€€
(☑ 0973 87 81 34; www.villacheta.it; Via Canonica 48, Acquafredda; r from €230; ⊙ Apr-Oct; P ❄ 🛜 🛏) Set in an art-nouveau villa in Acquafredda, this hotel is like a piece of plush Portofino towed several hundred kilometres south. Enjoy a broad terrace with spectacular views of the Gulf of Policastro, a fabulous restaurant (1pm to 2pm and 8pm to 9.30pm), a pool and large rooms where antiques mix seamlessly with modern amenities. Bright Mediterranean foliage fills sun-dappled terraced gardens.

✖ Eating

Il Sacello　　ITALIAN €€
(☑ 0973 87 61 39; www.facebook.com/ristoranteil sacellomaratea; Via Mazzei 4, Maratea Borgo; meals €40-45; ⊙ 12.30-2.30pm & 7.30-10pm; 🛜) The in-house *ristorante* of the Locanda delle Donne

Surprises of the South

In the Mezzogiorno, the sun shines on a magical landscape: dramatic cliffs and sandy beaches fringed with turquoise seas; wild mountains and gentle forested slopes; rolling green fields and flat plains. Sprinkled throughout are elegant *palazzi* (mansions), ancient cave dwellings and gnome-like stone huts.

Valle d'Itria

In a landscape of rolling green hills, vineyards, orchards and picture-pretty fields, conical stone huts called *trulli* sprout from the ground en masse in the Disney-esque towns of Alberobello (p153) and Locorotondo (p155).

Matera

A European Capital of Culture in 2019, the ancient cave city of Matera (p171) has been inhabited since Paleolithic times. Explore the tangled alleyways, ponder frescoes in rock churches, and slumber in millennia-old *sassi* (former cave dwellings).

Promontorio del Gargano

Along with its charming seaside villages, sandy coves and crystalline blue waters, the Gargano (p148) is also home to the Parco Nazionale del Gargano. It's perfect for hikers, nature trippers and beach fiends alike.

Salento

Hot, dry plains covered in wildflowers and olive groves reach towards the gorgeous beaches of the Ionian and Adriatic Seas. This is the unspoilt 'heel' of Italy, with Lecce (p158) as its sophisticated capital.

Parco Nazionale dell'Aspromonte

In this wild park (p188), narrow roads lead to hilltop villages such as spectacularly sited Bova. Meanwhile, waterfalls, wide riverbeds, jagged cliffs and sandstone formations set the scene for some unforgettable hikes.

1. Alberobello (p153) 2. Matera (p171) 3. A beach at Viente, Promontorio del Gargano (p148) 4 A Salento beach (p158)

Monache hotel, Il Sacello serves wonderful Lucanian fare and seafood, overlooking the red rooftops of Maratea Borgo. Try the pasta with local sausage, the beef tartare or delicately wrought desserts such as the buffalo-ricotta souffle. Il Sacello sometimes closes on Monday or Tuesday night in June.

Lanterna Rossa SEAFOOD **€€**

(☑ 0973 87 63 52; www.facebook.com/lanternaros samarateaporto; Via Arenile, Maratea Porto; meals €35-40; ☉ 11am-3pm & 7-11.30pm) This terrace restaurant, sitting above the Bar del Porto overlooking the marina, has been knocking out delightful Lucanian seafood for over 20 years. Sit either in the tastefully art-strewn interior or on the terrace to enjoy dishes such as *zuppa di pesce* (fish soup) and octopus with wild beans and fennel. Bookings are advised, especially in July and August.

ℹ️ Information

Maratea has two tourist offices: one in the **borgo** (☑ 0973 03 03 66; www.maratea.info; Piazza Vitolo 1, Maratea Borgo; ☉ 10am-1pm & 5-10pm Mon-Fri, daily Jul & Aug) and one above the **marina** (☑ 0973 87 71 15, 371 1446350; www. maratea.info; Via Arenile 35, Maratea Porto; ☉ 8am-1pm & 3-7pm Jun-Oct, shorter hours rest of year).

ℹ️ Getting There & Away

Maratea is easily accessed via the coastal train line. InterCity and regional trains on the Rome–Reggio line stop at Maratea train station. Some slower trains stop at Marina di Maratea.

Local buses (€1.20) connect the coastal towns and Maratea train station with Maratea Borgo, running more frequently in summer. Some hotels offer pickups from the station.

CALABRIA

If a Vespa-riding, siesta-loving, unapologetically chaotic Italy still exists, it's in Calabria. Rocked by recurrent earthquakes and lacking a Matera or Lecce to give it high-flying tourist status, this is a corner of Italy less globalised and homogenised. Its wild mountain interior and long history of poverty, Mafia activity and emigration have all contributed to its distinct culture, but there is so much more to Calabria than just its history - it is authentic, has great culinary experiences and utterly breathtaking landscapes. Calabria is unlikely to be the first place in Italy you'd visit. But if you're intent on seeing a candid

and uncensored version of *la dolce vita* that hasn't been dressed up for tourist consumption, look no further, *ragazzi* (guys).

Calabria's gritty cities are of patchy interest. More alluring is its attractive Tyrrhenian coastline, broken by several particularly lovely towns (Tropea and Scilla stand out). The mountainous centre is dominated by three national parks, none of them particularly well explored. Its museums, collecting the vestiges of a rich classical past are probably its greatest treasure.

History

Traces of Neanderthal, Palaeolithic and Neolithic life have been found in Calabria, but the region only became internationally important with the arrival of the Greeks in the 8th century BCE. They founded a colony at what is now Reggio Calabria. Remnants of this colonisation, which spread along the Ionian coast with Sibari and Crotone as the star settlements, are still visible. In 202 BCE the cities of Magna Graecia came under the control of Rome, the rising power in Italy. The Romans did irreparable environmental damage, destroying the countryside's handsome forests. Navigable rivers became fearsome *fiumare* (torrents) dwindling to wide, dry, drought-stricken riverbeds in high summer.

Post-Rome, Calabria's fortified hilltop communities weathered successive invasions by the Normans, Swabians, Aragonese and Bourbons, and remained largely undeveloped. Although the late 18th-century Napoleonic incursion and the later arrival of Garibaldi and Italian unification inspired hope for change, Calabria remained a disappointed, feudal region and, like the rest of the south, was racked by malaria.

A byproduct of this tragic history was the growth of banditry and organised crime. Calabria's Mafia, known as the 'ndrangheta (from the Greek for heroism/virtue), inspires fear in the local community, but tourists are rarely the target of its aggression. For many, the only answer has been to get out and, for at least a century, Calabria has seen its young people emigrate in search of work.

Northern Tyrrhenian Coast

The good, the bad and the ugly all jostle cheek-by-jowl along Calabria's northern Tyrrhenian coast. The *Autostrada del Mediterraneo* (A2), one of Italy's great coastal drives, ties them all together. It twists and turns through mountains, past huge swathes of dark-green forest and flashes of cerulean-blue sea. But the Italian penchant for cheap summer resorts has taken its toll here and certain stretches, particularly in the south, are blighted by shoddy hotels and soulless stacks of flats.

A 30km stretch of wide, pebbly beach runs south from the border with Basilicata, from the popular and not-too-garish resort town of Praia a Mare to Diamante, a fashionable seaside town famed for its chillies and bright murals painted by local and foreign artists. Inland are the precariously perched, otherworldly villages of Aieta and Tortora, reached by a tortuously twisted but rewarding mountain drive. Further south, Paola is worth a stop to see its holy shrine.

◉ Sights

Santuario di San Francesco di Paola   CAVE
(☑ 0984 47 60 32; www.santuariopaola.it; Via San Francesco di Paola, Paola; ☺ 6am-1pm & 2-8pm Apr-Sep, 6am-1pm & 2-6pm Oct-Mar) FREE Watched over by a crumbling castle, the Santuario di San Francesco di Paola is a curious, empty cave with tremendous significance to the devout. The saint lived and died in Paola in the 15th century and the sanctuary that he and his followers carved out of the bare rock has attracted pilgrims for centuries. The cloister is surrounded by naive wall paintings depicting the saint's truly incredible miracles. The original church contains an ornate reliquary of the saint.

Isola di Dino   ISLAND
Visible from the Praia a Mare seafront is an intriguing rocky chunk off the coast, the Isola di Dino. The tourist office has information on the island's sea caves; alternatively, expect to pay around €10 for a guided tour from the old boys who operate from the beach.

❶ Information

Just off the Praia a Mare seafront is the tourist office for the area, the **Consorzio Turistico del Tirreno** (Tyrrhenian Tourist Consortium; ☑ 0985 77 76 37; Via Amerigo Vespucci 4, Praia a Mare; ☺ 9am-noon Mon-Fri).

❶ Getting There & Away

Paola is the main train hub for Cosenza, about 25km inland. From Praia a Mare, **Autolinee Preite** (☑ 0984 41 30 01; www.autoservizipreite.it) buses go to Cosenza via Diamante and to Aieta and Tortora, (6km and 12km from Praia respec-

tively). **SITA** (☑ 0971 50 68 11; www.sitabus.it) buses run to Maratea and regular trains also pass through for Paola and Reggio Calabria.

Cosenza

☑ 0984 / POP 67,600 / ELEV 238M

Stacked atop a steep hill, Cosenza's old town epitomises the authentic, unkempt charm of southern Italy. Time-warped and romantically dishevelled, its dark weathered alleys are full of drying clothes on rusty balconies, old curiosity shops and the freshly planted shoots of an arty renaissance. Welcome to a no-nonsense workaday town where tourists are incidental and local life, with all its petty dramas, takes centre stage

Cosenza's modern city centre is a typically chaotic Italian metro area that serves as a transport hub for Calabria and a gateway to the nearby mountains of Parco Nazionale della Sila.

◉ Sights

In the new town, pedestrianised Corso Mazzini provides a pleasant respite from the chaotic traffic and incessant car honking. The thoroughfare serves as an open-air museum with numerous sculptures lining the *corso,* including *Saint George and the Dragon* by Salvador Dalí.

In the old town, head up the winding, charmingly dilapidated Corso Telesio, which has a raw Neapolitan feel to it and is lined with ancient tenements and antiquated shopfronts, including shops housing a musical instrument maker, a Dickensian shoe mender and shops selling traditional crafts. Enlivened by an ever-changing gallery of street art, the side alleys are a study in urban decay. At the top is Cosenza's 12th-century cathedral (☑ 0984 7 78 64; www.cattedraledicosenza.it; Piazza del Duomo 1; ☺ 8am-noon & 3-7.30pm).

Head further along the *corso* to Piazza XV Marzo, an appealing square fronted by the Palazzo del Governo and the handsome neoclassical **Teatro Rendano** (☑ 0984 81 32 27; Piazza XV Marzo; tickets from €5).

From Piazza XV Marzo, follow Via Paradiso, then Via Antonio Siniscalchi for the route to the restored Norman castle (☑ 0984 181 12 34; www.castellocosenza.it; Piazza Frederico II; adult/reduced €4/2; ☺ 9.30am-6pm Tue-Sat, from 10am Sun).

Cosenza's culture is low-key, but you can piece bits of it together at the refurbished Galleria Nazionale (☑ 0984 79 56 39; Via

PUGLIA, BASILICATA & CALABRIA COSENZA

PARCO NAZIONALE DEL POLLINO

Italy's largest national park, the Parco Nazionale del Pollino (Pollino National Park; www.parcopollino.it), straddles Basilicata and Calabria and covers 1960 sq km. It acts like a rocky curtain separating the region from the rest of Italy and has the richest repository of flora and fauna in the south.

The park's most spectacular areas are Monte Pollino (2248m), Monti di Orsomarso (1987m) and the canyon of the Gole del Raganello. The mountains, often snowbound, are blanketed by forests of oak, alder, maple, beech, pine and fir. The park is most famous for its ancient *pino loricato* trees, which can only be found here and in the Balkans.

Your own vehicle is needed to explore within Pollino. To get there, however, there's a daily SLA Bus (0973 2 10 16; www.slasrl.it) between Naples and Rotonda, while SAM Autolinee (0973 66 38 35; www.samautolinee.com) buses operate around some of Pollino's Basilicatan villages.

Basilicata

In Basilicata the park's main centre is Rotonda (elevation 626m), home to the official park office, Ente Parco Nazionale del Pollino (0973 66 93 11; www.parcopollino.gov. it/en/live-the-park; Strada Provinciale 28, Rotonda; 9am-1pm & 2-4pm Mon-Fri). It can recommend local guides, accommodation and nearby stores to buy good hiking maps.

Adjacent to the park office is the L'Ecomuseo del Pollino (www.parcopollino.gov.it/en/live-the-park/ecomuseum; Strada Provinciale 28, Rotonda; 9am-1pm & 2-4pm Mon-Fri), offering a brilliant overview of the park's cultural, geological and natural heritage. Based in Rotonda, English-speaking guide Guiseppe Cosenza (347 2631462; www.viaggiarenelpollino.it; Rotonda) offers hiking, birdwatching and walking tours to see the park's ancient *pino loricato* trees. Water sports including canyoning and river tubing can be booked with Info Pollino (338 2333888; www.infopollino.com; Strada Provinciale 4, Viggianello) near Rotonda.

The unique, isolated Albanian villages of San Paolo Albanese and San Costantino Albanese fiercely maintain their mountain culture and the Greek liturgy is retained in the main churches. For local handicrafts, visit the town of Terranova di Pollino for wooden crafts, Latronico for alabaster, and Sant'Arcangelo for wrought iron. The chalet-style Picchio Nero (0973 9 31 70; www.hotelpicchionero.com; Via Mulino 1, Terranova di Pollino; s/d €65/78; P) in Terranova di Pollino is a popular hotel for hikers and includes a recommended restaurant.

Two highly recommended restaurants include Luna Rossa (0973 9 32 54; www.federicovalicenti.it; Via Marconi 18, Terranova di Pollino; meals €35-40; noon-3pm & 7-10pm Thu-Tue) in Terranova di Pollino and Da Peppe (0973 66 12 51; Corso Garibaldi 13, Rotonda; meals €30-35; noon-3pm & 7.30-11pm Tue-Sun) in Rotonda.

Calabria

Civita was founded by Albanian refugees in 1746. Other towns worth visiting are Castrovillari, with its well-preserved 15th-century Aragonese castle, and Morano Calabro. Naturalists should also check out the wildlife museum Centro Il Nibbio (0981 3 07 45; www.ilnibbio.it; Vico II Annunziata 11, Morano Calabro; €4; 9am-6pm Jul & Aug, shorter hours rest of year) in Morano.

White-water rafting down the spectacular Lao river is popular in the Calabrian Pollino. Centro Lao Action Raft (0985 9 10 33; www.laoraft.it; Via Lauro 10/12, Scalea) in Scalea can arrange rafting trips as well as canyoning, trekking and mountain biking. Ferula Viaggi (p174) in Matera runs mountain-bike excursions and treks into the Pollino.

The park has a number of *agriturismi*. Agriturismo Colloreto (347 3236914, 0981 3 12 55; www.colloreto.it; Contrada Colloreto, Morano Calabro; half board per person €60) near Morano Calabro, and Locanda di Alia (339 8346881, 0981 4 63 70; www.alia.it; Via letticelle 55, Castrovillari; s/d €100/110; P) in Castrovillari are noteworthy.

Gravina; ⊙10am-6pm Tue-Sun) FREE. Close by is the **Museo dei Brettii e degli Enotri** (☑0984 2 33 03; www.museodeibrettiiedeglienotri. it; Salita Agostino 3; adult/reduced €4/3; ⊙9am-1pm & 3.30-6.30pm Tue-Fri, 10am-1pm & 3.30-6.30pm Sat & Sun).

🛏 Sleeping

B&B Via dell'Astrologo   B&B €

(☑338 9205394; www.viadellastrologo.com; Via Benincasa 16; s/d from €41/71; 🐾) A gem in the historic centre, this small B&B is tastefully decorated with polished wooden floors, white bedspreads and good-quality artwork. Host Marco is a mine of information on Cosenza and Calabria in general.

Royal Hotel   HOTEL €

(☑0984 41 21 65; www.hotelroyalcosenza.it; Via delle Medaglie d'Oro 1; s/d/ste from €60/75/85; P❄🐾) The best all-round hotel central Cosenza can provide, the four-star Royal is a short stroll from Corso Mazzini right in the heart of town. Rooms are fresh and businesslike, and there's a bar, restaurant and convenient parking on-site. Efficient and friendly front-desk service comes with good advice on where to eat in Cosenza.

🍴 Eating & Drinking

Gran Caffè Renzelli   CAFE €

(www.renzelli.com; Corso Telesio 46; cakes from €1.50; ⊙7am-9pm; 🐾) This venerable cafe behind the *duomo* has been run by the same family since 1803 when the founder arrived from Naples and began baking gooey cakes and desserts. Sink your teeth into *torroncino torrefacto* (a confection of sugar, spices and hazelnuts) or *torta telesio* (made from almonds, cherries, apricot jam and lupins).

Il Paesello   CALABRIAN €€

(☑349 4385786; Via Rivocati 95; meals €30; ⊙7-11pm Mon-Sat, noon-3pm Sun) Beloved of the locals, this unpretentious trattoria is one of Cosenza's best. Simple, robust dishes such as *fagioli con cozze* (beans with mussels), tagliatelle with porcini mushrooms and anything plucked from the sea are executed with care and skill.

Bulldog Ale House   BAR

(☑0984 181 14 43; www.facebook.com/bulldog cosenza; Corso Mazzini 39; ⊙6pm-2am; 🐾) More than 200 beers and a good selection of gin and whiskey combine at our favourite Cosenza bar. Grab a table outside on the city's main pedestrian thoroughfare and meet the friendly locals, including Cosenza's big stu-

dent population. The beer taps feature a rotating selection of always interesting brews.

ⓘ Getting There & Away

AIR

Lamezia Terme Airport (Sant'Eufemia Lamezia, SUF; ☑0968 41 43 85; www.sacal.it; Via Aeroporto 40, Lamezia Terme), 63km south of Cosenza, at the junction of the A2 and SS280 motorways, links the region with major Italian cities. The airport is served by Ryanair, easyJet and charters from northern Europe. A shuttle leaves the airport every 20 minutes for the airport train station, where **Autolinee Romano** (☑0962 2 17 09; www.autolineeromano. com) runs two buses a day to Cosenza (€7, 70 minutes).

BUS

Cosenza's main **bus station** (☑0984 41 31 24) is northeast of Piazza Bilotti. Services leave from here for Catanzaro and towns throughout La Sila. **Autolinee Preite** (☑0984 41 30 01; www.autoservizipreite.com) has buses heading daily along the north Tyrrhenian coast; **Autolinee Romano** serves Crotone as well as Rome and Milan.

TRAIN

Stazione Nuova (Via Vaglio Lise) is about 2km northeast of the centre. Regular trains go to Reggio Calabria (from €15, 2¾ hours) and Rome (from €54, four to six hours), both usually with a change at Paola, and Naples (from €119, three to four hours), as well as most destinations around the Calabrian coast.

Regular buses link the centre and the main train station, although they follow a roundabout route.

Parco Nazionale della Sila

'La Sila' is a big landscape, where wooded hills stretch to endless rolling vistas. Dotted with hamlets, it's cut through with looping roads that make driving a test of your digestion.

The park's 130 sq km are divided into three areas: the **Sila Grande**, with the highest mountains; the strongly Albanian **Sila Greca** (to the north); and the **Sila Piccola** (near Catanzaro), with vast forested hills.

The highest peaks, covered with tall Corsican pines, reach 2000m – high enough to generate enough winter snow to attract skiers. In summer the climate is coolly alpine; spring sees carpets of wildflowers; and there's mushroom hunting in autumn. Gigantic firs grow in the **Bosco di Gallopane** (Forest of Gallopane). There are several beautiful lakes, the largest of which is **Lago di Cecita o**

Mucone near Camigliatello Silano. There is plenty of wildlife here, including the light-grey Apennine wolf, a protected species.

◉ Sights

La Sila's main town, San Giovanni in Fiore (1049m), is named after the founder of its beautiful medieval abbey. Today, the abbey houses a home for the elderly and the Museo Demologico (☑0984 97 00 59; Abbazia Forense; adult/reduced €1.50/1; ☺8.30am-6.30pm Mon-Sat year-round & 9.30am-12.30pm Sun mid-Jun–mid-Sep). San Giovanni's handsome old centre is famous for its Armenian-style hand-loomed carpets and tapestry. See how it's done at the studio and shop of master carpet maker Domenico Caruso (☑0984 99 27 24; http://carusotessiture.it; Via Gramsci 195, San Giovanni in Fiore; ☺8.30am-8pm Mon-Sat).

A popular ski-resort town with 6km of slopes, Camigliatello Silano (1272m) looks much better under snow. A few lifts operate on Monte Curcio, about 3km to the south. Around 5.5km of slopes and a 1500m lift can be found near Lorica (1370m), on gloriously pretty Lago Arvo – the best place to camp in summer.

Scigliano (620m) is a small hilltop town located west of the Sila Piccola section of the park and 75km south of Cosenza.

🏃 Activities

Valli Cupe   TREKKING
(☑334 9174699, 333 8342866; www.riservanatura levallicupe.it) You can take fantastic trekking, 4WD or donkey trips with this cooperative in the area around Sersale in the southeast, where there are myriad waterfalls and the dramatic Canyon Valli Cupe. Specialising in botany, the guides also visit remote monasteries and churches. Check out their excellent English-language website for planning and contact information.

Cammina Sila   HIKING
(☑347 9131310; www.camminasila.com) Based in the town of San Giovanni in Fiore this outfit offers scheduled hiking and canoeing excursions in Parco Nazionale della Sila throughout June, July and August. Most tours are scheduled on Saturday or Sunday. Check the website for upcoming dates.

🎊 Festivals & Events

During August, Sila in Festa takes place, featuring traditional music. Autumn is mushroom season, when you'll be able to frequent mushroom festivals, including the Sagra del Fungo in Camigliatello Silano.

🛏 Sleeping & Eating

B&B Calabria   B&B €
(☑349 8781894; www.bedandbreakfastcalabria. it; Via Roma 7, Scigliano; s/d €40/60; ☺Apr-Nov; P🛜) This B&B in the mountains has five clean, comfortable and characterful rooms, all with separate entrances. Owner Raffaele is a great source of information on the region and can recommend places to eat, visit and go hiking. There's a wonderful terrace overlooking endless forested vistas. Mountain bikes are available and there's wi-fi in public areas. Cash only.

The B&B is west of the national park in the village of Scigliano, about an hour south of Cosenza by train.

Albergo San Lorenzo   HOTEL €
(☑0984 57 08 09; www.sanlorenzosialberga.it; Campo San Lorenzo; d/tr/q/ste €90/105/120/135; P❄🛜) Above their famous restaurant, the owners of La Tavernetta have opened the area's most stylish sleep, with 21 large, well-equipped rooms done up in colourful, modernist style.

★La Tavernetta   CALABRIAN €€€
(☑0984 57 90 26; www.sanlorenzosialberga. it; Campo San Lorenzo, near Camigliatello Silano; meals €50-55; ☺12.30-3pm & 7.30-11pm Tue-Sun) Among Calabria's best eats, La Tavernetta marries rough country charm with citified elegance in warmly colourful dining rooms. The food is first-rate and based on the best local ingredients, from wild anise seed and mushrooms to mountain-raised lamb and kid. Reserve ahead on Sundays and holidays.

🛍 Shopping

★Alta Salumeria Campanaro   FOOD
(☑0984 57 80 15; https://altagastronomiacam panaro.it; Piazza Misasi 5, Camigliatello Silano; sandwiches €4; ☺9am-1.30pm & 3.30-8pm Thu-Tue) Even among Italian delicatessens, this long-established *salumeria* is something special. It's a temple to all things fungoid (get your Sila porcini here), as well as an emporium of fine meats, cheeses, pickles, sweetmeats and wines.

ℹ Information

Good-quality information in English is scarce. You can try the national park **visitors centre** (☑0984 53 71 09; www.parcosila.it; Via Nazionale, Lorica; ☺10am-noon & 3-5pm Mon & Wed,

10am-noon Tue, Thu & Fri) at Lorica, 10km from Camigliatello Silano, or the **Pro Loco tourist office** (☑ 0984 57 81 59; www.prolococam igliatello.it; Via Roma, Camigliatello Silano; ⊙ 9.30am-6.30pm Tue-Sun) in Camigliatello Silano. A useful internet resource is the official park website (www.parcosila.it). The people who run B&B Calabria in the park are extremely knowledgeable and helpful.

For a map, you can use *La Sila: Carta Turistico-Stradale ed Escurionistica del Parco Nazionale* (€7). *Sila for 4* is a miniguide in English that outlines a number of walking trails in the park. The map and booklet are available at tourist offices.

❶ Getting There & Away

You can reach the park's two main hubs, Camigliatello Silano and San Giovanni in Fiore, via regular Ferrovie della Calabria buses from Cosenza or Crotone.

Ionian Coast

With its flat coastline and wide sandy beaches, the Ionian coast has some fascinating stops from Sibari to Santa Severina, with some of the best beaches around Soverato. However, it has borne the brunt of some ugly development and is mainly a long, uninterrupted string of resorts, thronged in the summer months and mothballed from October to May.

It's worth taking a trip inland to visit Santa Severina, a spectacular mountain-top town, 26km northwest of Crotone. The town is dominated by a Norman castle and is home to a beautiful Byzantine church. But the true glories of this long stretch of coast are its museums and archaeological sites, preserving what remains of the pre-Roman cities of Magna Graecia (Greater Greece).

Le Castella

☑ 0962 / POP 1103

This town is named for its impressive 16th-century Aragonese castle (☑ 0962 79 51 60; €3; ⊙ 9am-midnight Jul & Aug, shorter hours rest of year, closed Mon Oct-Mar), a vast edifice linked to the mainland by a short causeway. The philosopher Pliny said that Hannibal constructed the first tower. Evidence shows it was begun in the 4th century BCE, designed to protect Crotone in the wars against Pyrrhus. Le Castella is south of Capo Rizzuto, a rare protected area along this coast, rich not only in nature but also in Greek history. For further information on the park, try www.riservamarinacaporizzuto.it.

🛏 Sleeping

With around 15 campgrounds near Isola di Capo Rizzuto to the north, this is the Ionian coast's prime camping area.

La Fattoria CAMPGROUND €
(☑ 0962 79 11 65; Via del Faro, Isola di Capo Rizzuto; camping 2 people, car & tent €30, bungalow €65; ⊙ Jun-Sep) Around 1.5km from the coast, La Fattoria has 100 grass campsites (generally shaded), plus games and hot showers.

🍴 Eating

Trattoria La Bussola SEAFOOD €€
(☑ 329 2769164; Via Annibale Barca; meals €25-30; ⊙ 8-11.30pm) When your dad's a fisherman, it's easy to guarantee a good supply of the freshest seafood. There's nothing pretentious about this family-owned eatery, just a dedication to great seasonal dishes showcasing the best of local produce. Tables are limited, so try to book ahead. Don't leave without trying the hazelnut gelato and the homemade wild fennel and myrtle digestif.

❶ Getting There & Away

Autolinee Romano buses connect Le Castella with Crotone (€3.20, 20 minutes, three per day).

Gerace

☑ 0964 / POP 2650

A spectacular medieval hill town, Gerace is worth a detour for the views alone – on one side the Ionian Sea, on the other, dark, interior mountains. Blessed with numerous handsome churches, some dating back to the Byzantine 9th century, it's dramatically sited on a rocky fastness rearing up from the inland plain. On the highest point is the photogenic ruin of a Norman castle that seems to sprout from the jagged stones.

Further inland is Canolo, a small village seemingly untouched by the 21st century.

◉ Sights

Cathedral CATHEDRAL
(Via Duomo 28; adult/reduced €3/2; ⊙ 9.30am-12.30pm & 3-6.30pm) Gerace has Calabria's largest Romanesque cathedral. Dating from 1045, its three aisles are divided by columns salvaged from classical villas and temples in the area; later alterations have not robbed it of its majesty. The interior is wonderfully austere and admission includes entry to the attached Cathedral Treasury museum with a glittering array of tapestries and ecclesiastical riches.

🛏 Sleeping & Eating

L'Antico Borgo
B&B **€€**

(☑ 327 2330095; https://lanticoborgogerace.it; Via IV Novembre 38; d €70; ☎) L'Antico Borgo's five rooms are tucked away in Gerace's medieval labyrinth adjacent to the restaurant and pizzeria of the same name. Decor is relatively simple, but rooms are kept spotless and are a good option to enjoy the hill town's shadowed streets and laneways after the day trippers have departed.

Ristorante A Squella
CALABRIAN **€**

(☑ 0964 35 60 86; Via Ferruccio 21; meals €20-25; ☉ 12.30-2.30pm daily & 7.30-10.30pm Mon-Sat) For a taste of traditional Calabrian cooking, modest, welcoming Ristorante a Squella makes for a great lunchtime stop. It serves reliably good dishes, specialising in seafood and Calabrian pasta dishes. The views from just outside are spectacular and the service from the friendly family that owns the restaurant is warm and heartfelt. Try the delicious deep-fried doughnuts for dessert.

ℹ Getting There & Away

Buses connect Gerace with Locri and also Canolo with Siderno, both of which link to the main coastal railway line. To explore these quiet hills properly, you'll need your own transport.

Parco Nazionale dell'Aspromonte

Most Italians think of the **Parco Nazionale dell'Aspromonte** (www.parcoaspromonte.gov. it) as a refuge used by Calabrian kidnappers in the 1970s and '80s. It's still rumoured to contain 'ndrangheta strongholds, but you're extremely unlikely to encounter any murky business. The park, Calabria's second-largest, is dramatic, rising sharply inland behind Reggio. Its highest peak, **Montalto** (1955m), is dominated by a huge bronze statue of Christ and offers sweeping views across to Sicily.

Subject to frequent mudslides and carved up by torrential rivers, Aspromonte's mountains are awesomely beautiful. Underwater rivers keep the peaks covered in coniferous forests and ablaze with flowers in spring. It's wonderful walking country and is crossed by several colour-coded trails. **Gambarie** is the main town and the easiest approach to the park. The roads are good and many activities are organised from here – you can ski and it's also the place to hire a 4WD – ask around in the town.

Extremes of weather and geography have resulted in some extraordinary villages, such as **Pentidàttilo** and **Roghudi**, clinging limpet-like to the craggy, rearing rocks and now all but deserted. It's worth the drive to explore these eagle-nest villages. Another mountain eyrie with a photogenic ruined castle is **Bova**, perched at 900m above sea level. The drive up the steep, dizzying road to Bova is not for the faint-hearted, but the views are stupendous.

🏃 Activities

Misafumera
WALKING

(☑ 340 9024422, 347 0804515; www.facebook. com/www.misafumera.it; Via Nazionale 306d, Reggio Calabria Bocale 2; treks €690) Reggio-based Misafumera runs week-long trekking excursions (€690, April to November). Treks operate with a minimum of six participants.

Aspro Park
ADVENTURE SPORTS

(☑ 342 8065010; https://aspropark.wordpress.com; Strada Redentore Gambarie; adult/child €15/10; ☉ 10am-6pm Sun Jun–mid-Jul, 10am-6pm daily mid-Jul–Aug) Fifteen minutes' drive southwest of Gambarie is this outdoor adventure park with forested walking trails, mountain bike rental and tree-climbing and elevated ropes courses. A good option for travelling families.

🛏 Sleeping

Hotel Centrale
HOTEL **€**

(☑ 0965 74 31 33; www.hotelcentrale.net; Piazza Mangeruca 22, Gambarie; s/d €50/100; ᴾ❋☎) Hotel Centrale in Gambarie is a large all-encompassing place with a decent restaurant, a comprehensive modern spa, renovated wood-finished rooms and the best cafe in town. Centrale also helps organise treks and other activities, and offers full and half pension for €20/30 more per person. The attached bookshop is a good place to pick up maps and local information.

Azienda Agrituristica Il Bergamotto
AGRITURISMO **€**

(☑ 347 6012338; www.naturaliterweb.it; Via Amendolea, Amendolea di Condofuri; per person €25) You can stay among the olives, donkeys and eponymous bergamot trees at this peaceful *agriturismo*. Ugo Sergi can arrange excursions, the rooms are simple and the food delicious.

ℹ Information

Maps are scarce. Try the **national park office** (☑ 0965 74 30 60; www.parcoaspromonte.gov. it; Via Aurora 1, Gambarie; ☉ 10.30am-12.30pm

Mon & Fri & 3-6pm Tue) in Gambarie or ask at the bookshop at the Hotel Centrale in Gambarie.

The cooperative **Naturaliter** (☑ 347 3046799; www.naturaliterweb.it; Condofuri), based in Condofuri, is an excellent source of information. **Co-operativa San Leo** (☑ 347 3046799; https://coopsanleobova.it/i-nostri-trekking; Bova), based in Bova, also provides guided tours and accommodation. In Reggio Calabria, you can book treks and tours with Misafumera.

❶ Getting There & Away

To reach Gambarie, take ATAM city bus 319 from Reggio Calabria (€1, 1½ hours, up to six daily). Most of the roads inland from Reggio eventually hit the SS183 road that runs north to the town.

It's also possible to approach from the south, but the roads aren't as good.

FOOTPRINTS OF MAGNA GRAECIA

Long before the Romans colonised Greece, the Greeks were colonising southern Italy. Pushed out of their homelands by demographic, social and political pressures, the nebulous mini-empire they created between the 8th and 3rd centuries BC was often referred to as Magna Graecia by the Romans in the north. Many Greek-founded cities were located along the southern coast of present-day Puglia, Basilicata and Calabria. They included (south to north) Locri Epizephyrii, Kroton, Sybaris, Metapontum and Taras (now known, respectively, as Locri, Crotone, Sibari, Metaponto and Taranto).

Magna Graecia was more a loose collection of independent cities than a coherent state with fixed borders, and many of these cities regularly raged war against each other. The most notable conflict occurred in 510 BC when the athletic Krotons attacked and destroyed the hedonistic city of Sybaris (from which the word 'sybaritic' is derived).

Magna Graecia was the 'door' through which Greek culture entered Italy, influencing its language, architecture, religion and culture. Though the cities were mostly abandoned by the 5th century AD, the Greek legacy lives on in the Griko culture of Calabria and the Salento peninsula, where ethnic Greek communities still speak Griko, a dialect of Greek.

Remnants of Magna Graecia can be seen in numerous museums and architectural sites along Calabria's Ionian coast.

Locri

Museo Nazionale di Locri Epizephyrii (☑ 0964 39 00 23; www.locriantica.it; Contrada Marasà, Locri; adult/reduced €6/3; ⊙ 9am-8pm Tue-Sun; 🅿 👬) Situated 3km south of modern-day Locri, the Greek colony of Locri Epizephyrii was founded in 680 BC, later subsumed by Rome and finally abandoned following Saracen raids in the 10th century AD. The archaeological site is sprawling and full of interest, including harbour structures, the *centocamere* (hundred rooms) and the Casino Macri – a Roman bathhouse later repurposed as a farming villa. The attached museum is well curated, and includes artefacts found in the numerous nearby necropoli.

Sibari

Museo Archeologico Nazionale delle Sibaritide (☑ 0981 7 93 91; Località Casa Bianca, Sibari; €3; ⊙ 9am-8pm Tue-Sun) Founded around 730 BC and destroyed by the Krotons in 510 BC, Sybaris was rebuilt twice: once as Thurii by the Greeks in 444 BC, and again in 194 BC by the Romans, who called it Copia. Prehistoric artefacts and evidence of all three cities are displayed at this important (if underpatronised) museum, 5km southeast of the modern beach resort of Sibari. The nearby archaeological park has been affected by flooding in the past: check ahead to ensure it's open.

Crotone

Museo Archeologico Nazionale di Crotone (☑ 0962 2 30 82; Via Risorgimento 14, Crotone; €2; ⊙ 9am-8pm) Founded in 710 BC, the powerful city-state of Kroton was known for its sobriety and high-performing Olympic athletes. Crotone's museum is located in the modern town, while the main archaeological site is at Capo Colonna, 11km to the southeast. Votive offerings and other remnants of the famous Hera Lacinia Sanctuary at Cape Colonna are a highlight.

Reggio Calabria

☑ 0965 / POP 182,550

Port, transport nexus and the main arrival and departure point for Sicily, Reggio seems more functional than fascinating. That is up until the point you set foot inside its fabulous national museum, custodian of some of the most precious artefacts of Magna Graecia known.

The city's architectural eclecticism is a result of its tectonic liveliness: in 1908 the last big quake triggered a tsunami that killed over 100,000. By Italian standards, little of historical merit remains, although the *lungomare*, with its views across the Messina Strait to smouldering Mt Etna is, arguably, one of the most atmospheric places in Italy for an evening *passeggiata*.

Fortunately, there's no need to doubt the food. Reggio hides some of Calabria's best salt-of-the-earth restaurants. You can work up an appetite for them by hiking in the nearby Parco Nazionale dell'Aspromonte, or exploring the coastline at nearby seaside escapes along the Tyrrhenian and Ionian coasts.

◉ Sights

★ Museo Nazionale di Reggio Calabria   MUSEUM

(☑ 0965 81 22 55; www.museoarcheologicoreggio calabria.it; Piazza de Nava 26; adult/reduced €8/5; ☺ 9am-8pm Tue-Sun; 🅿) Over several floors in Southern Italy's finest museum you'll descend through millennia of local history, from Neolithic and Palaeolithic times through Hellenistic, Roman and beyond. The undoubted crown jewels are, probably, the world's finest examples of ancient Greek sculpture: the Bronzi di Riace, two extraordinary bronze statues discovered on the seabed near Riace in 1972 by a snorkelling chemist from Rome. You'll have to stand for three minutes in a decontamination chamber to see the bronzes, but they're more than worth the wait. Larger than life, they depict the Greek obsession with the body; inscrutable, determined and fierce, their perfect form is more godlike than human. The finest of the two has ivory eyes and silver teeth parted in a faint *Mona Lisa* smile. No one knows who they are – whether human or god – and even their provenance is a mystery. They date from around 450 BCE, and it's believed they're the work of two artists.

In the same room as the bronzes is the 5th-century-BCE bronze *Philosopher's Head,* the oldest-known Greek portrait in existence. Also on display are impressive exhibits from Locri, including statues of Dioscuri falling from his horse.

Museo Nazionale del Bergamotto   MUSEUM

(☑ 0340 7635968; www.facebook.com/museodel bergamotto; Via Filippini 50, Mercato Coperto; €3; ☺ 9am-noon & 5-7pm Tue-Sat, 10.30-noon Sun) Housed in Reggio's former covered market, this museum showcases the interesting 300-year-old history of the region's bergamot growing industry. The zesty citrus fruit is grown almost exclusively in the Reggio and Aspromonte area. Sample the essential oils and bergamot-infused teas before trying *bergamotto* gelato at Reggio's beloved gelateria Cèsare (☑ 0965 88 99 77; www.gelato cesare.it; Piazza Indipendenza 2; gelato from €2.50; ☺ 6am-1am).

Aragonese Castle   CASTLE

(Piazza Castello; ☺ 9am-1pm & 2-7pm Tue-Sun) FREE Only two towers, restored in 2000, remain of the Aragonese Castle damaged by earthquake and partially demolished in 1922. The site is used for events and performances today. It's worth a visit for the excellent views from the towers.

🛏 Sleeping

★ B&B Kalavria   B&B €

(☑ 347 5637038; ww.kalavriabb.com; Via Pellicano 21F; s/d €70/80; 🅰) Owner Domenico is a brilliant host at this modern and elegant B&B a few blocks from Reggio's waterfront *lungomare*. Bathrooms are particularly stylish, and in warmer months the rooftop terrace is a great place to relax. Breakfast features the best of local baked goods and Domenico can offer well-researched recommendations on where to eat and drink in his interesting hometown.

B&B Casa Blanca   B&B €

(☑ 340 9032992; www.bbcasablanca.it; Via Arcovito 24; s/d/tr €55/75/85; 🅿🅰) A little gem in Reggio's heart, this 19th-century *palazzo* has three floors of spacious rooms gracefully furnished with white-on-white decor. There's a self-serve breakfast nook, a small breakfast table in each room and two apartments available. Breakfast is a celebration of fresh pastries.

Reggio Calabria

⊙ 0 ————————— 500 m
Ⓝ 0 ————————— 0.25 miles

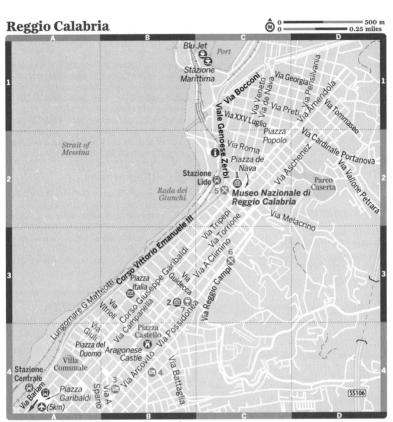

Reggio Calabria

⊙ Top Sights
1 Museo Nazionale di Reggio
Calabria...C2

⊙ Sights
2 Museo Nazionale del Bergamotto........B3

🛏 Sleeping
3 B&B Casa Blanca...................................B4

4 B&B Kalavria..B4

🍴 Eating
5 Cèsare..C2
   La Cantina del Macellaio ....(see 3)
6 La Vie del Gusto....................................C3

🍷 Drinking & Nightlife
7 Lievito...B3

🍴 Eating & Drinking

★ **La Cantina del Macellaio**   TRATTORIA €€
(☎ 0965 2 39 32; www.lacantinadelmacellaio.com;
Via Arcovito 26/28; meals €35; ⊙ 12.30-3pm &
7.30-11.30pm Wed-Mon) One of the best restaurants in Reggio, serving *maccheroni al
ragù di maiale* (handmade pasta with pork
sauce) and *involtini di vitello* (veal rolls)
in an open, tiled dining room with exposed
stonework and green flasks on the walls. The

mostly Calabrian wines are equally impressive, as is the service. Aficionados of excellent
meat dishes should order the mixed grill.

La Vie del Gusto   CALABRIAN €€
(☎ 324 8844025; Via II Settembre 55; meals €30-
35; ⊙ 7.30-11.30pm Tue-Sat, noon-4pm Sun) Local Calabrian flavours shine at this friendly
and informal spot where the menu changes
regularly on a seasonal basis. Meaty favourites like Calabrian sausage are a perennial

favourite and La Vie del Gusto's sprawling *antipasti* plates are famous in Reggio. Great ambience and also great value.

Lievito CRAFT BEER
(☑0965 81 30 88; www.pizzerialievito.it; Via dei Filippini 33; ☺7pm-midnight) Street art and excellent pizza made from Slow Food ingredients combine with Lievito's own range of craft beers – the 9% Belgian-style Tripel is a smooth heavy hitter – and there's also a fridge full of other interesting Italian brews. Check out the artisan food products on sale before you leave; a good option for tasty gifts and souvenirs.

ℹ Information

MEDICAL SERVICES

Hospital (☑800 198629, emergency 118; www.ospedalerc.it; Via Melacrino; ☺24hr) Reggio's main hospital has a 24-hour *pronto soccorso* (emergency department).

POST

Post Office (☑0965 31 51 11; Via Miraglia 14; ☺8.30am-7pm Mon-Fri, to 12.30pm Sat)

TOURIST INFORMATION

Tourist Information Kiosk (☑0965 2 11 71; http://turismo.reggiocal.it; Via Roma 3; ☺9am-noon & 4-7pm) There is also an information kiosk at the **airport** (☑0965 64 32 91; ☺9am-5pm).

ℹ Getting There & Away

AIR

Reggio's **airport** (REG; ☑0965 64 05 17; https://reggiocalabriaairport.it) is at Ravagnese, about 5km south. It has Alitalia flights to Rome, Turin and Milan.

BUS

Most buses terminate at the **Piazza Garibaldi bus station**, in front of the Stazione Centrale . Several different companies operate to towns in Calabria and beyond. Regional trains are more convenient than bus services to Scilla and Tropea.
ATAM (☑800 43 33 10; www.atam-rc.it) Runs to Gambarie (€1.50, 1½ hours, six daily) in the Aspromonte National Park.
Lirosi (☑0966 5 79 01; www.lirosiautoservizi.com) Buses to Rome (from €36, 9½ hours, two daily).

CAR & MOTORCYCLE

The A2 ends at Reggio, via a series of long tunnels. If you are continuing south, the SS106/

E90 hugs the coast around the 'toe', then heads north along the Ionian Sea.

TRAIN

Trains stop at **Stazione Centrale** (☑0965 32 41 91; Via Barlaam 1), the main train station at the town's southern edge. Of more use to ferry foot passengers and those visiting the Museo Nazionale is the **Stazione Lido** (Viale Zerbi), near the harbour. There are frequent trains to Milan, Rome and Naples. Regional services run along the coast to Scilla and Tropea, and also to Catanzaro and less frequently to Cosenza and Bari.

ℹ Getting Around

Orange local buses run by **ATAM** (☑800 43 33 10; www.atam-rc.it) cover most of the city including regular buses between the port and Piazza Garibaldi outside Stazione Centrale. The Università–Aeroporto bus, bus 27, runs from Piazza Garibaldi to the airport and vice versa (15 minutes, hourly). Buy your ticket at ATAM offices, tobacconists or newsstands.

Southern Tyrrhenian Coast

North of Reggio Calabria, along the coast-hugging **Autostrada del Mediterraneo (A2)**, the scenery rocks and rolls to become increasingly beautiful and dramatic, if you can ignore the shoddy holiday camps and unattractive developments that sometimes scar the land. Like the northern part of the Tyrrhenian coast, it's mostly quiet in winter and packed in summer.

Scilla

☑0965 / POP 4900
In Scilla, cream-, ochre- and earth-coloured houses cling on for dear life to the jagged promontory, ascending in jumbled ranks to the hill's summit, which is crowned by a castle and, just below, the dazzling white confection of the **Chiesa Arcipretale Maria Immacolata**. Lively in summer and serene in winter, the town is split in two by the tiny port. The fishing district of Scilla Chianalea, to the north, harbours small hotels and restaurants off narrow lanes, lapped by the sea. It can only be visited on foot.

Scilla's high point is a rock at the northern end, said to be the lair of Scylla, the mythical six-headed sea monster who drowned sailors as they tried to navigate the Strait of Messina. Swimming and fishing off the town's glorious white sandy beach is somewhat safer today. Head for **Lido Paradiso** from where you can squint up at the castle while sunbathing on the sand.

Sights

Castello Ruffo
CASTLE

(☎ 0965 70 42 07; Piazza San Rocco; admission €2; ⊙ 8.30am-7.30pm) An imposing fortress surmounting the headland commanding Scilla, this castle has at times been a lighthouse and a monastery. It houses a *luntre,* the original boat used for swordfishing, and on which the modern-day *passarelle* (a special swordfish-hunting boat equipped with a 30m-high metal tower) is based.

Sleeping

The old fishing village of Chianalea, on Scilla's eastern flank, holds some delightful sea-facing B&Bs.

B&B Sunshine
B&B €

(☎ 339 7980266; www.sunshinescilla.com; Via Garibaldi 13; d €80-120; ☎) Brilliant ocean views combine with friendly service from host Antonio at this sparkling hillside B&B around halfway between Chianalea and Scilla town. Sunshine's three colourful rooms have poetic names referencing Scilla's maritime climate. Our favourite is the romantic Rosa Dei Venti room. The Tramanto apartment includes a kitchen and accommodates up to five guests. Look forward to legendary breakfasts.

Hotel Principe di Scilla
HOTEL €€

(☎ 0965 70 43 24; www.ubais.it; Via Grotte 2; ste from €150; ❄☎) Get lulled to sleep by the sound of lapping waves in this grand old family residence on Scilla's seafront. Two suits of armour guard the front door while inside six individually themed suites are stuffed with countless antiques. In warm weather throw the windows open onto lovely views of the fishing village of Chianalea and, beyond, the sparkling Tyrrhenian.

Eating & Drinking

Osteria del Centro
ITALIAN €€

(☎ 392 6440208; www.facebook.com/osteria delcentroscilla; Via Bastia 7; meals €30-35; ⊙ 12.30-3pm & 8-11.30pm Tue-Sun) Providing an elegant upper town alternative to the cafes and restaurants in Chianalea, this place comes recommended by locals for its excellent meat dishes.

Blue of You
SEAFOOD €€

(☎ 0965 79 05 85; www.bleudetoi.it; Via Grotte 40; meals €35-40; ⊙ noon-3pm & 8pm-midnight Wed-Mon) Soak up the atmosphere at this lovely little restaurant, where blue lampshades, a Blue Note soundtrack and glimpses of the blue Tyrrhenian set the mood. It has a terrace over the water and excellent seafood dishes made with local ingredients such as Scilla's renowned swordfish, perhaps with fresh pasta and eggplant. Ask for the homemade Amaro (herbal liqueur) to finish.

Casa Vella
WINE BAR

(☎ 329 3649711; www.casavelascilla.it; Via Annunziata 18; ☎) Good-value sandwiches and flatbreads combine with Calabrian craft beer and wine at this spot in Chianalea's pedestrian main drag. The friendly owners also run an adjacent B&B (doubles €60 to €120) and can advise on local walks and excursions. Don't miss the array of Calabrian artisan produce on sale inside.

Getting There & Away

Scilla is on the main coastal train line. Frequent trains run to Reggio Calabria (€2.40, 30 minutes). The train station is a couple of blocks from the beach.

Tropea
☎ 0963 / POP 6400

Tropea, a puzzle of lanes and piazzas, is famed for its beauty, dramatic cliff's-edge site and spectacular sunsets. It sits on the Promontorio di Tropea, which stretches from Nicotera in the south to Pizzo in the north. The coast alternates between dramatic cliffs and icing sugar–soft sandy beaches, all edged by translucent sea. Unsurprisingly, hordes of Italian holidaymakers descend here in summer. If you hear English being spoken, it is probably from Americans visiting relatives: enormous numbers left to forge better lives in America in the early 20th century.

Despite the legend that Hercules founded the town, it seems this area has been settled as far back as Neolithic times. Tropea has been occupied by the Arabs, Normans, Swabians, Anjous and Aragonese, as well as being attacked by Turkish pirates. Perhaps they were all after the town's famous red onions, so sweet they can be turned into marmalade?

Sights & Activities

Santa Maria dell'Isola
CHURCH

(☎ 347 2541232; www.santuariosantamariadelliso latropea.it; garden & museum €2; ⊙ 9am-1pm & 3-7.30pm Apr-Jun, 9am-8.30pm Jul & Aug, shorter hours rest of year) Tropea's number-one photo opp is Santa Maria dell'Isola, a medieval monastic church given several facelifts over centuries of wear and tear (mainly attributable to earthquakes). Sitting on what was once its own rocky little island, it's now joined to the mainland by a causeway created by centuries of silt, and is reached via a flight of steps up the cliff face. Access to the church is free, but the small museum and garden costs €2.

Cathedral
CATHEDRAL

(Largo Duomo 12; ⏲ 7am-noon & 4-8pm) The beautiful Norman cathedral has two un-detonated WWII bombs near the door: it's believed they didn't explode due to the protection of the town's patron saint, Our Lady of Romania. A Byzantine icon (1330) of the Madonna hangs above the altar – she is also credited with protecting the town from the earthquakes that have pummelled the region.

CST Tropea
BOATING

(☑ 0963 6 11 78; www.csttropea.it; Largo San Michele 8-9) This Tropea-based company can arrange a wide variety of tours and activities around the area including boat trips and trekking on the island of Stromboli, mountain-bike rental, Vespa tours and horse riding. For travelling foodies options include cookery classes and excursions taking in the local wine and olive oil scene. Apartment rentals can be arranged through its website.

ⓘ ONWARD TO SICILY

Reggio is the gateway to Sicily, via the island's main port, Messina.

Note that there are two main departure ports for Sicily: the **Stazione Marittima** in Reggio Calabria, and the ferry port in the town of Villa San Giovanni, 14km north of Reggio and easily accessible by train. Passenger ferries operated by **Blu Jet** (☑ 0340 1545091; www.blujetlines.it) depart from both Stazione Marittima (€3.50, 20 minutes, 16 daily Monday to Friday and six daily on weekends) and Villa San Giovanni (€2.50).

Car ferries from Villa San Giovanni (€29 with vehicle, 20 minutes, 28 per day) are run by **Caronte & Tourist** (☑ 800 62 74 14; www.carontetourist.it). This is also the port used by Trenitalia's train-ferry – carriages are pulled directly onto the ferry.

🛏 Sleeping

Keep an eye on seasonal fluctuations: a reasonable B&B room may become exorbitant, or simply unavailable, during the high summer season of August.

Donnaciccina
B&B €€

(☑ 0963 6 21 80; www.donnaciccina.com; Via Pelliccia 9; s/d/ste €75/150/200; ✷ ❐) Look for the sign of a bounteous hostess bearing fruit and cake to find this delightful B&B, overlooking the main *corso*. The 17th-century *palazzo* retains a tangible sense of history with carefully selected antiques, canopy beds and terracotta tiled floors. There are nine restful rooms, a nearby suite (itself dating to the 15th century) and a chatty parrot at reception.

Residenza il Barone
B&B €€

(☑ 0963 60 71 81; www.residenzailbarone.it; Largo Barone; ste from €130; ✷ ❐) This graceful *palazzo* has six suites decorated in masculine neutrals and tobacco browns, with dramatic modern paintings by the owner's brother adding pizzazz to the walls. There's a computer in each suite and you can eat breakfast on the small roof terrace with views over the old city and out to sea.

🍴 Eating

Osteria del Pescatore
SEAFOOD €

(☑ 0963 60 30 18; Via del Monte 7; meals €22-25; ⏲ noon-2.30pm & 8pm-midnight Wed-Mon) *Pesce spada* (swordfish) is a speciality on this part of the coast and it rates highly on the menu at this simple seafood place tucked away in the backstreets. Also arranges fishing trips in good weather.

Genus Loci
ITALIAN €€

(☑ 345 5896475; Largo Vaccari; €35-40; ⏲ noon-2.30pm & 6.30-10.30pm) Dining options include a slender and modern dining room or an outside terrace with excellent views, both great locations to enjoy Genus Loci's light and innovative approach to the freshest of local seafood. Try the eggplant layered with shrimps and basil before a *secondi* course of baked grouper with anchovies. A concise wine list features mainly Calabrian varietals.

ⓘ Information

Tourist Office (☑ 347 5318989, 0963 6 14 75; www.prolocotropea.eu; Piazza Ercole; ⏲ 9am-1pm & 4-8pm) In the old town centre.

ℹ Getting There & Away

Trains run to Pizzo-Lamezia (€2.40, 30 minutes, 12 daily), Scilla (€4.80, 1¼ hours, frequent) and Reggio (from €6.40, 1¾ hours, frequent). **Ferrovie della Calabria** (☑ 0961 89 62 39; www.ferroviedellacalabria.it) buses connect with other towns on the coast.

Pizzo

☑ 0963 / POP 9300

Stacked high up on a sea cliff, pretty little Pizzo is the place to go for *tartufo*, a death-by-chocolate ice-cream ball, and to see an extraordinary rock-carved grotto church. It's a popular and cheerful tourist stop. Piazza della Repubblica is the heart, set high above the sea with great views. Settle here at one of the many gelateria terraces for a gelato fix.

◉ Sights

Chiesetta di Piedigrotta   CHURCH
(☑ 0963 53 25 23; Via Riviera Prangi; adult/reduced €3/2.50; ⊙ 9am-1pm & 3-7.30pm Jul & Aug, shorter hours rest of year) The Chiesetta di Piedigrotta is an underground cave full of carved stone statues. It was carved into the tufa rock by Neapolitan shipwreck survivors in the 17th century. Other sculptors added to it and it was eventually turned into a church. Later statues include the less-godly figures of Fidel Castro and John F Kennedy. It's a bizarre, one-of-a-kind mixture of mysticism, mystery and kitsch, especially transporting when glowing in the setting sun.

Castello Murat   CASTLE
(☑ 0963 53 25 23; www.castellomurat.it; Scesa Castello Murat; adult/reduced €3.50/2.50; ⊙ 9am-11pm Jul & Aug, to 7pm Apr-Jun, Sep & Oct, shorter hours rest of year) This neat little 15th-century castle is named for Joachim Murat, brother-in-law of Napoleon Bonaparte and briefly King of Naples, captured in Pizzo and sentenced to death for treason in 1815. Inside the castle, you can see his cell and the details of his grisly end by firing squad, which is graphically illustrated with waxworks. Although Murat was the architect of enlightened reforms, the locals showed no great concern when he was executed.

Chiesa Matrice di San Giorgio   CHURCH
(Via San Giorgio 1; ⊙ hours vary) In town, the 16th-century Chiesa Matrice di San Giorgio, with its splendid baroque facade and dressed-up Madonnas, houses the tomb of Joachim Murat.

WORTH A TRIP

CAPO VATICANO
··
There are spectacular views from this rocky cape, around 7km south of Tropea, with its beaches, ravines and limestone sea cliffs. Birdwatchers' spirits should soar. There's a lighthouse, built in 1885, which is close to a short footpath from where you can see as far as the Aeolian Islands. Capo Vaticano beach is one of the balmiest along this coast.

🛏 Sleeping & Eating

Armonia B&B   B&B €
(☑ 0963 53 33 37; www.casaarmonia.com; Vico II Armonia 9; s/d €45/60; @) Run by the charismatic Franco in his 16th-century family home, this B&B has three relaxing rooms and spectacular sea views.

Piccolo Grand Hotel   BOUTIQUE HOTEL €€
(☑ 0963 53 32 93; www.piccolograndhotel.com; Via Chiaravalloti 32; s/d €110/130; ❄ 🛜) This pleasant four-star boutique hotel is hidden on an unlikely and rather dingy side street. But its exuberant blue-and-white design, upscale comforts and panoramic rooftop breakfasts make it one of Pizzo's top sleeps. There's also a small fitness area and e-bikes to rent.

Pepe Nero   SEAFOOD €€
(☑ 348 8124618; www.facebook.com/pg/pepe neropizzo; Via Marconi; meals €30-35) This family-owned restaurant just off Pizzo's main square has a stylish outdoor deck, the ideal spot to enjoy local seafood like *spada* (swordfish), prawn and lobster. We can also recommend the *calamaretti ripieni* (stuffed baby squid) and tuna tartare. Wine selections of local Calabrian varietals are also excellent. An essential stop for seafood fans.

ℹ Getting There & Away

Pizzo is just off the major A2 autostrada. There are two train stations. Vibo Valentia-Pizzo is located 4km south of town on the main Rome–Reggio Calabria line. A bus service connects you to Pizzo. Pizzo-Lamezia is south of the town on the Tropea–Lamezia Terme line. Shuttle buses (€2) connect with trains or you can walk for 20 minutes along the coast road. Note the final walk up the hill is very narrow so consider taking a taxi (or a tuk-tuk during summer).

AT A GLANCE

POPULATION
4.88 million

CAPITAL
Palermo

BEST CONFECTIONARY
I Dolci di Nonna Vincenza (p231)

BEST MUSIC FESTIVAL
Ortigia Sound System (p240)

BEST BEACH
Riserva Naturale Torre Salsa (p258)

WHEN TO GO
Easter Colourful religious processions and marzipan lambs in every bakery window.

May Wildflowers, dreamy coastal walking and Syracuse's festival of classic drama.

Sep Warm weather and seaside fun without summer prices.

Teatro Greco (p224) Taormina
IORKFISHER/SHUTTERSTOCK ©

Sicily

O verloaded with art treasures and natural beauty, undersupplied with infrastructure, and continuously struggling against Mafia-driven corruption, Sicily's complexities sometimes seem unfathomable. To really appreciate this place, come with an open mind – and a healthy appetite. Despite the island's perplexing contradictions, one factor remains constant: the uncompromisingly high quality of the cuisine.

After 25 centuries of foreign domination, Sicilians are the heirs to an impressive cultural legacy, from the refined architecture of Magna Graecia to the Byzantine splendour and Arab craftwork of the island's Norman cathedrals and palaces. This cultural richness is matched by a startlingly diverse landscape that includes bucolic farmland, smouldering volcanoes and kilometres of island-studded aquamarine coastline.

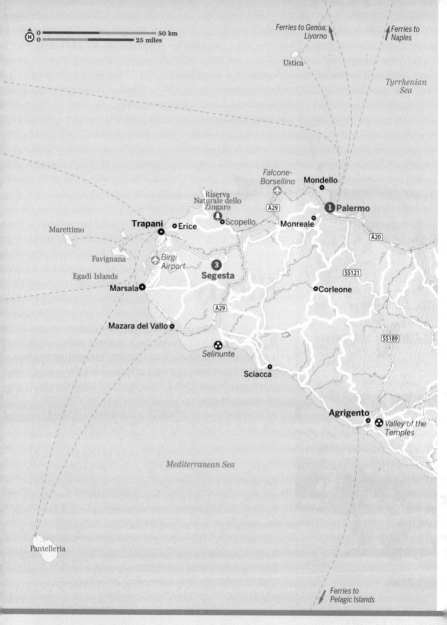

Sicily Highlights

1 Teatro Massimo (p209)
Joining the impeccably dressed opera-goers at this elegant theatre in Palermo.

2 Catania (p228)
Bargaining with fish vendors

at dawn, climbing sn active volcano in the afternoon, and returning to buzzing nightlife.

3 Segesta (p262)
Marvelling at the majesty of the 5th-century ruins.

4 Taormina (p224)
Watching stars perform against Mt Etna's breathtaking backdrop at summer festivals.

5 Aeolian Islands (p216)
Observing Stromboli's

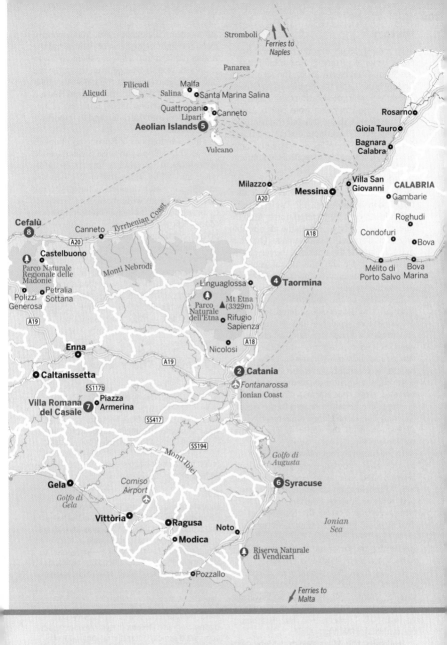

volcanic fireworks and hiking on these stunningly scenic islands.

6 Syracuse (p236) Wandering aimlessly in Ortygia's atmospheric alleys

or stepping back in time at an ancient Greek theatre performance.

7 Villa Romana del Casale (p251) Admiring prancing wild beasts and dancing bikini-

clad gymnasts on the mosaic floors.

8 Cefalù (p214) Being dazzled by Byzantine mosaics and splendid coastal sunsets.

History

Sicily's most deeply ingrained cultural influences originate from its first inhabitants – the Sicani from North Africa, the Siculi from Latium (Italy) and the Elymni from Greece. The subsequent colonisation of the island by the Carthaginians (also from North Africa) and the Greeks, in the 8th and 6th centuries BC respectively, compounded this cultural divide through decades of war when powerful opposing cities struggled to dominate the island.

Although part of the Roman Empire, Sicily didn't truly come into its own until after the Arab invasions of 831 CE. Trade, farming and mining were all fostered under Arab influence and Sicily soon became an enviable prize for European opportunists. The Normans, desperate for a piece of the pie, invaded in 1061 and made Palermo the centre of their expanding empire and the finest city in the Mediterranean.

Impressed by the cultured Arab lifestyle, Norman king Roger squandered vast sums on ostentatious palaces and churches and encouraged a hedonistic atmosphere in his court. But such prosperity – and decadence (Roger's grandson, William II, even had a harem) – inevitably gave rise to envy and resentment and, after two centuries of pleasure and profit, the Norman line was extinguished. The kingdom passed to the austere German House of Hohenstaufen with little opposition from the seriously eroded and weakened Norman occupation.

In the centuries that followed, Sicily passed to the Holy Roman Emperors, Angevins (French) and Aragonese (Spanish) in a turmoil of rebellion and revolution that continued until the Spanish Bourbons united Sicily with Naples in 1734 as the Kingdom of the Two Sicilies. Little more than a century later, on 11 May 1860, Giuseppe Garibaldi planned his daring and dramatic unification of Italy from Marsala on Sicily's western coast.

Reeling from this catalogue of colonisers, Sicilians struggled in poverty-stricken conditions. Unified with Italy, but no better off, nearly one million men and women emigrated to the US between 1871 and 1914 before the outbreak of WWI.

Ironically, the Allies (seeking Mafia help in America for the re-invasion of Italy) helped in establishing the Mafia's stranglehold on Sicily. In the absence of suitable administrators, they invited the undesirable *mafioso* (Mafia boss) Don Calógero Vizzini to do the job. When Sicily became a semi-autonomous region in 1948, Mafia control extended right to the heart of politics and the region plunged into a 50-year silent civil war. It only started to emerge from this after the anti-Mafia maxi-trials of the 1980s, in which Sicily's revered magistrates Giovanni Falcone and Paolo Borsellino hauled hundreds of Mafia members into court, leading to important prosecutions.

The assassinations of Falcone and Borsellino in 1992 helped galvanise Sicilian public opposition to the Mafia's inordinate influence, and while organised crime lives on, the thuggery and violence of the 1980s has diminished. A growing number of businesses refuse to pay the extortionate protection money known as the *pizzo*, and important arrests continue, further encouraging those who would speak out against the Mafia. On the political front, anti-Mafia crusader Leoluca Orlando, now serving his fifth term as mayor of Palermo, continues the fight.

Nowadays the hottest topics on everyone's mind are the island's continued economic struggles and conflict over Sicily's role as a major gateway for immigrants from northern Africa.

❶ Getting There & Away

AIR

A number of airlines fly direct to Sicily's two main international airports, Palermo's Punta Raisi (PMO) and Catania's Fontanarossa (CTA). A few also serve the smaller airports of Trapani (TPS) and Comiso (CIY). Alitalia (www.alitalia.com) is the main Italian carrier, while Ryanair (www.ryanair.com) is the leading low-cost airline serving Sicily.

BOAT

Hydrofoils and car ferries cross the narrow Strait of Messina between Sicily and the Italian mainland ports of Villa San Giovanni and Reggio di Calabria. Sicily is also accessible by ferry from Naples, Genoa, Civitavecchia, Livorno, Salerno, Cagliari, Malta and Tunis. Prices rise between June and September, when advanced bookings may also be required.

BUS

SAIS Trasporti (☑ 091 617 11 41; www.sais trasporti.it) and **Flixbus** (https://global.flixbus.com; Via d'Amico, Catania) run long-haul services to Sicily from Rome and Naples.

TRAIN

For travellers originating in Rome and points south, Intercity trains cover the distance from mainland Italy to Sicily in the least possible time, without a change of train. If coming from Milan,

Bologna or Florence, your fastest option is to take the ultra-high-speed Frecciarossa as far as Naples, then change to an Intercity train for the rest of the journey.

All trains enter Sicily at Messina, after being transported by ferry from Villa San Giovanni at the toe of Italy's boot. At Messina, trains branch west along the Tyrrhenian coast to Palermo, or south along the Ionian coast to Catania.

❶ Getting Around

BOAT

Efficient ferries and hydrofoils serve Sicily's outer islands. Main ports include Milazzo for the Aeolian Islands, Palermo for the island of Ustica, Trapani for the Egadi Islands and Porto Empedocle for the Pelagie Islands.

BUS

Buses are the best option for certain intercity routes, including Palermo–Trapani, Palermo–Syracuse and Catania–Agrigento. Also useful for some villages not served by train.

CAR & MOTORCYCLE

Having your own wheels is preferable for visiting smaller interior towns and remote archaeological sites (Segesta, Selinunte, Piazza Armerina etc). Car hire is readily available at airports and in many towns.

TRAIN

Trenitalia service is dependable and frequent along the Palermo–Messina and Messina–Syracuse coastal routes. Other well-served routes include Palermo to Agrigento, and Trapani to Marsala.

PALERMO & AROUND

Palermo

☑ 091 / POP 668,400

Having been the crossroads of civilisations for millennia, Palermo delivers a heady, heavily spiced mix of Byzantine mosaics, Arabesque domes and frescoed cupolas. This is a city at the edge of Europe and at the centre of the ancient world, a place where souk-like markets rub up against baroque churches, where date palms frame Gothic palaces and where the blue-eyed and fair have bronze-skinned cousins.

Centuries of dizzying highs and crushing lows have formed a complex metropolis. Here, crumbling staircases lead to gilded ballrooms, and guarded locals harbour hearts of gold. Just don't be fooled. Despite its noisy streets, Sicily's largest city is a shy

beast, rewarding the inquisitive with citrus-filled cloisters, stucco-laced chapels and crooked side streets dotted with youthful artisan studios. Add to this Italy's biggest opera house and an ever-growing number of vibrant, new-school eateries and bars and you might find yourself falling suddenly, unexpectedly in love.

◉ Sights

Via Maqueda is the main street, running north from the train station, changing names to Via Ruggero Settimo as it passes the landmark Teatro Massimo, then finally widening into leafy Viale della Libertà north of Piazza Castelnuovo, the beginning of the city's modern district.

◉ Around the Quattro Canti

Forming the centre of the old city, the busy intersection of Corso Vittorio Emanuele and Via Maqueda is known as the Quattro Canti (Four Corners). This crossroads neatly divides the historic nucleus into four traditional quarters – Albergheria, Capo, Vucciria and La Kalsa.

★Chiesa e Monastero di Santa Caterina d'Alessandria   CONVENT
(☑ 091 271 38 37; Piazza Bellini; church, convent & rooftop adult/reduced €10/9, church only adult/reduced €3/2; ⊙ church 9am-7pm, convent & rooftop 10am-7pm) Built as a hospice in the early 14th century and transformed into a Dominican convent the following century, this monastic complex wows with its magnificent maiolica cloister, surrounded by unique balconied cells and punctuated by an 18th-century fountain by Sicilian sculptor Ignazio Marabitti. The convent's rooftop terraces offer spectacular views of the surrounding piazzas and city, while the church's baroque interior harbours works by prolific artists, among them Filippo Randazzo, Vito D'Anna and Antonello Gagini.

La Martorana   CHURCH
(Chiesa di Santa Maria dell'Ammiraglio; ☑ 345 8288231; Piazza Bellini 3; adult/reduced €2/1; ⊙ 9.30am-1pm & 3.30-5.30pm Mon-Sat, 9-10.30am Sun) On the southern side of Piazza Bellini, this luminously beautiful 12th-century church was endowed by King Roger's Syrian emir, George of Antioch, and was originally planned as a mosque. Delicate Fatimid pillars support a domed cupola depicting Christ enthroned amid his archangels. The interior is best appreciated in the morning, when sunlight illuminates the magnificent Byzantine mosaics.

Palermo

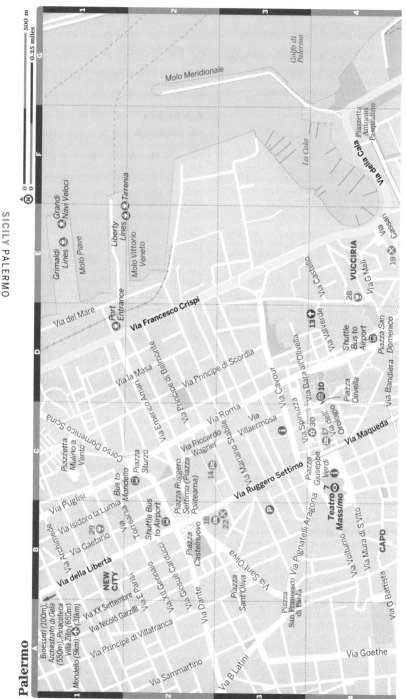

500 m
0.25 miles

Bioesseri (100m);
Archestrato di Gela
(550m); Pinacoteca
Villa Zito (650m);
Mondello (9km); (31km)

NEW
CITY

Via della Libertà

Via Achimede

Via Isidoro la Lumia

Via Gaetario

Via Puglisi

Bus to
Mondello

Via Torrearsa

Shuttle Bus
to Airport

Via XII Gennaio

Via E Parisi

Via Giosuè Carducci

Via Nicolò Garzilli

Via XX Settembre

Via Dante

Via Principe di Villafranca

Via Sammartino

Via B Latini

Piazzetta
Mulino a
Vento

Corso Domenico Scinà

Piazza
Sturzo

Piazza
Castelnuovo

Piazza
Sant'Oliva

Via Sant'Oliva

Via Francesco di Paola

Piazza
San Francesco
di Paola

Via Goethe

Piazza Ruggero
Settimo (Piazza
Politeama)

Via Riccardo
Wagner

Via Emerico Amari

Via la Masa

Via Principe di Belmonte

Via Principe di Scordia

Via Ruggero Settimo

Via Mariano Stabile

Via Roma

Via
Villaermosa

Piazza
Giuseppe
Verdi

Teatro 7
Massimo

Via Pignatelli Aragona

Via Voltuno di S Vito

Via Mura di S Vito

CAPO

Via G Battista

Via del Mare

Port
Entrance

Via Francesco Crispi

Via Cavour

Via Bara all'Olivella

Via Spinuzza

Via dell'
Orologio

Via Maqueda

Via Valverde

Shuttle
Bus to
Airport

Piazza
Olivella

Piazza San
Domenico

Via Bandiera

Via Maqueda

Piazza
Olivella

Molo Meridionale

Molo Piave

Liberty
Lines

Molo Vittorio
Veneto

Grimaldi
Lines

Grandi
Navi Veloci

Tirrenia

La Cala

Via della Cala

Golfo di
Palermo

VUCCIRIA

Via G Meli

Via Castello

Piazzetta
Antonio
Pasqualino

Via
Cassari

28

13

10

30

17

14

18

22

19

29

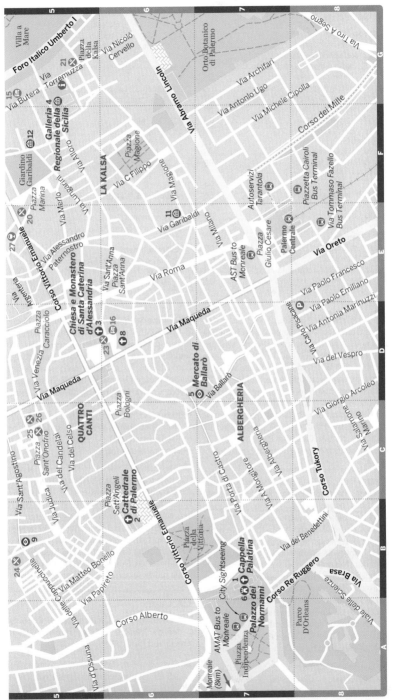

Palermo

◉ Albergheria

Once inhabited by Norman court officials, this neighbourhood southwest of the Quattro Canti has been poor and ramshackle since the end of WWII – you can still see wartime bomb damage scarring some buildings. The area is now home to a growing immigrant population that has revitalised the streets with its aspirations. By far the biggest tourist draws are the Palazzo dei Normanni and its exquisite chapel, Cappella Palatina, both at the far western edge of the neighbourhood,

★**Palazzo dei Normanni**   PALACE
(Palazzo Reale; ☑091 705 56 11; www.federicosecondo.org; Piazza del Parlamento; adult/reduced incl exhibition Fri-Mon €12/10, Tue-Thu €10/8; ⊙8.15am-5.40pm Mon-Sat, to 1pm Sun) Home to Sicily's regional parliament, this venerable palace dates back to the 9th century. However, it owes its current look (and name) to a major Norman makeover, during which spectacular mosaics were added to its royal apartments and magnificent chapel, the Cappella Palatina. Visits to the apartments, which are off-limits from Tuesday to Thursday, take in the mosaic-lined **Sala dei Venti** and King Roger's 12th-century bedroom, **Sala di Ruggero II.**

★**Cappella Palatina**   CHAPEL
(Palatine Chapel; ☑091 705 56 11; www.federicosecondo.org; Piazza del Parlamento; adult/reduced

incl Appartamenti Reali €9.50/7.50; ⊙8.15am-5.40pm Mon-Sat, to 1pm Sun) Designed by Roger II in 1130, this extraordinary chapel is Palermo's top tourist attraction. Located on the middle level of Palazzo dei Normanni's three-tiered loggia, its glittering gold mosaics are complemented by inlaid marble floors and a wooden *muqarnas* ceiling, the latter a masterpiece of Arabic-style honeycomb carving reflecting Norman Sicily's cultural complexity.

Note that queues are likely, and you'll be refused entry if you're wearing shorts, a short skirt or a low-cut top.

★**Mercato di Ballarò**   MARKET
(Via Ballaro 1; ⊙7.30am-8.30pm) Snaking for several city blocks southeast of Palazzo dei Normanni is Palermo's busiest street market, which throbs with activity well into the early evening. It's a fascinating mix of noises, smells and street life, and the cheapest place for everything from Chinese padded bras to fresh produce, fish, meat, olives and cheese – smile nicely for *un assaggio* (a taste).

◉ Capo

Northwest of the Quattro Canti, Capo is a densely packed web of interconnected streets and blind alleys.

★**Cattedrale di Palermo**   CATHEDRAL
(☑329 3977513; www.cattedrale.palermo.it; Corso Vittorio Emanuele; cathedral free, royal tombs €1.50,

treasury & crypt €3, roof €5, all-inclusive ticket adult/reduced €8/4; ⊙7am-7pm Mon-Sat, 8am-1pm & 4-7pm Sun; royal tombs, treasury, crypt & roof 9am-1.30pm Mon-Sat, royal tombs & roof also 9am-12.30pm Sun) A feast of geometric patterns, ziggurat crenellations, maiolica cupolas and blind arches, Palermo's cathedral has suffered aesthetically from multiple reworkings over the centuries, but remains a prime example of Sicily's unique Arab-Norman architectural style. The interior, while impressive in scale, is essentially a marble shell whose most interesting features are the **royal Norman tombs** (to the left as you enter), the **treasury** (home to Constance of Aragon's gem-encrusted 13th-century crown) and the panoramic views from the **roof**.

Mercato del Capo   MARKET

(Via Sant'Agostino; ⊙7am-8pm Mon, Tue & Thu-Sat, to 1pm Wed & Sun) Running the length of Via Sant'Agostino, Capo's street market is a seething mass of colourful activity during the day, with vendors peddling fruit, vegetables, meat, fish, cheese and household goods of every description.

⊙ Vucciria

Once the heart of poverty-stricken Palermo and a den of crime and filth, this neighbourhood northeast of the Quattro Canti illustrated the almost medieval chasm that existed between rich and poor in Sicily until the 1950s. Though it's still quite shabby, the winds of change are blowing.

Museo Archeologico
Regionale Antonio Salinas   MUSEUM

(☎091 611 68 07; www.regione.sicilia.it/bbccaa/salinas; Piazza Olivella 24; admission €3; ⊙9am-6pm Tue-Sat, to 1.30pm Sun) Situated in a Renaissance monastery, this splendid, wheelchair-accessible museum houses some of Sicily's most valuable Greek and Roman artefacts, including the museum's crown jewel: a series of original decorative friezes from the temples at Selinunte. Other important finds in the museum's collection include Phoenician sarcophagi from the 5th century BC, Greek carvings from Himera, the Hellenistic *Ariete di bronzo di Siracusa* (Bronze Ram of Syracuse), Etruscan mirrors and the largest collection of ancient anchors in the world.

Oratorio di Santa Cita   CHAPEL

(www.ilgeniodipalermo.com; Via Valverde; €4, incl Oratorio di San Domenico €6; ⊙9am-6pm) This 17th-century chapel showcases the breath-taking stuccowork of Giacomo Serpotta, who famously introduced rococo to Sicilian churches. Note the elaborate *Battle of Lepanto* on the entrance wall. Depicting the Christian victory over the Turks, it's framed by stucco drapes held by a cast of cheeky cherubs modelled on Palermo's street urchins. Serpotta's virtuosity also dominates the side walls, where sculpted white stucco figures hold gilded swords, shields and a lute, and a golden snake (Serpotta's symbol) curls around a picture frame.

⊙ La Kalsa

This quarter southeast of the Quattro Canti was long one of the city's most notorious neighbourhoods. A program of urban regeneration, however, has seen many of its long-derelict palazzos being restored and long-abandoned streets speckled with petite bohemian bars, trendy eateries, artisan studios and street art.

★Galleria Regionale della Sicilia   MUSEUM

(Palazzo Abatellis; ☎091 623 00 11; www.regione.sicilia.it/beniculturali/palazzoabatellis; Via Alloro 4; adult/reduced €8/4; ⊙9am-6.30pm Tue-Fri, to 1pm Sat & Sun) Housed in the stately 15th-century Palazzo Abatellis, this art museum – widely regarded as Palermo's best – showcases works by Sicilian artists dating from the Middle Ages to the 18th century. One of its greatest treasures is *Trionfo della morte* (Triumph of Death), a magnificent fresco (artist unknown) in which Death is represented as a demonic skeleton mounted on a wasted horse, brandishing a wicked-looking scythe while leaping over his hapless victims.

Museo dell'Inquisizione   MUSEUM

(Palazzo Chiaramonte-Steri; ☎091 2389 3788; Piazza Marina 61; adult/reduced €8/5; ⊙10am-6pm Tue-Sun) Housed in the lower floors and basements of 14th-century Palazzo Chiaromonte Steri, this fascinating museum explores the legacy of the Inquisition in Palermo. Thousands of 'heretics' were detained here between 1601 and 1782; the honeycomb of former cells has been painstakingly restored to reveal multiple layers of their graffiti and artwork (religious and otherwise). Visits are by one-hour guided tour only, conducted in English and Italian and departing roughly every 40 to 60 minutes from the ticket desk.

Museo delle Maioliche   MUSEUM

(Stanze al Genio; ☎340 0971561, 380 3673773; www.stanzealgenio.it; Via Garibaldi 11; adult/reduced

Delightful Desserts

From citrus-scented pastries filled with ricotta, to gelato served on brioche, to the marzipan fruits piled in every confectioner's window, Sicily celebrates the joys of sugar morning, noon and night.

Multicultural Roots

People from the Arabs to the Aztecs have influenced Sicily's culture of sweets: the former introduced sugar cane; the latter's fiery hot chocolate so impressed the Spaniards that they brought it to Sicily. The land also supplied inspiration, from abundant citrus, almond and pistachio groves to Mt Etna's snowy slopes, legendary source of the first *granita* (frozen fruit dessert).

Sweet Sicilian Classics

The all-star list of Sicilian desserts starts with *cannoli*, crunchy pastry tubes filled with sweetened ricotta, garnished with chocolate, crumbled pistachios or a spike of candied citrus. Vying for the title of Sicily's most famous dessert is *cassata*, a coma-inducing concoction of sponge cake, cream, marzipan, chocolate and candied fruit. Feeling more adventurous? How about an *'mpanatigghiu*, a traditional Modican pastry stuffed with minced meat, almonds, chocolate and cinnamon?

A SUGAR-FILLED ISLAND SPIN

I Segreti del Chiostro (p210) Scrumptious sweets using ancient recipes passed down by generations of Sicilian nuns.

Da Alfredo (p221) Dreamy *granita* made with almonds and wild strawberries.

Antica Dolceria Bonajuto (p249) Aztec-influenced chocolate with vanilla and hot peppers.

Caffè Sicilia (p246) Legendary Noto *gelateria* satisfying Sicilian sweet tooths since 1892.

Maria Grammatico (p262) Marzipan fruit, almond pastries and toasted-nut *torrone* (nougat).

1. 'Mpanatigghi 2. Cassatine (miniature cassate) 3. Cannoli
4. Granita

AROUND PALERMO

A few kilometres outside Palermo's city limits, the beach town of Mondello and the dazzling cathedral of Monreale are both worthwhile day trips. Just off shore, Ustica makes a great overnight or weekend getaway.

Monreale

In the hills 8km southwest of Palermo, **Cattedrale di Monreale** (☑ 091 640 44 03; www.monrealeduomo.it; Piazza del Duomo; cathedral free, Roano chapel, terrace & cloister adult/reduced €10/7; ⊘ cathedral 8.30am-12.30pm & 2.30-5pm Mon-Sat, 8-9.30am & 2.30-5pm Sun, cloisters 9am-7pm Mon-Sat, to 1.30pm Sun) is considered the finest example of Norman architecture in Sicily, incorporating Norman, Arab, Byzantine and classical elements. Inspired by a vision of the Virgin, it was built by William II in an effort to outdo his grandfather, Roger II, who was responsible for the cathedral in Cefalù and the Cappella Palatina in Palermo. The interior, completed in 1184 and executed in shimmering mosaics, depicts 42 Old Testament stories. Outside the cathedral, the **cloister** is a tranquil courtyard with a tangible oriental feel. Surrounding the perimeter, elegant Romanesque arches are supported by an exquisite array of slender columns alternately decorated with mosaics. To reach Monreale, take AMAT bus 389 (€1.40, 35 minutes, every 1¼ hours) from Palermo's Piazza Indipendenza or AST's Monreale bus (€2.40, 40 minutes, every 60 to 90 minutes Monday to Saturday) from in front of Palermo Centrale train station.

Mondello

Tucked between dramatic headlands 12km north of Palermo, Mondello is home to a long, sandy beach that became fashionable in the 19th century, when people came to the seaside in their carriages, prompting the construction of the huge art nouveau pier that still graces the waterfront. Most of the beaches near the pier are private (two sunloungers and an umbrella cost from €15 to €22); however, there's a wide swath of public beach opposite the centre of town with all the requisite pedalos and jet skis for hire. Given its easygoing seaside feel, Mondello is an excellent base for families. To get here, take AMAT bus 806 (€1.40, 20 to 30 minutes) from Piazza Sturzo in Palermo.

Ustica

A 90-minute boat trip from downtown, the 8.7-sq-km island of Ustica was declared Italy's first marine reserve in 1986. The surrounding waters are a playground of fish and coral, ideal for snorkelling, diving and underwater photography. To enjoy Ustica's wild coastline and dazzling grottoes without the crowds, try visiting in June or September.

There are numerous dive centres, hotels and restaurants on the island, as well as some nice hiking. To get here from Palermo, take the once-daily ferry (from €97 including vehicle, three hours) operated by **Siremar** (☑ 090 57 37; https://carontetourist.it/it/siremar; ⊘ ticket office 9.30am-1pm & 3-6.15pm) or the faster, more frequent hydrofoils (€26, 1½ hours) operated by **Liberty Lines** (☑ Ustica office 091 844 90 02, customer service 0923 87 38 13; www.libertylines.it; ⊘ ticket office 9.30am-1pm & 3-6.15pm). For more details on Ustica, see Lonely Planet's *Sicily* guide.

€9/8; ⊘ guided tours in English 3pm Tue-Fri, 10am Sat, 11am Sun, in Italian 4pm Tue-Fri, 11am Sat & Sun) Lovers of hand-painted Italian maiolica should make a beeline for this unique museum, which contains a superlative private collection of almost 6000 tiles, most from Sicily and Naples, and spanning the 15th to 20th centuries. Amassed over three decades by founder Pio Mellina, the tiles fill the walls and floors of the lovingly restored 16th-century Palazzo Torre-Piraino, itself a work of art with vaulted and frescoed ceilings. The museum also houses a small collection of vintage Italian toys.

◉ New City

North of Piazza Giuseppe Verdi, Palermo's streets widen, the buildings lengthen, and the shops, restaurants and cafes become more elegant (and more expensive). Glorious neoclassical and Liberty examples from the last golden age in Sicilian architecture give the city an exuberant, belle-époque feel in stark contrast to the narrow, introspective vibe of the historic quarter.

★ Teatro Massimo — THEATRE

(📋box office 091 605 35 80; www.teatromassimo.it; Piazza Giuseppe Verdi; guided tours adult/reduced €8/5; ⏰9.30am-6pm) Taking over 20 years to complete, Palermo's neoclassical opera house is the largest in Italy and the second-largest in Europe. The closing scene of *The Godfather: Part III,* with its visually arresting juxtaposition of high culture, crime, drama and death, was filmed here and the building's richly decorated interiors are nothing short of spectacular. Guided 30-minute tours are offered throughout the day in English, Italian, French, Spanish and German.

★ Pinacoteca Villa Zito — GALLERY

(📋091 778 21 80; www.villazito.it; Via della Libertà 52; adult/reduced €5/3; ⏰9.30am-7.30pm Tue-Sun) Elegant 18th-century Villa Zito houses a sharply curated collection of mainly Sicilian-themed art spanning the 17th to 20th centuries. You'll find a number of fascinating historical depictions of Palermo, numerous paintings by Ettore De Maria Bergler (considered the foremost Italian painter of the Liberty era), as well as works by 20th-century heavyweights Ugo Attardi, Fausto Pirandello, Filippo De Pisis, Carlo Carrà and Renato Guttuso.

★ Palazzina Cinese & Parco della Favorita — PALACE

(📋091 707 14 03; Via Duca degli Abruzzi 1; ⏰9am-6pm Tue-Sat, plus 9am-1pm 1st Sun of month) Once a retreat for King Ferdinand IV and his wife Maria Carolina, this pagoda-inspired pavilion exemplifies the popularity of 'Oriental exotica' in 18th-century Europe. Chinese, Egyptian, Islamic and Pompeiian motifs decorate its many rooms, with particular highlights including a trompe l'oeil 'collapsed' ceiling by Giuseppe Velazquez and a nifty dining table connected to the kitchen below via a lift. To get here, catch bus 107 to Piazza Giovanni Paolo II and then bus 615 or 645 to Duca degli Abruzzi – Palazzina Cinese.

⚜ Festivals & Events

Festino di Santa Rosalia — RELIGIOUS

(U Fistinu; ⏰Jul) Palermo's biggest annual festival celebrates patron saint Santa Rosalia, beloved for having saved the city from a 17th-century plague. The most colourful festivities take place on the evening of 14 July, when the saint's relics are paraded aboard a grand chariot from the Palazzo dei Normanni through the Quattro Canti to the waterfront, where fireworks and general merriment ensue.

🛏 Sleeping

A burgeoning crop of B&Bs in Palermo's historic centre offers an alternative to the city's established, oft-dated hotels. Be mindful that street noise can be a problem, and some accommodation occupies historic buildings where stairs rather than lifts provide the only access.

★ Stanze al Genio Residenze — B&B €

(📋340 0971561; www.stanzealgeniobnb.it; Via Garibaldi 11; s €85-100, d €100-120; ❄🖥) Speckled with Sicilian antiques, this B&B offers four gorgeous bedrooms, three with 19th-century ceiling frescoes. All four are spacious and thoughtfully appointed, with Murano lamps, old wooden wardrobes, the odd balcony railing turned bedhead, and top-quality, orthopaedic beds. That the property features beautiful maiolica tiles is no coincidence; the B&B is affiliated with the wonderful Museo delle Maioliche downstairs.

Palazzo Pantaleo — B&B €

(📋091 32 54 71; www.palazzopantaleo.it; Via Ruggero Settimo 74h; s/d/ste €80/100/150; 🅿🖥) Offering unbeatable comfort and a convenient location, Giuseppe Scaccianoce's elegant B&B occupies the top floor of an old *palazzo* (mansion) half a block from Piazza Politeama, hidden from the busy street in a quiet courtyard with free parking. Glowing with warm, earthy tones, five rooms and one spacious suite feature high ceilings, marble, tile or wooden floors, soundproof windows and modern bathrooms.

B&B Amélie — B&B €

(📋328 8654824, 091 33 59 20; www.bb-amelie.it; Via Prinicipe di Belmonte 94; s €40-60, d €60-80, tr €90-100; ❄@🖥) On a central, car-free street, affable, multilingual Angela has converted her grandmother's spacious 6th-floor flat into a cheery B&B. Rooms are simple, colourful and spotless. All have private bathroom (either as an ensuite or in the hallway) and two come with private terrace. Breakfast includes homemade cakes and jams, and Angela, a native Palermitan, is a font of local knowledge.

Massimo Plaza Hotel — HOTEL €€

(📋091 32 56 57; www.massimoplazahotel.com; Via Maqueda 437; d €140-250; 🅿❄🖥) The intimate Massimo Plaza sits in a prime location along vibrant, pedestrianised Via Maqueda.

Tie-back curtains and wooden furniture give rooms a classic feel. Seven of the rooms offer a prime view of the iconic Teatro Massimo across the street. Breakfast can be delivered directly to your room at no extra charge.

Butera 28
APARTMENT €€

(📋 333 3165432; www.butera28.it; Via Butera 28; apt per day €85-265, per week €570-1780; 🅿️ ❄️ 🛜) Delightful multilingual owner Nicoletta rents 12 apartments in the 18th-century Palazzo Lanzi Tomasi, the last home of Giuseppe Tomasi di Lampedusa, author of *The Leopard*. Graced with family antiques, the units range from 30 to 180 sq metres, most sleeping a family of four or more. Five apartments face the sea and all feature laundry facilities, well-equipped kitchens and soundproofed windows.

★ De Bellini Apartments
APARTMENT €€€

(📋 331 8836589; http://debellinipalermo.it; Piazza Bellini 5; apt from €200; ❄️ 🛜) In a 17th-century *palazzo* on one of Palermo's finest squares, these 10 architect-designed apartments are spectacular. Six have their own kitchen with high-tech appliances, and while all have different configurations and looks, all feature contemporary art, striking designer furniture, contemporary bathrooms and quality bedding. Bellini's balcony apartment is so close to the 12th-century La Martorana you can almost touch it from your private terrace.

Grand Hotel Villa Igiea
HOTEL €€€

(📋 091 631 21 11; www.villa-igiea.com; Salita Belmonte 43; d from €289; 🅿️ ❄️ @ 🛜 🏊) What can you say about an art nouveau villa that was designed by Ernesto Basile for the Florio family (of tuna and Marsala-wine fame)? This is Palermo's top hotel, located around 3km north of the city centre and with its own private beach, swimming pool, tennis court, spa centre, gym and restaurants. The rooms are predictably elegant, with blissful beds and palatial bathrooms.

✖️ Eating

Palermo's restaurant scene ranges from heirloom trattorias serving faithful classics like *bucatini con le sarde* (pasta mixed with sardines, wild fennel, raisins, pine nuts and breadcrumbs) to next-gen hotspots. Hit the markets and street-food stalls for delicious bargain bites.

★ I Segreti del Chiostro
SWEETS €

(📋 327 5882302; www.isegretidelchiostro.com; Monastero di Santa Caterina d'Alessandria, Piazza Bellini; sweets from €1; 🕙 10am-7pm summer, to 6pm winter; ✏️ 🎒) Countless blessings await at this extraordinary *pasticceria*, hidden away in a former convent. The culmination of endless hours of research, it uses once-secret recipes to bake rare sweet treats from numerous Sicilian convents. Everything is made from scratch using premium ingredients, including the *fedde del Cancelliere*, a reckless concoction of apricot jam and *biancomangiare* (almond pudding) encased in marzipan clam shells.

★ Trattoria al Vecchio Club Rosanero
SICILIAN €

(📋 349 4096880; Vicolo Caldomai 18; mains €3-12; 🕙 1-3.30pm Mon-Sat & 8-11pm Thu-Sat; 🛜) A veritable shrine to the city's football team (*rosa nero* refers to the team's colours, pink and black), cavernous Vecchio Club scores goals with its generous, bargain-priced grub. Fish and seafood are the real fortes here; if it's on the menu, order the *caponata e pesce spada* (*caponata* with swordfish), a sweet-and-sour victory. Head in early to avoid a wait.

Archestrato di Gela
PIZZA €

(📋 091 625 89 83; www.facebook.com/archestratodigelapalermo; Via Emanuele Notarbartolo 2f; pizzas €6.50-14; 🕙 7.45pm-midnight Tue-Sun; 🛜 ✏️) If you're serious about wood-fired pie, book at least two days ahead at what many consider to be the best pizzeria in town. The puffy, Neapolitan-style crusts are charred to perfection and topped with speciality, artisan ingredients from across Italy. Standouts include the Priolo, a turf-meets-surf smash of Bronte pistachio pesto, aged *prosciutto crudo, burratina* cheese (made from mozzarella and cream) and Cetara tuna. Libations include cocktails.

★ Aja Mola
SEAFOOD €€

(📋 091 611 91 59, 334 1508335; www.ajamolapalermo.it; Via Cassari 39; meals €35-40; 🕙 12.30-3pm & 7.30-11pm Tue-Sun; 🛜) On-point Aja Mola is among Palermo's top seafood eateries. The interior's smart, subtle take on a nautical theme is reflected in the open kitchen, which eschews stock-standard clichés for modern, creative dishes. The result: appetite-piquing options like teriyaki-style tartare with caperberries, or surf-turf *tagliolini* pasta with succulent shrimps and pork jowl. Bar seating available; ideal for solo diners. Book ahead.

Ristorante Ferro
SICILIAN €€

(📋 347 1618373, 091 58 60 49; www.facebook.com/ristoranteferropalermo; Piazza Sant'Onofrio 42;

PALERMO'S STREET FOOD

Bangkok, Mexico City, Marrakesh and Palermo: worldly gluttons know that Sicily's capital is a street-food heavyweight. Palermitans are obsessed with eating (and eating well), and almost any time is a good time to feast. What they're devouring is *buffitieri* – little hot snacks prepared at stalls and designed for eating on the spot.

Kick off the morning with *pane e panelle*, Palermo's famous chickpea fritters – great for vegetarians and a welcome change from a sweet custard-filled croissant. You might also want to go for some *crocchè* (potato croquettes, sometimes flavoured with fresh mint) or *quaglie* (literally translated as quails, they're actually aubergines/eggplants cut lengthwise and fanned out to resemble a bird's feathers, then fried). Other options include *sfincione* (a spongy, oily pizza topped with onions and caciocavallo cheese) and *scaccie* (discs of bread dough spread with a filling and rolled up into a pancake). In the warmer months, locals find it difficult to refuse a freshly baked brioche jammed with gelato or *granita* (crushed ice mixed with fresh fruit, almonds, pistachios or coffee).

From 4pm onwards the snacks become decidedly more carnivorous, and you may just wish you hadn't read the following translations: how about some barbecued *stigghiola* (goat intestines filled with onions, cheese and parsley), for example? Or a couple of *pani ca meusa* (breadroll stuffed with sautéed beef spleen). You'll be asked if you want it *'schietta'* (single) or *'maritata'* (married). If you choose *schietta,* the roll will only have ricotta in it before being dipped into boiling lard; choose *maritata* and you'll get beef spleen as well.

You'll find stalls and kiosks selling street food all over town, especially in Palermo's street markets. Top choices include **Francu U Vastiddaru** (Corso Vittorio Emanuele 102; sandwiches €1.50-4; ⊙ 9am-1am), **Friggitoria Chiluzzo** (☑ 329 0615929; Piazza della Kalsa; sandwiches €1-2.50; ⊙ 8am-5pm Mon-Sat, to 4pm Sun) and tiny **I Cuochini** (Via Ruggero Settimo 68; snacks from €0.70; ⊙ 8.30am-2.30pm Mon-Sat, plus 4.30-7.30pm Sat).

meals €30-40; ⊙ 8-11pm Mon-Sat) All clean lines, timber panels and tinted mirrors, intimate, family-run Ferro wouldn't look out of place in London or Sydney. Whether you're savouring a soup of squid and mussels, earthy ravioli stuffed with porcini mushrooms, or a flawless steak, the food here is superb in its simplicity, favouring prime produce cooked beautifully and without fuss. Alas, wines by the glass are limited.

Le Angeliche   SICILIAN €€
(☑ 091 615 70 95; www.leangeliche.it; Vicolo Abbadia 10; meals €25-35; ⊙ 9am-3pm Mon-Thu, to midnight Fri & Sat; 🛜) An oasis of potted plants and pastel hues, Le Angeliche is run by four women passionate about honouring and refreshing Sicily's rich, sometime obscure culinary traditions. Scan the menu and you might find a soup of cannellini beans, endive, chestnuts and pasta, or perhaps *cassatella di Montevago* – fried, ravioli-like pastries filled with sweetened sheep's milk ricotta, honey and lemon zest. Book ahead.

Bioesserì   HEALTH FOOD €€
(☑ 091 765 71 42; www.bioesseri.it; Via Giuseppe La Farina 4; pizza €7.50-14, meals €30-35; ⊙ 7.30am-11pm Mon-Thu, to 11.30pm Fri, 8.30am-11.30pm Sat, to 11pm Sun; 🛜) Organic fare with flair awaits at this stylish Milanese import. Part cafe,

part upmarket grocery store, its virtuous bites tap all bases, including vegan *cornetti* (croissants), smoothies and soy-milk *budini* (puddings), spelt-flour pizzas and well-executed, bistro-style dishes like *fregola* pasta in a fish-and-crustacean soup, or stuffed calamari paired with herbed potato purée.

Gagini   ITALIAN €€€
(☑ 091 58 99 18; www.gaginirestaurant.com; Via Cassari 35; meals €45, 4-/5-/8-course degustation menu €70/85/110; ⊙ 12.30-3pm & 7.30-11.30pm; 🛜) Expect sharp professionals and serious gastronomes at Gagini's rustic, candlelit tables. In the kitchen are Massimiliano Mandozzi and Elnava De Rosa, whose passion for season, region and fresh thinking might offer a Sicilian twist on the kebab, a playful take on classic *pasta con le sarde* (pasta with sardines), or seafood unexpectedly paired with cracked wheat and hazelnuts. Book ahead.

🍸 Drinking & Nightlife

Popular drinking spots include bohemian Via Paternostro, Piazza della Rivoluzione, Discesa dei Giudici, as well as cheap, gritty Via Maccherronai. Further north, lively bars line Via Isidora la Lumia. You'll also find bars in the Champagneria district due east of Teatro Massimo, centred on Piazza Olivella, Via

Spinuzza and Via Patania. Higher-end drinking spots are concentrated in the new city.

★ **Ferramenta** WINE BAR

(☑ 091 672 70 61; Piazza G Meli 8; ☉ 6.30pm-1am Tue-Sun) Once a hardware store, this genuinely cool, piazza-side bar-eatery now fixes long days with well-mixed cocktails and clued-in vino. Rotating wines by the glass might include a natural white from western Sicily or an organic red from Etna, best paired with a *tagliere* (board) of top-notch charcuterie, seafood or vegetables (€10 to €18). More substantial dishes are also available, including pasta.

★ **Hic! La Folie du Vin** WINE BAR

(☑ 349 2693038; www.facebook.com/hiclafoliedu vin; Via G Mazzini 46; ☉ 6.30-11.30pm, closed Sun mid-Jun–Jul & Sep, closed Mon Oct–mid-Jun, closed Aug) Hugely popular with 30- and 40-plus locals, Hic! is never short of a fun crowd, spilling out onto the footpath in a sea of banter and reasonably priced vino. The latter includes lots of Italian, French and German drops, each one approved by owner Giuseppe. Edibles include quality cheeses and cured meats, and the bar hosts live acoustic sets on Sunday evenings.

☆ Entertainment

★ **Teatro Massimo** OPERA

(☑ box office 091 605 35 80; www.teatromassimo. it; Piazza Giuseppe Verdi) Ernesto Basile's six-tiered art-nouveau masterpiece is Europe's second-largest opera house and one of Italy's most prestigious, right up there with La Scala in Milan, San Carlo in Naples and La Fenice in Venice. It stages opera, ballet and music concerts from September to June. Opera tickets range from around €20 to €140.

Teatro dei Pupi di
Mimmo Cuticchio THEATRE

(☑ 091 32 34 00; www.facebook.com/TeatroDell OperaDeiPupi; Via Bara all'Olivella 95) This puppet theatre is a charming low-tech choice for children (and the child within), staging traditional, one-hour shows using exquisitely handcrafted Sicilian *pupi* (puppets). Check the theatre's Facebook page for upcoming performances.

🛍 Shopping

In the new city, Via della Libertà is lined with high-end fashion stores. More atmospheric is Palermo's historic centre, where crumbly streets harbour artisan workshops selling everything from ceramics to leather goods. Many belong to ALAB (www.alab palermo.it), an association of artisans helping to revitalise the area. For fresh edibles, hit Mercato di Ballarò or Mercato del Capo. Come Sunday morning, trawl the Mercatino Antiquariato Piazza Marina for antiques and decorative objects.

ℹ Information

Micro² Tourist Information Centre (☑ 091 732 02 48; www.visitpalermo.it; Via Torremuzza 15; ☉ 10am-1pm & 2.30-5.30pm Mon-Sat, 10.30am-2pm Sun) Enthusiastic, privately run tourist-information office open seven days a week and able to book tours, transfers and accommodation.

Municipal Tourist Office (☑ 091 740 80 21; http://turismo.comune.palermo.it; Piazza Bellini; ☉ 8.45am-6.15pm Mon-Fri, from 9.45am Sat) Main branch of Palermo's city-run information booths. Other locations include **Via Cavour** (☉ 8.30am-1.30pm Mon-Fri), **Teatro Massimo** (Piazza Giuseppe Verdi; ☉ 9.30am-1.30pm Mon-Fri), the Port of Palermo and Mondello, though these are only intermittently staffed, with unpredictable hours.

Ospedale Civico (☑ 091 666 55 17; www.arnas civico.it; Via Tricomi; ☉ 24hr) Major hospital with 24-hour emergency department.

Police (Questura; ☑ 091 21 01 11; Piazza della Vittoria 8) Palermo's main station, located between Via Maqueda and Palazzo dei Normanni.

Tourist Information Office, Falcone-Borsellino Airport (☑ 091 59 16 98; www.gesap.it/en/ aeroporto/services/tourist-information-of-fice; ☉ 8.30am-7.30pm Mon-Fri, to 6pm Sat) Downstairs in the arrivals hall, run by Palermo Metropolitan City.

ℹ Getting There & Away

AIR

Palermo Falcone-Borsellino Airport (☑ 800 541880, 091 702 02 73; www.gesap.it) is at Punta Raisi, 31km northwest of Palermo on the E90 motorway. Alitalia and other major airlines such as Air France, Lufthansa and KLM fly from Palermo to destinations throughout Europe. Several cut-rate carriers also offer flights to/ from Palermo, including Ryanair, Volotea, Vueling and easyJet. Falcone-Borsellino is the hub airport for regular domestic flights to the islands of Pantelleria and Lampedusa.

BOAT

Ferry companies operate from Palermo's **port** (☑ 091 604 31 11; cnr Via Francesco Crispi & Via Emerico Amari), just east of the new city.

Grandi Navi Veloci (☑ 010 209 45 91, 091 6072 6162; www.gnv.it; Molo Piave, Porto Stazione Marittima) Runs ferries to Civitavecchia (from €43), Genoa (from €51), Naples (from €43) and Tunis (from €44).

Grimaldi Lines (☑ 081 49 65 55, 091 611 36 91; www.grimaldi-lines.com; Molo Piave, Porto Stazione Marittima) Operates twice-weekly ferries from Palermo to Salerno (from €25, 9½ to 11 hours) and Tunis (from €38, 10 to 13½ hours). Ferries run thrice weekly to Livorno (from €32, 18½ to 19½ hours).

Liberty Lines (☑ 091 32 42 55; www.liberty lines.it; Calata Marinai d'Italia) Operates one to five daily hydrofoil services (€26, 1½ hours) between Ustica and Palermo.

Siremar (☑ 090 57 37; https://carontetourist. it/it/siremar; ⏲ ticket office 9.30am-1pm & 3-6.15pm) Runs one daily car ferry (passenger including car from €95, three hours) between Ustica and Palermo.

Tirrenia (☑ 800 804020, 091 611 65 18; www. tirrenia.it; Calata Marinai d'Italia) Sails to Cagliari (from €45, 13 hours, once or twice weekly) and Naples (from €55, 10½ hours, daily).

BUS

Offices for all bus companies are located within a block or two of Palermo Centrale train station. The two main departure points are the Piazzetta Cairoli bus terminal, just south of the train station's eastern entrance, and the newer Via Tommaso Fazello bus terminal, beside the station's western entrance. Check locally with your bus company to make sure you're boarding at the appropriate stop.

AST (Azienda Siciliana Trasporti; ☑ 091 620 81 11; www.aziendasicilianatrasporti.it; Piazzetta Cairoli Bus Terminal) Services to southeastern destinations including Ragusa (€13.50, four hours, two to four daily) and Modica (€13.50, 4½ hours, two to four daily)

Autoservizi Tarantola (☑ 0924 310 20; www. facebook.com/groups/calecavincenzo; Via Paolo Balsamo) To Segesta (€7, 1¼ hours, three daily Mon-Sat Apr-Oct)

Cuffaro (☑ 091 616 15 10; www.facebook. com/cuffaro.info; Via Paolo Balsamo 13) To Agrigento (€9, two hours, three to seven daliy)

Interbus (☑ 091 616 79 19; www.interbus.it; Piazzetta Cairoli Bus Terminal) To Syracuse (€13.50, 3½ hours, two to three daily)

SAIS Autolinee (☑ 800 211020, 091 616 60 28; www.saisautolinee.it; Piazzetta Cairoli Bus Terminal) To Messina (€14, 2¾ hours, four to seven daily) and Catania (€14, 2¾ hours, 10 to 14 daily)

Salemi (☑ 0923 98 11 20; www.autoservizi salemi.it; Piazzetta Cairoli Bus Station) To Trapani airport (€11, 1¾ hours, four to six daily) and Marsala (€9.50, 2¼ hours, four to six daily)

AST, Salemi, Segesta, SAIS and Interbus tickets are sold at the bus terminal building at Piazzetta Cairoli.

Cuffaro tickets can be purchased from the Cuffaro ticket office at Via Paolo Balsamo 13, just east of the train station, or on board.

CAR & MOTORCYCLE

Palermo is accessible on the A20–E90 toll road from Messina, and from Catania (A19–E932) via Enna. Trapani and Marsala are also easily accessible from Palermo by motorway (A29), while Agrigento and Palermo are linked by the SS121, a good state road through the interior of the island.

TRAIN

Regular services leave from **Palermo Centrale train station** (Piazza Giulio Cesare) to the following destinations:

Agrigento (€9, two hours, six to 13 daily)

Catania (€13.50, three hours, five to six Monday to Saturday, transfers required Sunday)

Cefalù (from €5.60, 45 minutes to one hour, eight to 17 daily)

Messina (€12.80; 2¾ to three hours, six to nine daily)

From Messina, Intercity trains continue to Reggio di Calabria, Naples and Rome.

Inside the station are ATMs, toilets and left-luggage facilities (first five hours €6 flat fee, next seven hours €1 per hour, all subsequent hours €0.50 per hour; office staffed 8am to 8pm).

ⓘ Getting Around

TO/FROM THE AIRPORT

Prestia e Comandè (☑ 091 58 63 51; www. prestiaecomande.it; Via Tommaso Fazello Bus Terminal; 1-way/return €6.50/11) runs efficient, half-hourly buses between Palermo and the airport. From the airport, buses run from 5am to 12.30am (1am May to October; 50 minutes). From Palermo, airport-bound buses run from 4am to 10.30pm, departing from the Via Tommaso Fazello Bus Terminal beside Palermo Centrale train station and stopping at numerous points in central Palermo, including outside the Rinascente department store on Via Roma 289 and on Piazza Ruggero II. Purchase tickets on board or, for a small discount, online.

Trinacria Express (☑ 091 704 40 07; www. trenitalia.com) trains run between the airport (Punta Raisi station) and Palermo Centrale (€5.90, around one hour). Trains run every 15 to 60 minutes and tickets can be purchased online or at the station.

Societá Autolinee Licata (SAL; ☑ 0922 40 13 60; www.autolineesal.it) runs between the airport and Agrigento (€12.60, 2¾ hours, three daily Monday to Saturday).

SICILY PALERMO

There is a taxi rank outside the arrivals hall and the fare to/from Palermo is between €35 and €45, depending on your destination in the city.

All major car-hire companies are represented at the airport.You'll often save money by booking online before leaving home. Given the city's chaotic traffic and expensive parking, and the excellent public transport from Palermo's airport, it's generally best to postpone rental car pickup until you're ready to leave the city.

BICYCLE

Centrally located **Social Bike Palermo** (☑ 328 2843734; www.socialbikepalermo.com; Discesa dei Giudici 21; standard/electric bike half-day €8/15, guided bike tours €40-55; ☺ 9.30am-6.30pm) rents out folding, standard, electric and tandem bikes and runs bike tours of Palermo's *centro storico* (historic centre) and its Liberty (art nouveau) architecture.

CAR & MOTORCYCLE

Driving is frenetic in Palermo and best avoided. Many hotels have a *garage convenzionato*, a local garage that offers special rates to their guests (typically between €12 and €20 per day). Street parking spaces marked by blue lines require that you buy a ticket from a machine or a *tabaccheria* (tobacconist's shop); spaces marked by white lines are free.

PUBLIC TRANSPORT

Palermo's orange, white and blue city buses, operated by **AMAT** (☑ 091 35 01 11, 848 800817; http://amat.pa.it), are frequent but often overcrowded and slow. Tickets, valid for 90 minutes, cost €1.40 if pre-purchased from *tabaccherie* or from AMAT information kiosks, including one at Palermo Centrale train station. Tickets can also be purchased on board (€1.80). A day pass costs €3.50. Remember to validate your ticket at a machine when boarding. The free map handed out at Palermo tourist offices details the major bus lines; most stop at Palermo Centrale train station.

TAXI

Official taxis should have a *tassametro* (meter), which records the fare; check for this before embarking. The minimum starting fare is €3.81, with a range of additional charges, all listed at www.taxi.it/palermo. Hailing a passing taxi on the street is not customary; rather, wait at one of the taxi ranks at major travel hubs such as the train station, Piazza Ruggero Settimo, Teatro Massimo and Piazza Indipendenza, or order ahead by calling **Autoradio Taxi Palermo** (☑ 091 8481; www.autoradiotaxi.it) or using appTaxi (www.apptaxi.it).

TYRRHENIAN COAST

The coast between Palermo and Milazzo is studded with popular tourist resorts attracting a steady stream of holidaymakers, particularly between June and September. The best of these is Cefalù, a resort second only to the Ionian coast's Taormina in popularity. Just inland lie the two massive natural parks of the Madonie and Nebrodi mountains.

Cefalù

☑ 0921 / POP 14,300

Beautiful Cefalù offers a rare combination of tourist attractions: one of Sicliy's finest beaches side-by-side with one of its greatest Arab-Norman architectural masterpieces, all set against a dramatic mountain backdrop. Holidaymakers from all over Europe flock here to relax in resort hotels, stroll the narrow cobbled streets and sun themselves on the long sandy beach.

This popular holiday resort wedged between a dramatic mountain peak and a sweeping stretch of sand has the lot: a great beach, a truly lovely historic centre with a grandiose cathedral, and winding medieval streets lined with restaurants and boutiques. Avoid the height of summer when prices soar, beaches are jam packed and the charm of the place is tainted by bad-tempered drivers trying to find a car park.

◉ Sights & Activities

★ **Duomo di Cefalù**   CATHEDRAL

(☑ 092 192 20 21; www.cattedraledicefalu.com; Piazza del Duomo; towers & apse or treasury & cloisters €5, combo ticket incl towers, apse, treasury & cloisters €8; ☺ 8.30am-6.30pm Apr-Oct, 8.30am-1pm & 3.30-5pm Nov-Mar) Cefalù's cathedral is one of the jewels in Sicily's Arab-Norman crown, only equalled in magnificence by the Cattedrale di Monreale and Palermo's Cappella Palatina. Filling the central apse, a towering figure of Cristo Pantocratore (Christ All Powerful) is the focal point of the elaborate Byzantine mosaics – Sicily's oldest and best preserved, predating those of Monreale by 20 or 30 years.

★ **Spiaggia di Cefalù**   BEACH

Cefalù's crescent-shaped beach is one of the most popular along the whole Sicilian coast. In summer it's packed, so arrive early to get a good spot. Though some sections require a ticket, the area closest to the old town is public and you can hire a beach umbrella and deckchair for around €15 per day.

★ **La Rocca** HIKING
(adult/reduced €4/2; ⊙8am-7pm May-Sep, 9am-4pm Oct-Apr) Looming over Cefalù, this imposing rocky crag was once the site of an Arab citadel, superseded in 1061 by the Norman castle whose ruins still crown the summit. To reach the top, follow signs for Tempio di Diana, taking Vicolo Saraceni off Corso Ruggero or Via Giuseppe Fiore off Piazza Garibaldi. The 30- to 45-minute route climbs the **Salita Saraceni**, a winding staircase, through three tiers of city walls before emerging onto rock-strewn upland slopes with spectacular coastal views.

🛏 Sleeping & Eating

Bookings are essential in the summer.

★ **B&B Agrodolce** B&B €
(☑338 7250863; www.agrodolcebb.it; Via Gioeni 44; d €80-110, tr €100-120; 🛜) Three flights of old stone steps lead to this lovely upper-floor B&B in Cefalù's historic centre. Architect Rita Riolo offers four bright and airy rooms with cool tiled floors and bathrooms, along with delicious lemon cake and other home-baked goodies served on a tiny breakfast terrace looking towards the Duomo.

La Plumeria HOTEL €€
(☑0921 92 58 97; www.laplumeriahotel.it; Corso Ruggero 185; d €169-229; P❄🛜) Midway between the Duomo and the waterfront, this small hotel offers four-star service in a prime location. Rooms are mostly unexceptional but well appointed; the sweetest of the lot is

room 301, a cosy top-floor eyrie with checkerboard tile floors and a small terrace looking up to the Duomo.

Bottega Tivitti PIZZA €
(☑0921 92 26 42; www.bottegativitti.com; Lungomare Giardina 7; mains €6-15; ⊙11am-4pm & 7pm-midnight) This casual waterfront spot serves pizzas, salads and inventive 'Sicilian burgers' made with top-of-the-line local ingredients – like the Tivitti Burger, with sheep's-milk cheese, olive tapenade, sundried tomatoes and roasted eggplant. It's a great spot to watch the sunset while sampling Sicilian wines and microbrews and snacking on local cheese and meat platters.

Mandralisca 16 Bistrot SICILIAN €€
(☑0921 99 22 45; www.facebook.com/mandralisca16; Via Mandralisca 16; meals €25-35; ⊙noon-3pm & 7-11pm Tue-Sun) Picturesque setting combines with scrumptious Sicilian cuisine at this relative newcomer with sidewalk seating in an alley gazing towards the Duomo's bell towers. Start with a perfect *caponata* (eggplant, olives, capers, onions and celery in a sweet-and-sour tomato sauce), then move on to chickpea, chard and sage soup or *involtini* (roulades) of fish with citrus, bay leaves and breadcrumbs.

Locanda del Marinaio SEAFOOD €€
(☑0921 42 32 95; www.locandadelmarinaiocefalu.it; Via Porpora 5; meals €35-45; ⊙noon-2.30pm & 7-11pm Wed-Sun, 7-11pm Mon) Fresh seafood rules the chalkboard menu at this upscale eatery on the old town's main waterfront thoroughfare. Depending on the season, you'll find

SICILY CEFALÙ

WORTH A TRIP

THE MADONIE MOUNTAINS: CEFALÙ'S BACKYARD PLAYGROUND

Due south of Cefalù, the 400sq-km **Parco Naturale Regionale delle Madonie** incorporates some of Sicily's highest peaks, including the imposing Pizzo Carbonara (1979m). The park's wild, wooded slopes are home to wolves, wildcats, eagles and the near-extinct ancient Nebrodi fir trees that have survived since the last ice age. Ideal for hiking, cycling and horse trekking, the park is also home to several handsome mountain towns, including **Castelbuono**, **Petralia Soprana** and **Petralia Sottana**.

The region's distinctive rural cuisine includes roasted lamb and goat, cheeses, grilled mushrooms, and aromatic pasta with *sugo* (meat sauce). A great place to sample these specialties is **Nangalarruni** (☑0921 67 12 28; www.hostariananangalarruni.it; Via delle Confraternite 7; meals €29-45; ⊙12.30-3pm & 7-10pm Thu-Tue) in Castelbuono.

For information, contact the park headquarters in **Petralia Sottana** (Madonie Park Authority; ☑0921 68 40 11; www.parcodellemadonie.eu; Corso Paolo Agliata 16) or the branch office in **Cefalù** (☑0921 92 33 27; www.parcodellemadonie.eu; Corso Ruggero 116; ⊙8am-2pm Mon, to 6pm Tue-Sat).

Bus service to the park's main towns is limited; to fully appreciate the Madonie, you're better off hiring a car for a couple of days.

dishes such as red tuna carpaccio with toasted pine nuts, shrimp and zucchini on a bed of velvety ricotta, or grilled octopus served with thyme-scented potatoes, all accompanied by an excellent list of Sicilian wines.

ℹ️ Information

Tourist Office (☑️ 0921 42 10 50; www.turismocefalu.sicilia.it; Corso Ruggero 77; ⊙ 9am-7.30pm Mon-Fri, 8am-2pm Sat) English-speaking staff, lots of leaflets and good maps.

ℹ️ Getting There & Away

Hourly trains go to Palermo (€5.60, 45 minutes to 1¼ hours), and virtually every other town on the coast.

AEOLIAN ISLANDS

The Aeolian Islands are a little piece of paradise. Stunning cobalt sea, splendid beaches, some of Italy's best hiking and an awe-inspiring volcanic landscape are just part of the appeal. The islands also have a fascinating human and mythological history that goes back several millennia: the Aeolians figured prominently in Homer's *Odyssey*, and evidence of the distant past can be seen everywhere, most notably in Lipari's excellent archaeological museum.

The seven islands of Lipari, Vulcano, Salina, Panarea, Stromboli, Alicudi and Filicudi are part of a huge 200km volcanic ridge that runs between the smoking stack of Mt Etna and the threatening mass of Vesuvius above Naples. Collectively, the islands exhibit a unique range of volcanic characteristics, which have earned them a place on Unesco's World Heritage List. The islands are mobbed with visitors in July and August, but out of season things remain delightfully tranquil.

ℹ️ Getting There & Away

Liberty Lines (☑️ 0923 87 38 13; www.libertylines.it) operates the lion's share of hydrofoils to the islands, including summer-only services from Palermo that make stops on all seven islands. Check the Liberty Lines website for up-to-the-minute schedules.

Ferry service from Milazzo (cheaper but slower and less frequent than hydrofoil service) is provided by **Siremar** (☑️ 090 57 37; www.carontetourist.it/en/siremar) and **NGI Traghetti** (☑️ 090 928 40 91; www.ngi-spa.it).

From Naples, Siremar runs twice-weekly car ferries to the islands, while **SNAV** (☑️ 081 428 55 55; www.snav.it) operates summer-only hydrofoils.

ℹ️ Getting Around

Liberty Lines (www.libertylines.it) runs frequent hydrofoils connecting all seven islands; ferries ply the same routes, costing less but taking twice as long.

Lipari, Vulcano and Salina are the only islands with significant road networks. Bringing your own car by ferry is expensive; you'll often save money by garaging it at Milazzo or Messina on the mainland (from €12 per day) and hiring a scooter on-site, or better yet, exploring the islands on foot or bike.

Lipari

☑️ 090 / POP 12,800

Lipari is the largest, busiest and most accessible of the Aeolian Islands, yet still retains a charming, unhurried vibe. Visitors arriving from the mainland will likely experience it as a relaxing introduction to island life; on the other hand, if you've just come from the outer Aeolians, it may feel a bit like a big city!

The main focus is Lipari Town, the archipelago's principal transport hub and the nearest thing that islanders have to a capital city. A busy little port with a pretty, pastel-coloured seafront and plenty of accommodation, it makes the most convenient base for island-hopping. Away from the town, Lipari reveals a rugged and typically Mediterranean landscape of low-lying *macchia* (dense Mediterranean shrubbery), silent, windswept highlands, precipitous cliffs and dreamy blue waters.

👁️ Sights

Town Centre   AREA
One of Lipari Town's great pleasures is simply wandering its streets, lapping up the laid-back island atmosphere. Lipari's liveliest street is **Corso Vittorio Emanuele**, a cheerful thoroughfare lined with bars, cafes and restaurants. The street really comes into its own in early evening, when it's closed to traffic and the locals come out for their *passeggiata* (evening stroll). Equally atmospheric is **Marina Corta**, down at the end of Via Garibaldi, a pretty little marina ringed by popular bars and restaurants.

⭐ **Museo Archeologico Regionale Eoliano**   MUSEUM
(☑️090 988 01 74; www.regione.sicilia.it/beniculturali/museolipari; Via Castello 2; adult/reduced €6/3; ⊙9am-7.30pm Mon-Sat, to 1.30pm Sun) A must-see for Mediterranean history buffs, Lipari's archaeological museum has one of Europe's

finest collections of ancient finds. Especially worthwhile are the **Sezione Preistorica**, devoted to locally discovered artefacts from the Neolithic and Bronze Ages to the Graeco-Roman era, and the **Sezione Classica**, the highlights of which include ancient shipwreck cargoes and the world's largest collection of miniature Greek theatrical masks. Pay admission fees at the **ticket office**, about 100m north of the Sezione Classica.

★ **Quattrocchi**   VIEWPOINT

Lipari's best coastal views are from a celebrated viewpoint known as Quattrocchi (Four Eyes), 3km west of town. Follow the road for Pianoconte and look on your left as you approach a big hairpin bend about 300m beyond the turnoff for Spiaggia Valle Muria. Stretching off to the south, great cliffs plunge into the sea, while in the distance plumes of sinister smoke rise from the dark heights of neighbouring Vulcano.

★ **Spiaggia Valle Muria**   BEACH

Lapped by clean waters and surrounded by sheer cliffs, this dark, pebbly beach on Lipari's southwestern shore is a dramatically beautiful swimming and sunbathing spot. From the signposted turnoff, 3km west of Lipari town towards Pianoconte, it's a steep 25-minute downhill walk; come prepared with water and sunscreen. In good weather, Lipari resident **Barni** (☑ 339 8221583, 349 1839555) sells refreshments from his rustic cave-like beach bar, and provides memorably scenic boat transfers to and from Lipari's Marina Corta (€5/10 one-way/return).

☞ **Tours**

Numerous agencies in town, including the dependable **Da Massimo/Dolce Vita** (☑ 090 601 98 41; www.damassimo.it; Via Maurolico 2), offer boat tours to the surrounding islands. Prices run around €20 for a tour of Lipari and Vulcano, €45 to visit Filicudi and Alicudi, €45 for a day trip to Panarea and Stromboli, or €80 for a late-afternoon trip to Stromboli with a guided trip up the mountain and a late-night return to Lipari.

🛏 **Sleeping**

Lipari is the Aeolians' best-equipped base for island-hopping, with plenty of places to stay, eat and drink. Note that prices soar in summer; avoid August if possible.

★ **B&B Al Salvatore di Lipari**   B&B €

(☑ 335 8343222; www.facebook.com/bbalsalvatore; Via San Salvatore, Contrada al Salvatore; d €60-

120; ⊘ Apr-Oct; 🛜) Once you reach this peaceful hillside oasis 2km south of town, you may never want to leave. Artist Paola and physicist Marcello have transformed their Aeolian villa into a green B&B that works at all levels, from dependable wi-fi to a panoramic terrace where delicious home-grown breakfasts are served, featuring produce from the adjacent garden, fresh-baked cakes and homemade marmalade.

★ **Diana Brown**   B&B €

(☑ 338 6407572, 090 981 25 84; www.dianabrown.it; Vico Himera 3; s €35-65, d €50-80, tr €65-105; ❄🛜) Now run by the daughter and son-in-law of longtime Lipari innkeeper Diana Brown, this delightful warren of rooms tucked down a narrow alley sports attractive features including in-room kettles, fridges, clothes-drying racks, satellite TV and a book exchange. Units downstairs are darker but have built-in kitchenettes. Its excellent buffet breakfast is served on the sunny terrace and solarium with deck chairs.

Enzo Il Negro   GUESTHOUSE €

(☑ 090 981 31 63; www.enzoilnegro.com; Via Garibaldi 29; s €45-50, d €75-90, tr €90-120; ❄🛜) Family-run for nearly 40 years, and perfectly placed in the pedestrian zone near picturesque Marina Corta, Enzo and Cettina's down-to-earth guesthouse offers spacious, tiled, pine-furnished rooms with fridges and air-con. Two panoramic terraces overlook the rooftops, the harbour and the castle walls.

🍴 **Eating**

Gilberto e Vera   SANDWICHES €

(☑ 090 981 27 56; www.gilbertoevera.it; Via Garibaldi 22; half/full sandwiches €3.50/5; ⊘ 7.30am-11pm mid-Mar–mid-Nov) Still run by the friendly couple who founded it four decades ago (ably assisted by daughter Alessia), this beloved shop sells two dozen varieties of *panini,* many named for now-grown locals who once stopped by here on their way to school. It's the perfect stop for morning hiking and beach-hopping provisions, or afternoon glasses of wine on the street-side terrace.

★ **Sangre Rojo**   SICILIAN €€

(☑ 338 2909524; www.facebook.com/ristorantesangrerojo; meals €34-39; ⊘ noon-2.30pm & 7pm-midnight Wed-Mon Easter–mid-Oct) Dazzling vistas of Salina, Filicudi and Alicudi floating in the Tyrrhenian are reason enough to visit this hilltop restaurant near Lipari's northern tip. But the cuisine, based on fresh fish and classic Aeolian ingredients like wild fennel, capers,

Lipari Town

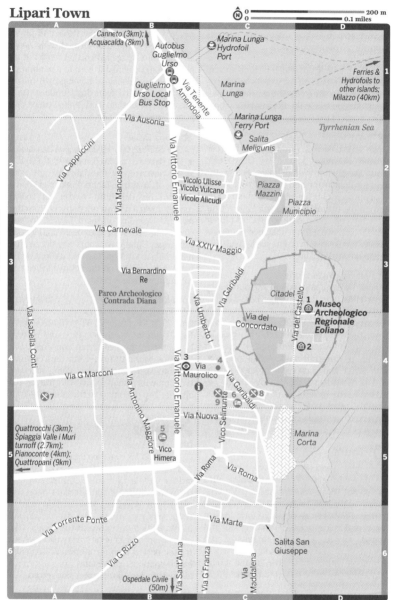

Canneto (3km);
Acquacalda (8km)

Autobus
Guglielmo
Urso

Marina Lunga
Hydrofoil
Port

Guglielmo
Urso Local
Bus Stop

Ferries &
Hydrofoils to
other islands;
Milazzo (40km)

Via Tenente Amendola

Via Ausonia

Marina
Lunga

Via Cappuccini

Via Mancuso

Via Vittorio Emanuele

Marina Lunga
Ferry Port

Salita
Meligunis

Tyrrhenian Sea

Vicolo Ulisse
Vicolo Vulcano
Vicolo Alicudi

Piazza
Mazzini

Piazza
Municipio

Via Carnevale

Via XXIV Maggio

Via Bernardino
Re

Parco Archeologico
Contrada Diana

Via Garibaldi

Citadel

Via del
Concordato

Via del Castello

1
Museo
Archeologico
Regionale
Eoliano

2

Via Umberto I

Via Isabella Conti

Via G Marconi

3
Via
Maurolico

4

7

Via Vittorio Emanuele

Via Antonino Maggiore

9

6

8

Via Garibaldi

Vico Selinunte

Via Nuova

5

Vico
Himera

Marina
Corta

Quattrocchi (3km);
Spiaggia Valle i Muri
turnoff (2.7km);
Pianoconte (4km);
Quattropani (9km)

Via Roma

Via Roma

Via Torrente Ponte

Via Marte

Salita San
Giuseppe

Via G Rizzo

Via Sant'Anna

Via G Franza

Via Maddalena

Ospedale Civile
(50m)

olives and mint, is the real clincher. Enjoy lunch on the gorgeous sun-drenched terrace or linger over dinner with a sunset view.

Kasbah MEDITERRANEAN €€
(☑090 921 37 42; www.kasbahlipari.it; Vico Selinunte 43; pizzas €10-12, meals €35, tasting menu

€45; ⊘7-10.30pm Apr-Oct) Tucked down narrow Vico Selinunte, with a window where you can watch the chefs at work, this place serves everything from fancy pasta, fish and meat dishes to simple wood-fired pizzas (try the Kasbah, with smoked swordfish, rocket, lemon and black pepper). The stylish dining

Lipari Town

◎ Top Sights
1 Museo Archeologico Regionale
   Eoliano..D3

◎ Sights
Museo Archeologico
   Eoliano (Sezione Classica)........(see 1)
2 Museo Archeologico Eoliano
   (Sezione Preistorica) D4
3 Town Centre...B4

◎ Activities, Courses & Tours
4 Da Massimo/Dolce Vita.....................C4

◎ Sleeping
5 Diana Brown...B5
6 Enzo Il Negro C4

◎ Eating
7 E Pulera...A4
8 Gilberto e Vera C4
9 Kasbah C4

room with its grey linen tablecloths is complemented by a more casual outdoor terrace.

E Pulera   MODERN SICILIAN €€
(☑ 090 981 11 58; www.pulera.it; Via Isabella Conti; meals €35-45; ⊙ 7.30-11.30pm late Apr–mid-Oct) With its serene garden setting, low lighting, tile-topped tables and exquisite food – from tuna carpaccio with blood oranges and capers for dinner to *cassata* (sponge cake, ricotta, marzipan, chocolate and candied fruit) served with sweet Malvasia wine for dessert – E Pulera makes an upscale but relaxed choice for a romantic dinner.

ⓘ Information

Tourist Office (☑ 090 988 00 95; Via Maurolico 17; ⊙ 9am-1pm Mon-Fri, plus 4-6pm Wed & Fri) Lipari's sporadically staffed office provides information covering all the Aeolian Islands.

ⓘ Getting There & Around

BOAT
Lipari is the Aeolians' transport hub. The main port is Marina Lunga, where you'll find the **ticket office** (☑ 090 981 24 48; ⊙ 5am-8.40pm) for hydrofoil operator Liberty Lines, and ferry operators NGI and Siremar. Hydrofoils run frequently to the mainland port of Milazzo (€16, one hour) and to the other Aeolian islands, including Vulcano (€6, 10 minutes), Salina (€9, 20 minutes) and Stromboli (€18, 1½ to 1¾ hours). Hydrofoil service to Messina (€26, 1½ to 3¼ hours) is less frequent. In summer (late May through early September), **SNAV** (☑ 081 428 55 55; www.

snav.it) also runs daily hydrofoils from Naples to Lipari (from €62, 6½ hours).

BUS
Autobus Guglielmo Urso (☑ 090 981 10 26; www.ursobus.com/Orario-ita.htm) runs buses from its stop opposite the Marina Lunga hydrofoil dock. One route serves the island's eastern shore, from Lipari Town to Canneto (five minutes) and Acquacalda (20 minutes); another runs from Lipari Town to the splendid Quattrocchi viewpoint and the western highland settlements of Pianoconte and Quattropani. Individual tickets range from €1.30 to €2.40; discounts are available for round-trip tickets or multiple rides (six/10/20 tickets for €10/14/28). Service is limited to nonexistent on Sundays.

CAR & MOTORCYCLE
Lipari's seafront road circles the entire island, a journey of about 30km. Various outfits at Marina Lunga, including **Da Marcello** (☑ 090 981 12 34; www.noleggiodamarcello.com; Via Amendola), rent out bikes (about €10 per day), scooters (€15 to €40) and cars (€30 to €70).

Vulcano

POP 720

With its visibly smoking crater and vile sulphurous fumes, Vulcano makes an indelible first impression. The island's volcanic nature has long impressed visitors: the ancient Romans believed it to be the chimney of the fire god Vulcan's workshop. Vulcano's most obvious attractions – climbing the crater, strolling over to the mud baths and the black beaches at Porto di Ponente – are easily managed on a day trip from Lipari. Visitors who linger and explore beyond drab, dated and touristy Porto di Levante will discover a whole different island, swimming off Gelso's volcanic beaches, kayaking the wild coast or enjoying the rural tranquillity of the central plateau, filled with vegetable gardens, birdsong and a surprising amount of greenery.

Boats dock at Porto di Levante. To the right, as you face the island, are the mud baths and the small Vulcanello peninsula; to the left is the volcano. Straight ahead is Porto di Ponente, 700m west, where you will find the black sands of **Spiaggia Sabbie Nere**.

◎ Sights & Activities

For spectacular sea and island views without the physical exertion of climbing Fossa di Vulcano, follow the signposted road to **Capo Grillo**, about 7km southeast of Vulcano port, near the mid-island settlement of Piano.

★ Fossa di Vulcano
HIKING

Vulcano's star attraction is the straightforward trek up its 391m volcano (no guide required). Start early if possible and bring a hat, sunscreen and water. Follow the signs south along Strada Provinciale, then turn left onto the zigzag gravel track that leads to the summit. It's a 30- to 60-minute climb to the lowest point of the volcano's rim (290m), where you'll be rewarded with fine views of the steaming crater encrusted with red and yellow crystals.

Sicily in Kayak   BOATING
(☑ 329 5381229; www.sicilyinkayak.com; excursions from €55) Kayaking enthusiast Eugenio Viviani heads this home-grown outfit offering everything from half-day explorations of Vulcano's sea caves to multiday paddling excursions visiting multiple islands in the Aeolian archipelago.

 Sleeping & Eating

Vulcano isn't a great place for an overnight stay; the town is pretty soulless and the sulphurous fumes really do smell. Most people visit on day trips from nearby Lipari.

★ Malvasia
SANDWICHES €

(☑ 346 6039439; www.ristorantemalvasiavulcano .it; Via degli Eucaliptus; sandwiches from €12; ◷ 11.30am-2.30pm & 7.30-11pm late Apr-early Oct) After years selling open-faced sandwiches from a cart near Vulcano's port, jovial owner Maurizio Pagano opened this popular restaurant and wine bar in 2015. Bask on the sunny front patio and enjoy his trademark *pane cunzatu eoliano* (tuna, olives, capers, tomatoes and buffalo-milk mozzarella on delectable toasted homemade bread drenched in extra-virgin olive oil), or go for salads and daily specials.

★ Trattoria da Pina
SEAFOOD €€

(☑ 368 668555; Gelso; meals €29-32; ◷ 12.30-2.30pm & 8-9.45pm Apr–mid-Oct) With sea-blue tablecloths and an intimate outdoor porch overlooking the black-sand beach at Vulcano's southern tip, this down-to-earth trattoria serves up delicious pasta and fresh-caught fish in a wonderful end-of-the-line setting. Two local men do the fishing, and their families do the cooking. Save room for scrumptious desserts such as pistachio *semifreddo*, or homemade biscotti and sweet Malvasia wine.

❶ Getting There & Around

BOAT

Vulcano is an intermediate stop between Milazzo (€15, 50 minutes) and Lipari (€5.80, 10 minutes). Both Liberty Lines and Siremar run multiple vessels in both directions throughout the day. The hydrofoil journey to or from Lipari takes only 10 minutes, making Vulcano an easy and popular day-trip destination.

CAR & MOTORCYCLE

Sprint da Luigi (☑ 347 7600275; www.nolo sprintdaluigi.com; Porto di Levante; bike/ electric bike/scooter/car rental per day from €7/20/25/50) Rent some wheels and get travel advice about the island from Luigi and Nidra, friendly multilingual owners of this well-signposted outfit just south of the port.

Salina
POP 4000

Ah, green Salina! In stark contrast to sulphur-stained Vulcano and lava-blackened Stromboli, Salina's twin extinct craters, Monte dei Porri and Monte Fossa delle Felci – nicknamed *didyme* (twins) by the ancient Greeks – are lushly wooded and invitingly verdant, a result of the numerous freshwater springs on the island. Wildflowers, thick yellow gorse bushes and serried ranks of grapevines carpet the hillsides in vibrant colours and cool greens, while its high coastal cliffs plunge dramatically towards beaches. The famous Aeolian capers grow plentifully here, as do the grapes used for making Malvasia wine.

HYDROFOILS TO THE AEOLIAN ISLANDS

FROM	TO	COST (€)	DURATION	FREQUENCY
Messina	Lipari	31	1½-3½hr	5 daily in summer, 1 daily in winter
Milazzo	Lipari	21	1hr	12-17 daily
Milazzo	Vulcano	20	45min	12-16 daily
Milazzo	Stromboli	26	1¼-3hr	3-7 daily
Milazzo	Salina	23	1½hr	12 daily

⊙ Sights & Activities

Salina's main villages are Santa Marina, on the east side of the island where most boats dock, and Malfa on the northwestern coast. Salina is famous for its dark-golden or light-amber sweet Malvasia wine. Wineries in Malfa and Lingua offer visits and tastings with advance notice.

Pollara   VILLAGE

Don't miss a trip to sleepy Pollara, sandwiched dramatically between the sea and the steep slopes of an extinct volcanic crater on Salina's western edge. The gorgeous beach here was used as a location in the 1994 film *Il Postino,* although the land access route to the beach has since been closed due to landslide danger.

★ Monte Fossa delle Felci   HIKING

For jaw-dropping views, climb to the Aeolians' highest point, Monte Fossa delle Felci (962m). The two-hour ascent starts from the Santuario della Madonna del Terzito, an imposing 19th-century church at Valdichiesa, in the valley separating the island's two volcanoes. Up top, gorgeous perspectives unfold on the symmetrically arrayed volcanic cones of Monte dei Porri, Filicudi and a distant Alicudi.

★ Signum Spa   SPA

(Salus Per Aquam; ✆ 090 984 42 22; www.hotel signum.it; Via Scalo 15, Malfa; €30, treatments extra; ⊙ 10am-8pm Apr-Sep) Enjoy a revitalising hot spring soak or a cleansing sweat in a traditional adobe-walled steam house at Hotel Signum's fabulous spa. The complex includes several stylish Jacuzzis on a pretty flagstoned patio, and blissful spaces where you can immerse your body in salt crystals, get a massage or pamper yourself with natural essences of citrus, Malvasia and capers.

🛏 Sleeping & Eating

Salina remains relatively undisturbed by mass tourism, yet offers some of the Aeolians' finest hotels and restaurants.

★ Hotel Ravesi   HOTEL €€

(✆ 090 984 43 85; www.hotelravesi.it; Via Roma 66, Malfa; d €90-190, ste €160-290; ⊙ mid-Apr–mid-Oct; ❄ 🛜 🏊) Star attractions at this peach of a family-run hotel beside Malfa's town square include the delightful grassy lounge and bar area and the outdoor deck with infinity pool overlooking Panarea, Stromboli and the Mediterranean. Sea views are especially nice from corner room 12 upstairs

and from the two honeymoon suites with antique furniture, decorative tiles and private terraces.

Capofaro   BOUTIQUE HOTEL €€€

(✆ 090 984 43 30; www.capofaro.it; Via Faro 3; d €260-680, ste €580-1200; ⊙ May–mid-Oct; ❄ @ 🛜 🏊) Immerse yourself in luxury at this five-star boutique resort surrounded by well-tended Malvasia vineyards, halfway between Santa Marina and Malfa. Sharp white decor prevails in the 20 rooms with terraces looking straight out to smoking Stromboli and six suites in the picturesque 19th-century lighthouse. Tennis courts, poolside massages, wine tasting and vineyard visits complete this perfect vision of island chic.

★ Da Alfredo   SANDWICHES, GELATERIA €

(Piazza Marina Garibaldi, Lingua; granite €3, sandwiches €10-14; ⊙ 8am-11pm Jun-Sep, reduced hours Oct-May) Straddling a sunny waterfront terrace in Lingua, Alfredo's place is renowned Sicily-wide for its *granite:* ices made with coffee, fruit or locally grown pistachios, hazelnuts and almonds. For an affordable lunch, try its *pane cunzato,* open-faced sandwiches loaded with smoked tuna carpaccio, citrus, wild fennel, almond-caper pesto, ricotta, tomatoes, capers, olives and more; split one with a friend – they're huge!

★ A Cannata   SICILIAN €€

(✆ 090 984 31 61; www.acannata.it; Lingua; meals €35; ⊙ 12.30-2.30pm & 7.30-10pm) Meals are built around locally sourced produce and seafood caught fresh daily by owner Santino at this unassuming but excellent restaurant, run by the same family for four decades. Expect dishes such as squid-ink risotto, *maccheroni* (macaroni) with eggplant, pine nuts, mozzarella and ricotta, fresh grilled fish, sautéed wild fennel, almond *semifreddi* (a light frozen dessert) and local Malvasia wine.

★ A Quadara   TRATTORIA €€

(✆ 389 1519650; www.aquadaratrattoria.it; Via Roma 88, Malfa; meals €25-39; ⊙ 6.30-11pm) Since opening in 2018, this restaurant has won a loyal following for its delicious, authentic Aeolian cuisine. The menu abounds in seasonal specials and enticing local recipes, from pasta with chickpeas and fennel, to rabbit stewed with veggies, pine nuts, almonds, lemon, cinnamon and capers. Scrumptious homemade *cannoli* and an excellent local wine selection are icing on the cake.

🍷 Drinking & Nightlife

⭐ **Maracaibo** — BAR

(☑ 331 6244981; Punta Scario, Malfa; ⊘ 8am-11pm late May-Sep) This palm-thatched beach bar on the rocky shoreline of Punta Scario (just below Malfa town) makes a dreamy spot for a sunset drink. The friendly owners also rent out loungers, beach umbrellas and kayaks.

ℹ️ Getting There & Around

BOAT

Hydrofoils and ferries serve Santa Marina Salina and the small southern port of Rinella from Lipari and the other islands. You'll find ticket offices in both ports.

BUS

CITIS (☑ 090 984 41 50; www.trasportisalina. it) provides dependable local bus service year-round from Santa Marina to Lingua (€2, five to 10 minutes), Malfa (€2, 15 to 20 minutes) and Rinella (€2.80, 40 minutes). From Santa Marina to Pollara (€2.50, 25 minutes to 1½ hours), a change of bus in Malfa is always required. See schedules online.

CAR & MOTORCYCLE

Just above Santa Marina's port, **Antonio Bongiorno** (☑ 338 3791209; Via Risorgimento 222, Santa Marina Salina; ⊘ 8am-8pm) hires scooters (from €20 per day) and cars (from €50 per day).

Stromboli

POP 500

For many the most captivating of the Aeolians, Stromboli conforms perfectly to one's childhood idea of a volcano, with its symmetrical, smoking silhouette rising dramatically from the sea. It's a hugely popular day-trip destination, but to best appreciate its primordial beauty, languid pace and the romance that lured Roberto Rossellini and Ingrid Bergman here in 1949, you'll need to give it at least a couple of days.

Volcanic activity has scarred and blackened much of the island, but the northeastern corner is inhabited, and it's here that you'll find the island's famous black beaches and the main settlement sprawled attractively along the volcano's lower slopes. Despite the picture-postcard appearance, life here is tough: food and drinking water have to be ferried in, there are no roads across the island, and until relatively recently there was no electricity in Ginostra, the diminutive second settlement on Stromboli's west coast.

👁️ Sights & Activities

⭐ **Stromboli Crater** — VOLCANO

For nature lovers, climbing Stromboli is one of Sicily's not-to-be-missed experiences. Since 2005 access has been strictly regulated: you can walk freely to 400m, but need a guide to continue any higher. Organised treks depart daily (between 3.30pm and 6pm, depending on the season), timed to reach the summit (924m) at sunset and to allow 45 minutes to an hour to observe the crater's fireworks.

The climb itself takes 2½ to three hours, while the descent back to Piazza San Vincenzo is shorter (1½ to two hours). All told, it's a demanding five- to six-hour trek up to the top and back; you'll need to have proper walking shoes, a backpack that allows free movement of both arms, clothing for cold and wet weather, a change of T-shirt, a handkerchief to protect against dust (wear glasses not contact lenses), a torch (flashlight), 1L to 2L of water and some food. If you haven't got any of these, **Totem Trekking** (☑ 090 986 57 52; www.totemtrekkingstromboli.com; Piazza San Vincenzo 4; ⊘ 9.30am-1pm & 3.30-7pm Mar-Nov) hires out all the necessary equipment, including boots (€6), backpacks (€5), hiking poles (€4), torches (€3) and windbreakers (€5).

⭐ **Sciara del Fuoco Viewpoint** — VIEWPOINT

(Path of Fire) An alternative to scaling Stromboli's summit is the hour-long climb to this viewpoint (400m, no guide required), which directly overlooks the Sciara del Fuoco (the blackened laval scar running down Stromboli's northern flank) and offers fabulous if more distant views of the crater's explosions. Bring plenty of water, and a torch (flashlight) if walking at night. The trail (initially a switchbacking road) starts in Piscità, 2km west of Stromboli's port; halfway up, you can stop for pizza at L'Osservatorio.

Volcano Climbs

To climb to the top of Stromboli you'll need to go on an organised trek. Maximum group size is 20 people, and although there are usually multiple groups on the mountain, spaces can still fill up. To avoid disappointment, book early – if possible a week or more before you want to climb. The standard fee for group climbs is €28 per person.

Beside the church in the heart of town, **Magmatrek** (☑ 090 986 57 68; www.magmatrek. it; Via Vittorio Emanuele) is one of Stromboli's longest-established and most professional agencies, with experienced, multilingual

(English-, German- and French-speaking) guides. Other agencies charging identical prices include **Stromboli Adventures** (📞 090 98 60 95, 339 5327277; www.stromboliad ventures.it; Via Vittorio Emanuele 17), **Stromboli Fire Trekking** (📞 090 98 62 64; www.stromboli firetrekking.com; Via Vittorio Emanuele) and **Il Vulcano a Piedi** (📞 090 98 61 44; www.ilvul canoapiedi.it; Via Pizzillo).

Boat Tours

Numerous operators down by the port, including **Società Navigazione Pippo** (📞 090 98 61 35, 348 0559296; www.facebook.com/pipponavigazi onestromboli; Porto Scari) and **Antonio Caccetta** (📞 339 5818200; Vico Salina 10), offer three-hour daytime circuits of the island (€25), 1½-hour sunset excursions to watch the Sciara del Fuoco from the sea (€20), and evening trips to Ginostra village on the other side of the island for dinner or *aperitivi* (€25).

Many private boat operators in Lipari offer day-trip packages including a guided excursion to the craters followed by return transport to Lipari the same evening.

Beaches

Stromboli's black sandy beaches are the best in the Aeolian archipelago. The most accessible swimming and sunbathing is at **Ficogrande**, about a 10-minute walk northwest of the hydrofoil dock. Further-flung beaches worth exploring are at **Piscità**, 2km to the west, and **Forgia Vecchia**, about 300m south of the port.

🛏 Sleeping

More than a dozen places offer accommodation, including B&Bs, guesthouses and fully fledged hotels.

⭐ **Casa del Sole**   GUESTHOUSE €
(📞 090 98 63 00; www.casadelsolestromboli.it; Via Cincotta; dm €25-35, s €30-55, d €60-110) This cheerful Aeolian-style guesthouse is only 100m from a sweet black-sand beach in Piscità, the tranquil neighbourhood at the west end of town. Dorms, private doubles and a guest kitchen all surround a sunny patio, overhung with vines, fragrant with lemon blossoms, and decorated with the masks and stone carvings of sculptor-owner Tano Russo. It's a pleasant 25-minute walk or a €10 taxi ride from the port 2km away.

Pensione Aquilone   GUESTHOUSE €
(📞 090 98 60 80; www.aquiloneresidence.it; Via Vittorio Emanuele 29; s €30-50, d €50-70) Convenience and a peaceful location come together at this cheerful, long-established guesthouse tucked away above Stromboli's main drag, just west of the hilltop church square. Guests love the sunny, flowery central garden patio and shared terraces with views to the volcano and Strombolicchio. Three rooms come with cosy cooking nooks; otherwise, friendly owners Adriano and Francesco – both Stromboli natives –provide breakfast.

🍴 Eating

⭐ **Lapillo Gelato**   GELATO €
(Via Roma; gelato €3-5; ⊙ 10am-1pm & 3.30pm-midnight Jun-Aug, 10.30am-12.45pm & 3.30-8pm Sep-May) On the main street between the port and the church, this artisanal gelateria is a great place to fuel up with homemade gelato before making the big climb. The pistachio flavour is pure creamy bliss.

L'Osservatorio   PIZZA €
(📞 090 958 69 91; www.facebook.com/osservatorio stromboli; pizzas €8-11; ⊙ 10am-10pm Apr-Jun & Sep–mid-Nov, to 2am Jul & Aug) Sure, you could eat a pizza in town, but come on - you're on Stromboli! On clear evenings, nothing compares to the full-on views of the volcano's eruptions from l'Osservatorio's panoramic outdoor terrace. From Piscità, 2km west of Stromboli's port, it's a 30-minute uphill trek or a bumpy ride on the free included shuttle (call ahead to be met at Piscità).

⭐ **Punta Lena**   SICILIAN €€
(📞 090 98 62 04; http://ristorantepuntalena.busi ness.site; Via Marina 8; meals €36-45; ⊙ 12.15-2.30pm & 7-10.30pm Thu-Tue, 7-10.30pm Wed May-Sep) For a romantic outing, head to this upscale waterfront restaurant with cheerful blue decor, lovely sea views and the soothing sound of waves lapping in the background. The food is among the island's finest, with signature dishes including fresh seafood, fish stewed with local olives and capers, and *spaghetti alla stromboliana* (with wild fennel, mint, anchovies, cherry tomatoes and breadcrumbs).

ℹ Information

Bring enough cash for your stay on Stromboli. Many businesses don't accept credit cards, and the village's lone ATM on Via Roma is sometimes out of service. Internet access here is limited.

ℹ Getting There & Away

Liberty Lines (📞 0923 87 38 13; www.liberty lines.it) offers daily hydrofoil service to Salina (€16, one to 1¼ hours), Lipari (€19, one to two hours) and Milazzo (€21, 2¼ to three hours). **Siremar** (☑ 090 57 37; www.carontetourist.it/en/siremar) also runs car ferries from Stromboli to Naples (from €48, 10 hours), Milazzo and the other Aeolians, and **SNAV** (☑ 081 428 55 55; www.snav.it) runs a summer-only hydrofoil to Naples (from €62, 4½ hours, late May through early September). In bad weather service is often disrupted or cancelled altogether. The **ticket office** (☑ 090 98 60 03; ⊙ 6-8am, 9.30am-12.30pm & 3-5.30pm) is 150m north of Stromboli's **ferry dock**.

IONIAN COAST

The Ionian Coast is studded with enough Sicilian icons to fill a souvenir tea towel. It's here that you'll find the skinny Strait of Messina, mighty Mt Etna and the world's most spectacularly located ancient Greek theatre. Catania is the region's centre, a gritty, vibrant city packed with students, bars and nightlife. Its black-and-white baroque Piazza del Duomo is World Heritage–listed, while its hyperactive fish market is one of Sicily's most appetising sights. Halfway up a rocky mountainside, regal Taormina is sophisticated and exclusive, a favourite of holidaying VIPs and day-tripping tourists. Brooding menacingly on the city's doorstep, Mt Etna offers unforgettable hiking and is also a vino-making hotspot, dotted with celebrated wineries.

Taormina

☑ 0942 / POP 10,900 / ELEV 204M
Spectacularly perched on the side of a mountain, Taormina is one of Sicily's most popular summer destinations, a chic resort town popular with holidaying high-rollers and those wanting a taste of Sicilian *dolce vita*.

Although unashamedly touristy and expensive, the town merits a couple of days for its stunning ancient theatre, people-watching and breathtaking vistas.

Founded in the 4th century BC, Taormina enjoyed great prosperity under the Greek ruler Gelon II and later under the Romans, but fell into quiet obscurity after being conquered by the Normans in 1087. Its reincarnation as a tourist destination dates to the 18th century, when northern Europeans discovered it on the Grand Tour. Among its fans was DH Lawrence, who lived here between 1920 and 1923.

Taormina gets extremely busy in July and August and virtually shuts down between November and Easter. Ideally, head up in April, May, September or October.

◎ Sights & Activities

A short walk uphill from the bus station brings you to Corso Umberto I, a pedestrianised thoroughfare that traverses the length of the medieval town and connects its two historic town gates, Porta Messina and Porta Catania.

Lido Mazzarò is the nearest beach to Taormina, located directly beneath the town. It's well serviced with bars and restaurants, though it gets very crowded in the summer.

★Teatro Greco   RUINS
(☑ 0942 2 32 20; Via Teatro Greco; adult/reduced €10/5; ⊙ 9am-1hr before sunset) Taormina's premier sight is this perfect horseshoe-shaped theatre, suspended between sea and sky, with Mt Etna looming on the southern horizon. Built in the 3rd century BC, it's the most dramatically situated Greek theatre in the world and the second largest in Sicily (after Syracuse). In summer, it's used to stage concerts and festival events. To avoid

---

SICILY'S OFFSHORE ISLANDS

Sicily is an island lover's paradise, with more than a dozen offshore islands scattered in the seas surrounding the main island. Beyond the major Aeolian Islands of Lipari, Vulcano, Stromboli and Salina, you can detour to the smaller Aeolians: Panarea, Filicudi and Alicudi.

Alternatively, cast off from Trapani on Sicily's western coast to the slow-paced Egadi Islands or the remote, rugged volcanic island of Pantelleria.

South of Agrigento, the sand-sprinkled Pelagie Islands of Lampedusa, Linosa and Lampione offer some fantastic beaches.

Liberty Lines (☑ 0923 02 20 22; www.libertylines.it) and **Siremar** (☑ 090 57 37; www.carontetourist.it/siremar) provide hydrofoil and/or ferry services to all of these islands. For further information, see Lonely Planet's *Sicily* guide.

the high-season crowds, try to visit early in the morning.

Corso Umberto I
STREET

Taormina's chief delight is wandering this pedestrian-friendly, boutique-lined thoroughfare. Start at the tourist office in **Palazzo Corvaja** (Piazza Santa Caterina; ⊙varies), which dates back to the 10th century, before heading southwest for spectacular panoramic views from **Piazza IX Aprile**. Facing the square is the early-18th-century **Chiesa di San Giuseppe** (⧉ 0942 2 31 23; ⊙ 8.30am-8pm). Continue west through the **Torre dell'Orologio**, the 12th-century clock tower, into **Piazza del Duomo**, home to an ornate baroque fountain (1635) that sports Taormina's symbol, a two-legged centaur with the bust of an angel.

Villa Comunale
PARK

(Parco Duchi di Cesarò; Via Bagnoli Croce; ⊙ 8am-midnight summer, to 6pm winter; ⟦♦⟧) Created by Englishwoman Florence Trevelyan in the late 19th century, these stunningly sited public gardens offer breathtaking views of the coast and Mt Etna. They're a wonderful place to escape the crowds, with tropical plants and delicate flowers punctuated by whimsical follies. You'll also find a children's play area.

Castelmola
VILLAGE

For eye-popping views of the coastline and Mt Etna, head for this cute hilltop village above Taormina, crowned by a ruined castle. If you're reasonably fit, head up on foot (one hour) for a good workout and sweeping panoramas. Alternatively, take the hourly Interbus service (one-way/return €1.90/3, 15 minutes). While you're up here, stop in for almond wine at **Bar Turrisi** (⧉ 0942 2 81 81; www.barturrisi.com; Piazza Duomo; ⊙ 10am-late; ⟦🛜⟧), a multilevel bar with some rather cheeky decor.

Isola Bella
ISLAND

(www.parconaxostaormina.com; adult/reduced €4/2; ⊙ 9am-7pm May-Aug, to 6.30pm Apr & early–mid-Sep, reduced hours rest of year) Southwest of Lido Mazzarò is the minuscule Isola Bella, a beautiful nature reserve set in a stunning cove with fishing boats. Reached on foot via a narrow sandbar (take your shoes off!), the island was once home to Florence Trevelyan, creator of the Villa Comunale.

Gole Alcantara
SWIMMING

(⧉ 0942 98 50 10; www.golealcantara.com; €1.50; ⊙ 8am-sunset; ⟦♦⟧) This series of vertiginous lava gorges with swirling rapids, 20km west of Taormina, is a pretty spot for cooling off on a summer day. That said, some may be put off by the crowds and the heavy layers of tourist infrastructure. If driving, park in the main Gole Alcantara car park (tip optional), then walk 200m further up the main road to the public entrance, where you'll find a ticket booth and stairs leading down to the gorge.

🎭 Festivals & Events

Taormina Arte
PERFORMING ARTS

(⧉ 391 7462146; www.taoarte.it; ⊙ Jun-Sep) Taormina Arte oversees a plethora of cultural events in town, including the annual **Taormina Film Fest** (http://taofilmfest.it; ⊙ Jun or Jul). The peak season for offerings is summer, when the Teatro Greco becomes a hub for world-class opera, dance, theatre and music concerts, with no shortage of internationally renowned acts. See the website for what's on.

🛏 Sleeping

Given its VIP reputation, it's not surprising that Taormina's accommodation scene tends towards the expensive. Still, there are a number of decent, centrally located midrange options. Book well in advance, especially if visiting during the summer, when demand (like the room rates) is at its highest.

Villa Nettuno
PENSION €

(⧉ 0942 2 37 97; www.hotelvillanettuno.it; Via Pirandello 33; s €35-44, d €60-78; ⟦❄🛜⟧) A throwback to another era, this conveniently located salmon-pink *pensione* has been run by the Sciglio family for seven decades. Its low prices reflect a lack of updates, but the inviting lounge, pretty gardens (complete with olive trees and potted geraniums) and the sea views from the breakfast terrace offer a measure of charm you won't find elsewhere at this price. Breakfast costs €4.

Médousa Suites
BOUTIQUE HOTEL €€

(⧉ 0942 38 87 38; www.medousa.it; Via Sesto Pompeo 1; junior ste €100-250, ste €150-600; ⟦❄🛜⟧) Set above a stylish garden bar-restaurant, these five high-end suites offer an on-point mix of oak panels, linen curtains, Milanese sofas and contemporary takes on Sicily's *cementine* (traditional cement floor tiles). The suites also include coffee machines, SMEG minibars, quality Parisian amenities and handy USB ports by the custom-made beds. Guests also have access to a small garden area dotted with citrus.

Taormina

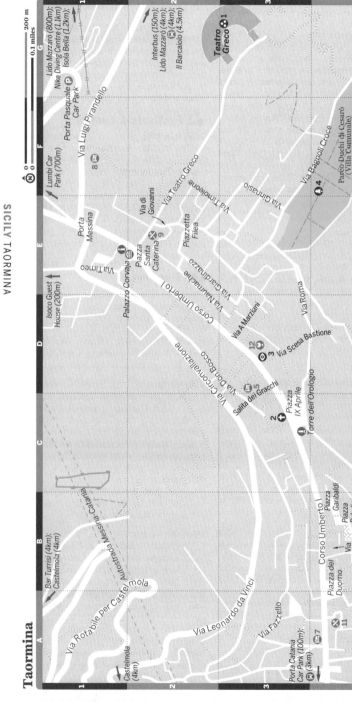

0   0.1 miles
0   200 m

Lido Mazzarò (800m);
Nike Diving Centre (1.1km);
Isola Bella (1.2km);

Interbus (150m);
Lido Mazzarò (4km);
Il Barcaiolo (4.5km);

Teatro Greco ⊗ 1

Porta Pasquale P
Car Park

Via Luigi Prandello

6

Lumbi Car
Park (700m);

Porta
Messina

Via Teatro Greco

Via Timoleone

Via Bagnoli Croce

Parco Duchi di Cesarò
(Villa Comunale)

F

Isoco Guest
House (200m);

Palazzo Corvaja 🏛

Piazza
Santa
Caterina ⊗ 9

Via di
Giovanni

Via Timeo

8 🏛

Via Gimnasio

4

E

Piazzetta
Filea

Via Naumachie

Via Giardinazzo

Corso Umberto I

Via Roma

D

Bar Turrisi (4km);
Castelmola (4km)

Via Rotabile Per Castelmola

Via Circonvallazione

Via A Marziani

Via Scesa Bastione

12 🏨
⊙ 3

Via Don Bosco

Salita dei Gracchi

🏨 5

Piazza
IX Aprile

C

Autostrada Messina-Catania

Castelmola
(4km)

Via Leonardo da Vinci

Via Fazzello

2

Torre dell'Orologio

Piazza
del
Duomo

Corso Umberto I

Via
Paladini

Piazza
Garibaldi

Piazza
Paladini

10 ⊗

Piazza San
Domenico

B

Porta Catania
Car Park (100m);
(3km)

🏨 7

⊗ 11

Via Pietro Rizzo

A

Taormina

Isoco Guest House   GUESTHOUSE €€
(☑ 0942 2 36 79; www.isoco.it; Via Salita Branco 2; r €78-220; ⊙ Mar-Nov; P ❄ @ 🛜) Each room at this welcoming, LGBTIQ-friendly guesthouse is dedicated to an artist, from Botticelli to Keith Haring. While the older rooms are highly eclectic, the newer suites are chic and subdued, each with a modern kitchenette. Breakfast is served around a large table, while a pair of terraces offer stunning sea views and a hot tub. Multinight or prepaid stays earn the best rates.

★ **Casa Turchetti**   B&B €€€
(☑ 0942 62 50 13; www.casaturchetti.com; Salita dei Gracchi 18/20; d €220-260, junior ste €360, ste €470; ⊙ late Mar-Oct; ❄ @ 🛜) Every detail is perfect at this painstakingly restored former music school turned luxurious B&B, on a back alley near Piazza IX Aprile. Vintage furniture and fixtures (including a giant four-poster bed in the suite), handcrafted woodwork and fine homespun sheets exude a quiet elegance. Topping it off is a breathtaking rooftop terrace and the warmth of Sicilian hosts Pino and Francesca.

★ **Hotel Villa Belvedere**   HOTEL €€€
(☑ 0942 2 37 91; www.villabelvedere.it; Via Bagnoli Croce 79; d €120-680, ste €390-890; ⊙ Mar-late Nov; ❄ @ 🛜 ⛱) Built in 1902, the distinguished, supremely comfortable Villa Belvedere was one of Taormina's original grand hotels. Well positioned with fabulous views, luxuriant gardens and wonderful service, its highlights include plush, communal lounge areas and a swimming pool complete with century-old palm. Neutral hues and understated style typify the hotel's 55 rooms, with parking costing an extra €20 per day.

🍴 Eating & Drinking

Eating in Taormina is expensive, and service can be lacklustre. That said, there are some excellent restaurants, serving quality local produce and wines. Avoid touts and tourist menus and reserve up to a week ahead in the summer.

★ **Minotauro**   PASTRIES €
(☑ 0942 2 47 67; Via di Giovanni 15; pastries from €1, cannoli €2.50; ⊙ 9am-8.30pm, to midnight mid-Jun-Aug, closed Dec–mid-Mar) Tiny Minotauro has an epic reputation for its calorific, made-from-scratch treats. Scan the counters for old-school tempters such as artful marzipan, sticky *torrone* (nougat) and *paste di mandorla* (almond biscuits) with fillings like orange or pumpkin. Top billing goes to the silky ricotta *cannoli*, filled fresh to order and pimped with pistachio, cinnamon and candied orange.

★ **Il Barcaiolo**   SICILIAN €€
(☑ 0942 62 56 33; www.barcaiolo.altervista.org; Via Castellucci 43, Spiaggia Mazzarò; meals €33-45; ⊙ 1-2.30pm & 7-10.45pm Wed-Mon Jun-Aug, to 10pm Wed-Mon Apr, May, Sep-early Jan) Book five days ahead come summer, when every *buongustaio* (foodie) and hopeless romantic longs for a table at this fabulous trattoria. Set snugly in a boat-fringed cove at Mazzarò beach, it's celebrated for its sublimely fresh seafood, such as sweet *gamberi rossi marinati agli agrumi* (raw Mazzara shrimps served with citrus fruits) and *sarde a beccaficu* (stuffed sardines).

★ **Osteria Nero D'Avola**   SICILIAN €€
(☑ 0942 62 88 74; www.facebook.com/osterianero davola; Piazza San Domenico 2b; meals €40-50; ⊙ 7-11pm daily mid-Jun–mid-Sep, noon-2.30pm & 7-11pm Tue-Sun rest of year; 🛜) Owner Turi Siligato fishes, hunts and forages for his smart *osteria,* and if he's in, he'll probably share anecdotes about the day's bounty and play a few tunes on the piano. This is one of Taormina's top eateries, where seasonality, local producers and passion underpin outstanding dishes, such as grilled meatballs in lemon leaves, and fresh fish with Sicilian pesto.

SICILY TAORMINA

Osteria RossoDiVino
SICILIAN €€€

(☑ 0942 62 86 53; www.osteria-rosso-divino.com; Vico De Spuches 8; meals €45-65; ☉ 7pm-midnight Jul-early Sep, noon-3pm & 7-11pm Wed-Mon Mar-Jun & mid-Sep–Dec; ☎) With seating on an intimate, candlelit courtyard, this coveted nosh spot (book ahead!) is the passion project of siblings Jacqueline and Sara Ragusa. The day's offerings are dictated by the season, the local fishers' catch, and the siblings' own morning market trawl. Expect anything from heavenly anchovy tempura (the secret: mineral water in the batter) to *paccheri* pasta with gorgonzola crema and dehydrated pears.

★ Morgana
COCKTAIL BAR

(☑ 0942 62 00 56; www.morganataormina.it; Scesa Morgana 4; ☉ 7.30pm-late daily Apr-Oct & mid-Dec–early Jan, 7.30pm-late Fri & Sat Nov–mid-Dec; ☎) This so-svelte cocktail-lounge sports a new look every year, with each concept inspired by Sicilian culture, artisans and landscape. It's the place to be seen, whether on the petite dance floor or among the prickly pears and orange trees in the dreamy, chi-chi courtyard. Fuelling the fun are gorgeous libations, made with local island ingredients, from wild fennel and orange to sage.

🛍 Shopping

Taormina is a window-shopper's paradise, particularly along pedestrianised Corso Umberto I, where you'll find a mix of high-end fashion, shoes and accessories, quality ceramic goods, lace and linen tableware and antique furniture, along with local culinary treats and wine. Side streets harbour some interesting boutiques and artisan studios.

ℹ Information

Tourist Office (☑ 0942 2 32 43; Palazzo Corvaja, Piazza Santa Caterina; ☉ 8.30am-2.15pm & 3.30-6.45pm Mon-Fri Jan-Dec, 9am-1pm & 4-6.30pm Sat summer) Handy for practical information, including transport timetables and town maps.

ℹ Getting There & Away

BUS

Bus is the easiest way to reach Taormina.
Interbus (☑ 0942 62 53 01; www.interbus.it; Via Luigi Pirandello) goes to Messina (€4.30, 55 minutes to 1¾ hours, one to five daily), Catania (€5.10, 1¼ to two hours, once or twice hourly) and Catania airport (€8.20, 1½ hours, once or twice hourly).

CAR & MOTORCYCLE

Taormina is on the A18 autostrada and the SS114. The historic centre is closed to nonresident traffic and Corso Umberto I is closed to all traffic. Some top-end hotels offer limited parking; otherwise, you'll have to leave your car in one of three car parks outside the historic centre: **Porta Catania**, **Porta Pasquale** or **Lumbi** (per 24hr €16 Jul & Aug, Sep-Jun €14). All three are within walking distance of Corso Umberto I, though Lumbi (the furthest) runs a free shuttle bus up to the centre.

TRAIN

Trains run frequently to Messina (from €4.30, 45 minutes to 1¼ hours) and Catania (€4.30, 35 minutes to one hour), but the awkward location of Taormina's station (a steep 4km below town) is a strong disincentive. If you arrive this way, catch a taxi (€15) or an Interbus coach (€1.90, 10 minutes) up to town.

Catania

☑ 095 / POP 311,600

For all the noise, chaos and scruffiness that hit the visitor at first glance, Catania has a strong magnetic pull. This is Sicily at its most youthful, a city packed with cool and gritty bars, abundant energy and an earthy spirit in sharp contrast to Palermo's aristocratic airs.

Catania's historic core is a Unesco-listed wonder, where black-and-white *palazzi* tower over sweeping baroque piazzas. One minute you're scanning the skyline from a dizzying dome, the next perusing contemporary art in an 18th-century convent. Beneath it all are the ancient ruins of a town with over 2700 candles on its birthday cake. Indeed, food is another local forte. This is the home of Sicily's iconic *pasta alla Norma* and the extraordinary La Pescheria market.

Keeping an eye on it all is Catania's skyscraping frenemy, Mt Etna, a powerful presence that adds another layer of intensity and beauty to Sicily's second-biggest city.

⊙ Sights

Piazza del Duomo
SQUARE

A Unesco World Heritage Site, Catania's central piazza is a set piece of contrasting lava and limestone, surrounded by buildings in the unique local baroque style and crowned by the grand Cattedrale di Sant'Agata. At its centre stands **Fontana dell'Elefante** (1736), a naive, smiling black-lava elephant dating from Roman times and surmounted by an improbable Egyptian obelisk. Another fountain at the piazza's southwest corner, **Fontana dell'Amenano**, marks the entrance to Catania's fish market.

⭐ **La Pescheria** MARKET
(Via Pardo; ⏰ 7am-2pm Mon-Sat) Catania's raucous fish market, which takes over the streets behind Piazza del Duomo every workday morning, is pure street theatre. Tables groan under the weight of decapitated swordfish, ruby-pink prawns and trays full of clams, mussels, sea urchins and all manner of mysterious sea life. Fishmongers gut silvery fish and high-heeled housewives step daintily over pools of blood-stained water. It's absolutely riveting. Surrounding the market are a number of good seafood restaurants.

⭐ **Teatro Massimo Bellini** THEATRE
(📞 095 730 61 35, guided tours 344 2249701; www.teatromassimobellini.it; Via Perrotta 12; guided tour adult/child €6/4) Completed in 1890 and made for homegrown composer Vincenzo Bellini, Catania's opera house is suitably lavish, from the stucco-and-marble extravagance of the foyer (dubbed the *ridotto*) to the glory of the theatre itself, wrapped in four tiers of gilded boxes. Its painted ceiling, by Ernesto Bellandi, depicts scenes from four of Bellini's best-known operas. The **Associazione Guide Turistiche Catania** (www.guidecatania.it; info@guidecatania.it) runs 45-minute guided tours; email to book a tour and call ahead to confirm times as the theatre isn't always open.

⭐ **Monastero delle Benedettine** CHURCH
(www.officineculturali.net/benedettine.htm; cnr Via Teatro Greco & Via Crociferi; adult/reduced €5/3; ⏰ 10am-5pm Tue, Fri & Sat, plus 11am-5pm 1st Sun of the month) The Monastero delle Benedettine covers two adjacent sites: a Benedictine convent and the **Chiesa di San Benedetto**. Top billing goes to the church, built between 1704 and 1713 and adorned with splendid stucco, marble and a late-18th-century altar made of Sicilian jasper. Standout artworks include Giovanni Tuccari's glorious ceiling frescoes and a graphic depiction of St Agatha being tortured in front of a curious sultan.

Parco Archeologico Greco Romano RUINS
(📞 095 715 05 08; Via Vittorio Emanuele II 262; adult/reduced incl Casa Liberti €6/3; ⏰ 9am-7pm) West of Piazza del Duomo lie Catania's most impressive ancient ruins: the remains of a 2nd-century Roman Theatre and its small rehearsal theatre, the Odeon. The ruins are evocatively sited in a crumbling residential neighbourhood, with vine-covered buildings that appear to have sprouted organically from the half-submerged stage. Adjacent to the main theatre is the **Casa Liberti** (closed Sundays), an elegantly restored 19th-century apartment now home to two millennia worth of artefacts discovered during the excavation of the site.

Cattedrale di Sant'Agata CATHEDRAL
(📞 095 32 00 44; Piazza del Duomo; ⏰ 7am-noon & 4-7pm Mon-Sat, 7.30am-12.30pm & 4.30-7.30pm Sun) Inside the vaulted interior of this cathedral, beyond its impressive marble facade sporting two orders of columns taken from the Roman amphitheatre, lie the relics of the city's patron saint. Its other famous resident is the world-famous Catanian composer Vincenzo Bellini, his remains transferred here in 1876, 41 years after his death in France. Consider visiting the **Museo Diocesano** (📞 095 28 16 35; www.museodiocesanocatania.com; Piazza del Duomo; adult/reduced €7/4, incl baths €10/6; ⏰ 9am-2pm Mon, Wed & Fri, to 2pm & 3-6pm Tue & Thu, to 1pm Sat) next door for access to the Roman baths directly underneath the church.

Castello Ursino CASTLE
(Piazza Federico II di Svevia) Catania's forbidding 13th-century castle once guarded the city from atop a seafront cliff. However, the 1669 eruption of Mt Etna changed the landscape and the whole area to the south was reclaimed by the lava, leaving the castle completely landlocked. The castle now houses the **Museo Civico** (📞 095 34 58 30; adult/reduced €6/3; ⏰ 9am-7pm), home to the valuable archaeological collection of the Biscaris, Catania's most important aristocratic family. Exhibits include colossal classical sculpture, Greek vases and some fine mosaics.

⭐ Festivals & Events

If you're visiting Catania in February or early March, don't miss Carnevale (www.carnevaleacireale.it) in nearby Acireale, one of Sicily's most colourful festivals.

Festa di Sant'Agata RELIGIOUS
(www.festadisantagata.it; ⏰ 3-5 Feb) In Catania's biggest religious festival one million people follow the Fercolo (a silver reliquary bust of St Agatha) along the main street of the city. On the evening of 3 February, spectacular fireworks are set to music, with some folk heading into the square early in the afternoon to secure a good vantage point.

Catania

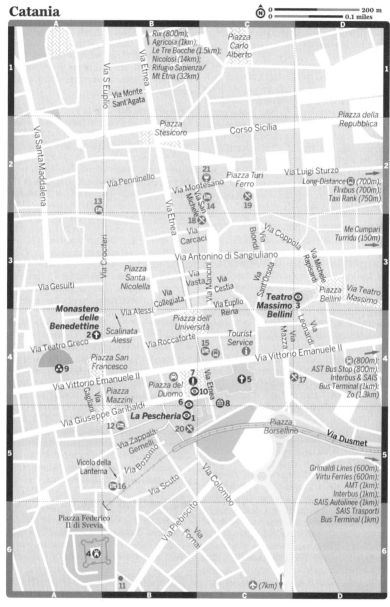

🛏 Sleeping

As Sicily's second-largest city, Catania offers a solid range of accommodation options, from chain and boutique hotels to unique B&Bs offering a taste of the city's creative and cultural spirit.

★ **Palazzu Stidda**   APARTMENT €

(📞338 6505133, 095 34 88 26; www.palazzu stiddacatania.com; Vicolo della Lanterna 2-5; d €80-100, q €140-160, main apt €150-300; ❄ 🤙) Creative hosts Giovanni and Patricia Manidoro have poured their hearts into creat-

Catania

ing these four family-friendly apartments on a peaceful dead-end alley, with all the comforts of home plus a host of whimsical touches. All are decorated with the owners' artwork, handmade furniture, family heirlooms and upcycled vintage finds. The largest apartment, Ammiraglia, accommodates up to eight people, with three bedrooms, a kitchen and lounge.

★ **B&B Crociferi** B&B €
(📞095 715 22 66; www.bbcrociferi.it; Via Crociferi 81; d €75-85, tr €100-110, apt €98-110, ste €120-140; ❄️🛜) Perfectly positioned on pedestrianised Via Crociferi, this B&B in a beautifully decorated family home affords easy access to Catania's historic centre. Three palatial rooms (each with a private, refurbished bathroom across the hall) feature high ceilings, antique tiles, frescoes and artistic accoutrements from the owners' travels. The B&B also houses two apartments, the largest (called Lilla) has a spectacular, leafy panoramic terrace. Book ahead.

B&B Faro B&B €
(📞349 4578856; www.bebfaro.it; Via San Michele 26; d/tr €80/100, apt €130-150; 🅿️❄️🛜) Artist couple Anna and Antonio own this urbane B&B, set in a vibrant quarter dotted with galleries and bohemian bars. Anna's custommade furniture graces the rooms, which feature double-glazed windows and modern bathroom fixtures. The fabulous apartments offer the convenience of kitchenettes, while the plush communal lounge makes for a wonderful spot to linger. Self check-in and nearby parking (€6) are available.

Ostello degli Elefanti HOSTEL €
(📞095 226 56 91; www.ostellodeglielefanti.it; Via Etnea 28; dm €19-26, d €55-70; ❄️🛜) Housed in a 17th-century *palazzo* a stone's throw from the *duomo*, this clean, friendly hostel offers incredible location and value. Three dorms (one female-only) and one private room have lofty frescoed ceilings and panoramic balconies, with reading lights and curtains for every bed. The marble-floored former ballroom doubles as a lounge, while the rooftop terrace-bar offers incomparable Etna vistas.

★ **Asmundo di Gisira** BOUTIQUE HOTEL €€
(📞095 097 88 94; www.asmundodigisira.com; Via Gisira 40; d from €125; ❄️🛜) Not many B&Bs welcome you with a 3m-high pink flamingo at reception, but then this is no ordinary slumber pad. Its six 'Art Rooms' are designed by renowned Italian and international artists, each inspired by local mythological figures. The remaining five rooms find their muse in the 18th-century's Grand Tour era. All are airy, with lofty ceilings, stylish bathrooms and excellent amenities.

🍽 Eating

Eating in Catania is a pleasure, whether by market stalls at La Pescheria or on trendy Via Santa Filomena. Classic street food bites include *arancini* (fried rice balls) and *cartocciate* (bread stuffed with ham, mozzarella, olives and tomato).

★ **I Dolci di Nonna Vincenza** SWEETS, GELATO €
(📞095 715 18 44; www.dolcinonnavincenza.it; Piazza San Placido 7; cannoli & arancini from €2.30;

⏱ 8.30am-8pm Mon-Sat, 9am-1.30pm Sun; ♿) Nuns taught a young Nonna Vincenza the art of baking. Today, her fragrant sweets are the stuff of glutinous dreams. Under huge chandeliers, counters gleam with irresistible treats, among them cinnamon- and lemon-flavoured *geli* (jellies) and crisp *cannoli* filled with combos like ricotta and hazelnut. Take-home treats include cult-status *cassatella di Agira,* shortcrust biscuits filled with cocoa, cinnamon, almond and citrus zest.

La Deliziosa SICILIAN €
(☑ 095 668 18 06; www.deliziosacatania.it; Via Crociferi 77; meals €20-25; ⏱ 12.30-4pm & 5.30pm-midnight Tue-Sun; �🍷) Affable Aurora and Carminia run this adorable little eatery, with alfresco tables on atmospheric Via Crociferi. The weekly-changing menu celebrates regional produce and modern takes on Sicilian cooking, with staples including *facciazza,* a pizza-style concoction topped with uncooked ingredients like tomatoes, cheese and prosciutto. Those wanting to graze can drop in for an afternoon *aperitivo* of Sicilian nibbles, vino, beer and *spritz.*

Agricolab SICILIAN €
(☑ 095 1693 2878; www.agricolab.it; Via F Crispi 258; meals €20-27; ⏱ 12.30-3pm & 6-10.30pm Mon, Wed & Thu, to midnight Fri & Sat, winter times vary; �🍷♿) 🖉 Small Sicilian farms and producers are showcased at this hip, upbeat cafe-bistro, run by Singaporean Fawn and her Sicilian partner Giuseppe. Tuck into anything from sourdough bread with homemade spreads, to Agricolab's signature *pasta aglio e olio* (pasta with olive oil and garlic). Service is friendly, and the option of bar seating makes it perfect for solo diners. Book ahead on weekends.

La Cucina dei Colori VEGETARIAN €
(☑ 095 715 98 93; Via San Michele 9; mixed plates €10-14, meals €20; ⏱ 12.30-3pm & 7.30-11pm, closed Sun mid-Jun–Sep; 🍷♿) Take away or dine in at communal tables at this contemporary ode to seasonal, organic, meat-free nosh. Scan the counters for the daily-changing options, which might include wholewheat pasta with artichokes, sautéed seitan (wheat gluten) with vegetables, or an egg, vegetable and *caciocavallo* cheese flan. Vegan and gluten-free options are available and drinks include organic wines.

★ Mè Cumpari Turiddu SICILIAN €€
(☑ 095 715 01 42; www.mecumparituriddu.it; Piazza Turi Ferro 36-38; meals €26-40; ⏱ 11.30am-

12.30am; �) Old chandeliers, recycled furniture and vintage mirrors exude a nostalgic air at this quirky bistro-restaurant-providore, where tradition and modernity meet to impressive effect. Small producers and Slow Food sensibilities underline sophisticated, classically inspired dishes like ricotta-and-marjoram ravioli in a pork sauce, soothing Ustica lentil stew or a playful 'deconstructed' *cannolo.* There's a fabulous selection of Sicilian cheeses, lighter bistro grub and cakes.

Pescheria Fratelli Vittorio SEAFOOD €€
(☑ 339 7733890; Via Dusmet 1; meals €25-40; ⏱ 11.30am-3.30pm & 7pm-midnight Tue-Sun, closed Sun dinner Nov–mid-May) Cats would kill for a table at Fratelli Vittorio, a cult-status eatery whose counter glistens with Catania's freshest fish and seafood. It's not surprising given that co-owner Giovanni is a fishmonger, handpicking the best ingredients from the nearby market. For an overview, order the *degustazione di antipasti del giorno,* or feel the love in the generous *zuppa di pesce* (seafood soup).

Le Tre Bocche SEAFOOD €€
(☑ 095 53 87 38; Via Ingegnere 11; meals €35-45; ⏱ 8.30-11.45pm, plus 1-3.30pm Sun) Reservations are essential at this Slow Food–recommended restaurant, which even has its own stand at La Pescheria market. The tasting of antipasti is a non-negotiable feast of fresh, vibrant coastal flavours. If you still have room, opt for a standout *primo* (first course), whether it be spaghetti soaked in sea urchins or squid ink, or perhaps a risotto of courgette and prawns.

🍷 Drinking & Entertainment

Catania has great nightlife. Dozens of cafes and bars dot town. Hubs include Piazza Bellini (a university-student favourite), Via Montesano, Via Santa Filomena, Via Penninello and Via Alessi. Catania's live-music and clubbing scenes are also notable, with regular live acts at many bars, plus dedicated venues serving up top-tier Italian and international names.

★ Mercati Generali CLUB
(☑ 334 9197095, 095 57 14 58; www.mercatigenerali.org; Strada Statale 417, Contrada Lungetto; 9pm-4am Sat; �) The 11km drive southwest of central Catania is worth it: this is one of Sicily's finest clubs, with top-tier Italian and international DJs and live-music acts, plus edgy exhibitions and other cultural

events. Then there's the enchanting setting, in a converted 19th-century wine-pressing warehouse, complete with summertime courtyard. Attention to detail extends to the drinks and food, which include decent wood-fired pizzas.

★**Bohéme Mixology Bar**   COCKTAIL BAR
(📞095 250 33 40; www.bohememixologybar.com; Via Montesano 27-29; ⊙7pm-3am; 🛜) There's no drinks list at this intimate cocktail den, decked out in mismatched furniture, gilded mirrors and the odd gramophone. Simply state your flavour and spirit preferences and let the barkeeps work their magic. While the cocktails aren't cheap (€8 to €12), they're better than most local offerings, with everything from the syrups to the grilled pineapple marmalade made from scratch.

★**Rix**   COCKTAIL BAR
(www.facebook.com/ritzcatania; Via Pantano 54; ⊙7pm-1.30am Mon-Sat summer, Tue-Sun winter; 🛜) Svelte, convivial, urbane Rix takes its cocktails seriously. Each is made with passion and precision, from punchy Aviations to a very local Etna Kir (spumante Brut rosé, Etna cherry-liqueur, hazelnut crust). The bar harbours some lesser-known local craft spirits, and almost half of the wines are natural. Food options are seasonal and top notch, with some especially memorable desserts.

★**Teatro Massimo Bellini**   THEATRE
(📞095 730 61 11; www.teatromassimobellini.it; Via Perrotta 12) Catania's premier theatre is named after the city's most famous son, composer Vincenzo Bellini. It's one of Italy's most glorious old theatres, staging annual seasons of world-class opera and classical music, as well as dance performances. Tickets, which are available online, start at around €20 and can rise to over €100 for a seat in the stalls.

ℹ Information

Airport Tourist Office (📞095 723 96 82; www.comune.catania.it/la-citta/turismo; ⊙8am-7pm, 8.30am-1.30pm Sun) In the arrivals hall.

Police (Questura; 📞095 736 71 11; Piazza Santa Nicolella 8) Just off Via Etnea.

Presidio Ospedaliero Garibaldi-Centro (📞095 759 11 11; www.ao-garibaldi.catania.it/presidio-osp-garibaldi; Piazza Santa Maria di Gesù 5) Major hospital with a 24-hour emergency department.

Tourist Office (📞095 742 55 73; www.comune.catania.it/la-citta/turismo; Via Vittorio Emanuele II 172; ⊙8am-7pm Mon-Sat, 8.30am-

1.30pm Sun) City-run tourist office just off Piazza del Duomo.

ℹ Getting There & Away

AIR

Catania Fontanarossa (📞095 723 91 11; www.aeroporto.catania.it; 🛜) is located 7km southwest of the city centre. It's Sicily's busiest airport, with regular non-stop connections to major Italian cities and numerous destinations in Europe, as well as to Dubai.

BOAT

From Catania's **ferry terminal** (Via Dusmet) at the southeast edge of the historic centre, **Grimaldi Lines** (📞095 586 22 30; www.grimaldi-lines.com; Via Dusmet) operates overnight ferries to Salerno (passenger/with car from €23/57, 13 hours, one nightly Monday to Saturday).

From May through September, **Virtu Ferries** (📞095 703 12 11; www.virtuferries.com) runs daily catamarans from Pozzallo (south of Catania) to Malta (1¾ hours, same-day adult return €90 to €141, open return €118 to €166). Coach transfer between Catania and Pozzallo (€14 each way) adds two hours to the journey. Frequency is reduced from October to April.

BUS

All long-distance buses leave from a **terminal** (Via Archimede) 300m northwest of the train station, with ticket offices across the street on Via D'Amico.

Tickets for SAIS Autolinee, Salemi and Big Bus services can also be purchased at **Nafè** (📞095 219 45 50; https://coffeebarnafe.business.site; Piazza Papa Giovanni XXIII 6; ⊙5.30am-8.30pm, closed Sun winter), a cafe-bar opposite Catania train station. Around the corner from Nafè, **TDS Service** (📞095 216 64 54; Via Sturzo 245; ⊙9am-8pm Mon-Sat) is a good-value, cash-only left-luggage office (per hour/day €2/6). It also sells bus tickets for numerous long-distance bus companies, including SAIS Autolinee.

As a rule, buses are quicker than trains for most destinations.

Interbus (📞095 53 27 16; www.interbus.it; Via d'Amico 187) Runs to Syracuse (€6, 1½ hours, 10 to 20 daily), Taormina (€5, 1¼ to two hours, 15 to 20 daily), Ragusa (€8.50, two hours, eight to 14 daily) and Piazza Armerina (€9, 1¾ hours, two to six daily).

SAIS Autolinee (📞800 211020, 095 53 61 68; www.saisautolinee.it; Via d'Amico 181) Serves Palermo (€14, 2¾ hours, 10 to 14 daily).

SAIS Trasporti (📞090 601 21 36; www.sais trasporti.it; Via d'Amico 181) Runs to numerous destinations, including Agrigento (€13.50, three hours, 10 to 14 daily) and overnight to Rome (€44, one daily, 10½ hours).

Flixbus (https://global.flixbus.com; Via d'Amico) Operates direct long-distance buses from Catania to Italian mainland destinations, including Taranto (from €20, 7½ hours, one daily), Bari (from €23, eight to nine hours, twice daily) and Naples (from €26, 8½ to nine hours, twice daily).

CAR & MOTORCYCLE

Catania is easily reached from Messina on the A18 *autostrada* as well as from Palermo on the A19. From the *autostrada*, signs for the city centre direct you to Via Etnea.

TRAIN

Frequent trains depart from Catania Centrale station on Piazza Papa Giovanni XXIII. Destinations include Messina (€7.50, 1¼ to 2¼ hours), Syracuse (€7, one to 1½ hours) and Palermo (€13.50, three hours). Train services are significantly reduced on Sunday.

ℹ Getting Around

TO/FROM THE AIRPORT

Shuttle-bus service **Alibus** (www.amt.ct.it; 🛜) runs to the airport from numerous stops in central Catania, including the train station (€4, 20 to 30 minutes, every 25 minutes). Tickets can be purchased on board using cash (carry the correct change) or credit card. A taxi will cost around €20 to €26. All major car hire companies have offices at the airport.

CAR & MOTORCYCLE

Driving in Catania is challenging due to limited parking and a complicated system of one-way streets. If you're bringing your own vehicle, consider a hotel or B&B with parking facilities; if you're hiring a car, you're best advised to pick up the car as you leave town and return it when you re-enter.

PUBLIC TRANSPORT

Several useful **AMT** (☏ 800 018696, 095 751 91 11; www.amt.ct.it) city bus routes terminate in front of Catania Centrale train station, including bus 2-5, which runs every 10 to 40 minutes from the station west to Via Etnea and southwest to Piazza Borsellino (just south of the Cattedrale di Sant'Agata). Also useful is bus D, which runs every 50 minutes from Piazza Borsellino to the local beaches south of the centre. Tickets, available from *tabacchi* (tobacconists), cost €1 and last 90 minutes. All-day tickets are also available (€2.50).

Catania's one-line metro currently has 11 stops, all on the periphery of the city centre. For tourists, it's mainly useful as a way of getting from Catania Centrale station to the Circu-

metnea train that circles Mt Etna. A 90-minute metro ticket costs €1. A two-hour combined metro-bus ticket costs €1.20.

TAXI

For a taxi, call **Radio Taxi Catania** (☏ 095 33 09 66; www.radiotaxicatania.org). You'll find taxi ranks at the train station and at the northwest corner of Piazza del Duomo.

Mt Etna

ELEV 3326M

Dominating the landscape of eastern Sicily, Mt Etna is a massive brooding presence. At 3326m it is Italy's highest mountain south of the Alps and the largest active volcano in Europe. It's in an almost constant state of activity and eruptions occur frequently, most spectacularly from the four summit craters, but more often, and more dangerously, from the fissures and old craters on the mountain's flanks. This activity, which is closely monitored by 120 seismic activity stations and satellites, means that it is occasionally closed to visitors. The park's varied landscape ranges from the severe, snowcapped mountaintop to lunar deserts of barren black lava, beech woods and lush vineyards where the area's highly rated DOC wine is produced.

⊙ Sights & Activities

The southern approach to Mt Etna presents the easier ascent to the craters. The AST bus from Catania drops you off at **Rifugio Sapienza** (1923m) from where the **Funivia dell'Etna** (☏ 095 91 41 41; www.funiviaetna.com; return adult/child €30/23, incl bus & guide adult/child €65/48; ⊙ 9am-4pm) cable car runs up the mountain to 2500m. Once you're out of the cable car you can attempt the long walk (3½ to four hours return) up the winding track to the authorised crater area (2920m). Alternatively, you can opt for a 4x4 minibus to take you up to (and back down from) the crater area; the minibus option includes a 40-minute guided tour of the crater area. If you plan on walking up to the crater, make sure you leave yourself enough time to get up and down before the last cable car.

The gateway to Etna's quieter and more picturesque northern slopes is **Piano Provenzana** (1800m), a small ski station about 16km upslope from Linguaglossa. Further down the volcano, there's lovely summer walking in the pine, birch and larch trees of the **Pineta Ragabo**, a vast wood accessible from the Mareneve road between

Linguaglossa and Milo. Note that you'll need your own car to get to Piano Provenzana and the Pineta Ragabo, as no public transport passes this way.

☞ Tours

Many operators offer guided tours up to the craters and elsewhere on the mountain. Tours typically involve some walking and 4WD transport. Recommended operators include **Etna Guided Tours** (☑ 340 5780924; www.facebook.com/EtnaGuidedTours), **Gruppo Guide Alpine Etna Nord** (☑ 348 0125167, 095 777 45 02; www.guidetnanord.com; Via Roma 81-83, Linguaglossa), **Gruppo Guide Alpine Etna Sud** (☑ 389 3496086, 095 791 47 55; www.etnaguide.eu) and **Etna Experience** (☑ 349 3053021, 347 6620341; www.etnaexperience.com; Piazza Federico di Svevia 32). **Etna Touring** (☑ 095 791 80 00; www.etnatouring.com; Via Roma 1, Nicolosi) also offers guided mountain bike tours.

🛏 Sleeping & Eating

There's plenty of B&B accommodation around Mt Etna, particularly in the small, pretty town of Nicolosi.

Shalai   BOUTIQUE HOTEL €€
(☑ 095 64 31 28; www.shalai.it; Via Marconi 25, Linguaglossa; d €162-200, d with frescoed ceiling €247-285; ☉ restaurant 7.30-10.30pm daily, plus 1-2.30pm Sat & Sun; [P] [✳] [🛜]) After a day tackling Etna, retreat to this luxe spa hotel. Softly lit and in muted shades, the hotel's 13 rooms are minimalist and contemporary, with crisp white linen, flowing drapes, designer lighting and (in rooms 101 and 102) original frescoed ceilings. Then there's the stucco-adorned 19th-century lounge, the candlelit spa (for that post-trek massage), bar and fine-dining, Michelin-starred restaurant. Bliss.

★**Monaci delle Terre Nere**   BOUTIQUE HOTEL €€€
(☑ 095 708 36 38; www.monacidelleterrenere.it; Via Monaci, Zafferana Etnea; d from €360; [P] [✳] [🛜] [≋])
🌿 This is one of Sicily's top boutique hotels, set in a winery on Mt Etna's eastern flank, halfway between Catania and Taormina. The 27 rooms and suites – spread between a main villa and outbuildings – impeccably balance rustic architectural elements with contemporary artworks, designer furniture and antiques. Bathroom amenities are chemical-free, and the fabulous in-house

SICILY MT ETNA

SAVOURING ETNA: WINE & HONEY TASTING

Mt Etna's rich volcanic soils produce some of Italy's finest wines. This is the home of Etna DOC, one of 23 Sicilian wines to carry the Denominazione di Origine Controllata denomination. While there are numerous wineries offering wine degustations, many (including those listed below) require that you book at least a day ahead.

Among the area's standout wineries is **Planeta Feudo di Mezzo** (☑ 0925 195 54 60; https://planeta.it; Contrada Sciara Nuova, Passopisciaro), a highly acclaimed estate located 3.2km southwest of Passopisciaro. Wine degustations take place in a historic pressing room, with a tasting of five wines (€30 per person) including samples of typical local bites. A lunch of traditional recipes (€55 to €65) is also available.

For an especially intimate winery experience, make time for **Cantina Malopasso** (☑ 393 9728960; www.cantinamalopasso.it; Via Sguazzera 25, Zafferana Etnea). Just south of Zafferana Etnea on Etna's eastern flank, its young, talented winemakers are making waves with nuanced, small-batch wines, often blended with less-common local varietals. Degustations (€22, with a first course €27) are offered from mid-April to December.

Zafferana Etnea itself has a long tradition of apiculture, producing up to 35% of Italy's honey. For a taste, visit **Oro d'Etna** (☑ 095 708 14 11; www.orodetna.it; Via San Giacomo 135, Zafferana Etnea; ☉ 8.30am-6.30pm), where you can try honey made from the blossoms of orange, chestnut and lemon trees.

The **Treno dei Vini dell'Etna** (Etna Wine Train; ☑ 392 6263404; www.stradadelvinodelletna.it/treno-vino-etna; train & tour adult €80, 11-17yr €40, 4-10yr €35) offers a handy way to explore Etna's wineries without a car. The train runs on selected dates from May to October, leaving Riposto train station at 9.15am and arriving in Randazzo at 10.24am. From here, a 'Wine Bus' service continues to a couple of wineries and towns on Etna's northern slopes. The tour includes wine tastings.

restaurant serves plenty of homegrown and organic produce.

★ **Cave Ox** SICILIAN €€
(📞 0942 98 61 71; www.caveox.it; Via Nazionale Solicchiata 159, Solicchiata; meals €25-30, pizzas €5-10; ⊗ noon-3.30pm & 7-11pm Wed-Mon) Modest Cave Ox is a fabulous spot to sample local produce, including *salumi* (charcuterie) made from local black pigs. Whether it's a bowl of carbonara tweaked with speck and asparagus, or spectacular pork and wild-fennel sausages, the dishes burst with flavour. Pizzas are available in the evenings and owner Sandro Dibella's impressive wine cellar includes his own collaboration with maverick local winemaker Frank Cornelissen.

ℹ️ Information

Nicolosi Tourist Office (📞 095 91 44 88; Piazza Vittorio Emanuele 32, Nicolosi; ⊗ 9am-1pm daily, plus 4-6pm Wed & Thu) In central Nicolosi on Etna's southern side.

Parco dell'Etna (📞 095 91 44 88; www.parcoetna.ct.it; Via del Convento 45, Nicolosi; ⊗ 9am-1.30pm Mon-Fri, also 4-6pm Wed & Thu) Offers specialist information about Mt Etna, including climbing and hiking information. About 1.3km north of the centre of Nicolosi.

Proloco Linguaglossa (📞 095 64 30 94; Piazza Annunziata 5, Linguaglossa; ⊗ 9am-1pm & 4-7pm Mon-Sat, 9am-noon Sun) In central Linguaglossa on Etna's northern side.

ℹ️ Getting There & Away

BUS

AST (📞 095 723 05 11; www.azienda sicilianatrasporti.it) runs daily buses from Catania to Rifugio Sapienza (one-way/return €3.40/6.50, two hours). Buses leave from the car park opposite Catania's train station at 8.15am, travelling via Nicolosi. The bus back to Catania departs Rifugio Sapienza at 4.30pm, arriving in Catania at 6.30pm.

CAR & MOTORCYCLE

Nicolosi is about 17km northwest of Catania on the SP10. From Nicolosi it's a further 18km up to Rifugio Sapienza. For Linguaglossa, take the A18 *autostrada* from Catania, exit at Fiumefreddo and follow the SS120 towards Randazzo.

TRAIN

Slow train **Ferrovia Circumetnea** (FCE; 📞 095 54 11 11; www.circumetnea.it; Via Caronda 352a, Catania) follows a 114km route around the base

of the volcano from Catania to Riposto, stopping at various small towns along the way. Most trains terminate at Randazzo (two hours, one-way/return €5.50/9) in the mountain's northern reaches.

SOUTHEASTERN SICILY

Sicily's southeast is the island at its most seductive. This is the cinematic *Sicilia* of TV series *Inspector Montalbano*, a swirl of luminous baroque hill towns, sweeping topaz beaches and olive-laden hillsides luring everyone from French artists to Milanese moguls in search of new beginnings.

The region's coastal protagonist is Syracuse (Siracusa), where Graeco-Roman ruins meet magnificent piazzas, boutique-studded side streets and crystalline waves. To the southwest lies the undulating Val di Noto, its string of late-baroque towns the most beautiful in Sicily. Noto, Modica, Ragusa and Scicli are the fairest of them all, each one a feast of architectural flourishes and gastronomic delights, from artisanal gelato and chocolate to Michelin-star-spangled chefs.

Then there is the region's countryside, a sun-bleached canvas of sleepy back roads lined with carob trees, rocky ravines pierced with prehistoric tombs, and rugged coastline dotted with crumbling *tonnare* (tuna fisheries), Mediterranean herbs and precious, migratory birdlife.

Syracuse

📞 0931 / POP 121,600

More than any other city, Syracuse (Siracusa) encapsulates Sicily's timeless beauty. Ancient Greek ruins rise out of lush citrus orchards, cafe tables spill onto dazzling baroque piazzas, and honey-hued medieval side streets lead down to the sparkling blue sea. It's difficult to imagine now, but in its heyday this was the largest city in the ancient world, bigger even than Athens and Corinth. Its 'once upon a time' begins in 734 BC, when Corinthian colonists landed on the island of Ortygia (Ortigia) and founded the settlement, setting up the mainland city four years later. Almost three millennia later, the ruins of that then-new city constitute the Parco Archeologico della Neapolis, one of Sicily's greatest archaeological sites. Across the water from the mainland, Ortygia remains Syracuse's most beautiful corner, a deeply atmospheric quarter with an ever-growing legion of fans enamoured with its beautiful streetscapes and attractive dining, drinking and shopping options.

Sights

Syracuse's showpiece square, **Piazza del Duomo**, is a masterpiece of baroque town planning. A long, rectangular piazza flanked by flamboyant *palazzi,* it sits on what was once Syracuse's ancient acropolis (fortified citadel).

Ortygia

★ Duomo   CATHEDRAL
(Map p238; Piazza del Duomo; adult/reduced €2/1; ⊙ 9am-6.30pm Mon-Sat Apr-Oct, to 5.30pm Nov-Mar) Built on the skeleton of a 5th-century BC Greek temple to Athena (note the Doric columns still visible inside and out), Syracuse's 7th-century cathedral became a church when the island was evangelised by St Paul. Its most striking feature is the columned baroque facade (1728–53) added by Andrea Palma after the 1693 earthquake. A statue of the Virgin Mary crowns the rooftop, in the same spot where a golden statue of Athena once served as a beacon to homecoming Greek sailors.

Castello Maniace   CASTLE
(Map p238; Piazza Federico di Svevia; adult/reduced €4/2; ⊙ 2.30-6.45pm Mon, 8.30am-1pm Tue-Fri & Sun, 8.30am-6.45pm Sat Apr-Sep, reduced hours rest of year) Guarding the island's southern tip, Ortygia's 13th-century castle is an evocative place to wander, gaze out over the water and contemplate Syracuse's past glories.

Built for Emperor Frederick II, it's an important example of Swabian (German) architecture, with a magnificent, vaulted central hall (Sala Ipostila). The grounds house a small antiquarium displaying archaeological objects from the site, including Norman-era ceramics and some curious-looking ceramic hand grenades from the 16th century.

Galleria Regionale
di Palazzo Bellomo   GALLERY
(Map p238; ☑ 0931 6 95 11; www.regione.sicilia.it/beniculturali/palazzobellomo; Via Capodieci 16; adult/reduced €8/4; ⊙ 9am-7pm Tue-Sat, to 1.30pm Sun) Housed in a 13th-century Catalan-Gothic palace, this art museum's eclectic collection ranges from early Byzantine and Norman stonework to 19th-century Caltagirone ceramics. In between there's a good range of medieval sculpture, as well as medieval, Renaissance and baroque religious paintings. Among the latter is *Annunciation* (1474), executed by Sicily's greatest 15th-century artist, Antonella da Messina. The museum also claims a couple of storybook 18th-century Sicilian carriages.

Mainland Syracuse

★ Parco Archeologico
della Neapolis   ARCHAEOLOGICAL SITE
(Map p240; ☑ 0931 6 62 06; Viale Paradiso 14; adult/reduced €10/5, incl Museo Archeologico €13.50/7; ⊙ 8.30am-1hr before sunset) For the classicist, Syracuse's real attraction is this archaeological park, home to the pearly **Teatro Greco**. Constructed in the 5th century BC and rebuilt in the 3rd century, the 16,000-capacity amphitheatre staged the last tragedies of

SICILY SYRACUSE

DON'T MISS

LA GIUDECCA

Simply walking through Ortygia's tangled maze of nougat-coloured alleys is an atmospheric experience, especially down the narrow streets of **Via della Maestranza**, the heart of the old guild quarter, and the gentrifying Jewish ghetto of Via della Giudecca. At the Alla Giudecca hotel you can visit an ancient Jewish **miqwe** (Ritual Bath; Map p238; ☑ 0931 2 14 67; Via Alagona 52; tours €5; ⊙ tours 10am-6pm May-Oct, reduced hours rest of year) some 20m below ground level. Blocked up in 1492 when the Jewish community was expelled from Ortygia, the baths were rediscovered during renovation work at the hotel.

A short walk away, Syracuse's much-loved puppet theatre, the **Teatro dei Pupi** (Map p238; ☑ 0931 46 55 40; www.teatrodeipupisiracusa.it; Via della Giudecca 22; ⊙ 6 times weekly Mar-Jul, Sep & Oct, 6 to 18 times weekly Aug, fewer Nov-Feb), stages puppet shows re-enacting traditional tales involving magicians, love-struck princesses, knights and dragons. Just down the road, the small **Museo dei Pupi** (Map p238; ☑ 328 5326600; www.museodeipupisiracusa.it; Palazzo Midiri-Cardona, Piazza San Giuseppe; adult/reduced €3/2; ⊙ 11am-1pm & 2-7pm Mon-Sat Mar-Nov) chronicles Sicily's rich history of puppet theatre.

Ortygia

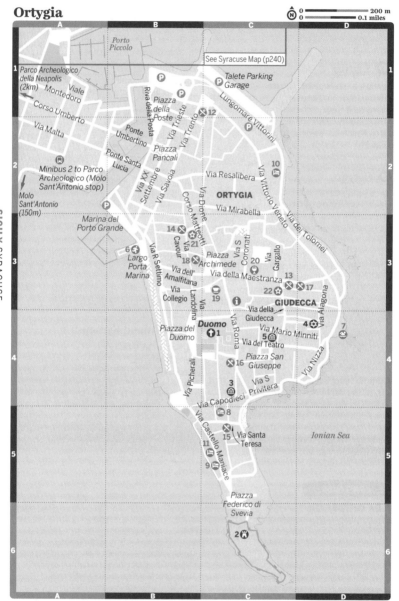

SICILY SYRACUSE

See Syracuse Map (p240)

Aeschylus (including *The Persians*), first performed here in his presence. From early May to early July it's brought to life with an annual season of classical theatre.

Beside the theatre is the mysterious **Latomia del Paradiso** (Garden of Paradise), a deep, precipitous limestone quarry out of which stone for the ancient city was extracted. Riddled with catacombs and filled with citrus and magnolia trees, it's also where the 7000 survivors of the war between Syracuse and Athens in 413 BC were imprisoned. The **Orecchio di Dionisio** (Ear of Dionysius), a 23m-high grotto extending 65m back into

Ortygia

the cliffside, was named by Caravaggio after the tyrant Dionysius, who is said to have used the almost perfect acoustics of the quarry to eavesdrop on his prisoners.

Back outside this area you'll find the entrance to the 2nd-century **Anfiteatro Romano**, originally used for gladiatorial combats and horse races. The Spaniards, little interested in archaeology, largely destroyed the site in the 16th century, using it as a quarry to build Ortygia's city walls. West of the amphitheatre is the 3rd-century-BC **Ara di Gerone II** (Altar of Hieron II), a monolithic sacrificial altar to Hieron II, where up to 450 oxen could be killed at one time.

To reach the park, take Sd'A Trasporti minibus 2 (€1, 15 minutes) from Molo Sant'Antonio, on the west side of the main bridge into Ortygia; purchase tickets on-board. Alternatively, walking from Ortygia will take about 30 minutes. If driving, there is limited free parking on Viale Augusto.

There are two ticket offices here: one office is located near the corner of Via Cavallari and Viale Augusto, opposite the main site, while the second outlet is located down the path leading to the actual ruins. Those wanting a break will find a cafe between the second ticket office and the Anfiteatro Romano.

★ **Museo Archeologico
Paolo Orsi** MUSEUM
(Map p240; ☑ 0931 48 95 11; www.regione.sicil ia.it/beniculturali/museopaoloorsi; Viale Teocrito 66; adult/reduced €8/4, incl Parco Archeologico €13.50/7; ◎ 9am-6pm Tue-Sat, to 1pm Sun) Located about 500m east of the archaeological park, Syracuse's archaeological museum claims one of Sicily's largest and most interesting collections of antiquities. Allow at least a couple of hours to investigate its various sprawling sections, which chart the area's prehistory, as well as the city's development from foundation to the late Roman period.

🏃 **Activities**

The **Forte Vigliena** (Map p238; Via Nizza) swimming platform, flanked by crenellated walls along Ortygia's eastern waterfront, is a favourite summertime hangout for swimming and sunbathing. Serious beach bunnies make the short trip south to **Lido Arenella** (Traversa Arenella), where sandy beaches await. In summer, **Compagnia del Selene** (Map p238; ☑ 347 1275680; www.com pagniadelselene.it; Foro Vittorio Emanuele II; 50min tour per adult/under 10yr €10/free) offers scenic sailing trips around Ortygia.

🎭 **Festivals & Events**

★ **Festival del Teatro Greco** THEATRE
(Festival of Greek Theatre; www.indafondazione. org; ◎ mid-May–early Jul) Syracuse claims the only school of classical Greek drama outside Athens, and from early May to early July it hosts live performances of Greek plays (in Italian) at the Teatro Greco, attracting Italy's finest performers. Tickets (from around €29 to €55) are available online, from the **Fondazione Inda ticket office** (Map p238; ☑ office 0931 48 72 48, tickets 800 542644; www.indafon dazione.org; Corso Matteotti 29; ◎ 10am-1pm

Syracuse

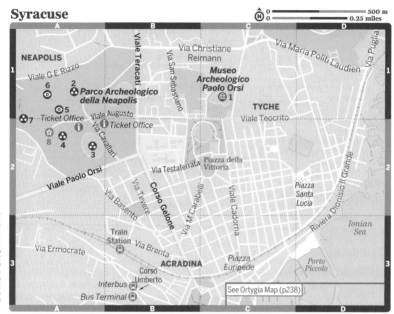

NEAPOLIS

Viale G E Rizzo

Parco Archeologico della Neapolis

Viale Teracati

Via San Sebastiano

Via Christiane Reimann

Museo Archeologico Paolo Orsi

Via Maria Politi Laudien

Via Puglia

Ticket Office

Viale Augusto

TYCHE

Viale Teocrito

Ticket Office

Via Cavallari

Viale Paolo Orsi

Via Tevere

Via Basento

Corso Gelone

Via Testaferrata

Piazza della Vittoria

Via M Carabelli

Viale Cadorna

Piazza Santa Lucia

Riviera Dionisio il Grande

Ionian Sea

Train Station

Via Ermocrate

Via Brenta

ACRADINA

Corso Umberto

Interbus

Bus Terminal

Piazza Euripede

Porto Piccolo

See Ortygia Map (p238)

SICILY SYRACUSE

Syracuse

Mon-Sat) in Ortygia or at the **ticket booth** (Map p240; ☑800 542644; ⊙10am-5pm Mon, to 7pm Tue-Sun) outside the theatre.

★ **Ortigia Sound System**   MUSIC
(www.ortigiasoundsystem.com; ⊙Jul) One of Sicily's top music festivals, OSS takes over Ortygia with five summery days of electronic music spanning various styles. Events take place across the island, with boat parties and a stellar lineup of top-tier Italian and international artists. Past guests have included Virgil Abloh (US), Danielle (UK) and Italy's own 'Father of Disco' Giorgio Moroder.

🛏 Sleeping

The best place to slumber is on the atmospheric island of Ortygia, the historic heart of Syracuse. Here you'll find everything from boutique hotels to atmospheric B&Bs and beautiful self-contained apartments in historic *palazzi*.

B&B Aretusa Vacanze   B&B €
(Map p238; ☑0931 48 34 84; www.aretusava canze.com; Vicolo Zuccalà 1; d €59-90, tr €70-120, q €105-147; P ❋ ☎) This great, family-run budget option, elbowed into a tiny pedestrian street in a 17th-century building, has large rooms and apartments with comfortable beds, kitchenettes and satellite TV. The recently refurbished bathrooms feature spacious showers and three of the 11 rooms come with small balconies. Parking costs €15 per day.

B&B dei Viaggiatori,
Viandanti e Sognatori   B&B €
(Map p238; ☑0931 2 47 81; www.bedandbreak fastsicily.it; Via Roma 156; d €55-70, tr €70-80; ❋ ☎) Enjoying a prime Ortygia location, this relaxed, TV-free B&B exudes an easy, boho vibe. It's a homely place, where books and antiques mingle with the owners' children's toys. Rooms are simple yet imaginatively decorated, and the sunny roof terrace – complete with sweeping sea views – is a fine

place for breakfast-time organic bread and marmalade.

★ Hotel Gutkowski   HOTEL €€
(Map p238; ☑0931 46 58 61; www.guthotel.it; Lungomare Vittorini 26; d €90-150, tr €150, q €160; ❄🛜) Book well in advance for one of the sea-view rooms at this stylish, eclectic hotel on the Ortygia waterfront, at the edge of the Giudecca neighbourhood. Divided between two buildings, its rooms are simple yet chic, with pretty tiled floors, walls in teals, greys, blues and browns, and a sharply curated mix of vintage and industrial details.

Palazzo Blanco   APARTMENT €€€
(Map p238; ☑342 7672092; www.casedisicilia.com; Via Castello Maniace; small apt per night €210-240, large apt per night €230-260; ❄🛜) Two elegant apartments await in this *palazzo*, owned by a Milanese art collector. The larger apartment is utterly decadent, with luxurious sofas, king-size bed, dining table, precious artworks and stone, vaulted ceiling. There's a sea-view terrace and bathroom with original stonework and hydro-massage shower. The smaller apartment features floor-to-ceiling artwork and a romantic four-poster bed. Both have kitchenettes and can accommodate up to four.

Henry's House   HOTEL €€€
(Map p238; ☑0931 2 13 61; www.hotelhenryshouse.com; Via del Castello Maniace 68; d €160-300, ste €260-400; ❄🛜) This waterfront 17th-century *palazzo* was restored by an antique collector. The period lounge is fabulously aristocratic, while the homely rooms blend antiques and modern art. If money isn't an issue, book one of the two upstairs suites (one with terrace, both with water views).

The hotel offers free bike use and, for those who book directly through the hotel website, complimentary minibar.

✖ Eating

Ortygia is the best place to eat. Its postcard-pretty streets heave with bustling trattorias, fashionable restaurants and cafes. While some are obvious tourist traps, many are not, and you'll have no trouble finding somewhere to suit your style. Expect plenty of seafood pasta and grilled catches of the day.

★ Caseificio Borderi   SANDWICHES €
(Map p238; ☑329 9852500; www.caseificioborderi.eu; Via Benedictis 6; sandwiches €6; ⊙7am-4pm Mon-Sat) No visit to Syracuse's market is complete without a stop at this colourful deli near Ortygia's far northern tip. Veteran sandwich-master Andrea Borderi stands out front with a table full of cheeses, olives, greens, herbs, tomatoes and other fixings and engages in nonstop banter with customers while creating free-form sandwiches big enough to keep you fed all day.

Fratelli Burgio   SICILIAN €
(Map p238; ☑0931 6 00 69; www.fratelliburgio.com; Piazza Cesare Battisti 4; panini €3.50-7.50, platters €12-20; ⊙7am-4pm Mon-Sat; 🍴) A hybrid deli, wine shop and eatery edging Ortygia's market, trendy Fratelli Burgio is all about artisanal grazing. Consider opting for a *tagliere*, a wooden platter of artful bites, from cheese, charcuterie and smoked fish, to zesty *caponata* (sweet-and-sour vegetables). If you're euro-pinching, fill up on one of the gourmet *panini*, stuffed with a range of seasonal veggies, herbs, cured meats and cheeses.

WORTH A TRIP

NECROPOLI DI PANTALICA

On a huge plateau above the Valle dell'Anapo, the **Necropoli di Pantalica** `FREE` is Sicily's most important Iron and Bronze Age necropolis, with more than 5000 tombs of various shapes and sizes honeycombed along the limestone cliffs. The site is incredibly ancient, dating to between the 13th and 8th centuries BC, and its origins are largely mysterious, although it is thought to be the Siculi capital of Hybla, which gave the Greeks Megara Hyblaea in 664 BC. Enshrined by Unesco as a World Heritage Site, Pantalica's ruins are surrounded by the beautifully wild and unspoilt landscape of the **Valle dell'Anapo**, a deep limestone gorge laced with walking trails.

Maps posted at the archaeological site's entrance allow you to find your way, but the site is remote, with no services; wear sensible hiking shoes and bring plenty of water.

You'll need your own wheels to get here. From Syracuse, head northwest on the SS124 towards Palazzolo Acreide. After about 36km, turn right towards Ferla; the Necropoli di Pantalica is 11km beyond the town.

★ Moon
VEGAN €€

(Map p238; ☑0931 44 95 16; www.moonortigia.com; Via Roma 112; meals €22-30; ⊙6-11.30pm Wed-Mon, also open 12.30-3pm Wed-Mon Apr-Jun, Sep & Oct, closed mid-Jan–mid-Mar; 🗟☑) This moody, boho-chic restaurant and bar makes vegan food so good even a hardcore carnivore could convert. A cast of mostly organic and biodynamic ingredients beam in balanced, intriguing dishes that might see a tower of thinly sliced pears interlayered with a rich, soy-based cashew cream cheese, or chickpea and tofu conspiring in a smokey carbonara pasta as wicked as the Roman original.

★ Sicilia in Tavola
SICILIAN €€

(Map p238; ☑392 4610889; www.siciliaintavola.eu; Via Cavour 28; meals €27-40; ⊙1-2.30pm & 7.30-10.30pm Tue-Sun) One of the longest established and most popular eateries on Via Cavour, this snug, wonderfully hospitable trattoria has built its reputation on delicious homemade pasta and seafood. To savour both at once, tuck into the *fettuccine allo scoglio* (pasta ribbons with mixed seafood) before sampling *secondi* (mains) like beautifully cooked octopus with chilli, garlic, potatoes and a sublime tomato *sugo*. Reservations recommended.

Retroscena
SICILIAN €€

(Map p238; ☑0931 185 42 78; www.facebook.com/retroscenaristorante; Via della Maestranza 108; meals €40; ⊙7.30-11.30pm Mon-Sat summer, to 10.30pm winter; 🗟) After running a restaurant in Greece for 18 years, Syracuse local Fabio and his Greek partner Kiri are pleasing palates at their hotspot Ortygia restaurant. Vintage mirrors, midcentury lighting and velvet in shades of blue and dusty pink set a fashionable scene for creative, rotating options like trofie pasta with pesto, ricotta, sun-dried tomatoes and crispy zucchini ribbons, or mandarin-and-honey glazed prawns.

Il Pesce Azzurro
SEAFOOD €€

(Map p238; ☑366 2445056; Via Cavour 53; meals €30-35; ⊙noon-3.30pm & 6.30-10.30pm) Seafood-loving locals swear by this easy-to-miss *osteria* (casual tavern), its white-and-blue interior somewhat reminiscent of a Greek-island taverna. The menu favours simplicity and top-notch produce, whether it's sweet, succulent Mazara shrimps drizzled in lime juice, plump *vongole* (clams) paired with spaghetti and garlic, or tender *polpo* (octopus) served *alla luciana* (in a rich tomato and onion sauce). Honest, flavour-packed goodness.

La Medusa
SICILIAN €€

(Da Kamel; Map p238; ☑0931 6 14 03; Via Santa Teresa 21-23; meals €26-45; ⊙noon-3pm & 7-11pm Tue-Sun) This friendly, family-run spot made its name serving delicious couscous, but chef-owner Kamel also knows his way around a fish – the must-try *fritto misto* (mixed fish fry) is wonderfully light. If there's more than one of you, order the *pasta fibus*, an epic, plate-licking serve of *pennette* pasta with seafood, cherry tomatoes, radicchio and crunchy *pangrattato* (toasted breadcrumbs). Book ahead.

★ Don Camillo
SICILIAN €€€

(Map p238; ☑0931 6 71 33; www.ristorantedoncamillo.it; Via della Maestranza 96; meals €45-75; ⊙12.30-2.30pm & 8-10.30pm Mon-Sat; 🗟☑) One of Ortygia's most elegant restaurants, Don Camillo specialises in sterling service and innovative Sicilian cuisine. Pique the appetite with a *crudo* of crustaceans paired with sweet-and-sour celery gelato, swoon over decadent braised-beef ravioli with butter, sage and *ragusano* cheese, or (discreetly) lick your whiskers over an outstanding *tagliata di tonno* (tuna steak) with red-pepper 'marmalade'. A must for Slow Food gourmands.

🍸 Drinking & Nightlife

A vibrant university and tourist town, Syracuse has a lively bar scene, with cafes, wine bars, pubs and cocktail hotspots spilling over the gorgeous streets of Ortygia.

★ Cortile Verga
COCKTAIL BAR

(Map p238; ☑333 1683212; www.facebook.com/cortilevergaortigia; Via della Maestranza 33; ⊙11am-midnight summer, from 5.30pm winter, closed Jan–mid-Mar; 🗟) Take an aristocratic courtyard, add an intimate interior kitted out in vintage coffee tables and a Chesterfield lounge, and you have Cortile Verga. This is one of Ortygia's top cocktail bars, crafting top-tier drinks like the Eleutheria, a blend of vermouth, mezcal, *amaro* (Italian herbal liqueur) and hibiscus tonic. While they're not cheap (€8 to €10), they're a cut above the competition.

Biblios Cafè
CAFE

(Map p238; ☑0931 6 16 27; www.biblioscafe.it; Via del Consiglio Reginale 11; ⊙5-11pm Wed-Sat) This beloved bookshop-cafe organises a whole range of activities, including Italian language courses and regular literary events. It's also a great place to drop in for a restorative *caffè* (coffee), an *aperitivo* or simply to mingle.

🛍 Shopping

Browsing Ortygia's quirky boutiques is great fun. Good buys include papyrus paper, ceramics and handmade jewellery. You'll find a concentration of interesting boutiques and galleries on Via Cavour, Via Roma and Via della Giudecca.

ℹ Information

Hospital (Ospedale Umberto I; ☑ emergency department 0931 72 42 85, switchboard 0931 72 41 11; www.asp.sr.it/default.asp?id=424; cnr Via Testaferrata & Corso Gelone) Located just east of the Parco Archeologico.

Tourist Office (Map p238; ☑ 800 055500; www.provincia.siracusa.it; Via Roma 31; ⏱ 7.30am-2pm Mon, Tue, Thu & Fri, to 4.30pm Wed) Offers a free city map and small selection of brochures.

ℹ Getting There & Away

Syracuse's train and bus stations are a block apart from each other, halfway between Ortygia and the Parco Archeologico.

BUS

Buses are generally faster and more convenient than trains, with long-distance buses arriving and departing from the **bus terminal** (Map p240; Corso Umberto I), 180m southeast of the train station.

Interbus (Map p240; ☑ 091 611 95 35; www.interbus.it) runs buses to Catania (€6.20, 1½ hours, one to two hourly) and its airport, Noto (€3.60, 55 minutes, three to seven daily) and Palermo (€13.50, 3½ hours, two to three daily). Tickets can be purchased at the ticket kiosk.

SAIS Autolinee (☑ 091 617 11 41; www.saistrasporti.it) runs an overnight service to Rome (€41, 12 hours, one nightly) and both daytime and overnight services to Bari (€40, 9½ to 11 hours, one to two daily). Purchase tickets from the train station *edicola* (newsagent).

Flixbus (https://global.flixbus.com) runs direct buses from Syracuse to numerous destinations on the Italian mainland, including Taranto (from €26, nine hours, one daily), Bari (from €26, 10½ hours, one nightly) and Naples (from €28, 10¼ hours, one nightly). Buy tickets on the Flixbus website.

CAR & MOTORCYCLE

The dual-carriageway SS114 heads north from Syracuse to Catania, while the SS115 runs south to Noto and Modica. While the approach roads to Syracuse are rarely very busy, traffic gets increasingly heavy as you enter town and can be pretty bad in the city centre.

If you're staying in Ortygia, the best place to park is the **Talete parking garage** (Parcheggio Talete; ☑ 0931 46 32 89) on Ortygia's northern tip, which charges a 24-hour maximum of €10 (payable by cash or credit card at the machine).

Note that most of Ortygia is a limited traffic zone, restricted to residents and those with special permission. On-street parking is hard to find during the week, less so on Sunday when it's often free.

TRAIN

From Syracuse's **train station** (Via Francesco Crispi), trains depart daily for Catania (€6.90, one to 1½ hours, 12 daily Monday to Saturday, six Sunday) and Messina (from €10.50, 2½ to 3¼ hours, 11 daily Monday to Saturday, five Sunday). Some go on to mainland Italy. Note that passengers travelling from Syracuse to Messina may need to change at Catania Centrale station.

There are also trains to Noto (€3.80, 30 to 45 minutes, seven daily Monday to Friday, six Saturday), Scicli (€6.90, 1½ to 1¾ hours, six daily Monday to Friday, five Saturday), Modica (€7.60, 1¾ to two hours, six daily Monday to Friday, five Saturday) and Ragusa (€8.30, 2¼ hours, five daily Monday to Friday, four Saturday).

ℹ Getting Around

Siracusa d'Amare Trasporti (☑ 0931 175 62 32; 90min ticket €1) runs inexpensive electric minibuses around Syracuse and Ortygia. To reach Ortygia from the bus and train stations, catch **minibus 1**. To reach the Parco Archeologico della Neapolis, take **minibus 2** (Map p238) from Molo Sant'Antonio (just west of the bridge to Ortygia). Buses run every 20 minutes between 8am and 8pm from March to June and every 30 minutes between 9am and 9pm from July to December. Tickets can be purchased on board. Be warned that during the Ciclo di Rappresentazioni Classiche (p28) festival, minibus 2 can get extremely crowded, with lengthy delays.

Noto

☑ 0931 / POP 24,000 / ELEV 152M

Noto is an architectural supermodel, a baroque belle so gorgeous you might mistake it for a film set. Located less than 40km southwest of Syracuse, the town is home to one of Sicily's most beautiful historic centres. The pièce de résistance is Corso Vittorio Emanuele, an elegant walkway flanked by thrilling baroque *palazzi* and churches. Dashing at any time of the day, it's especially hypnotic in the early evening, when the red-gold buildings seem to glow with a soft inner light.

The Noto you see today dates to the early 18th century, when it was almost entirely rebuilt in the wake of the devastating 1693 earthquake. Creator of many of the finest buildings was Rosario Gagliardi, a local architect whose extroverted style also graces churches in Modica and Ragusa.

◉ Sights

About halfway along Corso Vittorio Emanuele is the graceful **Piazza Municipio**, flanked by Noto's cathedral and a series of elegant palaces, including **Palazzo Landolina** and **Palazzo Ducezio** (☑ 0931 83 64 62; www.comune.noto.sr.it/la-cultura/la-sala-degli-specchi; Sala degli Specchi €2, panoramic terrace €2; ⊙ 10am-6pm).

Further west, **Piazza XVI Maggio** is overlooked by the beautiful **Chiesa di San Domenico** (☑ 327 0162589; www.oqdany.it; church free, guided tour of crypt €2; ⊙ 10am-2pm & 4.30-9pm Jul & Aug, 10am-6pm Sep-Jun) and the adjacent Dominican monastery, both designed by Rosario Gagliardi. On the same square, Noto's elegant 19th-century **Teatro Tina di Lorenzo** (Teatro Vittorio Emanuele; ☑ 0931 83 50 73; www.fondazioneteatrodinoto.it; general visit €2, theatre tickets adult/reduced from €10/8; ⊙ general visits 10am-6pm) is worth a look.

For sweeping views of Noto's baroque splendour, climb to the rooftop terrace at **Chiesa di Santa Chiara** (Corso Vittorio Emanuele; adult/reduced €2/1; ⊙ 10.30am-1pm & 2.30-4pm) or the campanile (bell tower) of **Chiesa di San Carlo al Corso** (Corso Vittorio Emanuele; campanile €2; ⊙ 10am-10pm Jul & Aug, to 8pm May, Jun & Sep, reduced hours rest of year).

★ Basilica Cattedrale
di San Nicolò   CATHEDRAL
(☑ 327 0162589; www.oqdany.it; Piazza Municipio; ⊙ 10am-2pm & 4.30-9pm Jul & Aug, 10am-6pm Sep-Jun) Pride of place in Noto goes to San Nicolò Cathedral, a baroque beauty that had to undergo extensive renovation after its dome collapsed during a 1996 thunderstorm. The ensuing decade saw the cathedral scrubbed of centuries of dust and dirt before reopening in 2007. Today the dome, with its peachy glow, is once again the focal point of Noto's skyline.

★ Palazzo Castelluccio   PALACE
(☑ 0931 83 88 81; http://palazzocastelluccio.it; Via Cavour 10; adult/child €12/free; ⊙ 11am-7pm, closed Mon & Tue winter) Abandoned for decades, this 18th-century *palazzo* found its saviour in French journalist and documentary filmmaker Jean-Louis Remilleux, who purchased the aristocratic pad and set about

restoring it. Now accessible by guided tour, it offers the most complete insight into how Noto's nobility once lived, its sumptuous rooms awash with original frescoes and tiles, faithfully reproduced wallpaper, as well as Sicilian and Neapolitan baroque furniture from the owner's collection.

Palazzo Nicolaci di Villadorata   PALACE
(☑ 338 7427022; www.comune.noto.sr.it/palazzo-nicolaci; Via Corrado Nicolaci; admission €4; ⊙ 10am-6pm mid-Mar–mid-Oct, 10am-1pm & 3-5pm rest of year) The fantastical facade of this 18th-century palace wows with its wrought-iron balconies, supported by a swirling pantomime of grotesque figures. Inside, the richly brocaded walls and frescoed ceilings offer an idea of the sumptuous lifestyle of Sicilian nobles, as brought to life in the Giuseppe Tomasi di Lampedusa novel *Il Gattopardo* (The Leopard).

Basilica del Santissimo Salvatore   CHURCH
(☑ 327 0162589; www.oqdany.it; Via Vincenzo Gioberti; ⊙ 10am-2pm & 4.30-9pm Jul & Aug, 10am-6pm Sep-Jun) Situated towards the grand Porta Reale is the Basilica del Santissimo Salvatore. Its recently restored interior is the most impressive in Noto, crowned by a glorious vault fresco by Antonio Mazza depicting the Holy Spirit's descent. Mazza is also responsible for the church's facade, completed in 1791 and showing influences of a more restrained neoclassical style. The adjoining Benedictine convent offers sweeping views from its bell tower.

🎊 Festivals & Events

Infiorata   CARNIVAL
(⊙ mid-May) Noto's big annual jamboree is the Infiorata, celebrated over three days with music concerts, parades and the breathtaking decoration of Via Corrado Nicolaci with designs made entirely of flower petals.

🛏 Sleeping

Ostello Il Castello   HOSTEL €
(☑ 320 8388869; www.ostellodinoto.it; Via Fratelli Bandiera 1; dm €20, s/d €35/70; P ✱ 🛈) Directly uphill from the centre, this renovated hostel offers excellent value for money and is a great option for families or groups. There's one dorm (mixed with 18 beds), with all other rooms private and capable of accommodating up to six people. Some rooms come with a terrace, delivering commanding views over Noto's cathedral and rooftops. Wi-fi in communal areas only. Breakfast included.

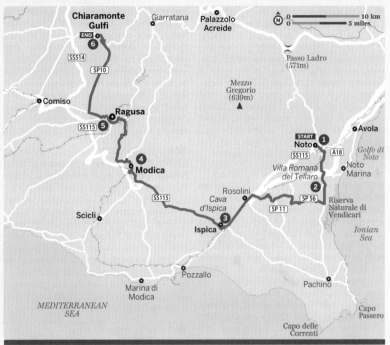

Driving Tour
Baroque Towns

START NOTO
END CHIARAMONTE GULFI
LENGTH 71KM; TWO DAYS

A land of remote rocky gorges, sweeping views and silent valleys, Sicily's southeastern corner is home to the 'baroque triangle', an area of Unesco-listed hilltop towns famous for their lavish baroque architecture. This tour takes in some of the finest, all within easy driving distance of each other.

Just over 35km south of Syracuse, **1 Noto** is home to what is arguably Sicily's most beautiful street – Corso Vittorio Emanuele, a pedestrianised boulevard lined with golden baroque *palazzi*. It's also home to a number of culinary hotspots, among them Ristorante Vicari and Manna. From Noto, head south along SP19, quickly pop into **2 Villa Romana del Tellaro** (☎0931 57 38 83; www.villaromanadeltellaro.com; ⊙8.30am-7.30pm, last entry 6pm) FREE to admire its Roman mosaics. Continue on to Ispica, a hilltop town overlooking a huge canyon, **3 Cava d'Ispica** (☎0932 95 26 08; www.cavadispica.org; Crocevia Cava Ispica; adult/

reduced €4/2; ⊙9am-6.30pm May-Oct, to 1.15pm Mon-Sat Nov & Dec), riddled with prehistoric tombs. Follow the SS115 for a further 18km to **4 Modica** (p247), a bustling town set in a deep rocky gorge. There's excellent accommodation and great restaurants, so it's a good place to stay overnight. The best of the baroque sights are up in Modica Alta, the high part of town, but make sure you have energy left for the *passeggiata* on Corso Umberto I and dinner at Accursio, Cappero or Ornato.

Next morning, a short, winding, up-and-down drive through rock-littered hilltops leads to **5 Ragusa** (p249). The town is divided in two – Ragusa Ibla is a claustrophobic warren of grey stone houses and elegant *palazzi* that opens up onto Piazza Duomo, a superb example of 18th-century town planning. Consider lunching at casual standout I Banchi, or save your appetite for **6 Chiaramonte Gulfi**, a tranquil hilltop town some 20km to the north along the SP10. Dubbed the Balcone della Sicilia (Sicily's Balcony) for its breathtaking panorama, it's famous for its coveted olive oil and blue-ribbon pork, the latter best savoured at Ristorante Majore.

★**Nòtia Rooms** B&B €€
(☑ 366 5007350, 0931 83 88 91; www.notiarooms.
com; Vico Frumento 6; d €130-150, tr €150-170;
🛜) In Noto's historic workers' quarter, this
sophisticated B&B is owned by the gracious
Giorgio and Carla, who gave up the stress of
northern Italian life to open this three-room
beauty. Crisp white interiors are accented
with original artworks, Modernist Italian
lamps and upcycled vintage finds. Rooms
seduce with sublimely comfortable beds
and polished modern bathrooms. Gorgeous
breakfasts maintain the high standards.

★**Seven Rooms**
Villadorata BOUTIQUE HOTEL €€€
(☑ 0931 83 55 75; https://7roomsvilladorata.it; Via
Cavour 53; d from €275; P❄🛜) This elegantly
appointed boutique hotel occupies a wing
of the 18th-century Palazzo Nicolaci, one of
Noto's most celebrated aristocratic palaces.
With their restrained colour palette, rooms
are tactile and sophisticated, with artfully
distressed furniture, beautiful artworks, al-
paca throws, Nespresso machines and luxurious bathrooms stocked with high-quality
amenities; the Deluxe Rooms are especially
impressive. Quality extends to the breakfast,
served at a communal table.

✖ Eating & Drinking

Noto has a vibrant food scene, with a mix
of innovative, sophisticated restaurants and
old-school trattorias serving unfussy classics. The best spots are in the *centro storico*
(historic centre), within walking distance of
Corso Vittorio Emanuele. The corso and its
piazzas constitute the town's social nerve
centre, with evening crowds partaking in the
evening *passeggiata* (stroll).

★**Caffè Sicilia** GELATO €
(☑ 0931 83 50 13; www.caffesicilia.it; Corso Vittorio Emanuele 125; pastries €2.50; ⏰8am-10pm
Tue-Sun, closed Nov & early Jan-early Mar; 🍦)
Dating from 1892 and especially renowned
for its *granite*, this beloved place vies with
its neighbour, Dolceria Corrado Costanzo,
for the honours of Noto's best dessert shop.
Frozen desserts are made with the freshest
seasonal ingredients (wild strawberries in
springtime, for example), while the delicious
torrone (nougat) bursts with the flavours of
local honey and almonds. It's also a good
spot for an *aperitivo*.

★**Manna** SICILIAN €€
(☑ 0931 83 60 51; www.mannanoto.it; Via Rocco Pir-
ri 15; meals €35-47; ⏰noon-2.30pm & 7-10.30pm
Wed-Mon Easter-Jul & Sep-Dec, 7-10.30pm daily Aug;
🛜) Divided into a hip front bar and sultry
back dining rooms, Manna wows with its
competent, contemporary creations. Premium produce dictates the menu, which
might see *tagliatelle* pasta paired with duck
ragù and Parmesan crisps, or mackerel fillet
served with aromatic herbs, seaweed and a
salted lemon *gelo* (Sicilian jelly). Staff are
competent and friendly, and the wine list is
focused on worthy drops.

★**Ristorante Vicari** SICILIAN €€€
(☑ 0931 83 93 22; www.ristorantevicari.it; Ronco
Bernardo Leanti 9; meals €45-60; ⏰12.30-2pm
Mon, Tue & Thu-Sat, plus 7-10pm daily Jul-Sep,
12.30-2pm Tue-Sat, plus 7-10pm Mon-Sat Oct-Jun)
Low-slung lamps spotlight linen-clad tables
at Vicari, and rightfully so. In the kitchen is
young-gun chef Salvatore Vicari, who thrills
with his whimsical takes on Sicilian produce:
succulent squid stuffed with tomato and almonds and served on a pistachio cream, or
ravioli stuffed with roast chicken and paired
with a carrot, lemon and spinach cream. Reservations highly recommended.

★**Anche gli Angeli** LOUNGE
(☑ 0931 57 60 23; www.anchegliangeli.it; Via A
da Brescia 2; ⏰8am-1am; 🛜) Sophisticated,
LGBTIQ-friendly and irrefutably cool, 'Even
the Angels' is *the* place to schmooze in Noto.
A cafe-bar, lounge, restaurant and concept
store in one, it's as fabulous for a cappuccino
and house-baked pastry as it is for browsing
books, *aperitivo* sessions, a smashing mod-
ern-Sicilian dinner (meals €32 to €60) or a
late-night tipple. Live music Wednesdays and
Fridays, with DJ sets Fridays and Saturdays.

ℹ Information

Infopoint Noto (☑ 339 4816218; www.notoin
forma.it; Corso Vittorio Emanuele 135; ⏰10am-
7pm Apr, May & Oct, to 8pm Jun & Sep, to 9pm
Jul, to 10pm Aug, to 6pm rest of year) Offers
maps, brochures, free computer access and a
complimentary left-luggage service. Visitors
can print boarding passes or other documents
(€1), and the enthusiastic, multilingual staff
also organise guided tours in Italian, English
and French.

ℹ Getting There & Away

BUS
Noto's bus station is conveniently located just
to the southeast of Porta Reale and the Giardini
Pubblici. Buy tickets from **Bar Flora** (Hotel Flora,
Via Pola 1), located at Hotel Flora, just west of
the bus stop.

AST (☎0931 46 27 11; www.aziendasiciliana
trasporti.it) runs to Syracuse (€3.60, one hour,
seven daily Monday to Saturday) and Catania
(€7.50, 1½ hours, six daily Monday to Saturday,
two Sunday). Buses to Catania stop at Catania
airport en route.

Interbus (☎091 611 95 35, 0935 2 24 60;
www.interbus.it) also runs to Catania (€8.40,
1½ to 2½ hours, eight to nine daily Monday to
Friday, six Saturday, three Sunday) and Syracuse
(€3.60, one hour, four to five daily Monday to
Friday, four Saturday, three Sunday).

TRAIN

Trains run daily except Sunday to Syracuse
(€3.80, 30 to 40 minutes), Scicli (€4.30, one
hour), Modica (€5.10, 1¼ hours) and Ragusa
(€6.20, 1½ hours), but the station is inconvenient-
ly located 1km downhill from the historic centre.

Modica

☎0932 / POP 54,500 / ELEV 296M

From early Greek and Roman roots, Modica rose to become one of Sicily's most powerful cities as the personal fiefdom of the
Chiaramonte family in the 14th century.
Modern-day Modica remains a superbly atmospheric town, with its medieval and baroque buildings climbing steeply up either
side of a deep gorge. The multilayered town
is divided into Modica Alta (Upper Modica)
and Modica Bassa (Lower Modica). A devastating flood in 1902 resulted in the wide ave-
nues of Corso Umberto and Via Giarrantana
(the river was dammed and diverted), which
remain the main axes of the town, lined by
palazzi and tiled stone houses.

⊙ Sights

Duomo di San Giorgio CHURCH
(☎0932 94 12 79; Corso San Giorgio, Modica Alta;
◑8am-12.30pm & 3.30-7pm) The high point of
a trip to Modica – quite literally as it's up in
Modica Alta – is the Duomo di San Giorgio,
one of Sicily's most extraordinary baroque
churches. Considered Rosario Gagliardi's
great masterpiece, it stands in isolated
splendour at the top of a majestic 250-step,
19th-century staircase, its sumptuous three-
tiered facade towering above the medieval
alleyways of the historic centre.

Duomo di San Pietro CATHEDRAL
(Corso Umberto I 159, Modica Bassa; ◑8.30am-
12.30pm & 2-7pm Mon-Sat, to 8pm Sun) In Modica, the Duomo di San Pietro plays second
fiddle only to the Cattedrale di San Giorgio.
The original 14th-century church was damaged in the earthquake of 1693, leading to its

reconstruction in 1697. Construction continued way into the 19th century; the rippling
staircase, lined with life-sized statues of the
Apostles, was only completed in 1876.

Chiesa di San Giovanni Evangelista CHURCH
(Piazza San Giovanni, Modica Alta; ◑hours vary)
Attributed to Rosario Gagliardi and marking
the top of Modica Alta is this grand baroque
church. Prefaced by a sweeping staircase, the
church underwent major restoration work
in the 19th century, its current facade completed between 1893 and 1901. If the church
is open, slip inside its elliptical interior for
beautiful, neoclassical stuccowork. Nearby,
at the end of Via Pizzo, a viewing balcony offers arresting views over the old town.

🛏 Sleeping

Sophisticated Modica offers a wide choice of
accommodation in both the upper and lower
towns; the latter is closer to the action, especially at night. Book ahead in summer and
during busy periods such as April's Festa di
San Giorgio.

★**Masseria Quartarella** AGRITURISMO €
(☎360 654829; www.quartarella.com; Contrada
Quartarella Passo Cane 1; s €40, d €75-80, tr €85-
100, q €90-120; P❄🏠🖥) Spacious rooms,
welcoming hosts and ample breakfasts make
this converted farmhouse in the countryside
south of Modica an appealing choice for anyone travelling by car. Owners Francesco and
Francesca are generous in sharing their love
and encyclopaedic knowledge of local history,
flora and fauna and can suggest a multitude
of driving itineraries in the surrounding area.

Palazzo Failla HOTEL €
(☎0932 94 10 59; www.palazzofailla.it; Via Blan-
dini 5, Modica Alta; s €55-65, d €69-125; ❄@🏠)
Smack in the heart of Modica Alta, this
four-star, family-run hotel in a nostalgic
18th-century palace has retained much of its
historical splendour, with original frescoed
ceilings, hand-painted ceramic Caltagirone
floor tiles, elegant drapes and heirloom
antiques. Start the day with the generous
breakfast buffet and end it at the hotel's
well-regarded restaurant.

★**Casa Gelsomino** APARTMENT €€
(☎335 8087841; www.casedisicilia.com; Via Raccomandata, Modica Bassa; per night €160-200, per
week €1000-1260; ❄🏠) It's easy to pretend
you're a holidaying celebrity in this beautifully restored apartment, its balconies and private terrace serving up commanding views

over Modica. Incorporating an airy lounge, fully equipped kitchen, stone-walled bathroom, laundry room, sitting room (with sofa bed) and separate bedroom, its combination of vaulted ceilings, antique floor tiles, original artworks and plush furnishings takes self-catering to sophisticated highs.

✖ Eating

Modica merits a stop on any Sicilian foodie trail, with both Slow Food trattorias and creative, high-end restaurants. The town is renowned for its grainy chocolate, a blend of bitter cocoa, sugar and spices worked at low temperature using an ancient method.

★ **Caffè Adamo** GELATO €
(☑ 0932 197 25 46; www.caffeadamo.it; Via Maresa Tedeschi 15-17, Modica Bassa; cup/cone from €2/2.50; ⊙ 6am-1am summer, to 11pm rest of year, closed Mon Sep-Mar; ☎) There is great gelato and then there's gelato made by Antonio Adamo. The affable *modinese* makes all his confections from scratch; even the Agrigento pistachios are ground on-site. The result is ice cream packed with extraordinarily natural flavour and freshness. Gelato aside, Antonio's *cremolate* (water ices), Modica chocolate blocks and take-home jars of *babà* (rum-soaked sponge cake) are also outstanding.

★ **Ornato** SEAFOOD €€
(☑ 0932 94 24 23; http://ornato-ristorante-di-pesce.thefork.rest; Via Pozzo Barone 30, Modica Bassa; meals €35-50, tasting menu €60; ⊙ noon-2pm & 7-10.30pm Tue-Sun Sep-Jul, 7-10.30pm daily Aug; ☎) The decorative tagines at stylish Ornato reflect Luca Ornato's love of global flavours, a fact also echoed in out-of-the-box dishes like *crudo* (raw seafood) with yuzu. The talented cook marries tradition and innovation with impressive skill, his menu as likely to offer flawless *spaghetti con frutti di mare* (spaghetti with seafood) as it is a sweet interpretation of the Caprese salad.

★ **Cappero** SICILIAN €€
(☑ 393 9078088; www.facebook.com/Cappero Bistrot; Corso Umberto I 156, Modica Bassa; meals €25-40; ⊙ noon-3pm & 7-10.30pm Fri-Wed, closed Aug; ☎ ☑) Small, quietly confident Cappero wows food lovers with beautiful cooking that's refined and comforting in equal parts. The house-made pasta is made using ancient grains, herbs are picked fresh from the restaurant's vertical herb garden, and the seasonal menu includes typically Modican dishes like broth with veal meatballs and noodles. If it's on the menu, sink your teeth into the succulent rabbit. Reservations recommended.

★ **Accursio** SICILIAN €€€
(☑ 0932 94 16 89; www.accursioristorante.it; Via Grimaldi 41, Modica Bassa; meals €80-90, tasting menus €90-150; ⊙ 12.30-2pm & 7.30-10pm Tue-Sat, 12.30-2pm Sun) While we love the modernist furniture and vintage Sicilian tiles, the food is the real thrill at this intimate,

---

WORTH A TRIP

SCICLI

About 10km southwest of Modica, Scicli is the most authentic and relaxed of the Val di Noto's showpiece baroque towns. Its relatively compact, quickly gentrifying historic centre is awash with cultural sights, from beautiful churches and aristocratic *palazzi* (mansions) to eclectic museums and a time-warped apothecary. The town makes regular cameos on the hit TV series *Inspector Montalbano,* and visitors can visit two of the show's sets inside **Palazzo Municipio**.

Overlooking the town is a rocky peak topped by an abandoned church, the **Chiesa di San Matteo**. It's not too hard a walk up to the church to take in the sweeping views – simply follow the yellow sign up from Palazzo Beneventano and keep going for about 10 minutes.

For those who wish to linger overnight, **Scicli Albergo Diffuso** (☑ 392 8207857; www.sciclialbergodiffuso.it; Via Francesco Mormina Penna 15; r €77-177; ❋ ☎) offers fabulous digs in numerous locations across Scicli's historic core. Options range from simple rooms in restored *dammusi* (traditional stone abodes) to breathtaking suites in 19th-century palaces. Top of the heap are the frescoed rooms inside the 18th-century Palazzo Favacchio Patanè.

Trains run daily except Sunday to Modica (€1.70, 10 to 14 minutes), Ragusa (€3.10, 30 to 40 minutes), Noto (€4.30, 50 minutes to one hour) and Syracuse (€6.90, 1½ hours).

Michelin-starred maverick. Head chef Accursio Craparo specialises in boldly creative, nuanced dishes inspired by childhood memories and emblematic of new Sicilian thinking. For a well-rounded adventure, opt for a tasting menu.

🛍 Shopping

Antica Dolceria Bonajuto · CHOCOLATE
(✷ 0932 94 12 25; www.bonajuto.it; Corso Umberto I 159, Modica Bassa; ⊙ 9am-8.30pm Sep-Jul, to midnight Aug) Sicily's oldest chocolate factory is the perfect place to taste Modica's famous chocolate. Flavoured with cinnamon, vanilla, orange peel and even hot peppers, it's a legacy of the town's Spanish overlords who imported cocoa from their South American colonies. Leave room for Bonajuto's *'mpanatigghi,* sweet local biscuits filled with chocolate, spices...and minced beef!

ⓘ Information

Tourist Office (✷ 0932 75 96 34, 346 6558227; www.comune.modica.rg.it; Corso Umberto I 141, Modica Bassa; ⊙ 8.30am-1.30pm & 3-7pm Mon-Fri, 9am-1pm & 3-7pm Sat) City-run tourist office in Modica Bassa.

ⓘ Getting There & Away

BUS

Modica's bus station is at Piazzale Falcone-Borsellino at the top end of Corso Umberto I. **AST** (✷ 0932 76 73 01; www.aziendasiciliana trasporti.it) runs to Noto (€3.90, 1½ to 1¾ hours, seven to 11 daily Monday to Saturday, one Sunday), Ragusa (€2.40, 25 to 30 minutes, 14 to 18 daily Monday to Saturday, two Sunday) and Catania (€9, 2¼ hours, seven to eight daily Monday to Saturday, four Sunday).

TRAIN

There are trains to Ragusa (€2.50, 20 to 30 minutes, nine daily Monday to Friday, seven Saturday), Scicli (€1.70, 10 minutes, six daily Monday to Friday, five Saturday) and Syracuse (€7.60, 1¾ hours, six daily Monday to Friday, five Saturday).

Ragusa

✷ 0932 / POP 73,600 / ELEV 502M

Set amid the rocky peaks northwest of Modica, Ragusa is a town of two faces. Crowning the hilltop is Ragusa Superiore, a busy workaday town with sensible grid-pattern streets and all the trappings of a modern provincial capital, while etched into the hillside further down is Ragusa Ibla. This sloping area of tangled alleyways, grey stone houses and baroque *palazzi* on handsome squares is effectively Ragusa's historic centre and it's quite magnificent.

⊙ Sights

★ **Ragusa Ibla** · AREA
Ragusa Ibla is a joy to wander, its labyrinthine lanes weaving through rock-grey *palazzi* to open onto beautiful, sun-drenched piazzas. It's easy to get lost but you can never go too far wrong, and sooner or later you'll end up at **Piazza Duomo**, Ragusa's sublime central square.

Facing the piazza, on Corso XXV Aprile, is **Palazzo Arezzo di Trifiletti** (✷ 339 4000013, 349 6487463; www.palazzoarezzo.it; 20min tour €5, tour & aperitivo €15-40; ⊙ guided tours 10.30am-7pm daily Jun-Sep, by appt rest of the year), built between the 17th and early 19th centuries. Guided tours of the aristocratic palace include its showpiece ballroom, graced with rare, late-18th-century Neapolitan majolica tiles and luminous 19th-century frescoes that have never needed touching up.

Opposite the palace, Via Novelli leads to the entrance of jewel-box **Teatro Donnafugata** (✷ 334 2208186; www.teatrodonnafugata.it; Via Novelli 3; guided tour €10; ⊙ guided tours Apr-Oct, shows year-round), a 99-seat theatre that looks like a grand Italian opera house in miniature form. The theatre is a stop on the A Porte Aperte walking tour of Ragusa Ibla.

Via Novelli leads to Via Orfanotrofio, home to **Cinabro Carrettieri** (✷ 340 8444804; www.cinabrocarrettieri.it; Via Orfanotrofio 22; 15/30min guided tour €3/5; ⊙ 10.30am-9pm), the colourful workshop of world-famous Sicilian cart craftsmen Biagio Castilletti and Damiano Rotella. The street continues south back to Corso XXV Aprile, where you're met by an eye-catching Gagliardi church, the elliptical **Chiesa di San Giuseppe** (Piazza Pola; ⊙ 9am-12.30pm & 3-7pm daily Jun-Sep, reduced hours rest of year), its cupola graced by Sebastiano Lo Monaco's fresco *Gloria di San Benedetto* (Glory of St Benedict, 1793).

Further downhill, the street to the right of the entrance of the **Giardino Ibleo** (✷ 0932 65 23 74; Piazza Odierna) harbours the Catalan Gothic portal of what was once the large **Chiesa di San Giorgio Vecchio** (Via dei Normanni), now mostly ruined. The lunette features an interesting bas-relief of St George killing the dragon.

At the other end of Ragusa Ibla, the **Chiesa delle Santissime Anime del Purgatorio** (✷ 0932 62 18 55; Piazza della Repubblica; ⊙ 10am-

7pm daily Jun-Sep, reduced hours rest of year) is one of the few churches in town to have survived the great earthquake of 1693. Step inside to admire Francesco Manno's *Anime in Purgatorio* (Souls in Purgatory; 1800) at the main altar.

Duomo di San Giorgio CATHEDRAL
(Piazza Duomo, Ragusa Ibla; ⊘10am-1pm & 3-6.30pm Apr-Oct & Dec, shorter hours rest of year) At the top end of the sloping Piazza Duomo is the town's pride and joy, the mid-18th-century cathedral with a magnificent neo-classical dome and stained-glass windows. One of Rosario Gagliardi's finest accomplishments, its extravagant convex facade rises like a three-tiered wedding cake, supported by gradually narrowing Corinthian columns and punctuated by jutting cornices.

Castello di Donnafugata PALACE
(☑0932 67 65 00; www.comune.ragusa.gov.it; Contrada Donnafugata; adult/reduced €6/3; ⊘9am-1pm & 2.30-7pm Tue-Sun summer, 9am-1pm & 2-4.45pm Tue-Sun winter) Located 18km southwest of Ragusa, this sumptuous neo-Gothic palace houses the Collezione Gabriele Arezzo di Trifiletti, an extraordinary fashion and costume collection. The easiest way to reach the *castello* is by car. From Monday to Saturday, trains run from Ragusa to Donnafugata (three to four daily, 20 to 25 minutes, €2.50), from where it's a 600m walk to the castle. Alternatively, Autotrasporti Tumino (☑0932 62 31 84; www.tuminobus.it; Via Zama) runs a very limited bus service from Ragusa (return €4.80); see the company website for times.

🏃 Activities

A Porte Aperte WALKING
(☑366 3194177; www.facebook.com/aporteaperte; guided tour €10; 🖳) Cultural association 'Iblazon' runs 50-minute walking tours of three historic sites in Ragusa Ibla: the 'Circolo di Conversazione' (a club for Ragusan aristocrats), the private garden Palazzo Arezzo-Bertini and the Teatro Donnafugata, a jewel-box 19th-century theatre. Tours are offered in Italian and English and must be booked at least a day ahead, either by email, SMS or calling.

🎉 Festivals & Events

★ **Scale del Gusto** FOOD & DRINK
(www.scaledelgusto.it; ⊘Oct) For three days, Ragusa's squares, streets and Unesco-listed buildings not usually open to the public become evocative settings for this buzzing celebration of Sicilian food and artisan food producers. The program includes master-classes by prolific chefs, talks, *aperitivo* sessions, pop-up restaurants, art exhibitions, live performances and light installations.

🛏 Sleeping

Tenuta Zannafondo B&B €
(☑0932 183 89 19; www.tenutazannafondo.it; Contrada di Zannafondo; d €79-89; 🅿 ❋ �) Set amid olive-sprinkled hillsides lined with stone walls, this converted 19th-century farmstead sits halfway between Ragusa and the coast (a 15-minute drive from each). Its charm lies in the tranquil cluster of independent stone-walled cottages, each with its own little patio; two rooms in the main house are less appealing. Dinner is available on request.

L'Orto Sul Tetto B&B €
(☑0932 24 77 85; www.lortosultetto.it; Via Tenente di Stefano 56, Ragusa Ibla; d €75-90; ❋ �) This sweet little B&B behind the Duomo di San Giorgio offers an intimate experience, with simple, tastefully decorated rooms and a leafy roof terrace where a generous breakfast is served. Service is warm and obliging.

🍴 Eating

★ **I Banchi** ITALIAN €€
(☑0932 65 50 00; www.ibanchiragusa.it; Via Orfanotrofio 39, Ragusa Ibla; panini €6-6.50, meals €40-50, tasting menus €30-70; ⊘8.30am-11pm; �) Michelin-star chef Ciccio Sultano is behind this contemporary, smart-casual eatery, which includes a dedicated bakery, specialist deli counter and the freedom to choose anything from *caffè* and just-baked pastries, to made-on-site gourmet *panini,* lazy wine-and-cheese sessions or more elaborate, creative dishes that put twists on Sicilian traditions, such as carob-glazed local pork with hummus and Modican chocolate salsa.

Agli Archi SICILIAN €€
(☑0932 62 19 32; www.facebook.com/agliarchi trattoria; Piazza della Repubblica 15, Ragusa Ibla; meals €25-30; ⊘12.30-3pm & 7.30-10.30pm Fri-Wed, closed Jan & Feb; � 🖳) With an outdoor terrace facing the pretty Chiesa delle Santissime Anime del Purgatorio, Agli Archi reveals a genuine passion for local ingredients and less-ubiquitous regional recipes. Rotating with the seasons, offerings might include *cavatelli* (elongated, shell-like pasta) with broccoli, anchovies and breadcrumbs,

VILLA ROMANA DEL CASALE

Near the town of Piazza Armerina in central Sicily is the stunning 3rd-century Roman **Villa Romana del Casale** (☑ 0935 68 00 36; www.villaromanadelcasale.it; adult/reduced €10/5, combined ticket incl Morgantina & Museo Archeologico di Aidone €14/7; ☺ 9am-11.30pm Apr-Oct, to 5pm Nov-May), a Unesco World Heritage Site and one of the few remaining sites of Roman Sicily. This sumptuous hunting lodge is thought to have belonged to Diocletian's co-emperor Marcus Aurelius Maximianus. Buried under mud in a 12th-century flood, it remained hidden for hundreds of years before its magnificent floor mosaics were discovered in the 1950s. Visit out of season or early in the day to avoid the crowds.

The mosaics cover almost the entire floor (3500 sq metres) of the villa and are considered unique for their narrative style, the range of subject matter and variety of colour – many are clearly influenced by African themes. Along the eastern end of the internal courtyard is the wonderful **Corridor of the Great Hunt**, vividly depicting chariots, rhinos, cheetahs, lions and the voluptuously beautiful Queen of Sheba. Across the corridor is a series of apartments, where floor illustrations reproduce scenes from Homer's Odyssey. But perhaps the most captivating of the mosaics is the so-called **Room of the Ten Girls in Bikinis**, with depictions of sporty girls in bikinis throwing a discus, using weights and throwing a ball; they would blend in well on a Malibu beach and are among Sicily's greatest classical treasures.

Travelling by car from Piazza Armerina, follow signs south of town to the SP15, then continue 5km to reach the villa. Getting here by public transport is more challenging. Buses operated by **Interbus** (☑ 095 53 27 16; www.interbus.it) run from Catania to Piazza Armerina (€9.20, 2 hours); from here catch a local bus (€1, 30 minutes, summer only) or a taxi (€20) for the remaining 5km.

or succulent pork fillet cooked with oranges and served in a carob salsa.

★ **Ristorante Duomo**   SICILIAN €€€
(☑ 0932 65 12 65; www.cicciosultano.it; Via Capitano Bocchieri 31, Ragusa Ibla; tasting menus €135-150; ☺ 12.30-2pm Mon, 12.30-2pm & 7.30-10.30pm Tue-Sat) Widely regarded as one of Sicily's finest restaurants, Duomo comprises a cluster of small rooms outfitted like private parlours behind its stained-glass door, ensuring a suitably romantic ambience for chef Ciccio Sultano's refined creations. The menu abounds in classic Sicilian ingredients such as pistachios, fennel, almonds and Nero d'Avola wine, combined in imaginative and unconventional ways. Reservations essential.

ℹ Information

Tourist Office (☑ 0932 68 47 80; www.comune.ragusa.gov.it; Piazza San Giovanni, Ragusa Superiore; ☺ 9am-7pm Mon-Fri year-round, 9am-2pm Sat & Sun Easter–mid-Oct & Dec) Ragusa's main tourist office, with friendly, helpful staff.

ℹ Getting There & Around

BUS

Long-distance and municipal buses share a terminal on Via Zama in the upper town (Ragusa Superiore). Buy tickets at the ticket kiosk at the terminal or from the bar **Tre Passi Avanti** (☑ 0932 191 00 60; Via Zama 24; ☺ 5am-9pm Mon-Sat), located 70m away.

AST (☑ 0932 76 73 01; www.aziendasiciliana trasporti.it; Via Zama) runs direct services to numerous destinations, including Modica (€2.70, 25 minutes, 15 to 17 daily Monday to Saturday, two Sunday) and Syracuse (€7.20, 3¼ hours, three daily Monday to Saturday).

Interbus (☑ 091 611 95 35; www.interbus. it; Via Zama) runs to Catania (€8.60, two hours, hourly Monday to Friday, every one to three hours Saturday, every one to two hours Sunday).

Flixbus (https://global.flixbus.com) operates direct services to the Calabrian port of Villa San Giovanni (from €14, 3¾ to five hours, three daily) on the Italian mainland.

Monday through Saturday, AST's city buses 11 and 33 (€1.20) run hourly between Via Zama bus terminal and Giardino Ibleo in Ragusa Ibla. On Sunday, bus 1 makes a similar circuit. Daily tickets are available (€2).

TRAIN

Trains run daily except Sunday to Modica (€2.50, 20 to 25 minutes), Scicli (€3.10, 30 to 35 minutes) and Syracuse (€8.30, two to 2½ hours).

1. Teatro Greco (p224), Taormina 2. Selinunte (p259) 3. Tempio della Concordia (p254), Valley of the Temples 4. Duomo (p237), Syracuse

STEFANO_VALERI/SHUTTERSTOCK ©

EDDY GALEOTTI/SHUTTERSTOCK ©

A Graeco–Roman Legacy

As the crossroads of the Mediterranean since the dawn of time, Sicily has seen countless civilisations come and go. The island's classical treasure trove includes Greek temples and amphitheatres, Roman mosaics and a host of fine archaeological museums.

Taormina

With spectacular views of snowcapped Mt Etna and the Ionian Sea, Taormina's Teatro Greco (p224) makes the perfect venue for the town's summer film and arts festivals.

Selinunte

Selinunte's vast ruins (p259) poke out of wildflower-strewn fields beside the sparkling Mediterranean.

Valley of the Temples

Crowning the craggy heights of Agrigento's Valley of the Temples (p254) are five Doric temples – including stunning Tempio della Concordia, one of the best preserved in all of Magna Graecia. Throw in the superb archaeological museum and you've got Sicily's most cohesive and impressive collection of Greek treasures.

Syracuse

Once the most powerful city in the Mediterranean, Syracuse (p236) brims with reminders of its ancient past, from the Greek columns supporting Ortygia's cathedral to the annual festival of classical Greek drama, staged in a 2500-year-old amphitheatre.

Villa Romana del Casale

Bikini-clad gymnasts and wild African beasts prance side by side in remarkable floor decorations in this ancient Roman hunting lodge (p251). Buried under mud for centuries and now gleaming from restoration work, they're the most extensive mosaics in Sicily and a Unesco World Heritage Site.

Segesta

Segesta's perfect Doric temple (p262) perches on a windswept hilltop above a rugged river gorge.

CENTRAL SICILY & THE MEDITERRANEAN COAST

Central Sicily is a land of vast panoramas, undulating fields, severe mountain ridges and hilltop towns not yet sanitised for tourism. Moving towards the Mediterranean, the perspective changes, as ancient temples jostle for position with modern high-rise apartments outside Agrigento, Sicily's most lauded classical site and also one of its busier modern cities.

Agrigento

☑ 0922 / POP 59,600

Situated about 3km below the modern city of Agrigento, the Unesco-listed Valley of the Temples is one of the most mesmerising sites in the Mediterranean, with the best-preserved Doric temples outside Greece. On the travel radar since Goethe sang their praises in the 18th century, the temples now constitute Sicily's single biggest tourist site, with more than 600,000 visitors a year. As impressive as the temples are, what you see today are mere vestiges of the ancient city of Akragas, which was once the fourth-largest city in the known world.

Just uphill, Agrigento has an attractive medieval core, but beyond the elegant old town, the modern city is a chaos of elevated motorways converging on a ragged hilltop scarred by brutish tower blocks and riddled with choking traffic. Focus on the city's attractive old town and the proximity to the Valley of the Temples to maximise your enjoyment of a sojourn here.

◎ Sights & Activities

For English-language tours of the ruins, contact **Associazione Guide Turistiche Agrigento** (**☑** 345 8815992; www.agrigentoguide.org). After a day among the temples, roaming the lively, winding streets of medieval Agrigento makes a pleasant counterpoint. Start your exploration on Via Atenea, an attractive strip lined with smart shops, trattorias and bars. From here, narrow alleyways wind upwards past tightly packed *palazzi* (mansions) interspersed with historic churches.

★ **Valley of the Temples**   ARCHAEOLOGICAL SITE
(Valle dei Templi; **☑** 0922 183 99 96; www.parco valledeitempli.it; adult/reduced €12/7, incl Museo Archeologico €15.50/9, incl Museo Archeologico & Giardino della Kolymbetra €17/11; ⊘ 8.30am-8pm, to 11pm mid-Jul–mid-Sep) Sicily's most

enthralling archaeological site encompasses the ruined ancient city of Akragas, highlighted by the stunningly well-preserved **Tempio della Concordia** (Temple of Concord), one of several ridge-top temples that once served as beacons for homecoming sailors. The 13-sq-km park, 3km south of Agrigento, is split into eastern and western zones. Ticket offices with car parks are at the park's southwestern corner (the main Porta V entrance) and at the northeastern corner near the Temple of Hera (Eastern Entrance).

★ **Museo Archeologico**   MUSEUM
(**☑** 0922 40 15 65; Contrada San Nicola 12; adult/reduced €8/4, incl Valley of the Temples €13.50/7; ⊘ 9am-7.30pm Tue-Sat, to 1.30pm Sun & Mon) North of the temples, this wheelchair-accessible museum is one of Sicily's finest, with a huge collection of clearly labelled artefacts from the excavated site. Noteworthy are the dazzling displays of Greek painted ceramics and the awe-inspiring reconstructed *telamon*, a colossal statue recovered from the nearby Tempio di Giove.

🛏 Sleeping

★ **PortAtenea**   B&B €
(**☑** 349 0937492; www.portatenea.com; Via Atenea, cnr Via Cesare Battisti; s/d/tr €50/70/90; ❋ 🖱) This five-room B&B wins plaudits for its panoramic roof terrace overlooking the Valley of the Temples, and its superconvenient location at the entrance to the old town, five minutes' walk from the train and bus stations. Best of all is the generous advice about Agrigento offered by hosts Sandra and Filippo.

★ **Fattoria Mosè**   AGRITURISMO €
(**☑** 0922 60 61 15; www.fattoriamose.com; Via Pascal 4a; r per person €55, incl breakfast/half board €65/93, 2-/4-/6-person apt per week €550/850/1100; ❋) If Agrigento's urban jungle has got you down, head for this authentic organic *agriturismo* 6km east of the Valley of the Temples. Four suites, six self-catering apartments and a pool offer ample space to relax. Guests can opt for reasonably priced dinners (€28 including wine) built around the farm's organic produce, cook for themselves or even enjoy cooking courses on site.

★ **Villa Athena**   HISTORIC HOTEL €€€
(**☑** 0922 59 62 88; www.hotelvillaathena.it; Via Passeggiata Archeologica 33; d €423-577, ste €505-1165; 🅿 ❋ @ 🖱 ❋) With the Tempio della Concordia lit up in the near distance and palm trees lending an exotic *Arabian Nights* feel, this historic five-star hotel in an aristocratic

Agrigento

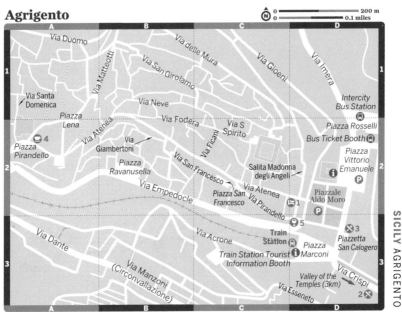

18th-century villa offers the ultimate luxury experience. The cavernous Villa Suite, floored in antique tiles with a free-standing spa bath and a vast terrace overlooking the temples, might well be Sicily's coolest hotel room.

✖ Eating & Drinking

On a hot day, head for **Caffè Concordia** (Piazza Pirandello 36; almond milk €2; ⊘ 6am-9.30pm Tue-Sat) near Teatro Pirandello for a chilled glass of almond milk made from Agrigento's famous almonds, mixed with sugar, water and a hint of lemon rind.

★**Aguglia Persa**   SEAFOOD €€
(☑ 0922 40 13 37; www.agugliapersa.it; Via Crispi 34; meals €30-40; ⊘ noon-3.30pm & 7-11pm Wed-Mon) Set in a mansion with a leafy courtyard just below the train station, this place is a welcome addition to Agrigento's fine-dining scene. Opened by the owners of Porto Empedocle's renowned Salmoriglio restaurant, it specialises in fresh-caught seafood in dishes such as citrus-scented risotto with shrimp and wild mint, or marinated salmon with sage cream and fresh fruit.

★**Kalòs**   SICILIAN €€
(☑ 0922 2 63 89; www.ristorantekalos.it; Piazzetta San Calogero; meals €35-45; ⊘ 12.30-3pm & 7-11pm Tue-Sun) For fine dining, head to this restau-

Agrigento

rant just outside the historic centre. Tables on little balconies offer a delightful setting to enjoy homemade *pasta all'agrigentina* (with fresh tomatoes, basil and almonds), grilled lamb chops or *spada gratinata* (baked swordfish in breadcrumbs). Superb desserts, including homemade *cannoli* (pastry shells with a sweet filling) and almond *semifreddi* (a light frozen dessert), round out the menu.

Caffè San Pietro   WINE BAR
(☑ 0922 2 97 42; www.spaziotemenos.it/sanpietro; Via Pirandello 1; ⊘ 7.30am-late Oct-Apr, from 11am May-Sep, closed Mon) This hip cafe serves excellent coffee, Sicilian wines and evening *aperitivi,* but what really sets it apart is the adjacent 18th-century San Pietro church, accessed through a doorway just beyond the

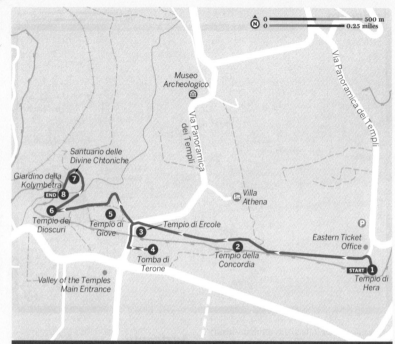

Archaeological Walking Tour
Valley of the Temples

START TEMPIO DI HERA
END GIARDINO DELLA KOLYMBETRA
LENGTH 3KM; THREE HOURS

Begin your exploration in the so-called Eastern Zone, home to Agrigento's best-preserved temples. From the Eastern Ticket Office, a short walk leads to the 5th-century-BC **1 Tempio di Hera**, perched on the ridge top. Though partly destroyed by an earthquake, the colonnade remains largely intact, as does a long sacrificial altar. Traces of red are the result of fire damage likely dating to the Carthaginian invasion of 406 BC.

Next, descend past a gnarled 500-year-old olive tree and a series of Byzantine tombs to the **2 Tempio della Concordia** (p254). This remarkable edifice, the model for Unesco's logo, has survived almost entirely intact since its construction in 430 BC, partly due to its conversion into a Christian basilica in the 6th century, and partly thanks to the shock-absorbing, earthquake-dampening qualities of the soft clay underlying its hard rock foundation.

Further downhill, the **3 Tempio di Ercole** is Agrigento's oldest, dating from the end of the 6th century BC. Down from the main temples, the miniature **4 Tomba di Terone** dates to 75 BC.

Cross the pedestrian bridge into the western zone, stopping first at the **5 Tempio di Giove**. This would have been the world's largest Doric temple had its construction not been interrupted by the Carthaginian sacking of Akragas. A later earthquake reduced it to the crumbled ruin you see today. Lying flat on his back amid the rubble is an 8m-tall *telamon* (a sculpted figure of a man with arms raised), originally intended to support the temple's weight. It's actually a copy; the original is in Agrigento's archaeological museum.

Take a brief look at the ruined 5th-century-BC **6 Tempio dei Dioscuri** and the 6th-century-BC complex of altars and small buildings known as the **7 Santuario delle Divine Chtoniche**, before ending your visit in the **8 Giardino della Kolymbetra**, a lush garden in a natural cleft near the sanctuary, with more than 300 (labelled) species of plants and some welcome picnic tables.

bar. Beautifully restored by the bar's owners over an eight-year period, the church sometimes serves as a lively venue for concerts, films and other cultural events.

ⓘ Information

Ospedale San Giovanni di Dio (☏ 0922 44 21 11; Contrada Consolida; ⊗ 24hr) North of the centre.

Tourist Office (☏ 0922 59 32 27; www.living agrigento.it; Piazzale Aldo Moro 1; ⊗ 8am-7pm Mon-Fri, to 1pm Sat) In the provincial government building.

ⓘ Getting There & Away

BUS

From most destinations, the bus is the easiest way to get to Agrigento. The intercity bus station and ticket booth are on Piazza Rosselli, just off Piazza Vittorio Emanuele.

Buses to Palermo (€9, two hours) are operated by **Cuffaro** (☏ 091 616 15 10; www.facebook. com/cuffaro.info) (eight Monday through Friday, six on Saturday, three on Sunday) and **Camilleri** (☏ 0922 47 18 86; www.camilleriargentoelat tuca.it) (five Monday through Friday, four on Saturday, one on Sunday), while **SAL** (Società Autolinee Licata; ☏ 0922 40 13 60; www.auto lineesal.it) serves Palermo's Falcone-Borsellino Airport (€12.60, 2¾ hours, three to four Monday through Saturday).

Lumia (☏ 0922 2 04 14; www.autolineelumia. it) runs to Trapani and its Birgi airport (€11.90, three to four hours, three daily Monday to Friday, two on Saturday, one on Sunday).

SAIS Trasporti (☏ 0922 2 60 59; www.sais trasporti.it) runs 10 to 14 buses daily to Catania and its Fontanarossa airport (€13.40, three hours).

CAR & MOTORCYCLE

Agrigento is easily accessible by road from all of Sicily's main towns. The SS189 and SS121 connect with Palermo, while the SS115 runs along the coast to Sciacca and Licata. For Catania, take the SS640 via Caltanissetta.

Driving and parking in Agrigento can be a nightmare. Via Atenea, the historic centre's main street, is closed to traffic from 9am to 8pm, with a short break during lunchtime when cars can pass through the centre (for loading luggage). There's metered parking at Piazza Vittorio Emanuele and on the streets around Piazzale Aldo Moro, although you'll have to arrive early to find a space.

TRAIN

Trains run regularly to/from Palermo (€9, two hours, hourly). For Catania, the bus is a better option as there are no direct trains. The train station has left-luggage lockers (per 12 hours €2.50).

ⓘ Getting Around

BUS

City bus 1, operated by **TUA** (Trasporti Urbani Agrigento; ☏ 0922 41 20 24; www.trasportiurba niagrigento.it), runs half-hourly from Agrigento's bus and train stations to the archaeological museum (15 minutes) and the Porta V entrance to the temples (20 minutes). 'Bus 2/', as distinct from 'bus 2' (which has a different route – watch out for the hard-to-spot slash!) runs every hour or so to the temples' eastern entrance near the Tempio di Hera (10 to 15 minutes). Tickets cost €1.20 if purchased in advance from a tobacconist, or €1.70 on board the bus.

CAR & MOTORCYCLE

From Agrigento's train station (Piazza Marconi), take Via Francesco Crispi downhill. After 1.5km, bear gently left onto Via Panoramica Valle dei Templi to reach the valley's eastern entrance and car park. To reach the main (Porta V) entrance and car park, bear right on Via Passeggiata Archeologica, then left on the SP4 and right on Viale Caduti di Marzabotto.

WESTERN SICILY

Situated directly across the water from North Africa and still retaining vestiges of the Arab, Phoenician and Greek cultures that once prevailed here, Sicily's windswept western coast is a feast for the senses – from Trapani's savoury fish couscous to the dazzling views from hilltop Erice and the wild coastal beauty of the Riserva Naturale dello Zingaro.

Marsala

POP 82,800

Many know about its sweet dessert wines, but few people realise what a charmer the town of Marsala is. Though its streets are paved in gleaming marble, lined with stately baroque buildings and peppered with graceful piazzas, Marsala has pleasures that are simple – a friendly *passeggiata* (evening stroll) most nights, plenty of *aperitivo* options and family-friendly restaurants aplenty.

⊙ Sights & Activities

Piazza della Repubblica   PIAZZA
Marsala's most elegant piazza is dominated by the imposing Chiesa Madre. Just across the way, on the eastern side of the square, is the arcaded **Palazzo VII Aprile**, formerly known as the Palazzo Senatorio (Senatorial Palace) and now the town hall.

SCALA DEI TURCHI & TORRE SALSA

With your own wheels, you'll find some dreamy beaches and beauty spots west of Agrigento, all within an easy 30- to 45-minute drive of the city via the SS115.

Scala dei Turchi

One of the most beautiful sights in the Agrigento area, this blindingly white rock **outcrop**, shaped like a giant staircase, juts into the sea near Realmonte, 15km west of Agrigento. It's a popular spot with local sunseekers who come to sunbathe on the milky-smooth rock and dive into the indigo sea. To escape the crowds, walk another few hundred metres north along the white rocky shelf, and descend to the long sandy beach below.

Riserva Naturale Torre Salsa

This stunning 761-hectare natural **park** (www.wwftorresalsa.com), administered by the World Wildlife Fund, is signposted off the SS115. Exit at Siciliana Marina (a small coastal settlement with its own great sandy beach) or continue 10km north to the second Montallegro exit and follow the signs for WWF Riserva Naturale Torre Salsa. There's plenty of scope for walkers here, with well-marked trails and sweeping panoramic views of the surrounding mountains and coast. The long, deserted Torre Salsa beach (reached from the northern entrance) is especially beautiful, although the access road is rough.

Cantine Florio   WINE

(☏0923 78 13 05; www.duca.it/en/florio/ospitalita; Via Vincenzo Florio 1; standard tour adult/reduced €13/5; ☺9am-6pm Mon-Fri, to 1pm Sat, English-language tour 10am & 4pm Mon-Fri, 10am Sat) These venerable wine cellars, in a huge walled complex east of the centre and on the seafront since 1833, open their vintage doors to visitors to explain the Marsala-making process and the fascinating history of local viticulture. Afterwards, visitors can sample the goods in the sharp tasting room: tasting of four wines, accompanied by hors d'oeuvres, are included in the standard 1½-long tour.

★ **Prokite Alby Rondina**   KITESURFING

(☏347 5373881; www.prokitealbyrondina.com; Via Passalacqua; 2/6hr lesson €150/370, 2hr lesson plus 1/2/5 days of equipment rental €200/330/440; ☺Mar-Oct; 🚣) Handily located just 10 minutes from Trapani's Birgi airport and 14km north of Marsala, this highly professional kitesurfing resort combining school, **hotel** (☏347 5373881; www.prokitealbyrondina.com; Via Passalacqua; s/d/tr from €60/85/115; ☺Mar-Nov; P🅿❄@🛜) and villa accommodation is a world-class spot to kite on a lagoon.

🍽 Sleeping & Eating

★ **Il Profumo del Sale**   B&B €

(☏0923 189 04 72; www.ilprofumodelsale.it; Via Vaccari 8; s/d €40/65; 🛜) Perfectly positioned in Marsala's historic city centre, this lovely B&B offers three attractive rooms – including a palatial front unit with cathedral views from its small balcony – enhanced by welcoming touches like almond cookies, fine soaps and ample breakfasts featuring homemade bread and jams. Sophisticated owner Celsa is full of helpful tips about Marsala and the surrounding area.

★ **Quimera**   SANDWICHES €

(☏349 0765524; www.facebook.com/quimerapub; Via Sarzana 34-36; sandwiches & salads from €5; ☺noon-3pm & 6.30pm-2am Mon-Sat, 6.30pm-2am Sun) Smack in the heart of Marsala's pedestrianised centre, this buzzy eating-drinking hybrid is the local hotspot for artisanal craft beers, gourmet sandwiches and meal-sized salads – all served with a big smile and bags of charm by the friendly young owners. Linger over a shared cutting board of cheeses or salami, or agonise over the choice of creatively filled *panini* and *piadine* (wraps).

🍷 Drinking & Nightlife

★ **Ciacco Putia Gourmet**   WINE BAR

(☏347 6315684; www.ciaccoputia.it; Via Cammareri Scurti 3; ☺noon-3pm & 7-11pm Mon-Sat; 🛜) Run by Tuscan-Sicilian couple Anna and Francesco, this irresistible *enoteca* is a gorgeous spot to quaff Marsala wines with locally sourced *salumi* (cold cuts), *panini* with *burrata* (cheese made from mozzarella and cream), anchovies and other snacks. The icing on the cake is the beautiful summertime terrace on a cobbled fountain-pierced square overlooking the showy baroque facade of 18th-century Chiesa del Purgatorio.

❶ Information

Tourist Office (☎ 0923 71 40 97, 0923 99 33 38; Via XI Maggio 100; ⊙ 8.30am-1.30pm & 3-8pm Mon-Fri, to 1.30pm Sat) Provides a limited range of maps and brochures, plus a list of wine cellars open by guided tour (but staff cannot make bookings for you).

❶ Getting There & Away

Operators from Marsala's **bus station** (Piazza del Popolo) include Lumia (www.autolineelumia. it) to Agrigento (€10.10, 2¾ hours) and Salemi (www.autoservizi salemi.it) to Palermo (€11, 2¼ to 2½ hours). Train is the best way to get to Trapani (€3.80, 35 minutes). To reach Marsala's historic centre from the train station, walk 800m up Via Roma, which meets Via XI Maggio at Piazza Matteotti.

Selinunte

The ruins of **Selinunte** (Selinunte Archaeological Park; ☎ 0924 4 62 77, 334 6040459; https:// en.visitselinunte.com/archaeological-park; Via Selinunte, Castelvetrano; adult/reduced €6/3; ⊙ 9am-6pm Mar-Oct, to 5pm Nov-Feb) are the most impressively sited in Sicily. The huge city was built in 628 BC on a promontory overlooking the sea, and over the course of two-and-a-half centuries became one of the richest and most powerful in the world. It was destroyed by the Carthaginians in 409 BC and finally fell to the Romans about 350 BC, at which time it went into rapid decline and disappeared from historical accounts.

The city's past is so remote that the names of the various temples have been forgotten and they are now identified by the letters A to G, M and O. The most impressive, **Temple E**, has been partially rebuilt, its columns pieced together from their fragments with part of its tympanum. Many of the carvings, particularly from **Temple C**, are now in the archaeological museum in Palermo. Their quality is on par with the Parthenon marbles and clearly demonstrates the high cultural levels reached by many Greek colonies in Sicily.

The ticket office and entrance to the ruins is located near the eastern temples. Try to visit in spring when the surroundings are ablaze with wildflowers. Escape the mediocre restaurants near the ruins by heading for **Lido Zabbara** (☎ 0924 4 61 94; www.face book.com/lidozabbara; Via Pigafetta, Marinella di Selinunte; buffet per person €12; ⊙ noon-3pm Mar-early Nov, plus 7.30-10.30pm Jun-Sep), a beach-front eatery in nearby Marinella di Selinunte that serves good grilled fish and a varied buffet. Alternatively, drive 15km east to **Da Vittorio** (☎ 0925 7 83 81; www.ristorantevittorio. it; Via Friuli Venezia Giulia, Porto Palo; meals €30-45; ⊙ 12.30-2.30pm & 7-10pm) in Porto Palo, another wonderful spot to enjoy seafood, sunset and the sound of lapping waves.

❶ Getting There & Away

Selinunte is midway between Agrigento and Trapani, about 10km south of the junction of the A29 and SS115 near Castelvetrano. Salemi (https://autoservizisalemi.it/tratte/selinunte) runs regular buses between Marinella di Selinunte and Castelvetrano train station (€1.50, 25 to 35 minutes), where you can make onward rail connections to Marsala (€4.30, 45 minutes) and Trapani (€6.20, 1¼ hours). For eastbound travellers, Lumia (www.autolineelumia.it) runs buses from Castelvetrano to Agrigento (€8.60, two hours, one to three daily).

CELEBRATING COUSCOUS

Couscous (or cuscus), the beloved North African culinary treat cooked with gusto all over Western Sicily, is the delicious focus of **CousCousFest** (www.couscousfest. it; ⊙ last week Sep), a six-day multicultural festival filling small-town San Vito Lo Capo with international chefs and foodies for one week in September. Food stands inviting festival goers to taste dozens of different couscous recipes from western Sicily, North Africa and the Mediterranean pop up on the beach and in town. Live cooking shows and music concerts fill the stage most evenings and the festival climaxes with – drum roll – the Couscous World Championships starring couscous chefs from 10 countries. Tickets (€15 to €25) are sold to be part of the tasting jury for the semifinals or finals. Otherwise, a 'tasting ticket' (€10) gives you access to dozens of stands on the beach and around town.

Trapani

POP 67,900

Hugging the harbour where Peter of Aragon landed in 1282 to begin the Spanish occupation of Sicily, the sickle-shaped spit of land occupied by Trapani's old town once sat at the heart of a powerful trading network that stretched from Carthage to Venice. Traditionally the town thrived on coral and tuna fishing, with some salt and wine production. These days, Trapani's small port buzzes with ferry traffic zipping to and from the remote Egadi Islands and the mysterious volcanic rock island of Pantelleria, not far from Tunisia.

◉ Sights

Trapani's historic centre, with its small but compelling maze of gold-stone *palazzi* and 18th-century baroque gems such as the **Cattedrale di San Lorenzo** (☑ 0923 2 33 62; http://cattedraletrapani.it; Corso Vittorio Emanuele; ⊘ 8am-4pm), is a mellow place to stroll, for both locals and travellers awaiting their next boat. From late afternoon onwards, car-free main street Via Garibaldi buzzes with what feels like the entire town out in force enjoying their lazy, absolute sacrosanct *passeggiata*. Join them.

Chiesa Anime Sante del Purgatorio   CHURCH
(☑ 329 7078896; Via San Francesco d'Assisi; by donation; ⊘ 7.45am-noon & 4-7pm Mon-Sat, 10am-noon & 4-7pm Sun) Just off the *corso* in the heart of the city, this church houses the impressive 18th-century *misteri*, 20 life-sized wooden effigies depicting the story of Christ's Passion, which take centre stage during the city's dramatic Easter Week processions every year. Explanatory panels in English, Italian, French and German help visitors to understand the story behind each figure.

🛏 Sleeping & Eating

★ **Room Mate Andrea**   DESIGN HOTEL €€
(☑ 912 179287; https://room-matehotels.com/en/andrea; Viale Regina Margherita 31; d €79-135; P ✳ @ 🛜 ⩒) Graceful Palazzo Platamone, with neoclassical caramel-coloured facade dating to the 1900s, is the grandiose setting for the Sicilian debut of Spanish urban hotel group, Room Mate. Andrea is predictably stylish, with the city's only rooftop pool. Beautifully decorated, vintage-chic rooms mix original neoclassical fittings and fix-tures with modern comforts. Breakfast costs €19.90 and is served until noon; the bar serves tip-top seasonal cocktails.

★ **La Bettolaccia**   SICILIAN €€
(☑ 0923 2 59 32; www.labettolaccia.it; Via Enrico Fardella 25; meals €35-45; ⊘ 12.45-3pm & 7.45-11pm Mon-Fri, 7.45-11pm Sat) Unwaveringly authentic, this on-trend Slow Food favourite, squirrelled away down a sleepy side street, is the hotspot to feast on spicy couscous with fried fish or mixed seafood, *caponata* (eggplant and sun-dried tomatoes with capers in a sweet-and-sour sauce), the catch of the day, and other traditional Trapanese dishes in a sharp, minimalist white space. Reservations essential.

ℹ Information

Tourist Office (☑ 0923 54 45 33; Piazzetta Saturno 3bis; ⊘ 9am-1pm Mon-Fri summer, 9am-2pm & 3-5pm Mon & Thu, 9am-2pm Tue, Wed & Fri winter) Just north of the port.

ℹ Getting There & Around

AIR

Trapani's **Vincenzo Florio (Birgi) Airport** (☑ 0923 61 01 11; www.airgest.it) is served by budget flights from mainland Italy and the rest of Europe. **AST** (Azienda Siciliana Trasporti; ☑ 0923 2 10 21; www.astsicilia.it; Via Virgilio 20) runs hourly buses (€4.90, 20 minutes) to/from Trapani's port. A taxi between Birgi airport and Trapani costs a fixed €30. Marsala-based Salemi (https://autoservizisalemi.it) operates buses between the Birgi airport and Palermo (€11, 1¾ to two hours, five to six daily); buy tickets online or on the bus.

BOAT

Trapani's busy port is the main departure point for the Egadi Islands and the remote Mediterranean island of Pantelleria. Ferry and hydrofoil schedules are available from **Liberty Lines** (☑ 0923 87 38 13; https://eng.libertylines.it; Via Ammiraglio Staiti) and **Siremar** (☑ 090 57 37; https://carontetourist.it/en/siremar; Stazione Marittima, Porto Trapani). See Lonely Planet's Sicily guide for more information on the islands themselves.

BUS

AST (Azienda Siciliana Trasporti; ☑ 0923 2 10 21; www.astsicilia.it; Via Virgilio 20) buses to/from Vincenzo Florio (Birgi) airport (€2.90, 55 minutes) use the bus stop in front of the hydrofoil docks. Buy tickets at **Egatour** (☑ 0923 2 17 54; www.egatourviaggi.it; Via Ammiraglio Staiti 13), located directly opposite. The same bus stop is used by Big Bus (www.

SCOPELLO & RISERVA NATURALE DELLO ZINGARO

Saved from development and road projects by local protests, the tranquil **Riserva Naturale dello Zingaro** (☑ 0924 3 51 08; www.riservazingaro.it; adult/child €5/3; ⊙ 7am-7.30pm Apr-Sep, 8am-4pm Oct-Mar) is the star attraction on the Golfo di Castellammare, halfway between Palermo and Trapani. Founded in 1981, this was Sicily's first nature reserve. Zingaro's wild coastline is a haven for the rare Bonelli's eagle, along with 40 other species of bird. Mediterranean flora dusts the hillsides with wild carob and bright yellow euphorbia, and hidden coves, such as Capreria and Marinella Bays, provide tranquil swimming spots. The main entrance to the park is 2km north of the village of Scopello. Several walking trails are detailed on maps available for free at the entrance or downloadable from the park website. The main 7km trail along the coast passes by the visitor centre and five museums that document everything from local flora and fauna to traditional fishing methods.

Once home to tuna fishers, the tiny town of **Scopello** has morphed into a popular weekend getaway. The town's vintage *tonnara* (tuna factory), on the waterfront 1km below town, now houses the unusual **Tonnara di Scopello** (☑ 388 8299472; www.la tonnaradiscopello.it; Largo Tonnara Scopello; adult/child €5/free; ⊙ 10am-7pm summer, shorter hours rest of year) museum, which documents traditional tuna fishing. In operation from the 13th century until its closure in 1984, the complex was greatly developed in the 15th and 16th centuries, and in 1874 the wealthy owners had the elegant, salmon-pink **Palazzina Florio** built right on the water. The setting alone – overlooking the fluorescent blue gulf, at the foot of dramatic rock formations capped by a medieval tower – makes it a worthwhile visit.

Pensione Tranchina (☑ 0924 54 10 99; www.pensionetranchina.com; Via Armando Diaz 7; B&B per person €35-50, half-board per person €60-75; ❄ 🤶) is the nicest of several accommodation options clustered around the cobblestoned courtyard at Scopello's village centre. Friendly owner Marisin offers comfortable rooms, a roaring fire on chilly evenings and superb home-cooked meals featuring local fish and home-grown fruit and olive oil.

bigbus.it) buses heading to/from Palermo train station (two hours), Marsala (50 minutes) and an overnight bus to/from Naples (13¾ hours, one daily) and Rome (14¼, one daily). Segesta Autolinee (www.segesta.it) buses connect Trapani with Palermo airport (€8, 65 minutes, at least hourly).

TRAIN

From Trapani's train station, 1km east of the centre on Piazza Umberto, 10 daily trains (five on Sunday) run to Marsala (€3.80, 25 to 40 minutes). For Palermo, the bus is a much faster option.

Erice

POP 27,900 / ELEV 751M

Medieval Erice watches over the port of Trapani from its giddy mountain perch atop the legendary peak of Eryx, spectacularly set 750m above sea level. It's a mesmerising, walled 12th-century village whose peculiar history, mountain charm and sensational sea-and-valley views are only enhanced by frequent unpredictable changes in weather

that take you from brilliant sunshine to thick fog in the space of minutes.

Allow ample time for losing yourself in the atmospheric maze of stone-paved streets – all the more cinematic when the piercing sun plays peekaboo with swirling mist – and savouring a sweet old-world moment at Sicily's most famous pastry shop.

⊙ Sights

The best views can be had from Giardino del Balio, which overlooks the turrets and wooded hillsides south to Trapani's saltpans, the Egadi Islands and the sea. Looking north, there are equally staggering views of San Vito Lo Capo's rugged headlands.

Castello di Venere   CASTLE
(Castle of Venus; ☑ 329 7823035; www.fondazi oneericearte.org/castellodivenere.php; Via Castello di Venere; adult/reduced €4/2; ⊙ 10am-8pm Aug, to 7pm Jul & Sep, to 6pm Apr-Jun & Oct, 10am-1pm Sat & Sun Nov-Mar) This 12th- to 13th-century Norman castle was built over the Temple of Venus, long a site of worship for the ancient

Elymians, Phoenicians, Greeks and Romans. Nowadays the castle's rooms are off-limits, but visitors can explore the grassy interior courtyard, filled with ruined foundations and flanked by an impressive stone wall allegedly built by Daedalus. Stealing the show are the spectacular panoramic vistas extending to San Vito Lo Capo on one side and the Saline di Trapani on the other.

Sleeping & Eating

Hotels, many with their own restaurants, are scattered along Via Vittorio Emanuele, Erice's main street. After the day-trippers have gone, the town assumes a beguiling medieval air.

Erice has a tradition of *dolci ericini* (Erice sweets) made by local nuns. There are numerous pastry shops in town, the most famous being Maria Grammatico (🎲 0923 86 93 90; www.mariagrammatico.it; Via Vittorio Emanuele 14; pastries from €2; ⊙9am-midnight May-Sep, to 9pm Oct-Apr), revered for its *frutta martorana* (marzipan fruit) and almond pastries. If you like what you taste, you can even stick around and take cooking classes from Signora Grammatico herself.

Hotel Elimo HOTEL €€
(🎲 0923 86 93 77; www.hotelelimo.it; Via Vittorio Emanuele 75; s €72-100, d €90-160, q €120; ❈ 🎧) Communal spaces at this atmospheric historic house are filled with tiled beams, marble fireplaces, intriguing art, knick-knacks and antiques. The bedrooms are more mainstream, although many (along with the hotel terrace and restaurant) have breathtaking vistas south and west towards the Saline di Trapani, the Egadi Islands and the shimmering sea.

❶ Getting There & Away

AST runs four to six buses daily between Erice and Trapani's bus terminal (€2.90, 40 minutes to one hour). Alternatively, catch the **funicular** (Cabinovia di Erice; 🎲 0923 56 93 06, 0923 86 97 20; www.funiviaerice.it; one way/return €5.50/9; ⊙1-8pm Mon, 8.30am-8pm Tue-Fri, 9am-9pm Sat, 9.30am-8.30pm Sun) opposite the car park at the foot of Erice village, across from Porta Trapani; the 10-minute descent drops you in Trapani near Ospedale Sant'Antonio Abate, where you can catch local bus 21 or 23 into the centre of Trapani.

Segesta

Set on the edge of a deep canyon amid desolate mountains, the 5th-century BC ruins of Segesta (🎲 0924 95 23 56; Contrada Barbaro, SR22; adult/child €6/free; ⊙9am-7.30pm Apr-Sep, to 6.30pm Mar & Oct, to 5pm Nov-Feb) are among the world's most magical ancient sites.

Long before the arrival of the Greeks, Segesta was the principal city of the Elymians, an ancient civilisation claiming descent from the Trojans that settled in Sicily in the Bronze Age. The Elymians were in constant conflict with Greek Selinunte, whose destruction (in 409 BC) they pursued with bloodthirsty determination. More than 100 years later the Greek tyrant Agathocles slaughtered over 10,000 Elymians and re-populated Segesta with Greeks.

Little remains of ancient Segesta today, save its hilltop theatre and the never-completed Doric temple, yet the ruins' remarkable state of preservation and the majesty of their rural setting combine to make this one of Sicily's enduring highlights. Occasional music concerts and cultural events held beneath the stars in the theatre on hot summer nights are nothing short of magical.

❶ Getting There & Away

Tarantola (www.tarantolabus.com) operates a limited service to/from Trapani bus station and Segesta (single/return €4/6.60, 40 to 50 minutes). From April to October only, it also operates services to/from Palermo (single/return €7/11.20, 80 minutes, three daily Monday to Saturday). Check schedules carefully as times posted are not necessarily reliable; there are no buses on Sunday.

Visitors with their own vehicles must use the car park 1.5km from the hilltop ruins and continue to the temple on foot or by shuttle bus (€1.50, every 15 minutes). A second bus (€1.50) shuttles visitors between the temple and the theatre, another 1.25km uphill again.

WESTEND61 / GETTY IMAGES ©

Syracuse (p236)

Understand Southern Italy

History

Italy's south is ancient, its history tracing back some 8000 years. Writer Carlo Levi called it 'that other world...which no-one can enter without a magic key'. Magical it may be, but there has been plenty to regret – invasions, feudalism and a centuries-long scourge of malaria that stunted the south's development. Venture here and expect to have your preconceptions of modern Italy challenged.

The Early Years

Southern Italy has been active for a very long time. The first inhabitant we know of is the Altamura Man, currently wedged in the karst cave of Lamalunga, Puglia, and slowly becoming part of the crystal concretions that surround him. He's about 130,000 years old.

Fast forward to around 7000 BCE, when the Messapians, an Illyrian-speaking people from the Balkans, were settling down in the Salento and around Foggia. Alongside them, other long-gone tribes such as the Daunii in the Gargano, the Peucetians around Taranto and the Lucanians in Basilicata were starting to develop the first settled towns – by 1700 BCE there is evidence that they were beginning to trade with the Mycenaeans from mainland Greece and the Minoans in Crete.

The first evidence of an organised settlement on Sicily belongs to the Stentillenians, who came from the Middle East and settled on the island's eastern shores sometime between 4000 and 3000 BCE. But it was the settlers from the middle of the second millennium BCE who radically defined the island's character and whose early presence helps us understand Sicily's complexities. Thucydides (c 460–404 BCE) records three major tribes: the Sicani, who originated either in Spain or North Africa and settled in the north and west (giving these areas their Eastern flavour); the Elymians from Greece, who settled in the south; and the Sicels, who came from the Calabrian peninsula and spread out along the Ionian Coast.

> It is commonly said that there is less Italian blood running through modern Sicilian veins than there is Phoenician, Greek, Arabic, Norman, Spanish or French.

TIMELINE	c 200,000–9000 BCE	3000–1000 BCE	750–600 BCE
	As long ago as 700,000 BCE, Palaeolithic humans like the Altamura Man lived precarious lives in caves. Painted caves like the Grotta dei Cervi are testament to this period.	The Bronze Age reaches Italy courtesy of the Mycenaeans of Eastern Europe. The use of copper and bronze marks a leap in sophistication, accompanied by a more complex social organisation.	The Greeks begin establishing cities all over southern Italy and Sicily, including Naxos and Syracuse in Sicily, and Cumae, Sybaris, Crotone, Metaponto, Eraklea and Taras in southern Italy.

Magna Graecia

Following the earlier lead of the Elymians, the Chalcidians landed on Sicily's Ionian coast in 735 BCE and founded a small settlement at Naxos. They were followed a year later by the Corinthians, who built their colony on the southeastern island of Ortygia, calling it Syracoussai (Syracuse). The Chalcidians went further south from their own fort and founded a second town called Katane (Catania) in 729 BCE, and the two carried on stitching towns and settlements together until three quarters of the island was in Hellenic hands.

On the mainland, the Greeks' major city was Taras, which dominated the growing region now known as Magna Graecia (Greater Greece). They exploited its harbour well, trading with Greece, the Near East and the rich colonies in Sicily and so built up a substantial network of commerce. Their lucrative business in luxury goods soon made them wealthy and powerful; by the 4th century BCE the population had swelled to 300,000 and city life was cultured and civilised.

Although few monuments survive, among them the ambitious temples of Paestum in Campania and Selinunte in Sicily, the Greek era was a golden age for the south. Art and sculpture, poetry, drama, philosophy, mathematics and science were all part of the cultural life of Magna Graecia's cities. Exiled from Crotone (Calabria), Pythagoras spent years in Metapontum and Taras; Empedocles, Zeno and Stesichorus were all home-grown talents.

But despite their shared Greekness, these city-states' deeply ingrained rivalries and parochial politics undermined their civic achievements, ultimately leading to damaging conflicts like the Peloponnesian War (431–399 BCE), fought by the Athenians against the Peloponnesian League (led by Sparta). Syracuse's decision to challenge the hegemony of mainland Greece led Athens to attack the Sicilian city in 415 BCE, mounting the 'Great Expedition' – the largest fleet ever assembled. Despite the fleet's size and Athens' confidence, Syracuse fought back and the mainland Greek army suffered a humiliating defeat.

Though Syracuse was celebrating its victory, the rest of Sicily was in a constant state of civil war. In 409 BCE this provided the perfect opportunity for the powerful city state of Carthage (in modern-day Tunisia) to seek revenge for its humiliation in 480 BCE, in which Carthaginian mercenaries, commanded by Hamilcar, were defeated by the crafty Greek tyrant Gelon. Led by Hamilcar's bitter but brilliant grandson Hannibal Mago, the Carthaginians wrought havoc in the Sicilian countryside, completely destroying Selinunte, Himera, Agrigento and Gela. The Syracusans were eventually forced to surrender everything to Carthage except the city of Syracuse itself.

Best Graeco–Roman Ruins

Pompeii & Herculaneum (Campania)

Paestum (Campania)

Selinunte (Sicily)

Segesta (Sicily)

Valley of the Temples (Sicily)

HISTORY MAGNA GRAECIA

Get to grips with the history, peoples and wars of Ancient Greece by logging on to www.ancientgreece.com, which gives potted histories of all the key characters and places. It also has an online bookstore.

264–146 BCE	280 BCE–109 CE	79 CE	300–337
The Punic Wars rage between the Romans and the Carthaginians. In 216 BCE Hannibal defeats the Romans at Cannae, but the Romans ultimately defeat the Carthaginians in 146 BCE.	The Romans build the Via Appia and then the Via Appia Traiana. The Via Appia Traiana covered 540km and enabled travellers to journey from Rome to Brindisi in 14 days.	Mt Vesuvius showers molten rock and ash upon Pompeii and Herculaneum. Pliny the Younger later describes the eruption in letters; the towns are only rediscovered in the 18th century.	After a series of false starts, the Roman Empire is divided into an eastern and western half just east of Rome. In 330 Constantine moves the imperial capital to Byzantium and refounds it as Constantinople.

During the 4th century BCE, the mainland's Greek colonies came under increasing pressure from other powers with expansionist ambitions. The Etruscans began to move south towards the major port of Cumae in Campania, and then the Samnites and Sabines started to capture the highlands of the Apennines in Basilicata. Unable to unite and beat off the growing threat, the Greeks had little choice but to make a Faustian pact with the Romans, long-standing admirers of the Greeks and seemingly the perfect allies. It was a partnership that was to cost them dearly: by 270 BCE the whole of southern Italy was under Roman control.

Eastern Influences

Roman control of southern Italy was to set the tone for centuries to come. While they turned the Bay of Naples into a holiday hotspot for Rome's elite and built the Via Appia (280–264 BCE) and later the Via Appia Traiana (109 CE) – the first superhighway to the south from Rome – the Romans also stripped the southern landscape of its trees, creating just the right conditions for the malarial scourge that the region would face centuries hence. Then they parcelled up the land into huge *latifondi* (estates) that they distributed among a handful of wealthy Romans, who established a damaging agricultural monoculture of wheat to feed the Roman army. Local peasants, meanwhile, were denied even the most basic rights of citizenship.

Despite the Romans' attempts at Latinising the region, this period actually had the effect of reinforcing Eastern influences on the south. As it was, the Romans admired and emulated Greek culture, the locals in cities like Neapolis (modern-day Naples) continued to speak Greek, and the Via Appia made Puglia the gateway to the East. In 245 CE when Diocletian came to power, he determined that the empire was simply too vast for good governance and split it in two. When Constantine came to power in 306 CE, the groundwork was already established for an Eastern (Byzantine) Empire and a Western Empire – in 324 CE he officially declared Constantinople the capital of Nova Roma.

With southern Italy's proximity to the Balkans and the Near East, Puglia and Basilicata were exposed to a new wave of Eastern influence, bringing with it a brand-new set of Christian beliefs. This new wave of influence would officially reach Sicily in 535 CE, when the Byzantine general Belisarius landed an army on the island's shores. Despite falling to the Visigoths in 470 CE after more than 700 years of Roman occupation, the island had a population that was still largely Greek, both in language and custom. The Byzantines were eager to use Sicily as a launching pad to retake of the lands owned by the combined forces of Arabs, Berbers and Spanish Muslims, collectively known as the Saracens, but their dreams were not to be realised.

Messages could be shot around the Roman Empire in days or weeks. At wayside inns, dispatch riders would have a bite and change mounts. The Romans even devised a type of odometer, a cogwheel that engaged with the wheel of a chariot or other vehicle.

Kingdom in the Sun by English historian John Julius Norwich offers a wonderful romp through the Norman invasions of the south, which led to their spectacular takeover of Sicily.

476	827–965	1059	1130
The last western emperor, Romulus Augustulus, is deposed. Goths, Ostrogoths and Byzantines tussle over the spoils of the empire.	A Saracen army lands at Mazara del Vallo in Sicily in 827. The island is united under Arab rule and Palermo becomes the second-largest city in the world after Constantinople.	Pope Nicholas II and Norman mercenary Robert Guiscard sign a concordat at Melfi, making Robert duke of Apulia and Calabria. Robert agrees to rid southern Italy of Saracens and Byzantines.	Norman invader Roger II is crowned king of Sicily, a century after the Normans landed in southern Italy; a united southern Italian kingdom is created.

In 827 CE the Saracen army landed at Mazara del Vallo, in Sicily. Palermo fell in 831 CE, followed by Syracuse in 878 CE. Under the Saracens, churches were converted to mosques and Arabic was implemented as the common language. At the same time, much-needed land reforms were made and trade, agriculture and mining were fostered. New crops were introduced, including citrus trees, date palms and sugar cane, and a system of water supply and irrigation was developed. Palermo was chosen as the capital of the new emirate and over the next 200 years it became one of the most splendid cities in the Arab world.

ARCHIMEDES & THE SIEGE OF SYRACUSE

Breaking into Italy via the Alps, the mighty Carthaginian military commander Hannibal Barca (247–183/181 BCE) would lead a number of victories against the Romans, including at the Battle of Cannae (216 BCE) in modern-day Puglia. Hannibal's gains led many in Sicily to question whether their allegiance to Rome was sensible. Among these doubters was teen tyrant Hieronymos (231–214 BCE), who became king of Syracuse in 215 BCE aged 15. While some Syracusans supported Hieronymos' courting of the Carthaginians, others did not, and the king's assassination in 214 BCE sparked a civil war between the city's pro-Roman and pro-Carthaginian factions. Rome, determined to maintain control of the Mediterranean, was hardly impressed by the pro-Carthaginians' victory in Syracuse, dispatching esteemed Roman general Marcus Claudius Marcellus (268–208 BCE) to gain control of the city. Little did it know what a long and arduous task it would be.

The source of Rome's frustration was Greek Syracusan Archimedes (c 287–212/211 BCE), considered the most brilliant mathematician and inventor in ancient Greece. Before Hieronymos' rise to power, his predecessor and grandfather Hiero II (died c 216/215 BCE) had assigned Archimedes the task of developing weapons to defend Syracuse. Archimedes did not fail, creating a series of ingenious war machines. Among these were catapults capable of hurling objects weighing in excess of 300kg and the extraordinary Claw of Archimedes, a giant wooden crane attached to a grappling hook. Dangling over the city walls of Ortygia (Syracuse's historic centre), the crane would reach down and grab Roman galleys by the prow, lifting them out of the water and causing them to capsize or sink. While many modern historians doubt it ever existed, legend persists that Archimedes even created a death ray. The invention reputedly used copper or bronze shields to reflect the sun's rays onto approaching Roman vessels, causing the wooden ships to catch fire.

Archimedes' clever contraptions managed to keep the Romans out of the city for two years, until lax defences during a festival in honour of Artemis allowed a small group of Roman soldiers to scale Ortygia's walls and enter the outer city in 212 BCE and, eventually, take control of the town. Despite the humiliation Archimedes' war machines had inflicted on the Romans, Marcus Claudius Marcellus could not help but admire Archimedes and his technical brilliance - so much so that he ordered his men not to harm the mathematician. Alas, it was too honourable an order for one Roman soldier, whose sword cut short Archimedes' life.

1215	1224	1270–1500	1516
Frederick II is crowned Holy Roman Emperor in Aachen, where he symbolically re-inters Charlemagne's body in a silver and gold reliquary. He takes the cross and vows of a crusader.	The Università degli Studi di Napoli Federico II is founded in Naples. The oldest state university in the world, its alumni include Catholic theologian and philosopher Thomas Aquinas.	The French Angevins and Spanish Aragonese spend the best part of two centuries fighting over southern Italy. Instability, warfare, the Black Death and overtaxation strangle the region's economic development.	Holy Roman Emperor Charles V of Spain inherits southern Italy. The region is strategically important to Spain in its battle with France. Charles invests in defences in cities like Lecce.

Pilgrims & Crusaders

Ever since Puglia and Basilicata's colonisation by the Greeks, multifarious myths had established themselves in the region. Many were related to the presence of therapeutic waters and the practice of *incubatio*, a rite whereby one had to sleep close to a holy place to receive revelations from a deity. In its early days the cult of the Archangel Michael was mainly a cult of healing forces based on the saint's revelations. It started to gain currency in the early 5th century, but it wasn't until the arrival of the Lombards in the 7th century that it really began to take off.

Sweeping down from the north, the Lombards found in St Michael a mirror image of their own pagan deity, Wodan. In Michael, they saw similar characteristics: the image of a medieval warrior, a leader of celestial armies. There is little doubt that their devotion to the saint was instrumental in their easy conversion to Catholicism, as they repeatedly restored and enlarged the Monte Sant'Angelo shrine, making it the most important centre of the cult in the Western world. Soon the trail of pilgrims along the Via Traiana became so great that the road was nicknamed the Via Sacra Langobardorum (Holy Road of the Lombards), and dozens of churches, hostels and monasteries were built to accommodate the pilgrims along the way.

Another group of pilgrims in this region were the Normans. Ruling over northern France, they arrived in southern Italy in the 10th century, initially en route from Jerusalem, and later as mercenaries attracted by the money to be made fighting for the rival principalities and against the Muslim Saracens in Sicily. By 1053, after six years of mercenary activity, Robert Guiscard (c 1015–85), the Norman conquistador, had comprehensively defeated the combined forces of the Calabrian Byzantines, the Lombards and the papal forces at the Battle of Civitate. Having established his supremacy, Robert turned his attentions to expanding the territories under his control. To achieve this, he had to negotiate with the Vatican. In return for being invested with the titles of duke of Apulia and Calabria in 1059, Robert agreed to chase the Saracens out of Sicily and restore Christianity to the island. He delegated this task – and promised the island – to his younger brother Roger I (1031–1101), who landed his troops at Messina in 1061, capturing the port by surprise. In 1064, Roger tried to make good on his promise and take Palermo, but he was repulsed by a well-organised Saracen army; it wasn't until Robert arrived in 1072 with substantial reinforcements that the city fell into Norman hands. Impressed by the island's cultured Arab lifestyle, Roger shamelessly borrowed and improved on it, spending vast amounts of money on palaces and churches and encouraging a cosmopolitan atmosphere in his court.

The Arabs introduced spaghetti to Sicily; 'strings of pasta' were documented by the Arab geographer Al-Idrissi in Palermo in 1150. They also brought couscous and sugar cane to the island.

1600	1647	1714	1737
Naples is Europe's biggest city, boasting a population of over 300,000. Among its growing number of residents is renegade artist Caravaggio, who arrives in 1606.	Gross mismanagement causes the southern Italian economy to collapse. In Naples, the Masaniello Revolt breaks out over heavy taxes. Revolt spreads to the provinces and peasant militias rule the countryside.	The end of the War of the Spanish Succession forces the withdrawal of Spanish forces from Lombardy. The Spanish Bourbon family establishes an independent Kingdom of the Two Sicilies.	Naples' original Teatro San Carlo is built in a swift eight months. Designed by Giovanni Antonio Medrano, it was rebuilt in 1816 after a devastating fire.

BORN TO RUMBLE

In the late 10th century Norman fighters began to earn a reputation across Europe as fierce and tough mercenaries. As inheritance customs left younger sons disadvantaged, younger brothers were expected to seek their fortunes elsewhere – and seek they did, with remarkable success.

According to one legend, Norman involvement in southern Italy began in 1013 at the shrine of St Michael at Monte Sant'Angelo, when Latin rebel Meles, chafing under Byzantine authority, invited the Normans to serve him as mercenaries. By 1030 what had begun as an offer of service in return for booty became a series of unusually successful attempts at wresting control from local warlords.

At the forefront of the Italian conquests were the Hauteville brothers: the eldest, William 'Bras de Fer' (Iron Arm; c 1009–46), who controlled Puglia, and Robert Guiscard (the Cunning; c 1015–85), who rampaged over Calabria and southern Campania. By 1053, after six years of incessant fighting, Robert had defeated the combined forces of the Calabrian Byzantines, the Lombards and the papal forces at Civitate.

Up to this point the Normans (as mercenaries) had fought both for and against the papacy as their needs had required. But Robert's relationship with the Vatican underwent a radical transformation following the Great Schism of 1054, which resulted in a complete break between the Byzantine and Latin churches. In their turn, the popes saw in the Normans a powerful potential ally, and so in 1059 Pope Nicholas II and Robert signed a concord at Melfi that invested Robert with the titles of duke of Apulia (including Basilicata) and Calabria. In return, Robert agreed to chase the Byzantines and Saracens out of southern Italy and Sicily and restore the southern kingdom to papal rule.

Little would the pope suspect that Roger would go on to develop a territorial monarchy and become a ruler who saw himself as detached from the higher jurisdiction of both western and eastern emperor – and even the pope himself.

By 1130 most of southern Italy, including Sicily, was in Norman hands and it was only a question of time before the prosperous duchy of Naples gave in to the inevitable. It did so in 1139 – the Kingdom of the Two Sicilies was thus complete.

The Wonder of the World

Frederick II, king of Sicily and Holy Roman Emperor, presided over one of the most glamorous periods of southern history. The fact that he came to wield such power and wear Charlemagne's crown at all is a quirk of history.

He inadvertently inherited the crown of Sicily and the south from his mother, Constance (the posthumous daughter of Roger I), in 1208 after William II died childless; the crown of the Holy Roman Empire came to him through his father, Henry VI, the son of Frederick Barbarossa.

1752	1798–99	1805	1814–15
Work commences on the Palazzo Reale in Caserta, north of Naples. Commissioned by Charles VII of Bourbon and designed by Luigi Vanvitelli, the palace would outsize Versailles.	Napoleon invades Italy and occupies Rome. Ferdinand I sends an army to evict the French, but his troops flee. The French counter-attack and take Naples, establishing the Parthenopean Republic.	Napoleon is proclaimed king of the newly constituted Kingdom of Italy, comprising most of the northern half of the country. A year later, he retakes the Kingdom of Naples.	After Napoleon's fall the Congress of Vienna is held to re-establish the balance of power in Europe. The result for Italy is largely a return of the old occupying powers.

History of the Italian People by Giuliano Procacci is one of the best general histories of the country in any language. It covers the period from the early Middle Ages until 1948.

The union of the two crowns in 1220 meant that Frederick II would rule over lands covering modern-day Germany, Austria, the Netherlands, Poland, the Czech Republic, Slovakia, southern France and southern Italy, as well as the rich Kingdom of Sicily and the remnants of the Byzantine world.

It was a union that caused the popes much discomfort. For while they wanted and needed an emperor who would play the role of temporal sword, Frederick's wide-reaching kingdom all but encircled the Papal States and his belief in the absolute power of the monarchy gave them grave cause for concern.

Like Charlemagne before him, Frederick controlled a kingdom so vast that he could realistically dream of reviving the fallen Roman Empire – and dream he did. Under his rule, Sicily was transformed into a centralised state playing a key commercial and cultural role in European affairs, and Palermo gained a reputation as the continent's most important city; most of the northern Italian city states were brought to heel. In 1225 he went on to marry Jolanda of Brienne and gained the title of king of Jerusalem, making him the first Roman emperor to bear that title. In 1228 the crusade he launched was not only nearly bloodless, but it saw the return of the shrines of Jerusalem, Nazareth and Bethlehem to the Christian fold.

As well as being a talented statesman, he was also a cultured man, and many of his biographers see in him the precursor to the Renaissance prince. Few other medieval monarchs corresponded with the sages of Judaism and Islam; he also spoke six languages and was fascinated by science, nature and architecture. He even wrote a scholarly treatise on falconry during one of the long, boring sieges of Faenza, and Dante was right to call him the father of Italian poetry.

Yet despite his brilliance, his vision for an international empire was incompatible with the ambitions of the papacy and he struggled throughout his reign to remain on good terms with increasingly aggressive popes. Finally, in 1243, Pope Innocent IV proclaimed him deposed, characterising him as a 'friend of Babylon's sultan' and a heretic. At the same time the northern Italian provinces were straining against his centralised control and years of war and strategising were finally taking their toll. Only in Puglia, his favourite province throughout his reign, did Frederick remain undisputed master.

In December 1250, after suffering a bout of dysentery, he died suddenly in Castel Fiorentino, near Lucera. His heirs, Conrad and Manfred, would not survive him long. Conrad died of malaria four years later in Lavello in Basilicata, and Manfred was defeated at the Battle of Benevento in 1266 by Charles of Anjou, the pope's pretender to the throne. Two

1848	1860	1861	1880–1915
European revolts spark rebellion in Italy. The Bourbons are expelled from Sicily but retake it in a rain of fire that earns Ferdinand II the epithet 'Re Bomba' (King Bomb).	In the name of Italian unity, Giuseppe Garibaldi lands with 1000 men, the Red Shirts, in Sicily. He takes the island and lands in southern Italy.	By the end of the Franco-Austrian War (1859–61), Vittorio Emanuele II controls Lombardy, Sardinia, Sicily, southern Italy and parts of central Italy, and is proclaimed king of a newly united Italy.	People vote with their feet; millions of impoverished southerners embark on ships for the New World, causing a massive haemorrhage of the most able-bodied and hardworking southern male youth.

years later another battle took the life of Manfred's 15-year-old nephew and heir, Conradin, who was publicly beheaded in Naples.

By 1270 the brilliant Hohenstaufen period was officially over. And while Frederick's rule marked a major stage in the transformation of Europe from a community of Latin Christians under the headship of two competing powers (pope and emperor) to a Europe of nation states, he had failed to leave any tangible legacies. The following ruling family, the Angevins, did not make the same mistake: Naples' Castel Nuovo (built by Charles of Anjou in 1279) and Castel Sant'Elmo (constructed by Robert of Anjou in the early 14th century) remain two of the city's iconic landmarks.

Sicily's Inglorious Slide

Under the Angevins Sicily was weighed down by onerous taxes, religious persecution of the island's Muslim population was the order of the day, and Norman fiefdoms were removed and awarded to French aristocrats. On Easter Monday 1282 the city of Palermo exploded in rebellion. Incited by the alleged rape of a local girl by a gang of French troops, peasants lynched every French soldier they could get their hands on. The revolt spread to the countryside and was supported by the Sicilian nobility, who had formed an alliance with Peter of Aragon. Peter had landed at Trapani with a large army and was proclaimed king. For the next 20 years the Aragonese and the Angevins were engaged in the War of the Sicilian Vespers – a war that was eventually won by the Spanish.

By the end of the 14th century, Sicily had been thoroughly marginalised. The eastern Mediterranean was sealed off by the Ottoman Turks, while the Italian mainland was off limits on account of Sicily's political ties with Spain. As a result, the Renaissance passed the island by, reinforcing the oppressive effects of poverty and ignorance. Even Spain lost interest in its colony, choosing to rule through viceroys. By the end of the 15th century the viceroy's court was a den of corruption, and the most influential body on the island became the Catholic Church (whose archbishops and bishops were mostly Spaniards). The Church exercised draconian powers through a network of Holy Office tribunals, otherwise known as the Inquisition.

Reeling under the weight of state oppression, ordinary Sicilians demanded reform. Unfortunately, their Spanish monarchs were preoccupied by the Wars of the Spanish Succession and Sicily was subsequently passed around for decades from European power to European power like an unwanted Christmas present. Eventually the Spanish reclaimed the island in 1734, this time under the Bourbon king Charles III of Sicily (r 1734–59).

Steven Runciman's *Fall of Constantinople 1453* provides a classic account of this bloody episode in crusading history. It manages to be academically sound and highly entertaining at the same time.

1889	1908	1915	1919
Raffaele Esposito invents 'pizza margherita' in honour of Queen Margherita, who takes her first bite of the Neapolitan staple on a royal visit to the city.	On the morning of 28 December, Messina and Reggio Calabria are struck by a 7.5-magnitude earthquake and a 13m-high tsunami. More than 80,000 lives are lost.	Italy enters WWI on the side of the Allies to win Italian territories still in Austrian hands after Austria's offer to cede some of the territories is deemed insufficient.	Former socialist journalist Benito Mussolini forms a right-wing militant group, the Fasci Italiani di Combattimento (Combat Squads), a precursor to his Fascist Party.

The Bourbon Paradox

Between January and August 1656, the bubonic plague wiped out about half of Naples' 300,000-plus inhabitants and much of the economy. The city would take almost two centuries to reach its pre-plague headcount again.

Assessment of Bourbon rule in southern Italy is a controversial topic. Many historians consider it a period of exploitation and stagnation. Others, more recently, have started to re-evaluate the Kingdom of the Two Sicilies, pointing out the raft of positive reforms Charles III implemented. These included abolishing many noble and clerical privileges, curtailing the legal rights of landowners within their fiefs and restricting ecclesiastical jurisdiction at a time when the Church was reputed to own almost a third of the land within the kingdom.

Naples had already begun prospering under the rule of Spanish viceroy Don Pedro de Toledo (1532–53), whose building boom attracted some of Italy's finest artistic talent. Under Charles, the city became one of the great capital cities of Europe, drawing hundreds of aristocratic travellers. On top of this, Charles was a patron of architecture and the arts. During his reign Pompeii and Herculaneum (both destroyed in the 79 CE eruption of Mt Vesuvius) were discovered and the Archaeological Museum in Naples was founded. He was responsible for the Teatro San Carlo, the largest opera house in Europe, and he built the huge palaces of Capodimonte and Caserta. Some subsequent Bourbon monarchs also made positive contributions, such as Ferdinand II (1830–59), who laid the foundations for modern industry, developing southern harbours, creating a merchant fleet and building the first Italian railway line and road systems, such as the dramatic Amalfi drive.

But where Charles might rightfully claim a place among southern Italy's outstanding rulers, later Bourbon princes were some of the most eccentric and pleasure-seeking monarchs in Europe. Charles' son, Ferdinand I (1751–1825), was by contrast venal and poorly educated. He spent his time hunting and fishing, and he delighted in the company of the *lazzaroni* (the Neapolitan underclass). He much preferred to leave the business of government to his wife, the ambitious and treacherous Archduchess Maria Carolina of Austria, whose main aim was to free southern Italy from Spanish influence and secure a rapprochement with Austria and Britain. Her chosen administrator was the English expatriate Sir John Acton, who replaced the long-serving Bernardo Tanucci, a move that was to mire court politics in damaging corruption and espionage.

For a wide-ranging general site on Italian history, check out www.arcaini.com. It covers everything from prehistory to the postwar period, and includes a brief chronology to the end of the 20th century.

When the French Revolution broke out in 1789, Maria Carolina was initially sympathetic to the movement, but when her sister Marie Antoinette was beheaded, she became fanatically Francophobic. The French invasion of Italy in 1799, and the crowning of Napoleon as king in 1800, jolted the south out of its Bourbon slumbers. Although Napoleonic rule was to last only 14 years, this brief flirtation with republicanism was to awaken hopes of an independent Italian nation. Returning to his beloved

1922	1927	1934	1940
Mussolini and his Fascists stage a march on Rome in October. Doubting the army's loyalty, a fearful Vittorio Emanuele III entrusts Mussolini with the formation of a government.	A study released by the Italian government puts the number of Italian citizens living abroad at around 9.2 million. Southern Italians make up over 60% of the Italian diaspora.	Screen siren Sophia Loren is born, and spends her childhood living in Pozzuoli and Naples. Her break would come in 1951, as an extra in Mervyn LeRoy's film *Quo Vadis*.	Italy enters WWII on Nazi Germany's side and invades Greece in October. Greek forces counter-attack and enter southern Albania. Germany saves Italy in March–April 1941 by overrunning Yugoslavia and Greece.

Naples in 1815, Ferdinand, who was once so at ease with his subjects, was now terrified of revolution and became determined to exert his absolute authority. Changes that had been made by the Bonapartist regime were reversed, causing widespread discontent. Revolutionary agitators sprang up everywhere, and the countryside, now full of discharged soldiers, became more lawless than ever.

Yet there was no putting the genie back in the bottle. The aggressive tactics of Ferdinand II only exacerbated the situation, and in 1848 Sicily experienced a violent revolt that saw the expulsion of the Bourbons from the island. Although the revolt was crushed, Ferdinand earned himself the nickname 'Re Bomba' (King Bomb) after his army mercilessly shelled Messina. From such a promising beginning, the last decades of Bourbon rule were so oppressive that the Bourbons were almost universally hated throughout liberal Europe. The seeds had well and truly been sown for the Risorgimento (reunification period), which would finally see the whole peninsula united into a modern nation state.

> Edward Gibbon's 18th-century *History of the Decline and Fall of the Roman Empire* is the acknowledged classic work on the subject of the empire's darker days. Try the abridged single-volume version.

Kingdom of Death

Although not commonly acknowledged, the widespread presence of malaria in the Italian peninsula during the 19th and 20th centuries is one of the most significant factors in the social and economic development (or lack of it) of the modern country. An endemic as well as epidemic disease, it was so enmeshed in Italian rural society that it was widely regarded as the Italian national disease. Even the word maleria itself comes from the Italian *mal aria* (bad air), as it was originally thought that the disease was caused by a poisoning of the air as wet earth dried out during the heat of summer.

The scale of the problem came to light in the decades following Italian unification in 1861. Out of 69 provinces, only two were found to be free of malaria; in a population of 25 million people, at least 11 million were permanently at risk of the disease. Most famously, Giuseppe Garibaldi, one of the founding fathers of modern Italy, lost both his wife, Anita, and a large number of troops to the disease. Thus stricken, Garibaldi urged the newly united nation to place the fight against malaria high on its list of priorities.

In the dawning era of global competition, Italian farming was dangerously backward. As a predominantly grain-producing economy, it was tragically ironic that all of Italy's most fertile land was in precisely the zones – coastal plains and river valleys – where malaria was most intense. To survive, farm workers had to expose themselves to the disease. Unfortunately, disease in turn entailed suffering, days of absence and low productivity.

More significantly, although malaria ravaged the whole peninsula, it was pre-eminently an affliction of the south, as well as the provinces of

HISTORY KINGDOM OF DEATH

1943	1944	1946	1950
Vittorio Emanuele III sacks Mussolini. He is replaced by Marshal Badoglio, who surrenders after Allied landings in southern Italy. German forces free Mussolini.	Mt Vesuvius explodes back into action on 18 March. The eruption is captured on film by United States Army Air Forces personnel stationed nearby.	Italians vote in a national referendum in June to abolish the monarchy (by about 12.7 million votes to 10.7 million) and create a republic. The south is the only region to vote against the republic.	The Cassa per il Mezzogiorno is established to help fund public works and infrastructure in the south. Poor management and corruption see at least one third of the money squandered.

Rome and Grosseto in the centre. Of all the regions, six were especially afflicted – Abruzzo, Basilicata, Calabria, Lazio, Puglia and Sardinia – earning the south the lugubrious epithet 'the kingdom of death'. Furthermore, Giovanni Battista Grassi (the man who discovered that mosquitoes transmit malaria) estimated that the danger of infection in the south was 10 times greater than in northern Italy.

No issue illustrates the divide between the north and south of the country quite so vividly as the malaria crisis. The World Health Organization defines malaria in the modern world as a disease of poverty that distorts and slows economic growth. In the case of the Italian south, malaria was a significant factor in the underdevelopment of the region at a critical time in its history. Malarial fever thrives on exploitative working conditions, substandard housing and diet, illiteracy, war and ecological degradation, and Italy's south had certainly had its fair share of all of these by the early 20th century. As late as 1918 the Ministry of Agriculture reported that 'malaria is the key to all the economic problems of the South'. Against this background of regional inequality, the fever became an important metaphor deployed by *meridionalisti* (southern spokesmen) such as Giustino Fortunato (1848–1932) and Francesco Nitti (1868–1953) to describe the plight of the south and to demand redress. Nitti attributed the entirety of southern backwardness to this single factor.

Between 1900 and 1907 the Italian parliament passed a series of laws establishing a national campaign – the first of its kind in the world – to eradicate or at least control the disease. But it was to take the best part of half a century to bring malaria under control, as two world wars and the Fascist seizure of power in 1922 were to overwhelm domestic policies, causing the program to stall and then collapse entirely amid military defeat and occupation.

HISTORY ON SCREEN

Il Gattopardo (The Leopard; Luchino Visconti; 1963) A Sicilian aristocrat grapples with the changes heralded by the 19th-century Risorgimento (reunification period).

Le quattro giornate di Napoli (The Four Days of Naples; Nanni Loy; 1962) Neapolitan courage shines through in this film about the famous popular uprisings against the Nazis in September 1943.

Il resto di niente (The Remains of Nothing; Antonietta De Lillo; 2003) Eleonora de Pimental Fonesca, heroine of the ill-fated Neapolitan revolution of 1799, is the protagonist.

Salvatore Giuliano (Francesco Rosi; 1963) A neorealist classic about the murder of Sicily's very own modern Robin Hood.

1950s–60s	1980	1999	2003
Soaring unemployment causes another mass migration of about two million people from the south to the factories of northern Italy, Europe and Australia.	At 7.34pm on 25 November, a 6.8-magnitude earthquake strikes Campania. The quake kills almost 3000 people and causes widespread devastation; the city of Naples also suffers damage.	Brindisi becomes a strategic base for the Office of the UN and the World Food Organization. The disused military airport's hangars are converted into storage space for humanitarian aid.	Sicilian *mafioso* Salvatore 'Totò' Riina is arrested in Palermo. Nicknamed 'The Beast', the 'boss of bosses' had ordered the bombing death of antimafia magistrates Giovanni Falcone and Paolo Borsellino.

Final victory against the disease was only achieved following the end of WWII, when the government was able to re-establish public-health infrastructures and implement a five-year plan that included the use of a new pesticide, DDT, to eradicate malaria. The designation 'malarial zone' was only officially lifted from the entire peninsula in 1969.

The Southern Question

The unification of Italy meant sudden and dramatic changes for all the southern provinces. The huge upsurge in *brigantaggio* (banditry) and social unrest throughout the last decades of the 19th century was caused by widespread disillusionment about the unification project. Though he is remembered as a leading figure in the push towards unification, it was never the intention of 19th-century Italian statesman Camillo Benso, Count of Cavour, to unify the whole country. Even later during his premiership, Cavour favoured an expanded Piedmont rather than a united Italy.

For southerners, it was difficult to see the benefits of being part of this new nation state. Naples was stripped of its capital-city status; the new government carried away huge cash reserves from the rich southern Italian banks; taxes went up and factories closed as new tariff policies, dictated by northern interests, caused a steep decline in the southern economy. Culturally, southerners were also made to feel inferior; to be southern or 'Bourbon' was to be backward, vulgar and uncivilised.

After WWI the south fared a little better, experiencing slow progress in terms of infrastructure projects like the construction of the Puglian aqueduct, the extension of the railways and the improvement of civic centres like Bari and Taranto. But Mussolini's 'Battle for Wheat' – the drive to make Italy self-sufficient in food – compounded many of the southern problems. It destroyed even more valuable pastureland by turning it over to the monoculture of wheat, while reinforcing the parlous state of the southern peasantry, who remained uneducated, disenfranchised, landless and at high risk of malaria. To escape such a hopeless future, many of them packed their bags and migrated to North America, northern Europe and Australia, starting a trend that was to become one of the main features of post-WWII Italy.

In the 1946 referendum that established the Italian republic, the south was the only region to vote no. In Naples, 80% voted to keep the monarchy. Still, change moved on apace. After the wreckage of WWII was cleared – especially that caused by Allied air raids in Sicily and Naples – the Cassa per il Mezzogiorno reconstruction fund was established to bring the south into the 20th century with massive, cheap housing schemes and big industrial projects like the steel plant in Taranto and the

Between 1944 and 1946 the German Wehrmacht systematically sabotaged the pumping systems that drained Italy's marshes and confiscated quinine from the Department of Health. The ensuing malaria epidemic proved as deadly as any WWI ground offensive.

2003	2004–05	2005	2011
The Campania government launches Progetto Vesuvia in an attempt to clear Mt Vesuvius' heavily populated lower slopes. The €30,000 offered to relocate is rejected by most in the danger zone.	Tension between rival Camorra clans explodes on the streets of suburban Naples. In only four months, almost 50 people are gunned down in retribution attacks.	Nichi Vendola, representing the Communist Refoundation Party, is elected president of Puglia. He is the first gay communist to be elected president of a southern Italian region.	Thousands of people fleeing the revolutionary chaos in northern Africa land on the island of Lampedusa. Italy grants 30,000 refugees temporary visas, creating tension with France.

Fiat factory in Basilicata. Yet constant interference by the Mafia in southern Italy's economy did much to nullify the efforts of Rome to reduce the gap between the prosperous north and the poor south. The disappearance of large amounts of cash eventually led the central government to scrap the Cassa per il Mezzogiorno fund in 1992.

Clean Hands, Dirty Politics

Hitting the headlines in 1992 was the Tangentopoli (Bribesville) scandal, which exposed the breadth and depth of institutionalised kickbacks and bribes in Italy (the country's modus operandi since WWII). Although it was largely focused on the industrial north, the repercussions of the widespread investigation into graft (known as *Mani pulite,* or Clean Hands) were inevitably felt in southern regions like Sicily and Campania, where politics, business and organised crime were longtime bedfellows.

The scandal eventually brought about the demise of the Democrazia Cristiana (DC; Christian Democrats), a centre-right Catholic party that appealed to southern Italy's traditional conservatism. Allied closely with the Church, the DC promised wide-ranging reforms while at the same time demanding vigilance against godless communism. It was greatly aided in its efforts by the Mafia, which ensured that the local DC mayor would always top the poll. The Mafia's reward was *clientelismo* (political patronage) that ensured it was granted favourable contracts.

In the meantime, things were changing in regard to how many southern Italians viewed the Mafia, thanks in no small part to Sicilian investigating magistrates Paolo Borsellino and Giovanni Falcone. The duo contributed greatly to turning the climate of opinion against the Mafia on both sides of the Atlantic, and they made it possible for ordinary citizens to speak about and against the Mafia more freely. When they were tragically murdered in the summer of 1992, it was a great loss for Italy and Sicily, but it was these deaths that finally broke the Mafia's code of *omertà* (silence).

Cultural Revival & COVID's Challenge

Until the development of COVID-19, tourist numbers were growing strongly in the region, especially in Naples and Puglia, and in Matera due to its tenure as a European Capital of Culture in 2019. Outside of tourism, unemployment rates, especially among young people, do remain significantly higher than in other parts of the country, although it's envisaged tech industry investment in Matera and Naples will help to alleviate this. Following a focused campaign to vaccinate 80% of Italy's eligible population against COVID-19 by late 2021, and the subsequent adoption of vaccination mandates and the country's Green Pass, tourist numbers in the region were again increasing by the year's end.

2016	2018	2019	2021
US tech giant Apple opens its first iOS Developer Academy in Naples. The centre's aim is to train both local and foreign app developers using Apple's iOS mobile operating system.	Palermo is crowned Italian Capital of Culture. The city hosts a number of special cultural events, including the 12th edition of Manifesta, Europe's most important biennial exhibition of contemporary art.	Alongside Plovdiv in Bulgaria, the city of Matera steps onto the European stage as the continent's official City of Culture in 2019. It's the first time the annual title has been given to a city in southern Italy.	Diverse and significant challenges impact the region throughout 2020 and 2021, including COVID-19, devastating wildfires, and a tragically increased stream of asylum seekers arriving by boat.

The Southern Way of Life

The Mezzogiorno, or land of the midday sun, is more than haunting ruins, poetic coastlines and peeling *palazzi* (mansions). Its true protagonists are the *meridionali* (southern Italians), whose character and nuances echo a long, nail-biting history of dizzying highs and testing lows. To understand the southern psyche is to understand the complexities and contradictions that have moulded Italy's most misunderstood half.

Dreams & Diasporas

Emigration to Immigration

Severe economic problems in the south following Italy's unification and after each of the world wars led to massive emigration as people searched for a better life in northern Italy, northern Europe, North and South America, and Australia. Between 1880 and 1910, more than

Above: Altar to Diego Maradona (p282), Naples

1.5 million Sicilians alone left for the US, and in 1900 the island was the world's main area of emigration. In Campania, a staggering 2.7 million people left the motherland between 1876 and 1976.

Today, huge numbers of young Italians, often the most educated and ambitious, continue to move abroad. According to official estimates, over 100,000 Italians leave the country annually in search of better opportunities abroad, with almost 70% of departing Italians remaining in Europe. This brain-drain epidemic is fuelled in part by a persistently high national youth unemployment rate – around 30.2% in mid-2019. Another factor is Italy's entrenched system of patronage and nepotism, which commonly makes landing a job more about who you know than what you know.

For southern Italians, the standard of education available is often another contributing factor. A commonly held belief that southern universities aren't up to scratch sees many parents send their children north or overseas to complete their studies. While some return after completing their master's degree, many become accustomed to the freedom and opportunities found in their host city or country and tend to stay.

And yet, somewhat ironically, southern Italy has itself become a destination for people searching for a better life. Political and economic upheavals in the 1980s brought new arrivals from central and Eastern Europe, Latin America and North Africa, including Italy's former colonies in Tunisia, Somalia and Ethiopia. More recently, waves of Chinese, Sri Lankan and Bangladeshi immigrants have made the presence of Asian grocery stores and businesses a common sight from Naples' Quartieri Spagnoli to Palermo's Ballarò market district.

From a purely economic angle, these new arrivals are vital for the country's economic health. Without immigrant workers to fill the gaps left in the labour market by pickier locals, Italy would be sorely lacking in tomato sauce and shoes. From hotel maids on the Amalfi Coast to fruit pickers on Calabrian farms, it is often immigrants who take the low-paid service jobs that keep Italy's economy afloat. Unfortunately, their vulnerability has sometimes led to exploitation, with several reported cases of farmhands being paid below-minimum wages for back-breaking work.

The North–South Divide

In his film *Ricomincio da tre* (I'm Starting from Three; 1980), acting great Massimo Troisi comically tackled the problems faced by southern Italians forced to head north for work. The reverse scenario was tackled in the comedy *Benvenuti al Sud* (Welcome to the South; 2010), in which a northern Italian postmaster is posted to a small southern Italian town, bulletproof vest and prejudices in tow. Slapstick aside, both films reveal Italy's enduring north–south divide. While the north is celebrated for its fashion empires and moneyed metropolises, Italy's south is commonly associated with high unemployment, crumbling infrastructure and organised crime. At a deep semantic level, the word *meridionale* (southern Italian) continues to conjure a series of unflattering stereotypes.

From the Industrial Revolution to the 1960s, millions of southern Italians fled to the industrialised northern cities for factory jobs. As the saying goes, *'Ogni vero milanese ha un nonno pugliese'* (Every true Milanese has a Pugliese grandparent). For many of these domestic migrants, the welcome north of Rome was anything but warm. Disparagingly nicknamed *terroni* (peasants), many faced discrimination on a daily basis, from everyone from landlords to baristas. While such overt discrimination is now practically nonexistent, historical prejudices linger. Some northerners argue that the rich north is unfairly burdened with subsidising the poor south, a belief that has fuelled a number of right-wing northern politicians.

A one-man Abbott and Costello, Antonio de Curtis (1898–1967), aka Totò, famously depicted the Neapolitan *furbizia* (cunning). Appearing in more than 100 films, including *Miseria e nobiltà* (Misery and Nobility; 1954), his roles as a hustler living on nothing but quick wits would guarantee him cult status in Naples.

Today, people of Italian origin account for more than 40% of the population in Argentina and Uruguay, more than 10% in Brazil, more than 5% in Switzerland, the US and Venezuela, and more than 4% in Australia and Canada.

THE OLD PROVERBIAL

They might be clichés, but proverbs can be quite the cultural revelation. Here are six of the south's well-worn best:

➡ *Cu si marita, sta cuntentu nu jornu, Cu' ammazza nu porcu, sta cuntentu n'annu* (Sicilian). Whoever gets married is happy for a day, whoever butchers a pig is happy for a year.

➡ *Aprili fa li ciuri e li biddizzi, l'onuri l'avi lu misi ri maju* (Sicilian). April makes the flowers and the beauty, but May gets all the credit.

➡ *A chi troppo s'acàla 'o culo se vede* (Neapolitan). He who kowtows too low bares his arse.

➡ *Cu va 'n Palermu e 'un viri Murriali, sinni parti sceccu e tonna armali* (Sicilian). Whoever goes to Palermo and doesn't see Monreale goes there a jackass and returns a fool.

➡ *Quannu la pulice se vitte a la farina, disse ca era capu mulinaru* (Pugliese). When the flea found itself in the flour, it said it was the master miller.

➡ *Lu mericu piatusu fa a chiaja virminusa* (Sicilian). A compassionate doctor makes the wound infected.

Yet prejudices and stereotypes exist on both sides of Rome. Many southerners view their northern compatriots as *freddi* (cold) and uptight. And it's not uncommon to hear southern Italians living in the north complain of life being isolated and anonymous.

The Southern Psyche
Beautiful Family, Beautiful Image

Family is the bedrock of southern Italian life, and loyalty to family and friends is usually non-negotiable. As Luigi Barzini (1908–84), author of *The Italians,* noted, 'A happy private life helps tolerate an appalling public life.' This chasm between the private arena and the public one is a noticeable aspect of the southern mentality, and has evolved over years of intrusive foreign domination. Some locals mightn't think twice about littering their street, but step inside their home and you'll get floors clean enough to eat from.

Maintaining a *bella figura* (beautiful image) is very important to the average southerner, and how you and your family appear to the outside world is a matter of honour, respectability and pride. Many continue to believe that you are better than your neighbour if you own more and better things. This mindset is firmly rooted in the past, when owning many things was necessary for attaining certain social roles and, ultimately, for sustaining one's family. Yet *fare bella figura* (making a good impression) goes beyond a well-kept house; it extends to dressing well, behaving modestly, performing religious and social duties and fulfilling all essential family obligations. In the context of the extended family, where gossip is rife, a good image protects one's privacy.

Any self-respecting Italian bookshelf features one or more Roman rhetoricians. To *fare la bella figura* (make a good impression) among academics, trot out a phrase from Cicero or Horace (Horatio), such as 'Where there is life there is hope' or 'Whatever advice you give, be brief'.

It's Not What You Know...

In Europe's most ancient, entrenched bureaucracy, strong family ties are essential to getting things done. Putting in a good word for your son, niece or grandchild isn't just a nice gesture but an essential career boost. According to Italy's Ministry of Labour, over 60% of Italian firms rely on personal introductions for recruitment. Indeed, *clientelismo* (nepotism) is as much a part of the Italian lexicon as *caffè* (coffee) and *tasse* (taxes) – a fact satirised in Massimiliano Bruno's film *Viva L'Italia* (2012), about a crooked, well-connected senator who secures jobs for his three children, among them a talentless TV actress with a speech impediment.

PELICETA/GETTY IMAGES ©

TETIANA TYCHYNSKA/SHUTTERSTOCK ©

Top: Parading the statue
of San Rocco, Puglia
(p142)
Bottom: Good-luck
charms for sale, Naples
(p68)

In 2016 Raffaele Cantone – president of the Autorità Nazionale Anti-corruzione (ANAC) – sparked a national debate after claiming that nepotism in Italian universities was playing a major role in the country's ongoing 'brain drain'. It's a sentiment also seen in a 2011 study conducted by the University of Chicago Medical Center. The study found an unusually high recurrence of the same surnames amongst academic staff at various Italian universities. As the satirist Beppe Severgnini wryly comments in his book *La Bella Figura: A Field Guide to the Italian Mind*, 'If you want to lose an Italian friend or kill off a conversation, all you have to say is "On the subject of conflicts of interest..." If your interlocutor hasn't disappeared, he or she will smile condescendingly.'

A Woman's Place

As in many places in the Mediterranean, a woman's position in southern Italy has always been a difficult one. In the domestic sphere, a mother and wife commands the utmost respect within the home. She is considered the moral and emotional compass for her family, an omnipresent role model and the nightmare of newly wedded wives. In the public sphere, however, her role has less frequently been that of a protagonist.

But times are changing. Only two generations ago, many southern men and women were virtually segregated. In many cases, women would often only go out on Saturdays, and separate beaches for men and women were common. Dating would often involve a chaperone, whether it be the young woman's brother, aunt or grandmother. These days, more and more unmarried southern women live with their partners, especially in the cities. Improvements in educational opportunities and more liberal attitudes mean that the number of women with degrees and successful careers is growing.

Yet true gender equality remains an unattained goal, both in southern Italy and in the country as a whole. The World Economic Forum's 2018 Global Gender Gap Report ranked Italy 70th worldwide in terms of overall gender equality, up from 82nd position in 2017. It ranked 118th in female economic participation and opportunity, 61st in educational attainment and 38th in political empowerment.

According to the report, only 55% of Italian women are in the workforce, compared to 86.1% in Iceland, 75.9% in Norway and 69.3% in Spain. On average, Italian women earn around 35% less than their male counterparts. And though successful Italian businesswomen do exist – among them Poste Italiane chairperson Maria Bianca Farina and Eni chairperson Emma Marcegaglia – almost 95% of public-company board members in Italy are male and, of these, approximately 80% of them are older than 55.

Italian women fare no better on the domestic front. OECD figures reveal that Italian men spend 130 minutes per day cooking, cleaning or caring (what the OECD labels unpaid work), compared to 306 minutes per day for Italian women.

The Sacred & the Profane

While almost 80% of Italians identify as Catholics, only around 15% of Italy's population regularly attends Sunday Mass. Yet, despite the Vatican's waning influence on modern Italian life, religious festivals and traditions continue to play a significant role in southern Italy. Every town has its own saint's day, celebrated with music, special events, food and wine. Indeed, these religious festivals are one of the best ways into the culture of the Mezzogiorno. Cream of the crop is Easter, with lavish week-long events to mark Holy Week. People pay handsomely for the privilege and prestige of carrying the various back-breaking decorations around the town – the processions are usually solemnly, excruciatingly slow.

Pilgrimages and a belief in miracles remain a central part of the religious experience. You will see representations of Padre Pio – the Gargano

---

THE SOUTHERN WAY OF LIFE THE SOUTHERN PSYCHE

John Turturro's film *Passione* (2010) is a *Buena Vista Social Club*-style exploration of Naples' rich and eclectic musical traditions. Spanning everything from folk songs to contemporary tunes, it offers a fascinating insight into the city's complex soul.

Turkish-Italian director Ferzan Özpetek explores the clash of southern tradition and modernity in his film *Mine vaganti* (Loose Cannons; 2010), a sitcom about two gay brothers and their conservative Pugliese family.

saint who was canonised for his role in several miraculous recoveries – in churches, village squares, pizzerias and private homes everywhere. Around eight million pilgrims visit his shrine every year. Three times a year, thousands cram into Naples' Duomo to witness their patron saint San Gennaro's blood miraculously liquefy in the phial that contains it. When the blood liquefies, the city is considered safe from disaster. When it doesn't – as was the case in December 2016 – the faithful see it as an ominous sign. Another one of Naples' holy helpers is Giuseppe Moscati (1880–1927), a doctor who dedicated his life to serving the city's poor. According to the faithful, the medic continues to heal from up above, a dedicated section inside the city's Chiesa del Gesù Nuovo heaving with *ex-voti* (including golden limbs) offered in thanks for miraculous recoveries.

Still, the line between the sacred and the profane remains a fine one in the south. In *Christ Stopped at Eboli,* his book about his stay in rural Basilicata in the 1930s, writer-painter-doctor Carlo Levi wrote: 'The air over this desolate land and among the peasant huts is filled with spirits. Not all of them are mischievous and capricious gnomes or evil demons. There are also good spirits in the guise of guardian angels.'

> Italy's culture of corruption and *calcio* (football) is captured in *The Dark Heart of Italy,* in which English expat author Tobias Jones wryly observes, 'Footballers or referees are forgiven nothing; politicians are forgiven everything'.

While the mystical, half-pagan world Levi describes may no longer be recognisable, ancient pagan influences live on in daily southern life. Here, curse-deterring amulets are as plentiful as crucifix pendants, the most famous of which is the iconic, horn-shaped *corno*. Adorning everything from necklines to rear-view mirrors, this lucky charm's evil-busting powers are said to lie in its representation of the bull and its sexual vigour. A rarer, but by no means extinct, custom is that of Naples' 'o Scartellat. Usually an elderly man, he'll occasionally be spotted burning incense through the city's older neighbourhoods, clearing the streets of bad vibes and inviting good fortune. The title itself is Neapolitan for 'hunchback', as the task was once the domain of posture-challenged figures. According to Neapolitan lore, touching a hunchback's hump brings good luck...which beats some of the other options, among them stepping in dog poop and having wine spilt on you accidentally.

Calcio (Football): The Other Religion

Catholicism may be Italy's official faith, but its true religion is *calcio*. On any given weekend from September through to May, you'll find millions of *tifosi* (football fans) at the *stadio* (stadium), glued to the TV, or checking the score on their mobile phone. In Naples' Piazzetta Nilo, you'll even find an altar to Argentine football star Diego Maradona, who elevated the city's Napoli team to its most successful era in the 1980s and early 1990s.

It's no coincidence that *tifoso* means both 'football fan' and 'typhus patient'. When the ball ricochets off the post and slips through the goalie's hands, when half the stadium is swearing while the other half is shouting '*Goooooooooooooool!*', 'fever pitch' is the term that comes to mind.

Indeed, nothing quite stirs Italian blood like a good (or a bad) game. Nine months after Neapolitan Fabio Cannavaro led Italy to victory in the 2006 World Cup, hospitals in northern Italy reported a baby boom. In February the following year, rioting at a Palermo–Catania match in Catania left one policeman dead and around 100 injured. Blamed on the Ultras, the violence shocked both Italy and the world, leading to a temporary ban of all matches in Italy, and increased stadium security.

Yet, the same game that divides also unites. You might be a Juventus-loathing Bari supporter on any given day, but when the national team Azzurri (the Blues) bag the World Cup, you are nothing but a heart-on-your-sleeve *italiano*. In his book *The 100 Things Everyone Needs to Know About Italy,* Australian journalist David Dale writes that Italy's 1982 World Cup win 'finally united twenty regions which, until then, had barely acknowledged that they were part of the one country'.

The Mafia

To many outside Italy, the Mafia means Sicily's Cosa Nostra, seared into popular culture thanks to Francis Ford Coppola's classic film *The Godfather*. In reality, Cosa Nostra has three other major partners in crime: Campania's Camorra, Calabria's 'ndrangheta and Puglia's Sacra Corona Unita. Apt at everything from loan sharking to trafficking narcotics, arms and people, these four criminal networks produce a staggering annual profit estimated at around €100 billion.

Origins

The concept of the *mafioso* dates back to the late 15th century, when Sicily's rent-collecting *gabellotti* (bailiffs) employed small gangs of armed peasants to help them solve 'problems'. Soon robbing large estates, the bandits struck fear and admiration into the peasantry, who were happy to support efforts to destabilise the feudal system. They became willing accomplices, protecting the outlaws, and although it was another 400 years before crime became 'organised', the 16th and 17th centuries witnessed a substantial increase in the activities of brigand bands. The peasants' loyalty to their own people resulted in the name Cosa Nostra (Our Thing). The early Mafia's way of protecting itself from prosecution was to become the modern Mafia's most important weapon: the code of silence, or *omertà*.

In the 1860s, a band of Sicilians exiled to Calabria began forming their own organised gangs, planting the seeds for the 'ndrangheta. For almost a century, these gangs remained a local menace, known for extortion, racketeering and rural banditry. But it was the murder of a local godfather in 1975 that sparked a bloody gang war, transforming the organisation and creating a rebellious faction infamous for holding northern Italian businessmen to ransom. With its profits invested in narcotics, the 'ndrangheta would transform itself into Italy's most powerful Mafia entity.

The powerful Camorra reputedly emerged from the criminal gangs operating among the poor in late 18th-century Naples. The organisation had its first big break after the failed revolution of 1848. Desperate to overthrow Ferdinand II, pro-constitutional liberals turned to *camorristi* to help garner the support of the masses – the Camorra's political influence was sealed. Dealt a serious blow by Mussolini, the organisation would get its second wind from the invading Allied forces of 1943, which turned to the flourishing underworld as the best way to get things done. The black market thrived and the Camorra slowly began to spread its roots again.

In turn, the Camorra would give birth to the Sacra Corona Unita (Sacred United Crown), created by Camorra boss Raffaele Cutolo in the 1970s to gain access to Puglia's seaports. Originally named the Nuova Grande Camorra Pugliese, it gained its current name in the early 1980s after its Pugliese members cut ties with Campania and strengthened their bond with Eastern Europe's criminal networks.

Mafia-affiliated loan sharks commonly offer struggling businesses cash with an average interest rate of 10%. An estimated 50% of shops in Naples are run with Camorra money. Mafia profits are often reinvested globally in legitimate real estate, credit markets and businesses in what is known as 'the Invisible Mafia'.

The Value of Vice

The combined annual revenue of Italy's four main mafia organisations is equal to around 10% of Italy's entire GDP. This is a far cry from the days of roguish characters bullying shopkeepers into paying the *pizzo* (protection money). As journalist Roberto Saviano writes in his Camorra exposé *Gomorra:* 'Only beggar Camorra clans inept at business and desperate to survive still practice the kind of monthly extortions seen in Nanni Loy's film *Mi manda Picone*' (Picone Sent Me).

The top money-spinner is narcotics. According to the United Nations Office on Narcotics and Crime, the drug trade makes over €32 billion annually for Italy's mafia clans. King of the scene is the Calabrian mafia, whose strong ties to Latin American crime syndicates has allowed it to control between 60% and 80% of Europe's cocaine market. Indeed, the 'ndrangheta is now also the main supplier of cocaine to Italy's rival mafia groups.

Other sources of revenue include the illegal trading of arms, the disposal of hazardous waste and Italy's ongoing refugee crisis. In May 2017, 68 people were arrested in relation to the mismanagement of a Calabrian migrant centre in the town of Isola Capo Rizzuto. According to Italian prosecutors, a powerful 'ndrangheta clan had infiltrated the centre a decade earlier, taking control of key services and skimming government funding allocated to the running of the complex. It's believed that at least €36 million of the circa €103 million in funding between 2006 and 2015 ended up in mafia coffers. The resulting shortfall impacted on the lives of those accommodated at the centre, with many migrants regularly missing out on meals.

Further north in Campania, illegal waste disposal has been one of the Camorra's biggest profit generators. According to the Italian environmentalist association Legambiente, the Camorra has illegally dumped, buried or burned close to 10 million tons of garbage in Campania since 1991. Alarmingly, this includes highly toxic waste, collected from northern Italian and foreign manufacturers lured by the cut-price rates of Camorra-owned waste-disposal companies. Abnormally high rates of cancer and congenital malformations of the nervous and urinary systems have led medical journal *Lancet Oncology* to nickname an area in Naples' northeast hinterland 'the triangle of death'.

The Greater Naples region is home to over 100 Camorra clans, with an estimated 10,000 immediate associates, and an even larger number of clients, dependants and supporters.

Backlash of the Brave

Despite the Mafia's global reach, the war against it soldiers on, with frequent police crackdowns and arrests. After five years on the run, kingpin 'ndrangheta cocaine dealer Nicola Assisi was arrested in Brazil in July 2019. In 2017, police arrested some 116 alleged members of the 'ndrangheta in Italy's largest coordinated operation against the Calabrian mafia to date. Further south in Sicily, the newly-elected head of the Cosa Nostra, Settimo Mineo, was captured in Palermo in December 2018, one of several recent blows to the Sicilian mafia.

Police crackdowns aren't the only concern for the mafia. In recent years a growing number of women within clan families have broken the sacred code of *omertà* (vow of silence) to collaborate with police. Statistics from Italy's Ministry of Justice reveal that the number of women turning their back on their own criminal relatives has more than doubled since 2005. Indeed, this growing defiance of *omertà* is a serious threat to all Italian mafia organisations, whose success relies on fear, loyalty and non-interference.

The *anti-pizzo* (anti protection money) movement was inspired by the defiance of a Palermitan shopkeeper called Libero Grassi, whose anonymous letter to an extortionist was featured on the front page of a local newspaper in 1991. Grassi was murdered seven months later.

AMY LAUGHINGHOUSE/SHUTTERSTOCK ©

Art & Architecture

Southern Italy is Western Europe's cultural attic – a dusty repository filled to the rafters with some of its most ancient and formative art and architecture. From sea to summit, its landscapes are punctuated with Hellenic and Roman ruins, proud medieval castles, Byzantine mosaics and glorious baroque frescoes, not to mention the brushstrokes and buildings of the south's modern milieu. It's an overwhelming heap, so why not start with the undisputed highlights?

Art

Classical Splendour

The Greeks had settled many parts of Sicily and southern Italy as early as the 8th century BCE, naming the region Magna Graecia (Greater Greece) and building great cities such as Syracuse and Taranto. These cities were famous for their magnificent temples, many of which were

Above: Baroque detail, Basilica di Santa Croce (p158), Lecce

Cappella Palatina (p204), Palermo

First published in 1950, Sir EH Gombrich's seminal work *The Story of Art* gives a wonderful, accessible overview of the history of Italian art.

decorated with sculptures modelled on, or inspired by, masterpieces by Praxiteles, Lysippus and Phidias.

The Greek colonisers were equally deft at ceramics, adorning vases with painted scenes from daily life, mythology and Greek theatre. Some of the most vivid examples are the 4th-century-BCE phylax vases, with larger-than-life characters and costumes that depict scenes from phylax plays, a type of ancient southern Italian farce.

In art, as in so many other realms, the Romans looked to the Greeks for examples of best practice, and sculpture, architecture and painting flourished during their reign. Yet, the art produced in Rome was different in many ways from the Greek art that influenced it. Essentially secular, it focused less on harmony and form and more on accurate representation, mainly through sculptural portraits. Innumerable versions of Pompey, Titus and Augustus all show a similar visage, proving that the artists were seeking verisimilitude in their representations, and not just glorification.

Wealthy Roman citizens also dabbled in the arts, building palatial villas and adorning them with statues looted from the Greek world or copied from Hellenic originals. You'll find many fine examples in Syracuse's Museo Archeologico Paolo Orsi, including the celebrated *Venere Anadiomene,* a 1st-century Roman copy depicting a voluptuous goddess of love. Status-conscious Romans didn't stop there, lavishing floors with mosaics and walls with vivid frescoes. Outstanding mosaics continue to enthral at Sicily's Villa Romana del Casale, Pompeii, Herculaneum and Naples' Museo Archeologico Nazionale. Pompeii itself claims the world's largest ancient wall fresco, a restored wonder inside the Villa dei Misteri.

The Glitter of Byzantine

In 330, Emperor Constantine, a convert to Christianity, made the ancient city of Byzantium his capital and renamed it Constantinople. The city became the great cultural and artistic centre of Christianity and it remained so up to the time of the Renaissance, though its influence on the art of that period was never as fundamental as that of the art of ancient Rome.

Artistically, the Byzantine period was notable for its extraordinary mosaic work and – to a lesser extent – its painting. Its art was influenced by the decoration of the Roman catacombs and the early Christian churches, as well as by the Oriental Greek style, with its love of rich decoration and luminous colour.

As a major transit point on the route between Constantinople and Rome, Puglia and Basilicata were exposed to Byzantine's Eastern aesthetics. Indeed, the art that most encapsulates these regions are its 10th- and 11th-century Byzantine frescoes, hidden away in locked chapels dotted across their expanse. There is an incredible concentration in Matera, the most fantastic of which are found in the monastic complex of Chiesa di Madonna delle Virtù and Chiesa di San Nicola del Greci. Impressive examples in Puglia include the lively frescoes inside Otranto's Chiesa di San Pietro.

In Sicily, Byzantine, Norman and Saracen influences fused to create a distinct regional style showcased in the mosaic-encrusted splendour of Palermo's Cappella Palatina inside the Palazzo dei Normanni, not to mention the cathedrals of Monreale and Cefalù.

Giotto & the 'Rebirth' of Italian Art

Italy's Byzantine painters were adept with light and shade, but it would take Florentine painter Giotto di Bondone (c 1266–1337) to break the spell of conservatism and venture into a new world of naturalism. He is best known for his frescoes in Padua and Assisi, but faded fragments of his work survive in Naples' Castel Nuovo and Basilica di Santa Chiara.

Giotto and the painters of the Sienese School introduced many innovations in art: the exploration of perspective and proportion, a new interest in realistic portraiture and the beginnings of a new tradition of landscape painting. The influx of Eastern scholars fleeing Constantinople in the wake of its fall to the Ottoman Turkish Muslims in 1453 prompted a renewed interest in classical learning and humanist philosophy. Coupled with the increasingly ambitious, competitive nature of northern Italy's city states, these developments would culminate in the Renaissance.

Centred in Florence in the 15th century, and Rome and Venice in the 16th century, the Renaissance was slower to catch on in southern Italy, which was caught up in the power struggles between its French and Spanish rulers. One of the south's few Renaissance masters was Antonello da Messina (1430–79), whose luminous works include *Virgin Annunciate* (1474–77) in Palermo's Galleria Regionale della Sicilia and *Annunciation* (1474) in Syracuse's Galleria Regionale di Palazzo Bellomo.

Bad Boys & the Baroque

With the advent of the baroque, it was the south's time to shine. Under 17th-century Spanish rule, Naples was transformed into Europe's biggest city. Swelling crowds and counter-Reformation fervour sparked a building boom, with taller-than-ever *palazzi* (mansions) and showcase churches sprouting across the city. Ready to adorn these new landmarks was a brash, arrogant and fiery league of artists, ditching Renaissance restraint for baroque exuberance.

Click on to www. exibart.com (in Italian) for up-to-date listings of art exhibitions across Italy. Exhibitions and events can be searched for by region, and the site also includes exhibition reviews, articles and interviews.

ART & ARCHITECTURE ART

Best for Baroque

Lecce (Puglia)

Noto (Sicily)

Ragusa (Sicily)

Naples (Campania)

MASTERS OF THE NEAPOLITAN BAROQUE

Michelangelo Merisi da Caravaggio (1573–1610) Bridging Mannerism and the baroque, Caravaggio injected raw emotion and foreboding shadow into his work. His greatest masterpiece the multiscene *Le sette opere di Misericordia* (Seven Acts of Mercy; 1607), in Naples' Pio Monte della Misericordia.

Giuseppe de Ribera (1591–1652) Though Spanish born, most of this bullying painter's finest work was created in southern Italy, including his dramatic *St Jerome* (1626) and *Apollo and Marsyas* (c 1637), both in the Museo di Capodimonte.

Cosimo Fanzago (1591–1678) This revered sculptor, decorator and architect cut marble into the most whimsical forms, producing luscious, inlaid spectacles. Naples' Certosa di San Martino aside, his beautiful high altar in Naples' Chiesa di San Domenico Maggiore is not to be missed.

Mattia Preti (1613–99) Dubbed 'Il Cavaliere Calabrese' (The Calabrian Knight), Preti infused thunderous, apocalyptic scenes with a deep, affecting humanity. Seek out his *Feast of Absalom* (c 1670) in the Museo di Capodimonte.

Luca Giordano (1632–1705) Affectionately nicknamed *Luca fa presto* (Luca does it quickly) for his dexterous ways with a brush. Fabulous frescoes aside, his canvas creations include *Apollo and Marsyas* (c 1660) in the Museo di Capodimonte.

Francesco Solimena (1657–1747) Lavish and grandiose compositions define this icon's work. One of his best is the operatic fresco *Expulsion of Eliodoro from the Temple* (1725) in Naples' Chiesa del Gesù Nuovo.

Giuseppe Sanmartino (1720–93) Arguably the finest sculptor of his time, Sanmartino's ability to breathe life into his creations won him a legion of fans, including the bizarre alchemist prince, Raimondo di Sangro.

The main influence on 17th-century Neapolitan art was Milanese-born Caravaggio (1573–1610). A controversial character, he escaped to Naples in 1606 after killing a man in Rome; although he only stayed for a year, his impact on the city was huge. Caravaggio's dramatic depiction of light and shade, his supreme draughtsmanship and his naturalist style had an electrifying effect on the city's younger artists. One look at Caravaggio's *Flagellazione* (Flagellation; 1607–10) in Naples' Museo di Capodimonte, his *Le sette opere di Misericordia* (Seven Acts of Mercy; c 1607) in the Pio Monte della Misericordia, or his swan song *Martirio di Sant'Orsola* (Martyrdom of St Ursula) in the city's Galleria d'Italia – Palazzo Zevallos Stigliano and you'll understand why.

One of Caravaggio's greatest fans was artist Giuseppe (or Jusepe) de Ribera (1591–1652), whose combination of shadow, colour and gloomy naturalism is brilliantly executed in his masterpiece *Pietà* (1637), which is hanging in Naples' Certosa e Museo di San Martino. Merciless to the extreme, Lo Spagnoletto (The Little Spaniard, as Ribera was known) reputedly won a commission for the Cappella del Tesoro in Naples' Duomo by poisoning his rival Domenichino (1581–1641), as well as wounding the assistant of a second competitor, Guido Reni (1575–1642). The Duomo would be adorned with the frescoes of a number of rising stars, among them Giovanni Lanfranco (1582–1647) and Luca Giordano (1632–1705).

A fledgling apprentice to Ribera, Naples-born Giordano found great inspiration in the brushstrokes of Mattia Preti (1613–99). By the second half of the 17th century, Giordano would become the single most important artist in Naples. His finest fresco, the *Triumph of Judith,* decorates the treasury ceiling of the Certosa di San Martino's church.

In *M: The Man Who Became Caravaggio,* Peter Robb gives a passionate personal assessment of the artist's paintings and a colourful account of Caravaggio's life, arguing he was murdered for having sex with the pageboy of a high-ranking Maltese aristocrat.

Certosa di San Martino (p75), Naples

Contemporary Movements

Of the many movements that shaped Italy's 20th-century art scene, few match the radical innovation of Arte Povera (Poor Art). Emerging from the economic and political instability of the 1960s, its artists aimed to blur the boundary between art and life. Using everyday materials, ranging from painting and photography to installations, they created works that put the viewer at the centre, triggering personal memories and associations. The movement would ultimately pave the way for contemporary installation art. Its leading practitioners included Mario Merz (1925–2003), Luciano Fabro (1936–2007) and Giovanni Anselmo (b 1934), the latter's sculptures inspired by the geological forces of Stromboli. Another icon of the scene was the Greek-born Jannis Kounellis (b 1936–2017), whose installations often focused on the disintegration of culture in the modern world. Naples' MADRE contains a fine collection of Kounellis' creations, as well as other Arte Povera works. Among the wittiest is Michelangelo Pistoletto's *Venere degli stracci* (Venus of the Rags), in which a Greek goddess contemplates a pile of modern hand-me-downs.

Reacting against Arte Povera's conceptual tendencies was the 'Transavanguardia' movement of the late 1970s and 1980s, which refocused attention on painting and sculpture in a traditional (primarily figurative) sense. Among its leading artists are Mimmo Paladino (b 1948) and Francesco Clemente (b 1952). Both of these Campanian artists are represented in Naples' Novecento a Napoli, a museum dedicated to 20th-century southern Italian art.

While most of Italy's current crop of internationally renowned artists are from northern and central Italy, one southern standout is Pietro Roccasalva (b 1970). The Sicilian artist is famous for using painting as the orbital centre in works that often also include sculpture, performance and video. Many of these creations focus on Roccasalva's fascination with iconography, motion and simulacrum in painting.

One of the few well-known female artists of the Italian Renaissance was Artemisia Gentileschi (1593–1652), whose style is reminiscent of Caravaggio's. One of her most famous paintings, the intensely vengeful *Judith and Holofernes*, hangs inside Naples' Museo di Capodimonte.

Top: Chiesa del Gesù Nuovo (p74), Naples

Bottom: Hilltop theatre, Segesta (p262)

Architecture

Ancient Legacies

One word describes the buildings of ancient southern Italy: monumental. The Greeks invented the architectural orders (Doric, Ionic and Corinthian) and used them to great effect in once-mighty cities like Akragas (modern-day Agrigento), Catania and Syracuse. More than two millennia later, the soaring temples of Segesta, Selinunte, the Valley of the Temples and Paestum confirm not only the ancient Greeks' power but also their penchant for harmonious proportion. This skill also underscored their sweeping theatres, the finest of which still stand in Syracuse, Taormina and Segesta.

Having learned a few valuable lessons from the Greeks, the Romans refined architecture to such a degree that their building techniques, designs and mastery of harmonious proportion underpin most of the world's architecture and urban design to this day. In Brindisi a brilliant white column marks one end of the Via Appia – the ancient cross-country road connecting Rome to east-coast Brindisi. In Pozzuoli the Romans erected the Anfiteatro Flavio, the empire's third-largest arena and the very spot where Roman authorities had planned to feed San Gennaro to hungry bears. (In the end, they opted to behead the Christian at the nearby Solfatara crater.)

Medieval Fusion

Following on from Byzantine architecture and its mosaic-encrusted churches was Romanesque, a style that found four regional forms in Italy: Lombard, Pisan, Florentine and Sicilian Norman. All displayed an emphasis on width and the horizontal lines of a building rather than height, and featured church groups with *campaniles* (bell towers) and baptisteries that were separate to the church. Surfacing in the 11th century, the Sicilian Norman style encompassed an exotic mix of Norman, Saracen and Byzantine influences, from marble columns to Islamic-inspired pointed arches to glass tessera detailing. The form is clearly visible in the two-toned masonry and 13th-century bell tower of Amalfi's Cattedrale di Sant'Andrea, but one of its greatest examples is the cathedral of Monreale, just outside Palermo.

With the 12th and 13th centuries came the Gothic aesthetic. The Italians didn't embrace this style as enthusiastically as the French, Germans and Spanish did. Its flying buttresses, grotesque gargoyles and over-the-top decorations were just too far from the classical ideal that was (and still is) bred in the Italian bone. This said, the Gothic style did leave its mark in southern Italy, albeit in the muted version encapsulated by Naples' Chiesa di San Lorenzo Maggiore and Chiesa di San Domenico Maggiore, and Palermo's Palazzo Bellomo. The south's most striking Gothic icon, however, is Puglia's Castel del Monte; its Italianate windows, Islamic floor mosaics and Roman triumphal entrance attest to the south's flair for absorbing foreign influence.

Baroque: the Golden Age

Just as Renaissance restraint redefined Italy's north, the wild theatricality of 17th- and 18th-century baroque revamped the south. Encouraging the makeover was the Catholic Church, for whom baroque's awe-inducing qualities were the perfect weapon against the Reformation and its less-is-more philosophy. Deploying swirls of frescoes, gilt and polychromatic marble, churches like Naples' Chiesa del Gesù Nuovo and Chiesa di San Gregorio Armeno turned Catholicism into a no-holds-barred spectacular.

ART & ARCHITECTURE ARCHITECTURE

Italy's dedicated art police, the Comando Carabinieri Tutela Patrimonio Culturale, tackles the looting of Italy's priceless heritage. It's estimated that over 100,000 ancient tombs have been ransacked by *tombaroli* (tomb raiders) alone; the contents are often sold to private and public collectors around the world.

ARCHITECTURE SPEAK: 101

Do you know your transept from your triclinium? Demystify some common architectural terms with the following bite-size list:

Apse Usually a large recess or niche built on a semicircular or polygonal ground plan and vaulted with a half dome. In a church or temple, it may include an altar.

Baldachin (Baldacchino) A permanent, often elaborately decorated canopy of wood or stone above an altar, throne, pulpit or statue.

Balustrade A stone railing formed of a row of posts (called balusters) topped by a continuous coping, and commonly flanking baroque stairs, balconies and terraces.

Impluvium A small ornamental pool, often used as the centrepiece of atriums in ancient Roman houses.

Latrine A Roman-era public convenience, lined with rows of toilet seats and often adorned with frescoes and marble.

Narthex A portico or lobby at the front of an early Christian church or basilica.

Necropolis Burial ground outside the city walls in antiquity and the early Christian era.

Oratory A small room or chapel in a church reserved for private prayer.

Transept A section of a church running at right angles to the main body of the church.

Triclinium The dining room in a Roman house.

Inlaid marble would become a dominant special effect, adorning everything from tombs and altars to floors and entire chapel walls. The form's undisputed master was Cosimo Fanzago (1591–1678), an occasionally violent sculptor whose masterpieces would include Naples' Certosa di San Martino's church, a mesmerising kaleidoscope of colour, geometry and arresting precision.

In Puglia's Salento region, *barocco leccese* (Lecce baroque) saw the style reach extraordinary new heights. Local limestone was carved into lavish decorative detail around porticoes, windows, balconies and loggias, themselves crowned with human and zoomorphic figures as well as a riot of gargoyles, flora, fruit, columns and cornices. The leading exponents of the style were Gabriele Riccardi (1524–82) and Francesco Antonio Zimbalo (1567-1631), but it was Francesco's grandson Giuseppe Zimbalo (1620–1710), nicknamed Lo Zingarello (The Little Gypsy), who was its most exuberant disciple. Among his greatest designs is the upper facade of Lecce's Basilica di Santa Croce.

It would take an earthquake in 1632 to seal Sicily's baroque legacy. Faced with destruction, ambitious architects set to work rebuilding the towns and cities of the island's southeast, among them Noto, Modica and Ragusa. Grid-patterned streets were laid and spacious piazzas were lined with confident, curvaceous buildings. The result was a highly idiosyncratic *barocco siciliano* (Sicilian baroque), best known for its cheeky stone *putti* (cherubs), wrought-iron balustrades and grand external staircases. Equally idiosyncratic was the use of dramatic, centrally placed church belfries, often shooting straight above the central pediment. Two of the finest examples are Ragusa's Cattedrale di San Giorgio and Modica's Chiesa di San Giorgio, both designed by the prolific Rosario Gagliardi (1698-1762).

Sicily's most celebrated baroque architect, however, was be Giovanni Battista Vaccarini (1702-68). Trained in Rome, Vaccarini would dedicate three decades of his life to rebuilding earthquake-stricken Catania, using the region's volcanic black rock to dramatic effect in Piazza del Duomo. His reputation would see him join forces with Neapolitan starchitect Luigi Vanvitelli (1700–73) in the creation of Italy's gargantuan baroque epilogue, the Reggia di Caserta, 30km north of Naples.

Sorrento (p105)

EL GRECO 1973 / SHUTTERSTOCK ©

Survival Guide

Directory A–Z

Accessible Travel

Southern Italy is not easy for travellers with disabilities. Cobblestone streets and pavements blocked by parked cars and scooters make getting around difficult for wheelchair users. While many buildings have lifts, they are not always wide enough for wheelchairs. Overall, not a lot has been done to make life easier for hearing- or vision-impaired travellers either.

That said, awareness of the importance of accessibility and a culture of inclusion is steadily spreading, and a growing number of museums and archaeological sites are becoming more accessible, with wheelchair-friendly ramps and pathways. Among these are Pompeii in Campania and Villa Romana del Casale and Valley of the Temples in Sicily.

If you have an obvious disability and/or appropriate ID, many museums and galleries offer free admission for yourself and a companion.

Resources

➡ Village for All (www.village forall.net/en) lists a small number of accommodation options in southern Italy suitable for those with limited mobility.

➡ Tourism without Barriers (www.turismosenzabarriere. it) has a limited database of accessible accommodation in southern Italy.

➡ You can find a list (in Italian) of accessible beaches at www.fondazioneserono. org/disabilita/spiagge-accessibili/spiagge-accessibili.

➡ Download Lonely Planet's free Accessible Travel guide from http://shop.lonely planet.com/accessible-travel.

Discount Cards

Italy's state museums and sites are free for EU citizens under the age of 18. Discounts also apply to people aged from 18 to 25, and to seniors over the age of 65.

Some cities or regions offer their own discount passes, such as the **Campania Arte-card** (www.campani artecard.it), which provides free public transport and free or reduced admission to many museums and archaeological sites.

In numerous places around southern Italy, you can also save money by purchasing a *biglietto cumulativo*, a ticket that covers admission to a number of associated sights.

Electricity

Italian plugs have two or three round pins; travellers from countries with a different plug type should bring an adapter.

The current is 230V, 50Hz.

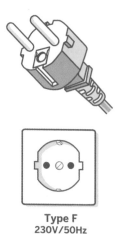

**Type F
230V/50Hz**

Type L
220V/50Hz

COVID-19 REGULATIONS

In 2021, Italy introduced the Green Pass, or *certificazione verde*, a digital or paper certificate showing that the holder has been vaccinated, tested negative or recovered from COVID-19. This pass allows for use of public transport, access to cafes and restaurants for dining indoors, visiting museums and galleries, and attending festivals and sports events.

At the time of writing travellers from other EU countries could use the EU Digital COVID Certificate, and certification of vaccination status for citizens of other nations including Canada, Israel, Japan, Australia, New Zealand, the UK and the US was also recognised. Check current details carefully on the Italian National Tourism Board's website (www.italia.it), including the need to complete a Passenger Location Form.

Health

Italy has a public health system (Servizio Sanitario Nazionale, SSN) that is legally bound to provide emergency care to everyone.

EU nationals are entitled to reduced-cost, sometimes free, medical care with a European Health Insurance Card (EHIC), available from your home health authority. Non-EU citizens should take out medical insurance.

If you need insurance, make sure to get a policy that covers you for the worst possible scenario, such as an accident requiring emergency repatriation.If you are paying for medical services out of your own pocket, always ask for a receipt as you will need to show this to your travel-insurance provider.

Also, check if there is a reciprocal arrangement between your country and Italy. If there is, you may be covered for essential medical treatment and some subsidised medications. Australia, for instance, has such an agreement; carry your Medicare card.

Availability & Cost of Health Care

Health care is readily available throughout southern Italy, but standards can vary significantly.

Pharmacists can advise on medical matters and sell over-the-counter medications for minor illnesses. They can also point you in the right direction if you need more specialised help. In large city-centre pharmacies *(farmacie)*, you're more likely to find someone who speaks a little English.

Pharmacies are marked by a green cross and generally keep shop hours (typically from 8.30am to 7.30pm Monday to Friday and on Saturday mornings). Outside these hours, they open on a rotational basis. When closed, a pharmacy is legally required to post a list of places open in the vicinity.

In the larger cities, English-speaking doctors are often available for house calls or appointments through private clinics.

For emergency treatment, head to the *pronto soccorso* (casualty department) of an *ospedale* (public hospital), where you can also get emergency dental treatment.

If you need an ambulance anywhere in Italy, call 118.

Environmental Hazards

Italian beaches are occasionally inundated with jellyfish. Their stings are painful but not dangerous. Dousing them in vinegar will deactivate any stingers that have not fired. Calamine lotion, antihistamines and analgesics may reduce the reaction and relieve pain.

Italy's only dangerous snake, the viper, is found throughout Puglia and Basilicata. To minimise the possibility of being bitten, always wear boots, socks and long trousers when walking through undergrowth where snakes may be present. Don't put your hands into holes and crevices, and be careful when collecting firewood. Viper bites do not cause instantaneous death and an antivenin is widely available in pharmacies. Keep the victim calm and still, wrap the bitten limb tightly, as you would for a sprained ankle, and attach a splint to immobilise it.

Always check all over your body if you have been walking through a potentially tick-infested area. Ticks can cause skin infections and other more serious complications such as Lyme disease and tick-borne encephalitis. If a tick is found attached, press down around the tick's head with tweezers, grab the head and gently pull upwards. Avoid pulling the rear of the body as this may squeeze the tick's gut contents through the attached mouth into the skin, increasing the risk of infection and disease. Lyme disease begins with the spreading of a bull's-eye rash at the site of the bite, accompanied by fever, headache, extreme fatigue, aching joints and muscles, and severe neck stiffness. If untreated, symptoms usually disappear, but disorders of the nervous system, heart and joints can develop later. Treatment works best early in the illness: medical help should be sought. Symptoms of tick-borne encephalitis include blotches around the bite, which is sometimes pale in the middle, and headaches, stiffness and other flu-like symptoms (as well as tiredness) appearing a week or two after the bite. Again, medical help must be sought.

Leishmaniasis is a group of parasitic diseases transmitted by sandflies and found in coastal parts of Puglia. Cutaneous leishmaniasis affects the skin and causes ulceration and disfigurement; visceral leishmaniasis affects the internal organs. Avoiding sandfly bites by covering up and using repellent is the best precaution.

Insurance

A travel-insurance policy to cover theft, loss and medical problems is highly recommended. It may also cover you for cancellation of and delays to your travel arrangements.

Paying for your ticket with a credit card can often provide limited travel accident insurance, and you may be able to reclaim the payment if the operator doesn't deliver. Ask your credit-card company what it will cover.

Internet Access

Public wi-fi hotspots are fairly common in cafes, bars and eateries, and most hotels and B&Bs offer free wi-fi. In accommodation listings the internet icon is used to indicate that there is a computer available for guest use, while the wi-fi icon indicates that there is wi-fi access. Wi-fi is specifically mentioned in reviews only when charges apply.

Language Courses

Italian language courses are run by private schools and universities throughout Italy. For a list of language schools around the country, see Saena Iulia (www.saenaiulia.it); click on 'Schools in Italy'.

Italian Foreign Ministry (www.esteri.it) publishes a list on its website of the 83 worldwide branches of the Istituto Italiano di Cultura (IIC), a government-sponsored organisation promoting Italian culture and language. It's an excellent resource for studying Italian before you leave or finding out more about language-learning opportunities in Italy. Locations include Australia (Melbourne and Sydney), the UK (London and Edinburgh), Ireland (Dublin), Canada (Toronto and Montreal), and the USA (Los Angeles, San Francisco, Chicago, New York and Washington, DC). Click on 'Foreign Policy', then 'Culture Diplomacy' and 'The Network of Italian Cultural Institutes'.

Legal Matters

Southern Italy is relatively safe and the average tourist will only have a brush with the law if they need to report a theft. If you do have something stolen and you want to claim it on insurance, you must make a statement to the police; insurance companies won't pay up without proof of a crime.

Drugs & Alcohol

➡ If you're caught with what the police deem to be a dealable quantity of hard or soft drugs, you risk a prison sentence.

➡ The legal limit for blood alcohol when driving is 0.05% and random breath tests do occur. Penalties for driving under the influence of alcohol can be severe.

Police

The Italian police force is divided into three main bodies: the *polizia,* who wear navy-blue jackets; the *carabinieri,* in a black uniform with a red stripe; and the grey-clad *guardia di finanza* (fiscal police), responsible for fighting tax evasion and drug smuggling. If you run into trouble, you're most likely to end up dealing with the *polizia* or *carabinieri*. If, however, you land a parking ticket, you'll need to speak to the *vigili urbani* (traffic wardens).

To contact the police in an emergency, dial 112 or 113.

POLICE DEPARTMENT	DEPARTMENT RESPONSIBILITIES
Polizia statale (state police)	Thefts, visa extensions and permits
Carabinieri (military police)	General crime, public order, drug law enforcement
Vigili urbani (local traffic police)	Parking tickets, towed cars
Guardia di finanza	Tax evasion, drug smuggling
Corpo forestale	Environmental protection

Your Rights

➡ You should be given verbal and written notice of the charges laid against you within 24 hours by arresting officers.

➡ You have no right to a phone call upon arrest, though the police will inform your family with your consent. You may also ask the police to inform your embassy or consulate.

➡ The prosecutor must apply to a magistrate for you to be held in preventive custody awaiting trial within 48 hours of arrest.

➡ You also have the right to a lawyer. If you do not know of any local lawyers, the police should ask the local bar council for a state-appointed lawyer *(difensore di ufficio)* to be appointed.

➡ You have the right not to respond to questions without the presence of a lawyer. If the magistrate orders preventive custody, you have the right to contest this within the following 10 days.

LGBTIQ+ Travellers

Homosexuality is legal and same-sex civil unions are recognised in Italy. Although attitudes towards LGBTIQ+ people have improved significantly in recent times, it remains fairly conservative and discretion is still wise. Overt displays of affection by LGBTIQ+ couples can attract a negative response, especially in smaller towns.

You'll find gay scenes in Naples, Catania, Palermo, Syracuse and Bari. Both Taormina in Sicily and Gallipoli in Puglia are popular gay holiday spots in the summer.

Summertime pride parades take place annually in Naples (www.napolipride. org), Bari, Palermo (www. palermopride.it), Catania (www.facebook.com/ Cataniagaypride) and Syracuse (www.facebook.com/ siracusapride).

Online resources include the following (mostly in Italian):

Arcigay (www.arcigay.it) Italy's largest gay organisation, with branches in numerous southern cities, including Naples, Salerno, Lecce, Bari, Reggio Calabria, Messina, Catania, Syracuse, Ragusa and Palermo.

Coordinamento Lesbiche Italiano (CLR; www.clrbp.it) The national organisation for lesbians, holding regular literary meetings, film festivals and other events.

Gay.it (www.gay.it) Website featuring LGBTIQ+ news, feature articles and gossip.

Guida Gay Italia (www.guidagay. it) Details on gay-friendly bars, clubs, beaches and hotels.

Pride (www.prideonline.it) National monthly magazine of art, music, politics and gay culture.

Spartacus World (www. spartacus.gayguide.travel/ goingout/europe/italy) Lists male-only venues in southern Italy and further afield.

Maps

Touring Club Italiano (www. touringclub.com) is Italy's largest map publisher and offers a comprehensive 1:200,000, 592-page road atlas of Italy (€54.90), as well as 1:400,000 maps of northern, central and southern Italy (€8.50). It also produces regional maps at 1:200,000 (€8.50), as well as a series of walking guides with maps (from €14.90).

Media

Newspapers Key national dailies include centre-left *la Repubblica* (www.repubblica.it) and its conservative rival *Corriere della Sera* (www.corriere.it). For the Vatican's take on affairs, *L'Osservatore Romano* (www. osservatoreromano.va) is the Holy See's official newspaper.

Television The main terrestrial channels are Rai 1, 2 and 3,

run by Rai (www.rai.it), Italy's state-owned national broadcaster, and Canale 5, Italia 1 and Rete 4, run by Mediaset (www.mediaset.it), the commercial TV company founded and still partly owned by Silvio Berlusconi.

Radio As well as the principal Rai channels (Radiouno, Radiodue, Radiotre), there are hundreds of commercial radio stations operating across the country. Popular Rome-based stations include Radio Capital (www. capital.it) and Radio Città Futura (www.radiocittafutura.it). Vatican Radio (www.radiovaticana.va) broadcasts in Italian, English and other languages.

Money

Currency

Italy's currency is the euro (€). The euro is divided into 100 cents. Coin denominations are one, two, five, 10, 20 and 50 cents, €1 and €2. Note denominations are €5, €10, €20, €50, €100, €200 and €500.

ATMs

➡ ATMs (known as 'Bancomat' in Italy) are widely available throughout the country and most will accept cards tied to the Visa, MasterCard, Cirrus and Maestro systems. The Italian term for international cash withdrawal is *prelievo internazionale*, although most ATMs have multilingual screens.

➡ If an ATM rejects your card, try another one before assuming the problem is with your card.

Credit Cards

Major cards such as Visa, MasterCard, Eurocard, Cirrus and Eurocheque are widely accepted. Amex is also recognised, although it's less common than Visa or MasterCard.

Opening Hours

Opening hours can vary throughout the year, especially at tourist attractions. 'Summer' times generally refer to the period from April to September or October, while 'winter' times generally run from October or November to March.

Banks 8.30am to 1.30pm and 2.45pm to 4pm Monday to Friday.

Restaurants noon to 3pm and 7.30pm to 11pm or midnight; many close one day per week.

Cafes 7am to 8pm, later if offering evening bar service.

Bars and clubs 10pm to 4am or 5am.

Shops 9.30am to 1.30pm and 4pm to 7.30pm or 8pm Monday to Saturday. Some also open Sunday and several close Monday morning.

Post

Poste Italiane (☏803 160; www.poste.it), Italy's postal system, is not particularly efficient, though letters and packages do generally arrive sooner or later.

Stamps (*francobolli*) are available at post offices and authorised tobacconists (look for the official *tabacchi* sign, a big 'T', often white on black), which you'll find in every town and village.

For more important items, use registered mail (*posta raccomandata*) or insured mail (*posta assicurata*); the cost depends on the value of the object being sent.

Postal Rates & Services

The cost of sending a letter by *aerea* (airmail) depends on its weight and size and where it is being sent. Most people use *posta prioritaria* (priority mail), Italy's most efficient mail service, guaranteed to deliver letters sent to Europe within three working days and to the rest of the world within four to nine working days.

Using *posta prioritaria*, mail up to 50g costs €3.50 within Europe, €4.50 to Africa, Asia and the Americas, and €5.50 to Australia and New Zealand. Mail weighing 51g to 100g costs €4.30 within Europe, €5.20 to Africa, Asia and the Americas, and €7.10 to Australia and New Zealand.

Public Holidays

Most Italians take their annual holiday in August, deserting the cities for the cooler seaside or mountains. This means that many businesses and shops close for at least part of the month, especially around the Feast of the Assumption (Ferragosto) on 15 August. Easter is another busy period, with many resort hotels opening for the season the week before Easter.

Italian schools close for three months in summer, from mid-June to mid-September, for two weeks at Christmas and for a week at Easter.

Individual towns have public holidays to celebrate the feasts of their patron saints. National public holidays include the following:

New Year's Day (Capodanno) 1 January

Epiphany (Epifania) 6 January

Easter Sunday (Pasqua) March/April

Easter Monday (Pasquetta) March/April

Liberation Day (Giorno della Liberazione) 25 April

Labour Day (Festa del Lavoro) 1 May

Republic Day (Festa della Repubblica) 2 June

Feast of the Assumption (Ferragosto) 15 August

All Saints' Day (Festa di Ognissanti) 1 November

Feast of the Immaculate Conception (Festa della Immaculata Concezione) 8 December

Christmas Day (Natale) 25 December

Boxing Day (Festa di Santo Stefano) 26 December

Telephone
Domestic Calls

➜ Italian area codes begin with 0 and consist of up to four digits. They are an integral part of all phone numbers and must be dialled even when calling locally.

➜ Mobile-phone numbers begin with a three-digit prefix starting with a 3.

➜ Toll-free numbers are known as *numeri verdi* and usually start with 800.

➜ Some six-digit national-rate numbers are also in use (such as those for Alitalia and Trenitalia).

International Calls

➜ To call Italy from abroad, dial your country's international access code, then Italy's country code (39), followed by the area code of the location you want (including the first zero) and the rest of the number.

➜ To call abroad from Italy, dial 00, then the country code, followed by the full number.

➜ Avoid making international calls from hotels, as rates are high.

➜ The cheapest way to call is to use an app such as Skype or Viber, connecting through the wi-fi at your accommodation. Wi-fi is also available at numerous cafes and bars.

Mobile Phones

➜ Italian mobile phones operate on the GSM 900/1800 network, which is compatible with the rest of Europe and Australia but not always with the North American GSM or CDMA systems – check with your service provider.

➜ The cheapest way of using your mobile is to buy a prepaid (*prepagato*) Italian SIM card. TIM (Telecom Italia Mobile; www.tim.it), Wind (www.wind.it), Vodafone (www.vodafone.it) and Tre (www.tre.it) all offer SIM cards and have retail outlets across southern Italy. You can then top up as you go, either online, at one of your provider's shops, or at tobacconists and bars selling recharge cards (*ricariche*).

➜ Note that by Italian law all SIM cards must be registered in Italy, so make sure you have your passport or ID card when you buy one.

Time

Italy is one hour ahead of GMT. Daylight-saving time starts on the last Sunday in March, when clocks are put forward one hour. Clocks go back an hour on the last Sunday in October. Italy operates on the 24-hour clock, so rather than 6.30pm, you'll see 18.30 on transport timetables.

Toilets

Beyond major tourist sites, archaeological parks and train stations, there are few public toilets in southern Italy. If you're caught short, the best thing to do is to nip into a cafe or bar. The polite thing to do is to order something at the bar. You may need to pay to use public toilets at some venues (usually €0.50 to €1). In many places public loos are pretty grim; go armed with some tissues.

Tourist Information

The quality of tourist offices varies dramatically. One office might have enthusiastic staff, another might be indifferent. Most offices offer at least a few brochures, maps and leaflets, even if they're uninterested in helping in any other way. Outside major cities and international tourist areas, it's fairly unusual for the staff to speak English.

Four tiers of tourist office exist: local, provincial, regional and national.

Local & Provincial Tourist Offices

Despite their different names, provincial and local offices offer similar services. All deal directly with the public and most will respond to written and telephone requests for information. Staff can usually provide a city map, lists of hotels and information on the major sights.

Main offices are generally open Monday to Friday; some also open on weekends, especially in urban areas or during the peak summer season. Subsidiary information booths (at train stations and airports, for example) may keep slightly different hours.

Regional Tourist Authorities

Regional offices are generally more concerned with planning, budgeting, marketing and promotion than with offering a public information service. However, they still maintain some useful websites.

Basilicata (www.aptbasilicata.it)

Calabria (www.turiscalabria.it)

Campania (http://incampania.com)

Puglia (www.viaggiareinpuglia.it)

Sicily (www.regione.sicilia.it/turismo)

Tourist Offices Abroad

The Italian National Tourist Office (www.enit.it) maintains offices in 28 cities on five continents. Contact information for all offices can be found on its website.

Visas

For up-to-date information on visa requirements, see www.esteri.it/visti.

EU citizens do not need a visa to enter Italy. Nationals of several other countries, including the post-Brexit United Kingdom, Australia, Canada, Israel, Japan, New Zealand and the USA, do not need visas for stays of up to 90 days.

Other people wishing to visit Italy have to apply for a Schengen visa, which allows unlimited travel in Italy and 25 other European countries for a 90-day period. You must apply for a Schengen visa in your country of residence and you cannot apply for more than two in any 12-month period. They are not renewable inside Italy.

Volunteering

Concordia International Volunteer Projects (www.concordiavolunteers.org.uk) Lists opportunities for short-term community-based projects covering the environment, archaeology and the arts.

European Youth Portal (http://europa.eu/youth) Has various links suggesting volunteering options across Europe. Navigate to the Volunteering page.

Legambiente (http://international.legambiente.it) Italy's best-known conservation group offers numerous environmentally focused volunteering opportunities.

World Wide Opportunities on Organic Farms (www.wwoof.it) For a membership fee of €35 this organisation provides a list of farms looking for volunteers.

Women Travellers

In general, southern Italy is a welcoming and safe place for women travellers, including those travelling solo. Cultural stereotypes of Italian men harassing lone foreign women are largely outdated and exaggerated.

That said, eye-to-eye contact remains the norm in Italy's daily flirtatious interplay, and with some men this may segue into overt staring. Usually simply showing a lack of interest is enough to nip unwanted attention in the bud. If ignoring such behaviour doesn't work, politely say that you're waiting for your *marito* (husband) or *fidanzato* (boyfriend) and, if necessary, walk away. If you are visibly in distress, people near you or passersby will generally step in to assist.

If you feel yourself being groped on a crowded bus or metro, a loud *'che schifo!'* (how disgusting!) will draw attention to the incident. Otherwise, take all the usual precautions you would in any other part of the world; avoid wandering around alone late at night, especially in parks and desolate urban areas.

You can report incidents to the police, who are required to press charges.

Work

EU citizens and nationals of Norway, Iceland, Switzerland and Liechtenstein are legally entitled to work in Italy. To stay in the country for more than three months you are simply required to register at your local registry office *(ufficio anagrafe)*.

Non-EU citizens will need a work visa to enter Italy, and a *permesso di soggiorno per lavoro* (permit to stay for work) to stay in the country.

For the visa, you'll first need to secure a job offer. Your prospective employer will then apply for work authorisation for you. If the application is successful, your local Italian embassy or consulate will be informed and you will be issued with a work visa. Note, however, that Italy operates a visa quota system for most occupations, so a visa will only be offered if the relevant quota has not been met by the time your application is processed.

Once in Italy, you'll need to apply for a *permesso di soggiorno* (permit to stay). You'll

have to do this within eight days of arriving in the country. See www.poliziadistato.it for details on the application process.

Italy has reciprocal working-holiday visa agreements with Canada, Australia, New Zealand and South Korea. With this type of visa you can stay in Italy for one year and work for six months. To be eligible you must be aged between 18 and 30. Contact your local Italian embassy for more information.

Popular jobs in Italy include English teaching, either at a language school or as a freelancer. While some language schools take on teachers without professional qualifications, the more reputable (and better-paying) establishments will require you to have a TEFL (Teaching of English as a Foreign Language) certificate.

Useful job-seeker websites for English-language teachers include ESL Employment (www.eslemploy ment.com) and TEFL (www. tefl.org.uk/tefl-jobs-centre).

Au pairing is another popular work option; check www.aupairworld.com for tips and more information on work opportunities.

Transport

GETTING THERE & AWAY

A plethora of airlines link Italy with the rest of the world, and cut-rate carriers have significantly driven down the cost of flights from other European countries. Excellent rail and bus connections, especially with northern Italy, offer efficient overland transport, while car and passenger ferries operate to ports throughout the Mediterranean.

Flights, cars and tours can be booked online at lonely planet.com/bookings.

Entering Italy

All passports should be valid for at least six months beyond your departure date from Italy.

Technically, all foreign visitors to Italy are supposed to register with the local police within eight days of arrival. However, if you're staying in a hotel or hostel you don't need to bother as the hotel will do it for you – this is why they always take your passport details.

By law you are supposed to have your passport or ID card with you at all times.

DEPARTURE TAX

Departure tax is included in the price of a ticket.

Air

Italy's main intercontinental gateways are Rome's **Fiumicino Airport** (Leonardo da Vinci International Airport; ☑06 6 59 51; www.adr.it/fiumicino) and Milan's **Aeroporto Malpensa** (MXP; ☑02 23 23 23; www.milanomalpensa-airport. com; ☒Malpensa Express). Venice's **Marco Polo Airport** (☑flight information 041 260 92 60; www.veniceairport.it; Via Galileo Gallilei 30/1, Tessera) is also served by a handful of intercontinental flights.

Most direct flights into southern Italy are domestic or intra-European, so you may need to change at Rome, Milan or Venice if arriving from outside Europe.

Handy airports in southern Italy include:

Naples International Airport (Capodichino), Naples (www. aeroportodinapoli.it) Alongside Catania Airport, this is southern Italy's busiest airport, with non-stop connections to numerous destinations in Italy, Europe and the UK, as well as to Dubai and (in season) New York. Serviced by Italy's national carrier, Alitalia, and several full-service and budget international airlines, including easyJet, Ryanair and Wizz Air.

Karol Wojtyła Airport, Bari (www.aeroportidipuglia.it) Puglia's main airport, with non-stop flights to numerous cities in Italy, Europe and the UK. Serviced by Alitalia, as well as both full-service and low-cost international carriers.

Brindisi Airport, Brindisi (www. aeroportidipuglia.it) Puglia's second-busiest airport, with non-stop connections to cities in Italy and a limited number of direct flights to European and UK destinations, several of which are seasonal. Flights mostly operated by Ryanair and Alitalia.

Lamezia Terme Airport, Cosenza (www.sacal.it) Calabria's principal airport, with non-stop flights to major Italian cities and a number of European and UK destinations, many of them seasonal. Also operates a summer-only service to Toronto, Canada. Year-round airlines include Alitalia, Ryanair and easyJet.

Fontanarossa Airport, Catania (www.aeroporto.catania.it) Along with Naples, the busiest airport in southern Italy. Offers non-stop flights to other Italian cities, and destinations within Europe and the UK, as well as to Dubai. Serviced by Alitalia and mainly low-cost European airlines.

Falcone-Borsellino Airport, Palermo (www.gesap.it) One of Sicily's two major airports, with frequent connections to other Italian cities as well as non-stop flights to numerous destinations in Europe and the UK, many of which are seasonal. Serviced by Alitalia and a handful of mainly low-cost European carriers.

Vincenzo Florio (Birgi) Airport, Trapani (www.airgest.it) Sicily's third-largest airport, with a handful of routes to other Italian destinations and summer-only flights to numerous European destinations. Flights operated mainly by Alitalia and Ryanair.

CLIMATE CHANGE & TRAVEL

Every form of transport that relies on carbon-based fuel generates CO_2, the main cause of human-induced climate change. Modern travel is dependent on aeroplanes, which might use less fuel per kilometre per person than most cars but travel much greater distances. The altitude at which aircraft emit gases (including CO_2) and particles also contributes to their climate change impact. Many websites offer 'carbon calculators' that allow people to estimate the carbon emissions generated by their journey and, for those who wish to do so, to offset the impact of the greenhouse gases emitted with contributions to portfolios of climate-friendly initiatives throughout the world. Lonely Planet offsets the carbon footprint of all staff and author travel.

Comiso Airport, Comiso (www.aeroportodicomiso.eu) Small airport in southeastern Sicily serviced mainly by Ryanair. Limited non-stop flights to Rome, Milan and Pisa, as well as to Frankfurt and Brussels.

Tickets & Discounts

The internet is the easiest way to locate and book reasonably priced seats.

Full-time students and those aged under 26 may qualify for discounted fares at agencies such as STA Travel (www.statravel.com). Many of these fares require a valid International Student Identity Card (ISIC).

Land

Reaching southern Italy overland involves travelling the entire length of Italy, which can either be an enormous drain on your time or, if you have plenty to spare, a wonderful way of seeing the country. Buses are usually the cheapest option, but services are less frequent and considerably less comfortable than the train.

Border Crossings

Aside from the coast roads linking Italy with France and Slovenia, border crossings into Italy mostly involve tunnels through the Alps (open year-round) or mountain passes (seasonally closed or requiring snow chains).

The list below outlines the major points of entry.

Austria From Innsbruck to Bolzano via A22/E45 (Brenner Pass); Villach to Tarvisio via A23/E55.

France From Nice to Ventimiglia via A10/E80; Modane to Turin via A32/E70 (Fréjus Tunnel); Chamonix to Courmayeur via A5/E25 (Mont Blanc Tunnel).

Slovenia From Sežana to Trieste via SR58/E70.

Switzerland From Martigny to Aosta via SS27/E27 (Grand St Bernard Tunnel); Lugano to Como via A9/E35.

Bus

Eurolines (☑0861 199 19 00; www.eurolines.eu) Italy-bound buses head to Milan, Venice, Florence and Rome, from where Italian train and bus services continue south.

FlixBus (☑02 9475 9208; www.flixbus.it) German-owned company offering both interregional and international routes. Interregional services reach numerous cities and towns in southern Italy, including Naples, Matera, Bari, Brindisi, Alberobello, Lecce, Potenza, Catania, Syracuse and Palermo.

Marozzi (☑080 579 02 11; www.marozzivt.it) Regular connections from Rome to Sorrento and the Amalfi Coast, and from Rome to numerous towns and cities in Puglia and Basilicata, including Bari, Alberobello, Taranto, Gallipoli, Otranto, Lecce and Matera.

Autolinee Miccolis (☑099 470 44 51; www.busmiccolis.it) Runs daily services from Naples to Bari via Pompeii, Salerno, Potenza and Matera. It also runs

from Naples to Taranto, Brindisi and Lecce via Potenza.

Marino (www.marinobus.it) Runs regular services from Naples to Bari, Brindisi, Matera, Lecce and Gallipoli.

Liscio (☑0971 5 46 73; www.autolineeliscio.it) Daily connections from Potenza to Rome. Also runs regularly between Rome and Matera.

Lirosi (☑0966 5 79 01; www.lirosiautoservizi.com) Daily services between Reggio Calabria and Rome.

SAIS Autolinee (☑800 211020; www.saisautolinee.it) Operates long-haul services to Sicily from numerous centres, including Rome, Naples and Bari.

Car & Motorcycle
FROM CONTINENTAL EUROPE

➡ Every vehicle travelling across an international border should display the nationality plate of its country of registration.

➡ Always carry the vehicle's registration certificate and evidence of third-party insurance. If driving an EU-registered vehicle, your home-country insurance is sufficient. Ask your insurer for a European Accident Statement (EAS) form, which can simplify matters in the event of an accident. The form can also be downloaded from http://cartraveldocs.com/european-accident-statement.

→ A European breakdown-assistance policy is a good investment and can be obtained through Italy's national automobile association, the **Automobile Club d'Italia** (ACI; ☑80 31 16, from a foreign mobile 800 116800; www.aci.it).

→ Italy's scenic roads are tailor-made for motorcycle touring, and motorcyclists swarm into the country every summer. With a motorcycle you can often enter restricted-traffic areas in cities. Crash helmets and a motorcycle licence are compulsory.

FROM THE UK

You can take your car to Italy, via France, by ferry or the Eurotunnel Shuttle rail service (www.eurotunnel.com). The latter runs up to four times per hour between Folkestone and Calais (35 minutes) at peak times.

For breakdown assistance, both the AA (www.theaa.com) and the RAC (www.rac.co.uk) offer comprehensive packages covering Italy.

Train

Regular trains on two western lines connect Italy with France (one along the coast and the other from Turin into the French Alps). Trains from Milan head north into Switzerland and on towards the Benelux countries. Further east, two main lines head for the main cities in Central and Eastern Europe. Those crossing the Brenner Pass go to Innsbruck, Stuttgart and Munich. Those crossing at Tarvisio proceed to Vienna, Salzburg and Prague. The main international train line to Slovenia crosses near Trieste.

FROM CONTINENTAL EUROPE

→ The comprehensive European Rail Timetable (UK£19.99, digital version UK£13.99), updated regularly, is available for purchase at https://www.europeanrailtimetable.eu, as well as at a handful of bookshops in the UK and continental Europe (see the website for details).

→ Reservations on international trains to/from Italy are always advisable, and sometimes compulsory.

→ Some international services include transport for private cars.

→ Consider taking long journeys overnight, as the supplemental fare for a sleeper will often cost less than an Italian hotel.

FROM THE UK

→ Trains to Italy from the UK involve a change in France.

→ The high-velocity Eurostar (www.eurostar.com) connects London with Paris, Lyon, Avignon and Marseille. Direct trains to Italy then run from Paris, Lyon and Marseille. Alternatively, you can get a train ticket that includes crossing the Channel by ferry.

→ For fare information and ticket bookings, check out Loco 2 (www.loco2.com), a clear and easy-to-use booking site.

Sea

→ Numerous ferry companies connect southern Italy with ports across the Mediterranean. Some routes only operate in summer, when ticket prices also rise. Fares for vehicles depend on the size of the vehicle.

INTERNATIONAL FERRY ROUTES FROM SOUTHERN ITALY

DESTINATION COUNTRY	DESTINATION PORT(S)	ITALIAN PORT(S)	COMPANY
Albania	Durrës	Bari	Ventouris Ferries, GNV, Adria Ferries
Croatia	Dubrovnik	Bari	Jadrolinija, Montenegro Lines
Greece	Igoumenitsa, Patras	Brindisi	Grimaldi Lines
Greece	Corfu, Igoumenitsa, Patras	Bari	Superfast, Anek Lines
Greece	Corfu, Igoumenitsa, Zakynthos, Cephalonia	Bari	Ventouris Ferries
Malta	Valletta	Pozzallo	Virtu Ferries
Montenegro	Bar	Bari	Montenegro Lines, Jadrolinija
Tunisia	Tunis	Palermo	GNV
Tunisia	Tunis	Palermo, Salerno	Grimaldi Lines

➔ Fares to Greece are generally more expensive from Bari than those available from Brindisi, although unless you're planning on travelling in the Salento, Bari is the more convenient port of arrival and also has better onward links for bus and train travel.

➔ The helpful website www.directferries.co.uk allows you to search routes and compare prices between international ferry companies. Another useful resource for Italy–Greece ferries is www.ferries.gr.

International Ferry Companies Serving Southern Italy

International ferry companies that serve southern Italy include:

Adria Ferries (☑071 5021 1621; www.adriaferries.com)

Anek Lines (☑071 207 23 46; www.anekitalia.com)

Grandi Navi Veloci (GNV) (Grandi Navi Veloci;☑010 209 45 91; www.gnv.it)

Grimaldi Lines (☑081 49 64 44; www.grimaldi-lines.com)

Jadrolinija (☑071 228 41 00; www.jadrolinija.hr)

Montenegro Lines (☑Bar +382 3030 3469; www.montenegro lines.net)

SNAV (☑081 428 55 55; www.snav.it)

Superfast (☑Athens +30 210 891 97 00; www.superfast.com)

Ventouris Ferries (☑080 876 14 51; www.ventouris.gr; Nuova Stazione Marittima di Bari)

Virtu Ferries (☑Catania 095 703 12 11; www.virtuferries.com)

GETTING AROUND

Air

A number of airlines compete with national carrier Alitalia (www.alitalia.com) on domestic routes, among them Air Italy (www.airitaly.

com) and low-cost foreign companies Ryanair (www.ryanair.com), easyJet (www.easyjet.com) and Volotea (www.volotea.com).

Useful websites for comparing fares include www.skyscanner.com and www.kayak.com. Airport taxes are factored into the price of your ticket.

Bicycle

Cycling may be more popular in northern Italy, but it can be just as rewarding south of Rome. Cyclo-trekking is particularly popular in the Murgia and the Promontorio del Gargano in Puglia. Cycling is also very popular in the Salentine cities of Lecce, Galatina, Gallipoli and Otranto, with more challenging itineraries in Basilicata's Parco Nazionale del Pollino and on Sicily's hilly terrain.

The following tips will help ensure a stress-free pedal:

➔ If bringing your own bike, you'll need to disassemble and pack it for the journey. You may need to pay an airline surcharge.

➔ Make sure to bring tools, spare parts, a helmet, lights and a secure bike lock.

➔ Bikes are prohibited on Italian autostrade (motorways).

➔ Avoid cycling in large cities like Naples, Palermo and Catania, where unruly traffic makes cycling dangerous. Cycling along the Amalfi Coast is another bad idea (blind corners and sheer drops).

➔ Bikes can be wheeled onto regional trains displaying the bicycle logo. Simply purchase a separate bicycle ticket (*supplemento bici*), valid for 24 hours (€3.50). Certain international trains also allow transport of assembled bicycles for €12, paid on board. Bikes dismantled and stored in a bag can be taken for free, even on night trains. For more information, see the

dedicated page on Trenitalia's website: www.trenitalia.com/en/services/travelling_with_yourbike.html.

➔ Bikes are sometimes free to transport on ferries. On some routes, you might have to pay a small supplement.

If you fancy seeing the south on a saddle, the following reputable organisations offer advice and/or guided tours:

Cycling UK (www.cyclinguk.org) can help you plan your tour or organise a guided tour. Membership costs £46.50 for adults, £29.50 for seniors and £22 for students.

Salento Bici Tour (www.salento-bicitour.org) offers bike rental and both guided and self-guided itineraries in Puglia's Salento region, including an Italian-language-course tour.

Bike Basilicata (☑0835 33 65 72; www.bikebasilicata.it; Via Cappelluti 34; ⊙9am-1.30pm & 3.30-7pm Mon-Sat) Matera-based outfit offering bike rental, maps and information for pre-planned tours of Matera and the surrounding country, as well as multi-day guided bike tours around Puglia and Basilicata.

Boat

Craft Domestic *navi* (large ferries) connect Sicily and Campania, while *traghetti* (smaller ferries) and *aliscafi* (hydrofoils) service the Bay of Naples islands, the Amalfi Coast and the Isole Tremiti in Puglia, as well as Sicily's Aeolian Islands, Egadi Islands, Pelagic Islands and Ustica. Most services are pared back between October and Easter, and some are suspended altogether during this period. Most ferries carry vehicles; hydrofoils do not.

Routes Ferries for Sicily leave from Naples and Salerno, as well as from Villa San Giovanni and Reggio Calabria. The main points of arrival in Sicily are Palermo, Catania, Messina and Trapani.

Timetables and tickets

Comprehensive website Direct Ferries (www.directferries.co.uk) allows you to search routes, compare prices and book tickets for Italian ferry services.

Cabins and seating Travellers can book a two- to four-person cabin or a *poltrona*, an airline-style armchair. Deck class (which allows you to sit/sleep in lounge areas or on deck) is available only on some ferries.

Bus

Numerous companies provide bus services in southern Italy, from meandering local routes to fast and reliable intercity connections.

➡ Buses are usually priced competitively with the train and are often the only way to get to smaller towns. If your destination is not on a main train line (trains tend to be cheaper on major routes), buses are usually a faster way to get around – this is especially true for the Salento in Puglia, for Basilicata and for inland Calabria and Sicily.

➡ Services are provided by a variety of companies. While these can be frequent on weekdays, they are reduced considerably on Sundays and holidays – runs between smaller towns often fall to one or none. Keep this in mind if you depend on buses as it is easy to get stuck in smaller places, especially at the weekends.

➡ It's usually possible to get bus timetables (*orari*) from local tourist offices and the bus companies' websites. In larger cities, most of the intercity bus companies have ticket offices or sell tickets through agencies. In villages and even some good-size towns, tickets are sold in bars – just ask for *biglietti per il pullman* – or on the bus itself.

➡ Advance booking, while not generally required, is a good idea in the high season for overnight or long-haul trips.

Car & Motorcycle

A car in southern Italy only really becomes useful if you want to get away from the main cities and take to the countryside.

Automobile Associations

Italy's national automobile association, the **Automobile Club d'Italia** (ACI; ☑80 31 16, from a foreign mobile 800 116800; www.aci.it) is a driver's best resource in Italy. It offers 24-hour roadside assistance, available on a pay-per-incident system, and its website has comprehensive information on driving in Italy: www.aci.it/laci/driving-in-italy/driving-in-italy-information-for-visiting-motorists.html.

Driving Licence

All EU driving licences are valid in Italy. Travellers from other countries should obtain an International Driving Permit (IDP) through their national automobile association.

A licence is required to ride a scooter – a car licence will do for bikes up to 125cc; for anything over 125cc you'll need a motorcycle licence.

Fuel & Spare Parts

➡ Staffed filling stations (*benzinai, stazioni di servizio*) are widespread. Smaller stations tend to close between about 1pm and 3.30pm and sometimes also on Sunday afternoons.

➡ Many stations have self-service (*fai da te*) pumps that you can use 24 hours a day. To use one insert a banknote into the payment machine and press the number of the pump you want.

➡ Unleaded petrol is marked as *benzina senza piombo*, diesel as *gasolio*.

➡ Prices vary from one station to another. At the time of writing, unleaded petrol was averaging €1.59 per litre, diesel €1.48 per litre.

TO DRIVE OR NOT TO DRIVE

Unless you're a masochist, avoid driving in larger centres such as Naples, Bari, Palermo and Catania, where unruly drivers and parking restrictions will quickly turn your holiday sour. Beyond these urban centres, however, having your own car is the easiest way to get around Italy's south. Buses and trains will get you to most of the main destinations, but they are run by a plethora of private companies, which makes buying tickets and finding bus stops a bit of a bind. Furthermore, the rail network in Salento is still of the narrow-gauge variety, so trains chug along at a snail's pace.

Your own vehicle will give you the most freedom to stray off the main routes and discover out-of-the-way destinations. This is particularly the case in the Parco Nazionale del Cilento, Vallo di Diano e Alburni in Campania, the national parks of Aspromonte, Pollino and Sila in Calabria and Basilicata, the Salento in Puglia and throughout much of rural Sicily.

This said, it's also worth considering the downside of driving. Aside from the negative environmental impact, petrol prices are notoriously high, and popular routes (including Campania's Amalfi Coast, the SS16 connecting Bari and the Salento in Puglia, and Sicily's Ionian and Tyrrhenian coastal routes) can be heavily trafficked during holiday periods and throughout the summer.

Hire

➡ Pre-booking via the internet often costs less than walking into a rental office when you're in Italy. Online booking agency **Rentalcars. com** (www.rental cars.com) compares the rates of numerous car-rental companies.

➡ Renters must generally be aged 21 or over, with a credit card and a home-country driving licence or IDP.

➡ Consider hiring a small car, which will reduce your fuel expenses and help you negotiate narrow city lanes and tight parking spaces.

➡ Check with your credit-card company to see if it offers a Collision Damage Waiver, which covers you for additional damage if you use that card to pay for the car. The following companies have pick-up locations throughout Italy:

Auto Europe (www.autoeurope. it)

Avis (www.avis.com)

Budget (www.budget.com)

Europcar (www.europcar.com)

Hertz (www.hertz.it)

Maggiore (www.maggiore.it)

Sixt (www.sixt.it)

MOTORCYCLES

Agencies throughout Italy rent motorbikes, ranging from small Vespas to large touring bikes. Prices start at around €35/150 per day/week for a 50cc scooter, upwards of €80/400 per day/week for a 650cc motorcycle.

Road Rules

➡ Drive on the right; overtake on the left.

➡ It's obligatory to wear seat belts (front and rear), to drive with your headlights on outside built-up areas, and to carry a warning triangle and fluorescent waistcoat in case of breakdown.

➡ Wearing a helmet is compulsory on all two-wheeled vehicles.

➡ Motorbikes can enter most restricted traffic areas in Italian cities, and traffic police generally turn a blind eye to motorcycles or scooters parked on footpaths.

➡ The blood-alcohol limit is 0.05%; it's zero for drivers under 21 and for those who have had their licence for less than three years.
Unless otherwise indicated, speed limits are as follows:

➡ 130km/h on autostrade (motorways)

➡ 110km/h on main roads outside built-up areas

➡ 90km/h on secondary roads outside built-up areas

➡ 50km/h in built-up areas

Local Transport

Bus & Underground Train

➡ Every city or town of any size has an efficient *urbano* (urban) and *extraurbano* (suburban) system of buses. Services are generally reduced on Sundays and holidays. Naples and Catania also have a metro system.

➡ Purchase bus and metro tickets before boarding. Validate bus tickets on board and metro tickets at the station turnstile.

➡ Tickets can be bought from a *tabaccaio* (tobacconist), newsstands, ticket booths or machines at bus stations and in underground stations, and usually cost €1–2. Some cities offer good-value 24-hour or daily tourist tickets.

Taxi

➡ There are taxi ranks outside most train and bus stations. Alternatively, phone for a radio taxi – the meters for these start the moment you call for them, not when you're picked up.

➡ Charges vary from one region to another. As a rough guide, most short city journeys will cost between €10 and €15. Generally, no more than four people are allowed in a single taxi.

➡ Uber is practically nonexistent in southern Italy. One common app is BlaBlaCar, which is a carpooling service.

Train

➡ Trains are convenient and relatively cheap compared with other European countries. The better train categories are fast and comfortable.

➡ Most trains are run by **Trenitalia** (☏892021; www. trenitalia.com), Italy's national operator.

➡ Privately owned competitor **Italo** (☏892020; www.italotreno.it) runs high-velocity trains from Salerno and Naples to major cities further north, including Rome, Florence, Milan and Venice.

Italy operates several types of train:

➡ Regionale – The slowest and cheapest trains, stopping at all or most stations.

➡ InterCity (IC) – Faster services operating between major cities.

➡ Alta Velocità (AV) – High-velocity Frecciarossa, Frecciargento, Frecciabianca and Italo trains, has speeds up to 300km/h and connections to the major cities.

There are also a number of private train lines operating throughout Italy's south.

➡ Circumvesuviana (www. eavsrl.it) – Links Naples and Sorrento, stopping at Ercolano (Herculaneum) and Pompeii.

➡ Ferrovia Cumana (www. eavsrl.it) – Connects Naples to the Campi Flegrei to the west. Stops include Pozzuoli.

➡ Ferrotramviaria (www. ferrovienordbarese.it) – Services towns in Puglia's Terra di Bari, including

Train Routes

Train Journey Durations:
Naples–Sorrento (1hr 8min)
Naples–Bari (4+hr)
Naples–Palermo (9hr 15min)
Bari–Brindisi (1hr 10min)
Bari–Lecce (1hr 30min)
Reggio Calabria–Catania (4hr)

—— Principal Train Lines
- - - Local Train Lines
—— Private Train Lines

Bitonto, Ruvo di Puglia, Andria and Barletta, as well as Bari airport. Replacement buses on parts of the network on Sundays.

➡ Ferrovie Appulo Lucane (www.fal-srl.it) – Links Bari province with Basilicata, including stops at Altamura and Matera. Replacement buses on Sundays.

➡ Ferrovie del Sud Est (www. fseonline.it) – The main network covering Puglia's Murgia towns and the Salento, servicing tourist hotspots like Castellana Grotte, Alberobello, Martina Franca, Lecce, Gallipoli and Otranto. Replacement buses on parts of the network on Sundays.

➡ Ferrovia Circumetnea (www.circumetnea.it) – A 114km line connecting the towns around the base of Mt Etna. No service on Sundays.

Classes & Costs

➡ Ticket prices vary according to type of train, class of service, time of travel and how far in advance you book.

➡ On Frecciarossa trains, 1st class is Business Class and 2nd class as Standard.

➡ Validate tickets in the green machines (usually found at the head of rail platforms) just before boarding. Failure to do so usually results in a fine.

Reservations

➡ Seat reservations are obligatory on InterCity, Frecciabianca, Frecciargento and Frecciarossa trains.

➡ Reservations can be made on the **Trenitalia** (www. trenitalia.com) and **Italo** (www.italotreno.it) websites, at railway-station counters, and at self-service ticketing machines, as well as through travel agents.

➡ Both Trenitalia and Italo offer advance-purchase discounts. Basically, the earlier you book, the greater the saving. Discounted tickets are limited, and refunds and changes are highly restricted. For all ticket options and prices, see the Trenitalia and Italo websites.

Language

Standard Italian is taught and spoken throughout Italy. Regional dialects are an important part of identity in many parts of the country, but you'll have no trouble being understood anywhere if you stick to standard Italian, which we've also used in this chapter.

The sounds used in spoken Italian can all be found in English. If you read our coloured pronunciation guides as if they were English, you'll be understood. The stressed syllables are indicated with italics. Note that ai is pronounced as in 'aisle', ay as in 'say', ow as in 'how', dz as the 'ds' in 'lids', and that r is a strong and rolled sound. Keep in mind that Italian consonants can have a stronger, emphatic pronunciation – if the consonant is written as a double letter, it should be pronounced a little stronger, eg *sonno son*·no (sleep) versus *sono so*·no (I am).

BASICS

Hello.	*Buongiorno.*	*bwon·jor·no*
Goodbye.	*Arrivederci.*	*a·ree·ve·der·chee*
Yes./No.	*Sì./No.*	*see/no*
Excuse me.	*Mi scusi.* (pol)	*mee skoo·zee*
	Scusami. (inf)	*skoo·za·mee*
Sorry.	*Mi dispiace.*	*mee dees·pya·che*
Please.	*Per favore.*	*per fa·vo·re*
Thank you.	*Grazie.*	*gra·tsye*
You're welcome.	*Prego.*	*pre·go*

WANT MORE?

For in-depth language information and handy phrases, check out Lonely Planet's *Italian Phrasebook*. You'll find it at **shop.lonelyplanet.com**.

How are you?		
Come sta/stai? (pol/inf)		*ko*·me sta/stai
Fine. And you?		
Bene. E lei/tu? (pol/inf)		*be*·ne e lay/too
What's your name?		
Come si chiama? (pol)		*ko*·me see *kya*·ma
Come ti chiami? (inf)		*ko*·me tee *kya*·mee
My name is ...		
Mi chiamo ...		mee *kya*·mo ...
Do you speak English?		
Parla/Parli		*par*·la/*par*·lee
inglese? (pol/inf)		een·*gle*·ze
I don't understand.		
Non capisco.		non ka·*pee*·sko

ACCOMMODATION

campsite	*campeggio*	kam·*pe*·jo
guesthouse	*pensione*	pen·*syo*·ne
hotel	*albergo*	al·*ber*·go
youth hostel	*ostello della gioventù*	os·*te*·lo de·la jo·ven·*too*
Do you have a ... room?	*Avete una camera ...?*	a·*ve*·te *oo*·na *ka*·me·ra ...
double	*doppia con letto matrimoniale*	*do*·pya kon *le*·to ma·*tree*·mo·*nya*·le
single	*singola*	*seen*·go·la
How much is it per ...?	*Quanto costa per ...?*	*kwan*·to *kos*·ta per ...
night	*una notte*	*oo*·na *no*·te
person	*persona*	per·*so*·na
air-con	*aria condizionata*	*a*·rya kon·dee·tsyo·*na*·ta
bathroom	*bagno*	*ba*·nyo
window	*finestra*	fee·*nes*·tra

DIRECTIONS

Where's ...?
Dov'è ...?   do·ve ...

What's the address?
Qual'è l'indirizzo?   kwa·le leen·dee·ree·tso

Could you please write it down?
Può scriverlo,   pwo skree·ver·lo
per favore?   per fa·vo·re

Can you show me (on the map)?
Può mostrarmi   pwo mos·trar·mee
(sulla pianta)?   (soo·la pyan·ta)

EATING & DRINKING

What would you recommend?
Cosa mi consiglia?   ko·za mee kon·see·lya

What's the local speciality?
Qual'è la specialità   kwa·le la spe·cha·lee·ta
di questa regione?   dee kwe·sta re·jo·ne

Cheers!
Salute!   sa·loo·te

That was delicious!
Era squisito!   e·ra skwee·zee·to

Please bring the bill.
Mi porta il conto,   mee por·ta eel kon·to
per favore?   per fa·vo·re

I'd like to reserve a table for ...	*Vorrei prenotare un tavolo per ...*	vo·ray pre·no·ta·re oon ta·vo·lo per ...
(eight) o'clock	*le (otto)*	le (o·to)
(two) people	*(due) persone*	(doo·e) per·so·ne

I don't eat ...	*Non mangio ...*	non man·jo ...
eggs	*uova*	wo·va
fish	*pesce*	pe·she
nuts	*noci*	no·chee

Key Words

bar	*locale*	lo·ka·le
bottle	*bottiglia*	bo·tee·lya
breakfast	*prima colazione*	pree·ma ko·la·tsyo·ne
cafe	*bar*	bar
dinner	*cena*	che·na
drink list	*lista delle bevande*	lee·sta de·le be·van·de
fork	*forchetta*	for·ke·ta
glass	*bicchiere*	bee·kye·re
knife	*coltello*	kol·te·lo

KEY PATTERNS

To get by in Italian, mix and match these simple patterns with words of your choice:

When's (the next flight)?
A che ora è   a ke o·ra e
(il prossimo volo)?   (eel pro·see·mo vo·lo)

Where's (the station)?
Dov'è (la stazione)?   do·ve (la sta·tsyo·ne)

I'm looking for (a hotel).
Sto cercando   sto cher·kan·do
(un albergo).   (oon al·ber·go)

Do you have (a map)?
Ha (una pianta)?   a (oo·na pyan·ta)

Is there (a toilet)?
C'è (un gabinetto)?   che (oon ga·bee·ne·to)

I'd like (a coffee).
Vorrei (un caffè).   vo·ray (oon ka·fe)

I'd like to (hire a car).
Vorrei (noleggiare   vo·ray (no·le·ja·re
una macchina).   oo·na ma·kee·na)

Can I (enter)?
Posso (entrare)?   po·so (en·tra·re)

Could you please (help me)?
Può (aiutarmi),   pwo (a·yoo·tar·mee)
per favore?   per fa·vo·re

Do I have to (book a seat)?
Devo (prenotare   de·vo (pre·no·ta·re
un posto)?   oon po·sto)

lunch	*pranzo*	pran·dzo
market	*mercato*	mer·ka·to
menu	*menù*	me·noo
plate	*piatto*	pya·to
restaurant	*ristorante*	ree·sto·ran·te
spoon	*cucchiaio*	koo·kya·yo
vegetarian	*vegetariano*	ve·je·ta·rya·no

Meat & Fish

beef	*manzo*	man·dzo
chicken	*pollo*	po·lo
herring	*aringa*	a·reen·ga
lamb	*agnello*	a·nye·lo
lobster	*aragosta*	a·ra·gos·ta
mussels	*cozze*	ko·tse
oysters	*ostriche*	o·stree·ke
pork	*maiale*	ma·ya·le
prawn	*gambero*	gam·be·ro
salmon	*salmone*	sal·mo·ne
scallops	*capasante*	ka·pa·san·t
shrimp	*gambero*	gam·be·ro

squid	*calamari*	ka·la·*ma*·ree
trout	*trota*	*tro*·ta
tuna	*tonno*	*to*·no
turkey	*tacchino*	ta·*kee*·no
veal	*vitello*	vee·*te*·lo

Fruit & Vegetables

apple	*mela*	*me*·la
beans	*fagioli*	fa·*jo*·lee
cabbage	*cavolo*	*ka*·vo·lo
capsicum	*peperone*	pe·pe·*ro*·ne
carrot	*carota*	ka·*ro*·ta
cauliflower	*cavolfiore*	ka·vol·*fyo*·re
cucumber	*cetriolo*	che·tree·o·lo
grapes	*uva*	*oo*·va
lemon	*limone*	lee·*mo*·ne
lentils	*lenticchie*	len·*tee*·kye
mushroom	*funghi*	*foon*·gee
nuts	*noci*	*no*·chee
onions	*cipolle*	chee·*po*·le
orange	*arancia*	a·*ran*·cha
peach	*pesca*	*pe*·ska
peas	*piselli*	pee·*ze*·lee
pineapple	*ananas*	*a*·na·nas
plum	*prugna*	*proo*·nya
potatoes	*patate*	pa·*ta*·te
spinach	*spinaci*	spee·*na*·chee
tomatoes	*pomodori*	po·mo·*do*·ree

Other

bread	*pane*	*pa*·ne
butter	*burro*	*boo*·ro
cheese	*formaggio*	for·*ma*·jo
eggs	*uova*	*wo*·va
honey	*miele*	*mye*·le
jam	*marmellata*	mar·me·*la*·ta

SIGNS

Closed	**Chiuso**
Entrance	**Entrata/Ingresso**
Exit	**Uscita**
Men	**Uomini**
Open	**Aperto**
Prohibited	**Proibito/Vietato**
Toilets	**Gabinetti/Servizi**
Women	**Donne**

noodles	*pasta*	*pas*·ta
oil	*olio*	*o*·lyo
pepper	*pepe*	*pe*·pe
rice	*riso*	*ree*·zo
salt	*sale*	*sa*·le
soup	*minestra*	mee·*nes*·tra
soy sauce	*salsa di soia*	*sal*·sa dee *so*·ya
sugar	*zucchero*	*tsoo*·ke·ro
vinegar	*aceto*	a·*che*·to

Drinks

beer	*birra*	*bee*·ra
coffee	*caffè*	ka·*fe*
juice	*succo*	*soo*·ko
milk	*latte*	*la*·te
red wine	*vino rosso*	*vee*·no *ro*·so
tea	*tè*	te
water	*acqua*	*a*·kwa
white wine	*vino bianco*	*vee*·no *byan*·ko

EMERGENCIES

Help!
Aiuto! — a·*yoo*·to

Leave me alone!
Lasciami in pace! — la·*sha*·mee een *pa*·che

I'm lost.
Mi sono perso/a. (m/f) — mee *so*·no *per*·so/a

Call the police!
Chiami la polizia! — *kya*·mee la po·lee·*tsee*·a

Call a doctor!
Chiami un medico! — *kya*·mee oon *me*·dee·ko

Where are the toilets?
Dove sono i gabinetti? — *do*·ve *so*·no ee ga·bee·*ne*·tee

I'm sick.
Mi sento male. — mee *sen*·to *ma*·le

SHOPPING & SERVICES

I'd like to buy ...
Vorrei comprare ... — vo·*ray* kom·*pra*·re ...

I'm just looking.
Sto solo guardando. — sto *so*·lo gwar·*dan*·do

Can I look at it?
Posso dare un'occhiata? — *po*·so *da*·re oo·no·*kya*·ta

How much is this?
Quanto costa questo? — *kwan*·to *kos*·ta *kwe*·sto

It's too expensive.
È troppo caro. — e *tro*·po *ka*·ro

There's a mistake in the bill.
C'è un errore nel conto. — che oo·ne·*ro*·re nel *kon*·to

ATM	*Bancomat*	*ban·ko·mat*
post office	*ufficio postale*	*oo·fee·cho pos·ta·le*
tourist office	*ufficio del turismo*	*oo·fee·cho del too·reez·mo*

TIME & DATES

What time is it?
Che ora è? ke o·ra e

It's (two) o'clock.
Sono le (due). so·no le (doo·e)

Half past (one).
(L'una) e mezza. (loo·na) e me·dza

in the morning	*di mattina*	dee ma·tee·na
in the afternoon	*di pomeriggio*	dee po·me·ree·jo
in the evening	*di sera*	dee se·ra
yesterday	*ieri*	ye·ree
today	*oggi*	o·jee
tomorrow	*domani*	do·ma·nee

Monday	*lunedì*	loo·ne·dee
Tuesday	*martedì*	mar·te·dee
Wednesday	*mercoledì*	mer·ko·le·dee
Thursday	*giovedì*	jo·ve·dee
Friday	*venerdì*	ve·ner·dee
Saturday	*sabato*	sa·ba·to
Sunday	*domenica*	do·me·nee·ka

TRANSPORT

boat	*nave*	na·ve
bus	*autobus*	ow·to·boos
ferry	*traghetto*	tra·ge·to
metro	*metropolitana*	me·tro·po·lee·ta·na
plane	*aereo*	a·e·re·o
train	*treno*	tre·no

bus stop	*fermata dell'autobus*	fer·ma·ta del ow·to·boos
ticket office	*biglietteria*	bee·lye·te·ree·a
timetable	*orario*	o·ra·ryo
train station	*stazione ferroviaria*	sta·tsyo·ne fe·ro·vyar·ya

... ticket	*un biglietto ...*	oon bee·lye·to
one way	*di sola andata*	dee so·la an·da·ta
return	*di andata e ritorno*	dee an·da·ta e ree·tor·no

NUMBERS

1	*uno*	oo·no
2	*due*	doo·e
3	*tre*	tre
4	*quattro*	kwa·tro
5	*cinque*	cheen·kwe
6	*sei*	say
7	*sette*	se·te
8	*otto*	o·to
9	*nove*	no·ve
10	*dieci*	dye·chee
20	*venti*	ven·tee
30	*trenta*	tren·ta
40	*quaranta*	kwa·ran·ta
50	*cinquanta*	cheen·kwan·ta
60	*sessanta*	se·san·ta
70	*settanta*	se·tan·ta
80	*ottanta*	o·tan·ta
90	*novanta*	no·van·ta
100	*cento*	chen·to
1000	*mille*	mee·lel

Does it stop at ...?
Si ferma a ...? see fer·ma a ...

Please tell me when we get to ...
Mi dica per favore quando arriviamo a ... mee dee·ka per fa·vo·re kwan·do a·ree·vya·mo a ...

I want to get off here.
Voglio scendere qui. vo·lyo shen·de·re kwee

I'd like to hire a ...	*Vorrei noleggiare una ...*	vo·ray no·le·ja·re oo·na ...
bicycle	*bicicletta*	bee·chee·kle·ta
car	*macchina*	ma·kee·na
motorbike	*moto*	mo·to

bicycle pump	*pompa della bicicletta*	pom·pa de·la bee·chee·kle·ta
child seat	*seggiolino*	se·jo·lee·no
helmet	*casco*	kas·ko
mechanic	*meccanico*	me·ka·nee·ko
petrol	*benzina*	ben·dzee·na
service station	*stazione di servizio*	sta·tsyo·ne dee ser·vee·tsyo

Is this the road to ...?
Questa strada porta a ...? kwe·sta stra·da por·ta a ...

Can I park here?
Posso parcheggiare qui? po·so par·ke·ja·re kwee

GLOSSARY

abbazia – abbey
agriturismo – farm-stays
(pizza) al taglio – (pizza) by the slice
albergo – hotel
alimentari – grocery shop
anfiteatro – amphitheatre
aperitivo – pre-dinner drink and snack
APT – Azienda di Promozione Turistica; local town or city tourist office
autostrada – motorway; highway

battistero – baptistry
biblioteca – library
biglietto – ticket
borgo – archaic name for a small town, village or town sector

camera – room
campo – field; also a square in Venice
cappella – chapel
carabinieri – police with military and civil duties
Carnevale – carnival period between Epiphany and Lent
casa – house
castello – castle
cattedrale – cathedral
centro storico – historic centre
certosa – monastery belonging to or founded by Carthusian monks
chiesa – church
chiostro – cloister; covered walkway, usually enclosed by columns, around a quadrangle
cima – summit
città – town; city
città alta – upper town
città bassa – lower town
colonna – column
comune – equivalent to a municipality or county; a town or city council; historically, a self–governing town or city
contrada – district
corso – boulevard
duomo – cathedral

enoteca – wine bar

espresso – short black coffee
ferrovia – railway
festa – feast day; holiday
fontana – fountain
foro – forum
funivia – cable car

gelateria – ice-cream shop
giardino – garden
golfo – gulf
grotta – cave

isola – island

lago – lake
largo – small square
lido – beach
locanda – inn; small hotel
lungomare – seafront road/ promenade

mar, mare – sea
masseria – working farm
mausoleo – mausoleum; stately and magnificent tomb
mercato – market
monte – mountain

necropoli – ancient name for cemetery or burial site
nord – north
nuraghe – megalithic stone fortress in Sardinia

osteria – casual tavern or eatery

palazzo – mansion; palace; large building of any type, including an apartment block
palio – contest
parco – park
passeggiata – traditional evening stroll
pasticceria – cake/pastry shop
pensione – guesthouse
piazza – square
piazzale – large open square
pietà – literally 'pity' or 'com-passion'; sculpture, drawing or painting of the dead Christ supported by the Madonna
pinacoteca – art gallery
ponte – bridge

porta – gate; door
porto – port

reale – royal
rifugio – mountain hut; accommodation in the Alps
ristorante – restaurant
rocca – fortress

sala – room; hall
salumeria – delicatessen
santuario – sanctuary; 1. the part of a church above the altar; 2. an especially holy place in a temple (antiquity)
sassi – literally 'stones'; stone houses built in two ravines in Matera, Basilicata
scalinata – staircase
scavi – excavations
sestiere – city district in Venice
spiaggia – beach
stazione – station
stazione marittima – ferry terminal
strada – street; road
sud – south
superstrada – expressway; highway with divided lanes

tartufo – truffle
tavola calda – literally 'hot table'; pre-prepared meals, often self-service
teatro – theatre
tempietto – small temple
tempio – temple
terme – thermal baths
tesoro – treasury
torre – tower
trattoria – simple restaurant
Trenitalia – Italian State Rail-ways; also known as Ferrovie dello Stato (FS)
trullo – conical house in Perugia

vaporetto – small passenger ferry in Venice
via – street; road
viale – avenue
vico – alley; alleyway
villa – town house; country house; also the park surrounding the house

Behind the Scenes

SEND US YOUR FEEDBACK

We love to hear from travellers – your comments keep us on our toes and help make our books better. Our well-travelled team reads every word on what you loved or loathed about this book. Although we cannot reply individually to your submissions, we always guarantee that your feedback goes straight to the appropriate authors, in time for the next edition. Each person who sends us information is thanked in the next edition – the most useful submissions are rewarded with a selection of digital PDF chapters.

Visit **lonelyplanet.com/contact** to submit your updates and suggestions or to ask for help. Our award-winning website also features inspirational travel stories, news and discussions.

Note: We may edit, reproduce and incorporate your comments in Lonely Planet products such as guidebooks, websites and digital products, so let us know if you don't want your comments reproduced or your name acknowledged. For a copy of our privacy policy visit lonelyplanet.com/privacy.

WRITER THANKS

Brett Atkinson

Exploring southern Italy and Sicily was a great experience thanks to Anna Rita in Bari, Luisa in Lecce and Domenico in Reggio Calabria. Thanks also to Amy in Matera for helping me negotiate the town's laneways, and to Tony in Vieste for securing me a boat to the Isole Tremiti. Special thanks to Anna Tyler for the commission, and to Carol.

Cristian Bonetto

Grazie infinite to all who shared their love and knowledge of the Mezzogiorno. In Sicily, special thanks to Ornella Tuzzolino, Giorgio Ferravioli and Carla Bellavista, Pierfrancesco Palazzotto, Lorenzo Chiaramonte, Rosario Fillari, Giorgio Puglisi, Gennaro Mattiucci, Ernesto Magri, Giovanni Gurrieri, Joe Brizzi, Giuseppe Savà, Luigi Nifosì, Antonio Adamo, Cesare Setmani, Norma Gritti and Cristina Delli Fiori. In Campania, *grazie di cuore* to my *Re e Regina di Napoli*, Federica Rispoli and Ivan Palmieri, as well as to Igor Milanese.

Gregor Clark

Grazie mille to the many people who shared their love and knowledge of Sicily with me, especially Fausto Ceschi, Fabiana Mariotti, Micol Beittel, Stefano Musaico, Mark, Giovanna, Angela, Francesco, Marcello, Paola, Carmelina, Marian, Diego and Patrizia. Back in Vermont, big hugs to Gaen, Meigan and Chloe, who always make coming home the best part of the trip.

Brendan Sainsbury

Many thanks to all the skilled bus drivers, helpful tourist information staff, generous hotel owners, expert cappucino makers, dogs-that-didn't-growl-at-me, and numerous passers-by who helped me, unwittingly or otherwise, during my research trip. Special thanks to my wife, Liz, and my son, Kieran, for keeping the home fires burning.

Nicola Williams

My chunk of Sicily is dedicated to my very own family-travel research team – Mischa, Kaya, Mathias (and Niko, vicariously from his desk) – who joined me for a 2000km+ road trip exploring every last nook, cranny, lemon grove and salt pan of the island's wild west. *Grazie mille* to the islanders who shared their knowledge with us, including Gaetana and Giuseppe at Favignana's La Casa del Limoneta and the team at Prokite Alby Rondina.

ACKNOWLEDGEMENTS

Climate map data adapted from Peel MC, Finlayson BL & McMahon TA (2007) 'Updated World Map of the Köppen-Geiger Climate Classification', *Hydrology and Earth System Sciences*, 11, 1633–44.

Cover photograph: Aerial view of Tropea, Naeblys/Shutterstock ©

Illustration pp102–3 by Javier Zarracina

THIS BOOK

This 6th edition of Lonely Planet's *Southern Italy* guidebook was researched and written by Brett Atkinson, Cristian Bonetto, Gregor Clark, Duncan Garwood, Brendan Sainsbury and Nicola Williams. This guidebook was produced by the following:

Destination Editor Anna Tyler

Senior Product Editors Kate Chapman, Elizabeth Jones

Regional Senior Cartographer Anthony Phelan

Product Editors Hannah Cartmel, Alison Ridgway, Claire Rourke

Cartographer Hunor Csutoros

Book Designers Aomi Ito, Virginia Moreno, Mazzy Prinsep

Assisting Editors Sarah Bailey, Andrea Dobbin, Gabrielle Innes, Anita Isalska, Kate Morgan, Lauren O'Connell, Fionnuala Twomey, Simon Williamson

Cover Researcher Brendan Dempsey-Spencer

Thanks to Bailey Freeman, Victoria Harrison, Karen Henderson, Sonia Kapoor, Fergus O'Shea, Kat Rowan

Index

Map Legend

Sights

- ⦿ Beach
- ⦿ Bird Sanctuary
- ⦿ Buddhist
- ⦿ Castle/Palace
- ⦿ Christian
- ⦿ Confucian
- ⦿ Hindu
- ⦿ Islamic
- ⦿ Jain
- ⦿ Jewish
- ⦿ Monument
- ⦿ Museum/Gallery/Historic Building
- ⦿ Ruin
- ⦿ Shinto
- ⦿ Sikh
- ⦿ Taoist
- ⦿ Winery/Vineyard
- ⦿ Zoo/Wildlife Sanctuary
- ⦿ Other Sight

Activities, Courses & Tours

- ⦿ Bodysurfing
- ⦿ Diving
- ⦿ Canoeing/Kayaking
- ● Course/Tour
- ⦿ Sento Hot Baths/Onsen
- ⦿ Skiing
- ⦿ Snorkelling
- ⦿ Surfing
- ⦿ Swimming/Pool
- ⦿ Walking
- ⦿ Windsurfing
- ⦿ Other Activity

Sleeping

- ⦿ Sleeping
- ⦿ Camping
- ⦿ Hut/Shelter

Eating

- ⦿ Eating

Drinking & Nightlife

- ⦿ Drinking & Nightlife
- ⦿ Cafe

Entertainment

- ⦿ Entertainment

Shopping

- ⦿ Shopping

Information

- ⦿ Bank
- ⦿ Embassy/Consulate
- ⦿ Hospital/Medical
- @ Internet
- ⦿ Police
- ⦿ Post Office
- ⦿ Telephone
- ⦿ Toilet
- ⦿ Tourist Information
- ● Other Information

Geographic

- ⦿ Beach
- ⋈ Gate
- ⦿ Hut/Shelter
- ⦿ Lighthouse
- ⦿ Lookout
- ▲ Mountain/Volcano
- ⦿ Oasis
- ⦿ Park
-)(Pass
- ⦿ Picnic Area
- ⦿ Waterfall

Population

- ⦿ Capital (National)
- ◉ Capital (State/Province)
- ● City/Large Town
- ● Town/Village

Transport

- ⦿ Airport
- ⦾ Border crossing
- ⦿ Bus
- ⦿ Cable car/Funicular
- ⦿ Cycling
- ⦿ Ferry
- Ⓜ Metro station
- ⦿ Monorail
- Ⓟ Parking
- ⦿ Petrol station
- ⦿ S-Bahn/Subway station
- ⦿ Taxi
- ⦿ T-bane/Tunnelbana station
- ⦿ Train station/Railway
- ⦿ Tram
- ⦿ U-Bahn/Underground station
- ● Other Transport

Routes

- Tollway
- Freeway
- Primary
- Secondary
- Tertiary
- Lane
- Unsealed road
- Road under construction
- Plaza/Mall
- Steps
- Tunnel
- Pedestrian overpass
- Walking Tour
- Walking Tour detour
- Path/Walking Trail

Boundaries

- International
- State/Province
- Disputed
- Regional/Suburb
- Marine Park
- Cliff
- Wall

Hydrography

- River, Creek
- Intermittent River
- Canal
- Water
- Dry/Salt/Intermittent Lake
- Reef

Areas

- Airport/Runway
- Beach/Desert
- Cemetery (Christian)
- Cemetery (Other)
- Glacier
- Mudflat
- Park/Forest
- Sight (Building)
- Sportsground
- Swamp/Mangrove

Note: Not all symbols displayed above appear on the maps in this book